HORATIO SEYMOUR
of
NEW YORK

LONDON : HUMPHREY MILFORD
OXFORD UNIVERSITY PRESS

Horatio Seymour

HORATIO SEYMOUR
OF
NEW YORK

STEWART MITCHELL

CAMBRIDGE, MASSACHUSETTS
HARVARD UNIVERSITY PRESS
1938

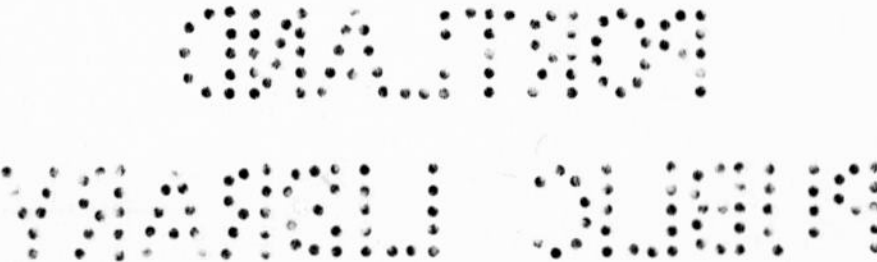

PRINTED AT THE HARVARD UNIVERSITY PRESS
CAMBRIDGE, MASS., U. S. A.

TO

GEORGINE HOLMES THOMAS

"Seymour had been Governor of New York, and though he was full of anxious misgivings during the war, he had not been backward in filling the requisitions which were made upon him for troops. . . . No man in the country was better equipped for the Presidency than Horatio Seymour": Hugh McCulloch (appointed secretary of the treasury by Abraham Lincoln, March 7, 1865), *Men and Measures of Half a Century*, 345.

". . . when the crisis of union or disunion was presented in the Civil War, he [Seymour] stood firmly for preserving the integrity of the Government and the unity of the country; and . . . amid all the changes of parties and of policies, and under all the difficulties of tremendous and trying events, he was always a patriot, always a gentleman, and, above all, always an honest man": Charles A. Dana (assistant secretary of war, 1862–1865): New York *Sun*, February 13, 1886.

Who are you that wanted only to be told what you knew before?
Who are you that wanted only a book to join you in your nonsense?

Walt Whitman, *By Blue Ontario's Shore*

ACKNOWLEDGMENTS

IN the preparation of this book, the author has received useful assistance and valuable advice from many persons. For permission to consult the Marcy Papers in the Library of Congress, he owes his thanks to the late J. Franklin Jameson. The collections of manuscripts, photographs, notes, and newspaper clippings at the New York State Library and the New York Historical Society were indispensable. That assembled at the latter institution was made available by the devoted niece of Horatio Seymour, the late Mrs. Charles Stebbins Fairchild, of Cazenovia, New York, by means of the good offices of Mr. Alexander J. Wall. The coöperation of Miss Edna L. Jacobsen, of the State Library, was constant and cordial. Mrs. William Gorham Rice, of Albany, generously copied and contributed important information from the journals of her father, John V. L. Pruyn, a lifelong friend of Seymour.

For sharing the drudgery of making this book, the author thanks three friends, Miss Marjorie M. Bruce (who also drew the maps from the rough drafts of the author), Mrs. Augusta Bruce Hitchcock, and Richard David Cowan. For transcriptions from newspapers and photostats he is indebted to Miss Doris Cobb, of Lockport, New York, and Miss J. L. O. Peirce, of Cambridge. Mr. Donald Born kindly read the proof in pages, and Mr. Waldo Emerson Palmer prepared the index.

Finally, except for the interest and encouragement of Arthur M. Schlesinger, this biography would never have been finished. Although Professor Schlesinger read the first draft and the last and was most generous with his time and helpful with his knowledge of the period, it is only fair to add that he was not always in complete agreement with all the opinions and conclusions of the author.

S. M.

CONTENTS

INTRODUCTION xv

I. HENRY SEYMOUR 3

II. TO SCHOOL WITH MARCY 25

III. THE FALL OF MARTIN VAN BUREN 46

IV. THE MANTLE OF DEWITT CLINTON 61

V. SPEAKER FOR THE HUNKERS 77

VI. THE DEATH OF SILAS WRIGHT 97

VII. TO BALTIMORE AND BACK 121

VIII. THE FORTS OF FOLLY 142

IX. AT SPRINGFIELD FOR BUCHANAN 169

X. THE CANAL ACROSS WISCONSIN 189

XI. CHARLESTON AND TWEDDLE HALL 202

XII. GOVERNOR AGAIN 231

XIII. FORCE, DISSOLUTION, OR COMPROMISE 259

XIV. MY FRIENDS 298

XV. THE DEVIL AND THE DEEP SEA 337

XVI. CHASE OR HENDRICKS 383

XVII. CANDIDATE BY COMPULSION 411

XVIII. DISGUISED AS A GENTLEMAN 443

XIX. THREE TROUBLESOME OLD FOOLS 487

XX. ELDER STATESMAN 517

XXI. OLD HUMBUG OF A FARMER 550

XXII. DEPARTURE IN PEACE 570

APPENDIX: "MY FRIENDS" 581

BIBLIOGRAPHY 587

INDEX 597

ILLUSTRATIONS

HORATIO SEYMOUR IN 1852 . . . . *Frontispiece*
By C. G. Crehen *Courtesy of the New York Historical Society*

HENRY SEYMOUR 4

THE ERIE CANAL 16

THE INTERIOR OF POMPEY ACADEMY 28

WILLIAM L. MARCY 34

AN EARLY VIEW OF UTICA 44

MRS. HENRY SEYMOUR 62

SILAS WRIGHT 84

DANIEL S. DICKINSON 112

JOHN VAN BUREN 112

NEW YORK ELECTION MAP: 1850 118

NEW YORK ELECTION MAP: 1852 134

WASHINGTON HUNT 142

MYRON H. CLARK 142

HORATIO SEYMOUR 150

SEYMOUR'S HOME IN ALBANY, 1853–1854 158

NEW YORK ELECTION MAP: 1854 166

HORATIO SEYMOUR 202

DEAN RICHMOND 246

JAMES S. WADSWORTH 246

NEW YORK ELECTION MAP: 1862 256

SEYMOUR'S HOME IN ALBANY, 1863–1864 260

CLEMENT L. VALLANDIGHAM 290

FRANCIS KERNAN 290

"MY FRIENDS" 324

THE DRAFT RIOTS 330
NEW YORK ELECTION MAP: 1864 382
SALMON P. CHASE 410
THOMAS A. HENDRICKS 410
HORATIO SEYMOUR 434
FRANCIS P. BLAIR, JR. 448
NEW YORK ELECTION MAP: 1868 474
NATIONAL ELECTION MAP: 1868 484
HORATIO SEYMOUR 522
SEYMOUR'S HOME AT DEERFIELD 550
MRS. HORATIO SEYMOUR 564
TWO BUSTS OF SEYMOUR 574
A GENEALOGY OF THE SEYMOURS 594

INTRODUCTION

THIS biography had its beginning in a desire to collect accurate information about the Democrat who polled an impressive popular vote for President of the United States against General Grant in the campaign of 1868. It was completed in the hope of providing an honest understanding of the character and the career of one of the best-loved and most sagacious sons of New York. A man who was nominated for governor of the greatest state of the Union no less than six times, and was twice elected to that office (with an interval of ten years between his terms) quite obviously exerted no little influence on the turbulent politics of his time.

In at least one respect, moreover, the experience of Horatio Seymour was unique — no man in American history other than he has received the presidential nomination of a major political party wholly against his own will. The action of the Democratic convention of 1868 was without precedent and has not been repeated. Candidates have been given nominations they did not seek, but Seymour, alone, was actually forced to accept one which he earnestly tried to escape. His sincerity was doubted and even denied; it has never been disproved. The delegates to that convention of 1868 were hot and tired and determined to have done; so they compelled Seymour himself to take what he had hoped to persuade them to give to Chief-Justice Chase or to Senator Hendricks.

At first sight Seymour looks like a born leader of lost causes. Such he may seem — in any short view of aims and issues. He looked a long way back, however, and even further forward. His opposition to Nativism — "America for the Americans," to abolition, and to prohibition was intelligent and tireless. In 1854, for instance, he was the most distinguished and forthright political victim of the mania for compulsory "temperance" which blazed over the northern states like a prairie fire — to burn itself out before the Civil War. The message in which he vetoed the Maine bill for New York contains practically all the wisdom which the American people would learn from bitter experience almost eighty years later. The presidential campaign of 1928, moreover, saw the revival of the same venomous feelings about race and religion which he defied and denounced in his own day.

Cried down as a "Dough-Face" in the late fifties because he did his level best to ward off the calamity of the Civil War, called a "Copperhead" in 1862 for openly questioning the methods demanded by a bloody conquest of the South, Seymour lived to see the complete collapse of the northern effort to reconstruct the states which had tried to leave the Union. His quarrel with the arbitrary acts of the administration of Lincoln was sound enough to be sustained by the Supreme Court in 1866, but victories like Gettysburg made his arguments unpopular if not impractical at the time he urged them on his fellow citizens. Curtis, Seymour, Tilden — any one of these men was probably too good a lawyer to have won the Civil War for the North; Abraham Lincoln was not.

Historians like to write as if the past could not have been other or better than it was. Even able scholars will imply that some specific event was inevitable. Looking back at unalterable facts, many of them slip into the error of forgetting the accidents of circumstances out of which men make fortune good or bad as they please. If the Civil War was not to be avoided, then scores of statesmen in both North and South lacked the good judgment they were once supposed to possess. Secession was not a conspiracy; nor was the notion a new one; the threat of it had been used by different sections of the country, and among these New England, almost from the first days of the Union. The basic cause of the Civil War was a common want of patience, confidence, good manners, and good will, and Seymour was one of millions of Americans who sensed this fact. If it be true that the split between North and South was a conflict of civilizations as well as sentiments, however, then his nomination at Charleston in 1860 would have only postponed the evil day.

Seymour's respect for Thomas Jefferson was much more than the idle lip service it has since become with men who would have fought the great Virginian tooth and nail as long as he lived. As a disciple in fact, not fancy, Seymour insisted that local government was of first importance as a true test of success at self-government. Such being the case, the only lasting kind of union for a large land, he argued, was a confederacy of states, and even communities, each managing its own immediate affairs. Gross inequalities in the representation of voters in the Senate would one day cause trouble, he believed, if any more than a necessary minimum of government were ever to gravitate to Washington, for a minority might then impose its will on the majority. This theory brought him into direct collision with the actual trend toward centralization of power, especially during his second term as governor of New York (1863–1864).

Holding fast to the doctrine of the sovereignty of states which were, after all, nothing more than historic accidents both as to bounds and being, Seymour was unwilling to foresee the change from a confederacy into a nation in which the springs of action would be frankly and not secretly sectional. He watched a federal government transform itself into a central government — most sensationally in the circumstances of the Civil War, but more subtly and steadily through increasing ease of transportation and communication. Even if he understood the transformation, it left him unconvinced. He died before the experiment of a central government began to feel the full force of the conflicts among eight or nine natural sections as determined by geography and economics. During his lifetime, however, the love of states, with most Americans, became secondary to the love of country — a very significant change.

Seymour's hostility to northern agitation for the abolition of slavery in the South was rooted in a distaste for what he called "malignant philanthropy" — a distrust of the "leprosy of hypocrisy." He was seven when his own state voted that the institution should go out of existence at the end of ten years, and there is no reason to believe that he ever regretted the reform or did not hope that other states would follow suit. If Marcy did not teach him his hatred of cant, he confirmed it. By 1856 Seymour would have agreed with Lee that the "holding of slaves was an evil, but that their emancipation would sooner come from the mild and melting influence of time than from the storms and contests of fiery controversy."[1] For "sooner" the famously unlucky Lee would have been wiser to write "better." In defiance of the clamor from New England and the Middle West, Seymour declared that the only proper place to work for emancipation was the South. In 1860, when both abolitionists and slave-holders were shouting for secession, Seymour brought nothing more against their deadly arguments than sound reason and the spirit of charity. Unlike many of the men who flourished in his prime he was never spectacular; he could not think of people as simply good or bad.

Although the active political career of Horatio Seymour coincided with the temporary decay of the Democratic party and its expulsion from a long lease of power, he lived to see one of his disciples, Grover Cleveland, President of the United States. By 1887 the husband of his favorite niece was secretary of the treasury. Seymour himself consistently declined national office; in 1875, for instance, he refused a senatorship which was his for the accepting and sent Francis Kernan to Washington in his place.

Critics of his career complain that it was wholly negative. The very phrasing of the criticism begs the question. Negative results are sometimes better than positive. Seymour, it is true, aroused widespread resentment by his good-tempered opposition to prohibition, but his judgment was sustained within two years by the highest court of his own state and much later, again, by the repeal of an eighteenth amendment. It has been said that his name was never connected with any important

1. *New England Quarterly*, VIII, 2 (June, 1935), 230.

piece of legislation. This objection ignores the salient fact that for more than forty years Horatio Seymour was the most able and active champion of the Erie Canal and all that it meant to the state of New York. In a very real sense he carried the great work of Clinton to its successful climax. Through lean years and fat, he predicted that the Erie Canal would continue to pay its own way, and he had the satisfaction of seeing the whole cost of the work and its improvements return to the treasury of the state. The foresight which planned, promoted, and maintained this canal was decisive in making New York City the eastern gateway of the country. Defense of the investment became a family tradition with the Seymours.

Most significant of all, perhaps, was the fact that Seymour lived through two of the four great American panics — those of 1837 and 1873. The first caused the nervous breakdown and the suicide of his father. It was then that the imminent collapse of state credit threatened the support and the improvement of the canal, and the youthful and sanguine son had to fight almost alone against the gloomy forebodings of such good but rigid Democratic leaders as Michael Hoffman and Azariah Flagg. Time proved that he was right and they were wrong. In the seventies his party was out of power, and he was limited to criticizing the loose finances of the Civil War and the insane prosperity which followed it. Three years after he had been defeated for President and had retired to private life he joined Tilden as first lieutenant in the long, stubborn, and successful fight to free the state and the city of New York from the control of the "canal ring" and the brazenly corrupt Tammany of Tweed.

By 1880, when General Hancock was ridiculed for quite accurately, if indiscreetly, calling the tariff "a local issue," Seymour definitely declared in favor of "freer trade" as against the easy prohibitory policy of the Republicans. Eight years later Grover Cleveland was to lose the electoral college on this very issue in spite of his popular majority of more than one hundred thousand votes. Shutting out imports, Seymour warned Americans as early as 1880, would lead to foreign retaliation, but his words were whistled down the wind. One nation after another followed the bad example of his countrymen until fifty years later international trade seemed likely to disappear from the oceans of the earth.

Scores of speeches are practically the only written record which Seymour left behind him, and speeches, as he himself observed, "make dull reading." [2] Even a half century after his death, however, the public utterances of Horatio Seymour, both in style and substance, stand up in honorable eminence against the turgid oratory of his day. Separated from the magnetism of his person they still have a dignity of their own. He liked short words; he preferred simple sentences, and his figures of speech were effective. Such of his correspondence as survives shows the wide range of his interests, his unfailing kindness, and his courteous humor. He was always an industrious reader of newspapers, and the printed reports of his interviews with journalists contain many of his most pungent remarks — as in 1884, when he doubted if the fact that Tilden had lost his voice would impair his success as a candidate for President.[3] His sharp sense of the absurd shut Seymour out from many of the tempting excitements of the time. He was fond of urging people to mind their own business and he tried his best to practise what he preached.

"If Horatio Seymour had only become a Republican," observed Edward Channing, "he would have died a great American statesman." One purpose of this biography is to show why Seymour did not choose to do so.

2. New York Historical Society: Seymour Papers: S. S. Nicholas to Horatio Seymour, October 19, 1867, protesting against Seymour's statement in a letter accompanying a present of a collection of his speeches.

3. New York *Mail and Express*, March 27, 1884.

HORATIO SEYMOUR OF NEW YORK

I

HENRY SEYMOUR: CANAL COMMISSIONER

1780–1837

IN 1786, when the representatives of New York and Massachusetts met at the halfway house in Hartford, Connecticut, to settle, once and for all, the question of the lands lying west of Seneca Lake, in New York, Henry Seymour was a boy of six. His father, Major Moses Seymour (1742–1827), who had served as an officer in the Revolution, had moved to Litchfield, in the western part of the state, but he still had intimate connections with Hartford, where the Seymours had long been an old and honorable family.[1] Frequently elected a member of the legislature, Major Moses Seymour was no stranger in the capital, and it is just possible that he may have witnessed one or two of the sessions at which the disposition of all the western territory of the state of New York was settled — the property rights going to Massachusetts, and the jurisdiction being vested in the government at Albany. The larger part of this land passed eventually into the hands of Dutch investors, being known as the "Holland Purchase." However that may be, with the close of the Revolution, the frontier of what was still the "Far West" began to attract the active and ambitious younger sons of New England. In that direction, then, Henry Seymour turned when, in 1801, he set out to make his fortune with the small capital his father had given him.

He was the sixth child and the fifth son of the major, all of whose children lived long and did well. The fourth son, Horatio (1778–1857), named in honor of General Horatio Gates, with whom the elder Seymour served at Saratoga,[2] emigrated to Middlebury, Vermont, succeeded in business, became a banker,

1. Seymour, *Richard Seamer or Semer of Hartford, Connecticut.*
2. Seymour, *Seymour Family in the Revolution.*

and sat in the Senate of the United States for two terms as a Republican (1821–1833). Stray references to him in the *Memoirs* of John Quincy Adams show resemblances of character in modesty and political tact to both the brother and the nephew who became prominently associated with the history of New York. Moses and Ozias, the first and second sons, remained with their father in their native town; Epaphroditus followed his brother to Vermont and became president of a bank at Brattleboro; the eldest child, a Mrs. Clarissa Marsh, of Litchfield, achieved the feminine distinction of living to be ninety-four.

As a rule, the Seymours of Connecticut had been shrewd and successful ever since they had left the Old World for the New. Richard Seamer (1605–1655) had emigrated in the company of Thomas Hooker, in 1636, leaving Cambridge for the site of what was to be called Hartford. Hooker, indeed, may have been responsible for his leaving England, for the Seymours probably heard him preach. The family can be traced back to the little town of Sawbridgeworth, sometime Sabsworth, in Hertfordshire, at the edge of Essex, just below Bishop's Stortford.[3] Because a certain Thomas Seymour, of Norwalk, Connecticut, drew up a will in 1712 to which he affixed a seal with wings that recalled those of the arms of the great house of Seymour of Penhow, an excess of family pride led certain of the Connecticut family to suppose that they were somehow connected with the Protector Somerset, the uncle of Edward VI. Thomas of Norwalk, in true colonial fashion, had probably used the first seal which came to hand, with never a thought of its significance or any knowledge of what it might resemble.

Sawbridgeworth, the ancestral home of Richard Seamer, or Semer, lay within the area of the influence of Hooker, who came out to America in 1633. Richard Seamer's father was buried at Sawbridgeworth in 1637; some time, then, before February, 1640, when he is first mentioned in the records of Hartford, the son left England with his wife, Mercy Ruscoe,

3. John Speed, *The Theatre of the Empire of Great-Britaine* (London, 1627), 39–40.

HENRY SEYMOUR

and two children. The Seymours of Hartford, Litchfield, and New York all derive from John (1639–1713), who married a Mary Watson, in 1665. This John was the fourth child and second son of the emigrant, a younger brother of Thomas, of Norwalk, to which town Richard had removed. Major Moses Seymour was the great-grandson of John Seymour of Norwalk. In 1763, at the age of twenty-one, Moses moved to Litchfield as a hat-maker's apprentice, and in 1771 married Mary Marsh, by whom he had the one daughter and the five sons already referred to.[4]

About the time New York put Thomas Jefferson in the White House, Henry Seymour set out for the western frontier, soon after his twenty-first birthday, carrying with him the three hundred dollars which his father, Moses, had given him. Arriving at one of the peaks of the watershed which divides the St. Lawrence River from the Susquehanna, he bought a patch of ground in what is now the southern part of Onondaga County, and put up a country store. A frame dwelling, obviously built about the middle of the nineteenth century, which now occupies the site at the southern end of the long village green, is still persistently, but inaccurately, pointed out as the birthplace of his son, Horatio, whose fame was one day to surpass his own. This little cross-roads village, originally called Butler's Hill after the first tavern-keeper, Ebenezer Butler of Connecticut, who settled there in 1792, is situated seventeen hundred and forty-three feet above tidewater. From this hill, perhaps the coolest, coldest, and most beautiful part of the country, one can look out into seven counties, now that the land has long been cleared of its forests.

Although the township had been named Pompey as early as 1790 by the commissioners of the land office in New York City, the village itself where Henry Seymour settled as a shopkeeper was not commonly called Pompey Hill until 1811.[5] The

4. Mary Marsh was the daughter of Ebenezer and Deborah (Buell) Marsh. She was commonly called "Molly."

5. Van Brocklin, *et al.*, *Old Town of Pompey*, 179; Clark, *Onondaga*, II, 241–282.

great world of to-day has gone by it on both sides. Before a passage was made through the low marshlands which surrounded the upper reaches of the Mohawk to the north, Pompey Hill was on the main highway east and west through New York, and Henry Seymour prospered as a merchant. The township slowly filled up with New Englanders, who took to the countryside just as the foreign immigrants were to settle in the cities along the river valleys.[6] By 1811 Seymour had put up his second windmill, "built mainly for his own convenience in the preparation of grain for distilling," a year after the inhabitants of the village had collected the money necessary for raising a new home for what was to become their well known academy.

As he prospered, young Henry Seymour began to figure prominently in the affairs of the growing village, which was still the chief point of Onondaga County, for Syracuse, which rose on the site of the salt-wells of Salina, was not yet thought of. In 1809, he was chosen clerk by the town-meeting. Nine years after he arrived at Pompey Hill, Seymour's one hundred dollars was the largest contribution in the list of subscriptions for a new building for Pompey Academy, founded about ten years before. His influence and efforts for the little school were constant. He was elected senior trustee, serving later as treasurer. He was a generous contributor, also, to the white-steepled New England meeting-house which still faces the green, and just before he left his adopted village to go down to Utica and start the construction of the first section of the Erie Canal, he gave the congregation the huge leather-bound Bible which can be seen in the old church to-day. Back in Connecticut Henry Seymour's father and mother had both become Episcopalians, largely as a result of pious and persistent quarrels among the Congregationalists of their neighborhood. Out on the frontier, however, freedom of choice among sects was limited, and so, in the records of the First Congregational Society of Pompey,

6. University of Wisconsin Library: Dissertation (1900): Winden, "Influence of the Erie Canal," 73–74.

New York, under the date of January 17, 1813, there is to be found this entry of baptism: "Horatio and Sophia Apollina, children of Henry Seymour." [7]

Within six years of the time he first settled at Pompey Hill the ambitious young store-keeper had taken a wife in Cazenovia, even to-day one of the most beautiful towns of Madison County, on the highway between Pompey Hill and Utica. The young lady was the daughter of Colonel Jonathan Forman, who had first come into the state from New Jersey as a member of the expedition which General James Sullivan led against the Indians. After the Revolution he settled down in the country, establishing himself and family on new land just within the western frontier. In the old family Bible, now at Albany, his record of the wedding reads as follows:

> On Thursday evening at candle-light, January the 1st. 1807, was the marriage of our only dear surviving daughter, Mary Ledyard Forman to Mr. Henry Seymour, merchant of Pompey (a native of Litchfield, Connecticut) by the Reverend Joshua Leonard, with my severe, lonely, but entire approbation.[8]

The bride was twenty-one; her husband was not yet twenty-seven. A little more than twenty years later their sixth and last child was born, completing a family of two boys and four girls: Mary Forman, Horatio, Sophia Apollina, Jonathan Forman, Helen Clarissa, and Julia Catharine, the youngest, who was one day to become the wife of the able and arrogant Roscoe Conkling. The Seymours kept up the connection with Cazenovia; years afterward, Helen Clarissa married Ledyard Lincklaen, son of a Dutchman who had settled in the district.

Henry Seymour's first adventure beyond his neighborhood came with the second war with England, when he served as brigade quartermaster for General Jacob Brown, going on duty

7. "First Congregational Society of Pompey, New York," 1 (1796–1815), 33. These parish records were (1929) in the possession of Charles W. Jerome, an elder of what is now the Presbyterian church of Pompey.

8. New York State Library: Seymour Papers. A copy made from the Forman Bible by Mrs. Helen Lincklaen Fairchild, granddaughter of the bride and groom, is to be found in the Seymour Papers in the New York Historical Society.

as early as September, 1812. His usefulness in the service was more important than it was spectacular, and Seymour might easily have remained nothing more than the leading citizen of a town so prolific in able men even as Pompey Hill, except for the decisive chance which led to his election to the legislature. At that time, state senators were chosen by the electors from four districts into which New York was divided for the purpose, the southern, the middle, the eastern, and the western. From the last, Henry Seymour and Stephen Bates were sent to Albany in April, 1815.[9]

Daniel D. Tompkins, political hero of the late war, was at the apex of his power. He was serving his third term as governor and was yet to be elected to his fourth, and every one of the senatorial districts except the eastern was Democratic. Tompkins was not only a hero of the war but the great northern ally of the "Virginia Dynasty." From the middle district came Martin Van Buren, of Kinderhook, in Columbia County, who sat in the state senate from 1813 to 1820. Van Buren was a supporter of the governor, and was already planning the overthrow of DeWitt Clinton, favorite nephew and secretary of Governor George Clinton — with whom he is often carelessly confused by generations which have all but forgotten both men. Having his future schemes in mind, Van Buren had allied himself with the Tammany men of New York City to form the nucleus of the Bucktails, once a famous faction of the Democratic party.[10] The first article of this alliance was hostility to the Clinton dynasty in the person of DeWitt. The second, which was to be written into the bargain at a later date, was opposition to the Erie Canal, derisively called "Clinton's ditch." Clinton was accused by these astute enemies of being self-

9. Hammond, *History*, 1, 401. For the complicated system of election to the state senate, see Werner, *Civil List*, 368–369.

10. Opposition to Clinton began in New York City among members of the Tammany Society. In the campaign of 1817 other opponents of DeWitt Clinton upstate joined these New Yorkers and took to wearing short tails of buck deer in their hats — "wherefore the anti-Clinton faction became known as the Bucktail party" — a name given by the Clintonians "in derision": Johnson and Smith, *History*, 1, 410.

seeking, hostile to the Virginians, and a Federalist at heart. The very year Henry Seymour was first elected to the senate, Clinton, who had opposed Madison for President in 1812 and Tompkins for governor in 1813, was ousted from his post as mayor of New York, in face of his vigorous support by the Irish, whose votes he sought consistently. This Clinton–Van Buren feud makes a long and elaborate story; in the course of it, however, the "Little Magician" began to look to the western part of the state for likely allies.[11]

The young merchant from Pompey Hill was just the kind of man Van Buren took delight in: he was able and active and, above all, suave. In 1816 and 1817, therefore, Seymour was safely reëlected to the senate from the western district. A first attempt to put him on the council of appointment was a failure, but on January 31, 1818, he took his seat for the one-year term to which service was limited.[12] The object of the management in this matter (once Clinton had become governor) was to select a council that "gave Clinton credit for controlling appointments without the slightest power of making them, so that the disappointed held him responsible and the fortunate gave him no thanks."[13] The moment the council was chosen Van Buren wrote to a friend in Columbia County: "All is safe. Seymour! Seymour! Seymour!"[14] The personnel and the powers of this council of appointment were the school, and often the scandal, of early New York politics.[15] Seymour remained a loyal Van Buren man through thick and thin: those who are interested in the squabbles and interminable intrigues

11. Hammond, *History*, I, 435–474; 489–490.

12. Hammond, *History*, I, 417.

13. Alexander, *History*, I, 261.

14. Hammond, *History*, I, 458–459.

15. This council of appointment supplanted under the first state constitution, 1777–1821, the executive council of the colonial period. It consisted of one senator from each of four great districts, openly nominated and appointed each year by the assembly, no senator being eligible for two years in succession. The governor was the presiding officer of the council and had a casting vote. This council filled up all the non-elective offices of the state, the several members of the council having concurrent power of nomination after 1801: Werner, *Civil List*, 367.

over appointments will find an amusing account, at first hand, in the history by Jabez Hammond.[16]

Clinton had been almost unanimously elected governor for the first of four times in the sensational campaign of the spring of 1817; taking office on July 1, he went to Rome, in Oneida County, where, on the fourth, he turned the initial spade of earth for the Erie Canal. Men whom Clinton could defeat in a canvass, however, often showed themselves his masters in a caucus, for the new governor's character was cold, and a certain confidence, perhaps arrogance, of manner made the people who worked with him feel a little too much like his errand boys.[17] While Clinton presided and looked on helplessly, Van Buren's men removed the secretary of state and generally got control of all appointments throughout New York. By the end of 1818 Van Buren, of the whole number of thirty-two senators, was leading his devoted faction of thirteen with such ability that a majority of the senate usually fell in with his plans. The gentleman from Kinderhook was determined to dispose of Clinton. Hammond, at one time the firm friend of the latter (who later accused him of treachery), comments as follows on Henry Seymour's part in the success of this scheme:

> I do not think his opposition to Governor Clinton originated from personal motives. I am inclined to believe that the apprehension that Mr. Clinton's policy, if sustained, would endanger the republican party, and his attachment personally to Mr. Van Buren, controlled him in his political action.[18]

Thus, by the end of 1818, Henry Seymour had become valuable to the founder of the system soon to be known as the "Albany Regency." The principles and the policies of this regency produced some of the most powerful personalities to be found in the history of New York. By 1822 this informal gov-

16. For 1818, the council of appointment consisted of Peter R. Livingston of Dutchess, Jabez D. Hammond of Otsego, Henry Yates, Jr., of Schenectady, and Henry Seymour of Onondaga. Livingston and Seymour were hostile to Clinton; Hammond was friendly (until the quarrel of 1826), and Yates resented the dictation and interference of Clinton's brother-in-law, Judge Ambrose Spencer. Livingston, Seymour, and Yates controlled most of the appointments: *Military Minutes of the Council of Appointment*, III, 1858–1859.

17. Alexander, *History*, I, Preface, iv.

18. Hammond, *History*, I, 455–456.

ernment within a government had gained recognition in Washington as the first agent and ally of the administration; it enjoyed the respect of President Monroe and was courted for its favor by more than one of the rivals who hoped to succeed him. DeWitt Clinton was left out in the cold, and thereafter, until his sudden death, early in 1828, he had to play a lone, if sometimes successful, hand. In and out of the governorship Clinton's policy was to build up a personal party out of disgruntled Democrats and hopeless Federalists, and, as he went about his work, his reputation and his power with the voters not only made the Erie Canal possible but were, in turn, greatly enhanced by its completion and its astonishing success.

The digging and the manning of the canal provided spoils for the politicians in the form of contracts and positions, and Van Buren was quick to see the implication. Of these spoils he would build up his machine for running the state of New York. His capture of the control of the canal was characteristically adroit. A majority of the canal board was the first objective, for with that would go the appointing power to thousands of posts all along the route of its construction and the awarding of profitable contracts from Albany right through to Buffalo. Van Buren's ultimate goal, of course, was an organization which should manage the government of the whole state. Everything fitted together neatly: in the round of his professional employment as a lawyer, Van Buren had acquired "an important estate near Oswego, whose value rapidly enhanced with the rapid growth of western New York and the development of the lake commerce from that port." [19] The Erie Canal was to transform this country from a wilderness into a land of farms and populous towns. The very men who had once opposed the canal suddenly became its champions and the dispensers of its prizes. They bought up real estate, for, as canals extended, land rose in value along the routes they followed. Although this waterway was to make New York City the chief port of the nation and the Hudson and the Mohawk rivers the thoroughfare to the Middle

19. Edward M. Shepard, *Martin Van Buren* (Boston and New York, 1888 and 1916), 26–31.

West, residents of the city were among the very last to be convinced of the great opportunity it offered to the state. Van Buren's first task, therefore, was to overcome the short-sighted hostility of his Bucktail allies at the mouth of the Hudson. How much the prospect of getting good contracts prevailed in this negotiation and how much Van Buren's eloquence, it is difficult to say, for one of the most persistent and practical traditions of the regency was a preference for talking things over in secret rather than writing letters.

Seymour would soon be ready for some new employment, for one year was a man's maximum length of service on the council of appointment; his term would come to an end early in 1819. He was eminently eligible for promotion. Though luck again favored Van Buren, his plans almost miscarried. During the summer of 1818 Joseph Ellicott, agent for the Holland Land Company, having sunk into a melancholia which was to end in suicide, suddenly resigned his post as canal commissioner. Governor Clinton seized the opportunity and temporarily filled the vacancy with one of his supporters, Ephraim Hart. The permanent appointment rested with the legislature, just as the election of senators to the Congress.[20] Hammond warned Clinton to beware, but the governor was confident, as always. When the legislature filled the office on March 24, 1819, Henry Seymour was chosen on a joint ballot by a majority of exactly one vote. Van Buren and his Bucktail allies had gained control of the commission of five members, and with that control went all the patronage and political power "which was felt along the whole line of country from Albany to Lakes Champlain and Erie." The editor of the Albany *Argus*, organ of the regency, openly rejoiced at the result:

> A majority of the canal commissioners are now politically opposed to the Governor, and it will not be necessary for a person who wishes to obtain employment on the canal as agent, contractor or otherwise, to avow himself a Clintonian.[21]

20. Werner, *Civil List*, 226.

21. For the intricate story of this political manœuvre, see Hammond, *History*, I, 495–497; Alexander, *History*, I, 261; and Van Buren, *Autobiography*, 91.

Jesse Buel's statement put the matter mildly: actually, the Erie Canal had become the political property of the enemies of Clinton. The governor's victory in the council of appointment for 1819 was cold comfort, for the vast majority of the jobs in the state were no longer given out by that body. The control of the canal commission by his opponents was to "annoy and prostrate" Governor Clinton, whether in or out of office, to the day of his death.

Once they were completed, canals were taken for granted; then, after the railroads had made them almost useless, they were filled up and forgotten. Yet, even to-day, what is now called the Barge Canal, dredged out along almost the same course as that which was laid out for the Old Erie from the Hudson River to Buffalo, remains the lasting monument of DeWitt Clinton. The development of the plans for the great canal has a much longer history than the eight years required to dig it, once it was actually begun. The fortunate fact that the Hudson River had cut through the northern extension of the Allegheny Mountains at what was called the Highlands gave free passage to ships as far as Albany. This river became the axis of the Dutch colony of New Netherland. The trading post called Fort Orange was planted at the eastern end of the convenient road which led over to the valley of the Mohawk and thence up to the portage and down again through Oneida Lake and its river to Oswego and Lake Ontario.

The slow growth of the idea by which the dream of a canal became a reality has been carefully set forth in the voluminous appendix which Dr. David Hosack attached to his *Memoir of De Witt Clinton*, published the year after the great governor's death.[22] Hosack was as diligent in his enquiries as he was loyal to the memory of Clinton, who never once, publicly or privately,

22. Hosack, *De Witt Clinton*, 209–504. In *Public Documents Relating to the New-York Canals . . . to Connect the Western and Northern Lakes with the Atlantic Ocean; with an Introduction*, by Charles G. Haines, students will find a valuable collection of reports and papers which were printed by the New York Corresponding Association for the Promotion of Internal Improvements. See, for instance, a detailed statement of contracts for the middle section of the Erie Canal, on pages 335 and 336.

spoke of himself as having been the author of the plan for such a canal. Perhaps the earliest document to call attention to the commercial and military value of the Hudson–Mohawk route by water to the region of the Great Lakes was a memorial addressed to Governor Burnet by Cadwallader Colden, in 1724. Colden was at the time surveyor-general of the province of New York and afterwards served as lieutenant-governor. His sole object was to show British colonials the ease with which the Indian fur-trade could be successfully diverted from the valley of the St. Lawrence to that of the Hudson.

George Washington visited the region of the Mohawk River shortly after the Revolution and, having viewed the portages and communications with Lake Ontario, was struck with the possibilities of the "vast inland navigation" of what was soon to be one of the greatest of the "United States." Gouverneur Morris indulged what were thought to be grandiose notions of boats going by water all the way from New York City to Lake Erie. General Philip Schuyler helped promote the Western Inland Lock and Navigation Company in 1792 and invested money in it. So far as can be discovered, the earliest legislative reference to what was to become the great work of the future occurs in the *Journals* of the assembly for Friday, March 17, 1786, on which date

> Mr. Jeffrey Smith moved for leave to bring in a bill entitled, "An act for improving the navigation of the Mohawk River, Wood Creek, and the Onondaga River, with a view to opening an inland navigation to Oswego, and for extending the same, if practicable, to Lake Erie."

The person deserving chief credit for first having drawn the attention of DeWitt Clinton to the plan is probably Jesse Hawley, who published a series of fourteen essays in the Genesee *Messenger* printed at Canandaigua, over the signature "Hercules" during the years 1807 and 1808. Hosack reprinted these articles in their entirety and added a letter from the author, who was living at Rochester in 1829, which tells how Simeon DeWitt, the surveyor-general, made use of his essays on a tour of exploration through the middle part of the state in

1810, DeWitt Clinton being one of the commissioners who accompanied him. In 1812, Clinton himself borrowed Hawley's essays from the latter's brother and had them in his hands for eight years. Clinton was dead when Jesse Hawley, or "Hercules," summed up his estimate of the governor's share in the famous achievement.

> The great merit of Mr. Clinton, in relation to the canal, consists in his having put his powerful mind to the investigation of the subject, and, probably with great labour, comprehending the magnitude of its utility and the splendour of its enterprise; and failing to render it a national work, he conceived the idea of rendering it a state undertaking and property — an idea which had escaped all others, from the supposed inadequacy of the state resources to accomplish it — resolutely shouldering the responsibility of the measure, at the hazard of his popularity and reputation — while others were confronting him with assertions that it would require the revenue of all the kingdoms of the earth, and the population of China, to accomplish it.
>
> Although others claim it for him, yet Mr. Clinton never claimed for himself the original idea of the canal. In his essays to Colonel Troup, written in 1820, he assigned that to me.[23]

It is amusing to remember and look back on the rancorous debate over the expense of a project which was to cost the "immense" sum of five million dollars. There were two chief differences of opinion among the disputants. In the first place, there was the usual chorus from those cautious or cowardly people who were sure that money would be wasted on work which would never be completed (or if it were completed would be found to be useless), that the credit of the state would never bear the burden, and so forth. In the second place, there was no general agreement as to the best course for the canal. All those who were not wholly opposed to any canal whatever, supported the project for a waterway from Albany as far as Oswego. Even allowing for a branch canal southwestward from Oswego to the salt-wells at Salina, a great many people felt that to parallel Lake Ontario with a trench of water from Salina to Buffalo would be an act of folly and extravagance.[24]

23. Hosack, *De Witt Clinton*, 303–304.
24. [Beach], *Considerations Against Continuing the Great Canal.*

Up to this point, the debates over plans for an Erie Canal read like ancient history.

Competition between the Hudson and St. Lawrence valleys for the rich trade of the Great Lakes is still very much alive even to-day. DeWitt Clinton's unanswerable objection to using Lake Ontario in place of digging a canal parallel to it sounds quite modern. Produce from the West which once reached the waters of that lake, he maintained, would almost certainly follow the course of the St. Lawrence on the way to Europe. In objection to his argument it was pointed out that ice would make the Canadian route impassable for almost half the year, and that if carriers became accustomed to going by way of Oswego and the New York route for six months, they would, in all probability, continue to use that means of passage for twelve. Clinton finally had his way, however, and the line of the great canal as laid out by 1817 covered three hundred and sixty-four miles between the Hudson and Buffalo.

Lake Erie is five hundred and fifty feet higher above sea-level than Albany, and this difference in elevation had to be overcome east of Utica, west of which extends a level stretch of seventy miles. The work on the canal was started in the midst of this plain, and Utica was the first centre of operations. There Henry Seymour made his headquarters, for he had been given the management of the construction of that section of the canal between Utica and Rome. This middle portion of "Clinton's ditch" was literally scooped out through marshlands by hundreds and thousands of "wild Irish," working half-naked. Swine were turned loose to kill off the rattlesnakes which infested the whole region. Year after year the work went forward with a persistence and a speed which public enterprises are vulgarly supposed to lack. In eight years' time a highway for water was hollowed out through plain and woodland from Albany north to Lakes George and Champlain and west to Buffalo. Locks carried the canal up the hills and down again, and bridges, or aqueducts, carried it over valleys. Whole colonies of workers and their descendants settled down in the cities which grew up along the route and soon made the more native inhabitants familiar with the speech and manners of foreigners, and with the spires of Catholic churches tipped with gilded crosses.

When Henry Seymour moved his wife and five children from Pompey Hill down to the little town of Utica early in 1820, his son Horatio was not yet ten years old.[25] The canal law of 1819, which authorized an annual loan of six hundred thousand dollars on the credit of the state, drove the work forward. Seymour helped to defeat Clintonian opposition to this measure with one of the last votes he cast in the senate at Albany. He was to serve twelve years on the canal commission, always as one of its most influential members.[26] Two terms in the assembly, to which he was elected in 1818 and 1821, completed his legislative career; thereafter, he seems to have acted in the capacity of a field-agent for the regency.[27] Slowly, but always more certainly, he became known as a firm opponent of DeWitt Clinton — affable in manner and always courteous but persuasive and effective.[28] Had he stayed on in politics, Henry Seymour might well have become governor one day, for the year that Yates was nominated (1822) he was mentioned for the office to which his own son was elected just thirty years later.[29]

As early as 1819 Seymour had the first part of his section of the canal in navigable condition. On October 22 the first boat set out from Rome; the next day Governor Clinton and

25. Fort Schuyler, named for Colonel Peter Schuyler, an uncle of General Philip Schuyler, was built on the present site of Utica in 1758. According to French, *Gazetteer*, 469, this fort was a stockaded work which stood between Main and Mohawk Streets, below Second Street.

26. Terms of the five commissioners were indeterminate; death or resignation usually ended a man's service. DeWitt Clinton was removed by the vote of the legislature on April 12, 1824, and Samuel Young was treated likewise as late as 1840: Werner, *Civil List*, 226–227.

27. New York Historical Society: Seymour Papers: See a characteristic letter to Perry G. Childs, of Cazenovia, October 28, 1820.

28. Hammond, *History*, I, 496.

29. Hammond, *History*, II, 97–98.

the five commissioners, "attended by about seventy ladies and gentlemen," embarked at Utica for the return trip.[30] James Schouler gives a pleasant picture of what travel by canal was soon to be.

> Old people and slow have recalled with a sigh those peaceful days when a family party might charter the entire cabin of an Erie canal boat, and glide at leisure on the safest voyage of its length ever projected by civilized man, eating and sleeping on board, and varying the monotony by striding the tow-path in advance of the horses, and sitting at the next lock to see the boat come up and take its new level. The dust and jolting of the stage were avoided, though the journey should consume more time. But the anxious business man who made one of twenty-five passengers whose majority, excluded from the red-curtained sanctuary of the fair sex, were compelled to eat, dress, and sleep in an outer saloon, gave a less pleasing picture of life by such conveyance. One wearied of being drawn incessantly through tame meadow scenery by horses whose jog-trot at the end of a long rope was sobriety itself; of delays at the locks; of low bridges which passengers on the deck had to shun by lying flat at the steersman's call; of the berths which were swung at night in tiers like hanging book-shelves, for which passengers drew lots. Had canal boats continued much longer in fashion they would have been propelled by steam.[31]

John Quincy Adams painted a less cheerful picture. In 1843 he crossed Ohio on the *Rob Roy*, keeping a careful record of his trials and tribulations. Twenty-one passengers were crowded into a boat eighty-three feet long and fifteen feet wide, with a compartment in the bow for the ladies and side settees about an iron stove in the centre where the men slept, "feet to feet." The windows of the cabins had to be kept closed against "the driving snow," and the stoves in the different compartments, crammed with "billets of wood," made the whole boat "uncomfortably warm." "So much humanity crowded into such a compass," wrote the former President, "was a trial such as I had

30. Good accounts of the planning and completing of the Erie Canal are to be found in Clark, *Onondaga*, II, 54–65; Turner, *Holland Purchase*, 617–637; Wager, *Our County* [Oneida], 215–223; and Winden, "Influence of the Erie Canal." Several descriptions of travel on the canal will be found in Thwaites, *Historic Waterways*, *passim*. For a brief statement of the way in which the canal transformed New York, see J. T. Adams, in Wright, *New England's Prospect*, 8–9. A particularly good narrative of the digging of the Erie Canal is that in Durant, *Oneida County*, 177–183.

31. James Schouler, *Eighty Years of Union* (New York, 1903), 268.

never before experienced, and my heart sunk within me when, squeezing into this pillory, I reflected that I am to pass three nights and four days in it." In spite of a "comfortless evening," Mr. Adams found his fellow travellers "well-bred persons and pleasant companions." They could see that they were in "a beautiful country, with a deep, rich soil," but the stumps of former forests gave "an aspect rather of desolation than of plenty." The New Englander had difficulty in "keeping up with the flight of time" by posting his journal, and he beguiled some of his "supernumerary hours" with "card-parties at whist and eucre — a game of which I had never heard before." He wrote amidst "perpetual interruptions" in the presence of other passengers who seemed to think him "a strange, sulky person." What most annoyed Mr. Adams was the bumping of the boat through the "numberless" locks — "careless and unskilful steering" — which made the vessel stagger along "like a stumbling nag." [32]

The brick house which was Henry Seymour's dwelling in Utica stood almost on the bank of the original route of the canal, which then passed directly through the city by what is now known as Oriskany Street. The commercial remains of the old residence can be seen to-day in Whitesboro Street facing south with the Mohawk River at the back. Just north lie the Barge Canal and the main line of the great railroad which was one day to push the canal into second place. In the twenties and thirties of the last century, however, water was still the more important means of travel and trade, and Henry Seymour's son may be said to have inherited his lifelong loyalty to the great canal of Clinton's dream. Until the close of the Civil War the advantages and the success of the achievement to which the father contributed with distinction more than justified the traditional interest of the son and that son's nephews. As in all cases involving courage and imagination the supporters of the canal had to encounter the complaints of critics and skeptics, and the

32. *Memoirs of John Quincy Adams*, Charles Francis Adams, Editor, (Philadelphia, 1874–1877), XI, 417–420.

prophets of calamity. Farmers living in remote regions saw no good reason why they should be taxed to pay the interest on loans which would be spent on public works that would benefit limited areas. Once the financial success of the parent system had silenced these protests, however, a clamor for canals rose from every county in the state, and waterways were extended extravagantly. Still other farmers complained of the competition of western wheat in the markets of New York City and Europe. Why should easterners tax themselves to provide cheap carriage through the country for the products of the farms of Ohio and Illinois? Canals, their length, width, depth, and then their tolls, were genuine political issues in New York for over forty years, and no matter what aspect of the subject might be under discussion Horatio Seymour was completely at home. The persistence of these problems accounts for much of his reputation and success. Political opponents might call him the champion of rum, but wiser men knew that Seymour was the best friend water ever had.

In the autumn of 1825 the Erie Canal was officially opened from Buffalo to Albany, and Governor Clinton performed a pompous wedding of the waters, emptying a cask he had filled at Lake Erie into the harbor of New York. The contemptible "ditch" was completed, but Henry Seymour held on to the lucrative office of canal commissioner for more than five years until the growth of his investments in real estate and stocks drew him out of politics and into business. In 1833 he served one year, by appointment, as mayor of Utica, and then performed his last public service when Governor Marcy made him one of a commission of three, with Benjamin Franklin Butler and Peter Augustus Jay, to join with a like commission from New Jersey and run the disputed boundary line between the two states.[33] Because Jabez Hammond, the historian, was not

33. A copy of this letter of appointment, March 12, 1833, is in the Seymour Papers, at the New York Historical Society. For the settlement of the boundary question, see *Report of the Regents of the University on the Boundaries of the State of New York*, 1, 235–239. The six commissioners signed in New York City, September 16, 1833; the legislatures of New York and New Jersey ratified on

only an actual participant in New York politics but a factional foe of Henry Seymour, his favorable opinion of Van Buren's canal commissioner is important. His occasional comments on Seymour's character and person foreshadow fair judgment of the more famous son.

He was a well bred man, and very gentlemanly in his deportment. His great native shrewdness and sagacity had been improved and highly cultivated by an association with genteel society. As a politician, he was cautious and wary. His opponents charged him with being jesuitical, but of this I cannot speak from my own knowledge; for he certainly never gave me any proofs of a want of sincerity and candor.

And again, at the time of Seymour's resignation from the canal board in 1831, Hammond ushered him out of his history with as plain a compliment as one politician can ever pay another:

It is due to the memory of Mr. Seymour to say, that notwithstanding the immense amount of moneys which passed through his hands, and the many and vastly important contracts made by him on the part of the state, that not the least suspicion has ever been breathed against the purity of his character and conduct. He was in all respects a correct business man.[34]

Already, a century ago, the lure of making money had begun to draw ability from the public service of politics to the private gain of business. Instead of waiting to be a governor Henry Seymour became a banker. In 1835 he was made president of the Farmers' Loan and Trust Company, and settled in New York City, leaving his family in Utica.[35] At first he put up at an old-fashioned hotel on lower Broadway kept by a man and wife from Nantucket — the famous Bunker's Mansion House, where New Yorkers of the late nineteenth century could still remember having occasionally seen a little old bright-eyed gentleman with a round head, who was pointed out with caution and some awe to strangers as Mr. Aaron Burr, late Vice-President of the United States, the "murderer" of Alexander Hamilton, and

February 5 and 26, respectively, 1834; the settlement was ratified by the United States on June 28, 1834.

34. Hammond, *History*, I, 455; II, 367.

35. Lanier, *Century of Banking in New York*, 275–287. The company was incorporated by the New York legislature on February 28, 1822, as the Farmers' Fire Insurance and Loan Company.

more recently the unhappy spouse of the "Widow Jumel," the man whose trial at Richmond for treason had made even Thomas Jefferson look vengeful and ridiculous. Seymour lived at Bunker's a little more than two years, and then he left the city, never to return.

He had entered New York banking in the midst of the Jackson boom: people were prosperous, happy, and improvident. Gambling in land was the favorite folly of the time. Seymour was growing rich, and the future looked serene. Then suddenly, after his long success, every circumstance seemed to conspire against him. The bank of which he was head had started out as a kind of insurance company, heavily committed in the real estate of the city. During his first winter in New York occurred the disastrous fire of 1835, which burned out a large section of the business district and destroyed confidence and credit as well. Quick on the heels of one disaster came another. Early in the morning of March 31, 1837, a great fire at Utica burned away the central part of the city which was still his home. Van Buren replaced Jackson in the White House, but less than two months later prosperity collapsed from one end of the country to the other; banks suspended payments, and by the summer of 1837 business was a wreck. The President was torn by divided counsel; then, taking his courage in both hands, he called a special session of the Congress for the autumn. Fear was in the air, and as usual the rich were most afraid of all. The legislature of New York gave the state banks one year's grace in which to resume payments before they should lose their precious charters.

In August of 1837 Henry Seymour hurried back to Utica for a rest from hot, anxious days and sleepless nights. Although his son Horatio had been handling his business upstate, and making what was soon to prove the best of a bad situation, the father had put too many irons in the fire to manage them all. Years of constant work had probably made him incapable of taking vacations, and he began to brood. Before long he was obsessed with the notion that he was ruined: the rich man's nightmare of the poorhouse broke him. Soon his "singular conduct" caused him to be watched. All his life he had been subject to occasional "depression of spirits," but now the "calmness of mind and decision of character for which he was conspicuous" seemed to have been "palpably impaired." He could only sit and wait. Late in August, however, he grew so silent and quiet that he was left unguarded for a short time. In that moment, about seven o'clock in the morning of August 26, he shot himself to death in his own dwelling.[36] He was buried respectably at Utica, on Tuesday, at eleven, officially lamented — an object of envy, perhaps — the most distinguished local victim of the first great American plague of a panic.

Suicide a hundred years ago caused rather more shock and scandal than it does to-day, when the strain of life and the fight for success have made it common and condoned. Over thirty years afterward the fact that Henry Seymour had killed himself was dug up and dwelt upon by Republican journalists and stump-speakers, as a plausible means of explaining the "softening of the brain" which made a Democratic candidate for President unfit for the White House. The good people of the United States were solemnly warned against voting for a man who might suddenly give them Frank Blair for his successor. Although Horatio Seymour never publicly referred to his father's unhappy death, the tragedy left its mark on his character. The psychological effect of the misfortune shows in his belief that life should be lived pleasantly. He was faithful in office and could work hard when he would, but his father's fate had taught him that success can sometimes cost a man too much for peace of mind. Friends were to think of him as courteous and gracious, always serene, even in the midst of their own excitement. His mastery of the art of not seeming to be annoyed was to irritate those of his enemies who liked to be annoyed.

Henry Seymour had exaggerated his misfortune. His widow

36. Utica *Observer*, August 29, 1837. A good miniature of Henry Seymour is reproduced in Wall, *Seymour*, 13, in which book will also be found pictures of his father and mother.

and six children eventually received comfortable sums out of the widely scattered and involved estate he left them. Although this favorable upshot was due largely to Horatio's cautious handling of the assets during many years of anxiety, the ground-work for success had been well laid — money had only to be saved and managed — not made. Thus, at the age of twenty-seven, young Seymour was left in charge of two families at the same time. Long afterward, Mrs. Roscoe Conkling — she who had been the baby sister, Julia — loved to recall her brother's industry and even temper during the doubtful days when "there never seemed to be much money" for the eight people who lived together in the late Henry Seymour's lead-colored brick dwelling, under the two big elms on Whitesboro Street in Utica. That reliable brother was learning how to live without anger, and yet persist and prevail — qualities of character which would stand him in good stead when he heard the howls of rage at his veto of the Maine bill, or the roar of rioting against the draft, or the wild cheers which welcomed him to his gallant battle against hatred, greed, and gullibility, and the brittle glory of General Grant.

II

TO SCHOOL WITH MARCY

1833–1839

HORATIO SEYMOUR'S earliest surviving letter deals, characteristically enough, with the management of land, a subject with which has father's absence made him well acquainted after 1835.[1] He was not yet twenty-five, but the tone and content of this letter show that the young lawyer was being encouraged to acquire that experience which suddenly became necessary to him in the midst of the tragic summer of 1837. He was the second child — his sister Mary was the first — but the elder of two sons; and the admiring fashion in which his younger brother, Jonathan Forman — or John F. — played second fiddle to Horatio was sometimes the cause of unkind ridicule among people who did not like the Seymour family or the politics of its most distinguished member. Even their friends called them "Big Pomp" and "Little Pomp" — a picturesque reminder of their native village and their disparity of stature, for Horatio was tall and slender, and Jonathan was not. Perhaps the affectionate nicknames had reference, as well, to their respective achievements.

Horatio took his name from an uncle, his father's older brother, Whig senator from Vermont, on whose birthday he happened to be born. In so far, he might be said to have been the indirect beneficiary of his grandfather's admiration for the ambitious general to whom the dramatist, Burgoyne, surrendered his sword at Saratoga. The coincidence of his birth and the fact that Senator Seymour was very much the most successful member of the family at the time made the choice of a name for him obvious. Looking forward to the criticism which the New York

1. New York State Library: Manuscript Section: Horatio Seymour to John T. Cooper, Albany, April 4, 1835.

Horatio was one day to encounter, it is interesting to observe that this uncle from Vermont displayed certain of the very characteristics which led those who disagreed with his nephew to call him a hypocrite. Although the senator had the advantage of a college education, having been graduated from Yale in 1797, and represented Vermont for twelve years (1821–1833), he never once made a speech in the Senate. It was this same shyness which had made it impossible for him to deliver the commencement part on which President Dwight vainly insisted — a dereliction which did not prevent his receiving a doctorate of laws from his college in 1847, fifty years later. A local historian described the senator's character in words that sound familiar to a student of the life of his nephew:

> Mr. Seymour was constitutionally diffident and distrustful of himself. So far from seeking for office, we think he never accepted one but with reluctance and through the solicitation of his friends.[2]

Shy men who get what other men want are not infrequently called sly. Senator Seymour did not carry this constitutional diffidence into his private life, apparently, for he would seem to have been friendly and familiar with such diverse persons as John Quincy Adams, Clay, Webster, and Marcy. It was his habit to stop off in New York State on his way to and from Washington in order to pick up political information which might be of use. In May, 1824, Adams recorded in his diary:

> With Seymour, Crowninshield, and Taylor I had particular conversations — with the two former concerning the Presidential election, with the latter relative to the proceedings of the committee. Seymour, on his way home, will stop some time in the State of New York. His main anxiety is to make friends by giving assurances of a *Republican* Administration; Crowninshield's, to give at home correct views of facts.[3]

2. Samuel Swift, *History of the Town of Middlebury, in the County of Addison, Vermont* (Middlebury, 1859), II, 255–256.

3. Adams, *Memoirs*, VI, 363. In the spring of 1828 Senator Horatio Seymour urged Adams (*Memoirs*, VII, 540–541) not to remove his postmaster-general, McLean, because western senators had told him that "McLean was a Methodist preacher, and that all the Methodists in the United States felt a deep interest for him." It is plainly to be seen how easily New Englanders like Dix and Marcy learned the arts of the politicians of the Albany Regency.

The elder Horatio's "anxiety" to "make friends" passed by inheritance to his nephew. One gets an interesting glimpse of him from the *Memoirs* of the second Adams on the exciting eve of the choice of a President by the House of Representatives in 1825, when, according to the successful candidate, he "came to give me advices respecting the prospects of election." [4] Although he was an active Jeffersonian when he left Connecticut in 1799, his neighbors in Vermont and his associates in the Congress directed his affections toward the side of Clay. In 1831, for instance, he helped to defeat Benton's resolution that the charter of the Bank of the United States ought not to be renewed — by the close vote of 23 to 20.[5] By 1832, when he voted against the confirmation of Van Buren as minister to England in the famous tie which Vice-President Calhoun resolved with his casting vote, Horatio of Vermont could no longer have been politically intimate with his own brother, Henry, who was an active and staunch supporter of the victim of this famous and foolish act of revenge.

Until he was almost ten years old, the second Horatio Seymour lived at Pompey Hill, then the focal point of the county. In addition to a thriving and handsome church, the village took pride in its academy, over which the Reverend Joshua Leonard presided during the years 1815–1819. Leonard had come out to Onondaga from Connecticut, and he it was who had the good fortune to teach half a dozen of the ablest men of the next generation when they were boys. Years afterward, the earliest memories of Horatio's older sister, Mary, went back to the little country school where she and her brother sat on the same bench, with their father's little slave-boy, Ambrose, squeezed in between them. "The good people strongly opposed to blacks and slavery," according to the recollection of the caustic Mrs. Miller, "were not willing to have their children sit next him"; but "Horatio, Mary, and Ambrose" were always called together on the roll.[6] The experience of the child was

4. Adams, *Memoirs*, VI, 501. 5. Hammond, *History*, II, 349.
6. New York Historical Society: Seymour Papers. Slavery was not finally

not without significance, perhaps, for the man: all his life Seymour thought, spoke, and acted with a certain suspicion of the louder friends of freedom.

In 1820, when Henry Seymour moved to Utica to take charge of the construction of the middle section of the Erie Canal, Horatio was put to school in that town. At first he attended Oxford Academy, which was kept by David H. Prentice, "a noted teacher";[7] at one time, too, he studied under Fay Edgerton, who was an enthusiast on geology and mineralogy, and took his students on long excursions through New York and neighboring states.[8] The interest Edgerton inspired in one of his school-boys lasted to the end of the pupil's life, for if Horatio Seymour was ever consciously proud of any part of his learning, his comparatively thorough knowledge of the geography and the history of his own state was the source of that pride. He seems, first and last, to have attended several schools in Utica. For a period he studied with a retired British officer, Charles Stuart by name, a Scotsman of large stature, who persisted in wearing his national costume in the streets of a country town of North America and was known as a great stickler for discipline and correct carriage. This Scot with the noble name must have been also a successful teacher, for Seymour — until he grew stout a year or so before his death — was always noticeable for his erect and so-called "military" bearing. For two years, 1822–1824, Seymour attended Geneva Academy, now called Hobart College, where no trace of him can be found on the records except for the note of his having once been fined twelve and one-half cents for attending a circus.[9]

---

abolished in New York until 1827, when there were but few slaves to be set free. The present three-story stone building of Pompey Academy was put up in 1833, on the site of the old yellow wooden school-house. Its windows command a wide view of the country of the Iroquois and the fabled land of Hiawatha.

7. Utica *Weekly Herald*, February 16, 1886.

8. New York Historical Society: Seymour Papers: Box 3, Bundle VI.

9. Letter of the librarian of Hobart College to the author, December 28, 1929. On June 23, 1886, the Honorable Delano C. Calvin, LL.D., delivered before the associate alumni of Hobart College and the Phi Beta Kappa Society, *An Address in Memory of the Honorable Horatio Seymour, LL.D.*

THE INTERIOR OF POMPEY ACADEMY

The boy was delicate, however, and in the autumn of 1824 his father decided to send him to the American Literary Scientific and Military Academy, conducted by Captain Alden Partridge at Middletown, Connecticut.[10] At this school, where his first cousin, Thomas H. Seymour, was a cadet at the same time, Horatio Seymour spent about two years, returning to Utica healthier, if not much the wiser, for his experience. Captain Partridge had once been a "master of the sword" at West Point, of which he was a graduate, and then he set up his own academy. For some years he met with considerable success, drawing students from all over the Union. Slowly, however, the growing prestige of West Point put him out of business. To judge by the reports of two English ladies who happened to visit Partridge's academy during the same year, the captain (or, as one lady called him, the "colonel") was a "clown and a miser"; the buildings were "filthy and neglected," and the students were in an "uproar." Mrs. Basil Hall's sense of refinement was offended by what she saw at Middletown:

> I can judge of their manners and appearance and I must say that those are sadly backward. They all walk with a slouch and with their hands in their breeches' pockets. . . . They helped themselves to butter, stewed onions, salt, or potatoes, all with their own nasty knives, with which the moment before they had been eating, and spit to the right and left during their meal.[11]

Mrs. Anne Royall left posterity an even less complimentary description of this Connecticut boarding-school. The town itself, she graciously acknowledged, was beautiful, and she approached the grounds and buildings of the American Literary Scientific and Military Academy with high hopes. Her visit was hardly a success. The captain was a boor, and the boys

10. See the *Dictionary of American Biography*, XIV (1934), 281–282, for a sketch of Captain Alden Partridge (1785–1854). See, also, Field, *Cromwell . . . Middletown and its Parishes*, 108–110. The two oldest buildings of Wesleyan University were purchased for that institution at the time of the removal of the academy to Vermont, in 1829.

11. Hall, *Aristocratic Journey*, 112. For the complete text of Mrs. Anne Royall's opinion of the American Literary Scientific and Military Academy, see the *Black Book*, II, 75–80.

were barbarians. She was all but mobbed by the curious cadets, who were "romping and squealing all through the rooms"—who stared and shouted at her and blew horns in her angry ears. Mrs. Royall was leaving "in despair" when she encountered one of the faculty:

> He took me, at my request through some parts of the building, all corresponding with what I had seen; independently of the rudeness and vulgarity contracted at the academy, the cadets run the risks of their lives, from the danger of contagion, arising from the filth of the place. It is said of this C[aptain] P[artridge], that he is such a penurious wretch, that he would not advance as much money as would scour a room, if the whole building was to rot down. He is very unpopular in the town, and very deservedly so, no doubt. He is said to be the greatest miser in the world, a character that is always despised. He dresses like a sweep, from pure love of money, which he is making off of the infatuated people, equal to coining. He has upwards of 200 scholars, from all parts of the Union, and even the West Indies! Nothing but that unaccountable propensity in man for novelty, could ever have thought of patronizing a man of such appearance. He is, I am told, accumulating vast sums of money, in this way, and not contented with one, it seems, he is enabled to establish another academy in one of the adjoining states. . . . I saw, by looking over the catalogue, it had a great number of professors, and amongst other things, a professor of Belles Lettres!

Captain Partridge seems to have been something of a martinet, whose lack of proper management or good manners made trouble. If Horatio Seymour never quite learned to trust the military mind, it is possible that his life at Middletown, Connecticut, may account for his suspicion of soldiers. He was not yet fifty-one when Fort Sumter was fired on, and though never sympathetic with the extremists at the South, he did not join the army which would conquer them after four years. He liked to make fun of a political general like Dix, who had "gone to the war poor and had come back rich." His keen sense of the fitness of things may have prevented him from adding himself to the burden which a Banks, a Butler, or a Burnside was to make for the weary shoulders of Lincoln. He gave both time and money to the business of recruiting men for the armies of the Union, not only in New York but in his second state of Wisconsin. A Republican governor, Morgan, put him in charge of the work in his own county of Oneida and there he served with distinguished success. He seems never to have thought of rushing off to the war in person. As a former governor of New York, Seymour would have had to be some kind of general, sooner or later, but his knowledge of his own limitations, it may safely be supposed, saved the distracted government of the United States from an additional misfortune.

Captain Alden Partridge had mastered the art of advertisement. During the winter of 1826 he took his boys on a trip to Baltimore and Washington, parading and manœuvring them at various stops along the way — partly as a means of drawing attention to his school. Their reception at the capital was cordial, for the most part: Henry Clay, in particular, delighted the cadets with the charm and warmth of his welcome. President Adams left behind him the following record of this visit:

[December 19, 1826] Captain Partridge came with the detachment of his cadets at one o'clock. He first drew them up in front of the house, where they paid me a military salute, after which I sent my son John to him and invited them all into the house, where they were individually introduced to me and shook hands with me. Refreshments were handed to them, and the Captain intimated an expectation that I should address them in a speech — which I declined.

Messrs. Gales and Seaton, and Force, the editors of the National Intelligencer, and Journal, were here, probably with the same expectation; but on the part of Partridge it is a mere expedient of quackery to drum up recruits for his school, which is already quite as successful as it deserves. He has now nearly three hundred scholars at Middletown, many of whom are withdrawn from colleges and universities, to be drilled into soldiers, marched about the country laying the people under contributions of hospitality, and getting puffed by newspapers into fashion and popularity. It is well that the modes of education should be varied; that a competent number of surveyors, engineers, and military officers should be formed among the youth of the country; but I felt no inclination to extol the system of military education, nor to discountenance it by remarking how much more suited to usefulness and respectability in after-life is a college education than that of a military academy can possibly be. I therefore barely thanked them for their visit as they were going away, told them I should be glad to see them again occasionally while they should remain here, and that I wished them all prosperity and success in their studies and pursuits. Their visit was of about half an hour, and at their departure they were again drawn up and gave me a marching salute. They are very well drilled to the manual exercise and marching to time.[12]

12. Adams, *Memoirs*, VII, 214.

It was during this trip, inaccurately remembered years afterward as having taken place in June, that Seymour and one of his friends got lost in Baltimore and were left behind without money or acquaintance. They resolved to see the President according to plan and packed their belongings on their backs and walked to Washington over night.[13]

Nor is it wholly fanciful to suppose that the contrast between Henry Clay and John Quincy Adams left a lasting impression on more than one of these youths — the grim man from New England who was President of the United States and, by his side, the gracious and obliging gentleman from Kentucky. They were, indeed, a strange pair of bed-fellows. In neither victory nor defeat were they divided. By his fatal appointment of Clay, Adams set a double seal to his doom. Among his political enemies this odd error of tact in regard to the man whose supporters in the House of Representatives had made him President laid him open to the unjust accusation of having made a shady bargain with the fourth man in order to beat the first. A secretary of state, moreover, according to the practice of the time, was supposed to have been picked as a President's eventual successor. Even the friends of Adams must have noticed the glaring contrast between his harsh self-righteousness and the charm of Clay — of whom men would remember the trifling fact that he walked like an Indian, with his toes straight forward.[14] Seymour always feared and ridiculed all sectional pretensions to superiority. He was not infrequently accused of prejudice against New England, the country where his father had been born and his uncles and cousins had flourished. Men like Sumner and Garrison, he came to believe, were national nuisances nagged on their way by notions of "malignant philanthropy." His initial encounter with the very incarnation of the spirit of New England at Washington could hardly be called fortunate. The first President of the United States he ever saw sourly refused to make a speech.

13. New York Historical Society: Seymour Papers.
14. Joseph M. Rogers, *The True Henry Clay* (Philadelphia, 1902), 165.

Seymour returned to Utica in the summer of 1827, when he was just past seventeen. Although his younger brother was to go to Yale, where he was graduated with the class of 1835, Horatio completed his education in the office of two lawyers distinguished in the history of central New York, Greene C. Bronson and Samuel Beardsley, and was admitted to the bar in 1832. It was Bronson, oddly enough, who, running as a "Hard" in 1854, and coming out fourth in a field of four candidates, drew away a sufficient number of votes to defeat Governor Seymour for reëlection.[15] Seymour practised law only for a year or two after leaving their office, for personal business took up all his time. His abandoning the law was something more than accident, however. Shortly after his death his friend, the Reverend Isaac S. Hartley, observed: "It is questionable whether he ever possessed a natural fondness for the law, or for that close application which success in the more learned professions plainly requires."[16] His sense of what he could not do was always shrewd: unlike the second Adams he was adequate to his ambition, and had no cause for complaint.

Young Seymour, however, was still to begin the most important part of his training for life. In 1832, William Learned Marcy was elected governor of New York for the first of his three terms. Marcy and Van Buren were confederates, and the sharp eye of the latter had already lighted on the son of his canal commissioner: Horatio Seymour should be appointed to the post of military secretary to the new governor. For the next six years (1833–1839) he lived in Albany at the right hand of Marcy, learning the ropes of the politics of the regency from a clever manager of men. The affectionate friendship between governor and secretary lasted for twenty-four years. Each man learned from the other. In the course of time, Seymour was to

15. Werner, *Civil List*, 167.

16. *Magazine of American History*, xv (May, 1886), 417–432: Isaac S. Hartley, *Horatio Seymour*, 422. Hammond writes of him in 1844:

> He had read law, but having had a large estate cast upon him, as one of the heirs of his father, and in right of his wife, who is a daughter of one of the wealthiest men in Albany, the care of his property engrossed so much of his time that he paid little attention to his profession, and never distinguished himself in it: Hammond, *History*, III, 378.

lure Marcy away from the Hunker half of the Democratic party — or, more accurately — would keep him a "Soft" when the "Hards" seceded from the reunited party in 1853.[17] Not until Marcy's death in 1857 did Horatio Seymour make his plans apart. The loss of the best friend he had in public life, his dream of playing Clinton to Wisconsin, and finally the death of his mother in 1859 turned his attention to his private affairs on the momentous eve of the Civil War.

Marcy became governor of New York when Jackson was at the pinnacle of his success. His election for his second term planted him firmly in the favor of the country. Only Grover Cleveland divides with him the distinction of having three times been the choice of the people of the United States for President. From all appearances the Democrats had dug in safely both at Albany and Washington. The shrewd old general had able lieutenants and loyal supporters in every section of the nation. Underneath the surface of strength and union in New York, however, there flowed circuitous currents of discontent and division. Two senators were to be elected — just as twelve years later, on the eve of Polk's inauguration — for Dudley's term was coming to its legal end, and his colleague, Marcy, had resigned his seat when he was chosen governor. The upshot showed that there were really two Democratic parties in the state, not one — conservative and radical factions, about equally balanced in strength. The same conflict would come to the surface again in 1845, by which time men would be calling one another "Hunkers" and "Barnburners." Under one name or

17. Much of what seems to modern readers the "mystery" of New York politics is accounted for by the confusion and the conversions at the outbreak of the Civil War. Vigorous and even venomous friends of the South in New York, like Daniel S. Dickinson, "Scripture Dick" (who lost his seat in the Senate largely because he helped to make the Compromise of 1850), became violent enemies of secession. John Adams Dix, on the other hand, who had followed the Barnburners with Van Buren in 1848 and then had voted for Breckinridge in 1860, found himself in the camp with Dickinson in 1861. Seymour was too much of a Hunker for Dix in 1848 and too much of a "Soft" for Dickinson in 1854, but, once the Civil War had broken out, these former enemies united in calling him a "Copperhead."

William Paige *New York City Hall*

WILLIAM L. MARCY

another, these two factions continued to exist until the time of the Civil War. The "money men," that is the investors and speculators who saw that their state banks would profit from President Jackson's war against the Bank of the United States, were "conservative." These men were the Hunkers. Nathaniel P. Tallmadge, of Poughkeepsie, was their choice for senator in 1833, and Tallmadge went to Washington for two full terms.

The hero of the radicals — the small farmers and the artisans (men suspicious of business and banking) — was Silas Wright of Canton, in St. Lawrence County, who had sat in the state senate from 1827 to 1831. The "radicals" elected him to the seat Governor Marcy had vacated and they sent him back to Washington in 1837 and again in 1843. Tallmadge and Wright supplied a perfect equilibrium within the state for twelve years. The truce was one of politics, not principles: New York became neutral on all great issues before the Senate, for the vote of one man usually negatived that of the other. Their going out of office together — Tallmadge to accept appointment as the governor of Oregon Territory and Wright to go to Albany — let loose the rivalry which was to be the plague of Polk's four years in the White House. A study of New York's dual election of senators in 1833 and again in 1845 provides a key to the politics of the state before the Civil War.

Thus Horatio Seymour began his long acquaintance with the legislature of his state at the very moment when Albany was full of plotting and pulling of wires. The new governor was a conservative: could he have had his way, Silas Wright would not have succeeded him at Washington. His sympathies and his surroundings were characteristic of leaders of a party long in power; in person and ability he was typical of the best product of that respectable statesmanship which the Democrats supplied until the morning of the Civil War. Then, bankrupt and caught between abolition and secession, it committed suicide.

Running errands for the governor, however, did not take all of Seymour's time. State capitals had a social life of their own, and that of Albany was not the least distinguished. The town was old, and the prosperous families were proud. From one of these Seymour chose his wife. Less than eighteen months after going to Albany, he was married to one of the six children of John Rutger Bleecker, the youngest daughter, Mary.[18] He was twenty-five on his wedding day. The Bleeckers were Dutch and rich in land. Rutger, the father of John R., had bought, in company with General Philip Schuyler and two others, at a sheriff's sale on July 4, 1772, the Oneida County, or western half of what was known as Cosby's Manor in the valley of the Mohawk.[19] Rutger Bleecker's four children, John and three sisters, inherited their father's quarter of this purchase — some 5,500 acres. The second of these sisters, Maria, married Morris Miller of Utica. The young woman Seymour married was her niece. A study of a good map of the neighborhood will show how valuable this land became, for the present city of Utica comprises almost precisely the southern half of the purchase of 1772. As the town grew, the fortune of the family increased; even to-day half a dozen streets in Utica recall the given names of its members.

Seymour acted as the local agent for John R. Bleecker even before he married his daughter, and after the death of his father in 1837 he had to give his whole time to the care of the property for which he was responsible — his wife's and Henry Seymour's. Nor was that quarter-share of the western half of Cosby's Manor all the land acquired by Rutger Bleecker: there is record of at least two grants in Montgomery County, totalling 8,600 acres in which he had an interest.[20]

All his life Seymour believed that the best investment for money was land, and this conviction fell in with his enthusiastic and persistent support of the Erie Canal. By the forties, the surplus funds of his own family were being spent in Michigan;

18. For the Bleecker family, see Schuyler, *Colonial New York*, II, 380.

19. A map and the history of Cosby's Manor — approximately ten miles long and six miles wide, 43,056 acres, granted to the colonial governor (1732–1736), Colonial William Cosby, in 1734 — will be found in Durant, *Oneida County*, 53 and 55–59. See, also, Burr, *Atlas*, Oneida County.

20. French, *Gazetteer*, 49–53.

by the fifties, Seymour was buying land for himself in Wisconsin. A canal, it is interesting to notice, was connected with each of these enterprises. At the time of his death in 1886, the farm which was his home had been in the possession of the family of his wife for more than one hundred years.

The Seymours had no children — Horatio Seymour, Jr., who often got votes as the son of his uncle, was the child of Jonathan. Lack of issue was the sole unhappy aspect of an affectionate partnership which lasted more than fifty years. Seymour, so far as can be discovered, never referred to his disappointment in public but once. After one of his many nominations, he was caught sight of, on his way back from the convention, seated in a train which had stopped at a station. Acting on the principle that a governor is always public property, a crowd filed in at one door of the car and out the other, each of the voters determined to shake his hand. It was summer, and before long the patient victim of this American ritual became flushed with fatigue and the heat; whereupon one of his companions ordered the car windows to be opened, calling out that what the governor needed was a little air. Seymour smiled at the sound of the words and then repeated them and nodded his assent. He had turned his loss of hope into a pun.

When New York passed Virginia in total population and was called the Empire State for the first time, Horatio Seymour was a boy of nine. Although the territory of the nation has been more than doubled since that day, although twenty-six states have been added to the Union as it was then, New York has held that proud title for well over a century. One of forty-eight members of the Union is the home of one-tenth of the total population of all. The axes of the state, moreover, are the natural highways not only between the East and the West, but north to Canada as well. It was no accident that decisive battles of both the wars with Great Britain were fought on the soil of New York. Geography, again, made the adhesion of this state vital to the success of the reform of 1787; the close vote by which New York ratified the Constitution made a hopeful experiment of the great adventure of 1788. Without New York, New England would have been isolated. Yet the division of opinion among the delegates at Poughkeepsie determined the separation between political parties in the state for almost fifty years. The rise of Jefferson and the vice-presidential alliance with the Virginia Dynasty gradually brought about a re-grouping of the citizens along the Hudson and the Mohawk. Both Aaron Burr and DeWitt Clinton threatened this alliance, and the bitter suspicion which their ambitions aroused is a measure of the strength of the tie to the men who feared and fought the Federalists.

By the time Seymour reached manhood, however, Jackson was in the saddle, and Martin Van Buren was working out his plan to succeed him at Washington. When the first son of New York was inaugurated in 1837, the Empire State had waited forty-eight years to see one of its citizens at the head of the federal government. The first lieutenant of the President in his own state was the political tutor of Seymour, Governor Marcy, a man chiefly remembered to-day for the words which fastened the phrase "spoils system" in the language of American politics. Lovers of the Adirondacks will recollect that the highest mountain in the state still bears his name.

During the years that Seymour lived in Albany as the military aide to Marcy the capital of any state was far more important than such places are to-day. Officials could not dash in and out of the city between dawn and darkness; they lived there, and during sessions of the legislature the social life of Albany, in particular, with its Dutch aristocracy, had some interest and much charm. When Seymour was born, it was already the second of the four cities of New York, with a population of almost ten thousand and 1,450 houses and stores clustered along the river bank and the steep street which led up to the new classic capitol, surmounted with an image of Justice and her inseparable scales. Travellers passed through on their way both east and west, for before the days of Clinton's great canal they avoided the seventy-two-foot falls at Cohoes, just opposite the head of the tide and sloop navigation in the Hudson, going straight across the country over the fifteen miles which separated Schenectady from Albany. The capital was also a convenient point of departure for those who took the water route to Canada.

The less-used road which turned west north of Albany passed through the Shaker village of Niskayuna, the "Valley of Wisdom," near Watervliet. There Ann Lee, of Manchester, England, had settled in September, 1784, with her "United Society of Believers in Christ's Second Appearing," a group of Shakers, quiet, industrious folk who held property in common, did not marry or have children, danced together with decorum at stated times according to their ritual, grew prosperous, and slowly disappeared. Although the lady of Niskayuna had never been to school and could not even write, her devoted followers believed that she could speak fluently no less than seventy-two languages. Ann Lee and her community were at home in that country. The sporadic appearance of religious freaks in New York is one of the most interesting aspects of the history of that state. The story of the founders of Mormonism and spiritualism are well known, but certain other fanatics, famous in their day, are all but forgotten. It was John Humphrey Noyes, first cousin of President Hayes, who fled from New England to establish his community of perfectionists at Oneida. Though bitter dispute raged about his alarming gospel of holding women, as well as other property, in common, Noyes was tolerated for a time and did not leave for Canada until shortly before he died in 1886.

Hard work from sunrise to sunset in little cities and on lonely farms left people scant time for relaxation and amusement. Daily newspapers were almost unknown, and organized sport was still a thing of the future; what slight leisure or surplus energy was left from gaining a livelihood went into politics and religion. Churches and taverns were the places where men met to talk and argue. Liquor was the swiftest means of escape from the monotonous round of familiar faces and constant toil — it was a long time, indeed, before the water of the rapidly growing cities could be drunk with safety. Camp-meetings supplied the excitement now provided by the annual visits of the circus. If human beings were happy, it was only because they had no chance not to be.

Yet the people of Seymour's youth found compensations for what may look to us like the emptiness of their lives — lack of opportunity for indulging their emotions. The men took their politics with an earnestness that was so fierce and unreasonable that the feuds between the Clintonians, the Hamiltonians, and the Livingstonians seem foolish to their sophisticated and indifferent descendants. In 1840, for instance, a national election was made the convenient occasion for a national spree; those who loved Clay shed tears at his defeat in 1844; the absorbing desire to make money had not yet drawn the skill of the best men of the country from politics to business. A judge, a member of the legislature or the Congress, even a governor, was still the envy of his town or country, an object of admiration to his neighbors. Politics belonged to lawyers in days when lawyers learned their skill in offices and courtrooms — not in schools.

There was a dark side to the fancy for religion, even more doubtful and dangerous to the reason than the comet-like appearances of itinerant preachers or the panic spirit of annual camp-meetings. Impostors and self-deluded humbugs came and went across the country, preaching strange doctrines dug out of the Bible. Almost invariably these people believed, or professed to believe, that God had deigned to visit the earth once more in their persons. Jemima Wilkinson, for instance, was much talked of in her time; yet the passing of a hundred years has hardly left her name behind her. This remarkable woman was born in Cumberland, Rhode Island, in 1753, and died for the first time in 1776 to rise again as the "Universal Friend," not to leave the world finally till 1819 at Jerusalem, New York.[21]

21. Hudson, *Wilkinson.* See, also, Barber and Howe, *Historical Collections of New York,* 605–607; and Carmer, *Listen for a Lonesome Drum,* 165–175: "The Woman Who Died Twice."

The body that had once been hers walked the earth in a long, loose robe of white linen and a broad-brimmed, low-crowned, white beaver hat, or rode in an open coach shaped like a crescent moon, or sat astride a beautiful horse, with silver-studded saddle and stirrups, preaching the love of God.

At the centre of six square miles of land in western New York, this reincarnation established her community in 1791, built a large house, and lived in what was then thought luxury. Envy had it that the "Universal Friend" was really neither man nor woman — and masculine manners, a grum voice, and an air of authority seemed to confirm the gossip. When she preached to the faithful, she stood in the door of her own bed-chamber, with a waistcoat, stock, and white cravat added to her customary costume. Tradition makes her a striking-looking person who grew stout in her old age, and suppressed the single portrait that was ever painted of her. She taught the Shaker doctrine of celibacy, often as she had to overlook, if we are to believe the hostile Hudson, the birth of children among her followers. She promised to walk on the waters of Seneca Lake one Sunday more than a century ago, and then discreetly gave up the experiment as not necessary to the great faith of the crowd that had come to see a miracle — riding off in her coach in full sight of a wicked and perverse generation that sought for a sign. Her dead body, so it was said, was appropriately taken at night from the vault in the cellar of her home, where she had been buried, and concealed. According to the historian of Yates County, who talked with contemporaries, Jemima Wilkinson was an able, earnest woman, and most of the picturesque stories which cling to her name were the work of hatred and malice.[22]

22. For many years all available accounts of this extraordinary woman stemmed from hearsay or the enmity of David Hudson, who, so it is said, had quarrelled with her over some business having to do with real estate. For more accurate information on Jemima Wilkinson, see the *Journal of American History*, IX, Number 2 (April–May–June, 1915), 249–263: Reverend John Quincy Adams, "Jemima Wilkinson, the Universal Friend"; and the *Quarterly Journal*, New York State Historical Association, XI, Number 2 (April, 1930), 158–175: Robert P. St. John, "Jemima Wilkinson." The second article contains an excellent bibliography. For a cynical contemporary account, see the Duc de la Rochefoucault Liancourt,

The year before the "Universal Friend" settled in New York, Robert Matthews was born there in the town of Cambridge, in Washington County.[23] This son of Scotch immigrants was trained as a carpenter, but went into business for himself, only to fail as a country merchant. At twenty-three he married and had children, after which he began to roam about the state calling down destruction on wicked cities like Albany — whose inhabitants had laughed at him. To his distracted wife and his hard-working, respectable brothers "Matthias" — as Matthews called himself — was only a lazy lunatic at large. In the city of New York, however, he attracted some attention to himself, riding through the streets on a raw-boned horse, spouting Isaiah, and stroking his luxuriant beard. Before long he had worked his way into the home of Elijah Pierson, who lived on Bowery Hill, and having mastered the household, had to go to law over the ownership of the property the husband left when he suddenly died of what neighbors said was poison.

In days when the Battery was still a favorite spot for the fashionable loungers of New York, Matthias would drive up on summer afternoons, step out of a "handsome, black carriage," and walk about with stately tread among the marvelling multitude. He was "tall and well-made"; his "face was sharp, his complexion sallow, his thick hair the color of ashes, and his eyes a cold, light grey." He got himself up in a black cap of japanned leather "in shape like an inverted cone with a shade," a green frock coat lined with pink satin, a vest of figured silk, green pantaloons, and a crimson sash around his waist. Now and then his feet were shod in sandals; at other times he

---

Travels Through the United States of North America, the Country of the Iroquois, and Upper Canada (London, 1799), I, 110–118.

The best source of dispassionate information is Stafford C. Cleveland, *History and Directory of Yates County* (Penn Yan, New York, 1873), 38–138, chapters III, IV, and V, containing pictures of Jemima Wilkinson and her dwellings. See, also, an introduction, "Illustrations to Volume I," *passim.* See the *Dictionary of American Biography*, XX (1936), 226–227.

23. Stone, *Matthias and His Impostures.*

wore "Wellington boots," which were polished until they glistened. As he paced to and fro with the attentive Mr. Pierson at his side, Matthias would twist his slender fingers through the curls of his beard or the hair which hung down to his shoulders, for he believed, with Tertullian, that shaving was a blasphemous effort to improve on the handiwork of God. Haled into court in connection with the sudden death of his host, this latter-day saint added lace ruffles to his wrist-bands and sported "a silver sun upon the left side of his breast and stars of the same metal on the right." The people of New York, it will be seen, had no good reason not to know something about native saints.

In 1810 New York comprised forty-five counties with a total population of 960,052, of which it was estimated that one hundred thousand persons were free-holders. The value of all the property of the state was reckoned at half a billion dollars; the tonnage of the great port was a quarter of a million annually, and no less than one-fourth of the whole federal revenue from tariffs was collected on what was still called York-Island. Napoleon Bonaparte had been a good friend of American business: during the summer of 1811, for instance, nearly two hundred thousand dollars' worth of coarse grain bound for Europe was bought up at Troy alone. The trade of the Great Lakes brought increasing profits annually; one cargo of furs which arrived at Buffalo that same year was valued at $150,000. Once the exciting Corsican had been permanently deposited on St. Helena, the accumulated capital of Europe began to move westward across the Atlantic in search of investment at good rates of interest.

Daniel D. Tompkins was the handsome head of the state in 1810, at a time when the governor of New York was still styled "captain-general," "commander-in-chief," and even "admiral of the navy" — all this on a salary of $3,750 and his Albany rent. It was Tompkins who talked the people of New York into voting the abolition of slavery; his pet amendment to their constitution was carried in 1817 to become effective in 1827. Once their state was free soil, enemies of slavery could fix their critical eyes on the South. There was danger, as well as hope, in this shift of interest.

The famous rich radical, Gerrit Smith, was born at Utica, and there, too, according to Artemus Ward, occurred that "high-handed outrage" an account of which Lincoln read to his solemn, self-important Cabinet just before he sprang emancipation on the country. At Utica Seymour was to pass most of his life in a neighborhood that was almost the centre of the state he loved. Sooner or later he came to understand the interests and ideals of almost every element of an increasingly conglomerate population. Yankees had begun to cross over to the Hudson Valley and the country beyond immediately after the Revolution; by the thirties and the forties immigrants from Ireland were crowding into New York City and making little communities for themselves along the water route to Buffalo. His abiding interest in the history of his state, his wide acquaintance with its people and its famous places, fed his love of dwelling on the various contributions which the Dutch, the English, and the Irish layers of population had made to the thought, well-being, and spirit of New York. During the summers he mingled with the rich southerners who used to come north to the fashionable watering-places in the easy days before the rebellion. Because wide reading and friendship had made him civil, in the very best sense, he remained singularly free throughout his life of the strenuous notions that dogged many of his neighbors.

To call him cool and inconsiderate is to miss the import of his experience; as often as other men worried or scolded or raged, he was wise enough to remember not to fret himself against the ungodly. When abolitionists railed against slavery, he pointed to the plain example of New York; when Americans threatened one another with secession, he reminded them that compromise had made their Union, and that compromise was probably the best means of living in it. He had seen and heard enough of freaks and fanatics to have his fill of them. The six

Courtesy of Earl Widtman, Utica

AN EARLY VIEW OF UTICA

years he spent at Albany with Marcy seem to have made a deep and lasting impression on his character. Time and again he was called in to unite the factions of his own party — to make peace between men who quarrelled over little causes to the detriment of matters far more important. The feuds of Cass and Van Buren bored him when he was young and served as a warning when he had grown old.

Because he was ready to give as well as take, because he remained keenly alive to the conflicting interests of one of the most diverse populations of all the states in the Union, Horatio Seymour was justly popular and powerful in his day — one of the ablest exponents, first and last, of that great tradition of American statecraft which both North and South abandoned for the savage folly of the Civil War.

III

THE FALL OF MARTIN VAN BUREN

1840

In 1838 Marcy accepted a fourth nomination for governor from the Democrats, only to be defeated for that office by William H. Seward, chiefly as the result of the political upheaval which followed the great panic of the spring of 1837. Marcy, as will be seen, had hopes of being President, and his willingness to stand for governor again is to be laid to this ambition. A fourth election would have made him a national figure and perhaps the acknowledged leader of the Democratic party, but this was not to be. His defeat in 1838 was the storm-signal of the hurricane which swept Harrison into office in 1840.

Van Buren's four years in the White House had suffered blight at the very beginning, and the financial policies he honestly felt obliged to follow in the autumn of 1837 lost him much of the conservative support he had inherited in 1836. Jackson had destroyed the national bank, and state banks had a way of sprouting up like mushrooms. The "pet" banks got deposits of the federal funds, and many of them promptly joined in the general gamble in stocks and land. Easy banks lent money rashly till the bottom dropped out of the bucket in the spring of 1837: credit disappeared; assets froze, and the state banks were forced to suspend payment. Hard cash went into hiding, and hard times loomed ahead. It was obvious that if a national bank might have become an octopus, hundreds of quickly chartered and badly managed state banks were a snare and a delusion. A third course for the handling of federal money yet lay open, and this Van Buren took boldly in the autumn of 1837: the federal government would establish an independent treasury and take care of its own funds in the future. This policy seems to have been popular with the masses, but it cost

Van Buren the support of the business men of the Democratic party in New York.

The triumph of Jackson in 1828 had created an embarrassment of riches for his party in the Empire State. During the intrigue of the national election of 1824, the Van Buren faction, always at war with DeWitt Clinton, had flirted with the candidacy of Crawford, although general opinion in the state supported Adams.[1] Four years later the scene had shifted: the upright Adams, who could never even grant a favor with so much grace as a President of the United States should be able to refuse one, was no equal for the glamorous Jackson. The tactless appointment of Clay as secretary of state was very like the naming of Evarts by Hayes in 1877: in each case the man who was offered the office lacked the considerate good taste to refuse it. Four men divided the electoral vote in 1824: Jackson, Adams, Crawford, and Clay. The legend of a dirty bargain between the second candidate and the fourth against the interest of the first was false, but so seasoned a politician as Clay can not be excused for ignoring its incalculable power for mischief. More important still, however, for the state of New York, was the sudden disappearance from the scene of the ambitious DeWitt Clinton. Triumphantly elected governor for a third time immediately after his spectacular and unpopular removal as canal commissioner by concurrent resolution of the legislature in 1824, the father of the Erie Canal had narrowly succeeded in winning a fourth term in 1826. It was difficult to predict what he would do at the next national election. Then, early in 1828, he died. Van Buren's dangerous rival was gone, and the following autumn New York joined the victorious procession of Jackson states.

The "Little Magician" got himself elected governor in 1828 and almost immediately resigned the office he had gained to join the Cabinet at Washington. His successor at Albany was the

1. For Van Buren's story of how Clay and Webster persuaded General Van Rensselaer to vote for Adams in the House instead of for Crawford, thus swinging the deciding vote of New York to Adams in 1825, see Van Buren, *Autobiography*, II, 150–152. See, also, Hammond, *History*, II, 177–178.

earnest but unexciting Enos T. Throop, who served two terms before the six years of Marcy. Thus, for ten years the Democrats of New York State had everything their own way. The Albany Regency was at the heyday of its power and glory: there was no person or party sufficiently strong to dispute for the spoils of office and the lucrative contracts for canals. Behind the scenes, pulling the strings, sat the able and acquisitive Edwin Croswell, publisher of the Albany *Argus*, who, soon and late, was to collect half a million dollars as state printer.[2] This once-famous Croswell was the Democratic counterpart to Thurlow Weed, that is, he was an inveterate promoter and investor who always subordinated politics to business, and thus forecast the future. Both men were advance agents of the era when the best energies of Americans were to be drawn off from statecraft to the making of money. Before very long the business man would use the politician as his puppet, but Croswell and Weed, although neither ever held an important office, were both active participants in the game of politics. They had mastered the art of managing men. While Seward was governor, Weed himself enjoyed the handsome profits of the state printer. For years these two publishers were familiar and almost permanent opponents at Albany.

In New York the name of Jackson Democrats was legion, and, as might have been expected, there were not enough rewards in the whole state to satisfy the faithful. Yet it would be unjust to lay all faction to ingrates in office and envious persons out of it. Real differences of opinion began to appear among the victors, and these disagreements were to divide the Democratic ranks — or, more accurately, to drive the conservative, or business, Jacksonians into temporary alliances with the Whigs. Throop, and then Marcy, came from the conservative wing, and Marcy, in particular, was an exceptionally gifted leader of men. During the eight years of Jackson's presidency, however, things went swimmingly. The Bank of the United States was put out of business, and the state banks inherited the

2. Gillet, *Wright*, II, 1802.

federal deposits. The whole system presented the pleasing appearance of one of those unbroken circles which are the delight of finance. Internal improvements were to open up the country for new population, but promoting canals and railroads cost money; therefore, the states issued "stocks" or, as we should say, bonds, which became the basis of the organization of state banks. These state banks accepted deposits from the people, and received national money if they were so lucky or influential as to get it. The power, or the privilege, of putting money to work is an easy way of making more. Thus it was that the eight years of Jackson at Washington were crowded with that rash confidence which always makes for a feeling of general well-being. Americans were taking in one another's washing. The favorite forms of speculation were canals, railroads, and, as a natural result of these ventures, land. Profits grew by leaps and bounds, and great numbers of people grew rich — or thought they did.

The startling success of the Erie Canal encouraged agitation through the southern tier of counties for the New York and Erie Railroad, in which enterprise New York would ultimately lose three million dollars.[3] The year 1862 saw the peak of canal tolls: $4,792,535.96; thereafter, Cornelius Vanderbilt, having captured control of what is now the New York Central Railroad, consolidated that new system of transportation which was slowly but surely to make the waterway of Clinton superfluous. Railroads did not freeze over four months of the year.

It would have been difficult, if not impossible, to control the opulent optimism of the period of 1829–1837, for, if the obvious success of one canal had disarmed its critics and contradicted prophets of disaster, any number of canals, it might be argued, could do as well or even better. To retain control of the legislature, it was necessary to please as many counties as possible; so plans were drawn, laws were passed, and bonds were issued with a rash disregard for real earning power. It took some time for the credit of the state to show signs of cracking.

3. French, *Gazetteer*, 70; Gillet, *Wright*, II, 1781.

The state printer, Croswell, controlled the most influential Democratic organ in New York, and he could always count on Whig votes when he needed them, for the Whigs, as a party, were lively supporters of internal improvements, as the rash borrowing and spending under Seward would soon show. As time went on, Croswell and his confederates encountered a growing opposition within the Democratic party. This came chiefly from what may fairly be described as the Jeffersonians, that is, the old-fashioned anti-Federalist Republicans. In a sense, this opposition was largely rural, for, though farmers saw the values of land rise as canals and railroads opened up communications through the country, they felt the competition of the agricultural products of the Middle West which poured through the Mohawk Valley and down the Hudson from the direction of Buffalo. The adored and distinguished leader of these farmer Democrats was Silas Wright, "man of the millions," from the town of Canton, in remote St. Lawrence County.[4] Slowly, however, these Jeffersonians were to lose their share of control of the national Democratic party: as in the case of the Republicans who supported Lincoln many years later, the more frequently the name of Jefferson was called on, the less obvious became the force of the example of the great Virginian.

In the meantime, Martin Van Buren was adroitly making himself inevitable as the successor of Jackson. During all of eight years he kept his eyes on 1836. Just how artfully the gentleman from Kinderhook had consolidated the support of his own state can be seen in the electoral vote of New York over a period of years.[5] Governor Marcy had defeated William H. Seward in 1834, and in 1836 the national victory of Van Buren returned him to Albany by a plurality of almost thirty thousand. Hardly, however, had Van Buren been inaugurated, when the

4. See the poem of Whittier published at the time of the death of Silas Wright.

5. In the electoral college of 1825, Adams received 26 of the votes of New York, Crawford 5, Clay 4, and Jackson 1. In 1829, the 36 votes of New York divided, 20 for Jackson, and 16 for Adams. In 1833, New York cast 42 electoral votes, and Jackson got them all, as did Van Buren in 1837. In 1841, however, all the electoral votes of New York went to Harrison: Werner, *Civil List*, 593–594.

Jackson boom blew up. Senator Silas Wright, as chairman of the committee on finance, reported and advocated the bill which was designed to carry into effect Van Buren's message recommending the establishment of an independent treasury.[6] Wright had opposed the national bank, and at first favored the transfer of federal funds to the state banks. Now he urged a second removal. His colleague, Senator Tallmadge, fought the bill bitterly, however, and Governor Marcy himself was accused of being cool to the new departure. Van Buren and Wright saw their reform go through the Senate only to be defeated in the House of Representatives by a union of Whigs and disgruntled Democrats — half a dozen of the latter coming from New York. The bill lay dormant, therefore, except for an interval, until the days when President Polk declared that an independent treasury and the tariff act of 1846 would be the double test of a genuine and national Democrat.[7]

Differences of opinion between the "credit" and the "anti-credit" leaders of the Democratic party in New York State over the proper method of financial readjustment aroused resentments which rankled there for years. How to repair the ruin of good times was the rub. Long afterward, former Senator Tallmadge told President Polk that

> . . . when he took his ground against the Independent Treasury scheme, he consulted with Governor Marcy, who was then Governor of New York, who concurred with him in opinion, but that the Governor afterwards en-

6. For the effect of Van Buren's message on the Democrats of New York, see the *American Historical Review*, XXIV, 3 (April, 1919): William Trimble, "Diverging Tendencies in New York Democracy in the Period of the Locofocos," 396–421; and the Albany *Atlas*, as quoted in Gillet, *Wright*, II, 1793–1818. In the Albany manifesto of 1837, Tallmadge, Croswell, and Marcy backed the "Credit Men"; while Wright, Dix, and Flagg favored the "Anti-Credit" policy, later advanced by Van Buren. By 1835 the independent-treasury Democrats were dubbed "Locofocos," a nickname which, like "Bucktail" of fifteen years before, originated in New York City. Their war-cry was "a clear field and no favors." The Hunker Democrats lined up behind the state banks, a policy of internal improvements, and the expansionist desires of the South.

7. State banks were made depositories of the federal government by the act of June 23, 1836. Acting for the administration, Senator Wright succeeded in putting through the independent-treasury bill of July 4, 1840, but this the Whigs repealed in 1841.

dorsed the scheme in his message to the Legislature of New York, and that he was left by many of those leading Democrats in New York who had at first approved his course, to stand alone.[8]

Governor Marcy's public, if not wholly loyal, support of Van Buren's famous message must have cost him some heart-burning, for, as Trimble observes:

> The pith of the progressive Democracy's opposition to the credit system was the issuance by the banks of a currency not strictly redeemable in specie. The great evil was the want of a fixed measure of value, and the prime remedy was the "separation of the two distinct functions of creating and lending the currency."

The Barnburners, or farmer Democrats, were more genuinely Jeffersonian than the Hunkers, or business Democrats, but the latter enjoyed the advantage of occupying the middle ground between the Whigs, who were always ready to borrow too much money on the credit of the state, and the "strict construction" men who were rarely, if ever, willing to borrow any. These Barnburners believed that the cost of internal improvements should be taken out of taxes, and that the test of any such improvement was its ability to "pay its way." The success of the Erie and Champlain Canal system vindicated the Hunkers, but losses in the lateral canals and the Erie Railroad certainly gave the Barnburners good reason for thinking that their doubts had firm ground. Just how persistent was this deep difference of opinion in the party is to be seen in the eleven-point program which John Adams Dix drew up for ideal Democrats as late as 1845. In setting forth his creed Dix, it is interesting to notice, touched the burning issue of slavery only twice; for him, the important points to be emphasized were just three — protection of state rights, a proper policy for internal improvements, and the fitting management of the federal treasury.[9] When Horatio Seymour entered the assembly, he was quick to take advantage of the possibility that the Hunkers, or conservative Democrats, could play the part of moderate men as between the cautious Barnburners on the one hand and the spendthrift

8. Polk, *Diary*, I, 57.
9. Dix, *Memoirs*, I, 231.

Whigs on the other. The advantage of this position was the secret of his political success.

The first of the four major American panics doomed Van Buren to defeat. In the autumn of 1837, he saw his party lose control of the New York legislature, the "bank" Democrats boasting openly of having voted for the Whigs. In the following fall Seward ousted Marcy from the office of governor by a majority of over ten thousand. The Whigs were now in complete control of the state, and the canal and bank men had everything their own way. In 1840, Seward was reëlected governor and Thurlow Weed, of the *Evening Journal*, was chosen state printer; yet he was not to reign for long, for the collapse of the credit of the state cost the Whigs control of the legislature in the elections of 1841. The chastened Democrats immediately stopped all expenditures on public works, issued bonds for the sums owing to canal contractors, and levied taxes to pay for the current cost of government and the interest on the state debt. This was the famous "stop and tax" law of 1842, which set up a sinking fund, the purpose of which was to extinguish the whole debt of New York in about twenty-two years.[10] It was calculated that the state would eventually have to pay, in principal and interest, more than forty million dollars.[11]

Within two months of the enactment of this radical remedy the seven per cent. bonds of New York sold at par; within fifteen months thereafter the five per cent. bonds had reached that level. It was the arguments over this bill, however, and

10. The story of the "stop and tax" law will be found in Hammond, *History*, III, 249–285.

11. By the time Silas Wright took office as governor in 1845, the following bonds had been issued on the credit of New York (Werner, *Civil List*, 157):

Purpose of Issue	Issued	Redeemed	Outstanding
Erie and Champlain Canal	$ 7,737,771	$7,737,771	....
Other canal issues (profitless)	14,472,257	2,949,531	$11,522,726
Preserving the State credit	5,422,136	346,006	5,076,130
General Fund	909,500	.....	909,500
Bankrupt companies	3,665,700	.....	3,665,700
Solvent companies	1,563,000	500,000	1,063,000
Total	$33,770,364	$11,533,308	$22,237,056

the proposed amendments to it which made a public show in the legislature of the differences of opinion between the radical Democrats, or Barnburners, and the conservatives, or Hunkers.[12] The radicals had their way, and the reappointment of Azariah C. Flagg as comptroller, on February 7, 1842, was itself an endorsement for the future of the credit of the state. Flagg was a friend of Wright, who was later to recommend him to Polk as secretary of the treasury.[13] It looked as if the Democrats were coming back to the complete political control of the state, but Edwin Croswell had his own plans as to what should happen if they did.

Martin Van Buren lost the presidency chiefly as the result of the collapse of the prosperity which Jackson's policies had fostered. Van Buren, it will be remembered, was the first New Yorker to live in the White House; if the Adamses of Massachusetts had been compelled to mark time for the Virginia Dynasty, sons of New York had been forced to wait even longer. Although the rise of Jackson's heir-apparent had caused bickering and jealousy, Van Buren was a prince among politicians, and he had a great hold on the northern vote. What Senator Wright called the humbug of the campaign of 1840 was exceptional, and the sudden death of Harrison and Whig quarrels with Tyler were certain to encourage natural hopes in the breasts of Van Buren and his noticeably faithful fol-

12. The probable origin of the names "Hunker" and "Barnburner" has given rise to a good deal of guess-work. The parable of the Dutchman who burned down his barn to get rid of the rats seems a more reasonable explanation of the second name than "hankering" after offices as a source for the first. Among Dutch children in local New York, "Hunk" means a goal, home, or den; "Old Hunks" is found in use in 1840 at Schenectady to denote a "surly, crusty or stingy old fellow," or one who sticks to his home or post. The *Oxford English Dictionary* suggests that "Hunker" is derived from a popular nickname for a self-satisfied, surly, rich man; a descendant of "Old Hunks," in fact. It seems curious that the German and Dutch words for farmer should never have been brought forward as the origin of "Hunker."

13. Gillet, *Wright*, II, 1644. Flagg had succeeded Wright as comptroller in 1834 and served for five years. His second appointment to that office kept him at the post until 1848. In November, 1847, and thereafter, comptrollers of the state were elected by popular vote in accordance with the new constitution, which was ratified in 1846.

lowers. At the time of the famous Baltimore convention of 1844, Van Buren was not yet sixty-two. New York had had one chance at the presidency and eagerly wished to have another; the ex-President was the obvious man. The consequence of Van Buren's failure to win a third nomination that year was to make history in the politics of his state. The feud which grew out of his loss of a chance for vindication in 1844 and his questionable candidacy on a third ticket in 1848 was widespread, and personal, and venomous.

New York politics were notoriously a maze to observers at Washington, but much of this mystery is imaginary. Ransom Gillet relates how President Polk on several occasions showed him "papers strongly recommending applicants, signed by men in New York standing high in the estimation of the democracy, which were followed or sometimes preceded by letters from some of the signers, requesting that no attention be paid to their names because obtained under the pressure of circumstances, and not because the appointment ought to be made."[14] Working at a distance with such men must have seemed difficult, but a survey of the scene, years after, shows that the setting was simpler than it once appeared — even to President Polk.

For about twenty years, it will be remembered, two professional manipulators worked from their rival headquarters at Albany: Croswell of the *Argus*, for the Democrats, and Weed of the *Evening Journal*, for the Whigs. The prizes of politics were state printing, contracts for canals and railroads (and jobs on both), charters of banks, issues of state bonds, and the rising value of land. As a rule, the Democrats were the dominant party, but of these, the radicals, or Barnburners, while more numerous, were less influential in their party than the conservatives, or Hunkers. These last could always fall back on the Whigs, with whose support they could punish the more idealistic Democrats and further their own business interests at the same time. The confusing cross-currents between Barnburners and Hunkers were caused by the ambitions of their respective

14. Gillet, *Wright*, II, 1662, note.

leaders, many of them governors or senators in the Congress at one time or another.

For many years before the Civil War the division of opinion in the delegations which New York sent to Democratic national conventions was notorious. Often two sets of men would put in an appearance, each claiming to be the true representatives of the party. Daniel D. Tompkins, DeWitt Clinton, Van Buren, Marcy, Silas Wright, Dickinson, John A. Dix — and perhaps Horatio Seymour at one time — were none of them unwilling to be made President of the United States. They were ready to ride into the White House on one horse or the other of the Democratic team, or, better still, on both. Only Van Buren arrived at the goal, and his singular success was to make matters more difficult for those who tried to follow him. The penalty has had peculiar power. Only six New Yorkers have ever become President of the United States and of these, Fillmore and Arthur were both accidents, and Theodore Roosevelt, the fifth, first took office as one. In a century and a half of Union only three men from that state — Van Buren, Cleveland, and Franklin Roosevelt, if we omit Tilden — have been nominated and elected President on their own reputations.

The associations of Horatio Seymour and his family drew him toward the conservative section of the Democratic party from the very first. His father's estate consisted of land and bank stocks, and he himself, as we have seen, had married an heiress to more land. Whatever he might think of the network of lateral canals as laid out over the state, loyalty to the great Erie and Champlain system was a tradition in his family. His father, however, had been a favorite lieutenant of Van Buren, and the endorsement from the future President had sent the son to Albany for six years' service with Governor Marcy. At that time the duties of military aide to a governor were rather those of a decorated messenger than a soldier. He acted as a confidential agent. Thus, in six years, young Seymour had met every important Democrat in the state and more than one from outside it. Then, early in 1839, when Seward became governor, he returned to Utica, the county seat of "self-seeking Oneida," a thriving town situated at the very centre of New York. The house which had been his father's stood in sight of Clinton's canal and, later on, the great New York Central Railroad would pass its doors.

As Hunkers and Barnburners began to divide in the battle over banks, Horatio Seymour watched his friends go into both camps. The interests of his family and his wife were one thing, but the long and intimate connection with Van Buren and his faction was another. Like Marcy he was unwilling to leave the middle ground, for time after time it became obvious that neither half of the distracted Democratic party could hold New York against the Whigs. The political power Seymour built up was so personal, at last, that it puzzled his enemies, who ridiculed his preference for private life as hypocritical. Seymour's slow growth from a local politician to a national statesman is all the more interesting in view of the fact that the party to which he remained attached lost control of the state and then the nation while he was trying to prevail upon the members of it to adjust themselves to changing conditions — to use foresight and practise forbearance. Always contemptuous of faction, he it was who negotiated the financial arrangements by which the famous editorial feud between the two wings of the Democrats was brought to an end at Albany in 1856. In the rise of the Republican party he saw a new and powerful sectional opposition come into view and against this he urged the factions of his party to combine. Within less than a year New York would elect its first Republican governor, John A. King. The *Argus* of Croswell and the *Atlas* of Cassidy must be merged, and merged they were by means of Seymour's money.

Eminently respectable, called rich in his time, well-read and widely interested in the history and geography of his native state, always an orator well above the average of his day, Horatio Seymour moved about the streets of Utica and Albany a handsome figure, familiar to all men and famous for his grace of speech and the easy charm of his manner. He never seemed to have an axe to grind; perhaps it was his independent means that put him above suspicion. Nor did he flaunt that love of humanity which goads men to reform their fellows — always for their own good. The drudgery of office tempered love of power. Lack of zeal for the causes and the fierce campaigns which other men concocted out of what they called moral issues made Seymour offensive to many of his contemporaries. This lack of interest was not selfish, but sincere and considerate. He distrusted the philanthropy which tours the world to find and root up wrong. He was apt at reminding men that their first duty was to sweep before their own doors — that railing at remote evils was an easy way of excusing their neglect of their own business. For him good life, like good government, was a question of neighborhood.

The party to which he remained loyal all his life had a curious history in his own state. From the time when Aaron Burr won the electors of New York for Jefferson in 1800, and thus defeated the dream of Hamilton and the hope of Adams, the state had been a favorite battle-ground for American politicians. Its politics became complicated and even notorious. Both East and South began to bid for the support of the voters of the Hudson Valley; thus George Clinton and Daniel Tompkins became Vice-Presidents from the North for the Virginia Dynasty from the South. DeWitt Clinton had his own visions of the White House, and, because there seemed to be no way of his arriving there as a Democrat, he was accused of being a Federalist in disguise. His enemies, therefore, looked for allies against him beyond the borders of their state. First they chose Crawford of Georgia, and then in 1828 they fastened on Andrew Jackson.

The partnership of Jackson and Van Buren was less strange than it appears. For all his unorthodox spelling and his stubborn notions, Old Hickory was neither illiterate nor unwise, and many educated men would do well to study the shrewdness of his judgment. Learned people like to lament his ignorance of history and what is now called economics, but Jackson, like Lincoln, had the knack of hiding the knowledge he used with rare skill. Of the thirty men who have been President of the United States, this "ignoramus" makes one of the half dozen who have owned a good library. His copy of Shakespeare shows that the story of his fondness for reading that author was not fiction. He was more familiar with the Bible than nine men out of ten to-day. He spelt, it is true, very much as he pleased, but so did the Pilgrim and Puritan fathers of New England. Standard ways of spelling, it should be remembered, are the comparatively recent products of dictionaries and public schools — in the old days they who could write used the alphabet not by the eye but the ear. Jackson's skill at guessing right, moreover, amounted to genius, and to choose Van Buren for his successor out of all the huge circle of his supporters showed ability in valuing men. He has been accused of making public office political spoil, but the practice was already a system in more states than New York by 1829, and Marcy was the unwary man who put it into words.

If Jackson's manners are at issue, the record of his meeting with President Adams after the roundabout election of 1825 will show that the soldier from Tennessee carried off the honors as against the gentleman from Massachusetts. General Jackson had stood at the top of the electoral vote in a field of four candidates; had he, instead of Adams, gone into the White House as the second man and made one of his three rivals for the office his secretary of state, resentment would have died hard in the North. The duplicity of his success would have become a legend, and the "trickery" of the South a tradition. He made his last appearance in politics to nominate and elect a second favorite disciple to the presidency — James Knox Polk, and the man of his choice was by no means the least able or successful chief executive of the United States. His hostility to Henry Clay was epic, but it was more soundly reasoned, on the whole, than Jefferson's unjust suspicions of Burr.

It was Burr and then Van Buren who consolidated the support of New York for the Republican-Democratic party twenty-five years apart. These two expert politicians built better than they knew. By 1828, it was obvious that the old hopes of Federalism were a lost cause in the Hudson Valley. DeWitt Clinton, the only unreliable person with power, died suddenly at the very beginning of that year, and thereafter the union of New York with the South West was secure. Slowly and secretly, almost shame-facedly perhaps, citizens slipped into the party ranks behind Van Buren — merchants and bankers, contractors, promoters, and speculators in land. Victory had made too many friends, and the commercial crash of 1837 divided this army, rank and file. Rivalry between business men and farmers explains most of the mystery and manipulation in the politics of New York from the panic to the Civil War. During all that time the Democrats of the state were never able to unite as a party behind a government at Washington — as Polk and Pierce and Buchanan were to find to their vexation and sorrow. The first cause was a difference of opinion over the questions of finance, but the first occasion of the long feud was the ambition of Van Buren for a third nomination and a second election. By 1848 "Little Van" was to show himself "a used-up man" in a much more serious way than the Whigs of 1840 had ever affected to believe.

IV

THE MANTLE OF DeWITT CLINTON

1844

IN January, 1839, Seymour returned to Utica after six years at Albany and took up his permanent residence in the prevalently Whig and alternatively Hunker county of Oneida. Since his father's death sixteen months before, he had been shouldering the management of the estate in all the time he could spare; henceforth he was to give his attention not only to the Seymour property but to that part of the Bleecker land on which the city of Utica was growing up rapidly. Henry Seymour had been shrewd enough, for one thing, to buy land along the course of that canal which Clinton had conceived and Van Buren had controlled, but the real value of what he had acquired during fifteen years at his post on the commission was problematical. He had dabbled in banks, moreover, and died a stockholder of the Farmers' Loan and Trust Company. One of his most profitable ventures had been his purchase of the Rochester Bank, which he managed so well that he sold half his stock for what he had paid for the whole — a gain of one hundred per cent.[1]

His son had no personal reason to regret the defeat of Marcy for a fourth term as governor. The younger brother, Jonathan, had gone to Yale and been duly graduated in June, 1835, but Horatio always bore the main burden of family affairs. As early as 1838, he had his hands full, according to a letter to his cousin, Origen Storrs Seymour, of Litchfield, Connecticut:

As it regards the business of the estate I can only say that I am getting along very well. Although there is still a good deal of money to be raised, yet the amounts have been so much reduced that there is no longer any

1. See Bagg, *Pioneers of Utica*, 481–482, for a brief but effective description of the father and mother of Horatio Seymour.

apprehension of our being compelled to submit to sacrifices to raise money. A little time will reduce the liabilities very much. Business begins to revive and our Banks will soon commence making dividends, and debts will be collectable. The $64000 note at the Rochester Bank has been reduced by a dividend to $12000 — The western purchase is doing very well — and although there are some troublesome questions connected with it which are to be adjusted yet the more troublesome matter of raising money is disposed of. The next time I go to New York I will go to Litchfield when I can give you a detailed statement of affairs which it is impossible to do in a letter.[2]

A last sentence, "I am at present very much engaged in my garden," shows the taste he got from his mother, who was known quite as well in Utica for the cultivation of flowers as for the kind acts of an old-fashioned lady with a good heart. Caring for the property of his father and that of his wife took him all over the state. Almost to the end of his life the governor was a great traveller through New York; at one time or another he visited practically every scene of historic interest and loved to tramp and camp in the Adirondacks. His knowledge of botany and geology surprised the learned Miss Amelia Murray, from England, quite as much as his wide acquaintance with books. He was never a specialist, never much of what is called a scholar, but he picked up that general information about things and people which often makes lawyers the most companionable of men. He seems to have been successful at the business in hand, for as late as 1844 he was still managing the Seymour estate and paying out shares of its income to his brother and four sisters.[3] For seven years, at least, he must have shown great skill or used even greater tact.

The Utica to which Seymour returned in 1839 was a city of something over twelve thousand inhabitants. Only a quarter of a century before it had been a frontier village.[4] The great fire in the spring of 1837 was not, perhaps, an unmixed evil; how-

2. New York State Library: Seymour Papers: Horatio Seymour to Origen Storrs Seymour, May 15, 1838.

3. New York Historical Society: Seymour Papers: Horatio Seymour to Sophia A. Shonnard, of Yonkers, October 15, 1844.

4. For the growth of Utica, a typical Erie Canal town, see French, *Gazetteer*, 468–469.

New York Historical Society

MRS. HENRY SEYMOUR

ever that may be, the record of the steady growth of the community shows only one interruption — according to the census of 1845 the population had fallen off six hundred from the total of five years before. Travellers noticed an air of business and bustle about this town on the site of Fort Schuyler at the ford of the Mohawk. A mile or two to the west was the somewhat older tavern-town of Whitesboro, which lost out in the race to be the local centre.[5] Utica became the county town of Oneida and remained such, though Rome was obviously more convenient, geographically. The little city was situated in the very midst of the state, almost exactly half way between New York and Buffalo. With the digging of canals and the laying down of roads and railways it became a favorite focal point for conventions of every kind. Abolitionists, prohibitionists, all the cranks, all the converts to the odd beliefs which sprang up on the strangely fertile soil of western New York roamed its streets and crowded its public halls for the next twenty-five years. The sight of these visitors and what they said was broadening.

Foreigners streamed in to work and live — Germans, Welshmen, and, finally, the Irish, who dug the canals and paid for the Catholic churches. Surplus New Englanders settled down all over the state, seeming to prefer the country to the town, and made themselves leaders in politics and industry. Of statesmen, for instance, Marcy, Wright, Dix, Dickinson, and Morgan, to name only some of the most notable, were all born in or east of the Berkshires or the Green Mountains. Greeley came from New

5. Hugh White, selectman of Middletown, Connecticut, led the settlers who founded this town in the spring of 1784: Wager, *Our County* [Oneida], 53–93. For other references to Utica, see the index volume to Thwaites, *Early Western Travels, 1748–1846*. A journal of the Reverend John Taylor, who passed through the country in 1802, together with the earliest map of Utica, will be found in O'Callaghan, *Documentary History*, III, 1107–1150. Although Taylor found the Mohawk Valley a babel of languages, heavy drinking, and superstitious Dutch, he describes Utica as "a very pleasant and beautiful village" — a garden spot in a waste land. He noticed the leasehold system and concluded: the land was good — too good for such inhabitants. Taylor was born and reared in Westfield, Massachusetts, went to Yale, and died in Michigan.

Hampshire, Bryant from Massachusetts, Rufus King from Maine. The Europeans, however, crowded into the cities; by 1845 Utica, for example, had a foreign population of almost thirty per cent., and a quarter of all the inhabitants were of Irish birth.[6] Francis Kernan, one of the first Catholic senators from New York, was a fellow townsman of Horatio Seymour, who urged his election (to the seat he himself had declined) as a matter of public policy.

Factories sprang up in the Mohawk Valley early in the century; the cotton and woollen mills of present-day Utica have long histories behind them. The commercial stake in these investments offers another instance of the clash of interests with the national politics of the Democratic party. The tariff Polk forced through the Congress in 1846 caused as much uneasiness in central New York as in New England or Pennsylvania, for spinning and weaving and manufacturing had come to stay. In 1808, Wolcott & Company set up the first cotton factory in the state at the village of New York Mills near Whitesboro; by 1848 the Utica Steam Woollen Mills had been organized with a capital of one hundred thousand dollars; the following year the Utica Globe Mills Woollen Company and the Utica Steam Cotton Mills Company were established — the latter with a capital of two hundred and thirty thousand dollars. Horatio Seymour was a director in both the latter companies, and he served on the boards of the Utica Bank and the Utica Water Works Company. His brother represented the family as a director of the Utica Gas Company — stores on Genesee Street being first lighted with gas in September, 1850.[7] It is interesting to remember that these commercial contacts never made a Whig or a Republican of Seymour.

He continued to hold land, to buy more and improve it; in 1846 he was acting as treasurer for a company of proprietors

6. Winden, "Influence of the Erie Canal," 66. In 1845 Albany had a total foreign population of 53.9 in the hundred.

7. Records of these companies, with their first boards of directors, are to be found in Jones, *Oneida County*, 603–617.

who were draining the great Canaseraga swamp in Madison County.[8] It was his lifelong conviction that land was the best use for capital. As late as 1868 a by-no-means friendly critic who went to Utica to look over the Democratic nominee for President reported that Seymour made a success at farming chiefly because of his good judgment in choosing his tenants.[9] At one time or another the governor called himself a dairy farmer. The fact that he was widely known as a land owner was probably the cause of Seymour's narrow defeat by Washington Hunt in his first campaign for governor in 1850, for anti-rentism was the issue of the hour in the northern part of the Hudson Valley.

In 1840, as we have seen, President Van Buren was punished for the collapse of the prosperity which had sprung from the financial policies of his less judicious predecessor. Even his own state swelled the avalanche of electoral votes against him. Then General Harrison died after one month in office, and the Whig government broke up under the firm will and cool ambition of that Virginian who was a Democrat on every issue but the independent treasury. Now, after it was too late, the unwisdom of the vote-catching coalition of 1840 was self-evident, and once he had discovered he could not manage Tyler, Clay waged relentless war against him. By the autumn of 1841 the voters of New York were ready for political repentance. Luck favored the Democrats in national politics from the days of Jefferson down to the Civil War: twice the Whigs succeeded in sending a President to Washington, and both elderly generals died on their hands. When Tyler took the place of Harrison, the Virginia Dynasty seemed likely to return to Washington for another long lease of power. First the Cabinet broke up and resigned; then the President began to quarrel with the Congress, which

8. New York Historical Society: Seymour Papers: See the letter of May 25, 1846.

9. See the letter of George Alfred Townsend, dated Utica, July 16, in the Hartford *Post*, July 21, 1868. After 1864, John F. Seymour occupied the Henry Seymour home in Whitesboro Street; while Horatio, who kept an office in Utica, lived at Deerfield.

took its orders from the embittered leader of the disappointed Whigs.

Nor were the Whigs more successful at Albany. In the spring of 1841, during Seward's second term, the credit of the state broke down under the strain of the expenses of canals and railroads. The Democrats saw their opportunity; victory was in the air, and Horatio Seymour became a candidate for the assembly. He was comfortably elected from the traditionally Whig city of Utica and went back to Albany in January, 1842, after an absence of three years. He was classed as a Hunker. The Barnburners, or anti-bank Democrats, took the lead in the legislature, however, and all work on internal improvements suddenly ceased as the famous "stop and tax" law of Michael Hoffman was pushed through both houses in order to restore the finances of the state. Peace reigned for the moment, for the party was not yet in power. Then, one year later, Edwin Croswell recovered from Weed the desirable office of state printer — defeating William Cullen Bryant, of the New York *Evening Post*, for the nomination — and radical Democrats like Comptroller Flagg and Senator Silas Wright began to fear that their strenuous "stop and tax" measure would be administered out of existence by the wily Hunkers.[10]

In the spring of 1842, while he was sitting as a member of the assembly, Seymour was elected mayor of Utica — the office to which his father had been appointed nine years before. The contest was sharp: Seymour secured a majority of only 130 votes over the incumbent, Spencer Kellogg, whose defeat was a severe setback for the Whigs. The new mayor actually served for only ten months, for he was busy at Albany during the first part of his term. He inherited a financial mess and he suffered the common fate of politicians who are called in to clean up a city during a "spasm of virtue." The ordinary expenses of Utica

10. For a thorough and interesting account of the intrigue of this office, see Donovan, *Barnburners*, 38–42. This quarrel in the caucus in January, 1843, made open enemies of the editors of the *Argus* and the *Atlas*. Thirteen years later Seymour managed to negotiate the union of the two Democratic papers.

averaged less than ten thousand dollars a year, but when a committee appointed to examine the municipal finances found it necessary to ask the legislature to pass a bill permitting the raising of $3,500 to meet the floating debt, the fat of reform was in the fire. The young mayor soon found that forcing a city to pay its way was not popular with voters, and in 1843 the Whigs elected Frederick Hollister mayor "by the narrow majority of 16, after a contest which was phenomenal in those days for its spirit and excitement."[11] Seymour was left with the odium of honor.

Taxes were not the only trouble of his one-year term as mayor. During November and December of 1842 he first came into official contact with abolitionists. As early as October, 1835, the Utica Anti-Slavery Society had called a state convention to that city, and Gerrit Smith was present. The meeting was the occasion for an uproar, and the convention adjourned to Smith's broad acres at Peterboro.[12] While Seymour was still serving his first term in the legislature a resolution came into the assembly from the senate declaring that stealing a slave contrary to the laws of Virginia was a crime within the meaning of the Constitution, and directing that a copy of the resolution be transmitted to the chief executive of that commonwealth. Seymour moved that the resolution be referred to the judiciary committee, but his motion was lost, and the assembly concurred with the senate by a vote of 62 to 35.[13] The member from Utica probably hoped that the resolution would die in the committee, for he was always urging New Yorkers to "mind their own business." By 1847, he would have agreed with President Polk that the slavery question was "assuming a fearful and most important aspect," and that northern agitation on that subject was "not only unwise but wicked."[14] He had learned much since the day when, at the age of twenty-one, he had joined a mass

11. Utica *Weekly Herald*, February 16, 1886.
12. Wager, *Our County* [Oneida], 313–315.
13. Hammond, *History*, III, 292.
14. Polk, *Diary*, II, 305.

meeting in Utica which drew up resolutions of sympathy for the rebellious Poles, when protests to the Romanoffs were fully as effective as a papal bull against a comet.[15] Eleven years later he would need the wisdom of experience which time had taught him.

William Lloyd Garrison arrived at Utica on a lecture tour of New York State in the winter of 1842. An anti-slavery convention was to meet there for three days beginning Tuesday, November 29. Lucretia Mott was among those present, and a Presbyterian church was thrown open for the sessions. Until the evening of December 1 the only violence was verbal; then an uproar broke out while a Mr. J. C. Fuller was speaking his mind on the eleventh article of the resolutions — that which condemned the attitude of the churches toward slavery, and particularly the non-aggressive spirit of the Baptist and the Quaker sects. However Christian may have been the logic of the speakers the taste of their language as printed in the *Liberator* was certainly none too good. While Mr. Fuller lashed the quietism of his fellow Christians some of those who heard him began to howl and jeer. In a moment the meeting was a bedlam.

Seymour, who was in the audience, rose to protest against the discourtesy of his fellow citizens, and in the short silence which followed the sight of him the mayor told them that their conduct "disgraced" them:

> This Convention [he declared] had a perfect right to assemble here and discuss any subject they chose without molestation; and he hoped that they would be permitted to proceed. He came there *armed with no authority* other than a citizen of Utica; but he would earnestly request the audience to be quiet, and listen to the gentleman in the pulpit.

His words were greeted with respect, and a Reverend Mr. Allen was "heard for a short time in silence." Order did not reign for long, however, and when some extravagant statement of the speaker started a second tumult, Seymour faced the noisy audience again:

15. Jones, *Oneida County*, 549–550.

This was the first request of the kind he had ever made to his fellow-citizens. Would they listen to him? — Never did he feel so disgraced before; the disgrace rested upon him, as the first officer of the city. On being asked by one of the Secretaries if he had not power, as Mayor, to preserve the peace? he replied, *he had no power, any more than any other citizen.*[16]

Nevertheless, when the Reverend D. Plumb and Jacob Snyder insisted that he was responsible, together with the police of the city, for keeping the peace of the meeting, Seymour promised to prosecute any persons whose names were given to him. "On this announcement," according to the *Liberator*, "the disturbance immediately subsided." The abolitionists talked themselves out and went home, heard and unharmed, but the mad course their pride of opinion set for them would cost their country dear.

The mayor had made his mark, however, and in November, 1843, he was elected to the assembly for a second time. In January, 1844, he was back in Albany. The Democrats had regained complete control of the state in the elections of the autumn of 1842. William C. Bouck, "the farmer of Schoharie," had been put up as a compromise candidate between the Barnburners and the Hunkers. Bouck had served on the canal commission, and the radicals knew that he needed watching; so his one term as governor was a tug-of-war between the two Democratic factions. His first message was the work of Martin Van Buren, who was living in ambush at Kinderhook, waiting for his chance to be sent back to the White House.[17] The Barnburners were a long time in coming to trust the former President, for Van Buren had a way of seeming to be all things to all men. His casual lack of interest in promoting public works and the national appeal of his name finally won them over to the task of making him their man. Van Buren's notion of the political ideal was a party united behind himself. Partly as a result of his ambition the only Democrat who achieved this ideal for the quarter of a century which followed 1844 was Horatio Seymour.

16. *Liberator*, XII, 52.
17. Donovan, *Barnburners*, 35.

Although Governor Bouck's first year in office had been vexed with quarrels and suspicions, the Democrats did well at the elections that autumn when Seymour was sent to the legislature for a second time. They captured ninety-two out of the one hundred and twenty-eight seats in the assembly; and elected twenty-six senators out of thirty-two. Seymour sat with an enormous majority, but a majority divided against itself. Those who find the politics of New York puzzling should remember that if Belgium is the cockpit of Europe, the Empire State was the strategic battle-ground for every great national issue before the Civil War. Banks, tariffs, internal improvements, nativism, temperance, and abolition — all these questions divided men more evenly and fiercely in New York than elsewhere. New Englanders had come into the state by thousands, and year by year the power of their opinions became more and more pronounced, but the conservative tradition of the descendants of the Dutch up and down the Hudson, the votes of the foreigners who settled along the route of the canal, and the great commercial connections of the merchants of New York City, served as a make-weight to the restless notions brought in from the East.

Agitation against slavery slowly but surely changed the political complexion of New York. A glance at the future will show the effect. Polk and Pierce were bedevilled with the elaborate feuds of the disgruntled Democrats of that state, and keeping their experience in mind, Seymour urged Buchanan to promise him that if he were elected President in 1856, he would not put any citizen of New York in his Cabinet or send one abroad as a minister.[18] He himself, it is said, declined the chance to go to England in 1857. If this be so, he must have been embarrassed either with the pledge he had tried to extort or the fact that though the "Softs" had supported Buchanan, they had failed to carry the state. By 1856, then, for the first time a Democrat had been elected President without the aid of New York. Dickinson, the fanatical leader of the "Hards," sent Buchanan an interesting explanation of this significant fact:

18. Flick, *New York*, VII: *Modern Party Battles*, 81.

I had no rational hope of this state after the "free soil" swing of the softs joined the "Republicans," but it was necessary to contest it for many and abundant reasons. Beyond the cities, wherever the *New England* people have sway, they came down like an avalanche, — men, women and children, — priest, and people, and churches, aggregate, and a train of frightened Buffaloes would be no more deaf to reason or argument.[19]

In Albany, Seymour naturally allied himself with Marcy and the Hunkers, who tried to make such headway as they could against the financial policy of "strict construction," as presented by the Barnburners behind their brilliant leader, Michael Hoffman. Comptroller Flagg assembled facts and figures for them; while John A. Dix acted as deputy for Martin Van Buren, and Senator Wright, at Washington, defended the doctrines of the old-fashioned Democrats. Differences as to principles ended in personalities, and Albany became the focal point of the furious contests which led directly to the national defeat of 1848. These fights of pygmies in the legislature seem to have been as tedious to Seymour as to posterity; the party had got control of the state again and its proper business was to govern it. Years afterward, in looking back on the beginnings of the spiteful split which would cost Lewis Cass the presidency, Seymour declared:

I tell the young men, when the opportunity is given to me, not to busy themselves with old men's quarrels. It is foolish, it is wasteful, it is damaging. When I was a young man we engaged in the quarrels of Lewis Cass and Martin Van Buren, and when they were in their graves, we continued the contest. Quarrels always outlive their cause. Thus I say to young men, take no heed of old men's quarrels, for when their causes are in their graves they are apt to continue and become heritages of woe.[20]

When he reëntered the assembly, Seymour was mentioned for the post of speaker, but Edwin Croswell laid his finger on Elisha Litchfield, who was immediately nominated and elected.[21] Seymour, writes Hammond, was probably the preference of "the most intelligent men of the hunker party," but "declined to be a competitor" against the editor's favorite, who hailed from Onondaga.[22] The young member from Utica, however,

19. Flick, *New York*, VII, 87: Dickinson to Buchanan, 1856.
20. Brooklyn *Daily Eagle*, March 13, 1878.
21. Alexander, *History*, II, 60.
22. Hammond, *History*, III, 382.

received the very important chairmanship of the committee on canals, a post in which he made his name.[23] The Democrats were almost equally divided, but the Whigs, it will be remembered, always supported the policy of internal improvements; thus the minority in both houses might be of value to the Hunkers, even though Whig management had been rejected by the voters. Seymour saw the advantage of urging a middle course of action: Hoffman and his Barnburners would fight any resumption of work on the canals, but the Whigs could be counted on to vote for as much as they could get.

Governor Bouck blew hot and cold on the subject. Robert Denniston, of Salisbury Mills, was chairman of the canal committee in the senate, to which he presented a gloomy statement of the situation. Seymour saw his chance and prepared a report in which he shrewdly took care not to contradict or antagonize the Barnburners.[24] He agreed that a sinking fund should be established to extinguish the state debt and that public works should be discontinued if they meant an increase in the debt or even inability to decrease it. He endorsed Flagg's policy of using only the surplus revenue of the canals for new works; the Democrats must not continue the careless spending of the Whigs. To abandon all improvement, however, would, he pointed out, lead to the eventual loss of the earning power of the vast investment which the state had already made.[25] The real difference of opinion between the report which Denniston brought into the senate and that which Seymour offered the assembly rose from a disagreement as to what should be done with the surplus revenues of canals over and above the require-

23. There were three great committees of the assembly: ways and means, canals, and judiciary. There were, however, four candidates for these three chairmanships. For the story of how Seymour got one of the three posts, see Hammond, *History*, III, 389–391.

24. Seymour's Canal Report, Number 177, comprising seventy-one pages, will be found in the New York *Assembly Documents*, *1844*, VII, 177. Because it was an essay on the commercial prospects of New York Seymour's report was frequently printed and became famous. The state debt stood at $23,847,167.62 in 1844, and the annual interest on it amounted to $1,377,261.84.

25. Donovan, *Barnburners*, 48–50.

ments of the act of 1842. Denniston urged that any extra money should be applied to a reduction of the state debt. Seymour, looking to a continual increase of the total receipts from canals, recommended that the surplus every year should be spent on completing unfinished work and improving the canals already in use. Just because the Whigs had been pound foolish the Democrats should not be penny wise.

Seymour saw a great future for the Erie Canal and he insisted on his optimism. The fact that he guessed right makes men looking back from this distance forget how excellent his judgment was at the time, for historians delight in dwelling on the inevitableness of what they know. As in all periods of depression, the very people who had once thought they would be "rich" for ever now talked as if they would always be "poor." Wildcat banking had damaged the credit of the state, but the country was recovering, and the only real danger ahead was the grave risk of another scramble for speculation. The land was full of alarmists, however: three millions of the tax payers' money had gone into the Erie Railroad (never to come out again) — what sound reason was there to suppose that enlarging the Erie Canal would not result in huge losses, also, if not ruin.

In the dark days of the "stop and tax" law, men had talked of having to go to Holland to borrow enough money to carry on the business of New York. Seymour looked west, and, watching the growth of the new states on the Great Lakes, calculated that the tolls of grain moving one way and manufactures moving the other would amply provide for the cost of deepening the canal and widening and lengthening the locks. He presented his case with such skill and persuasion that even Michael Hoffman, one of the most effective debaters in the assembly, refused to vote in the negative on the final roll-call.[26] Thus the chairman of the canal committee of the assembly carried the day, and his triumph was to be all the more personal and com-

26. Hammond, *History*, III, 403–418; and Alexander, *History*, II, 61–65.

plete because the Democrats were almost equally divided between the two factions.

Alexander, historian of New York State according to the gospel of Chauncey Depew, remarks of Seymour's achievement:

It [the canal report] was the first display of that mastery of legislative skill and power, which Seymour's shrewd discerning mind was so well calculated to acquire. The young Oneida statesman had been a favorite since his advent in the Assembly in 1842 . . . a kind, social nature, peculiarly fitted him for public life; and, back of his fascinating manners, lay sound judgment and great familiarity with state affairs. Like Seward, he possessed, in this respect, an advantage over older members, and he was now to show something of the moral power which the Auburn Senator displayed when he displeased the short-sighted partisans who seemed to exist and to act only for the present.[27]

Quite another sort of man, Henry B. Stanton, looking back over forty years through the activities of a life intimately concerned with the bewildering maze of politics and reform, offers at first hand evidence of how Seymour compared at this time with the man who was believed to be one of the ablest speakers of his day — John Van Buren, son of Martin.

Mr. Seymour was then among the most effective and eloquent platform orators in New York. Less electrical than John Van Buren, he was more persuasive; less witty, he was more logical; less sarcastic, he was more candid; less denunciatory of antagonists, he was more convincing to opponents. . . . These two remarkable men had little in common except lofty ambition and rare mental and social gifts. Their salient characteristics were widely dissimilar. Seymour was conciliatory, and cultivated peace. Van Buren was aggressive, and coveted war.[28]

That a Barnburner and an abolitionist should write well of Seymour is not surprising, for he made and kept good friends in both camps of the Democrats. During his first term in the assembly, he had earnestly supported the drastic "stop and tax"

27. Alexander, *History*, II, 61.

28. Stanton, *Random Recollections*, 178. Henry B. Stanton, journalist, lecturer, Barnburner, and abolitionist, married the daughter of the New York jurist, Daniel Cady. All his adult life Stanton was known as little more than the husband of his prominent wife, Elizabeth Cady Stanton. His *Random Recollections*, first published privately in 1885 and 1886, and finally put on sale in a third edition in 1887, is one of the most interesting of all books of reminiscence as to the history of the state.

law, a statute which was far less popular in the legislature than the state. It was he who persuaded Bouck to abandon his plan for "sending a mission to Holland to borrow money" at a time when the future governor hurried up to Albany in the hope of heading off that Barnburner bill for reforming the finances. Seymour, indeed, did so well by the radicals in 1842 that he earned the undying hatred of a prominent resident of Binghamton, Daniel Stevens Dickinson, ardent and eminent advocate of the Erie Railroad, which passed through his town. Dickinson was put on the ticket with Bouck in 1842, and after one term as lieutenant-governor went to Washington as senator. The grudge he nursed against Seymour for having helped in the making of the "stop and tax" law he never forgot. Until secession blasted his last hope of reaching the White House, Dickinson's fierce and effective opposition to both Marcy and Seymour was the chief personal cause of the ruin of the Democratic party in New York.[29] It probably gave the American people Pierce, instead of Marcy, for President in 1853.

Seymour's report to the assembly on April 23, 1844, became the basis for the canal policy of the state for over twenty years. "We do not hesitate," writes Hammond, "to pronounce it one of the ablest and best-written documents ever presented to a legislative body. . . . It ought to be read by every statesman and legislator, who desires to be acquainted with the situation of the public works and the financial condition of the state in the year 1844."[30] The chairman of the canal committee staked his reputation for good judgment on his estimates, for without impairment of the principle of the "stop and tax" law he calculated that the surplus revenues from canals already in operation would provide for the improvement of the Erie and for the completion of the Black River and Genesee Valley canals.

29. Dickinson was not in the legislature at the time the bill was passed, but when the Democratic state ticket was made up in the autumn of 1842, he was named for second place with Bouck, of Schoharie, in first, as a means of angling for the votes of those interested in railroads as well as those committed to canals: Jenkins, *History of New York*, 449–450.

30. Hammond, *History*, III, 410–411.

The timid were probably not persuaded at the time, but one has only to look at the record to see that Seymour was magnificently right. His only error was in underestimating the rise in revenue from the Erie.[31] Actual results surpassed his predictions.

A bill embodying his recommendations passed the assembly by a vote of 67 to 38 — the Whigs voting with the Hunkers. It went through the senate by the close vote of 17 to 13. The noise of the victory and the vindication of the future marked the young member from Utica as the foremost champion of the Erie Canal. What DeWitt Clinton had begun Horatio Seymour was determined to continue. Of the ninety-two Democrats who sat in the assembly of 1844, he alone was returned to the legislature at the elections in November of that year.

31. See the tables of tolls collected (1823–1858) in French, *Gazetteer*, 57; and *Manual . . . of the Legislature . . . 1864*, 514–515.

V

SPEAKER FOR THE HUNKERS

1845

THE Erie Canal was safe for the future because Horatio Seymour had been shrewd enough to unite the Hunker Democrats and the Whigs in support of a moderate policy of continuing to develop it. The Barnburners were beaten for the moment, but they had more than one card up their sleeves. A very able Whig, moreover, was soon to make use of the division in the Democratic majority in the legislature. This Whig was John Young. As leader of the opposition in the assembly Young had learned his lesson from Seymour's skill and decided to reverse the process — with what success, we shall see. Hunkers and Barnburners were agreed on one object, at least: the desire to retain control of the state and to replace Tyler with a Democrat in 1844. Neither faction wished to go out into the wilderness where they wandered when Seward was governor. The quarrels of the President with his adopted party gave the Van Buren men great hopes of sending their favorite back to the White House. Van Buren was, after all, the sponsor for the independent-treasury plan of 1837; and the author of it, Silas Wright, was still the champion of that plan in the Senate. Not only did the victim of the humbug about log cabins and hard cider deserve vindication, but a second election would return the North to power at Washington, and place New York in a position of advantage. Wright's colleague, Tallmadge, who had bolted on the issue of state banks, would soon be leaving the Senate; perhaps a more convenient successor could be found. When, therefore, by the spring of 1844, a majority of the delegates to the Democratic national convention to be held at Baltimore were known to be pledged to Van Buren, everything looked rosy for his restoration.

Texas was to account for a sudden and complete shift of the national scene; yet Texas was the occasion and not the cause of what happened at Baltimore in 1844. Clay, it was commonly believed, was certain to be nominated by the Whigs. The joint thought that they would be the candidates led these two men to make the blunder which was to cost the Democrat from New York the nomination and the Whig from Kentucky the election. It is interesting to notice that two of the ablest politicians our country has ever produced put their heads together, and without success, to block an embarrassing question as to which Americans were not only excitedly divided but determined to express an opinion at the first opportunity. Both Clay and Van Buren were afraid of the issue of the annexation of Texas and both were too clever by half. Their mutual agreement of 1843 recalls the frantic and futile efforts to save prohibition after 1929. While they tried to eliminate Texas it was Texas that eliminated them. Van Buren's miscalculation led him first to regret his folly and then to seek a respectable revenge for his own blunder. Thus it was that New York became the centre of the circumstances which made Taylor President in place of Cass.

Years afterward Tilden, a devoted lieutenant of Van Buren, told a curious story of his leader's fatal opposition to union with Texas. His decision, it appears, was partly an accident. The moment it seemed likely that the question would have to be answered during the campaign of 1844, Churchill C. Cambreleng, one of the ablest and most enthusiastic advocates of the renomination of the former President, wrote him a letter in which he warned him not to come out in the negative if he wished to be elected. Cambreleng had represented the third district of New York in the Congress from 1821 through 1837. He was Van Buren's recognized spokesman on the floor of the lower house, and the President never had any reason to doubt his personal loyalty or his political skill. Follower was wiser than leader in the spring of 1844. The Democrats were determined to have Texas, and Jackson was ready to strike in their favor. According to Tilden the long letter which Cambreleng wrote was almost illegible, and Van Buren laid it aside to decipher at leisure. Before he found the time and the patience to read it through, however, the former President had made the declaration which destroyed his hopes. If Tilden is to be believed, Van Buren acknowledged that the arguments of Cambreleng would have probably altered his decision.[1]

The "crime" of 1844 against Van Buren is a fiction, an elaborate legend invented to explain his misfortune. Out of it sprang the myth of a partisan conspiracy in favor of Polk — a southerner pledged to steal Texas from Mexico. Annexation was accomplished, of course, by joint resolution just before Tyler left the White House, but the conquest of the South West and the Pacific Coast, bringing all the troubles of the Wilmot Proviso and the Compromise of 1850 in its train, tempted northerners to persuade themselves that the Mexican War and its plunder were quietly plotted for in the interest of slavery. This plausible simplification of a very complicated story is unjust — by the same token southerners might have accused Polk of grabbing Oregon for free soil. It has taken a long time to discover that he had much more on his mind than slavery and free soil rolled into one.[2]

1. Tilden, *Letters and Literary Memorials*, II, 608.

2. For Van Buren's personal reactions (1843–1845), see *Proceedings*, Massachusetts Historical Society, XLII: "Van Buren–Bancroft Correspondence, 1830–1845," 381–442. Bancroft's acceptance of the department of the navy from Polk is explained by the fact that Van Buren seems to have had a friendly feeling for the President-elect as late as January 30, 1845:

> I am well satisfied that the President elect goes to Washington with the most upright intentions. How far the Intriguers will be able to bamboozle him remains to be seen. I have, however, strong hopes that their success will not be great in that way, but it is not an easy matter to resist them.

For a late statement of the obstinate story of a Democratic plot against Van Buren, see the volume written by the son of Benjamin F. Butler, William Allen Butler, *A Retrospect of Forty Years: 1825–1865*, 141:

> In a series of letters, written by Silas Wright, from his seat in the Senate Chamber, to my father between May 15 and June 3, 1844, under the strictest seal of confidence, and which have therefore never yet been published, I have very conclusive and interesting evidence of the development of the plans to destroy Mr. Van Buren's candidacy, notwithstanding the fact that a majority of the delegates to the convention had been instructed, and were pledged, to vote for him.

Polk was neither a schemer nor the tool of schemers. His enemies talked like the foes of Hildebrand: he "came in like a fox, ruled like a lion, and died like a dog." After four hard and memorable years in the White House Polk died soon enough to let all those whose heroes he had beaten declare that he deserved his sudden end. The publication of his diary and the scholarship of Professor McCormac show that the gentleman from Tennessee was both a shrewd and conscientious man, more completely successful in achieving what he planned to accomplish, perhaps, than any other President of the United States. He was direct, diligent, and determined in the great office which he filled with rare distinction. Because he kept his own counsel men whom he disappointed called him a liar. His judgment of people was discriminating — as witness his able estimate of Buchanan's strength and weakness. Above all Polk knew what he meant by the word "Democrat." He never failed to act accordingly. The secret of his selection lies in the fact that he suddenly succeeded to first place in the favor of Andrew Jackson.[3]

Van Buren committed political suicide in 1844. The man who got what he himself desired was a candidate only for Vice-President on the ticket with him and his loyal supporter to the last.[4] It was on April 20, 1844, that Van Buren, after waiting for almost a month, wrote his famous letter to Representative Hammet, of Mississippi, in reply to the latter's enquiry as to his position in regard to the proposal to annex Texas. Tyler brought in his treaty with three objects in view: he would gain territory; he would persuade the Democrats to put him up for President in 1844; and he would confound the man he hated more than any other — Henry Clay. Cass, of Michigan, and Buchanan, of Pennsylvania, in answer to similar letters, had each come out in favor of annexation; Polk and Jackson pronounced for what they called "reannexation." Van Buren de-

3. Jackson, *Correspondence*, VI.

4. McCormac, *Polk*, 212–251, *passim*. See *Proceedings*, American Antiquarian Society, XLV (October, 1935), 267–287: Stewart Mitchell, "Four Legends About President Polk."

clared against "immediate" annexation six weeks before the Baltimore convention. Instantly the "field" combined against him, and all his rivals for first place united to elect the chairman and force the re-adoption of the two-thirds rule, which had been invented in 1832.

The majority vote by which this rule was imposed on the whole convention showed that sixty-three delegates had deserted, to this extent, the man for whom they were instructed: if Van Buren could not win the support of two-thirds of the Democratic delegates, he ought not to receive the nomination. To call this "treachery" is far from fair, however happy the delegates who shifted to support the rule may have been over the chance to vote in favor of it. Nor was it discarded until after one hundred years. In 1860 it defeated Douglas, and in 1912, at Baltimore again, Speaker Clark, who surpassed the performance of Van Buren by actually receiving a majority of the convention on eight ballots, was denied the nomination of his party. For a second time the cry of treachery was raised, in face of the fact that to maintain that any Democrat who obtains a majority is thereby entitled to two-thirds would make the rule superfluous. It has been called into question and quarrelled over as often as the Democrats have felt they had a chance to elect a President.

The adoption of the rule did not necessarily defeat Van Buren, or him alone. On the fifth ballot Lewis Cass went ahead of him, and the New Yorkers made up their minds that if their choice should not have the nomination, neither should the gentleman from Michigan. When certain American historians dwell on what they call the growing arrogance of the South before the Civil War, they forget that Presidents like Polk and Taylor, for instance, were the direct result of the North's having failed to unite behind one of its own men for a national nomination. It was no fault of the southerners that the Democrats in 1844 and the Whigs in 1848 went south for the head of the ticket. The upright Benjamin F. Butler of New York was chief of the Van Buren managers at Baltimore, and, although his tactics were criticized, he seems to have been guided by loyalty first to the former President and then to his own state. Butler had authority to withdraw Van Buren's name from the contest at his discretion. The moment Cass took first place he planned a diversion in favor of Senator Wright, but a friend of the latter made this move impossible by declaring that Wright would not take what Van Buren could not gain. Then, at last, Butler turned to Polk, who was unanimously nominated on the ninth ballot.

Hammond's account of Van Buren's loss of the nomination, as told in the fifteenth chapter of the third volume of his *History*, presents a story long believed in the North. This book is practically a life of Silas Wright, and Hammond, it must be remembered, shared the bitter disappointment of the Barnburners at the defeat of Van Buren at Baltimore. Wright's biographer believed that there was a southern conspiracy against the New Yorker, though "Hunker" Croswell was treacherous, and dwelt on the fact that Cass declared for the annexation of Texas only after Van Buren had come out against it. He insisted on the common bond slavery supplied to the southern states, and supposed that Robert Walker, of Mississippi, who became Polk's secretary of the treasury, used Cave Johnson, later postmaster-general, to spy on the New York delegation, "composed indiscriminately of radicals and Hunkers."

In discussing the adoption of the two-thirds rule in 1844, Hammond pointed to the important fact that the imposition of the unit rule on the delegations from Massachusetts and Pennsylvania would have resulted in the defeat of the manœuvre. The same question as to the practice of some states, but not all, of voting their representatives in accordance with the will of the majority of each delegation, especially on measures as to procedure and platform, was to wreck the convention at Charleston in 1860. When some states could split their votes and others could not, a minority had the chance to control a convention. The conspiracy at Baltimore in 1844 was not southern but northern, for while Cass and Van Buren cut each other's throats, Polk walked away with the prize.

According to the first plan of the Democrats their national ticket was to be Van Buren and Polk. The campaign would be a hard one, for Henry Clay would head the Whigs. When Van Buren dropped out and Polk took his place, the managers of the convention turned to the pivotal state of New York and chose Silas Wright for his running-mate. The senator refused the nomination for three reasons: he resented the defeat of his friend; he was unwilling to be accused of having traded Van Buren to his own advantage; and he did not wish to give up an office which he liked — and in which he had still five years to serve. Butler had already accepted the nomination for him when the news of his withdrawal forced the convention to reassemble and substitute Dallas, of Pennsylvania.

The results at Baltimore in 1844 were far-reaching in the state of New York. In the first place, the Barnburners were disgruntled, if not vindictive, even though the Hunkers could hardly be said to have gained anything in the choice of Polk. In point of fact, they lost, for the failure of Van Buren made "Hunker" Governor Bouck, who had been chosen as a compromise between the factions in 1842, no longer acceptable for a second term. New York had lost both places on the ticket, and Democrats felt that something drastic had to be done to prevent its electoral vote from going to Clay. Silas Wright must save the day. Enormous pressure was brought to bear on him by all but the loyal friends who refused to abandon Governor Bouck. The senator wrestled with advice and doubt: only if the Barnburners had the chance to recover control of the state in his person, would they turn out in full strength for Polk. Without New York, however, the election would be lost; Clay would be President. Wright tried to find a way out but he yielded at last, sacrificing himself to his party. He accepted the nomination for the office he did not desire, and "Farmer Bouck" was sent back to Schoharie.[5] Though Seymour stood

5. A good biographical sketch of William C. Bouck, with a portrait, will be found in Jenkins, *Lives of the Governors*, 689–721. This old-fashioned volume contains sketches, with portraits, of all the elected governors of New York from George Clinton to Hamilton Fish; many of these are interesting.

with the governor to the last, he was the first to move that the choice of Wright be made unanimous.[6]

The national election of 1844 was one of the greatest battles of American politics. Henry Clay was known from one end of the land to the other. The sarcastic question "Who is James Knox Polk?" which the Whigs asked up and down the country during the campaign could not have been quite serious at a time when politics was still the favorite sport of the people. The person who twice had been Speaker of the House of Representatives, once governor of Tennessee, and first the left and then the right-hand man of Andrew Jackson, could not have been unknown in any part of the United States. Those who affected to forget who he was had good reason to remember soon enough. Both Jackson and Van Buren hoped to manage him, and neither was successful at the task. Dr. Jameson has called his mind "cool" and "dry" — which means, by implication, that it was never hot or wet.[7] Rhodes has graphically described the discouragement of Clay's supporters at the result; Whigs wept at the news of his defeat, and many of his life-long followers left politics for ever. Their disgust was epic. Yet the chief responsibility for Clay's never having been President lies directly at the door of his own party; twice, in a hopeful year, it passed him by for far less able men — two elderly generals, both of whom happened to win. Even if it be allowed that Harrison deserved his second chance in 1840, no such argument applies to the whimsical preference for Taylor in 1848. Wright more than doubled Polk's plurality in New York, and because New York's vote was decisive it is probable that his sacrifice saved the Democrats from defeat.

Utica returned Seymour to the assembly in the autumn of 1844. In view of the fact that he was the sole Democrat to succeed himself, it seems odd that there should have been a dispute over the speakership. He had put through the canal bill for the Hunkers and had moved the unanimous nomination

6. Gillet, *Wright*, II, 1568.
7. Jackson, *Correspondence*, VI, Preface, v.

SILAS WRIGHT

of Silas Wright at Syracuse in September. He had the important support of Edwin Croswell. The Barnburners, however, pushed their candidate, Crain, for the place, and there ensued one of those factional fights which Democrats had made familiar. The rival groups tried to enlist the support of Governor Wright, who coldly refused to interfere. Although the party was in control of both houses of the legislature, it was split down the middle, as usual, between radicals and conservatives. At the caucus of the sixty-eight Democrats Seymour received thirty-five votes, as against thirty for Crain, and was duly elected speaker.[8] Years afterward Alexander wrote of this contest:

> In the midst of all Horatio Seymour remained undaunted. No one had better poise, or firmer patience, or possessed more adroit methods. The personal attractions of the man, his dignity of manner, his finished culture, and his ability to speak often in debate with acceptance, had before attracted men to him; now he was to reveal the new and greater power of leadership. Seymour's real strength as a factor in state affairs seems to date from this contest. It is doubtful if he would have undertaken it had he suspected the fierceness of the opposition. He was not ambitious to be speaker. So far as it affected him personally, he had every motive to induce him to remain on the floor, where his eloquence and debating power had won him such a place. But, once having announced his candidacy he pushed on with energy, sometimes masking his movements, sometimes mining and countermining; yet always conscious of the closeness of the race and of the necessity of keeping his activity well spiced with good nature. Back of him stood Edwin Croswell. The astute editor of the *Argus* recognised in Horatio Seymour, so brilliant in battle, so strong in council, the future hope of the Democratic party.[9]

Edwin Croswell's support of Seymour calls for explanation. By 1844, in spite, or perhaps because of his industrious speculations, the publisher of the *Argus* was sadly in need of money. Not very long after he became speaker, Seymour was giving Croswell financial aid, going surety for the *Argus*, which was

8. Jenkins, *History of New York*, 532: Appendix to the second edition. Students of the political history of New York should supplement Hammond with Jenkins. These two historians began as friends but ended as enemies. Without reading both authors it is not possible to form a fair opinion of men and issues in New York between 1777 and 1850: Hammond, *History*, III, 518; Donovan, *Barnburners*, 61.

9. Alexander, *History*, II, 91.

doing the state printing free of charge in order to prevent Cassidy's *Atlas* from getting the work. The two men continued their business relations for some years, and early in 1848 Seymour and his friend, Erastus Corning, each advanced five hundred dollars to help Croswell purchase one-half of the three-quarter interest in the *True Sun*, of New York City — a paper with seven thousand daily subscribers, and three thousand by the week. By June of 1848 Croswell was in a corner. A bank failure in Albany threw his affairs in confusion, and again he turned to Seymour and secured the latter's endorsement on a note for five thousand dollars payable in one year. The facts and figures of the finances of editors at Albany are not easy to come by, but Seymour's interest in the eventual union of the *Atlas* and the *Argus* in 1856 was probably as much financial as political.[10]

The assembly over which he was called to preside in 1845 was divided into thirds — Hunkers, Barnburners, and Whigs, not to mention sixteen anti-renters and Native Americans. There were thus four parties represented, and the Democrats were split into two almost equal factions. The Whigs could muster forty-four votes, and before long their brilliant leader, John Young, who ousted Wright from the office of governor, saw his opportunity. Throwing the Whig vote now to the right with the Hunkers and now to the left with the Barnburners, he managed to control the session. His tactics were successful because the Democrats would not stand together.

Four different contests embittered the radicals and conservatives against each other after the Hunkers named their speaker. The first two were of national importance. Both senators in the Congress had resigned immediately after the election, Silas Wright to become governor, and Tallmadge to take charge of the territory of Wisconsin. Governor Bouck replaced them by appointment with two Hunkers — Foster and Dickinson, for the latter had declined a second term as lieutenant-governor.

10. Croswell's letters to Seymour (1844–1848) are in the Seymour Papers, in the New York Historical Society.

On January 17, 1845, the Democratic members of the legislature met in caucus, presumably to ratify Bouck's choices. An elaborate squabble resulted in a compromise as a consequence of which the Barnburners put in John A. Dix for the remainder of Wright's term, and the Hunkers chose Dickinson to serve the six weeks which remained of the term of Tallmadge. Then, by an adroit manœuvre, Dickinson was given a new full term of six years. Once again, as in 1833, New York's delegation in the Senate was deliberately divided — and the Hunkers got the better of the bargain. On the first of the following February, the Democratic caucus balloted for the state officers. It was Seymour's failure to support "Prince" John Van Buren, who was finally nominated for attorney-general, that made the sharp-tongued son of the former President his lifelong enemy.

The second controversy grew out of the making of Polk's Cabinet. The feeling that the state was entitled to a seat was unanimous, and Polk himself seems to have taken this for granted. Jackson, it will be remembered, was still active — having lived long enough to see the last defeat of his bitter rival from Kentucky. When Polk turned to him for advice, Jackson, it is interesting to observe in view of future recriminations among the Democrats, urged that Governor Wright should not be asked into the Cabinet.[11] Polk, however, had already offered Wright the treasury in a letter of December 7, 1844.[12] The governor-elect found himself duty-bound to decline the offer — perhaps he remembered that Van Buren's sudden resignation, after two months at Albany in 1829, had not been well received by the voters of New York. The friendly correspondence between the governor and the future President as published thirty years later, in Ransom H. Gillet's *Life and Times of Silas Wright*, shows the mutual confidence and cordiality of their relations. Wright generously attributed his "surplus" vote in New York to the support of Manhattan Whigs, who wished no more

11. Library of Congress: Polk Papers: Andrew Jackson to James K. Polk, December 16, 1844. See Jackson, *Correspondence*, VI, 342–343.

12. Gillet, *Wright*, II, 1631–1632.

money wasted on canals. This notion of his was significant — as we shall see later.

Polk consulted Van Buren, also. Not only did his influence entitle him to attention, but the two men had a joint friend in Bancroft, who was soon to become secretary of the navy. Van Buren approved of the offer made to Wright and suggested Benjamin F. Butler as secretary of state and Comptroller Flagg as secretary of the treasury. At this point, according to the legend, the wily Edwin Croswell is supposed to have appeared on the scene and persuaded Polk to offer Butler the war office, knowing he would decline.[13] Polk, however, we happen to know, had his own way of doing things. He did, indeed, ask Butler to become his secretary of war, but Butler declined for the reason that he thought the duties of the office unfamiliar — and perhaps beneath his dignity. Then Polk turned to William Learned Marcy, who jumped at the chance to go into the government and made a national name for himself during the Mexican War — partly as a result of a controversy with the pompous General Scott.

As late as March 1, however, Van Buren believed that a Barnburner would go into the new Cabinet, but Polk decided that Flagg's national reputation did not warrant his being made secretary of the treasury.[14] In their resentment the radical Democrats of New York were less than just to President Polk, for their only actual grievance was his failure to offer Flagg a place. Two Barnburners turned him down; then he appointed a Hunker. Marcy was still intimate with both Van Buren and Wright in the spring of 1844.[15] Van Buren himself was offered the ministry to England as late as May, 1845.

If Polk had ever really been the dupe of the New York politicians, the ancient story of Edwin Croswell's successful plot would be more plausible. For many years most of this President's

13. For the conventional account of the choice of New York's representative in Polk's Cabinet, see Alexander, *History*, II, 94–95.

14. McCormac, *Polk*, 296.

15. *Proceedings*, Massachusetts Historical Society, XLII: "Van Buren–Bancroft Correspondence, 1830–1845," 381–442.

policies were explained by what was supposed to be his secret hope for a second term. The publication of his diary shows that the suspicion is false; his singular independence of the desire to be reëlected largely accounts for his remarkable success during four years. The sincerity of the following two entries can not be called into question. Polk backed neither Hunker nor Barnburner.

> I will do, as I have done, Mr. Martin Van Buren's friends full justice in the bestowal of public patronage, but I cannot proscribe all others of the Democratic party in order to gain their good will. I will adhere sternly to my principles without identifying myself with any faction or clique of the Democratic party.
>
> I am perfectly disgusted with the petty local strife between these factions [Barnburners and Hunkers of New York]. There is no patriotism in it on either side. I have in many instances refused to lend myself to either and have alternately given offense to both.[16]

Gillet, the devoted friend of Wright, adds his testimony to the balance in favor of the honesty of Polk:

> Mr. Polk was highly indignant that any one should have been made to believe that his friendship for Governor Wright had cooled or abated, and especially that he could be supposed to desire his defeat or the overthrow of the democracy of the State. The Author used every possible means to counteract the mischief which had spread from the false assumptions concerning Mr. Polk's designs and wishes, but with very little success.[17]

The Barnburners, however, were furious at having lost a place in the new Cabinet — and all the more so for the fact of Hunker Marcy's having got it.[18]

The approach of a Democratic administration at Washington had not improved the political situation of the Democrats of

16. Polk, *Diary*, I, 104; II, 405.

17. Gillet, *Wright*, II, 1671. See Polk, *Diary*, II, 218, for a full refutation of the falsehood to which Gillet refers.

18. As late as 1856 James Buchanan, in a talk with John V. L. Pruyn, repeated substantially the usual story of the formation of Polk's Cabinet. Buchanan, however, laid the suggestion that Marcy be appointed to John Cramer, then at Washington, and added that Butler tardily decided to accept after Marcy had been offered the post: *Magazine of History*, XVI, 1 (January, 1913), 28. Gillet, *Wright*, II, 1646, defends the uprightness of Polk's intentions in appointing Marcy to his Cabinet but falls in with the Barnburner opinion that the consequences were disastrous both to Governor Wright and the Democratic party.

New York. In a sense, the two factions had broken even: each had a senator, and the governor was a Barnburner; while the state's representative in the Cabinet was called a Hunker. Marcy, however, was undergoing a conversion, for his controlling ambition made him hope for an end of the feud which paralyzed the power of New York in national conventions. Ill-natured gossip made mischief all during Governor Wright's two years of office: the Hunkers accused him of scheming to succeed Polk, and the Barnburners believed that Marcy and his friends were using all their influence with the President in order to head him off. Silas Wright's misfortune was chiefly owing to his character, for however successful he may have been at Washington, at Albany he was so inept in action as to make common enemies of mutually hostile men. His governorship was a painful example of just how much a man of high principles should not sacrifice to his sense of honor. New York has had no chief executive more honest than Silas Wright and none less lucky.

As soon as the legislature went to work, it was obvious that the Democratic majority was at the mercy of the Whigs. They were clever enough to see their opportunity. Although Seymour was never so able as when he was losing a fight — at his very best whenever the odds were against him — he had little or no reason to look back on the session of 1845 with any sense of pleasure or success. Two very important measures came before the assembly. First there was the question of canals, and the speaker took the floor in the committee of the whole to discuss the governor's message.[19] During the election of 1844 Seymour's brother-in-law, R. B. Miller, wrote to Wright to enquire as to his attitude toward the unfinished canals of the state — particularly the improvement projected along the Black River. The Democratic nominee replied that in view of the steady increase in canal revenues there would be no "two opinions in the Legislature upon the question of recommencing and completing" unfinished canals so long as the pledges of the "stop

19. Albany *Argus*, March 1, 1845.

and tax" law were lived up to.[20] Seymour, also, approached Wright on the subject and received a letter which served to quiet the fears of the Hunkers for a time.[21] Much depended on just how the "stop and tax" law was to be administered. Seymour presented the case so successfully that a bill to continue the Genesee Valley and Black River canals was carried through both houses, John Young throwing the Whig votes in favor of this Hunker policy. The bill appropriated almost two hundred thousand dollars for the work and made only partial provision for the redemption of the principal part of the debt. Wright promptly returned the bill with his veto.[22] The Hunkers were astonished and angry.

In the meantime, the legislature had been considering the question of the constitution of 1821. There was a general agreement throughout the state as to the need for certain changes, but differences of opinion on policy boiled down to one of method — should the existing constitution be amended, or would it be wiser to make a new one? There was no provision for amendment other than action by the legislature or a convention of the people by which the first government had been organized.[23] Sticklers for legal propriety, chiefly Hunkers, pointed out that the legislature had no authority to call a constitutional convention. Their lawyers urged the etiquette of dancing-masters on the representatives. They might have done

20. Gillet, *Wright*, II, 1573–1574.

21. New York Historical Society: Seymour Papers: Letter of Silas Wright to Horatio Seymour, October 28, 1844. Seymour, alarmed at charges that Silas Wright was hostile to all internal improvements, got this letter from Wright through the mediation of Jabez D. Hammond. In 1844 Wright received a majority of 821 in Oneida County; in 1846 John Young, the Whig candidate, beat him in that county by 1,337 votes: Gillet, *Wright*, II, 1813. Wright was defeated for reëlection as governor not at Washington but in New York.

22. Hammond, *History*, III, 555–561. Barnburners accused Seymour of having pushed the bill in order to force Governor Wright to veto it. Seymour's denial of any such intention is strengthened by the fact that the canal bill passed the senate by a vote of 14 to 9, six Barnburners having suddenly and mysteriously absented themselves, although their votes would have spared Wright the necessity of his veto. Five of the six truant senators were well known to be opposed to the bill.

23. Lincoln, *Constitutional History*, II, 210.

better to remember that the national convention which framed the federal Constitution in 1787 assembled with specific instructions to do no more than amend the Articles of Confederation but submitted, instead, a wholly new basis of government for the thirteen states. In this dispute John Young voted his Whigs with the Barnburners and forced through a call for the constitutional convention of 1846. The conservative Democrats, however, foolishly played into the hands of the radicals during the five or six years when the vexing question was under discussion. Declaring that a constitutional convention could properly be called only after a mandate from the sovereign people, they failed to insist on their policy of merely amending the old constitution of 1821. As early as the "stop and tax" law of 1842, the radicals had thought up a means of protecting the people of New York from its legislature — the electorate should have the final voice on any issue of bonds. Governor Bouck and his Hunker friends had shelved measures looking toward such an amendment in 1844.[24]

The finances of the state, it was felt, however, were not the only matters which stood in need of reform. The constitutional convention of 1821 had abolished the council of revision and vested the veto power in the governor. It had done away with the more famous, or infamous, council of appointment without a dissenting voice, providing that department officers were to be chosen by means of open and separate nomination by the two houses of the legislature and subsequent election on joint ballot. The remaining offices of the state were to be filled by appointment by the governor with the consent of the senate. In 1846, two hundred and eighty-nine offices were at their disposal.[25] The constitution of 1821, in other words, had greatly increased the power and importance of the governor. By 1842 it was felt that the chief executive had grown too strong.

There was, in addition, agitation for an extension of the elective franchise and a reconstruction of the courts. Those who

24. Donovan, *Barnburners*, 43–44 and 68–69; Hammond, *History*, III, 385–389, and see, also, 424–427 and 535–546.

25. Werner, *Civil List*, 128.

openly or secretly desired a constitutional convention had a twofold task before them — not only must they prove that amendments were necessary but they had to convince the people of New York that the amendments they desired would never be put through according to the methods provided by the constitution of 1821. In this the Whig minority completely outwitted both Hunkers and Barnburners. Their general was John Young.

At the same time Seymour was presenting his canal report in 1844 he sat as one of a committee on constitutional amendments, the four other members of which were so divided as to give him the decisive vote. Although a meeting of radicals at Albany in the autumn of 1843 had shown strong sentiments in favor of calling a constitutional convention, Governor Bouck devoted a large part of his second message to an argument against the wisdom of such a course. A few months later the committee of five of which Seymour was a member declined to report a convention bill to the assembly in spite of the protests of two of the five — one of whom was a Barnburner, Michael Hoffman. The Whigs held a meeting of protest at the Eagle Tavern in Albany.[26] Ultimately, however, the legislature of 1844 submitted to the people six amendments, all of which were approved at the election in the autumn of that year. To become effective these six amendments had to receive a two-thirds vote in both houses of the legislature which would sit in 1845. Governor Wright found these six proposed amendments satisfactory and urged that they be tacked on to the constitution of 1821. Their defeat would make a constitutional convention inevitable.

John Young made up his mind to kill them. By skillful management he succeeded in uniting enough of the Whig, the anti-rent, and the Native American vote in the legislature to throw out four of the six. Then Crain, Seymour's rival for the speakership, brought in a bill for a convention. It was referred to the committee on constitutional amendments which delayed action in the vain hope of preparing some measure that should

26. Hammond, *History*, III, 424–426.

have the united support of the Democrats. John Young, however, forced legislative action before the majority could arrive at any agreement. The bill for a convention, it was decided, should be made a special order at noon each day until it was disposed of. Governor Wright failed to hold the Barnburners in check; enough of them voted with the Whigs to pass a resolution which directed the committee to report on the bill Crain had brought in.

In the great debate which followed during the spring of 1845 Speaker Seymour was pitted against Young, the leader of the opposition. Croswell's *Argus* and Weed's *Evening Journal* made a partisan issue of their arguments.[27] "Dorr's Rebellion" in Rhode Island was the subject of heated dispute: New York, it was agreed by both sides, should learn by example. Seymour used all his "skill and ability" to show that if only all those who desired amendments rather than a new constitution would unite, a convention could be avoided. As politely as possible, he questioned the sincerity of the Whigs. They had lost the national election of 1844 and now they hoped to "produce a new order of things" which might be more favorable to their designs and objects.[28] Young countered by accusing Seymour of supporting the constitution of 1821 because it kept the Democrats in power. His closing words to the speaker were prophetic of the reproaches Seymour was to meet almost twenty years later during the Civil War:

> I have a single word to say to him. There is much of him to cultivate for good. He has shown himself the possessor of high and brilliant talents, and if he would forget party, and turn aside his passion for place and power, and the narrow path of party discipline and tactics — tear away the drapery he has thrown around himself, and stand out his own living self, breathing out the purposes of his generous heart, I hope I shall [*sic*] live to see that gentleman occupying the highest station that his ambition may desire.[29]

The convention bill passed both assembly and senate, much to the disgust of the Hunkers. Much to their dismay Governor

27. Hammond, *History*, III, 544–554.
28. Hammond, *History*, III, 545–546.
29. Hammond, *History*, III, 553–554.

Wright signed it.[30] The vote of the people was overwhelmingly in favor of calling a convention: 213,257 as against 33,860.[31] At the same election, however, the Democrats gained six members in the assembly and lost only three in the senate.[32] Young landed on the top of the heap. He had forced the governor to veto a canal bill which the Hunkers desired and sign a convention bill which they hated, and he had made his own reputation over night. Seymour was defeated, but Wright was doomed. The speaker, in fact, emerged from the session with honor, if not prestige.

> Horatio Seymour led his party, and, though other Hunkers participated with credit, upon the Speaker fell the brunt of the fight. He dispensed with declamation, he avoided bitter words, he refused to crack the party whip; but with a deep, onflowing volume of argument and exhortation, his animated expressions, modulated and well balanced, stirred the emotions and commanded the closest attention. Seymour had an instinct "for the hinge or turning point of a debate." He had, also, a never failing sense of the propriety, dignity, and moderation with which subjects should be handled, or "the great endearment of prudent and temperate speech" as Jeremy Taylor calls it; and, although he could face the fiercest opposition with the keenest blade, his utterances rarely left a sting or subjected him to criticism. This gift was one secret of his great popularity, and daily rumours predicted harmony before a vote could be reached.[33]

The gentleman from Utica had presided over an assembly which was really divided among three major parties. For all his integrity (or perhaps because of it) Silas Wright was neither a suave nor a quick-witted confederate. He had earnestly preferred to stay in the Senate, and his party had compelled him to become a governor. Even though he saw that the Democrats were divided, his conscience and his principles would not permit him to lure them into union. Yet all was not lost to the Hunkers — Dickinson was in the Senate for seven years, and Marcy sat in the Cabinet of President Polk.

The disappointments of the session of 1845 persuaded

30. For a clear digest of the struggle for the constitutional convention of 1846, see Donovan, *Barnburners*, 68–69.

31. Werner, *Civil List*, 129.

32. Donovan, *Barnburners*, 70–71.

33. Alexander, *History*, II, 99.

Seymour to leave the legislature. He refused to offer himself as a candidate that autumn and returned to eight quiet years of private life at Utica. Though he retired from office, he did not quit the councils of his party. It was alarmingly obvious that what the Democrats of New York needed was some sound basis for unanimous action in order to control the state. Without the support of New York no party could govern the nation for long. Seymour set to work to find this basis. By 1856 he felt that he had failed. Just as often as he repaired the damage of defeat and faction some new trouble would tear the Democrats asunder. Thomas Jefferson and then Andrew Jackson had left the party too large an inheritance of power in New York. The Democrats reigned there but they could not govern.

VI

THE DEATH OF SILAS WRIGHT

1847

THE constitutional convention met at Albany on the first of June and adjourned the ninth of October. This convention was dominated by Michael Hoffman, the Barnburner, and John Young, soon to be Whig governor. Seymour was not a member — in fact, many of the Hunkers were noticeable by their absence. Lincoln's *Constitutional History* contains a thorough and judicious study of the work of this body as preserved in the third constitution, which lasted until 1867.[1] On the same day that Silas Wright was defeated for reëlection, it was ratified by a vote of more than two to one. Apparently those who had tried to head it off misinterpreted popular opinion or endeavored to deny it a right to be heard. At best, the Hunkers had guessed wrong. The new instrument forbade the legislature to borrow money without a vote of the people; extended the elective franchise; provided for the popular election of most of the general and local officers who had formerly been chosen or appointed by the legislature or the governor; and created an independent court of appeals. Thus the year 1846 marks the real dividing line between the old state and the new.[2]

One of the most powerful agents in procuring the new constitution was an active group of agitators from a limited area in the state. The capital was at the centre of the disturbance, and the common grievance was the ownership and tenure of land.

1. Lincoln, *Constitutional History*, II, 9–217.

2. Partly as a consequence of having been deprived of the important powers of appointment no governor of New York between Silas Wright (1845–1847) and Edwin D. Morgan (1859–1863) was reëlected to office. The influence of Dorr's Rebellion in Rhode Island on the debates before and in the convention is significant. The young democracy of the Locofoco campaign was coming into its own at last.

During Governor Wright's term the trouble came to a head, and he was forced to proclaim martial law in the farming county of Delaware. The legal complications of what is known as anti-rentism were not all unravelled until long after the Civil War, but the main issue was fought out in the forties and fifties. The whole trouble originated in the Dutch patroon system of leasehold, as practised in the great domain which was founded on the upper Hudson by Kiliaen Van Rensselaer, merchant prince of Amsterdam, and director of the Dutch West India Company. When New Netherland and Rensselaerwyck became an English province in 1664, Dutch titles to land were confirmed. By 1839 the descendants of Van Rensselaer controlled a huge feudal estate in the heart of New York.

Readers interested in the details of this manorial system will find an illuminating description in Lincoln.[3] At this day it seems odd that the system should have survived as long as it did. The actual ownership of land continued in the proprietor; settlers were tenants of farms they had to improve and develop themselves. In 1786 Stephen Van Rensselaer III, the sixth patroon, assumed the management of the manor, and on the advice of his brother-in-law, Alexander Hamilton, devised a new form of conveyance, giving an absolute title, but requiring annual rent in grain, fowls, and personal service. If the tenant sold, Van Rensselaer had the first right to buy, and if a third person were the purchaser, Van Rensselaer received one-quarter of the purchase price. It was this quarter-sale provision, in Albany, Rensselaer, and Columbia counties, which was to cause most of the discontent called anti-rentism.[4] The sixth patroon was an easy landlord, but when he died in 1839 and his two sons tried to collect the rents which their father had allowed to fall in arrears, the trouble began. Sheriffs were of no avail, and Governor Seward had to call on the militia; whereupon the

3. Lincoln, *Constitutional History*, II, 10–27.

4. Cheyney, *Anti-Rent Agitation in the State of New York*; and Howell and Tenney, *The County of Albany*, 277–285. In 1852, in the De Peyster Case, the court of appeals declared the system of collecting quarter-sales illegal and forbade leases in perpetuity, citing the law of 1787, which had abolished "feudal tenure."

rioters dispersed. Seward's message of 1840, while urging law and order, showed that he regarded the system of leasehold and quarter-sales with no favorable eye.

As if Governor Wright had not trouble enough already in disloyalty at Albany and envy at Washington, the anti-renters became violent again during his term. Delaware County, as we have seen, was put under martial law and, after several clashes between farmers and militia, a number of people were lodged in jail. Wright, like most governors before and after him, was a lawyer, and it must be allowed that he leaned backward a little to be legal. Unluckily for him, the constitutional convention of 1846 which abolished the leasehold system for the future was no help till after he was out of office. This new constitution and victories in two out of three famous lawsuits were to do much to remove the grievances of the anti-renters, so that after 1850 they exerted little influence on the state elections. Their hostility to Governor Wright, however, was undoubtedly a contributing cause to his tragic defeat in the autumn of 1846.

The people of New York got their new constitution, and the farmers would get their land, but still another and a terrifying issue came on the scene as a result of the Mexican War. Polk added an empire to the Union and gained the finest harbors on the Pacific Coast of North America for the United States; yet the quarrel over the extension of slavery which ensued on these triumphs almost destroyed the country he loved. On August 8, 1846, a Democrat of Pennsylvania, David Wilmot, offered his famous proviso to the House of Representatives.[5]

5. There was more to Wilmot's act than met the eye. In 1846 he had voted for the Walker Tariff and was promptly dubbed a "Doughface," a northern man of southern principles. In thus supporting President Polk, Wilmot had disregarded the instructions which the legislature of Pennsylvania had sent to the representatives and senators from that state. He pushed his proviso as a means of rebuilding his political fences in the district he represented — he wished to curry favor with the sentiment for "Free Soil" in his part of the country. Wilmot became the Republican candidate for governor of Pennsylvania in 1857 and served as a senator in the Congress from 1861 to 1863. See the *Mississippi Valley Historical Review*, XVIII: Richard R. Stenberg, "The Motivation of the Wilmot Proviso."

The New York delegation was split wide open on the vote by which it passed — Preston King, of Wright's own county of St. Lawrence, led the Barnburners in the cause of Free Soil. These men looked on the Wilmot Proviso as a pledge to maintain free soil in Texas — where slavery, it was believed, had been abolished by Mexico — rather than as a challenge to the growth of the South. If Mexican soil had been free soil, so it must remain if it became American.[6] The Hunker, Dickinson, disregarding instructions from the legislature at Albany, aided in the narrow defeat of the proviso in the Senate. For three years national politics revolved around this vexing measure, representatives passing it, and senators defeating it.

As early as 1845, though he was serving as speaker for the Hunkers, Horatio Seymour, as appears in a letter from Silas Wright to John A. Dix, took his stand for free soil:

> The Speaker (Mr. Seymour) told me he did not think he could support any proposition for annexation which tolerated slavery in any part of the territory. I told him, what I believe to be true, that I did not think our democracy wished to go to that extent; that they would be willing to make a fair and liberal compromise upon that point, if a corresponding spirit was met with from the south; but that there was danger, if extreme demands were made and persisted in there, they might, by and by, lead to extreme demands from the north, with an equally uncompromising spirit.[7]

For the moment, it will be remembered, only the annexation of Texas was under discussion, and that was an accomplished fact before President Tyler left office. Seymour, however, stuck to his guns on this subject. In 1848, after the defeat of the Democratic national ticket in November, the historian, Hammond, wrote to him by way of negotiation for a reunion between the Democratic factions: "You claim to be in favor of a Declaration by Congress against the intrusion of slavery in the Territories. So are we [that is, the Barnburners]."[8]

By 1854, Seymour, who was then governor, privately expressed the opinion that the expense of slavery would finally

6. Dix, *Memoirs*, I, 205.

7. Gillet, *Wright*, II, 1625.

8. New York Historical Society: Seymour Papers: Jabez D. Hammond to Horatio Seymour, November 22, 1848.

exterminate a system which could never survive the competition of free labor in the North. He was talking to his house-guest, Miss Amelia Murray, who had met him at Newport during the summer, and was starting out on one of those tours of the United States which learned ladies from England were once very fond of making. Before she returned home Miss Murray had gone as far as Canada and Cuba, sketching landscapes and botanizing. Although politics, in the language of Artemus Ward, was not her "forte," this inquisitive blue-stocking was not by any means the pretentious fool which one reviewer of her book of travels would have had the readers of the *Times* believe. Miss Murray thought the governor described the institution "graphically":

"If the early settler wanted to buy beef, he must buy the whole ox — hide, horns, and tail; then comes a time when he can procure a quarter; and at last, as population increases, he can go to market and purchase a beef-steak, or any joint most pleasing to his taste. Now the same thing occurs in the case of labour, which, after all, is a marketable commodity. At first it may be necessary to take the whole man; then you can hire part of a man; and in due time you may be able to get so much of the time of a man as may just suit your purpose, without being burthened by his infancy or his old age." Thus we, who have been seeking to check the institution of Slavery by violent means, have unintentionally been prolonging it; but time will repair this mistake, by rendering the possession of slaves an expensive mode of cultivation — that is, if cotton can be cultivated without it.[9]

Doubt has recently been raised as to whether slavery was actually doomed by the laws of economics, for the able managers among the very small percentage of southerners who held slaves seem to have been making a success of the system on the large plantations. Free labor could not compete with the skillful use of slaves on a large scale.[10] Once the abolitionists and the free soilers had joined forces, however, Seymour was alarmed,

9. Murray, *Letters from the United States*, 129. For a contemptuous review of Miss Amelia Murray's book of travels, see the London *Times*, January 29, 1856. An anonymous reviewer expressed the opinion that Miss Murray was "ignorant and vain," and "frequently imposed upon," concluding: "she has spread her slender substance into a couple of volumes. She has done her best to make slavery popular and botany tedious, but she has principally succeeded in the latter department. Thus we kiss hands and part."

10. See, especially, Gray, *Agriculture in the Southern United States to 1860*, I, 462–480: Chapter XX, "Economic Efficiency and Competitive Advantages of Negro Slavery under the Plantation System."

for he argued that the only proper place in which to agitate for emancipation was the South. It was one thing to keep free soil free; it was quite another thing, in his opinion, to attack the institution of slavery as legally established — except from inside the states concerned.

Slavery is often used as the acid test of a statesman before the Civil War. Hindsight, however, distorts historical judgment of the men and the issues that lived and pressed for settlement before it. Hatred of foreigners, especially Catholics, and causes like prohibition dropped out of sight during the confusion of the great war and remained hidden for a long time. People are likely to forget that both the abolitionists and the slave-holders talked and threatened secession for years. Some northerners hoped to have a Union of their own without slavery; some southerners wished to found a separate nation on it. In both the North and South these men were in the active and mischievous minority. Many good people believed that it would be best for the two great sections to separate in peace — Horace Greeley, for instance. As early as 1820 the dangerous bargain of the Missouri Compromise had begun the plausible but doubtful practice of admitting states to the Union two at a time, one slave and one free, just as Maine and Missouri came in together.

If this balance could be maintained indefinitely, the Senate would remain evenly divided, what though the more rapid growth of the North would give Free Soil the advantage in the House of Representatives. Soon, however, it would be Senate against House. The seed of hatred had been sown in the Constitution of 1787. According to this first bad compromise, three-fifths of the slaves might be counted for seats in the House, and before long this dodge festered like a thorn in the side of the North. If slaves were only property it was obviously unjust to count any of them; if, on the other hand, they were persons, then they should all have been counted, as other non-voters like women and children. The upshot of the Civil War can hardly be said to have resulted in disadvantage to the South, in this respect, for now the southern states not only count all their negroes for representation but allow few or none of them to vote. They have gained strength, not lost it.

Looking backward to the Civil War men are tempted to assume that the outcome of the argument between slavery and Free Soil was certain to be violent. There were dangerous signs, to be sure — quite apart from the irritating activities of the abolitionists. The political excitement of the campaign of 1844 pushed into the background the alarming sectional split in the Methodist church. These Christians quarrelled over slavery and they remain separate to this day. *Uncle Tom's Cabin*, moreover, was to excite the sentiment of a whole generation in the North. Many people tried to forget that owners of slaves were hardly likely to be cruel or careless with expensive pieces of their own property. Though some men beat their horses, and abuse their automobiles, that sort of shiftless person seldom owned a slave. The fact that Mrs. Stowe's story was fiction (even if not pure in motive) did not make it any the less irritating and outrageous to good citizens of the South. It is hard for Americans to remember the great importance of a book which very few of them care to read at this day. Public opinion was changing, however: in 1846 New York rejected equal suffrage for negroes by a vote of 223,834 to 85,306. Exactly fourteen years later the returns stood 337,934 to 197,505 against the innovation.[11]

About a week before the constitutional convention adjourned, the Democratic state convention met at Syracuse on the first of October, 1846. It was a hard-fought affair — both Seymour, the Hunker, and John Van Buren, the Barnburner, were seated after contests. "Prince" John, son of the ex-President, so called because he had danced with the future Queen Victoria while his father was momentarily minister to England in 1832, was to play a spectacular part in the politics of New York for the next twenty years.[12] Governor Wright was renominated, and after

11. Werner, *Civil List*, 130–131.

12. Six John Van Burens played parts in the politics of New York. Two of them are commonly confused: the first of these was John Van Buren, son of Martin — "Prince John," who died at sea in 1866 while returning from England.

the first ballot Seymour moved that the choice be made unanimous, but one Crocker, of Oneida County, objected. Four of the fourteen votes against renaming the governor came from this same county.[13] The radicals, however, controlled this convention two to one. Addison Gardiner was named for lieutenant-governor, and then the delegates expressed their approval of the Oregon Settlement with Great Britain, the tariff of 1846, and the reënactment of the independent-treasury law. After voicing their desire for a "speedy and honorable" end to the Mexican War and endorsing the new constitution, the members of the convention voted a "handsome eulogy" on Governor Wright, and dispersed.[14]

The Whigs put up John Young, of Genesee, who had wrecked the legislative program of the Democrats in 1845 and was commonly regarded as the man who had made the new constitution possible. President Polk was disappointed with the outcome of the election in New York but his personal and political loyalty to Wright does not make it impossible that certain members of his Cabinet were glad to have the governor out of their way. A reëlection in 1846 would have made him the obvious heir to the President. Wright himself was dubious if not discouraged: his party had been out-manœuvred in the legislature, and all the fury of its folly had descended on his head. His handling of the anti-rent riots had been ungracious, even harsh. Silas Wright was the sort of man who tempts shallow people to believe that only scamps can stay in office. His integrity fairly bristled. His worst fears were to be realized — John Young was triumphantly elected governor in his stead.

In 1845 he was appointed attorney-general of New York and served until 1847 — his successors being elected. The son of Martin Van Buren was always a rival of Seymour — with the single exception of 1862. Colonel John Dash Van Buren came from Newburgh, in Orange County, and was an intimate friend and political assistant of Horatio Seymour, who used him on private and important business as late as 1868.

13. Albany *Atlas*, October 10, 1846. The Utica *Observer* repeatedly warned the Democrats not to nominate Wright again in 1846. The attitude of this paper and others is one argument against the possibility of Hunker treachery, for "conspirators" would hardly speak and act openly.

14. Hammond, *History*, III, 677–680.

Hammond printed a letter which Wright sent to one of his best friends a day or two after the election. He refers to his defeat as not "wholly unforeseen" nor any cause for "severe personal unhappiness." One sentence refers to the suspicions of his supporters: "Hereafter I think . . . our enemies will be open enemies, and against such the democracy ever has been able, and ever will be able, to contend successfully." Wright's further reference to his "errors" shows that he realized that he had been taken advantage of.[15] Between the defeat of Wright in 1846 and the election of Hoffman in 1868 on the ticket with Seymour, a stretch of twenty-two years, the Democrats were to elect a governor only twice, and each time Horatio Seymour was their successful candidate.

During December 1846 the Albany *Atlas* published a post-mortem analysis of the Democratic defeat. This remarkable series of articles was reprinted in Barnburner papers all over the state; it was brought out as a pamphlet for popular distribution. Although the articles were unsigned, they were subsequently attributed to Wright himself, but his letter of November 8 carries the implication that he can not have been the author — or did not intend to be, at least, one month before they appeared. It is not easy to fix the responsibility for his defeat. In the first place, the total vote fell off one hundred thousand from that of 1844. The decline in the governor's vote accounted for more than half of this loss. Addison Gardiner, however, Democratic candidate for lieutenant-governor, was elected, but Gardiner shared with Young the endorsement of the anti-renters.[16] Conservative Democrats had predicted Wright's failure to be re-elected; secretly, perhaps, they were pleased at the outcome, but there were many cross-currents in 1846.[17] In 1848 so shrewd

15. Hammond, *History*, III, 757.

16. Donovan, *Barnburners*, 76.

17. Dr. Donovan came to the conclusion that the "weight of evidence seems to sustain the contention of the radicals that their factional opponents were willing to see Wright sacrificed." An examination of the vote in the town of Western, Oneida County, makes it appear that "more than six-sevenths of the Democratic voters in that town cut Wright's name": Donovan, *Barnburners*, 80. Gillet observed of Wright's defeat, "There is no avoiding the conclusion that

a politician as Tilden declared publicly that the Hunkers were to blame for the overthrow of Wright two years before.[18] The campaign had national repercussions, also, for out of the thirty-four representatives from New York the Whigs elected twenty-three, and Polk found himself with a hostile House on his hands.

After Silas Wright piled a wagon high with his belongings and drove his wife and himself back to Canton in the dead of winter, peace between Hunkers and Barnburners was never to be more than a truce. Twice before the Civil War Horatio Seymour would negotiate a compromise between these factions, and on the very eve of secession it looked as if he might restore the party to control of the state. The Charleston convention put an end to these hopes. After 1846 New York habitually sent rival delegations to the national conventions of the Democratic party. At one of these all the contesting delegates were seated with half a vote apiece. Three defeats — 1848, 1856, and 1860 — in the state in the next four national campaigns were to leave the party prostrate by the time Lincoln entered the White House.

Seymour withdrew to what cynical enemies would one day call his "pent-up Utica" in the summer of 1845. His single term as speaker had ended in fatigue and disappointment, as is shown in a confidential and revealing letter he sent to former Governor Bouck, whom Polk was soon to make assistant-treasurer in New York City. The former speaker echoed Democratic anger at the general destruction of the legislative program of the preceding spring: "I fear I am devoting more time to these matters than I should, but I feel exceedingly anxious to see some gentlemen exposed and punished."[19] He corresponded regularly with Marcy at Washington. The conclusion of one of the letters he received from the harassed secretary of war is characteristic:

---

this was the work of treachery by a portion of those calling themselves 'conservative democrats' ": Gillet, *Wright*, II, 1793.

18. Tilden, *Public Writings*, I, 234.

19. New York Historical Society: Seymour Papers: Horatio Seymour to W. C. Bouck, February, 1846.

"I should have been pleased to have a personal interview with you, in which I could have gone into explanations that can not be made in a letter" — Marcy did not care to set down a story of the administration which, looked at from a distance, must have seemed confusing.[20] The chronic quarrel concerned the doling out of jobs. Seymour took the initiative. Early in 1846 he made a visit to Washington, where he found Secretary Marcy and the rival senators — Dix and Dickinson — pestering the plodding patience of President Polk.[21] The petty politics of the capital seem to have disgusted him.

In not standing for the legislature in the autumn of 1845 Seymour chose wisely, for the session of 1846 accomplished nothing in the way of promoting peace between Barnburners and Hunkers. The party had gained six seats in the assembly, and the radicals had increased their numbers in the senate. The latter body witnessed a violent debate on Texas and the question of endorsing the national administration, the Hunkers lashing out at Preston King, who had deserted Polk and was soon to vote for the Wilmot Proviso. The trouble-making resolution evaporated in vituperation. Edwin Croswell, the perpetual state printer, was the occasion of a second tug-of-war. Three years before, it will be remembered, Thurlow Weed had been turned out of the office. First Croswell prevented its being given to his former partner, Van Dyck, who had gone over to the *Atlas*, and then he blocked the appointment of W. C. Bryant, editor of the radical New York *Evening Post*. The Barnburners were determined, however, to keep Croswell from coming back. An enquiry into the cost of state printing led to a bill in the assembly which named William Cassidy of the Barnburner *Atlas* state printer. By skillful negotiation with the senators Croswell pushed through another bill to abolish the office and then offered

20. New York Historical Society: Seymour Papers: W. L. Marcy to Horatio Seymour, June 15, 1845.

21. Polk wrote down carefully an account of the absurd circumstances of the strife over his appointment of a single brigadier-general from New York in 1847. His story gives no credit to any of the three New Yorkers involved — Marcy, Dickinson, or Dix: Polk, *Diary*, II, 399–405.

to do the printing of the state free of charge. Both radicals and conservatives had lost the prize — to the profit of New York.[22]

During the years 1846 and 1847 Seymour devoted his time to his private affairs. It must have been difficult for him to keep his hands, if not his eyes, off politics, for the summer of 1847 saw exciting changes in his state. At the end of August came sudden and painful news. At eight o'clock on the morning of the twenty-seventh Silas Wright had walked to the post-office at Canton for his mail. He had hardly sat down among his neighbors to look over his letters when he spoke of feeling ill: his ruddy face turned pale, and he complained of a "sense of suffocation about the heart." Friends called a physician, who gave him medicine and walked home with him at nine. One hour later he was dead. Hard work on his farm in the heat of summer had brought on a stroke of apoplexy.[23] That two such very different persons as Whittier and Polk should have lamented the loss of Silas Wright is proof of the character and the appeal of this almost forgotten man.[24] So long as Wright lived there was still hope of revenge, first on Croswell, whom Barnburners accused of a nefarious league with Thurlow Weed the year before; then on John Young, who was said secretly to have promised to pardon all the anti-rent leaders whom Wright had put in prison [25] — and finally on the Democratic traitors at

22. Minute and complete information by counties of the newspapers and periodicals of New York State to 1859 is given in French, *Gazetteer*. The *Argus* was founded in 1813 by Jesse Buel. It became a daily in October, 1825, when Croswell took control. The *Atlas* first appeared in 1841.

23. Hammond, *History*, III, 730–731.

24. Polk, *Diary*, III, 153:

Intelligence reached the City to-day of the sudden death by apoplexy of the Honorable Silas Wright, late Governor of New York. He was a great and a good man. At the commencement of my administration I tendered to him the office of Secretary of the Treasury, which he declined to accept. I was intimate with him when he was in Congress. He was my personal and personal [political] friend, and I deeply regret his death.

The honesty of the sentiment of this entry is corroborated by the important correspondence Wright and Polk exchanged between December 7, 1844, and October 30, 1846.

25. Gillet, *Wright*, II, 1807.

Washington. The radicals had lost their leader, but the Hunkers had made a martyr.

In the stormy state convention which met at Syracuse for five days in September, 1847, it was James S. Wadsworth, of Geneseo, who first shouted the word "murderers" at the Democratic enemies of Silas Wright. Radicals and conservatives struggled for control, and when the Hunker majority refused to adopt resolutions sustaining the Wilmot Proviso, the out-numbered Barnburners declined to accept the proceedings as a "true index of Democratic sentiment," and arranged for a convention of their own in February, 1848. In the meantime, the Whigs carried off the bone of control of the assembly. The Hunkers, in order to anticipate the Barnburners, gathered at Albany on January 26, 1848, and appointed delegates to the national convention which would meet at Baltimore the following May. On February 16, the Barnburners met at Utica according to schedule, and after hearing Tilden tell the true story of the loss of the election of 1846, named a rival delegation to go to Baltimore in their behalf. Thus a double quota of New Yorkers put in an appearance, each half denouncing the other as a fraud. When the perplexed managers of the party proposed to divide the vote equally between these delegations, the outraged Barnburners went home. After a parley at Albany they assembled at Utica, on June 22, 1848, and chose an independent ticket of Van Buren for President and John A. Dix for governor.[26]

General Dix maintains that both Van Buren and he were personally opposed to the extreme measure of a separate ticket in 1848. According to him, they yielded their better judgment to the voice of the majority of the rebellious Barnburners. After the Free Soil convention at Buffalo, a second gathering of Democrats at Utica ratified the nominations of Martin Van Buren and Charles Francis Adams and proceeded to insist that Senator Dix run for governor. Lewis Cass of Michigan was the

26. The story of this revolt is told concisely in Johnson and Smith, *History*, II, 362–366.

national nominee of the Democrats, and on the ticket with him the Hunkers named Reuben H. Walworth for chief executive of the state. Once again, it seemed likely, the electoral vote of New York would be decisive. By dividing their numbers the Democrats had lost the election before they began to campaign.

This third-party movement of 1848 reflects very little credit on any of the participants. If the one purpose of it was to keep Cass out of the White House, its success can not be denied. Webster's jibe that the movement ought properly to be called the "Free Spoil" party was not altogether unjust. In Polk's opinion Mr. Van Buren was the "most fallen man" he had ever known.[27] Before long the President openly defied the Barnburners by summarily removing Van Buren's friend, Benjamin F. Butler, as United States attorney in New York.[28] Twice had Martin Van Buren accepted national nominations at the hands of the Democratic party; in 1844 he had sought a third in vain. Whatever principle it was which forced him to head the Free Soil ticket in 1848, the extremely short life that principle enjoyed provokes surprise. The sincerity of the Democratic rebels of 1848 is not beyond doubt, for men who could support Pierce in 1852 and Buchanan in 1856 must have bolted Lewis Cass for reasons not remote from spite and envy.

Prince John Van Buren, for instance, pitched into the fight of 1848 in behalf of his father and stormed up and down the state; yet two years later he accepted the Compromise of 1850, and from 1853 to 1861 supported the supposedly pro-southern administrations of Pierce and Buchanan. Senator Dix openly avows that his heart was not in the cause; in 1860 Dix voted for Breckinridge. So far as Polk is concerned the passage of time and the publication of his diary have cleared him completely of the ugly suspicions which were partly responsible for the Democratic revolt of 1848. When the Duc de Broglie watched his enemies unite to turn him out of the premiership, he observed: "This is not an opposition; it is a coalition of hatreds."

27. Polk, *Diary*, IV, 67.
28. Polk, *Diary*, IV, 114–115.

It seems clear that in 1848 the Barnburners tricked the Free Soilers into supplying the disguise of reform for their own political revenge on Polk and Cass. The Van Burens, both father and son, were famous dandies in their day; all that their gay enterprise wanted in respectability was provided by the bleak countenance and stern conscience of Charles Francis Adams. The Whigs carried New York, but the rebels ran second. Cass came in a close third. Once more a divided North had given a united South a President.

Immediately after the catastrophe of 1848, Seymour was approached with proposals looking toward a reunion of the party in New York. In this he took the lead of his lifelong partner, for Marcy had been a member of the hated Cabinet of Polk. The ticklish part of the business was to make advances to John Van Buren, who acted in the capacity of political trustee for his distinguished father. Seymour was suave, and Prince John was sarcastic and spectacular. The compromise which these two men arranged between themselves was to hold together for several years — partly, perhaps, because the Democrats were out of power both at Albany and Washington. The result justified the long and elaborate negotiations for a truce — as early as November, 1848, Jabez Hammond, in behalf of the radicals, had sounded out Seymour as a leader of the Hunkers.[29] By the following May, Seymour was sending out feelers through the state.[30] According to Dix, who had run second for governor, two classes of Democrats were hostile to any reunion with the Barnburner supporters of Free Soil — the extreme southern Democrats, and "those at the North who relied for success on a close alliance with them." [31]

A compelling appetite for office drew Barnburners and Hunkers together. The Democratic state convention held at Rome in July, 1849, was suspiciously harmonious: the delegates

29. New York Historical Society: Seymour Papers: Jabez D. Hammond to Horatio Seymour, November 22, 1848.

30. New York Historical Society: Seymour Papers: D. A. Ogden to Horatio Seymour, May 30, 1849.

31. Dix, *Memoirs*, I, 261.

smelled sweetness and saw light. Two conventions sat side by side and soon became one. Union was easy, at the moment, for there was no Democratic national administration to discuss and quarrel over. Endorsement of the policies of Washington was now the concern of the Whigs. Seymour had been patient and serene: he knew that if he only let John Van Buren get all the glory of the reunion conventions at Rome, the party could be knit together again.[32] Alexander found this famous reconciliation puzzling, particularly in view of all the high and mighty principles which were preached in the campaign of 1848.

It is difficult to realise the arguments which persuaded the Barnburners to rejoin their adversaries whom they had declared, in no measured terms, to be guilty of the basest conduct; but, after infinite labour, Horatio Seymour established constructive harmony and practical co-operation. . . . Seymour and Van Buren did not unite easily. From the first they were rivals. As an orator, Seymour was the more persuasive, logical, and candid — Van Buren the more witty, sarcastic, and brilliant. Seymour was conciliatory — Van Buren aggressive. Indeed, they had little in common save their rare mental and social gifts, and that personal magnetism which binds followers with hooks of steel. But they stood now at the head of their respective factions. When Van Buren, therefore, finally consented to join Seymour in a division of the spoils, the two wings of the party quickly coalesced in the fall of 1849 for the election of seven state officers.[33]

The Barnburners had punished Polk and Cass and had avenged the disappointment of Van Buren and the death of Wright. The source of that summer reunion at Rome was not spirit but earth. At least one of the leaders openly acknowledged that he knew what he was doing:

John Van Buren described it, in his graphic style: "We are asked to compromise our principles," said he. "The day of compromise is past; but, in regard to candidates for state offices, we are still a commercial people. We will unite with our late antagonists," he added. Then, paraphrasing the Declaration of Independence, he said: "And we will hold them as we hold the rest of mankind — enemies in war, in peace friends." [34]

Alexander took words too seriously: so far as the Democrats were concerned the third ticket of 1848 had been designed to

32. Johnson and Smith, *History*, II, 374–375.
33. Alexander, *History*, II, 149–150.
34. Stanton, *Random Recollections*, 165.

DANIEL S. DICKINSON

JOHN VAN BUREN

defeat Cass. The Hunkers accepted Free Soil in principle, but the "spirit" of the crusade of 1848 was "absent": once John Van Buren had avenged "the insult to his father," his horror at slavery would "vanish like a breath."

Hunkers like Edwin Croswell believed that Seymour let the Barnburners get the better of the bargain at Rome. The disgruntled editor of the Albany *Argus* lamented Seymour's refusal to run for the legislature in the autumn and deplored what was announced as his definite retirement from public life. "It is," he wrote, "a matter to be regretted on every *public* ground."[35] It is odd, however, that the Hunkers should have been angry at the light punishment which their leader served out to the seceders, for the Free Soil ticket had captured the larger part of the Democratic vote in 1848. The conservatives were even more irritated at the result of the November elections, for of the seven men they had nominated for the state offices on the Barnburner–Hunker ticket only four were elected. The Democrats carried the assembly by a margin of two, but the great Whig majority in the senate gave that party control of the legislature on joint ballot.

The compromise at Rome is significant for quite another reason. From the summer of 1849 the factional names Hunker and Barnburner drop out of the political history of New York. When the Democrats next divided, they called each other "Hards" and "Softs." The casual use of these nicknames by men who were familiar with what they meant confuses present-day students of the history of New York. Allowing for all the personal ambition involved in the second split in the fifties, it is safe to say that the "Hards" were conservative Democrats who seceded from the union Seymour and Van Buren patched up at Rome in 1849. These "Hards" were the extreme Hunkers who complained that Seymour had allowed the radicals to get the better of him and capture the Democratic party. In their

35. A series of letters from Edwin Croswell to Horatio Seymour written in the summer and autumn of 1849 will be found in the Seymour Papers in the New York Historical Society.

desperate resentment they looked south for a political alliance with the slave states. The "Hards" received financial support from the great merchants of New York, who sold supplies to the plantations. When the "conscience" Whigs, moreover, rebelled against Fillmore's having signed the Fugitive Slave Law, many of the "cotton" Whigs voted for the "Hards." The rise of the American party in the meantime complicated politics even more with its campaigns against foreigners and Catholics. By the fifties Maine exported the very popular policy of prohibition. The bogies of rum, Romanism, and slavery knocked foolish heads together all over the North. In 1854 four candidates for governor set up for themselves in New York: Clark, the Whig, who was "dry"; Seymour, the "Soft," who was "wet"; Ullman, the "American"; and Bronson, the "Hard." This election washed away the last political vestiges of the great days of Thomas Jefferson and Andrew Jackson.

The Wilmot Proviso and Free Soil had divided the Democrats of New York in 1846. The Compromise of 1850 saved the Union for the moment, and killed the Whigs for good. The state was hostile to the compromise — savagely so on the subject of the Fugitive Slave Law. Taylor died in the midst of the discussion, but when Fillmore of Buffalo signed the measures on which the Congress had agreed, he opened a destructive feud with Seward, who had succeeded Dix in the Senate in January, 1849. It is interesting to notice that every effort to maintain the Union was fatal to the party which happened to be in power at Washington at the time. For twenty years before the Civil War control of the national administration exploded in the hands of each party by turn, and in every case the fuse was lighted in New York.

The Compromise of 1850 had the last and beneficent blessing of both Webster and Clay, who were soon to disappear. Men of good will thought that it would take slavery out of politics — if not for ever, at least for as long a time as the dodge of the Missouri Compromise had brought quiet to the country. Pierce was to benefit by the national sense of relief. By 1856, however, Buchanan became President of the United States on a minority of the popular vote, and New York was carried by Frémont. That the result was partly due to the fact that once again a former President from the Empire State, Fillmore, was running for President on the American ticket ought not to have deafened the Democrats to the alarming state of popular opinion. The time was coming — it was, in fact, at hand — when control of New York would be essential to control of the nation.[36]

The Compromise of 1850 offered many Democrats in New York a convenient chance to climb back into the fold of the united party which issued from the conventions at Rome in 1849. The everlasting Edwin Croswell paid a visit to Washington during the summer of 1850. Writing to Seymour shortly after the death of President Taylor, he shrewdly predicted that the succession of Fillmore to the White House would fatally divide the Whigs. The Democrats in Washington were hoping for the return of Dickinson to the Senate. The Free Soil Democrats at the capital, he added, favored the nomination of Seymour for governor in order that the party might recover control of the House of Representatives by means of gains in the delegation from New York.[37] The sudden shift of scene caused by the death of the President, the apparent success of the Compromise of 1850, and the prestige he had gained from his bargain at Rome, seemed to have lured Seymour back to public life.

In the summer of 1850, according to the disillusioned Alexander,

Men deemed it politic and prudent to affect to believe that the slavery question, which had threatened to disturb the national peace, was finally laid at rest. The country so accepted it, trade and commerce demanded it, and old political leaders conceded it. In this frame of mind, delegates found

36. Since 1856, New York has cast her electoral vote for a losing candidate for President only twice — if we omit the exceptional circumstances of 1876. Seymour in 1868 and Hughes in 1916 received the support of New York, and both were citizens of the state. Even if it be thought that Tilden was really defeated, New York has voted with the losing side only three times. In each case the defeated candidate was one of her own sons.

37. New York Historical Society: Seymour Papers: Edwin Croswell to Horatio Seymour, July 18, 1850.

it easy to nominate Horatio Seymour for governor and Sanford E. Church for lieutenant-governor. . . . resolutions favoring a vigorous enforcement of the fugitive slave law were adopted; and a coalition ticket with Seymour at its head was agreed upon.[38]

Seymour's intimate friend, Hamilton Fish, a man whom he much resembled, was rounding out his one respectable term as governor and was soon to go into the Senate. Less than twenty years later this same Fish would enjoy the distinction of being the only able man whom the dazzled Grant chose for his Cabinet. Seymour and he were good companions all their lives; their characters and tastes were congenial; they wore their whiskers in the same style. Both Whigs and Democrats sneered at the rich respectability of these two amiable men. Hamilton Fish and Horatio Seymour are an interesting instance of the artificial nature of political divisions in fair weather — they were fast friends and lifelong political foes. The salt of difference had lost its savor.

Seymour was named for governor in September, 1850, to the almost general delight of his party. The *Argus* called him a "Democrat without variableness or shadow of turning." The candidate had his doubts as to what might happen. He was rarely, if ever, sanguine in appealing to the people.

I do not regard the result of the election as certain, on the contrary I think it is very doubtful. . . . Our difficulties are yet imperfectly healed and the quarrel among the Whigs has not diffused itself throughout the masses. . . . I have great faith that the politics of this state are hereafter to be more respectable than they have been heretofore. . . . I am the poorest of letter writers, and the extent of my correspondence of late has quite bewildered my head.[39]

The mutually hostile Seward and Fillmore Whigs had met at Utica and united on Washington Hunt of Lockport as their candidate for governor. The only issue in 1850 was which of two gentlemen should go to Albany for the next two years. Seymour had good reasons for his lack of confidence. The feud

38. Alexander, *History*, II, 155–157.

39. New York State Library: Manuscript Section: Letter of Horatio Seymour, October 10, 1850.

of 1848 was only two years behind his party, and the lawsuits arising from the ownership and sale of land were still unsettled by the courts of the state. He and his wife were both heavily interested in real estate — the Bleecker property was at the very centre of the trouble. In 1850 the anti-renters endorsed every candidate on the Democratic ticket except himself. On October 10 the *Argus* declared that

> The Loco Foco party of this State is once more a unit. A somewhat turbulent session of three days, terminated in the nomination of a ticket which will be acceptable to the great mass of both sections. Mr. Seymour, though classed with the Hunkers, is less obnoxious to the Barnburners than many other prominent members of the party. He is a gentleman of fair talents and enjoys considerable personal popularity. There are many greater men in the Loco Foco ranks, but there are few better adapted to the crisis, or who would receive a stronger vote.[40]

The campaign of 1850 was not a duel; it was a fencing match. Washington Hunt and Horatio Seymour bore themselves with a dignity and a consideration for each other which made victory something for which to apologize. They repeated their stately act in 1852. In 1850 the vote was practically a tie: Hunt, 214,614; Seymour, 214,352. It is not easy to estimate the effect of the anti-rent vote, but the Democrat who had the endorsement of the cause, Sanford E. Church, was elected lieutenant-governor, running a little less than four thousand votes ahead of Seymour. The result was not certain until late in November.

There was still another complication to the campaign of 1850. On October 30 a mass-meeting of merchants assembled at Castle Garden in New York City and appointed a union safety committee of fifty members, to nominate a fusion state ticket, headed by Horatio Seymour. By this method, the conservative business men of the city intended to rebuke the Whigs for their unseemly quarrels over "conscience" and "cotton" in regard to slavery. These merchants decided to serve notice on

40. Albany *Argus*, September 14 and 23, 1850. The use of Locofoco is amusing, as well as the cool endorsement of the candidate; there were greater Democrats in New York, but Seymour, it would seem, was merely the most available partisan for the office.

Senator Seward that they stood by the Compromise of 1850; they would show their southern customers that slavery had been taken out of politics in the North. "These rich gentlemen," writes von Holst, "thought themselves entirely sure of victory, and the Whigs, without allowing their own courage to fail, granted that they had not worked in vain in the city." Horace Greeley, however, comforted the upstate districts with the prediction that any shift of votes in Seymour's direction would not come up to the expectations of the "followers of King Cotton," and that the drift of the "adopted citizens" in the opposite direction would cost the Democrats more than they gained.[41]

With the loyal support of New York City Seymour might have pulled through in 1850, but the local trouble there cut his plurality to 705. Fernando Wood was running for mayor, and the respectable Democrats who rebelled against the rowdy methods of Wood and Tammany voted for the Whig candidate, Ambrose C. Kingsland, who was elected.[42] Senator Dickinson was also a drag on the state ticket. In 1846, it will be remembered, he had disregarded the instructions of the New York legislature and had voted against the Wilmot Proviso in the Senate. Dickinson served on the committee which framed the famous Compromise of 1850, and he came back to the state toward the end of his seven years at Washington confident of reëlection. But the convention which nominated Seymour for governor refused to endorse the record of New York's Hunker senator, and Dickinson was furious, as only Dickinson could be.[43] Ever afterward he was the enemy of Seymour, whether he pleaded for the South until 1860 or raged against the rebels during the Civil War. The Whigs held the legislature in 1850 on joint ballot, and Hamilton Fish took Dickinson's seat in the Senate.[44]

41. Von Holst, *History of the United States*, IV, 13.

42. Myers, *Tammany Hall*, 152.

43. New York Historical Society: Seymour Papers: Edwin Croswell to Horatio Seymour, October 26, 1850.

44. Senator Dickinson had a grievance, for he was really defeated for reelection by a legislative trick. No choice could be made for several weeks. The

The closeness of the vote in 1850 was a compliment to Seymour. His greatest triumph was personal, for he carried his home city of Utica, which had voted Whig consistently since 1828 — except for 1830, when Governor Throop carried it against Francis Granger.[45] The support of Seymour by his own neighbors was a peculiar source of pride. He had always stressed the power and the importance of the community; for him, the great stage of public life was local. If towns would take care to govern themselves well, the several states and the Union, he believed, could not fail to follow suit and flourish. The post of path-master at Deerfield, he once declared, was the only office he had ever asked for, and in doing the duties it called for he suffered his sunstroke of the summer of 1876. Seymour took his cue from Jefferson — yet not always. In 1846, for example, he opposed the radical Democrats who were pressing for a new constitution for the state in the very name of Thomas Jefferson and his theory of periodic revision. The words and acts of the author of the Declaration of Independence, like those of Lincoln, supply arguments and convenient quotations for every kind of politician. Few men seem disposed to master, or even remember, the whole doctrine of either.

Seymour must have closed his first campaign for governor with a sense of satisfaction: he had showed the Democrats that he could divide the vote of New York with the Whigs in a two-party contest; he had run well ahead of those defeated Whigs who shared with him the disapproval of the anti-renters; and he had reversed the usual result in his own city and county by carrying them safely.[46] His ability to run ahead of his ticket was soon depended on by the Democrats. Three out of six times — 1850, 1852, and 1854 — he brought Utica and Oneida

moment two Democratic members had to go to New York the Whigs forced through a resolution to proceed with the election, and Thurlow Weed's candidate, Hamilton Fish, was finally chosen senator after a continuous struggle of fourteen hours: Johnson and Smith, *History*, II, 385. Dickinson always believed that he had been defeated by connivance.

45. Jones, *Oneida County*, 34–35. Seymour carried Utica by a vote of 1201 to 1059.

46. See Map 1.

County over to his side. In 1862, in 1864, and again in 1868 he lost them. Even Horace Greeley could describe him in 1850 as "an able and agreeable lawyer of good fortune and competent speaking talent, who would make a highly respectable governor."[47] Not to have the editor of the *Tribune* rail at him might have seemed the most durable satisfaction of all to another kind of man than Seymour. Four years later Greeley was calling him a public enemy because of his cool distrust of the methods of the men and women who were preaching "temperance" and abolition.

Apart from their candidate, however, the Democrats had little or no reason to feel satisfied with the result of the election of 1850. For a third time in succession the Whigs had sent a governor to Albany, and now, at last, for the first time since 1800 neither senator in the Congress belonged to the party of Jefferson and Jackson. The Compromise of 1850, coupled with the fact that a Whig President from New York would sign the Fugitive Slave Law, was to give them still another chance before the confusion of the Civil War. That they failed to make the most of their last opportunity was largely owing to the jealousy of Daniel Stevens Dickinson and the easy-going good nature of Franklin Pierce. Yet the name of a third man was at work, also: Silas Wright seemed to be even more powerful now that he was dead than when he was alive.

47. Alexander, *History*, II, 158.

VII

TO BALTIMORE AND BACK

1852

ACCORDING to James Buchanan the Compromise of 1850 "ought never to have been disturbed by Congress."[1] Apart from whatever sense of justice it may lack, this judgment is at least plausible, for though the immediate effect of the bargain which Clay and Webster worked for was the destruction of the Whig party, the Kansas–Nebraska bill by which Douglas planned to "repeal" the Missouri Compromise of 1820 was to break the Democratic party in half throughout the North. James Buchanan, as Polk could not forget, was a reformed Federalist who had come over to the old Republican party as a youngish man in the days of the era of good feeling. The President for whom he served as secretary of state from 1845 to 1849 found Buchanan something of an "old maid." For all his real ability the only President from Pennsylvania showed the professional politician's passion for trying not to answer questions which the public insisted on asking.

If the compromise had stood, however, it would have been difficult to build up a national opposition to the Democrats on nothing more than nullification of the Fugitive Slave Law, no matter how annoying such nullification might be to the South. The Kansas–Nebraska proposal was all the more effective in the North because men who professed to be disciples of Jefferson found it very difficult to deny the claims of Douglas for local sovereignty on the subject of slavery. The settlement of 1820 was specious, as Abraham Lincoln himself acknowledged. Though Seymour believed that slavery would disappear in competition with free labor, though he resented agitation against slavery where it did not exist as causing more trouble than

1. Buchanan, *Works*, XII, 14.

slavery itself, the Douglas doctrine of allowing the citizens of territories to add more slave states to the Union if they chose was hard to counter. Both men took refuge in their foresight that new states from the North West would come in free.

For the moment, however, the political advantage lay with the Democrats. For a second time an old general had died on the hands of the Whigs, who treated Fillmore like the accident he was. In New York the summer and winter of 1851 were filled with plans for the national campaign of the next year. Democrats were out of office everywhere and eager to get back. Most picturesque, perhaps, of them all, Daniel Stevens Dickinson had retired to Binghamton after more than six years in the Senate to brood over the wrongs he had suffered from ingratitude and treachery. This son of Connecticut was a curious man — he wore his white hair long and wrote poetry. Years before, as lieutenant-governor and thus president of the state senate, he it was who ruled that the bill by which the state presented his beloved Erie Railroad with three millions of dollars was not a financial measure and did not, therefore, need the two-thirds vote required by the constitution.[2] His platform manner appealed to the public, for he made vituperation a fine art. From 1851 until secession and Fort Sumter Dickinson was the champion of the South in New York. Once the southern states seceded, however, he who had been the follower of Andrew Jackson breathed out blasts of fire and slaughter on the rebels. In 1861 the Republicans elected him attorney-general of New York; in 1864 he came within an ace of going on the Union ticket with Lincoln. As President of the United States instead of Andrew Johnson he would have proved an interesting experiment. As for New York every circumstance combined to confirm and intensify his hatred of Horatio Seymour: the Utican would veto a bill for prohibition and, worse still, leave the Hunkers for the "Softs."

Marcy was in temporary retirement, but he had made a name for himself as Polk's secretary of war, and his eye was on the

2. Hammond, *History*, III, 352–353.

future. Seymour and he corresponded regularly, and their letters constantly refer to conversations in a vague and tantalizing way. They saw too much of each other to make their correspondence a matter of primary importance. During the summer and autumn of 1851 Marcy began to feel confident that the Barnburner faction had been won over for good and insisted that the Democratic state convention at Rochester should stand on a "national platform" and endorse the whole Compromise of 1850 or nothing.[3] Some of the former Hunkers and Barnburners, united since 1849 in what would soon be called "Soft-Shell" Democrats, or "Softs," saw difficulties in the way. Dickinson, for one, stood in Marcy's path to the presidency and would divide the delegation of New York if he could. Then, too, Judge Greene C. Bronson, the irascible old gentleman with whom Seymour had studied law, had handed down a decision against the canal law of 1850 — Bronson was a Democrat, and his party suffered as a consequence. The Whigs must not be permitted to pose as the exclusive friends of the canals. Marcy's conversion to the "Softs" was the subject of jealous speculation. As late as 1847 he had denounced the Barnburners bitterly; he fought their third ticket in 1848 and refused to join Seymour in 1849, when the latter made "heroic efforts to re-unite the party" at Rome. Hardly had union been achieved, however, when the sudden death of President Taylor and the exciting prospect of succeeding Fillmore reconciled Marcy to the new situation. Why should not Polk's secretary slip in between Cass and Buchanan in 1852? Seymour and the Van Buren men are commonly supposed to have persuaded Marcy that he could.[4]

However that may be, William Learned Marcy was an earnest candidate for the nomination in 1852, and to suppose that his efforts to obtain it were only a means of making his appointment to Pierce's Cabinet inevitable in 1853, is absurd.[5] Dix

3. New York Historical Society: Seymour Papers: W. L. Marcy to Horatio Seymour, July 28 and September 7, 1851.

4. Alexander, *History*, II, 169–170.

5. Dix, *Memoirs*, I, 266–267.

brought this charge, but Dix wrote without knowledge of the confidential letters which passed between Marcy and Seymour during the winter and spring of 1851–1852. The correspondence leaves no reasonable doubt as to the serious intentions of both men.[6] Marcy's failure can not be laid to any lack of earnestness and effort on the part of both himself and his friends.[7] In describing the struggle for control of the New York delegation to Baltimore in 1852, Professor Nichols concludes that Marcy was probably the first preference of a majority of the Democrats. He and his supporters hoped that he would have the vote of New York in the convention by means of the choice of Themistocles — every rival aspirant would place Marcy second to himself.[8] The strategy of Dickinson and his men was to accuse Polk's secretary of war of having been a traitor to Cass in 1848; and then secretly to try to prevent the New York delegation from being instructed for him in 1852. Marcy, in their eyes, was a turncoat Hunker who could never carry New York with him in a national election. The denunciation which, for opposite reasons, both Seymour and Marcy suffered from the extremely radical and conservative sections of their party, is confusing; but it might be offered as excellent evidence of their common sense and moderation.

Marcy chose Seymour to act as his confidential agent and general manager at Baltimore in 1852. His was the delicate task of winning the support of the state for his friend in spite of the clamor of the mutually hostile "Dough-Face" and Free Soil Democrats. At the same time Marcy must not allow him-

6. Seymour's letters are in the Marcy Papers in the Library of Congress, and copies of Marcy's letters are to be found in the Seymour Papers, New York Historical Society. See especially Seymour's letters of August 7 and December 1, 9, and 25, 1851, and February 18 and March 26, 1852. The last letter, written from the political hot-bed of Washington, is a superior specimen of the diplomacy of New York politicians. Seymour writes: "I have been very guarded and conciliatory in my language and treat these attacks [on Marcy] as the natural result of disappointment and have avoided any appearance of annoyance. — Among strangers, cheerfulness and composure imply strength and confidence."

7. *Magazine of History*, xv, 1 (January, 1912), 78–79: W. L. Marcy to John V. L. Pruyn, May 31, 1852.

8. Nichols, *Democratic Machine*, 98–99.

self to be put in the position of seeming to deny Cass, the victim of 1848, a second chance at the presidency. A great number of the delegates in the national convention would demand another nomination for the senator from Michigan. It was Seymour's belief that to run Cass a second time would only revive the furious feud with Van Buren. Marcy, on the other hand, had served Polk well, and had worked with Van Buren. His only weakness in New York derived from the baseless charge that he had been jealous of Silas Wright and disloyal to him at the time of his defeat in 1846. Barnburners repeated the accusation, but it has gone without evidence to this day. Although Seymour was shrewd enough to know that the Democratic party in New York was nothing more than a temporary union of two halves, his desire to see Marcy President drove him on to do his best to get the office for him. Hindsight, if not foresight, probably made him realize that for Democrats to win a national election would be dangerous if not disastrous to the party in New York, for they squabbled over offices and then quarrelled about policies the moment they got into power.

In April, 1852, Seymour and his friend, John V. L. Pruyn, went to Washington together to promote the candidacy of the man they hoped to make at least the favorite son of New York. Just before he left Utica to sound out the members of the Congress, Seymour wrote, "I have no resentments nor commitments, to embarrass me beyond my relationship to Governor Marcy."[9] Already his friend had two-thirds of the delegates.[10] Dickinson, however, who was supporting Cass for the nomination in the secret hope of inheriting his strength, was represented in Washington by his son-in-law, Birdsall, and the champions of Buchanan and Douglas were not unwilling to see the two rivals from New York devour each other. Seymour carried a letter of introduction from Marcy to Senator Downs,

9. New York State Library: Manuscript section: Horatio Seymour to an unnamed correspondent, April 15, 1852.

10. New York was entitled to thirty-six votes in the Baltimore convention. The state convention in January chose twenty-three delegates for Marcy and thirteen for Cass.

of Louisiana, by means of which he was supposed to get in touch with southern Democrats; thus Pruyn and he planned to checkmate Marcy's enemies at Washington.

The capital was filled with intrigue during the spring of 1852, for it was the popular feeling that the Democrats were going to carry the country in the autumn. Seward and Fillmore Whigs were tearing their party asunder, and it was doubtful if Cass could get a second nomination. Careful respect, however, had to be paid to his friends. What chiefly irritated Marcy was the vexatious Dickinson's charge that he had compromised his principles in order to court the Free Soil vote. Time and again he returned to this subject in his letters to both Pruyn and Seymour, reminding them that the whole truth about his record would "show Southern men what sort of a friend I am and have been to them."[11]

On May 24, Marcy, writing from Albany, sent Seymour, John B. Skinner, and Erastus Corning, three of his best friends, a letter which committed to their discretion the control of the use of his name at the Baltimore convention. Corning was the delegate from Marcy's own district; Seymour and Skinner were delegates-at-large, and the Utican was the leader of the delegation. Marcy's instructions are an interesting example of the devious measures which are not uncommon in national conventions even at this late day. "You will as a matter of course," he wrote, "freely and fully consult and advise with all my friends in the delegation and respect their wishes in regard to the course to be taken; but in the event there should be a contrariety of views among them, the final and absolute decision will rest with you." Accompanying this letter was another, marked "confidential," written the same day and containing suggestions for every contingency which had occurred to Marcy.

11. New York Historical Society: Seymour Papers: Copy of a letter of W. L. Marcy to Horatio Seymour, May 29, 1852; *Magazine of History*, xv, 2 (February, 1912), 78–79: Letter of W. L. Marcy to J. V. L. Pruyn, May 31, 1852. On April 25, Congressman Dean spoke in favor of Marcy's nomination in the House of Representatives. Seymour helped to revise this speech which hailed Marcy as the choice of New York for President: Nichols, *Democratic Machine*, 103.

He forbade all trading of votes: "My chance of success depends upon two results. 1st. The failure of the nomination of either C[ass] or B[uchanan] and their friends seeing the necessity of throwing their votes on some other candidate." Marcy felt, and rightly, that grave doubt among the Democrats as to the ability of Cass to carry New York in 1852 would cost the man from Michigan the nomination. Buchanan's name, he believed, would be "coldly received"; the choice of Douglas, who was only thirty-nine, would be "an experiment of somewhat doubtful result." He shrewdly advised his committee of three friends to assume that General Scott was going to be the Whig candidate for President and reminded them that the "controlling influence" on the nomination he ardently desired would be the "qualification for getting elected."

Above all, he urged his representatives at Baltimore to keep their tempers, to stay out of arguments, and to make it plain to the national convention that he favored the whole Compromise of 1850 and wished "to have the settlement regarded as permanent," and would "deprecate agitation." Any attempt to "metamorphose" the party into an organization holding any other view of the settlement of 1850 would result in a loss of the election. These letters of Marcy show all the skill of the seasoned politician. He foresaw everything but his own failure —his oversight was caused by his ambition.

Lastly, Marcy reminded his three friends that he could not allow his name to be used "otherwise than in connection with the Presidency." "*Aut Cæsar aut Nullus* is the maxim to be acted on," he wrote, as his agents left Washington for Baltimore. Then, as late as June, he sent a third letter, addressed to Seymour alone, which contained his last suggestions as to strategy together with "confidential notes of introduction" to Caleb Cushing, of Massachusetts, and Henry A. Wise, of Virginia. In these two notes, so Marcy wrote Seymour, he had assured the gentlemen from Massachusetts and Virginia that the chairman of the New York delegation might be "depended on as reflecting my views more fully than any other person, and that what you might represent as to myself would be very likely to be sanctioned by me." Cushing and Wise, thought Marcy, would be "very controlling" in the convention, and he hoped that Seymour would "establish very confidential relations with them." Marcy wrote from New York City; then, having given his closest friend the sole power to make promises for him at Baltimore, concluded, "I shall go up the river to-night. With every wish for an auspicious result, *etc.*" [12]

The outcome at Baltimore should not have been surprising in New York. Before many years had passed the failure of the favorite sons of the state to win national nominations at the hands of the Democrats was to become a familiar misfortune. New York's inability to unite in 1852 lost her the prize of what was destined to be the presidency. The victor would need 188 votes. On the first ballot Cass had 116, Buchanan 93, Marcy 27, and Douglas 20. Nine New Yorkers, it will be seen, would not support Marcy, the choice of their chairman. These men were the nucleus of the faction called "Hards." Dickinson was their leader, and Dickinson was ostensibly for Cass. Seymour held Marcy's vote together for thirty-three ballots; then, on the thirty-fourth, Virginia threw fifteen votes to Dickinson, who expressed his thanks for the compliment but declined to "desert" Cass. According to Henry B. Stanton, he himself, as an active aspirant to the nomination, had secretly arranged for this switch. On the forty-fifth ballot Marcy reached 97, and the New York delegation retired for a conference in which Seymour proposed that it unite on Marcy. Astonishing though it may seem, an explosion of protests from the "Hards" led the chairman to withdraw his motion. Oliver Charlick, "a super-heated Hunker from Long Island, threatened to throw Seymour out of the window." [13] Yet the twenty-three Marcy men, had the unit rule been used, could have forced the delegation to cast

12. New York Historical Society: Seymour Papers: Copies of three letters from W. L. Marcy, two of which (dated May 24, 1852) were addressed to Horatio Seymour and his associates, and the third (dated in June, 1852) was for Seymour, alone.

13. Stanton, *Random Recollections*, 180–182.

all its thirty-six votes for their candidate. New York returned to the floor of the convention with its delegation still divided. Marcy had lost what would be his last chance to gain the office he desired above all others.

North Carolina and pivotal Virginia joined forces and started a stampede for Franklin Pierce, of New Hampshire — the President whom New Englanders often conveniently forget to list among their own. The result was a memorable instance of the importance of the baleful pettiness of politics. Marcy, if not a master of men, was an expert manager of them; it can hardly be doubted that he was the superior of Pierce in his grasp of national affairs. Though it is idle to imagine what might have happened if this apt pupil of the Albany Regency had governed the country from 1853 to 1857, it is equally idle to declare that the Civil War was not to be escaped. Marcy failed in 1852, not for want of friends, for when Seymour took the chairmanship of the delegation it was already too late to checkmate the designs of Dickinson.

Some time before the convention the supporters of Marcy had suggested that New York vote solidly at Baltimore for Dickinson or Marcy according as either could command the larger number of votes from outside the state. This diplomatic offer did not reach Dickinson until his leading friends had already pledged themselves to a second choice. In 1862, Dickinson told Thurlow Weed that he would have made the bargain (had he got news of it in time) although he realized, ten years later, that the agreement would have meant the nomination and election of his enemy.[14] Marcy might more wisely have chosen as his chief representative some man toward whom Dickinson was less hostile.

Marcy had missed the peak of his ambition, and his loss was more than personal, but he turned his attention immediately to seeking the consolation of a seat in the Cabinet. To win a place from Pierce the Democrats must make sure of New York;

14. Alexander, *History*, II, 172. For Pruyn's version, see the *Magazine of History*, XV, 3 (March, 1912), 97.

therefore the selection of their candidate for governor was of first importance. The "Softs" came back from Baltimore with empty hands and aching hearts. Seymour was the obvious first choice for nomination at the state convention. Like Bouck in 1842 he had to his credit the close vote of two years before. Although Dickinson hated him, the former senator's success at blocking Marcy satisfied his desire for revenge for the moment. Not that he intended to go along with the "Softs"; he joined with John Van Buren, on the contrary, in an effort to name John P. Beekman, of New York City, for the head of the ticket. Sentiment upstate seemed to favor Erastus Corning. The divided opposition was no match for an heir of the regency. Seymour outwitted his antagonists and won a second nomination.

> As Roscoe Conkling said of him many years later, he had sat at the feet of Edwin Croswell and measured swords with Thurlow Weed. He was one of the men who do not lose the character of good fighters because they are excellent negotiators. . . . Seymour could cut deeply when he chose to wield a blade.[15]

At Syracuse, on the first of September, Seymour had 59 votes to Beekman's 7, with 64 necessary to a nomination. The second ballot settled the contest, and Sanford E. Church was put up for lieutenant-governor again. Thus the Democratic ticket was the same as that of 1850.

Seymour is supposed to have worked hard for his victory; yet he refused to fight until he was convinced that he was the free choice of his party. In a confidential letter of July 10, 1852, he wrote to Marcy:

> You wish me to "write to you frankly" my views about the nominations. I have said so frequently that I do not desire a nomination myself that it is not necessary to repeat any thing on that point. Unless it is deemed important to nominate me again I am averse to going upon the ticket.[16]

Corning, he had discovered, did not wish to run but would do so "if pressed," and Seymour thought the party might be wise to force him. Marcy, however, insisted that Seymour accept,

15. Alexander, *History*, II, 172–173.

16. Library of Congress: Marcy Papers: Horatio Seymour to W. L. Marcy, July 10, 1852.

and by the middle of August he seems to have persuaded his friend that he ought to save the governorship from the unnatural alliance of Dickinson and John Van Buren. By the twentieth Seymour was active at rounding up delegates; while Marcy, stationed at Albany, was using all the arts at his command to gain control of the state convention. Trips to and from Concord, New Hampshire, punctuated their plans, and some time during the autumn a definite arrangement was arrived at — Seymour should go to Albany as governor, and Marcy should go into the Cabinet. Much to the chagrin of both conservatives and radicals that was just what happened.

In his second campaign for governor Seymour confronted two candidates. Three weeks after the Democrats had left Syracuse, the Whigs met there to renominate Governor Washington Hunt, who had supported Fillmore and the Compromise of 1850. The Whig delegates decided to dodge the subject of slavery and voted a state platform which endorsed that of Philadelphia indirectly — "an honest acquiescence in the action of the late national convention on all subjects legitimately before it" was expected of every Whig. "Legitimately" was the one important word. As with every dying party, the leaders of the Whigs tried to face two ways at once. The Free Soil party had nominated John P. Hale for President, and, in view of the neutrality of the New York Whigs on the hated Fugitive Slave Law, put up Minthorne, son of Daniel D. Tompkins, for governor. The resentment of this active minority was aimed directly at the party in power, and the Democrats carried twenty-seven states out of thirty-one. In New York the vote for governor was eminently satisfactory to Seymour, who polled a slight majority of the total cast for all three candidates: 264,121 to 241,525 and 19,299, respectively, for Hunt and Tompkins.[17]

17. The state vote for President stood: Pierce, 262,083; Scott, 234,882; Hale, 25,329. In the legislature the 32 senators were divided equally between the Whigs and Democrats; in the assembly there were 86 Democrats to 42 of their opponents. Of 33 representatives in the Congress, the Democrats elected 21, the Whigs 10, the Free Soilers 1, and the Land Reformers 1.

Dickinson contributed the only note of anger to this easy campaign, for the tempting sight of federal offices waiting to be filled united all but the most bitter leaders of the "Hards" and "Softs." Once again Hunt and Seymour paraded against each other with a mutual courtesy reminiscent of the good manners of the polite armies of the eighteenth century. Addressing the man who would oust him from office, the governor wrote:

You must not imagine that you can offend me by refusing to give me your vote. If my feelings were revengeful I would seek my satisfaction in voting for you, and if I should retaliate to that extent you must not take it amiss. . . . One point must be understood between us. I will not allow friend or foe not even you, to disparage my competitor. I appreciate his high qualities and feel a true affection for him. One who bears defeat so nobly deserves a triumph; and if he don't [*sic*] achieve it the fault shall not be mine.[18]

Though a convention of anti-renters had endorsed every name on the Democratic ticket this time — thus removing Seymour's last cause for anxiety, he plunged into the campaign with vigor and travelled all over the state. He hoped for a decisive victory and spoke and acted as if he believed that if the Democrats could once get back to Albany and Washington, the good management of new men might serve to keep them there. Dickinson he ignored, but he was suspicious of the dashing John Van Buren. Cassidy and the Barnburner *Atlas* seemed cold to his candidacy; yet he encountered agents of the paper everywhere in his tour through the state. A letter to Marcy is characteristic:

I am working very hard and I think with some effect. I have addressed six meetings this week and have seen a great number of persons. I have also written out and published my canal views in English and Welch [*sic*] and I think I shall put it into German. The Germans are very much opposed to debt and taxation.

I am going day after tomorrow into the southern tier of counties. I have appointments in Allegany, Cattaraugus, and Steuben Counties.[19]

Then, almost at the eleventh hour in this serene campaign, there bobbed up the issue of "temperance." The real question

18. New York Historical Society: Seymour Papers: Washington Hunt to Horatio Seymour, September 7, 1852.

19. Library of Congress: Marcy Papers: Horatio Seymour to W. L. Marcy, October 16, 1852.

was prohibition going under another name. In 1851 Maine had passed a law abolishing the sale of alcoholic liquors, and for eighty-three years thereafter that state was to remain loyal to what might be called its prohibitory tariff in favor of hard cider. Neal Dow and his experiment at making men over caught the fancy of the country — a great editor like Horace Greeley, for instance, open-minded victim of every fad from spiritism to phrenology, became an ardent advocate of the cause. Sooner or later it was worked into the statutes or the constitutions of a dozen states. Then the disaster of the Civil War drew popular attention in another direction; if fear of secession made the Know-Nothing party, the outbreak of civil war diverted Americans, if only for the time being, from their vulgar obsessions on the subject of rum and the Pope. In October, 1852, the corresponding secretary of the New York Temperance Alliance addressed letters of enquiry to all three candidates for governor: Hunt, Seymour, and Tompkins, whose distinguished father, it was said, had died of drink. Seymour's attitude is especially interesting in view of the storm he was to raise over the question once he was governor. On October 11, he wrote Marcy from Utica, "I think I shall not answer the letters of the State Temperance Alliance. If I should do so I will give you timely notice so that you may advise Governor Hunt." [20]

A week later he returned to Utica from a tour of speaking to discover that Governor Hunt had already replied to a duplicate of the letter which he had received; whereupon he sent off the answer which he had already prepared in advance, dating it October 18. This letter was printed far and wide in the newspapers of the state. Explaining — not quite frankly — that he had delayed his reply because of absence from home, Seymour called attention to the obvious fact that the legislature soon to be elected was certain to take up the question of temperance. What law that legislature might pass was quite unknown to any one, and he objected to pledging himself as to what he might do with such a bill if he were elected. A governor, he declared,

20. Library of Congress: Marcy Papers: Horatio Seymour to W. L. Marcy, October 11, 1852.

should enter upon the high and responsible duties of the station free to act on every question submitted to him, according to his convictions of duty at the time. In other words, a man should seek office on his character and person, not his promises. An election, he reminded the ardent advocates of prohibition, was hardly conducive to "considerate and conscientious action." Thus Seymour politely but firmly refused to commit himself in any way.[21] Governor Hunt had taken the same stand.

The candidate was anxious up to the very last moment: as late as October 29 he wrote Marcy of his fear that "improperly printed" tickets and plans to "cut" his name would cost him many votes. Readers will remember that the Australian system was still a thing of the future: parties prepared their own ballots, and any one who wished might watch to see how any one else would vote. "I think there should be some one at each Poll to attend to the State ticket. I will make it right," he added. On November 3, a gallant letter from Governor Hunt congratulated him on his victory.[22] In the darkest days of the Civil War, this old-fashioned Whig would leap to Seymour's aid and publicly urge his second election as governor in 1862. The first citizen of Utica carried his city and his county, but the sweetest part of his success must have been his triumph in Broome County, the home of Daniel Stevens Dickinson.[23]

Two days after his election Seymour wrote George Washington Newell, father of Marcy's second wife, factotum of

21. New York State Library: Seymour Papers: Horatio Seymour to the New York Temperance Alliance, October 18, 1852.

22. In 1852 Seymour carried 43 counties out of 59, gaining 10 counties over his total in 1850: *Whig Almanac*, 37. New York City was in the throes of a mayoralty campaign, the Democrats being determined to take the city patronage from the Whigs. Tammany nominated Jacob A. Westervelt, a moderate Hunker, a wealthy ship-builder, and the pink of respectability, who campaigned on the national issues of Pierce and peace. On the eve of the election, the Wigwam found "eighty thousand tickets" purporting to be Democratic ballots but carrying no Democratic names. These were borne off in triumph from the post-office, and the Democrats got a plurality in New York City of over 11,000: Myers, *Tammany Hall*, 159–160.

23. Broome County gave Seymour 3,084 votes as against 2,766 for Hunt: *Whig Almanac*, 37.

the canal board at Albany, and hub of the system by which the Democrats had once controlled the state:

My Dear Sir, If I am elected Governor of the State of New York, you must aid me in getting together the material for a Message. I have not the least information on the points that should be touched. Will you see Governor Marcy on the subject? I am particularly anxious to be informed about the condition of our Canal finances, *etc.* My motto is "Constitutional law and Legislative parity" — Get me the material to make a point in that respect.[24]

Evidently the governor-elect thought he knew little of the duties of the office he was soon to occupy. He was a faithful chief executive, hard-working and conscientious, staying at the capitol late at night, even when the legislature was not in session. The constitution of 1846 had greatly diminished the power of the position, the state offices being filled by popular choice. The salary was four thousand dollars in addition to rent until the state built the mansion on Eagle Street in the eighties. The routine plague of his first term was the use of the pardoning power from which Seymour developed decided and advanced ideas on questions of crime and punishment.

Though the new governor went into office as the champion of the waterways of the state, one of the first bills he signed in the spring of 1853 brought into being three-quarters of the great corporation which would ultimately make the canal system superfluous. In 1831, the Albany and Schenectady Railroad had been opened for traffic. Twenty-one years later one could travel all the three hundred and sixty-four miles from Albany to Buffalo by rail.[25] During this time, however, the Erie Canal was carrying an increasing tonnage year by year, and the revenues from tolls were rapidly retiring the debt and meeting the cost of constant improvements such as widening and deepening.[26] The ultimate goal of making the canal free was already in sight. Though it froze up for five months of every year, on

24. New York State Library: Manuscript Section: Marcy Papers: Horatio Seymour to G. W. Newell, November 4, 1852. This letter is marked "Private."

25. Winden, "Influence of the Erie Canal," 11.

26. In 1825 the maximum depth of the Erie Canal was three feet, accommodating boats of from sixteen to forty tons; by 1856, the average depth was

an average, the canal had one great advantage over railroads — boats could tie up for loading or unloading almost anywhere; while steam carriage on land had to build and use fixed stations. If Seymour signed the bill which made the New York Central, he never gave up his belief that canals were important supplements to railroads — as necessary regulators of their rates, if nothing else.[27]

Ten upstate railroads, for three of which Seymour's close friend, John V. L. Pruyn, acted as attorney, were consolidated into one by the law which Seymour signed on April 2, 1853. May 17 saw the formation of the New York Central Railroad, the total capital of which amounted to more than twenty-three millions with a bonded debt of almost two millions.[28] Dean Richmond, of Buffalo, future Democratic state chairman, John Pruyn, of Albany, and their associates controlled this railroad until 1867, when Cornelius Vanderbilt, who owned the Hudson River Railroad, captured it suddenly by means of buying stock in the open market. Vanderbilt's road ended at Rensselaer, and years of squabbling over freight had led the New York Central men to back a line of boats on the Hudson River in order to compete with him all the way to the city of New York. The union of the rival systems as the New York Central and Hudson River Railroad, in 1869, offered a new challenge to the Erie Canal, which never surpassed the tonnage of 1862.

Competition with railroads which competed with one another was one thing, but competition with a corporation which would spread out all over the state was something different. Seymour was wrong in supposing that canals could regulate the rates of railroads, for the improvement of traffic by land and the system of rebates to influential shippers were to push the canals out of

five feet, and boat tonnage between forty and seventy; by 1883, the canal could accommodate boats of two hundred and fifty tons and averaged a depth of seven feet: Howell and Munsell, *County of Schenectady*, 207.

27. Lincoln, *Constitutional History*, II, 647–648. Lincoln is quoting Seymour's letter of February 27, 1882, on canals, sent to the New York legislature in support of the abolition of tolls.

28. French, *Gazetteer*, 69.

the picture. Although tolls were abolished in 1882, the great canal of DeWitt Clinton had already started on its decline. Ultimately the legislatures of the states and finally the Congress had to regulate railroad rates by law. That the heir of DeWitt Clinton should have signed the act incorporating the New York Central Railroad was an odd coincidence; yet this fact was not more curious than the sight of a free-trader holding stock in the cotton and the woollen mills of Utica.[29] The passion for the economic interpretation of history assumes that men know much more about their business than is actually the fact.

For New York a Democratic victory had come to mean a free-for-all fight for offices among the victors. The year 1853 was no exception. Soon after election day Marcy set out for Florida because of the ill health of a member of his family, but his removal from the scene did not spell any lack of interest or ambition as to the Cabinet of President-elect Pierce. In the two months of freedom before his own inauguration as governor, Seymour worked faithfully in Marcy's behalf. The New Hampshire brigadier-general was the centre of anxiety — did he favor the "Hards" in New York or that precarious union of Hunkers and Barnburners called "Softs"? Shortly before the election, Marcy had met Pierce in Boston, and the two men had talked together satisfactorily for an hour.[30] Just after he took office Seymour wrote Pierce an interesting letter, the original draft of which is now at Albany.

The new governor stated that he had talked with Mr. Pruyn, who had recently returned from Concord, and that while he

29. During the campaign of 1852, the Whigs accused Seymour of being inimical to canals because, so it was said, he had one hundred and sixty thousand dollars invested in railroad stock. As a matter of fact, his total stock was worth just four thousand dollars; it consisted of shares, which had been "awarded" to him, in the Utica and Syracuse Railroad. The Bleecker money was largely in land situated in Herkimer, Montgomery, Onondaga, and Steuben counties; the bulk of the three hundred thousand dollars Henry Seymour left his widow and six children was invested in real estate, bank stocks, and mortgages. See the Rochester *Daily Union*, September 9, 1852.

30. New York Historical Society: Seymour Papers: copy of a letter from W. L. Marcy to Horatio Seymour, October 31, 1852.

was reluctant to be thought "obstinate or indelicate" in urging the name of any man on Pierce, he had "no hesitation" in saying that if Marcy went into the Cabinet, his appointment would "tranquillize" the state. Seymour informed Pierce that his position as leader in New York gave him a better opportunity to understand the situation than any other person. In a "population of more than three millions," it was "an easy matter" to impress an outsider with petitions which people would sign without reading. Men who really preferred Marcy had been persuaded that New York's representation in the Cabinet was a question of choice between Dix and Dickinson. Yet the very Democrats who opposed Marcy had been disloyal to the state tickets for the "last three years." While Seymour hoped the President would treat these men with "kindness and respect" and award them "a fair share of the fruits of victory" in order to "reconcile" them to the restoration of the Democratic ascendency in the state, he found it "somewhat annoying" to have those "who created the greatest obstacles in the way of success" claim "the right to control and denounce them who bore the weight of the contest."[31]

Professor Nichols has told the whole story of the intrigues at Concord in the *Democratic Machine*.[32] Seymour and Erastus Corning visited Pierce late in November for the purpose of urging Marcy's name and persuading him to announce the members of his Cabinet before January, when the new administration would take charge in New York. Seymour, in particular, felt that this would help him to control his legislature. The President-elect refused, however, to give out the names before he went on to Washington in March, and Seymour left Concord with the uneasy feeling that John A. Dix would go into the Cabinet. By the first of December, nevertheless, he seems to have found reasons for changing his mind, for he wrote Marcy

31. The text of this letter is in Seymour's handwriting and shows much correction and consideration.

32. Nichols, *Democratic Machine*, 173 and 218–219. The intimate side of the negotiations in behalf of Marcy can be found in Seymour's letters to Marcy, December 1, 1852, to February 20, 1853.

from Albany, "If General Pierce should make his Cabinet to-day, I have but little doubt he would select you for the position of Secretary of State." In view of the fact that this is what actually happened, the beleaguered Pierce may have decided silently and stuck to his decision. It was his genial fashion of listening as if he agreed with every visitor in turn that kept the rival aspirants for office guessing and plotting.

On December first, the day he wrote to Marcy, Seymour had attended the session of the electoral college of New York. The question of dispatching recommendations for his Cabinet to Pierce at Concord resulted in a dangerous difference of opinion. Dickinson's friends went about asking for signatures endorsing his name, but twenty-two out of the thirty-five electors present were supporters of Marcy and delegated Pruyn to perform the difficult feat of writing a letter to Pierce which should recommend Marcy without mentioning his name. Pruyn subsequently was accused of having composed a letter that read like an endorsement of Dix. In the midst of all this wrangling Pierce lost his only son, and almost his own life, in a railroad accident, and Seymour hesitated to write him thereafter. The despondent statesman had to receive so many delegations from New York that he wearily thought of asking them to come to see him all at once. On January 18, 1853, John Pruyn entered in his journal:

> I left for Concord to see General Pierce again on the subject of the member of the Cabinet from our state. Governor Seymour and Mr. Corning were desirous that I should go. Had two interviews with General Pierce which were quite free and full. Although he did not say whom he would appoint, and indeed left the matter quite open, not meaning as he said to promulgate his cabinet until the 4th of March, I came to the conclusion that he intended to ask Governor Marcy to take the State Department. General Pierce asked me for Governor Marcy's address (he being south), which I sent him on my return. I was satisfied from this and other things that the matter was settled in his own mind.[33]

Complaints against Marcy, even from New Yorkers, did not persuade Pierce. He would give the first post to the greatest

33. *Magazine of History*, XVI, 1 (January, 1913), 25.

state. Marcy left Florida for Washington and spent an evening alone with the President-elect on Washington's birthday — after which he wrote Seymour that he had been led to believe that he was going to be secretary of state. Some time between the election and the inauguration, John A. Dix was offered this post, Pierce asking later to be excused from his promise. Dix hoped for the consolation of the mission to France, but of this office, also, he would be deprived.[34]

Contempt for President Pierce as a "northern man of southern principles" has begun to give way before critical examination of his character and his policy. The biography by Professor Nichols presents the most that can be said for an expert state politician who liked the bottle a little too much and acquired a fictitious reputation as a soldier for having been a political general in the Mexican War.[35] He was a kind man, at heart, and a handsome one, and his nomination for a post too difficult for his abilities was the unhappy gift of a party over-confident and even arrogant from its long possession of power. Like Harding, he was quite unequal to his task, but unlike him he gave the best that was in him to the stormy days ahead. In 1853 he had to choose among three able and ambitious candidates for his Cabinet from the single state of New York — Dickinson, Dix, and Marcy, the favorites of the three great factions of his decaying party. The circumstance that two of these factions pretended to be united into one, the "Softs," did not make his choice any the less perplexing.

If he had known that no party can govern the nation long without the good will of New York, he might have done better to take all three of these men into his administration. It so happened that he chose the moderate man, and it is hard to believe that his choice was not the best. Yet a shrewd politician like Tilden urged the name of Dix on him with weighty argu-

34. Dix, *Memoirs*, I, 271–277.

35. For a spirited defense of President Pierce, see J. G. Randall's review of R. F. Nichols's *Franklin Pierce*, in the *Mississippi Valley Historical Review*, XIX, 1 (June, 1932), 120.

ments.[36] Once again, however, as in 1845, Marcy was picked as the man to go to Washington, but this time he received the first post. The selection of him disappointed Democrats both to the left and the right. It was the bitterness of this double disappointment — the resentment of the friends of Dickinson on one hand and Dix on the other — that was soon to make New York a Republican state.

36. Tilden, *Letters and Literary Memorials*, I, 80–99.

VIII

THE FORTS OF FOLLY

1854

AT ten o'clock in the morning of Saturday, New Year's Day, 1853, in the vestibule of the old capitol, torn down in 1886, Horatio Seymour took the oath of office as governor of New York. At two o'clock he was still receiving the congratulations of his fellow citizens. Among the more distinguished visitors was his cousin, Colonel Thomas Hart Seymour, an over-eminently successful veteran of the Mexican War and Democratic governor of Connecticut from 1850 to 1853. Hailed as a "ripe scholar, a citizen of great personal worth and purity of character, a courteous and accomplished gentleman," Seymour was expected to give New York an able administration.[1] No one predicted the distracting days before him. The whole nation, apparently, had accepted the Compromise of 1850, and the tension between North and South was relieved. Three Whig governors had preceded him in office, John Young, Hamilton Fish, and Washington Hunt — all men of charm and skill. Now, after six years, the Democrats were to gather their rewards both at Albany and Washington. Even as diminished in power by the constitution of 1846 the governorship of New York was a post of importance and dignity. Yet if Horatio Seymour could have foreseen the violent storm which would burst over his head, he might have insisted on remaining no more than the first citizen of Utica in 1852.

His personal associations with Albany were pleasant and familiar. Here, while still a young man, he had served six years on Marcy's staff, watching how the regency worked. His wife had been born and reared there, and something of that tight

1. New York State Library: Seymour Papers: *True National Democrat*, January 3, 1853.

C. L. Elliott *New York City Hall*

WASHINGTON HUNT

F. B. Carpenter *New York City Hall*

MYRON H. CLARK

Dutch family feeling seems to have made her always happy to settle down among the Bleeckers. The new governor rented a comfortable residence which still stands at the corner of Elk and Eagle Streets a few steps from his office — a three-story brick dwelling, where Governor Throop had lived before him. In the midst of his moving Seymour wrote Marcy at Washington:

> On the first of January when I was receiving calls I could not realise [*sic*] that twenty years had rolled away since I had called as one of your aids [*sic*] on a similar occasion (in the next house to the one I occupy) — I felt that I was one of the staff and was looking around for you. Twenty years more will dispose of us. While I am gratified with my recent election and particularly with the kindness of my friends I sometimes regret the comfort of private life. Poor General Pierce's triumph is made a mockery by [the] death of his only child.[2]

Marcy was to be gone in less than five years, but Seymour would live longer than he pretended to believe — in 1873 his sixth nomination for governor was still ahead of him, and implacable gossips were accusing him of laying plans to be President. He was not yet forty-three when he took the oath of office — tall, lean, alert, of swarthy complexion, with hazel eyes and a wide mouth that could smile with success. Friends always spoke of what they called his charm, but his disarming grace of manner never failed to irritate his enemies. His soft answers seldom turned away their wrath.

Seymour's power of appointment was slight, but he suffered abuse for the few offices he filled. The new governor was accused of proscribing that remnant of the Hunkers called "Hards." Within six weeks of taking office he was writing Marcy:

> Great pains have been taken to create the impression that my appointments have been exclusive in their character that none but Barn Burners were given any offices. Although I have but one Free Soiler on my staff (General Temple) it is boldly asserted that they are all of that character although they are seven to one the other way. I allude to these things to shew you the kind of attacks which are made to create prejudices against you.[3]

2. Library of Congress: Marcy Papers: Letter of Horatio Seymour to W. L. Marcy, January 7, 1853.

3. Library of Congress: Marcy Papers: Letter of Horatio Seymour to W. L. Marcy, February 20, 1853.

He went on doing his best to live up to the spirit of the union he had made at Rome with John Van Buren in the summer of 1849. He saw that the Democrats of New York must stand for Free Soil or give up all hope of holding the state. This the extreme conservatives could not or would not see: in obstinate spite of the warning of 1856 they voted for Breckinridge in 1860 and then railed and ranted at secession. As soon as Prince John, whom Marcy called "an itinerant orator," saw all the glory of reunion going to his rival, Seymour, he began to make a nuisance of himself.

The new governor secretly urged Marcy to use all his influence to prevent President Pierce from granting any of the rewards of office to the crowd who controlled the Albany *Argus*. Eight years before he was lending Edwin Croswell money, but times and policies had changed. This once stalwart Democratic paper had tried to betray the state ticket at the election of 1852 by publishing false statements as to the candidate — in particular a "low personal attack" on Seymour which "the Editors knew to be untrue." Even the faithful Utica *Observer* had not been loyal, and the governor felt that these two papers between them had done "more to aid the Whig party than any two Whig papers in the State." He asked Marcy to make it plain to Pierce that he would not "object to any one's appointment because he has been a friend of Mr. Dickinson's or for any difference of opinion about questions of policy." There his feeling of forgiveness ended, however — to show favor to the *Argus* or the *Observer* would be "mischievous and mortifying." [4]

On March 19, the new secretary of state having asked his advice as to some appointment in his department, Seymour wrote Marcy with what was perhaps unconscious humor: "Get an honest and capable man [even] if you have to take a Whig." The Democrats were faced with the old danger of making one

4. Library of Congress: Marcy Papers: Letter of Horatio Seymour to W. L. Marcy, March 5, 1853. Seymour wrote three letters to Marcy on this date, two of them marked "Private." Johnson, of the *Argus*, and Lyon, of the *Observer*, were trying to be made postmasters of their respective cities.

ingrate and nine enemies. The governor had connections to look out for, moreover — several times during the spring he requested that his "kinsman," namesake, and "kind of a cousin," Horatio Seymour of Buffalo, be taken care of. It was a casual way for him to describe his first cousin — the son of his father's older brother who had sat twelve years in the Senate for Vermont. His Uncle Horatio had ruined himself by kindly endorsing the notes of his friends, and his son had left Vermont to start over again in what was still called the West. The phrase "kind of a cousin" may have been the innocent subterfuge of a man who was unwilling to seem to make a family convenience of the department of state; yet more than once were the Seymours called proud of purse and blood. Connecticut, for instance, honored the family so often that Republicans there poked fun at its constant claim to public office. In a letter to James Campbell, Pierce's postmaster-general, the governor urged that "excellent citizens, and undeviating Democrats" be named to office — adding, however, that he thought it was only "right that the supporters of Mr. Van Buren should have a fair share of the offices in New York, as our party was re-united upon the principle that the past was to be overlooked."[5]

The tone of all the letters he sent from Albany to Washington during 1853 shows that he had learned much in the troublesome seven years since he had served one term as speaker for the Hunkers. Although he was not unacquainted with southerners, for he often went to Newport, where they liked to summer, the split ticket of 1848 had taught him a lesson. He won and he held the respect of the sentiment for Free Soil in New York. The Kansas–Nebraska bill embarrassed him, for he knew well that people in his part of the country looked with suspicion on any proposal which would open the way, even if only in theory, to the spread of slavery. In 1845, as we have seen, he was ready to shut it out of the South West. Yet Douglas's

5. New York Historical Society: Seymour Papers: Horatio Seymour to James Campbell, March 19, 1853.

doctrine of popular sovereignty was hard for a Democrat to deny. Northern agitation for abolition was, on the other hand, an impertinence which was certain to anger the South.

In 1853 Seymour's hope was to consolidate the moderate opinions of the state against the hostile extremes of both Seward and Dickinson. In this work he needed the help of the national administration. Caleb Cushing, however, seemed to have got the ear of President Pierce, who soon had good reason to regret his failure to "starve out" the rebels in the ranks of his own party. Neither the chief executive nor his attorney-general had any intimate knowledge of the tangled politics of New York, and Pierce, like Polk, was to suffer for his want of it. Many of the appointments made from Washington were to outrage Seymour, to whom Marcy could only write apologetically:

> I cannot now explain the condition of things in relation to the New York appointments. I have had and am having a *hard time* of it. Don't infer from this that I have not the influence and consideration which I deserve for I assure you I have both — and yet I may not be able to do what ought to be done.[6]

On January 4 Seymour sent his first annual message to the legislature.[7] Presumably the facts and figures of these forty-one printed pages were put together by Newell, to whom Seymour had written immediately after the election. About half the message is devoted to routine reports on the business of the state. The second half concerns the canals, which were

6. New York Historical Society: Seymour Papers: W. L. Marcy to Horatio Seymour, March 7, 1853. Copy. Dozens of Seymour's letters to Marcy during the years 1853 and 1854 will be found in the Marcy Papers. It is interesting to note that amid all the doubt as to the attitude of Pierce while he was still President-elect, Caleb Cushing, soon to be his attorney-general, accurately described his attitude in a letter to Horatio Seymour. New York Historical Society: Seymour Papers: February 19, 1853.

> My conviction is that there has not been that uncertainty in the mind of General P. on some great points, which many suppose. He has had a delicate and difficult task to perform in hearing every body dealing with so many aspirations and susceptibilities, and arriving at fixed conclusions. I do not know any man, who could have gone through all this with the same discretion and wisdom which he has manifested. What may have seemed to be indecision has in fact been a determined purpose to decide deliberately, and to keep his own counsel until the proper time for disclosing it to the country.

7. Lincoln, *Messages*, IV, 640–681.

once more a subject of angry dispute. The Whig statute of 1851 had been unsuccessful, and the finances of New York were in bad shape. Once more the Democrats had to repair the damage their opponents left behind. Seymour proposed that taxes be laid to enlarge the canal in order to increase the return from tolls. Tracing the history of Clinton's ditch from 1817 to 1853, the governor called to the attention of the legislature the fact that less than half the canal had been sufficiently enlarged so as to accommodate boats of one hundred and twenty tons. Every six inches which were added to the draft of a canal boat, he pointed out, increased its capacity by twenty-five tons. Seymour's plan was to provide for canal boats of one hundred and fifty tons. New York contained taxable property of the assessed valuation of a billion dollars, and on this Azariah C. Flagg, pay-as-you-go Barnburner, proposed an immediate levy of a half million.[8] Part of the reunion at Rome in 1849 had provided that the canal system of the state should not suffer. This, so it was said, was the price which the Hunkers demanded of the Barnburners for swallowing the principle of Free Soil.[9] It is important to remember, in this connection, that Dickinson's interest was not the Erie Canal but the Erie Railroad.

When, on April 13, the legislature adjourned without having acted on the question of canals, Seymour called it back into special session the same day and sent in his message on the fourteenth. A governor of New York enjoys the great power of limiting the business of a special session to the subject or subjects of his message. The legislators took a recess till May 24 and then sat until July 21, by which time the governor had forced action on the canals. The Whigs proposed a law author-

8. New York Historical Society: Seymour Papers: Letter of Azariah C. Flagg to Horatio Seymour, December 31, 1852. Flagg's letter, written after a talk with Dean Richmond, of Buffalo, shows how successfully the Barnburners had been converted to a belief in the future of the canals.

9. For Marcy's vigorous approval of this message and the delight with the way in which Seymour went about the business of being governor, see his letters to John V. L. Pruyn of January 19 and February 9, 1853, in the *Magazine of History*, XVI, 1 (January, 1913), 26–27.

izing a loan of nine million dollars for the enlargement of the Erie Canal, and Seymour felt that the matter of ways and means should be settled before the annual elections in November, when a new assembly would be chosen. In place of Flagg's scheme for the half-million tax, he urged a constitutional amendment authorizing a loan of ten and one-half millions to complete the lateral canals and enlarge the Erie. In June the legislature voted to submit this amendment to the people. At a special election on February 15, 1854, it was carried by more than three to one.[10]

"Barnburner" Flagg favored raising the taxes, but Seymour turned to a loan which should be repaid from profits on tolls. His calculations were correct, for nine years later, it will be recalled, revenue from the Erie Canal reached its peak, and the debt was redeemed. Yet the old difference of opinion as to how to get money for public improvements showed how unreal, in this respect, had been the reunion of 1849. Seymour knew that he must force the issue, however, if the "Softs" were to hold together.

> The importance of the adjustment does not arise merely from the fact that an agitating question is disposed of, but because the Canal question was to have been made the basis of a coalition with the Whigs at the next election. Every effort was made in certain quarters to prevent an agreement. If nothing unforeseen occurs we shall get through with the Extra Session with advantage to our party. All of the discontent disaffection and factious feeling have been "Hived" in the Canal question. When we found the Swarm had settled on that point we put a box over them and I am mistaken if the plans of the Conspirators are not threatened. . . . No one can complain of the proposed amendment of the Constitution as it has been assented to by the leading Barn Burners; indeed they have taken the lead in the matter.[11]

In his victory at the special election of February, 1854, Seymour won his second battle for the Erie Canal. In spite of his having called a special session he got on well enough with both senate and assembly: his two vetoes were sustained — indeed not once in eight times during his first term was he overridden. The day

10. Werner, *Civil List*, 131.

11. Library of Congress: Marcy Papers: Horatio Seymour to W. L. Marcy, June 12, 1853.

was saved at Albany; in Washington, however, all was not serene.

No sooner had Pierce been inaugurated than bitterness over the choice of his Cabinet burst out in New York. This the new governor had done his best to avoid. Before he had been in office three months, he was working on a plan to merge the *Argus* and the *Atlas*, for he realized that the peace patched up at Rome would never last if Croswell and Cassidy continued their feud. Seymour and his friends determined on buying Croswell out of his *Argus*. Although his scheme to unite the papers was not to be successful until 1856, he urged the great importance of his plan on Marcy. Success at Washington must come by way of Albany:

> Is it possible to work an adjustment out of the storm that rages at Washington? Every thing will go on harmoniously in this State if we get rid of the two papers here. While we have two contending papers we shall have trouble. If the Argus could be got into the right hands all would be well. *If you can disarm the two extremes in the State by depriving them of their organs here and get a paper under proper control it will be a great achievement. You then have every thing in your own hands.* Cannot the disposition of the patronage be made to produce this result? It appears to me the power of the Administration can now compel an adjustment of difficulties. The whole power of the opposition to you now is with Croswell. Without him and his press the rest of the concern could do nothing.[12]

The merger fell through for a very practical reason, and poor President Pierce paid the penalty. Dix, as we have seen, lost the mission to France to a Virginian; then Dickinson declined the collectorship of the port of New York as a reward less than his desert or beneath his dignity; so Pierce gave the office to Greene C. Bronson of Utica, an old Hunker. The great fees of this office made it a financial prize. When James Guthrie, however, became secretary of the treasury in 1853, he set about a business-like reform of the administration of his department — a reform he carried through with small regard for politicians. One of his measures was to put collectorships on a salary basis, and as soon as Bronson discovered the fact his anger at his loss

12. Library of Congress: Marcy Papers: Horatio Seymour to W. L. Marcy, March 20, 1853.

of income turned into a difference of principles. He felt he had been duped, and his friends were as furious as he. The moment this little group of influential men saw that the Hunkers and Barnburners were likely to get together on the question of canals they dragged national issues into the state in such a way as to break up the union which Seymour and Van Buren had made at Rome four years before.[13] Croswell helped them at their mischief with the *Argus*, for his rival, Cassidy, had the ear of both the governor and Marcy. Before long political explosions were taking place all over the state.

Governor Seymour went out to the state convention at Syracuse in the middle of September in order to exact from it an endorsement of the canal policy which would come before the voters in February. Control of this convention depended on thirty-six seats which were contested between "Hards" and "Softs," and an unseemly riot ensued. The "Softs" seized the seats and held them. A recess was taken after which the "Hards" withdrew in a body to hold a separate convention. Having shrewdly approved the proposed canal amendment, they endorsed the leadership of former Senator Dickinson, who railed at the governor's presence in Syracuse. Ignoring Seymour and his "Softs," they nominated a separate ticket for the state offices to be filled at the election in the autumn. The "Softs" organized their convention in the hall they had captured and put up a regular ticket under the leadership of the governor and John Van Buren. Thus the Democrats entered the campaign divided. It was a question of persons, not principles. Those federal office-holders in New York City who refused to ratify the ticket of Seymour and Van Buren were removed by President Pierce on the advice of Secretary Marcy.

In this house-cleaning, Greene C. Bronson, a "nervous crotchety old man with a bad cough," was put out of the collec-

13. Nichols, *Democratic Machine*, 202–212. Pierce enraged the Barnburners by sending Mason, of Virginia, to France instead of Dix; he alienated Seymour and the "Softs" by the appointment of Sickles and Sanders; and after Bronson was ousted as collector, the "Hards" were his deadly enemies.

C. L. Elliott *New York City Hall*

HORATIO SEYMOUR

torship for a "Soft." Seymour always believed that the real cause of Bronson's rebellion was Guthrie's financial reform.

A great effort will now be made to give Mr. Bronson the honors of martyrdom. If the facts are as I understand them they should be made public. I never doubted from the moment Mr. Guthrie decided that the Collector at New York was not entitled to fees Mr. Bronson determined to get out of the office and as he could not decently resign he resolved upon a quarrel. When he was at Washington last spring and when he made up his mind to accept the position of Collector he supposed the place was worth twenty or twenty five thousand dollars. He *then* intended to carry out the policy of the Administration. The loss of the fees changed his feelings. You will see the importance of this point. If I am correct, it should be pressed *now* for it gives a key to his policy.[14]

As might have been expected, the Democrats lost the state offices and the assembly in 1853, for their total vote was almost equally divided between the two factions.[15] All they saved from the Whigs were two places on the court of appeals, for which the "Hard" and "Soft" nominations were identical. The result was doubly disheartening, for there was no real principle involved — the "Hards," "having little to gain and nothing to lose," aimed only at punishing Seymour and Pierce.

Until the nomination of a separate ticket by the "Hards" Seymour had hopes for the campaign. Probably at his suggestion, the seceders at Syracuse were invited to return to the convention but they would not. In October the governor went down to New York to negotiate in behalf of Pierce for the support of one of the great newspapers. When the proposed purchase of the *Express* fell through, Seymour suggested that it would be wise to win the favor of one of the neutral papers by means of "early information" and "advertising." Writing to Marcy during his visit, he tried to diagnose the disease of which the Democratic party was dying in New York:

Dickinson is simply a fool. Unless I am entirely mistaken before two years have passed by it will be clearly seen that the national feelings of

14. Library of Congress: Marcy Papers: Horatio Seymour to W. L. Marcy, October 24, 1853.

15. The average vote in New York in 1853 stood: Whigs, 161,933; "Softs," 96,698; "Hards," 95,529. Johnson and Smith, *History*, II, 400.

some gentlemen which are so unappeasable have reference solely to the *National Treasury* and *the National Domains.* Their wild schemes of plunder will soon bring disgrace upon themselves and their friends. We have reached "the beginning of the end." The developments of Wall Street begin to throw a chill over certain interests. The Democratic party is always troubled when speculations are rife in the land and it always gathers strength when the reaction comes. You will have in Washington this winter a horde of hungry speculators. They may rob the Treasury and they may quarrel among themselves — in any event they will alarm and disgust all thinking and responsible citizens. Before the close of the next session of Congress it will be known why the Democratic party of this State is divided. We shall have similar scenes in this State when the Canal contracts are divided. For one I am entirely satisfied with my political position at this time and have no fear for the future.[16]

The bungling way in which the obstinate Bronson was removed from his office by the President probably accounts for the fact that the "Hards" got half the party vote in the autumn of 1853. The comparatively small vote they received a year later would seem to confirm this explanation.[17] Such, in any case, was Seymour's theory when, on November 5, "sitting this morning at your desk in your library," he wrote Marcy a carefully considered opinion of what might be expected to happen on election-day.[18] Yet the actual result astonished the governor. It puzzled him to find the "Hards" drawing their heaviest vote from the very districts which had deserted Cass for Van Buren in 1848, and he concluded that the Whigs, being confident of victory, were voting for the "Hards" wherever they dared. His explanation was probably sound as far as it went, but the contradictory result pointed to a reason lying deeper — a punishment which involved an inconsistency. The Pierce administration was already being called pro-southern, and merely because the "Hards" were hostile to the President, the Democratic vote of protest went to them in spite of the fact that Dickinson was at their head.

16. Library of Congress: Marcy Papers: Horatio Seymour to W. L. Marcy, October 17, 1853. See, also, Alexander, *History*, II, 184–185.

17. Nichols, *Democratic Machine*, 208–212.

18. Library of Congress: Marcy Papers. The election fell on Tuesday, the seventh. Seymour's letters of November 5, 11, 13, 15, and 24 show that he himself had underestimated the vote the "Hards" would receive.

In January, 1854, Seymour faced a Whig legislature. Seizing the opportunity offered by the late election, he devoted a large part of his second annual message to a careful discussion of the political issues of the day.[19] He filled six pages with what was really a lecture on the nature of the federal Constitution. The nation, he declared, was a union of "sovereign states" and had grown great and been happy under a strict construction of the compact of 1788. Three popular errors threatened its peace and safety — agitation in free states against slavery in slave states, propaganda for a protective tariff, and lobbying for the spending of federal money on internal improvements. Years before, New York had asked national aid for the Erie Canal, and had been turned down at Washington. Now that the state had gone ahead and done the work itself, good Democrats saw no reason for Pierce to reverse the Jeffersonian policies which Madison had stoutly maintained to their detriment by his veto of 1817.[20]

The governor's opinion as to the proper management of public lands can be taken without question as sincere. Land was always his favorite form of investment, and soon after he left office at Albany, he devoted much of his time and money to promoting a canal to connect the Great Lakes with the Mississippi. Clinton's enterprise had made his father rich and successful; the Fox and Wisconsin Canal would do as much for him if he bought up land along the way.[21] In 1854 he advocated the granting of public lands to "actual settlers" who would pro-

19. Lincoln, *Messages*, IV, 709–751. Seymour's sense of proportion in this second annual message is interesting: recommendations as to routine state business fill seventeen pages; the anti-rent troubles occupy three; to canals are given twelve; intemperance got one paragraph; and the state of the nation, six pages.

20. Seymour's message provoked comment from both Thurlow Weed and Horace Greeley. The Albany *Evening Journal*, January 3, 1854, found the message long, but "not verbose or turgid, like the President's." Greeley declared it "barren of valuable suggestions, timid and twaddling in treatment of subjects on which public sentiment is divided," but praiseworthy insofar as it urged strict enforcement of the existing laws against liquor. New York *Tribune*, January 5, 1854.

21. For the story of this venture see *Proceedings*, State Historical Society of Wisconsin (Madison, Wisconsin, 1900), 186–194: John B. Sanborn, "The Story of the Fox-Wisconsin Rivers Improvement." This address was delivered at Green Bay, Wisconsin, on September 7, 1899.

mote necessary improvements, for increasing population would provide for the cost of public works. Granting lands to actual settlers would head off speculators and supply homes for the destitute and work for the unemployed. Such a policy would create wealth by means of increasing the products of the soil. Seymour was always a champion of the immigrant, as we shall see from his hostility to Nativism, and he urged on the federal government the advisability of filling up the western lands with people. One of his favorite observations was that the shifting of population from the Old World to the New was the greatest spectacle in history. Before long, he liked to predict, North and South America would lie at the centre of power in the world. In this message of 1854 Seymour put in his first appearance on the stage of national politics.

Whatever they may have thought of his advice on the state of the Union, the Whigs snatched eagerly at one opportunity which this second message offered them. Seymour had devoted a paragraph to a suggestion that the legislature take some action to abate the evils of intemperance and the abuses of the traffic in liquor. In 1852, it will be remembered, he had refused to give any pre-election pledge to the corresponding secretary of the New York Temperance Alliance, but his recommendation of 1854 was not wholly voluntary. Compulsory abstinence was in the air. It was in 1846 that Maine first enacted a dry law; in 1851 the legislature passed a stricter statute. Riots in Neal Dow's city of Portland led to the repeal of the second law in 1855, but a third dry law was put on the books in 1858. One state after another played with the reform until Maine laws were being argued over almost everywhere.

In January, 1854, the state of New York was by no means what would be called "wet," for the sale of liquor in quantities of less than five gallons, except in genuine inns or hotels under license, or in grocery stores, where it might not be consumed, was already forbidden by law.[22] During the election of 1853,

22. For good summaries, see Johnson and Smith, *History*, II, 401; and Alexander, *History*, II, 199–204.

Myron H. Clark, who began as a cabinet-maker and grew as a merchant into a reformer and a governor, had been returned to the state senate as an ardent advocate of a Maine law for New York. Clark sympathized cordially with both Nativists and abolitionists, but his hobby was "temperance" — perhaps for that reason Alexander describes him as one of "the class of men generally known as fanatics." However that may be, Clark displayed a talent for talk, tact, and industry in the legislature. According to his promise to his constituents he introduced a Maine law at the beginning of his second term. Guided by the Whigs, the bill was pushed through the senate and the assembly, but on March 31, 1854, Horatio Seymour sent it back to the legislature with his veto.[23]

The special message with which Seymour returned this "Act for the Suppression of Intemperance" focused the attention of the whole state, for Maine laws were the talk of every household as prohibition appeared and disappeared again all over the Union. Here and there a paper agreed with the governor's contention that the bill was not only unwise but unconstitutional, as well. Far and wide, however, the veto was greeted with a roar of disapproval — Greeley of the *Tribune* being one of the noisiest and most effective critics. Supporters of the measure declared that the veto had been dictated by the liquor interests of the state, and some of them descended to personal abuse of the governor. Seymour, it was said, was addicted to the bottle — he was, in point of fact, a teetotaler. The conservative press was pleased, as a rule, for prohibition was generally associated in the public mind with other radical schemes of reform.[24]

Seymour's reasons for his veto of the Maine bill deserve a careful examination. He acknowledged that he did not believe that the control of the traffic in liquor was by any means ideal. It was in hope of improving that control that he had recom-

23. Lincoln, *Messages*, IV, 753–754.

24. Governor Seymour made an extensive collection of clippings on the subject of this famous veto, both complimentary and otherwise. New York State Library: Seymour Papers.

mended legislative action looking toward a more stringent enforcement of existing statutes. In 1854 New York already had a system which permitted what was practically local option, for the state law allowed the sale of liquor in small quantities only through such tavern-keepers and grocers as were licensed by the county supervisors or justices of the peace. The excise officers of all towns were elected, and it was legally possible for these officers to grant no licenses whatever. Such, in fact, was the situation in many different parts of the state. Seymour was a positive and persistent believer in the importance of local government; therefore local option, which banned or permitted liquor by what was practically a neighborhood vote, fitted in neatly with his notion of what was the proper method.

Myron Clark's bill, on the other hand, was designed, he declared, to compel abstinence by means of severe fines and penalties, search and seizure, and wholesale destruction of liquor. Five sections of the bill, in his opinion, violated the eleventh section of the Bill of Rights in the Constitution of the United States.[25] Seymour vetoed the measure first, because New York had only to avail itself of local option as it might please; second, because the issuing of "general warrants" was unusual and dangerous; and third, because the law assumed not the innocence, but the guilt of the accused. He had, he wrote, "given to the bill the respectful consideration due to the importance of the subject, and the deliberate action of the two branches of the legislature," but he could not sign it, for he believed its provisions were "calculated to injure the cause of temperance, and impair the welfare of the state." [26]

The resentment Governor Seymour aroused by his act lasted for years; the approval was less vociferous and, men being what they are, perhaps not so long-lived. The whispers against

25. The sections to which Governor Seymour took particular objection were: IX, XIII, XIV, XVII, and XXXII. These sections provided for the issue of search warrants as late as a month after the alleged offense of sale; authorized the forfeiture and destruction of liquor under suspicion; made a fact of sale prove unlawful sale; and delivery of liquor proof of the payment for it.

26. Lincoln, *Messages*, IV, 753.

Seymour's personal motives were silenced by a public statement from one of the most prominent of the prohibitionists. E. C. Delavan, of Ballston Spa, had long been known as an ardent advocate of temperance. No intoxicating liquor had ever been sold in the famous hotel which he owned at Albany in spite of the fact that Daniel Webster is known to have stayed there — at least once. "Dr. Delavan," as he was called, took issue with the reasoning of the governor, but openly praised his courage and conviction. Seymour, he declared, was sincere, and his intentions were good. The cause of temperance would triumph in the end, but temperance was not the only cause, and no earnest advocate should be harshly impatient of differences of opinion on the subject. Delavan's defense of Seymour was dangerous to himself and not very helpful to the governor.

Brewers, distillers, and tavern-keepers, moreover, were injudicious in their jubilation at the return of the bill. An eyewitness describes the celebration on the "memorable day" at Albany when Seymour's veto was announced. The enemies of the bill hauled out a cannon and fired it three hundred and sixty-five times in honor of a "veto long enough to veto the world." "But the triumphing of the wicked is short," wrote a pious student to his brother, just after returning from a "temperance" meeting at the city hall, where what he calls the "gases" had been turned off in the midst of an old-fashioned mass-meeting row.[27]

Seymour insisted that the measure he vetoed was unconstitutional, and the courts of the state from the lowest to the highest agreed with him, once they were given a chance to pass on the law. The bill went through again in 1855 as "An Act for the Prevention of Intemperance, Pauperism, and Crime." Governor Clark signed it on April 9, and it became effective on July 4.[28]

27. New York State Library: Manuscript Section: Letter from William W. Merritt to D. H. Merritt, March 31, 1854.

28. The vote on the reënactment of the Maine Law was: senate, yeas 21, nays 11; assembly, yeas 81, nays 44, absent 4.

Two test cases were carried through the courts, and the decision of the supreme court of the first judicial district, Justices Brown, Strong, and Rockwell went against the law. This decision was upheld by the supreme court of appeals in March of 1856.[29]

Men like Rufus Choate publicly opposed the law in principle, and before very long the cause of prohibition was forgotten, if not lost, in the growing gloom of the eve of the Civil War.

Seymour faced the storm of disapproval of his veto good-naturedly. In the very midst of the angry uproar he welcomed a delegation of distinguished visitors from New England with a banquet at his home at Albany and surprised some of his guests by taking nothing to drink, remarking that he had never been able to tell one wine from another and disliked the taste of liquor. His digestion was never good; all during his life he seems to have suffered from some organic trouble which probably caused his fatigue and attacks of low spirits. Years afterwards, speaking at Rome, just after his second election as governor in 1862, he apologized to his audience for not presenting the ruddy appearance of the heavy drinker he was commonly supposed to be. He had stopped to thank his enemies for always fighting him with falsehoods about himself rather than putting him to the pain of having to hear the simple truth.[30]

The veto of the Maine bill had caused trouble enough, but there was more around the corner. In 1854 a papal nuncio, Monsignor Bedini, put in his appearance at Albany to celebrate pontifical high mass in honor of the dedication of the altars of the new Roman Catholic Cathedral of St. Peter. Seymour entertained Bedini at his home one evening together with many of the Protestant clergy of the city. Everything went off well enough, but the fact that the governor of New York had received the foreign delegate of Pius IX did not help Seymour in certain parts of New York at the next election. It is interesting to notice that his lifelong affection for the Irish and the

29. Wynehamer versus People, 13 New York, 378: court of appeals: Lincoln, *Messages,* IV, 771.

30. Seymour, *Public Record,* 363.

HORATIO SEYMOUR'S HOME IN ALBANY

1853–1854

Catholics was the only sentiment he shared with Seward. He could not work with the latter, he once told Governor Andrew during a talk in Boston, because the gentleman from Auburn, so far as he had been able to discover, was utterly lacking in principles.[31]

It was Seward, oddly enough, who started the long-lived nuisance of Nativism in New York — perhaps unwittingly — by inserting a paragraph on education in his second annual message as governor in January, 1840. In this paragraph he recommended "the establishment of schools in which [foreigners] may be instructed by teachers speaking the same language with themselves and professing the same faith." At once the Whig governor was accused of trying to draw the Irish vote away from the Democrats. If such was his effort, it was doomed to failure. The "immediate response" to his message was the demand of Roman Catholics in New York City for a share of the public-school fund. Twice in 1840 this request was rejected by a common council controlled by the Democrats. Opponents of the Catholics fell in behind an organization called the Public School Society, and a bitter fight began.[32] From this seed sprouted Nativism.

Cowardly fear of Roman Catholics and jealousy of the Jews were not confined to the so-called uneducated classes. In 1841, for instance, the painter, S. F. B. Morse, was the nativist candidate for mayor of New York. Dr. Scisco's study of the movement in the state describes the cause of its sudden rise and its no less sudden disappearance. "It placed itself before the people," he discovered, "as an exponent of good citizenship only." There was no hostility to race or creed on the surface, but in New York City the "antagonism toward the clannishness of Irishmen and Irish ways" could not be concealed for long. The American Protestant Union, of which Morse was president, was organized on May 30, 1841, as a semi-religious protest against the balance of power which the Irish Catholics

31. Pearson, *John A. Andrew*, II, 158–159.
32. Scisco, *Nativism in New York*, 32–33, *passim*.

controlled in the elections in New York City. When Bishop Hughes unwisely countered with the organization of the Carroll Hall Ticket the following October, his rash action was condemned by every newspaper in New York.

In 1842 Governor Seward signed a new school bill, which set up an elective board of control for the public schools. Members of this board were to be chosen annually in June. The Whigs of the city promptly went nativist, and the Democrats split, putting up "anti-foreign" tickets in many of the wards. On election-night in April, 1842, mobs raided the Irish areas and stoned the residence of Bishop Hughes. Mayor Morris called out the militia and stationed soldiers at the Roman Catholic churches. By this time the soil was well seeded and watered for the bitter crop of the next twelve years. Secret societies rose overnight — the Order of United Americans, or "O. U. A.," in 1845, and that of the Star Spangled Banner in 1850 — first called "Know-Nothings" in the New York *Tribune* of November 10, 1853. These Know-Nothings put up their first state ticket that very autumn.

Because Seward had sowed the dragon's teeth, there was poetic justice in the fact that the Know-Nothings drew most of their votes from the Whigs. Then in May, 1854, James W. Barker, a shrewd organizer, began to build his political machine. On the first of June, Barker had ninety-one councils at his command; by August, he had two hundred and one. A state convention of the Star Spangled Banner nominated Daniel Ullman for governor. Ullman was not the first of the strange creatures who have caught the votes of Americans, nor was he the last. Although this graduate of Yale was a native of Delaware, his political enemies insisted that he had really been born in India and had even posed as a Hindoo in New Haven; whereupon the followers of Barker were called "Hindoos." [33] Mr.

33. Daniel Ullman, or Ullmann, though often called a Harvard man, was graduated from Yale in 1829, and took up the practice of law in New York City. He became a Silver-Gray, or anti-Seward, Whig, and was frequently an aspirant for office. In 1861 he raised a regiment of volunteers in New York and later enlisted negroes with the aid and consent of Lincoln. In November, 1865, he

Scisco ascribed much of the phenomenal strength of what came to be called the "American" party to that love of novelty which still pervades back-country counties of the United States and the pleasure people take in playing practical jokes on their leaders. Nativism not only kept the politicians of New York guessing for six years; in Massachusetts it made a man named Gardner governor of the state for three terms. It flourished wherever Catholics were strong: in 1856, for instance, Millard Fillmore carried Maryland as its candidate for President. Seymour's veto had united the drys against him, and their leader, Myron Clark, was a Whig. The rise of Barker and his friend, Daniel Ullman, added a second complication; Stephen Arnold Douglas made a third.

In 1854 came the Kansas–Nebraska Act, which brought up the issue of slavery once more in the form of what was called the "repeal of the Missouri Compromise." With the revival of this argument confusion in New York was worse confounded. The Compromise of 1850 had split the Whigs into "Woolly-Heads," or "Conscience" Whigs, who followed Seward, and "Silver-Grays," or "Cotton" Whigs, who followed Fillmore. The ineptitude of President Pierce, meanwhile, was dividing the Democrats into "Softs," like Marcy and Seymour, and "Hards," like Dickinson, who still hoped the South would make him President one day. Whigs and Democrats alike were afraid of the Know-Nothings. Into these sleepless camps of warriors Senator Douglas carelessly tossed the bomb of his bill for organizing the territories of Kansas and Nebraska. For the moment, Myron Clark's crusade for prohibition held the mutually hostile Seward and Fillmore Whigs together, and thus it was that there were only four (and not five) state conventions in the summer and autumn of 1854 and three live issues — Temperance, Free Soil, and Nativism. Of these four conventions only that of the Democratic "Softs," which nominated Seymour on September 7, united to condemn all three campaigns against alcohol,

retired from the service with the rank of major-general. He was born in 1810 and died in 1892, with an LL.D. from Colgate University.

slavery, and foreigners. On this firm platform the governor stood proudly through one of the most exciting contests the state of New York has ever seen.

Of the four candidates at the election, Clark, author of the Maine bill, was a total abstainer, an abolitionist, and a Whig. Daniel Ullman had been a follower of Fillmore, who was to run for President as a Nativist in 1856. Greene C. Bronson was an old Hunker Democrat — the recently dispossessed collector of the port of New York. Primarily, in fact, he was the tool of Dickinson. Horatio Seymour represented the federal government — as well as he could. He suffered, however, from two kinds of embarrassment. In the first place, the political appointments of President Pierce had brought not peace but war to New York; and the ill-managed removal of Bronson had made the old Hunker a martyr. In the second place, Douglas, with his doctrine of "popular sovereignty," had carried Free Soil onto dangerous ground. The Kansas-Nebraska Act provided for popular sovereignty even in advance of statehood.

No Democrat who preached the Jeffersonian theory of government by community feeling could deny the right of territories to settle the question of slavery for themselves even before, as well as at the time, of coming into the Union as sovereign states — and be consistent. Yet how could he explain the failure of the federal government to protect property rights in negroes in the territories which it still controlled? These territories were the common possessions of the American people. There was much to be said in favor of the argument that the convenient bargain of the Missouri Compromise had been shady, and it looked as if Seymour would be forced to acknowledge that charge as a fact. It was one thing to urge men not to agitate against slavery as it existed in the South; it was quite another to support a law which might allow slavery to spread through the West. Seymour could speak more openly than Douglas, for the senator from Illinois was ambitious. New Yorkers, so their governor told them, had no reason not to let the West vote as the West might please, for the new states, he predicted, would come into the Union free.

Governor Seymour accepted his third nomination unwillingly, for his disgust with President Pierce's management in New York tempted him to step out of office after the single term which was now becoming a respectable tradition in New York. In the spring of 1854, shortly after he vetoed the Maine bill, he wrote Secretary Marcy that he would take the governorship of Nebraska were it offered to him; otherwise, he hoped to spend the next two years in Europe — a natural desire he was never to fulfill. Marcy might think his willingness to go West "a strange idea" but he had "some purposes political pecuniary and scientific connected with the project."[34] The secretary of state was amazed and urged Seymour to seek a second term — possibly as a means of keeping him out of the political graveyard of Nebraska. A few weeks later the governor and his wife went to Washington and then retired to Newport to escape the heat of the summer. Dean Richmond and William Cassidy of the *Atlas* brought pressure to bear to force Seymour to accept a renomination. In Newport, however, he talked of flowers and stones with the Honorable Amelia Murray, blue-stocking botanist from Great Britain, who wrote home of her surprise at finding an American governor (and a Democrat at that) both intelligent and charming.

Some time in August the Seymours returned to Albany, shortly before the state convention was to meet at Syracuse. On September 7 came a telegram from Richmond and Cassidy: "You must not say or write anything on the subject of Governor till we see you. Keep still by all means." According to one story the telegraph wires from the capitol were cut in order to prevent the dispatch of Seymour's refusal to run a third time. However that may be, he found himself before long with the nomination of 1854 on his lap. The anxious Marcy wired him

34. Library of Congress: Marcy Papers: Horatio Seymour to W. L. Marcy, May 25, 1854:

If General Pierce will offer me the position of Governor of Nebraska, I will take it. You will think this a strange idea, but I have some purposes political pecuniary and scientific connected with the project. Of course I would not be a candidate for any place but I shall spend the next two years in Europe unless I can get away from home by engaging in some pursuit in the West. It is possible that I shall be in Washington in the course of a few weeks.

from Washington to be sure to accept, but Seymour's letter of September 9 shows that he was still undecided as to what he ought to do.

> It is a very great sacrifice for me to be a candidate. I cannot explain all my difficulties in a letter. To what end do I expose myself to the abuse and discomforts of a canvass which is to be bitter beyond all precedents? I must formally destroy my relationship with a great number of friends in the Hard organisation. If I am badly beaten, I injure myself and friends, for it is folly to talk of any gratitude for sacrifices. If I get a complimentary vote, it will draw down upon myself and friends the hostility of the National Administration. For myself I am indifferent to results. I should have preferred to have retired quietly from political life, but defeat has no terrors for me.[35]

Seymour allowed himself to be persuaded and accepted a renomination which meant nothing but denunciation, and, as it so happened, defeat. Not only were there prohibitionists to face, but he had to fight in New York for a man who was, in his opinion, "a fool who aspires to be a knave." Clark attacked him in front; while Ullman and his Know-Nothings struck at one flank, and Bronson, heading the "Hards," at the other. Dickinson stormed up and down the state, jeering at President Pierce and denouncing Seymour as the tool of the liquor interests.[36] As between the Democrats, Bronson and Seymour, Horace Greeley thought the only question was "as to whether the contempt universally felt for President Pierce should be openly expressed, or more decorously cherished in silence."[37] Greeley hit nearer the mark than he may have imagined, for a year earlier, when Seymour still thought that the Democrats "would insist upon a common ticket next autumn," he had written to Marcy:

> I have very little confidence in the manhood of General Pierce. His miserable policy of neglecting every one who made active efforts in this State last fall has discouraged the best men of the party, but if he will take a firm position in favor of a strict construction of the Constitution, we can tri-

35. Library of Congress: Marcy Papers: Horatio Seymour to W. L. Marcy, September 9, 1854.

36. Daniel S. Dickinson, *Speeches, Correspondence, etc., of the late Daniel S. Dickinson*, John R. Dickinson, Editor, (New York, 1867), I, 496–507.

37. Alexander, *History*, II, 202.

umphantly sustain his Administration against all his mistakes and against all the unworthy schemes of the miserable profligates who constitute his Kitchen Cabinet. The friends of Dickinson and Beardsley are making fools of themselves, and I have an abiding confidence they will continue to do so. Although we cannot always depend upon the wisdom of our friends in this State, we can count with confidence upon the folly of our enemies.[38]

For confusion, if not for bitterness, the state campaign of 1854 had never been equalled, even in New York. For days the result was in doubt — Ullman looked like the winner at first, owing to the surprising strength of his vote, but one week later Seymour was commonly believed to have been reëlected. Slowly, as returns trickled in from the western counties, the Whig vote mounted, and for some time Clark and Seymour ran neck and neck. Eleven days after the election, Clark was declared the victor.[39] The certified vote gave him the advantage of 309 votes out of a total poll of 469,431.[40] The Know-Nothings were amazed at their own showing; in view of the almost equally divided Democratic vote of 1853, Bronson had made a laughing-stock of himself: Clark squeezed into the governor's chair by virtue of the thirty-three thousand votes he collected. Horatio Seymour had made a magnificent showing — in the face of tremendous odds.

According to a shrewd observer who watched him close at hand the serenity of Seymour was surprising. Miss Amelia Murray was his guest at Albany all during the exciting two weeks when the totals for Clark and Seymour were mounting and changing places day by day. The governor went about his work with "a calm indifference" which his excited friends could

38. Library of Congress: Marcy Papers: Horatio Seymour to W. L. Marcy, November 5, 1853.

39. Scisco, *Nativism in New York*, 124–128.

40. The certified vote stood: Clark, Whig, 156,804; Seymour, "Soft" Democrat, 156,495; Ullman, American, 122,282; Bronson, "Hard" Democrat, 33,850: Werner, *Civil List*, 167. For a good description of the effects of the Maine bill and Seymour's veto of it on the election of 1854, see *New York History*, XVII, 3 (July, 1936), 260–272: John A. Krout, "The Maine Law in New York Politics," especially for Greeley's charge that Weed betrayed him as to a nomination for the governorship in 1954, and that Seymour promised, prior to his election in 1852, to sign a prohibitory bill!

not share. When they urged him to petition for a recount, he refused. Once the official decision had been announced, Seymour wrote to his brother:

As it regards the election I am perfectly satisfied with the matter as it stands. I received a larger number of votes than Mr. Clark and I could set aside the returns from a number of counties if I wished to do so — But it is for my interest personally, pecuniarily and politically not to go into the office of Governor again. I know that the leading Whigs would like to have a democratic Governor to relieve them from responsibilities. I have made up my mind to stand upon the present issues, and in the end my policy will be vindicated. It is a great matter to get out of office pleasantly. This I have done. I am about 30,000 ahead of my ticket; I have been counted out of an election by canvassers; my position has given the organisation to which I belong a great triumph. I have secured a majority of 1,200 in this Whig city — in fine, every aspect of the matter is agreeable to me. I could not hope to stand as well at the end of another term — The Maine Law will be tried and will fail.[41]

Perhaps Seymour was too diplomatic, too discreet in 1854. According to one of his allies he was too clever by half. Francis E. Spinner was running for the Congress as a Democrat. Years after, he became a Republican and served as registrar of the treasury for a long period. In the letter he wrote from Jacksonville, Florida, Spinner took Seymour to task for his tactics. If we are to believe the author of it, he was an eye-witness of an attitude not unknown in modern politics: the governor refused to speak out.

You are quite correct, the ticket I sent you was for the year 1854, when I was Elected to Congress, and when Honorable Horatio Seymour was defeated for governor by a very small majority, 300 or less. At that time, the Know Nothings were in their glory, and there were Silver Greys, and Wolley [*sic*] heads, in the Whig Party; and Hunkers and Barnburners, and Hards and Soft Shells in the Democratic Party. — Then, there was an abolition and a Temperance Party. — A pretty mess it was. — They all enquired, by letter of me, what my Political Opinions were relating to all the Subjects on which these Parties were founded. — I answered every One of them, *fairly and squarly* [*sic*]. — Governor Seymour came to see me, and begged me not to write any more letters, and said that I was ruining my prospects of an Election, and his as well. — I told him that he must permit me to manage my own campaign in my own way. — He kept *mum*; and I kept on

41. New York Historical Society: Seymour Papers: Horatio Seymour to John F. Seymour, November 22, 1854.

answering all enquiries. The result was, that if he had got within *a thousand* as many Votes in Herkimer and St. Lawrence, as I did, *he would have been Elected.*[42]

And last, but not least, the shrewd strategy of the Whigs contributed the decisive factor to the result. If Thurlow Weed had not managed matters so well as he did, Seymour might have been reëlected in spite of the defection of Bronson and the craze for Ullman. Greeley had pushed prohibition for all it was worth in New York, for he hoped that he himself would be the Whig nominee for governor in 1854. Weed, however, insisted on the choice of an upstate man, and Myron Clark, the author of the bill which Seymour had vetoed, was the obvious person. Then the editor of the *Tribune* tried to argue himself into the second place on the ticket, but although the Whig manager agreed that this must go to a resident of the city, he declared for a wet in order to balance the dry at the top of the ticket. The choice fell on Henry J. Raymond, a former employee of Greeley and his bitter rival at the moment, for Raymond had become editor of the New York *Times*. Thus the *Times* could not support Seymour, and the *Tribune* could not bolt Clark. Weed's generalship won the day in 1854 but it may have cost Seward the Republican presidential nomination in 1860. The immediate result of the manœuvre, however, was to hold just enough wet Whigs in line for Clark to carry the election.

Seymour's veto of Senator Clark's Maine bill probably lost him many more votes than it gained for him. His act was unpopular, and wet Whigs were hardly likely to vote in such a way as might seem to give endorsement to the "southern" policies of President Pierce. Yet the language of that veto expressed what would one day come to be the well considered opinion of a solid majority of the American people. Over three-quarters of a century after Seymour had phrased the case against compulsory abstinence, his fellow citizens of the future would sit in judg-

42. Francis E. Spinner to Thomas Cunningham, February 19, 1885. Letter in possession of the author.

ment on an "experiment noble in motive and far-reaching in consequence." At the very first opportunity craven politicians would grant them, they would decide that, whatever might be said of the motive, the consequence of prohibition was not quite to their hearts' desire.

Defeat did not shake his serenity. He fought on two fronts at once in 1854: Myron Clark commanded the fanatical foes of liquor, and Daniel Ullman led all those who feared and hated foreigners and Roman Catholics. Spite, if not treachery, moreover, divided the Democrats. Seymour's showing, in the circumstances, was astonishing; the decision hung on a handful of extremely doubtful votes. A protest would probably have returned him to the office he gave up without complaint. Looking at the result, he would have murmured with Matthew Arnold:

Charge once more, then, and be dumb!
Let the victors, when they come,
When the forts of folly fall,
Find thy body by the wall!

IX

AT SPRINGFIELD FOR BUCHANAN

1856

REPUBLICANS have always apologized for their first nominee for President. As a young man, John Charles Frémont, of Savannah, Georgia, handsome and curly-headed, had run off with Jessie Benton, daughter of Thomas Hart Benton, perpetual senator from Missouri — a notorious deed in days when elopements were still unusual. While not yet thirty, he explored the Rocky Mountains, and then helped in the conquest of California, for which state he sat as senator one year. Discovery of gold on the West Coast made him extremely wealthy. He liked to be known as "The Pathfinder," but Democrats fastened on the sound of his first two initials and the noise of his wedding to call him by the first name of his adoring and vivacious spouse. On August 31, 1861, his proclamation to the effect that he would confiscate all slaves of those persons in rebellion, confronted Lincoln with an excellent instance of doing the right thing the wrong way. The order was promptly annulled. Frémont travelled at full speed — one of the most incautious fathers of the party of caution. It was eminently fitting that this light-hearted son of romance should lose all his money and die poor.

Though Pierce hoped for a renomination in 1856, the Cincinnati convention hesitated and then turned to Buchanan. The dapper-legged bachelor from "Wheatland," Pennsylvania, was rich in the political experience which his Republican opponent lacked. Polk never quite trusted the man he made his secretary of state — he was a reformed Federalist, for one thing, and a tattler of tales. His life was one of waiting. He had sat in the House and the Senate and served at St. James's under Pierce. Like Cass, he was a wheel-horse of the party and accepted his last nomination as payment of a debt long overdue. All his friends were dead, he lamented, and all his enemies were friends. Because he was President at the unlucky moment when the southern states seceded, Buchanan has suffered unreasonable abuse at the hands of heroes with hindsight. The feud with Douglas and the fierce dissensions of the fatal winter of 1860–1861 conspired to make as difficult and doubtful a time as any President of the United States has ever had the misfortune to face; yet the only way to avoid Buchanan was to take Frémont — or Fillmore.

Buchanan was nothing if not respectable. Ambition and his keen sense of propriety led him to resign the ministry to England in January, 1856, and Marcy immediately sounded out Seymour on the subject of succeeding him.[1] It was not certain that Pierce would take his secretary's recommendation, but Marcy asked for the liberty of making the suggestion. Seymour had played with the notion of going to Europe. When Marcy's letter reached him, he was staying at the St. Nicholas Hotel in New York City, from which he wrote a characteristic reply: if Marcy thought he was fit for the post, and if it were clearly understood that he was not a candidate for it, the offer would be "agreeable" to him. Writing again the next day, he sent a second letter emphasizing the fact that he would consent to go to England only in case the President should ask him to do so:

> I was influenced in my reply by the feeling that if I remained at home during the coming year my whole time would be consumed by vexations and profitless excitement — I fear however that my conclusion will only make me a foot ball for the fickle head of our government and if my name should in any way be brought forward, I should be dropped as Dix and Miller were under similar circumstances — I fear I have let myself down from safe ground by consenting to take an appointment if one is tendered to me which I think is very doubtful.[2]

The ministry to England had an added importance at the moment, for Great Britain was at war with Russia, and mutual

1. New York Historical Society: Seymour Papers: Copy of a letter of S. B. Gavin to Horatio Seymour, January 3, 1856.

2. New York Historical Society: Seymour Papers: Horatio Seymour to S. B. Gavin, January 7 and 8, 1856.

complaints and misunderstandings had arisen between the two English-speaking powers. In November, 1855, for instance, Seymour and Marcy were seriously discussing the possibility of having to face a war with Great Britain and France.[3] Seymour suspected that the alliance between Victoria and Napoleon III had reference to both hemispheres and that the war against Russia was designed to check that nation's growth of power and its dream of becoming a commercial nation. "A contest with France and Great Britain would involve enormous losses to us," he wrote Marcy, "but if it must come, let it come now." There was some doubt as to whether the successor to Buchanan would be received; yet Seymour thought danger ought not to affect his decision.[4] As soon as he learned from Marcy that the English mission would be offered to Dallas, Seymour withdrew his name "in the most unqualified manner," writing from Utica, on January 27, that he was "very much pleased over the result" which kept him "out of public life." He had business enough of his own at home and in February he would have to go to Illinois and Wisconsin for several weeks. He was, moreover, negotiating the long-deferred union of the *Argus* and *Atlas* by which "the only obstacle to permanent peace would be removed from the path of the Democratic Party in New York."[5] Before he received this letter of withdrawal Marcy telegraphed that Dallas was hesitating, but that he feared he would accept.

A little more than a week later, Seymour was again in New York, at the St. Nicholas, when a second telegram from Marcy called him to Washington on "public business." The secretary wrote two letters to his friend; the first he sent to New York, the second to Utica. Kansas was the question at hand, and the distracted Pierce had decided to send out two commissioners —

> . . . the highest men he can get — one from the North and one from the south to the Territory of Kansas for the purpose of adjusting if it be prac-

3. Library of Congress: Marcy Papers: Horatio Seymour to W. L. Marcy, November 17, 1855.

4. Library of Congress: Marcy Papers: Horatio Seymour to W. L. Marcy, January 22, 1856.

5. Library of Congress: Marcy Papers: Horatio Seymour to W. L. Marcy, January 27, 1856.

ticable, the difficulty there — The President and all his cabinet are anxious to have you for one of them — I hope you will not hesitate about going.[6] Although he might have merged the interest of his business trip with service on this commission, Seymour refused to accept it. Kansas was no place to make a reputation. He was forty-six years old, financially independent, and there were no children for whose sake he might have changed his plans. He had made a good governor of New York, and its highest court was to vindicate the reasons for his veto of the Maine bill within less than a month. As the time for the Cincinnati convention approached, the possibility of a duel between Franklin Pierce and James Buchanan led to the suggestion of his name being used as a compromise. Persistent rumors that he might be offered as a candidate forced him to take an action which puts his refusal to go out to Kansas above any suspicion as to his sincerity.

In April he indulged in one of the fashionable formalities of American public life; he wrote an open letter to his friend, Calvert Comstock, of Rome, definitely putting aside all thought of his name at Cincinnati:

I am aware that my name has been mentioned in connection with the nominations to be made by the Democratic National Convention at Cincinnati. I have not deemed it worth the while to notice any harmless speculations about a matter so improbable. I am now exclusively engaged in attention to my own affairs, and the neglected duties of private life. I have no aspirations for any office; nor would I consent to take any position, either in the State or national government. I have had enough of public life, and more than my share of public honors.

Although I shall not hereafter hold official position, I do not feel indifferent to the questions which now agitate the public mind. Cant, bigotry and intolerance obstruct the progress of temperance, religion and prosperity in our own State, while fanaticism threatens the welfare, if not the continued existence of the institutions of our country. Against the spreading leprosy of hypocrisy, which makes an outward whiteness because there is inward impurity and corruption, I shall at all times contend.

. . . I do not know of any one from this State, who wishes to be nominated either for the office of President or Vice-President, at Cincinnati; and most assuredly I cannot, with a decent degree of self-respect, wish to be placed

6. New York Historical Society: Seymour Papers: Copies of two letters from W. L. Marcy to Horatio Seymour, February 10, 1856.

upon the National ticket, while I am a delegate to the Convention, and the condition of our political organization constitutes the only hope of our opponents for the defeat of our party and its principles.[7]

Seymour concluded with the statement that he could not doubt that the electoral vote of New York would be given to the Cincinnati nominee, but from this confidence he would have a rude awakening.

He attended the national convention as a member of one of the rival delegations which habitually turned up from New York — an equal number of "Softs" and "Hards." During the contest for seats he proposed that the twin sets of delegates be admitted in proportion to the votes they had cast in the last election in New York.[8] This arrangement would have given the "Softs" three-fifths of the coveted seats, but according to the final decision all the mutually hostile Democrats were invited into the hall each with half a vote. Seymour was selected as "key-noter" and made a very favorable impression. As the balloting began, the "Softs," under the leadership of Marcy, supported Pierce, in the secret hope of nominating Douglas. The "Hards" went for Buchanan at the very beginning and voted for him steadily until first Pierce, and then Douglas, withdrew. Pierce was expected to fall by the way, but that the senator from Illinois should bow himself out was an embarrassment. The "Softs," however, jumped for the Buchanan band-wagon a little more quickly than dignity should have allowed, Seymour declaring that they desired to do all in their power to harmonize their vote in the convention and to promote political peace in New York.[9] As a consequence of his diplomacy, "Hards" and

7. New York State Library: Seymour Papers: Horatio Seymour to Calvert Comstock, April 3, 1856.

8. In 1855 the Native Americans elected their entire state ticket and secured the balance of power in the legislature. For secretary of state the vote stood: Know-Nothings, 148,557; Republicans, 136,698; "Softs," 91,336; "Hards," 59,353. This vote was typical: the state senate consisted of sixteen Republicans, eleven Know-Nothings, four Democrats, and one Prohibitionist. Fifty Democrats (Softs and Hards), forty-four Know-Nothings, thirty-three Republicans, and one Whig sat in the assembly: Johnson and Smith, *History*, II, 413–414.

9. Alexander, *History*, II, 226–228.

"Softs" sat down together in a single state convention at Syracuse:

> In this crisis Horatio Seymour assumed the leadership that had been his in 1852, and that was not to be laid down for more than a decade. Seymour was now in his prime — still under fifty years of age. He had become a leader of energy and courage; and, although destined for many years to lead a divided and often a defeated organisation, he was ever after recognised as the most gifted and notable member of his party. He was a typical Northern Democrat. He had the virtues and foibles that belonged to that character in his generation, the last of whom have now passed from the stage of public action.[10]

To head their state ticket the Democrats put up Amasa J. Parker, an "eminent lawyer" and a "cultivated New Englander," who had sat in the Congress and had been a member of the supreme court of New York. The Whigs softly set aside their rabid prohibitionist and nominated John Alsop King — the first Republican governor of the state.

After his spectacular defeat in 1854, Seymour was relieved to be "in the minority and out of power." He found "numerous consolations" in his "political retirement"; he was "quite enamoured of savage life."[11] As he wrote Postmaster-General Campbell about the same time he felt that the election of 1854 had been a "triumph" for the Democratic party, for his opponent, Clark, had received "*ten* nominations" altogether to his one, and yet the difference between the two high men was "nominal."[12] He suspected that the Whigs would have been happy to have the Democrats carry all the responsibility for government until the national election of 1856, and he thought that Clark's narrow and accidental success would work to the detriment of his own party. Yet the last Whig would be followed by the first Republican.

From Syracuse Seymour returned to Utica to seek the "savage life" he loved. His language was not a pose. He knew his state

10. Alexander, *History*, II, 232.

11. New York Historical Society: Seymour Papers: Horatio Seymour to an unnamed correspondent, in 1854.

12. New York State Library: Manuscript Section: Horatio Seymour to James Campbell, November 17, 1854.

from one end to the other and took pride in his knowledge of its geography and history. He never tired of pointing out the strategic and commercial importance of the water-level route which DeWitt Clinton had carried on into the heart of the Middle West. Burgoyne's failure to split the colonies by way of Lake Champlain and the Hudson in 1777, was, he always insisted, the turning-point of the American Revolution. The decisive battle of that war had fittingly been fought on the soil of New York. He liked to dilate on the influence of the mixed population of the state on the growth of its civilization and the development of its jurisprudence — Dutch, English, Yankee, and Irish, all these people had contributed to a healthful conflict of opinion and a firm love of freedom. Dutchmen and New Englanders, in particular, had brought into New York their age-old genius for governing themselves. His fellow citizens had only to become acquainted with their own state to realize how wonderfully its inhabitants had made use of the natural advantages of the land.

Seymour did not limit his love of New York to working up elaborate lectures and writing out speeches to be delivered at the dedications of public memorials. In the autumn of 1854 the Honorable Amelia Murray arrived at Albany in the very midst of the exciting returns of the election. She saw a good deal of the governor and his wife, first and last, staying as their house-guest in both Albany and Utica, and visiting New York with them and then going on to Washington, where they joined her. Before she sailed from Boston in the autumn of 1855 this good lady had spent more than two months' time in the company of the Seymours. The result of her passion for travel and talk appeared in print early in 1856.[13]

The governor and his wife seem to have liked this lady quite as well as she did them. Late in November they set out for

13. *Letters from the United States, Cuba and Canada* was reprinted in one volume in New York in 1856. Because the book has no index readers who may wish to consult the author's more important contacts with, and opinions of, Horatio Seymour are referred to pages 35, 125–126, 128–130, 133–137, 139–141, 144–148, 180–181, 371–384, and 397.

New York City together. The people with whom they dined she found various and interesting. She witnessed a polite disagreement between her host and Henry Ward Beecher; she toured the alms-houses and the penitentiaries and watched the governor review the militia from the very steps of that city hall where almost nine years later he would make an impromptu speech which became notorious among his political enemies. She was struck with the contrast between Seymour's "tranquillity of manner and simple dignity" and his bustling staff of officers gorgeous in full regimentals. The troops, thought Miss Amelia, "manœuvred with great precision." They visited the "print-shops and galleries," but the Landseer picture which her amiable host "wished much to see" had already been packed up and sent off to Boston. She sat at dinner beside William Cullen Bryant, editor of the *Evening Post*, an imposing man with "grey head and beard," and allowed her love of literature to overcome her suspicions and dislike of abolitionists.[14]

Returning from her tour of the "United States, Cuba, and Canada," Miss Murray stopped off to visit the Seymours in Utica, in the summer of 1855. Her host was no longer governor; he was, in fact, planning one of his tramps through the Adirondacks, and the distinguished visitor was delighted to be asked to join the company of his niece and two guides. Seymour met the ladies at Elizabethtown, from which point the party of five travelled through the mountains for ten days, heading southwest for Utica in a leisurely fashion. Canoeing, riding, and walking, and camping out at night, they covered altogether more than one hundred miles. It was not a "dude" expedition — they slept in the open, and cooked their own food. The intimate and pleasant picture which this naïve narrative gives of Horatio Seymour shows the variety of his general information and his unfailing good nature, even under the strain of fatigue and petty misfortune. Once she had got over her surprise that every state should have its own governor, Miss Murray condescendingly concluded that the choice of such a

14. Murray, *Letters from the United States*, 142–148.

gentleman as Seymour had done credit to the voters of New York. She would have read Matthew Arnold's praise of Chester Alan Arthur without a smile: the President of the United States would have graced a British Cabinet. The two travellers talked over slavery together, and her host explained that difference between American parties which Englishmen still find confusing. The lady was a good listener and an eager convert.

Within a week and a day of his return from these rambles in the Adirondacks, Seymour was explaining America and Americans to a larger, if no more appreciative audience, at Tammany Hall, in New York City. This address was something more than a former governor's annual hack contribution to a state election. He had been out of office for less than a year but he had no thought of ever going back. He felt free to speak his mind on several subjects and he set about doing so. All his life he trusted the ultimate good judgment of the people, for he was a genuine follower of Jefferson and unwilling to despair of any of the principles of the agile Virginian. In January, 1855, he had gone to Washington to find the "Softs" regarded with respect, and the administration "moving on very harmoniously." Writing from the capital, he tried to make it clear that he had taken himself out of public life.

> The reports with respect to myself are equally absurd. No appointment will be tendered to me nor would I accept any office. I am "discharged cured" of all ambition for official stations. I could not be persuaded again to give up the comfort and respectability of private life.[15]

Marcy had been using his magic on his favorite pupil. The old secretary of state still had hopes that his friend was not yet "discharged cured." "I am glad that you are to address a mass meeting at Tammany Hall," he wrote; "I however regard it as a delicate task." [16] Seymour was never quite at home in the city of New York; before many years had passed he would associate

15. New York Historical Society: Seymour Papers: Letter of Horatio Seymour to an unnamed correspondent, January 30, 1855.

16. New York Historical Society: Seymour Papers: Copy of a letter of W. L. Marcy to Horatio Seymour, September 12, 1855. For the text of this speech of Friday, September 28, see the New York *Herald* of Saturday, September 29, 1855.

a convention at Tammany Hall with what he regretted as the greatest mistake of his whole career. In the autumn of 1855, however, he felt that some one ought to speak out for the Democrats on three abominations and believing that he was through with holding office for ever, he was ready and willing to undertake the unpopular task.

The Tammany Hall speech is a short and not so elaborate version of the address he gave in New England less than one year later. The sum and substance of both is a carefully reasoned case against three pet obsessions of the North — Nativism, or hatred of Catholics; temperance, or compulsory abstinence; and abolition, or agitation against slavery from the safe distance of free soil. He was not a Catholic; he never drank; and slavery, he believed, was doomed. If the success of his effort surprised him, it could hardly have failed to please him. Seymour's cousin wrote from Washington that he had read the speech in the New York *Herald* with the "utmost satisfaction" — his denunciation of the various "isms" would go far toward removing odium from New York and prove that the state was "still a virtuous community."

> Your speech, as reported in the Herald, has created a sensation such as no effort of the kind has produced for a long time and I feel proud to see that the sentiments it contains have met with such universal approbation.[17]

Morris Miller's praise was not all due to pride in a family commonly accused of being unusually proud; Seymour's speech at Tammany Hall drew favorable comment from as far west as Wisconsin and Iowa and as far south as New Orleans.[18] Shortly after the state election he declined "a flattering invitation" to speak at the Maryland Institute, being bound west on his private business. On December 8 the Appleton *Crescent* hailed him as the most plausible Democratic candidate for President in 1856. Republicanism, so the Wisconsin editor persuaded himself to believe, had "run its race" and future con-

17. New York Historical Society: Seymour Papers: Morris S. Miller to Horatio Seymour, October 3, 1855. Miller asked Seymour to send him fifteen or twenty copies of the speech for distribution in Washington.

18. See the clippings in the Seymour Scrap-Books in the New York State Library.

tests for the political control of the United States would be confined to Know-Nothings and Democrats — in which case Seymour was the only man who could beat the people who called themselves "Americans." The optimism of the editor was largely personal, for the orator at Tammany Hall was well known in Wisconsin.

Once Buchanan had squeezed out Pierce and Douglas at Cincinnati in the summer of 1856, the three-sided campaign was on. The new Republican party had named Frémont; the Know-Nothings persuaded former President Fillmore to head their national ticket. Seymour turned down an invitation from Philadelphia in order to speak at Springfield, Massachusetts, on the Fourth of July. Buchanan came from Pennsylvania, but New England was debatable ground. He preferred the enemy's country. The radio has disciplined public speakers in our own day; eighty years ago political candidates could tour the country repeating the speeches they had learned by heart. Repetition made reputation. Now one day wears out the magic of the spoken word. Seymour's speech at Springfield was a revised and extended version of the address he had made at Tammany Hall nine months before. Thus must his party think and vote if it would survive. Readers can imagine him still: tall, immaculately dressed, with golden voice and "large, luminous eyes," right hand tucked into his tightly-buttoned frock coat, facing a critical audience of poker-faced Yankees in a county town of the Connecticut Valley. In the autumn of 1855 he had spoken at a country fair in the neighborhood; now they would hear this New York Stater again.[19] Remembering, perhaps, that *Hudibras* was the favorite poem of Charles II, he did not venture to irritate the sons of Puritans with Samuel Butler's description of

> Such as do build their faith upon
> The holy text of pike and gun
> Call fire and sword and desolation
> A Godly thorough reformation.

19. As early as October 19, 1853, Seymour had spoken at the National Horse Fair at Springfield. See the *Connecticut Valley Farmer and Mechanic* (November, 1853).

The words of the satire which the Merry Monarch knew by heart went down better with the Irish of New York, and before very long the United States would have their fill of "fire and sword and desolation."

Shortly before he reached sixty Seymour ventured the opinion that an appeal to the ear rarely, if ever, seems equally good to the eye. What he wrote is true in so far as it is almost always difficult to recover the atmosphere of oratory — the circumstance of time, and place, and personality. Webster could move men to tears, but few of the grand-children of those who heard him weep over his words to-day. Distance and a change of fashion have robbed his great paragraphs of their emotional power. Edmund Burke's "Conciliation with America" survives as a set exercise, and school-boys do not find it exciting. Read aloud, Seymour's speech at Springfield runs on smoothly. In view of the public style of the time the absence of flowery language is noticeable. The content of the speech is a cool appeal to reason; yet no one of the three subjects of dispute greatly concerns Americans any longer. Abolition of slavery has been accomplished; prohibition has been tried and found wanting; and the Ku Klux Klan is in temporary retirement. The spirit of the speech, however, is still important. Seymour argued with all the eloquence at his command against the meddlesome desire to reform men by coercion. Temperance by compulsion, hatred of Roman Catholics and foreigners, and restless suspicion of the South — against these three sources of national misfortune he brought all his futile powers of persuasion in 1856.[20]

Starting from the old-fashioned Democratic theory that the most important power of government is local because men know best how to manage their own affairs — better than "seven watchmen on a high tower" — Seymour went on to maintain that "distributed jurisdiction not only makes good government, but also makes good manhood." From disregard of this principle, morals, religion, and liberty would all three lose out at

20. Seymour, *Public Record*, 1–21.

long last. In the United States, the Senate held "in check every other department of government," but surely the six states of New England had no reason to complain of their share of power in that body. New York, with only two senators, had a population equal to the whole section. He warned New England to beware; for if too much authority were ever to be centralized at Washington, the filling up of the West and the forming of new states might one day make the people east of the Hudson the victims of the very interference which some of their leaders were planning to impose on the South. Retention of the control of their own affairs would protect the people of every state from any and all unforeseen growth of the Union.

Coercive temperance was doubly objectionable. It not only violated constitutional guarantees but it was certain to increase the very evils it was designed to abolish. Men ought to remember that constitutions protected the whole public from the "peculiar views" of parts of the public. Prohibition would mean laws not only against drinking, but against thinking, as well — it was a form of "lazy philanthropy." Maine laws, such as the bill he had vetoed, flattered man's love of power and drew evil spirits out of his heart like the touch of Ithuriel's spear. The real victims of coercion of any kind were its advocates. A prohibition law would create "a spirit of resistance which increases the evil it claims to root out"; sooner or later, it would become a dead law, and "like a dead limb upon a living man" it would have to be cut off, or it would "carry decay and corruption into every part of the system."

> The vital principle of the Christian religion is persuasion, in opposition to restraints. It makes temperance and all other virtues something positive. It aims to make men unwilling, not unable to do wrong. It educates alike the feelings and the understanding, the heart and the head. All experience shows that mere restraints from vice do not reform. Our prisons are the examples of the perfect system of restraint. Their inmates, for a long series of years, are entirely prevented from indulging in intemperance or any kindred evil. They lead lives of perfect regularity, industry, and propriety, because they are compelled to do so. Yet few are reformed by this. Our instincts teach us that forced propriety of conduct gives no assurance of

future virtue; on the contrary, the very fact that they have been subjected to it, is by courts and communities regarded as evidence of depravity.

Students of history would discover that the progress of civilization brought with it the contraction of coercive laws. To look to government to evolve virtue was no less ignorant than to believe that thermometers regulated temperature. Good motives and wrong principles, according to Seymour, had lain at the root of almost every evil which had ever oppressed and afflicted mankind.

In 1856 Millard Fillmore was the nativist "American Party" candidate for President. He polled a handsome vote; he carried Maryland, and put Buchanan in the White House without a majority. The time was appropriate for Seymour to pay his respects to Know-Nothings. Nativists and Republicans agreed in this: the Fillmore men would disfranchise "those who come"; supporters of Frémont would take the vote from "those who go" — which was Seymour's way of summing up northern opposition to immigration and the "popular sovereignty" doctrine of Douglas. Nothing could surpass the folly of trying to make good mechanics, lawyers, and doctors by denying them citizenship and the right to vote. Massachusetts protested against the treatment received by the emigrants her aid societies sent out to Kansas, but she ought to remember that the border men of Missouri were only enforcing in the West the very laws which many voters in the East wished to impose on emigrants from Europe.

Absurd efforts are made to trace all the virtues of the American character back to the early colonists; to find the germs of our institutions in their first acts after landing upon our shores, and thus to make a distinction between them and the modern emigrant. It is assumed that the former were models of virtue and wisdom, and that we get from them our ideas of civil and religious liberty. Nothing can be more fallacious.

To cut off immigration to the United States would be to kill the goose which laid the golden eggs. Three great nations of Europe, he pointed out, were in the throes of the Crimean War; the misery of southern Russia as compared with the spectacle of a constant stream of people pouring peacefully into the New World was amazing. No Alexander, no Caesar had ever made such conquests as the steady drift of population was sending into North America year after year.

The charges of pauperism and criminality made against our foreign citizens are unjust. Their violations of law while they are not familiar with our institutions, and when placed under circumstances of great and novel temptations, are no more frequent than the commission of crimes by those of American birth, when removed from the conventional restraints of mankind and friends, in California, or on the shores of the Gulf of Mexico or the Caribbean Seas.

To immigration the North owed its numerical superiority to the South, and time would increase this surplus of numbers. Since the Revolution, the lion's share of the national soil had become free — witness Virginia's cession of the whole Northwest Territory to the Union. In view of the preponderance of population in its favor, Seymour thought that it was high time for the North to show consideration, rather than suspicion, of the South. In the days of the Virginia Dynasty, there had been a balance of power, but now the country had passed into the control of the free states; therefore, the preservation of the Union depended upon their good will. The new Republican party, however, threatened to array one section of the country against the other.

It will now be seen if the North will use its power fairly. If it does not, the South has the ability, and I hope the spirit to resist injustice. If it does not do so, it will be untrue to itself, to us, and to the whole country.

The threat of this ardent language is the least judicious statement Horatio Seymour ever made. It echoed war and the rumors of war. It was doubly indiscreet in view of the unfortunate decision of the South in 1861.

In passing judgment on Seymour's comments on the Kansas–Nebraska bill, it ought to be remarked that in the New York State convention of 1854 the "Softs" had adopted a "cunningly worded" resolution to the effect that though the repeal of the Missouri Compromise was inexpedient and unnecessary, it would benefit the territories, and therefore the convention opposed any attempt to tamper with it. This plank was part of the platform on which Seymour stood in his exciting and dramatic third campaign for governor. Two years later at Springfield he endorsed the doctrine of Senator Douglas in regard to Kansas and Nebraska.

It is true that the repeal of the Missouri Compromise was condemned by many, regretted by others, and approved by a third class. Many deemed its repeal as a great wrong; others regretted it as inexpedient; others again believed that the only way to dispose of agitating questions, dangerous to the peace of our country, was to leave them to the disposal of the communities particularly concerned. I believe there are few who wish for the restoration of the Missouri Compromise. It has been the singular fortune of this act of Congress to have been denounced at the North and the South at the time of its adoption; to have been generally condemned during the period of its existence, and to have created a political convulsion by its repeal.

Of the two possible tribunals to which territorial questions might be referred — the federal government or the people of the territories — Seymour made his Jeffersonian preference plain:

I agree with those who prefer territorial tribunals. The policy of local self-government has been adopted, and I believe there is a disposition on the part of all classes of Democrats to have it fairly tested; and it is demanded with justice that there should be no interference with its action from any quarter.

Slavery, he insisted, was primarily a question of patience. Immigration, preponderance of population, and hunger for land were extending the area of free soil every year, for emigrants poured out from the populous states to the cheaper lands of the West. By the census of 1850 the North exceeded the South by four millions of people, and was gaining by over a third of a million annually. Calculated on the basis of the square mile, the northern population was double; one acre of land in the North was worth three in the South. Unoccupied soil in the free states was dearer and in the slave states cheaper than in the national territories. The inference was plain: before long three-quarters of the Union would be free. Though for the moment slavery seemed to be moving into the South West, "excitements about Kansas" were "made to order," for the territories of Oregon, Washington, and Minnesota were certain to be carved out into free states. Easterners would do well to trust to the native genius of the settlers:

> Hitherto, emigation there has been controlled by a desire to secure town lots. When agricultural emigration commences, it will be governed by rules which prevail elsewhere. But few have gone from Missouri or other States to get farms — most expect to get cities. The true pioneers will soon make their appearance; the men who till the soil and subdue the earth — men of strong arms and clear heads — who know how to govern themselves, and who will direct their own affairs. Let not all our virtuous indignation be poured out upon border life. When you go among the sturdy men who, in advance of improvements, have chopped, and hoed, and ploughed their way almost across this continent, you will find they have generous and noble qualities.

Lastly, Seymour paid his respects to what he denounced as "the leprosy of hypocrisy." To this easy state of mind he laid all the great evils that visited his country in his lifetime. People who waxed uncharitable to white men in behalf of black men needed to look into their own hearts, he argued, for meddling with the lives of others was a subtle and convenient way of escaping personal responsibility for one's own. Experience taught Seymour that the spirit of reform wanted watching: in strong men it worked wonders in the world, but it made Pharisees of weak men and gave them false standards of value. People who dealt harshly with their neighbors were happy to "fancy themselves benevolent" as they complained of evils in some far corner of the country. The poor in the next street they forgot, so busy were they buying rifles for Kansas. Both pulpit and press were yielding to the vulgar satisfaction of scolding at slave-holders rather than sweeping before their own doors.[21]

21. Seymour did not attack sectional feeling only in public and for political effect. In *Harper's* for October, 1860, A. Oakey Hall, in "A Dinner at the Mayor's," contributed a description of one of Fernando Wood's fashionable parties in the year 1855. The dinner, which was served by Delmonico, was sumptuously wet, but Seymour seems to have had a good time in spite of his abstinence and amused the company (among whom were Martin Van Buren, Washington Irving, George Bancroft, Commodore Perry, and Winfield Scott) with "humorous remarks" on the "curiosities of political personalities." All the gentlemen present laughingly agreed that to differ with Horace Greeley even over porridge was to

No form of fanaticism, Seymour warned his hearers, ever gave its subjects rest; its very nature was to drive its victims on from one excitement to another. Yet vindictive piety and malignant benevolence were at odds with every principle of Christianity. The Roundheads, he reminded the good people of Springfield, were always followed by the Cavaliers.

Seymour's comparison of the make-up of the respective conventions which had nominated Frémont and Buchanan could not have been wholly ineffective even in New England, where he found the battle-line of the Democrats was "thinnest." The Republican convention contained men from only half the states of the Union — the country of the battle-fields of Yorktown, Camden, and New Orleans was not represented; no delegate spoke for the land where Washington and Jefferson, Marion, Sumter, and Morgan, or Jackson lay buried. To Cincinnati, on the other hand, had come representatives of every state and district in the Union. The one party was sectional; the other was national.

Having done his best for Buchanan, Seymour spent the summer in the West.[22] When he returned to Utica in September, he found that he was not a prophet in his own country. Paying a visit to relations at Cazenovia, a village not far from his birthplace, Pompey Hill, he found the town hall crowded on the evening he had promised to make a speech. Among a very large number of his neighbors there was a feeling of uneasiness at his failure to denounce "the pro-slavery position of Buchanan and his party." Men who had heard him urge the election of Polk from the same platform twelve years before questioned his prophecies as to the beneficence of Democratic rule. Slav-

make him a mortal enemy. Seymour, after having launched into an elaborate description of Moultrie's defense of Charleston, is reported to have remarked: "I place that defense of Charleston next to Bunker Hill in point of interest, valor, and importance; and yet some of our Anti-Nebraska orators will have it that South Carolina had no hand in '76 patriotism or in fighting."

22. New York State Library: Manuscript Section: Horatio Seymour to Kennedy Furlong, September 1, 1856.

ery would not down, and even prohibition was forgotten. Dickinson's "train of buffaloes" was on the move.[23]

The election of Buchanan in 1856 must have made the wiser leaders of the Democrats ponder. Were the great days of the party over? Only one of the three candidates, Fillmore, came from New York, and New York went Republican.[24] Buchanan's popular vote fell far behind the combined total of Frémont and Fillmore. The important question in 1856 was where the third-party men would go in 1860. These Know-Nothings could hardly be expected to prefer the Democrats — at least so far as New York State was concerned — for Horatio Seymour, the "unchallenged leader" of the reunion, the "most competent and masterful figure in the party," had publicly avowed his shame and humiliation at the victory of the so-called "Americans" at the state election of 1855.[25] Yet without the support of New York no party had been able to control the nation for long.

The election of Buchanan left Seymour free. New York was on the outside, and in 1857 he quite properly declined the offer of a foreign mission. He had urged the successful candidate to fight shy of New York and its feuds. A personal loss cut him off from politics even more suddenly. Marcy went out of office with Pierce in March; the early summer found him resting at Ballston Spa, not far from Albany. On the evening of July 4 he

23. New York State Library: Manuscript Section: Seymour Scrap-Books, I, 33: Speech at Cazenovia in 1856. See, also, the letter of D. S. Dickinson to Buchanan, page 71.

24. The Know-Nothing vote prevented a clear-cut decision: Frémont polled 276,007 votes; Buchanan, 195,878; and Fillmore, 124,604. King ran behind Frémont, and Parker ran ahead of Buchanan: King, 264,400; Parker, 198,616; Brooks, 130,870: Johnson and Smith, *History*, II, 417–419.

25. On Saturday, November 3, 1855, the year the Know-Nothings carried New York, the *Catholic Sentinel*, after stating that the advice of Horatio Seymour could be relied on because he was no bigot, added for the benefit of its bolder readers: "If any Catholic gets drunk on that day, and is swearing and rowdying around the city, he must blame no one if he gets well-licked by those who will be watching for such stray birds. And we advise everyone to take but very little trouble how the election goes, to keep clear of rowdys and demagogues, to attend to their work, and recommend the liberties of America to the merciful Providence of God": New York State Library: Seymour Papers.

was found dead, lying on a couch, a volume of Bacon's *Essays* open under his hand. Only a week before, in the course of a long talk with Seymour, he had confessed that finding a way to get out of life was much more difficult for him than getting on in it had ever been.[26] The memory of that shrewd remark died hard, for Seymour came back to it time after time during the next thirty years. In 1858 he flatly refused to allow the state convention of which he was temporary chairman to put him up for governor again. All the evidence supports the sincerity of his statement that he was through with public life for ever. In September, 1859, his mother died, and not long afterward his good friend, John Pruyn, sat down one evening in Albany to enter in his journal for December 6:

Governor Seymour called this evening. We had quite a long conversation about the present condition of things — the Harpers Ferry (John Brown) affair, the questions between the North and the South, the next Presidency, etc. Governor Seymour is tired of public life and wishes retirement. The ambition he once had, has, he says, passed away, and he certainly philosophizes well on this point. He does not wish or desire the Presidency could he have it — and he would by every means avoid it. He stated that he had a long conversation with Governor Marcy about a week before his death, in regard to his (Governor Seymour's) position and future in life and public affairs generally. Governor Marcy said that the trouble with him was *to know how to die*; how, after so long and active a career, to sit down quietly to meet the coming future. What a commentary on ambition! [27]

26. For an excellent appraisal of Marcy's work and character, see the *Political Science Quarterly*, XXX (September, 1915), 377–396: J. B. Moore, "A Great Secretary of State." Mr. Moore dwells on Marcy's wide reading, his sense of humor, and his hatred of cant. According to him Marcy was a good judge, an able secretary of war, and a great secretary of state.

27. Manuscript journal of John V. L. Pruyn, in possession of his daughter, Mrs. William Gorham Rice, of Albany, New York.

X
THE CANAL ACROSS WISCONSIN
1857–1859

SEYMOUR'S reasons for declining the dangerous post of commissioner to Kansas in 1856 and a fourth nomination for governor in 1858 were not political but personal. His unyielding loyalty to the Democratic party made him unwilling to see that it was on the verge of breaking up as a national power — however anxious he might be about the situation in his own state. Though President Pierce hailed the triumph of Buchanan as a repudiation of sectionalism, and an endorsement of his own administration, the Democratic victory of 1856 was specious: his successor had won office on a minority, and New York had given most of her votes to the Republicans. Hardly had Buchanan been inaugurated, when the Dred Scott Decision of March, 1857, gave the extreme southerners reason to believe that even without the House or the Senate they could still rely on the Supreme Court for the defense of their rights. Men began to count the gray heads of the court and calculate on the expectation of life of the nine justices: the inflexible Taney was an old man, holding over from the days of Andrew Jackson, but the new President could be depended on to fill up any vacancies which might occur during the next four years satisfactorily. With foreknowledge of the famous decision, Buchanan was able to adjust his inaugural message to the bold, legalistic interpretation of the right of property in slaves. The bitterly argued decision was to wait a long time for a judicial examination of its content and significance.[1] In the meantime the Civil War had "recalled" it.

1. Warren, *The Supreme Court*, III, 1–41: The Dred Scott Case. The nine justices of the Supreme Court in March, 1857, were: Taney, of Maryland; Wayne, of Georgia; Daniel, of Virginia; Catron, of Tennessee; Campbell,

The real significance of Taney's pronouncement of 1857 was its effect on the division and inheritance of the Fillmore vote of 1856. The American party was strongest and most evenly distributed in the South, but the total, both North and South, was "a protest against a sectional party, against radicalism, against the possibility of war." [2] The Dred Scott Decision, moreover, made the popular-sovereignty doctrine of Senator Douglas look like defiance of the Supreme Court. If slavery might go everywhere in the national territories until such time as parts of those territories might choose to abolish the system when they came into the Union as sovereign states, then to exclude slavery by merely neglecting to provide ordinances for its continued existence in those territories, as Douglas was driven to propose in 1858, was trickery. As has often been the case, the expounding of the Constitution by the Supreme Court made the amendment of the Constitution inevitable. Sooner or later, General Washington had remarked as he left office in 1797, the people of the United States could change the articles of their Union however they might please.

Seymour had told Pruyn that he was "tired of public life" and that the "ambition he once had" was "past away." Among several good reasons for believing in the sincerity of this statement was his financial interest in the West, where he spent much of his time between 1857 and 1861. We must go back for a moment to discover how it was that he came to plan a canal and buy land in Wisconsin. His interest in the topography of New York was lifelong—as a boy he had lived in a village where the roof of the tavern divided the rain water between the great valleys of the Susquehanna and the St. Lawrence. He liked to point out that the phenomenal strength of the Iroquois was owing to their having occupied the uplands of central New York, whence rivers flowed north, east, south, and west into the lands of their enemies. That the Hudson River should have cut

---

of Alabama; Grier, of Pennsylvania; Nelson, of New York; Curtis, of Massachusetts; and McLean, of Ohio, these last two dissenting from the majority opinion.

2. Beveridge, *Lincoln*, II, 442–520.

its way through the northern spur of the Alleghenies during the dim ages of the unknown past, that salt water should reach Poughkeepsie, and the tide be visible at Albany were facts of first importance to him in the happy history of the United States.[3] He was old-fashioned enough to believe that the British failure to split the colonies by way of Lake Champlain and the Hudson in 1777 was owing to supernatural intervention — possibly because that failure was incomprehensible. "This is one of those strange occurrences recognized in the lives of individuals as well as in the affairs of nations," he indiscreetly declared, "showing that there is an over-ruling Providence that watches over both" — an utterance all the more odd coming twelve years after the close of the Civil War.

Partly as a result of his speech at Tammany Hall, Seymour was invited to address the New York Historical and Geographical Society in January, 1856. His paper was published as a pamphlet, and the fact that Seymour saved all the letters of thanks from those to whom he sent complimentary copies, as well as his willingness to give it over again fourteen years later at Cornell, shows that the author was proud of his production.[4] John Jay believed that if the author would "fill up" the outline, he could make "an invaluable text book for our district schools." Even Gerrit Smith, by no means a congenial spirit, thought highly of it, writing that "We Dutchmen should thank this Yankee for the justice he has done to the Dutch."[5] Smith's comment is significant, for, as often as Seymour touched on the history of New York, he delighted to enlarge on the beneficial mixture of races and religions in the state. He loved the Dutch

3. For a good summary of Seymour's ideas, see the address at Schuylerville, delivered in 1877, at the celebration of the centenary of Burgoyne's surrender: *Proceedings*, New York State Historical Association, XII (New York, 1913), 205–225, especially 210–215.

4. *A Lecture on the Topography and History of New York* (Utica, 1856), 1–41. Fourteen years later, on June 30, 1870, Seymour, at the request of President White of Cornell, delivered a slightly revised version of this lecture at the commencement of that university: *History and Topography of New York: A Lecture by Horatio Seymour at Cornell University* (Utica, 1870).

5. New York Historical Society: Seymour Papers: Gerrit Smith to J. B. Miller, February 11, 1857.

as earnestly as Washington Irving, and much more soberly. That Holland should have sent "rights of conscience" to the harbor of New Amsterdam was, he thought, a scene of great "moral beauty." Whenever the Nativists, or Know-Nothings, began to see ghosts, Seymour would call the roll of the famous sons of his state — Schuyler, a Dutchman; Herkimer, a German; Jay, a Frenchman; Livingston, a Scotsman; Clinton and Morris, from Ireland and Wales; Hamilton, from the West Indies; and Steuben, who came from Prussia.

In view of the fact that Seymour was often bitterly abused for being unfair to the New England of Garrison and Sumner, his comparison of Dutch and Puritan character is interesting. His description of the early settlers of the section where his own father was born is more illuminating than much that has been written on the subject since his death.

> The Puritan colonists have been the objects of indiscriminate ridicule, and of equally indiscriminate praise; yet their characters and views are clearly defined in their own transactions and histories. They had been engaged in long and bitter controversies. . . . They were made gloomy by the belief that they were contending not only against men, but against spiritual foes in bodily forms, and they fenced themselves round with a charmed circle of austerities. They wished to be let alone in their remote retreats, and they resisted what they deemed the intrusions of heresy. They made no pretences to the views of religious toleration now claimed for them. . . . They were made harsh by suffering and sacrifices. But this is the dark side of their character. They were vigorous and self-reliant. A common poverty destroyed distinctions of rank. None were rich enough to establish the manorial estates or privileges which were created in New York. They were industrious and enterprising. Their religious doctrines led them to value education as a means of spiritual and intellectual improvement . . . none do so much injury to their characters as those who, with bad taste, try to soften their stern aspects with inconsistent adornments and graces, or, with still worse logic, insist that they had principles of toleration with practices of persecution. Let them alone in their clear and decided characters, as men of robust virtues and grave faults. Let the circumstances of their history excuse their wrong doings. From them we get many virtues and advantages; we get elsewhere our best conceptions of civil and religious liberty.[6]

This seasoned judgment has stood the test of time; it was written the very year that Peter Oliver's *Puritan Commonwealth*

6. Seymour, *Topography* (1856), 19, 20, and 21.

came off the press to outrage the uneasy pretensions of the filiopietistic historians of Boston and Cambridge.

To the Dutch influence, it is interesting to note, Seymour traced the root of the revolutionary notion of no taxation without consent. He believed, moreover, that the United States of the Netherlands had been the model for the United States of America. At the moment of the formation of the Union, the influence of New York had been decisive, for equal representation of the several states, large and small, in the Senate was thought to be the only possible security against a centralization of political power. When Virginia, Pennsylvania, and Massachusetts had insisted that both representatives and senators should be apportioned among the members of the Union by population, only New York of the great states intervened in favor of the little ones — "the noblest passage," thought Seymour, in its history. British management of America from a distance had broken down, and the genius of the settlers for self-government made the growth of a powerful central government superfluous and dangerous. If power were to gravitate toward Washington, he warned Americans, the people of the different states and sections would demand proportional representation in both the houses of the Congress: great states would complain of the undue power of small ones.

Seymour's observation on the settlers and the institutions of the western states takes us back to his visits to Wisconsin.[7] His father had made his fortune and his mark in the world by helping in the work which gave New York the water route to the West. Along that route, land-hungry Americans and immigrants from Europe had poured into the country of the Great Lakes which it was Seymour's dream to connect with the Mississippi. A portage of only one mile separated the headwaters of the Fox from those of the Wisconsin River. A canal like the Erie was by no means impossible — from Lake Michigan to Lake Winnebago the total ascent was 170 feet, part of it through rapids; from Winnebago up to the portage, another 65 feet. Thence down to the Mississippi River the

7. Seymour, *Topography* (1856), 24.

descent totalled 200 feet. Development of this famous route of the fur traders was first talked of as early as 1834. The history of the work has three chapters. Wisconsin began it; private capital continued it; and the United States completed it. During twenty-five years of scheming and squabbling the railroads superseded the canals as common carriers. Years afterward a western railroad manager thought that the whole investment ought to be "lathed and plastered." [8]

It was in 1835 that the territorial legislature of Michigan incorporated the Portage Canal Company, after a meeting at Green Bay to memorialize the Congress for aid in the construction of a canal had procured no response. The authorized capital of the company was fifty thousand dollars.[9] In 1839, the war department directed a survey of the proposed route, and three years later "Barnburner" Silas Wright of New York spoke against the bill for the canal which passed the Senate by a vote of 31 to 7.[10] In 1846, the United States granted lands for the promotion of the improvement of the Fox and Wisconsin rivers. The measure was typical — one-half the land, to an extent of three miles on each side of the canal, the Fox River, and the lakes through which it passed, was to go to the pro-

8. Ellis B. Usher, *Wisconsin: its History and Biography, 1848–1913* (Chicago, 1914), 312. At the time of this pessimistic remark it was estimated that digging this canal from the Great Lakes to the Mississippi had cost the public 680,000 acres of land and the investors two million dollars — not counting the money spent by the state.

9. The full story of the whole scheme to make a navigable waterway between the Great Lakes and the Mississippi will be found in the *Proceedings* of the State Historical Society of Wisconsin, XLVII (Madison, Wisconsin, 1900), 186–194. The Seymour Papers in the State Library at Albany contain a great number of plans and notes relating to the Sault Sainte Marie and Fox-Wisconsin Canals. Seymour seems to have looked even farther West: by 1857, he and Erastus Corning were consulting about "Iowa and Wisconsin affairs." New York State Library: Manuscript Section: Letter of Horatio Seymour to Erastus Corning, May 20, 1857. Seymour's brother, John F. Seymour, was president of the Fox River Improvement Company as late as 1862. New York State Library: Seymour Papers.

10. See Gillet, *Wright*, II, 1435–1437. The proposal was that the federal government should finance the improvement of the Fox and Wisconsin Rivers in Wisconsin Territory. Wright was a Jackson Democrat.

moters. Alternate sections were thus given away with the expectation that once the price of the land which remained to the government had doubled, the people of the whole country would have suffered no loss. Two years later, the legislature of Wisconsin passed a bill accepting this grant of land from the government, hoping to carry out the improvement without the appropriation of public money.

Captain Cram, who had made the war-department survey of 1839, estimated that a navigable waterway of 166 miles would cost less than half a million dollars. The legislature planned on an improved waterway of 200 miles. Optimism must have been in the air, for it was calculated that the sale of the 384,000 acres of land granted by the government at an average price of a dollar and twenty-five cents an acre would meet the cost of the whole public work. Perhaps the wish was father to the thought, for the constitution with which Wisconsin came into the Union in 1848 forbade the incurring of debt for internal improvements. The canal was to be dug under the supervision of a board of public works consisting of five members elected annually by the legislature.

In 1849, Wisconsin received sixty thousand dollars from the sale of lands; the next year fifty thousand dollars came in. In 1851, there were no purchasers, and the board found itself facing debts of seventy-five thousand dollars — with only eight thousand dollars in the treasury. There followed what Marcy of New York called "crimination and recrimination," and Morgan L. Martin took over the work, with the understanding that the state should meet the deficit when it pleased — paying twelve per cent. interest on the money in the meantime. Governor Farwell stopped the issue of scrip to Martin in 1853, because his contract anticipated on the sale of land and therefore violated the constitution by creating a debt for internal improvements. The legislature continued to issue the scrip in spite of Farwell's veto. Then the governor recommended private development of the whole work, at an estimated cost of half a million dollars. By this time, the value of Wisconsin's equity in land still unsold was calculated at something less than a quarter of a million dollars.

Largely as a result of the governor's recommendation, the Fox and Wisconsin Improvement Company was incorporated in 1853.[11] One of the members of the state senate of Wisconsin in 1852 was Orson S. Head, a native of Oneida County, who had studied law under Seymour at Utica. In 1841 he went out to Wisconsin, settled at Kenosha, and became successful and distinguished.[12] Orson Head probably supplied what was later to be the connecting link of the interest between Albany and Madison. The new company received all the rights of the state and all the property in unsold land. Wisconsin reserved the right to repurchase both after a period of twenty years. The state had never received all the public lands granted to it as a territory in 1846, but in 1854 an act of Congress authorized the substitution of any public lands in Wisconsin for any shortage of lands along the waterway. This act of 1854 was to be a source of trouble, for it stated that the same principle was to apply in this public work in Wisconsin as in the grant to Indiana for the Wabash and Erie Canal. But Indiana had been given alternate sections to the extent of five miles on either side of the canal. Wisconsin, it will be remembered, had been granted only three.

Immediately the question was raised as to whether the Congress had intended to increase the Fox–Wisconsin grant. Did the Congress mean to give the state a strip of land six miles wide, or ten? In 1855, a congressional resolution declared that Wisconsin was entitled to land "equal mile for mile of its improvement" to that granted Indiana. At once both Wisconsin and the corporation claimed the right to this increase of land. The state had the upper hand and forced the company to reconstruct a part of the work. It appointed trustees for the management of both the land and the whole public improvement. By 1856, the company found that its capital of a quarter of a

11. A good map of the area bordering on the investments of this company is to be found in the *Wisconsin Gazetteer* (Madison, Wisconsin, 1853).

12. *Collections*, Wisconsin Historical Society, VII, 466.

million dollars was insufficient for the work it had to carry through; it must raise more money or give up the whole enterprise.

At this point the New Yorkers stepped in with money which they were ready to invest. The most prominent of these were Horatio Seymour; Erastus Corning, a manufacturer of Albany; and Hiram Barney, later the intimate friend of Salmon P. Chase, and collector of the port of New York under Lincoln. Ultimately, as a result of loans and mortgages, the Wisconsin corporation was forced to sell out all its lands and improvements through the trustees to the capitalists from the East. The price of sale covered the expense for the execution of the trust and the estimated cost of the work through 1856. The New Yorkers organized the Green Bay and Mississippi Canal Company, and it was the oversight of this speculation that drew Seymour out of politics and into the West in 1857.

Grave doubt has been expressed as to the sincerity of the intention of the eastern men to carry on the improvement of the waterway.[13] It was thought that the New Yorkers were planning to unload the canal on the federal government and meanwhile hold onto the land they had bought in the hope of profiting from its certain rise in value as settlers crowded into the country. So far as Seymour is concerned, his lifelong interest in canals, the letters he wrote, and the many visits he made to the West leave no question as to his earnest interest. His dream was to match the success of his father, if not that of DeWitt Clinton himself. He became president of the company and interested his friend, John Pruyn, who seems in turn to have enlisted the support of William Allen Butler, son of that Benjamin Franklin Butler who had battled in vain for a third nomination for Martin Van Buren at Baltimore in 1844. When the governor's ill health prevented his going to Wisconsin as often as the business required, his younger brother, John F. Seymour, succeeded him as head of the company. The influence of these capitalists at Albany can be seen in a general puff for

13. *Proceedings*, Wisconsin Historical Society, XLVII, 192.

Wisconsin and its great future which appeared in the *Atlas and Argus* in April, 1857. According to this account Daniel C. Jenne, an engineer well known in New York, foresaw a handsome revenue from the stock of the canal company, which had a franchise permitting it to charge tolls. Proceeds from the sale of the company's land would result in "a clear profit."[14]

The outcome of the whole venture was not very satisfactory so far as the investors were concerned. Not long after the Civil War the Forty-Second Congress intervened and ordered an appraisal of the three kinds of property of the Green Bay and Mississippi Canal Company — locks, water-power, and land.[15] By 1871 the board of appraisal had brought in its findings, and in 1873 the Congress appropriated $145,000 to pay for the purchase of all improvements — leaving to the company the possession of the water-power and the property of unsold land. In the long run Seymour seems to have become land poor largely because of his heavy investments in the West. Writing to his brother-in-law, Senator Roscoe Conkling, in 1874, he dwelt on his lifelong interest in canals. It was almost twenty years since he had first become a stock-holder in the Green Bay and Mississippi Canal Company, and now the question of such a waterway was before the Congress again. The partial purchase had been negotiated, but there was a chance that the whole business would be reopened, and if so, it ought to be settled with wisdom and national foresight.

After assuring Conkling that he owned not an acre of land in Wisconsin that he did not "pay for in cash," he went on to remark that he had "lost heavily" in trying to improve the Fox and Wisconsin Rivers because of "the unjust action" of both the Congress and the state legislature. He hoped the senator would not feel that he was "an interested witness"; he wished merely to explain his point of view.

14. This write-up was reprinted in *Collections*, Wisconsin Historical Society, III, 496–499.

15. *Forty-Second Congress: Second Session, House Executive Documents*, Number 185.

I have for many years studied the question of transportation. I know that a steamboat route from the Mississippi to the Great Lakes is the first and greatest want of our country. I know that a small sum of money will enable the river boats to unload their freights directly into lake vessels. The moment this is done all rail road freights between the two channels of navigation will be put down. This will benefit every lake port and every farming region of the West. It will even help the rail roads by giving wealth prosperity and population to the country through which they run. The destruction of the Erie Canal would be a heavy blow to the Central Rail Road for the canal carries many things the road does not and thus makes business and travelling for the roads — The great Mississippi and Missouri system of rivers should have an outlet to the lakes as well as into the Gulf of Mexico — I do not think you have anything before Congress so important as this. To the state of New York this is vital. The public mind is now and will be in the future stirred up on this question.[16]

This notion was by no means a new one with Seymour. Eleven years before, in the midst of the Civil War and the hard work of his second term as governor, he urged his good friend, Sidney T. Fairchild, whose son was to marry his favorite niece, and who had been delegated by the legislature to represent New York at a canal convention at Chicago, to "recommend suitable measures to secure adequate and uninterrupted navigation between the Great Lakes and the Mississippi River."[17] The recommendation seems to have borne fruit, for in May, 1864, the Northwestern Ship Canal convention, meeting in Chicago, appointed a committee with instructions to request all the senators and representatives from Iowa, Minnesota, and Wisconsin to unite at Washington in order to obtain an appropriation for the survey of the Fox and Wisconsin rivers with the view to making them a ship canal — that route being far the most desirable for the country.[18] Iowa was interested because the digging of such a canal would have sent up the price of its land. In 1867 Seymour criticized the railroads in the region of the Great Lakes for not being far-sighted enough to help at getting grain to their shores by cheap routes.

16. New York Historical Society: Seymour Papers: Horatio Seymour to Roscoe Conkling, January 6, 1874.

17. New York Historical Society: Seymour Papers: Horatio Seymour to S. T. Fairchild, May 13, 1863. 18. Dubuque, Iowa, *Daily Times*, May 5, 1864.

By and large, Seymour wasted his time and lost much of his money on his dream of an Erie Canal in Wisconsin. He suffered in reputation, as well. He had spent the last three months of 1857 in Wisconsin, visiting the canal company's property and making friends in the towns of Green Bay and Appleton. He went to and fro more than once during the next four years. Early in 1861 business called him West again, and the fact that he happened to be far off in Wisconsin at the time of the actual outbreak of the Civil War was used as the basis for the absurd accusation that he took to the woods when he heard the guns at Fort Sumter. Daniel Stevens Dickinson, for instance, never tired of repeating this spiteful falsehood in those heady days when he raged furiously at the rebellious South he once had been supposed to have served too well for reëlection to the Senate.

By 1879, his associate William Allen Butler wrote Seymour that his canal stock was for sale and would be auctioned off within one month unless it were purchased privately before that time.[19] Just two weeks later Seymour wrote that he believed that his plan to open up the Great Lakes to the Atlantic Ocean so that steamers from Europe might tie up at Chicago was the most important issue of the century so far as North America was concerned.[20] Half a century later this very proposal was still a bone of contention between the North East and the Middle West. One year after Seymour's death, Reuben G. Thwaites, who paddled all the way up the Fox River in a canoe, found the waterway navigable and "highly improved" with locks, and the national government in full control. The traveller noticed, however, that railroads were crowding out canals even through the farming regions of Wisconsin.[21]

19. New York Historical Society: Seymour Papers: William Allen Butler to Horatio Seymour, May 5, 1879. Butler owned 1074 shares in the Green Bay and Mississippi Canal Company.

20. New York Historical Society: Seymour Papers: Letter of Horatio Seymour, May 19, 1879.

21. Thwaites, *Historic Waterways*, 144. For an interesting description of Wisconsin fifty years ago readers are referred to the second and third sections of this book: "The Fox River," 143–234, and "The Wisconsin River," 237–293.

Seymour's dream of Chicago as a seaport has enjoyed a long life. To-day the Middle West is demanding the very access to the ocean which he urged. The old dispute which Clinton faced as to whether the traffic of the Great Lakes should go down Lake Ontario and through the St. Lawrence River to the sea, or across New York to the Hudson, has become an important political issue. The West insists on a waterway through Canada, but the railroads from Chicago to the East Coast have opposed the enterprise with skill, and so far with success. In 1928, for instance, Alfred Emanuel Smith as a candidate for President was forced to eat the words he had spoken as governor of New York and acknowledge (while campaigning in the Middle West) that the St. Lawrence route was better than the Erie–Hudson route he had formerly favored.

President Hoover negotiated a treaty with Canada according to which the St. Lawrence River was to be jointly improved by the two nations, a bargain Governor Roosevelt watched with a jealous eye. When President Roosevelt submitted his predecessor's treaty to the Senate in 1933, it failed of ratification — both the senators from the state of New York (men of his own party) voting in the negative against his recommendation. So far, the railroads have prevailed, but if the dream of Seymour should ever come true, the valley of the St. Lawrence rather than the Hudson would thenceforth be the highway from the Atlantic Ocean to the West. Such a victory for internationalism would seem to grow less likely day by day. Ours is a world in which whole countries cut off their noses in the name of national independence.

XI

CHARLESTON AND TWEDDLE HALL

1860–1861

SEYMOUR spent the last three months of 1857 away from home. Part of the time he passed in New York City attending to the business of the Green Bay and Mississippi Canal Company. When he returned to Utica, he knew "very little about the movements at Washington."[1] Just after he left home in October, he wrote directly to the censorious Horace Greeley to deny that editor's casual accusation that he had come down to the city to act as attorney for the country banks of the state in an effort to persuade Governor John A. King to call an extra session of the legislature. The panic of 1857, it will be remembered, had struck the country in August — just over twenty years after its great forerunner. Seymour, according to his own account, went to New York City at "the request of some gentlemen from the interior . . . for the purpose of devising some plan for bringing forward the grain of the West to prevent the great calamities which threaten this city if its unemployed population shall be compelled to pay high prices for food." The suspension of specie payments, he assured Greeley, he regarded as a necessary evil, and he stood ready to support Governor King in any action he might feel obliged to take.

Greeley had published his suspicions in a paragraph in the *Tribune*, and Seymour took up the baseless charge. This editor's hostile attitude toward the "friend of rum" is important to keep in mind in passing judgment on the part he was to play in reporting evidence six years later during the New York draft riots. Greeley saved his spirit of charity for cranks and impostors, and leaders from upstate were never much to his liking;

1. New York Historical Society: Seymour Papers: Horatio Seymour to S. T. Fairchild, December 31, 1857.

New York State Capitol

HORATIO SEYMOUR

his feud with Thurlow Weed was notorious, and his itch for office was a constant cause of vexation to the Whigs. As early as 1857, then, the *Tribune* gratuitously accused Seymour of deliberate duplicity in a matter where public welfare was at stake. Memory of the veto of 1854 died hard. If the editor feared that the Democrats would try to make capital out of hard times, Seymour reassured him, their loyalty to a man like Judge Denio might be offered as a pledge to the contrary. The former governor referred to a bitter fight in the Democratic state convention at Syracuse on September 10, when he himself had stood up to propose the renomination of the very member of the court of appeals who had only recently "felt it his duty" to make a decision "unwelcome and injurious" to his own party. If the Democrats could be persuaded to defend the gallant independence of a judge, Greeley might be kind enough to consider the possibility that they would stand behind the courage of Governor King in time of trouble.[2]

James Buchanan had been in the White House less than a year. The panic had started in the summer after his inauguration, and now the "Hards" and "Softs" of New York were quarrelling over federal offices. Though the "Softs" were in the great majority in the state, the "Hards" had the personal advantage, for they had backed President Buchanan for the nomination at Cincinnati from the first. On the eve of going out of office, Secretary Marcy thought that the President-elect had stumbled "at the threshold" in managing his party. The South would demand much of him — perhaps more than it "ought to have." Only if he could keep it divided would he be safe in office.[3]

Little as he knew or seemed to care about current politics, Seymour was persuaded to go on to Washington in February, 1858. The cause for his visit was the endless factional feud between the "Hards" and "Softs." He succeeded in seeing

2. New York State Library: Seymour Papers: October 1, 1857.

3. New York Historical Society: Seymour Papers: W. L. Marcy to Horatio Seymour, December 25, 1856.

Buchanan and the attorney-general, whose recommendation was said to be important for all appointments in New York. Buchanan he found "very tenacious about adhering to his positions" but "very cordial in his interview" and "well disposed." These two men were tackling the old problem which both Polk and Pierce had tried to solve without success. When the President mildly proposed to balance his gifts between the Kilkenny cats, Seymour objected that "he had in no instance given an office to one of [his] friends," and went on to assure an unnamed correspondent that he had told Buchanan that he would regard the choice of a friend "as a personal favor." Just as he left Washington the implacable Daniel S. Dickinson arrived at the head of the "Hards."[4] The Democratic party was sick unto death in New York.

The Wisconsin canal and the panic left Seymour very little time for state politics. When Amasa J. Parker was put up for a second time in 1858, the "Hards" offered no candidate, but the nativist vote made Morgan governor by a minority. Just about this time Seymour came into personal contact with Samuel Jones Tilden, who had taken an interest in the western investments of the Green Bay and Mississippi Canal Company. Writing to him from Appleton, Wisconsin, in August, 1859, Seymour described his tour in the company of their joint friend, Erastus Corning, and the ardent prohibitionist, Delavan — he who had vouched for the sincerity of the unpopular veto of 1854. Among other things Seymour urged Tilden to use his influence with the railroads he served to turn immigration onto the canal company's lands in northern Wisconsin, even though their officers might prefer to book people the full length of their lines into Minnesota and Iowa.[5]

Although these two men were in their forties, both Democrats, and familiar with the politics of the state, this friendship which began in business was never to be intimate. It

4. New York Historical Society: Seymour Papers: Horatio Seymour to an unnamed correspondent, February 10, 1858.

5. Tilden, *Letters and Literary Memorials*, I, 110–111.

lasted, indeed, a long time; it survived the Civil War and continued until 1886, when both men died. Seymour sought the legal advice of Tilden on public affairs — as in the case when he wrote his veto of the Broadway Railroad franchise — and at one time he even borrowed money from him.[6] Friends of the two men, as well as enemies of both, accused them of mutual jealousy and fear of each other's success. When Seymour, for instance, suffered a sunstroke in the summer of 1876, he was suspected of sulking over Tilden's triumphant nomination for President at the very moment when he was too ill to speak in his behalf. Tilden, moreover, had no charm, and his most intimate biographer had very little charity. A sense of humor might have modified John Bigelow's hero worship very much to the advantage of the man he admired, for this worship took the unpleasant form of spite toward all who were not of the inner circle. In humor, however, Mr. Bigelow was sadly deficient — as readers of his absurd comments on Sammy Tilden's celibacy can never forget.[7]

During his business trip in the West with Corning and Delavan, Seymour was good natured enough to address "a grand mass meeting of the Democracy" at St. Paul. Minnesota was in the midst of an election in 1859, and the visiting statesman took for his text "Mind Your Own Business" in order to assail the "meddling" principles of the young Republican party. His speech is an able exposition of the national doctrines of the Democrats just before the gloomy sundown of their power. Starting as he nearly always did, with the statement that the most important part of all government was local, Seymour turned to rebuke the New Englanders from whom he himself was descended by remarking that the North was not only "unjust," but not "courageous" in its treatment of the South.

6. Tilden, *Letters and Literary Memorials*, I, 311.

7. One sentence of this extraordinary explanation is only a sample: "He seemed to have been betrothed in early life to his country, and the Democratic party occupied with him the place of offspring, until it was too late to think of having any other." Collectors of ridiculous trifles should consult the whole three pages which Bigelow devoted to this subject: Bigelow, *Tilden*, II, 372–375.

He went on to express wonder that people should pretend to be shocked by Chief-Justice Taney's opinion that a black man had no political rights, for such precisely had been the historical fact in the United States. The North, to be sure, had no slaves; but very few of its merchants had been backward about importing and selling them into the South. He offered his audience the evidence of a bill of sale by which a man from Massachusetts sold a negro to a New Yorker, and observed that the love of freedom some people professed reminded him of the "Feejee" islander who, by way of reform in his desire to join the church, ate up all his wives but one.[8] The ancestors of the abolitionists, at least, had not liked black men better than white.

He went on to point out that before long the North would elect two-thirds of the House of Representatives and an overwhelming majority of the Senate. Keeping in mind this inevitable control of the Congress, he could see no cogent reason for any "irrepressible conflict" between a strong North and a weak South. Slavery, in fact, was upheld by the great business firm of "Weaver, Wearer, and Planter"—only one of the three partners of which resided in the South—"but for the looms of New England and Old England [slavery] could not live a day." Abolitionists were shouting for secession of the free states from a Union which they denounced as a league with death and a covenant with Hell; but to destroy the United States because of slavery would be as mad as to drag all Europe into war in order to abolish serfdom in Russia or polygamy in Turkey.[9]

It was the public success of this almost impromptu speech at St. Paul which probably persuaded people that Horatio Seymour was still an aspirant for political office. Within less than six months, according to John Pruyn, he would make it plain, while talking confidentially with one of his best friends, that he was

8. Seymour owned this bill of sale, which he found among some old papers he had purchased. Two years before this speech at St. Paul, he had sent it to a friend with a letter in which he had asked for its safe return: New York Historical Society: Seymour Papers. Horatio Seymour to an unnamed correspondent, March 5, 1857.

9. St. Paul, Minnesota, *Pioneer and Democrat*, August 24, 1859.

not. The files of his correspondence for this period are littered with invitations to go here and there, to speak, preside, or lend the "support of his presence." Most of these he declined on the plea of ill health, although the only ailments he ever specifically mentioned at any time during his whole life were headaches, deafness as he grew old, and sore throats from too much speaking. People did not seem to tire of hearing him repeat himself in various parts of the country. Even a casual comparison of the texts of the four best-known speeches he gave before the outbreak of the Civil War will show that the burden of them all is the same.[10] These speeches covered a period of six years at the end of which Seymour could only express the futile hope that abolitionists and slave-holders would not destroy the whole country with their mutual suspicion and hatred.

Buchanan had been President for little more than two years when the Democrats were disputing angrily among themselves as to who should succeed him in office. Cassidy, of the *Atlas and Argus*, had scolded the New Yorkers for quarrelling over delegates to the coming convention at Charleston when the state had no candidate for the nomination. Early in June, 1859, the New York *Herald* jeered at what it called the "transparent dodge" of Cassidy — every one knew, declared Bennett, that Dean Richmond had tucked Horatio Seymour up his sleeve as the card with which to beat Dickinson, the "venerable champion of the Hards." Comparing the two men, the cynical Bennett concluded:

> Horatio Seymour is a much younger man and will not be fossilized, perhaps for ten years to come. Genial and fascinating, modest and generous in his manners, he quietly wins his way as a politician, and can wind about his finger, somewhat after the fashion of Thurlow Weed, the more noisy and rampant managers of his party. But we fear that Mr. Seymour will never touch bottom at Charleston: first, from being the candidate only of a local clique; and second, in being the stalking horse of the "Little Giant." [11]

The convention at Charleston, thought the *Herald*, would probably leave both Dickinson and Seymour high and dry, and the

10. Tammany Hall, New York, (1855); Springfield, Massachusetts, (1856); St. Paul, Minnesota, (1859); and Tweddle Hall, Albany, (1861).

11. New York *Herald*, June 4, 1859.

Democratic party in New York as "conveniently small" as it had became in Massachusetts.

Horace Greeley took up the cry of alarm in August: Seymour was to be put in training to receive the nomination at Charleston, "a contingency very likely to arise in that body." The game was to have the New York delegation act as a unit and "talk softly" in favor of Douglas, of Hunter, or of Guthrie, offering thirty-five votes for the support of any one of these three in exchange for a seat in the Cabinet for Seymour. The *Atlas and Argus*, according to the *Tribune*, was obviously the personal organ of Seymour, and if New York were called upon to name its choice at Charleston, it would be extremely painful, added Greeley with a sneer, for the delegation to express a preference between such "equally beloved statesmen" as Horatio Seymour and Daniel S. Dickinson. By December 15, the *Tribune* was declaring that Seymour would be played for either first or second place at Charleston. Greeley advised him to stop dealing in "specious generalities and shining sophistries" and come out frankly for slavery and disunion.[12] The editor's attitude is interesting in view of the fact that we now know that he was already planning to defeat Seward at Chicago, and the very possibility of Lincoln's nomination there was supposed to improve Seymour's chances at Charleston. If Seward lost out, his disgruntled friends might allow a native son to carry New York.[13]

By March 10, 1860, Edward Bates, future member of Lincoln's Cabinet, in commenting on the rumor that "a combination of Democratic powers not to be withstood" would force the ticket of Breckinridge and Seymour on the Charleston convention, thought that such a choice would be "very weak" and "easily beaten," if the Republicans would nominate a "conservative." A third ticket would probably throw the election into the House.[14] The Baltimore *Patriot* failed to specify what men were to make this combination, but presumably the editor

12. New York *Tribune*, August 20 and December 15, 1859.
13. Alexander, *History*, II, 294.
14. Bates, *Diary*, 108.

foresaw a union of the South with New York. This union was not unthinkable. In 1860 the chairman of the party in New York was Dean Richmond of Buffalo, originally a native of Virginia. Peter Cagger, an Albany lawyer, was secretary of the state committee, and these men, together with William Cassidy of the *Atlas and Argus*, worked as a triumvirate at headquarters.[15] Erastus Corning, iron manufacturer and president of the New York Central, and August Belmont, American agent of the Rothschilds in New York, supplied and managed the party funds. To these men should be added Samuel J. Tilden, once a Barnburner and now an expert reorganizer of railroads, and Fernando Wood, a Quaker, who began his career as a cigar-maker and rose from a grocer to be mayor of New York and a member of the Congress. The sacred circle of the Albany Regency had been broken into; by 1860 only Seymour and Dickinson survived as its heirs. Van Buren was still alive at Lindenwald but he was seventy-eight and out of public life, at last, for ever.

It was said that Richmond's plan of action at Charleston was to vote the delegation for Senator Douglas until the latter withdrew and then nominate Seymour with the aid of the South and the consent of the North West. By the spring of 1860 the New York *Herald* thought that the nomination of a New Yorker was extremely unlikely because the Democrats felt that they could never carry the state in November. A southern man, on the other hand, was impossible — the real battleground in 1860, according to Bennett, was Pennsylvania and the middle states. The South had only 120 electoral votes, and 154 were needed to elect a President — where would they ever get the necessary 34? [16] The *Herald's* belief that New York was certain to go Republican was based on the bitterness of Democratic feuds, particularly in the city. In his war on Tammany Fernando Wood had set up a rival organization called Mozart

15. Brummer, *History*, 25–26.

16. For interesting gossip and guess-work as to what would happen at Charleston, see the New York *Herald* for April, 1860.

Hall, and the two factions fought each other constantly and fiercely for control of place and plunder.

The so-called "respectable" Democrats like John A. Dix and John Van Buren refused to work with Wood, who must have seemed shady to them if they preferred Tammany. The usual struggle for delegates resulted, as of old, in New York's sending rival sets of representatives to Charleston. Seymour was not a member of either, but Belmont and Tilden inclined toward Tammany, and the suspicious *Herald* christened him the "Magnus Apollo" held in reserve by the clique headed by Richmond, Cagger, and Cassidy. With his fatal love for making trouble, Dickinson had flirted with Fernando Wood, for he hated Seymour, and President Buchanan had failed to satisfy his surly and often eccentric sense of political propriety. He still had his eye on the sole object of his ambition, but he always acted on the principle that an "opponent" was "necessarily a blockhead or a scoundrel."[17] Dean Richmond, however, knew how to handle Dickinson: apparently the chairman played up to the vanity of the former senator by hinting that he himself was not impossible as the national choice of the party at Charleston. This business man from Buffalo was not a bad judge of men. When Ben Butler of Massachusetts submitted his scheme for compromise at Charleston by asking Richmond if it were not "an honest and fair proposition," the chairman of the New York delegation replied that he had never in all his life seen but three men with casts in their eyes who could be trusted — and Butler was one.[18]

Murat Halstead, of Cincinnati, made his reputation as a journalist by reporting all eight of the national conventions of 1860 for the Cincinnati *Commercial*. *Caucuses of 1860*, as he called the book in which he reprinted all these dispatches, is a lively account at first hand of a most politically exciting spring and summer. One has only to read the record of this eye-

17. Alexander, *History*, II, 303.

18. *Letters of John Hay and Extracts from his Diary*, Clara S. Hay, Editor, (Washington, D. C., 1908), I, 373.

witness to imagine the atmosphere in which the Democrats assembled at Charleston in May, 1860. The heat was extreme, even for South Carolina, and the hotels were over-crowded. For a time there was fear of an epidemic of dysentery among the delegates. Supporters of Douglas were the most spectacular members, but the southerners were determined and silent to the point of sullenness. It looked like Douglas or nothing, and the slave states would not have Douglas. As in 1844, a combination of the unit rule for some states and the two-thirds rule for the nomination were to cause trouble. Sixteen years before, the working of these rules together had beaten Martin Van Buren for the third nomination he coveted; now they were to wreck the Democratic party.[19]

As we have seen, two delegations from New York arrived at Charleston. Dean Richmond and the "Softs" set out by boat on April 18. In the excitement of the send-off the dignified American agent of the Rothschilds was struck in the waist-band of his trousers by an orange thrown by some one in the crowd to which he was waving farewell from the deck. Richmond's failure to declare for Douglas openly has been laid to the fear of being refused admission to the convention. Fernando Wood and his Mozart Hall delegates, although they professed to represent the whole state, probably hoped for nothing better than a compromise like that at Cincinnati four years before which would give them half of New York's thirty-five votes. On April 22, the New York *Herald* announced that the Richmond and Tammany Hall men had been seated in the convention, and that Jefferson Davis had left Charleston after naming Dickinson, of New York, as one of the six candidates acceptable to the South. The absence of Seymour was noticeable, for Charleston was the only national convention of his party from 1844 to 1868 which he failed to attend. That he should have remained in

19. For the Charleston convention and its sequence, see, in addition to Halstead, *Caucuses of 1860*, Dumond, *Secession Movement*, 35–91. The latter book contains an excellent analysis of the state of mind which provoked the secession of the Gulf States, 113–145. For a summary of public opinion in the United States in 1860, see, also, Dumond, *Southern Editorials on Secession.*

Utica in 1860 made it commonly believed that he was secretly a receptive candidate. The "if" of the nomination that never took place is fascinating to reflect on: a two-man contest between Abraham Lincoln and Horatio Seymour might have changed the course of American history.

It is not altogether unfair to lay the blame for the breaking-up of the Charleston convention on Dean Richmond and the New York delegation. In all close votes an apparent contradiction of practice became evident, for the states could impose the unit rule or not as they pleased. When important matters like the two-thirds rule and the platform were settled by a majority vote, it was obvious that a partial use of the unit rule might easily enable a smaller part of the convention to dominate the larger. The state convention had directed that the delegation which was seated should vote as a unit; but for that fact the minority in that delegation of "Softs" could have saved the platform which the South demanded. Only Clancy, Savage, and Belmont of the city followed the lead of the Douglas men from upstate. Thus twenty votes controlled the other fifteen. Had New York divided her vote in proportion to the opinions of her representatives and let the South have its platform, the convention might never have dissolved.

The vote of New York was decisive a second time. The South contended that the nominee must receive two-thirds of the whole number of delegates — not merely of those voting. In this contention it was supported by New York, which hoped to avoid the withdrawal of the slave states. Richmond's strategy in these two important contests seems to show that he hoped to nominate Seymour in the end, whatever the latter might think. Neither President Buchanan, at the time, nor Professor Fite, years later, told the story of this convention in such a way as to imply that the secession of the southern delegates at Charleston was a pre-arranged conspiracy. It was tactless but it was not wholly unjustifiable in view of the circumstances. Had all the states imposed the unit rule or had all of them discarded it, the majority of the convention would have accepted the platform which the committee on resolutions had submitted to them.[20] To decide questions of procedure, to draw up the policies of a platform by majority votes and then require a two-thirds vote for the nomination only added to the difficulties and dangers.

In 1860, Seymour had never been farther south than Washington. Casual acquaintance with southerners during visits to the capital, meetings with them at national conventions of the party, and occasional summer vacations at Newport had been the only means by which he had become known to politicians of the slave states. Yet as early as the autumn of 1859 his name was bracketed in second place with that of Robert M. T. Hunter, of Virginia, by stray papers through the South.[21] There seems to have been a decided feeling in his favor in Louisiana, and on April 23 the New York *Herald* published a rumor that Slidell had withdrawn his own name and was offering to support Dickinson or Seymour of New York, Senator Lane of Oregon, or Vice-President Breckinridge of Kentucky. Benjamin Butler, one of the leaders of the Massachusetts delegation, let it be known that his personal preference was Seymour. Twenty-five years later, John Cochrane, of the New York delegation, wrote of having witnessed Slidell's offer — at the Baltimore convention — to nominate Seymour with a guarantee of the support of the South, if the northern Democrats would lay aside Douglas. Richmond went into consultation with his delegation, which refused to desert Douglas by a vote of 20 to 15.[22] This was the proportion in which New York divided at both Charleston and Baltimore, and the majority of twenty, it would seem, held on to Douglas for fear of getting Dickinson while they voted for Seymour.

After the break-up of the Charleston convention in May, two sets of Democrats gathered at Baltimore in June. The southern

20. Buchanan, *Works*, XII, 56 and 69–70; and E. D. Fite, *The Presidential Campaign of 1860* (New York, 1911), 106–107.

21. See, for instance, the Tuscumbia, Alabama, *Democrat*, October 12 and November 23, 1859.

22. *Magazine of American History*, XIV (1885): John Cochrane, "The Charleston Convention."

seceders nominated Vice-President Breckinridge, of Kentucky, then only thirty-nine years of age, and the northern Democrats — a convention of almost two-thirds — nominated Douglas, just past forty-seven. Then while Seward waited at Auburn for good news from Chicago, the Republican convention named Abraham Lincoln, who was fifty-one. The Union party nominations of Bell of Tennessee with Everett of Massachusetts completed the field. The two major candidates both came from Illinois; New York, it is worthy of remark, had none of the eight places on the four tickets. The case for the Democrats looked hopeless there, for Frémont had carried the state in 1856 over two opponents, Buchanan and Fillmore, and now three were in the lists against Lincoln. The Seward Republicans, to be sure, were sulking: they accused Greeley of spite and conspiracy and might stay at home, it was whispered, on election day. The stench of corruption in canal contracts, moreover, had permeated the first term of Governor Morgan. The *Herald* accused the Republicans of rushing through appropriations in April, 1860, in order that they might use the canal funds to carry the state in November.[23] People who dreaded Lincoln saw that the New York vote against him would be divided three ways and looked around for some method of throwing the choice of the next President into the House of Representatives. The makeshift of the fusion electoral ticket which resulted was one of the oddest political contraptions that has ever been devised.

Seymour's absence from the national conventions of 1860 looks less suspicious when it is remembered that he took no active part in the electoral campaign. On May 15, he was privately doubtful and discouraged with the outlook for his party, and more importantly, for his country, but he was "disposed to take results philosophically." Reports of the action of the New York delegation at Charleston made him sorry for the character of his state, but so far as Buchanan was concerned, the fact that "not one man" in New York held office by his

23. New York *Herald*, April 18, 1860.

recommendation left him free of any feeling of "responsibility to the Administration." "I suppose," he concluded bitterly, "Presidents love to be cheated."[24]

Within less than one month of writing this letter Seymour had published a second letter confirming the definite withdrawal of his name from the Baltimore convention to meet on June 18. This letter of June 5 was written for publication in the Utica *Observer*, and naturally sounded a more confident note than his private correspondence as to the outcome of the election.[25] Seymour explained the purpose of it to a friend a few days later:

> I wrote my letter to place myself in a position to aid if possible in getting the democratic party out of its troubles—While I do not suppose there was any probability of my nomination in any event, I found many supposed I wished to be placed upon [the] ticket. This misapprehension weakened my influence with the delegation.[26]

After the nomination of Douglas, he allowed himself to think that the senator from Illinois had a good chance to carry New York. He clutched at the straw of popular disgust with the record of the Republican legislature.

> If I am not mistaken Mr. Douglas will get the electoral vote of this State. The legislation of last winter has broken down the Republican party. I trust Mr. Breckenridge [*sic*] will not suffer his friends to be guilty of the extreme folly of running an electoral ticket in New York—it would not get one quarter of the votes of his friends and would make up a record of weakness against him and them which would be [inviting trouble] in the future.[27]

But the "extreme folly" he thought Breckinridge would avoid was persisted in; the "Hards" put up their ticket in the state and nominated James T. Brady for governor. This was the last and almost desperate act of Daniel S. Dickinson before the outbreak of the Civil War. This faction polled less than twenty thou-

24. New York Historical Society: Seymour Papers: Copy of a letter of Horatio Seymour to S. L. M. Barlow, May 15, 1860.

25. New York *Tribune*, June 6, 1860, quoting the Utica *Daily Observer* of June 5.

26. New York Historical Society: Seymour Papers: Copy of a letter of Horatio Seymour to S. L. M. Barlow, June 8, 1860.

27. New York Historical Society: Seymour Papers: Copy of a letter of Horatio Seymour to S. L. M. Barlow, July 26, 1860.

sand votes — too few even to affect the result as between Republicans and "Softs."[28] Brady was one of the best lawyers in the city of New York, and his supporters justified their course in putting up a separate state ticket on the basis of what they called Dean Richmond's tyrannical use of the unit rule at Charleston. Although their fifteen votes could have saved the day for the opinions and policies of the South, running a state ticket can not be taken as representing anything more than the bitter feeling of a hopeless minority determined to make mischief. Dickinson had done his best to destroy the disabled party he was soon to desert and denounce.

The state convention of the "Softs" met at Syracuse on August 15 and nominated William Kelly for governor. Although he was not a delegate, Seymour put in an appearance, and when he was discovered on the floor of the hall, he was hustled up to the platform to make a speech of welcome to the party. Referring to the enthusiasm with which New York had received the nomination of Douglas, he dwelt on the bitter lessons to be learned from neglect of the principle of home rule. What was good for the cities of New York and the states of the Union could certainly not be bad for the territories of the nation. After a brief reference to the extravagant policies of the Morgan administration, Seymour closed his short speech with the optimistic statement that the Douglas Democrats would win in November because they "ought" to win.[29] On what experience Seymour based this counsel of hope and happiness does not appear. In 1840, for instance, when he was thirty years old, he had heard the battle-cry of "Tippecanoe and Tyler, Too" catch the fickle fancy of the country and had seen his father's good friend, Martin Van Buren, go down in a sea of hard cider on the shoals of hard times. Again, eight years later, he had watched an unholy alliance between revenge and reform demolish Democratic chances in both New York and the nation to give Taylor the presidency over Lewis Cass. In 1854 he had

28. Werner, *Civil List*, 167.
29. New York *Herald*, August 16, 1860.

lost his own brave battle against every political mania he hated by the narrowest of doubtful margins. "Ought," he should have learned by the time he was fifty, is not always a safe take-off for prediction.

Seymour went to Syracuse that August of 1860 in the hope of smoothing out the wretched rivalry between Tammany Hall and the Mozart organization of Mayor Fernando Wood. Having named Kelly, the "Softs" had ratified the choice of Douglas at Baltimore and adroitly endorsed his doctrine of "non-intervention." The utter personal confusion in the politics of New York in 1860 is beautifully illustrated by the fact that William Kelly himself had bolted Cass for Van Buren in the feud of 1848. John A. Dix, who had joined him in that revolt and headed the third ticket for governor, was now supporting Breckinridge for President. On the other hand, Washington Hunt, a Whig who supported Fillmore in 1856, was now campaigning for the Union ticket of Bell and Everett. Tilden, a Barnburner in 1848, published a powerful plea which pointed out the danger which would result from the election of Lincoln, and voted for Douglas.

Partly through the influence of the latter, Washington Hunt and Horatio Seymour — good friends, though they had run against each other twice for governor — arranged what was called the "Syracuse juggle" — a fusion of the Douglas and the Bell electoral tickets. Ten Union party names were put on the Douglas list of electors, and Greeley had no sooner dubbed it the "confusion ticket" than arguments arose as to how the electors would vote if the amalgamation were victorious. The *Tribune* declared that the ten Bell electors were put up to catch the Know-Nothings; while the Douglas electors, it was hoped, would draw the Irish and the Germans. Hunt, so ran the rumor, planned to throw the election into the House so that John Bell of Tennessee would be chosen President.[30] Senator Lane, of Oregon, had been named for Vice-President with Breckinridge, and there is evidence that Seymour believed that, in the event of

30. Alexander, *History*, II, 324–327.

no candidate receiving an electoral majority, the vote of the House would light on him.

Inactive as he was during the campaign of 1860, Seymour was careful not to seem uninterested in the result. On October 8 the Douglas Democrats held a huge ratification meeting in the city of New York to which Seymour was duly invited. Although he did not attend this meeting, he sent a courteous explanation of his inability to be present. Much as he "detested political speech-making" and in spite of the fact that he never felt at home in that city, he assured the supporters of Douglas that he would have been "governed by the wishes" of his "friends" and have come down to do what he could if that had been possible. Unluckily the invitation had arrived while he was away from Utica, and a three-weeks absence from home had ended in a bad cold.[31] This ratification meeting he was unable to attend foreshadowed a second and still more surprising fusion of Democratic tickets. Douglas and Bell men were already on one list, and now a last desperate move to deprive Abraham Lincoln of the thirty-five votes of New York resulted in the addition of seven supporters of Breckinridge to that electoral ticket. The "Hards" resisted the arrangement to the bitter end, but the merchants and bankers of the city forced the union by promising money for the Democratic campaign only if it were effected. The ticket as finally completed represented Douglas, Bell, and Breckinridge in the proportion of 18, 10, and 7.[32] The *Tribune* warned Republicans that rich Democrats were raising a fund of a million dollars, and Lincoln himself seems to have been disturbed at the news of the fusion. The October elections in Pennsylvania and Indiana, however, confirmed the quiet confidence of Thurlow Weed. In New York in November the result showed that the Fillmore vote of 1856 had gone to the Republicans. Lincoln beat the Democratic union electoral ticket by 50,136 and Governor Morgan polled a handsome majority over the total vote for both Kelly and Brady.

31. New York Historical Society: Seymour Papers: Copy of a letter of Horatio Seymour to S. L. M. Barlow, October 9, 1860.

32. Alexander, *History*, II, 331.

The momentous election of Abraham Lincoln has been studied from every angle. It is well to disregard the providential aspect of the outcome. Seventeen years ago Mary Scrugham made a careful examination of the returns. Her *Peaceable Americans of 1860–1861* shows how ridiculously the machinery of the electoral college misrepresented American opinion in this critical campaign. To question the constitutionality of Lincoln's election is absurd, but to criticize the system by which one of four candidates could carry the electoral college decisively with a large third of the popular vote is pertinent.[33] In thirty-seven presidential campaigns elections have been thrown into the House just twice, even if we count the accidental tie vote between Jefferson and Burr in 1801. At the first two meetings of the electoral college, Washington was chosen without contest. Thereafter, as every one knows, the growth of parties put an end to the deliberative character of the body, for each political organization put up its own list of electors in every state — where the legislatures did not choose them. Reporting the popular result became automatic. Even if the contradiction of 1888 be taken into account, the method works well enough while the field of candidates is limited to two.

In the thirty-seven elections for President there have been more than two major candidates only six times. Four times there have been three; and twice, only, have there been as many as four. At the first of these elections the electoral vote was divided in such a way among Jackson, Adams, Crawford, and Clay that the House of Representatives was called upon to choose among the three highest. It is impossible to compare the electoral result with the popular vote in 1824, because many of the states still chose their electors in the legislature. The second of these elections was that of 1860, when it will be noticed that the decision did not fall to the House. Polling not a vote in almost one-third of the states, obtaining not a single elector

33. The popular vote in 1860 was as follows: Lincoln, 1,866,452; Douglas, 1,376,957; Breckinridge, 849,781; and Bell, 588,879. Of 303 electoral votes Lincoln received 180. The division of the popular vote closely resembles that of the election of 1856.

from the South, and receiving a noticeable minority of the popular suffrage, a sectional candidate was chosen President of the United States — and all this according to the Constitution. What may happen in the future can only be imagined — should this dangerous system survive. It is fashionable to jeer at political parties nowadays; but they, and they alone, have made the Constitution work.

Miss Scrugham's analysis of the election of 1860 should open our eyes. Lincoln had no votes in ten states of the Union; while Breckinridge received more than 6,000 in Maine, 2,000 in Vermont, and 14,000 in Connecticut. According to the "acid test of geographical membership," the Republican was the only "out-and-out sectional party." Some accused the southern Democrats of splitting their party for the sake of forcing the election of Lincoln and thus finding a compelling excuse for secession. If the entire opposition to Lincoln, however, had been united on one candidate, the electoral college would still have given him the presidency "regardless of the fact that the popular vote against him was a million more than that for him." In 1860, then, according to the returns, it would have been impossible for a majority of the American people to choose a President even if they had united their votes on a single hypothetical candidate. In the face of the vote which both Douglas and Bell received in the southern states, "it is folly to assert," continues Miss Scrugham, that the South was "aggressively pro-slavery and bent on maintaining slavery" even at the cost of the Union.[34] Tilden saw the fearful danger of the victory of Lincoln before it had occurred. Laying his finger on the political menace of any man's being made President without one electoral vote from the South, he urged his fellow citizens to defeat him by any means possible.[35]

The foresight of his long letter on the subject was shrewd and prophetic, for when the result of the election was announced, the Gulf States began to go out of the Union. The

34. Scrugham, *Peaceable Americans*, 35, 41, and 52.

35. New York *Evening Post*, October 30, 1860; Tilden, *Public Writings*, I, 289–330.

situation was unprecedented, and it is worse than idle, it is presumptuous, to rail at Buchanan for his failure to act. Eight months elapsed between the election and the special session of the Congress which met on July 4, 1861. For the first half of that time Buchanan was President and for the second, Lincoln. Secession began under one and continued under the other. Charleston fired on Fort Sumter in April. The inaction of Buchanan received the sincere flattery of imitation on the part of his successor. The used-up gentleman who had no time for his prayers has been made the scape-goat of the calamity of the Civil War. President Polk found him an "old maid," as early as the eighteen-forties, but Polk was a very remarkable American. Buchanan's record is an unalterable matter of fact: he supported the Compromise of 1850 and opposed the Kansas–Nebraska Act; he used his influence as President against both Douglas and Yancey; he accepted the Dred Scott Decision and favored the Lecompton Constitution for Kansas; he opposed the withdrawal of the Democratic delegates from the conventions at Charleston and Baltimore; he urged the Crittenden Compromise on the Congress, and believed the secession of South Carolina was a tragic act of outrage.[36]

On November 10, 1860, South Carolina called a state convention to meet at the capital on December 17. Delegates were elected on December 6, and eleven days later the convention ad-

36. See Buchanan, *Works*, XII, 263–285: W. U. Hensel, "Buchanan's Administration on the Eve of the Rebellion." John Tyler was to follow Virginia out of the Union, but even before the election of Lincoln he blamed both the Douglas men and the eight states which left the Democratic convention for the schism at Charleston:

> The Country is undoubtedly in an alarming condition. While I think you are too bitter on Douglass [*sic*], yet I consider his course, and that of his friends, unfortunate. In truth, I see nothing to approve on either side. The eight Southern States, had they remained in the Charleston Convention, might easily have defeated him, and, making a proper selection, might have waived a platform altogether. Bell becomes stronger every day, as is proven in the Missouri election; but still I persuade myself that Breckinridge will carry majorities in most of the Southern States and the plurallity [*sic*] in Virginia; but of course every thing is in doubt by the division in the Democratic ranks. Let things result as they may, I fear that the great Republic has seen its best days.

Proceedings, Massachusetts Historical Society, LXI, 220–221: John Tyler to his son, August 14, 1860.

journed to Charleston because of an epidemic of smallpox in Columbia. The first ordinance of secession was passed on December 20, 1860. In the meantime the city of New York took alarm. Men who had supported the fusion electoral ticket against Lincoln felt that some expression of opinion from the North might avert or delay any action in South Carolina. Conservative citizens signed the resolutions which led to what is called the Pine Street Meeting, on December 16. Charles O'Conor presided, and ten days later John A. Dix wrote Seymour that the committee appointed at the meeting "are very desirous that you should go to Washington with some other gentlemen, and if necessary to the South to induce, if possible, our southern friends to pause in their secession movement till we can do something to restore harmony. I hope you will not decline."[37] There is no evidence to show whether or not Seymour ever sent Dix the telegram for which he was asked. His frequent absence from Utica during the secession winter probably prevented his receiving this request until after the time for action had gone by. Dix and he were on the eve of a deep division of opinion which was never to be bridged. In two different ways, however, Horatio Seymour was to throw his influence on the side of compromise. He felt it was primarily the duty of the victors in the late election to act in such a way as to block the hot-heads of the South.

From Buffalo, on January 18, 1861, he wrote Senator Crittenden of Kentucky in support of his scheme of compromise. It was his opinion that this "great measure of reconciliation" struck "the *popular heart*." Bigler of Pennsylvania had proposed that the Crittenden Compromise be submitted to popular vote, and Seymour assured the senator that Bigler's suggestion was "here regarded as vastly important." He thought the measure would carry New York by 150,000 votes in a referendum, for many people had supported Lincoln in November only because they found Republicanism more tolerable than Yanceyism.

37. See Dix, *Memoirs*, I, 347–360; New York Historical Society: Seymour Papers: John A. Dix to Horatio Seymour, December 26, 1860.

Republican congressmen who feared to support the compromise would be glad of the chance to throw the responsibility on their constituents. In the event of the northern vote going against the compromise measures of Crittenden, the middle states "would be amply justified, before the world to posterity in casting their lot with their more southern brethren." In such a case the duty of northern conservatives would be obvious. If only the people were given "a chance *to vote* on that bill," however, the contingency, thought Seymour, would "never occur."[38]

James Ford Rhodes fortified one's belief in the good judgment of Seymour when he studied the defeat of Senator Crittenden's proposals. In view of the appalling consequences the responsibility of both Lincoln and Seward for that defeat is heavy, if not dark — in spite of all that historians of the inevitable have written of "this best of all possible worlds." The committee to which Crittenden's bill for compromise was referred consisted of thirteen men. Crittenden himself was the most prominent of the three representatives for the Border States. Of three northern Democrats, Douglas, of Illinois, was the leader; of five Republicans, Seward was the moving spirit. Only two men sat from the Cotton States, Davis and Toombs. Commenting on the fateful vote of the committee, Rhodes observed:

> No fact is clearer than that the Republicans in December defeated the Crittenden compromise; few historic probabilities have better evidence to support them than the one which asserts that the adoption of this measure would have prevented the secession of the cotton States, other than South Carolina, and the beginning of the civil war in 1861. . . . It is unquestionable, as I have previously shown, that in December the Republicans defeated the Crittenden proposition; and it seems to me likewise clear that, of all the influences tending to this result, the influence of Lincoln was the most potent.

In January the House refused, by a vote of 113 to 80, to submit the Crittenden Compromise to the people. About the same time the Senate joined this action by a vote of 20 to 19. Two-thirds of each House, however, recommended to the states a

38. Coleman, *Crittenden*, II, 254–255.

compromise thirteenth amendment to the Constitution, as follows: "No amendment shall be made to the Constitution which will authorize or give to Congress the power to abolish or interfere, within any State, with the domestic institutions thereof, including that of persons held to labor or service by the laws of said State." Conservative Republicans voted with the Democrats to carry this measure of which Lincoln approved in his inaugural address. Virginia, North Carolina, and Tennessee had not yet seceded, but they considered the amendment not "a sufficient concession." "As bearing on the question on whom rests the blame for the Civil War," observes Rhodes, this proposed thirteenth amendment and its fate is of the "highest importance." [39]

It was Horatio Seymour, it appears, who drew up the call for the famous convention held at Tweddle Hall in Albany early in 1861. The Crittenden Compromise having failed in the Congress, the resort to this convention of moderate men was his second definite move to do what he could to check secession and avert the Civil War. His speech at that gathering on January 31, 1861, is a plea directed to the North rather than the South. Six states, he reminded his hearers, had already "withdrawn from this confederacy," but secession, he declared, was revolution, and to call it by any other name or to argue that it was not constitutional would not "stay its progress or mitigate its evils." Wrangling over slavery hurt the North more than the South; the particular subject of controversy at the moment was the question of national territories. The North had got the lion's share, and it could not honestly be said that the South asked to extend slavery when the Supreme Court had decided that it legally existed in all territories until the formation of free states should exclude it. In the making of states, however, emigration from the East and from Europe was certain to consolidate the great gains of the North.

Six states had already seceded, but to use force against the South would merely unite it. Military conquest and naval

39. Rhodes, *History*, III, 41–43, 54–55, and 200–201.

blockade were impossible. "Let us see," he cautioned, "if successful coercion by the North is less revolutionary than successful secession by the South." At Tweddle Hall the question for Seymour was simply this: "Shall we have compromise after the war, or compromise without war?" Lincoln, it ought to be remembered, was a constitutional but a minority choice, and compromise would hold the Border States. The famous and long-lived Missouri Compromise had been a victory not for the South, but the North — even Abraham Lincoln acknowledged that "opposition to the admission of Missouri [in 1820] was unjustifiable." The federal Constitution, continued Seymour, was " based upon and made up of compromises." Now it was the duty of New York to demand the chance to vote on another compromise and to save that Constitution by supporting the remedies proposed. Seymour ended his address at Tweddle Hall by asking for "an appeal to the Republicans and to the Legislature of this State, to submit the proposition of Senator Crittenden to the vote of the people of New York."[40]

The convention at Albany was made up of distinguished men, but the very name of philanthropist Tweddle lent itself to ridicule.[41] Horace Greeley always called it "Twaddle" Hall. Readers of Senator Beveridge's *Abraham Lincoln* will realize how sorely the nation stood in need of the civilized spirit of mutual forbearance which these men who met at Albany urged on their fellow citizens at the very eve of the war. Yet the Democrats had controlled the presidency for eight years, and now the country was crumbling to pieces before their eyes. Seymour, it is plain, began by doubting the possibility of a conquest of the South but he lived to question the wisdom of that conquest. According to Alexander, of all men who met at Albany,

> Horatio Seymour received the heartiest greeting. Whether for good or evil, according to the standards by which his critics may judge him, he swayed the minds of his party to a degree that was unequalled among his

40. Seymour, *Public Record*, 22–32.

41. For an analysis of the membership of the convention and Seymour's speech at Tweddle Hall, see Brummer, *History*, 117–121.

contemporaries. For ten years his name had been the most intimately associated with party policies, and his influence the most potent. The exciting events of the past three months, with six States out of the Union and revolution already begun, had profoundly stirred him. He had followed the proceedings of Congress, he had studied the disposition of the South, he understood the sentiment in the North, and his appeal for a compromise . . . earned him enthusiastic commendation from friends and admirers.[42]

Both compromise and amendment were destined to fail; Lincoln was inaugurated and addressed the already rebellious southerners as "my friends" without evoking any hostile comment among loyal men; then Fort Sumter was fired on, and the President called for soldiers and the Congress. Writing to an unnamed correspondent in Rochester several weeks after Lincoln went into office, Seymour made the most of his philosophy.

How unfortunate it is that the people of this country will not think and learn more and talk less about matters which they do not understand. After all the excitement about Slavery how little is known about its history, causes, remedies *etc. etc.* Some good will grow out of our present troubles. We shall be compelled to inform ourselves about matters vital to the interests and progress of our country.[43]

Just nine days before he wrote this letter, Seymour had attended a dinner in New York City at which Tilden, George Bancroft, and William Howard Russell, the correspondent of the London *Times*, were also guests. Russell was staying at the Astor House, and the "banker" with whom he took dinner was probably August Belmont. His report of the opinions of his host and his fellow guests assembled in New York City on the eve of the outbreak of the Civil War is sufficiently significant to be quoted in full:

Among the guests were the Honorable Horatio Seymour, a former Governor of the State of New York; Mr. Tylden [*sic*], an acute lawyer; and Mr. [George] Bancroft; the result left on my mind by their conversation and arguments was that, according to the Constitution, the Government could not employ force to prevent secession, or to compel States which had seceded by the will of the people to acknowledge the Federal power. In fact, according to them, the Federal Government was the mere machine put

42. Alexander, *History*, II, 355.
43. New York Historical Society: Seymour Papers: Letter of March 28, 1861.

forward by a Society of Sovereign States, as a common instrument for certain ministerial acts, more particularly those which affected the external relations of the Confederation. I do not think that any of the guests sought to turn the channel of talk upon politics, but the occasion offered itself to Mr. Horatio Seymour to give me his views of the Constitution of the United States, and by degrees the theme spread over the table. . . . There was not a man who maintained the Government had any power to coerce the people of a State, or to force a State to remain in the Union, or under the action of the Federal Government; in other words, the symbol of power at Washington is not at all analogous to that which represents an established Government in other countries. . . . Although they admitted the Southern leaders had meditated "the treason against the Union" years ago,[44] they could not bring themselves to allow their old opponents, the Republicans now in power, to dispose of the armed force of the Union against their brother democrats in the Southern States.

Mr. Seymour is a man of compromise, but his views go farther than those which were entertained by his party ten years ago. Although secession would produce revolution, it was, nevertheless, "a right," founded on abstract principles, which could scarcely be abrogated consistently with due regard to the original compact.[45]

In what would now be called this timid opinion, these gentlemen were publicly supported by Thurlow Weed. What might have surprised them even more, perhaps, was the fact that Horace Greeley could agree with them. Long afterward so great a student of the history and government of the United States as Lord Bryce thought that the cabinet system of his own country would have prevented the Civil War. However that might have been, the researches of Miss Scrugham and Dr. Dumond show the startling suddenness with which the fatal conflict broke out between the states.[46]

Perhaps it will be asked why, with the outbreak of the Civil War, Seymour did not cast in his lot with the party which gov-

44. For an interesting discussion of whether or not the South thought of secession in 1850 and carried out the plan ten years too late, see the *American Historical Review*, XXVII (January, 1922), 245–270: H. D. Foster, "Webster's Seventh of March Speech and the Secession Movement, 1850." Mr. Foster points out that what Webster did for the North in 1850 Foote, Stephens, Toombs, and Cobb did for the South at the same time.

45. Russell, *My Diary North and South*, I, 28–31. Russell died a knight in February, 1907, at the age of 86. See the Boston *Herald*, February 11, 1907.

46. Scrugham, *Peaceable Americans*, 11; Dumond, *Southern Editorials on Secession, passim.*

erned the North — and seemed likely to continue to do so for many years to come. Ambition would have led him that way, as the careers of War Democrats like Dickinson and Dix and John Van Buren were to show; he, too, would have been welcomed with open arms. Why did he turn down his chance to "die a great American statesman"? What was it that made him distrust the coalition that had shaped itself into the Republican party? For the past ten years he had fought the Know-Nothings, and the Know-Nothings were now Republicans; in 1854 he had been the shining mark for the slings and arrows of the ardent friends of temperance, and the Whigs, both wet and dry, were now Republicans; time and again he had told the professional preachers of abolition to go south, where there were vineyards to be worked in, and the abolitionists were now Republicans. Secession left men like him to face these enemies alone — and they who were deserted must have wondered at the short sight of the South.

Seymour always refused to consider any aspect of slavery a paramount issue: whether or not it was to be maintained, extended, or exterminated were questions subordinate to the peace and welfare of the whole people. For seventy years the Union had existed with slavery; it need not perish overnight because of it. If this patience shows lack of moral force, then scores of great Americans shared that want with Seymour. Truth is, a certain inert smugness has dulled most of the pages which American historians have devoted to slavery, free soil, and abolition. It is not always remembered, for instance, that agitation against slavery served more than one purpose in the North.

By the 1830's the great strength of the Locofoco faction of the dominant Democratic party showed a strong feeling in favor of what were called "radical" reforms throughout the free states. The rural sections, in particular, were waxing suspicious of those bankers and promoters who fattened on speculation in land and contracts which were the consequence of the popular policy of internal improvements. The chartering of banks had better stop; state debts should be paid off, not piled up year by year. The great panic of 1837 gave impetus to this feeling — would a combination of farmers and artisans get out of hand? It is interesting to mark the decline of this sentiment as the agitation against secret societies and then Catholics, alcohol, and slavery slowly but surely increased. Although Horatio Seymour was the son of what was once called a rich man and married the daughter of another, it is pleasant to remember that he never encouraged any one of these diversions in the interest of his class. To a certain section of the conservatives these campaigns were convenient safety-valves for popular opinion — better that reformers should preach reform against slave-holders in the South rather than against speculators in the North.

Possibly there was still another reason why Seymour never joined the crusade against slavery. His admiration for Burke had taught him to prize and to praise the expedient: he distrusted grand notions as thoroughly as he disliked big words. Search for evidence that any man — black, yellow, or white — is *entitled* to freedom can safely be left to those confident persons who delight in dwelling on abstract and inalienable rights. The liberty of any man depends largely on the welfare of the country where he lives, and his economic status in that country. Quite against his own will the negro had left the jungles of Africa for fields of sugar, rice, and cotton in the South — how soon, then, would he be free to crowd the black ghettos of Philadelphia, Chicago, and New York? Just how much blood and treasure and good will were free soil, abolition, and emancipation worth? Was the danger of buying them too dear wholly imaginary?

As one looks back on the wild words and the mad antics of the abolitionists — Garrison burning a copy of the Constitution in a public square; Gerrit Smith playing "possum" at an asylum while the John Brown he had encouraged was found guilty of treason and hauled out to be hanged; self-righteous ranters pleading from their pulpits for the export of rifles to Kansas; industrious Mrs. Stowe embalming the slippery sentimentality of her half-truths in the lachrymose pages of *Uncle Tom's Cabin*;

even Democratic David Wilmot trying to repair, with his famous proviso, the political fences he had broken down with his vote for a lower tariff — there come to mind the words of the ancient philosopher which a president of Yale was always happy to remember: "Virtue is more dangerous than vice because the excesses of virtue are not subject to the restraints of conscience."

XII

GOVERNOR AGAIN

1862

SHORTLY after his speech for conciliation at Tweddle Hall in Albany, Seymour accepted the empty honor of standing as the candidate of the Democratic caucus for senator. Power to fill that office rested with the Republican majority in the legislature, but the majority was not united. The upshot was the spectacular battle in which Thurlow Weed defeated Horace Greeley with Ira Harris, who became such an eager hunter of patronage in Washington that patient President Lincoln declared that he never dared to get into bed without first looking underneath it for the junior senator from New York. Oddly enough, the Democratic minority took two ballots to name their candidate on February 4.[1] Seymour did not even wait at Albany to assist at the perfunctory compliment of the vote. It was the first of the two nominations for federal office which he ever received. Almost eight years later the second would be forced upon him against his better judgment.

When Fort Sumter was fired on, Seymour was headed west on the business of the Wisconsin Canal, a venture in which he proposed, so he told Abram S. Hewitt, to give up "ambition for avarice."[2] Years afterward, his absence from the state in April, 1861, became the subject of venomous ridicule: Dickinson, once called a "Doughface," professed to believe that the former governor had taken to the woods in terror, roaming among the lakes and rivers of Wisconsin, his voice silent for nearly half a year, until such time as he found it safe for him to come back to the councils of schemers.[3] During the presidential canvass of

1. Brummer, *History*, 135.
2. Allan Nevins, *Abram S. Hewitt* (New York, 1935), 265.
3. Dickinson, *Dickinson*, II, 196.

1868, one George W. Allen, in a political speech which was printed and circulated widely as a Republican campaign document, gave out what purported to be a description of Seymour's conduct when the news of Sumter reached Milwaukee. The apocryphal incident was located at the Newhall House, a hotel of that city. According to Allen, when it was learned that the former governor of New York was in town, Allen was delegated to ask Seymour to step out on a balcony and publicly denounce the firing on Fort Sumter from the usual safe distance. The gentleman from New York, though "in apparent health and fondling his hat," replied, however, that he would not leave the parlor where he was seated. On being urged a second time to lend his rhetoric to the rescue of the Union, the stately visitor was said to have answered: "Tell them I am sick. I don't know how this thing is going to turn out yet." Oddly enough, Allen did not mention the "infamous" speech to the draft rioters of which Horace Greeley was to make much, although he referred to Secretary Stanton's praise of Seymour's loyalty in supplying soldiers to the Union army on the eve of Gettysburg as killing the fatted calf for the prodigal son.[4]

News of the fall of Sumter actually reached Seymour when he was not yet in Wisconsin. He stopped off and spoke at Lansing, Michigan, and a few days later addressed the legislature at Madison. In both speeches, according to his nephew, Horatio Seymour, Jr., he called for unanimous support of the Lincoln administration, there being "but one course to follow."[5] From Madison, Seymour went on to Appleton, the centre of the activities of the Green Bay and Mississippi Canal Company, and thence north to Green Bay itself, where he helped

4. Allen, *Seymour*. When in Milwaukee, Seymour stayed at the Newhall House, as a business letter of August 31, 1861, will show: New York Historical Society: Seymour Papers.

5. New York Historical Society: Seymour Papers: Horatio Seymour, Jr., writing from Marquette, Wisconsin, to Benson J. Lossing, February 23, 1889. Seymour's nephew was undoubtedly making use, in this letter, of the manuscript of his own biography of his uncle. As late as 1929, this manuscript was in the possession of Horatio Seymour of Santa Monica, California, grandson of John F. Seymour, younger brother of the governor.

raise a company of artillery called the Oconto River Drivers. On July 4, 1861, he made a speech at Green Bay.[6] A little more than a year later Henry S. Baird, "neither a Democrat nor a politician," described this speech as "chaste, eloquent, and patriotic." Seymour, so Baird remembered in October, 1862, had in no way expressed himself as opposed to the government of the United States — on the contrary, he had explicitly declared that the administration ought to be sustained, and that the rebellion must be put down.[7] Contemporary evidence confirms the fact of Seymour's having been at Green Bay on July 4, 1861.

> Yesterday was the 4th of July — and we was [*sic*] there — and staid [*sic*] all night — and hav'nt [*sic*] been so well since. It was a beautiful day — bright and beautiful. The arrangements were well appointed, and executed. The oration of Governor Seymour was a splendid effort — the most splendid extempore speech we ever heard. And there was another presentation address by Mrs. Martin — and other interesting ceremonies — concluding with a grand display of fire-works in the evening, under the direction of Major Anderson.[8]

In every one of the three campaigns during which he was a candidate thereafter — 1862, 1864, and 1868 — Seymour's political opponents persistently put him in flight toward the woods and wildernesses of Wisconsin during the first days of the Civil War. He was annoyingly good-natured on the subject and was fond of making public references to the fact that he had sought refuge from the terrors of rebellion in the forests of the far West.[9] When he spoke at the Cooper Institute in the autumn of 1862, however, he was quite definite as to what he had been doing in Wisconsin eighteen months before.

6. This speech is usually located at Madison, from confusion with the one he delivered in the spring. See Wall, *Seymour*, 92. Mr. Wall's "List of the Addresses, Speeches and Writings of Horatio Seymour (1844–1886)" is most convenient and valuable.

7. If Baird was neither a Democrat nor a politician, he must have been a Republican, for he was mayor of Green Bay. Baird understood that Seymour came to Wisconsin "for his health." He objected to a New Yorker's referring to the vicinities of Madison, Milwaukee, and Green Bay as "wilderness": New York State Library: Seymour Papers.

8. Green Bay, Wisconsin, *Bay City Press*, July 6, 1861.

9. Seymour, *Public Record*, 363.

I was gratified that, while I was in a remote part of the great West, it was in my power to promote the formation of a company of as bold and as sturdy men as ever rallied in defence of our country's flag. I recall with pride their array when, drawn up before my lodging, they expressed through their commander, their good-will toward myself, and their obligations for such assistance as I had been able to give them.[10]

The childish charge was dug up for the last time when he ran for President; whereupon, the *National Intelligencer* published an affidavit of the captain and the surviving members of the Oconto River Drivers.[11] The truth seems never to have caught up with the lie.

Seymour not only made speeches for recruits; he spent his money on them. According to a minutely circumstantial story, while the former governor was staying in Green Bay the company of lumbermen which was to form the Oconto River Drivers arrived in town only to find that they were too late to be received under the first call for volunteers. The men were eager to enlist but they found themselves stranded without money either to go on or to return home. When he learned the facts, Seymour called the officers of the company into his hotel and not only paid the way of all the men to Washington but met the bill for a public dinner to the would-be soldiers at the Beaumont House.[12] The legend that at the fall of Fort Sumter Seymour was found hiding in the parlor of a hotel nervously handling his hat was a partisan fiction.

In 1862 a state senator named Maxon declared that when the news of the bombardment was spreading through Wisconsin, he and several of his colleagues called upon the former governor, who stated that the "Democrats should take high Union grounds," adding that "the personal liberty law and the seces-

10. Seymour, *Public Record*, 60.

11. In this statement both Democratic and Republican soldiers expressed "their gratitude to the man who gave his money, his counsel, and labor to the defence of the Government." The letter is dated Green Bay, September 20, 1868, and is addressed to the editor of the Green Bay *Associate*. It carries the signatures of J. F. Loy, late captain of Company H, Fourth Wisconsin Infantry, Oconto River Drivers, and the eighteen surviving soldiers of the original company: *National Intelligencer*, October 6, 1868.

12. *National Intelligencer*, September 29, 1868, quoting the Milwaukee *News*.

sion resolutions passed by the Republican Legislature in 1859 ought to be repealed, but that it [*sic*] *should not be made a condition* required by the Democrats for their support of the Administration." Mr. Maxon remembered Seymour's having expressed the fear that the government did not realize the magnitude of the rebellion and would have to wage a long war if the Union were ever to be restored by force of arms alone. Maxon could remember nothing that led him to suspect anything but zealous support of the federal power on the part of Seymour. According to him, the New Yorker's aid in organizing the 9th Wisconsin Battery was practical and prompt.[13] If this Democrat was ever honestly supposed to be privately disloyal to the Union, it is strange indeed that Edwin D. Morgan, the Republican governor of New York, should have appointed him, as late as 1862, chairman of the committee for recruiting in Oneida County. Many letters in his own hand survive to-day as evidence of his interest and his active service in this work.[14] Unreconstructed southerners had good reason to be cool toward his candidacy in 1868.

Why Seymour never served in the northern armies is a question less easy to answer nowadays than it was then. In April, 1861, he was only fifty years of age; he was independent and he had no children. He had spent two years at a military academy which enjoyed a good reputation at one time. His political prestige was great, and the force of his example was strong. So far as is known, however, he never even thought of going into the army and moreover he never saw fit to excuse or explain the fact that he remained a civilian all through the war. Two difficulties may have kept him from joining in the fight. In the first place, he suffered from ill health all his life: he seems to have been subject to attacks which prevented him from getting

13. Rochester *Union and Advertiser*, Oct. 27, 1862.

14. As early as January 23, 1862, Seymour went to Albany and addressed the New York State Military Association, in support of the plan to develop the militia: Seymour, *Public Record*, 351–358. Seymour's speech in favor of recruiting in the county so as to "secure volunteers, not conscripts," and his contribution to the bounty fund will be found in the *Public Record*, 43–45.

about for days at a time. It is not unlikely that he had some ailment of the liver; his grandmother, it will be remembered, had died in agony from what was thought to be a cancer of it. In 1868 the Republicans made political capital of his physical frailty, insisting that he was too delicate to be put in the White House — the fire-eater, Blair, they warned the voters, would himself be President before the term of office had expired.

If Seymour had enlisted, moreover, his distinction as a former governor would have lifted him at once into the long list of political generals. John Adams Dix, for instance, who traded on his military glory for the rest of his life, never saw any active service. After telegraphing a customs officer in 1860 to shoot on the spot any one who hauled down the American flag (though flags are not infrequently lowered at sunset) Dix sat guard at Fortress Monroe, where, according to Welles, his venal staff made a profitable business of selling passports and permits to trade to persons who went to and fro between the lines. As a further contribution to the suppression of the rebellion, General Dix spent whole days wrangling with Governor Seymour over the latter's use of the word, "conscription," at the time when he was stationed in New York City in command of soldiers detailed to suppress a riot which never occurred.[15]

As soon as he came east in the autumn of 1861, Seymour was asked by Dean Richmond, chairman of the Democratic state committee, to address the convention of the party at Syracuse. The political scene in New York had shifted somewhat during his long absence: at the great Union Square meeting on April 20, both Republicans and Democrats had united in denouncing the tragic act of Charleston in firing on Fort Sumter. With the change from passive to active resistance the South lost that advantage of position and policy which it never recovered. Fernando Wood — he who had suggested that New York City withdraw from both the North and South at once and make itself a free state — swelled the verbal uproar of nonsense, and

15. Seymour, *Public Record*, 142 and 286. As to "the gang of rotten officers" on the staff of John A. Dix and Lincoln's weakness in respect to the enforcement of the blockade at Norfolk, see Welles, *Diary*, I, 177 and 183.

Daniel S. Dickinson, the "Doughface" of old days, suddenly discovered that he knew "but one section, one Union, one flag, one government." Late in the summer of 1861 the Republican state committee proposed to the Democrats that the two parties unite in putting up a common ticket for the state offices; whereupon Dean Richmond consulted Seymour and other leaders who had not gone to Union Square — men like Peter Cagger and Sanford E. Church, holdovers from the second generation of the regency. The answer which Richmond sent in reply was amusing but evasive — to put good men in office was a laudable purpose toward which the government at Washington might first set the fashion. Principles, not politics, were important. The Democrats would unite with all citizens opposed to any war (and equally to any peace) based on a separation of the states. They would support all those who regarded it as the duty of the administration to hold out terms of conciliation and accommodation to the southern states at all times. The Union had been founded on compromise, with compromise it had been maintained, and only with compromise could it be restored. Secession was unrighteous, but sectional policy was also a very "present danger." [16]

The Democrats held their convention alone at Syracuse on September 4, with Francis Kernan, a Roman Catholic, a leader of the Oneida County bar, and subsequently senator of the United States (1875–1881), as temporary chairman. Kernan's fine speech gave the cue: the nation should bury abolition in the North and secession in the South. A week later the Republicans met at Syracuse, side by side with what was called a People's Convention, and the two groups of delegates nominated a composite ticket. It is interesting to notice that the Republicans united with the "people" on all the nominations except those for the offices of canal commissioners. Contracts for work on the canals were sources of profit to the politicians, and the use of them remained the peculiar and constant scandal of New York

16. Alexander, *History*, III, 15–16, quoting the New York *Herald* of August 9, 1861. Greeley thought this answer used "the livery of Democracy to serve the cause of treason": New York *Tribune*, August 10, 1861.

State until the days of Governor Tilden. It was easier to rail at the rebels than to split the spoils. Thus it was that the Democrats elected the commissioners. When Daniel S. Dickinson was put up for attorney-general, New York was treated to the spectacle of Greene C. Bronson, James T. Brady, and John A. Dix — all of whom had supported Breckinridge for President in 1860 — backing a Union ticket together with the hodge-podge party which editor Weed was trying to pull one way and editor Greeley the other.

Taking Richmond's reply to the Republican proposals as his text, Seymour contributed a single speech to the campaign of 1861. Years afterward he wrote to a niece that Americans were so busy making speeches for themselves that no one had time to read what any one said.[17] Back in Utica again, however, in his own county and among his own people, Seymour made a contribution to the oratory of the period of the Civil War which is not uninteresting reading even to-day. It was his belief, he declared, that if people asked themselves why the United States had split asunder in civil war, they had only to read Washington's Farewell Address for their answer and find out how completely they had neglected the warnings of their first President. Men who were loyal to nothing less than the whole Union both North and South would have to fight the spirit of both North and South alike, for people who made their prejudices and their passions "higher" laws than the laws of the land were by no means confined to the eleven states which had arrogated to themselves the dangerous right to secede.

A majority of the American people, he reminded his hearers, had not preferred Lincoln for President, and a large part of the voters had deplored his election as a calamity, but Lincoln had been chosen constitutionally and deserved a "just and generous support" — so long as he kept himself within the limits of that very Constitution by which he was entitled to his office. What would it profit the North to conquer the South if it destroyed the compact of government in the process? The Constitution was not a "fair-weather thing," giving no security to men in

17. Seymour, *Public Record*, 32–43. See page 565.

times of violence, for such were the very times when people needed the protection of the civil and religious rights which it was supposed to guarantee. Alexander Stephens, though he disapproved of secession, had followed his Georgia out of the Union; Seymour, though he disapproved of abolition and did not vote for Lincoln, stayed in the Union with New York. The bitterness between the two sections of the country sprang from intrigue and bigotry; soldiers, it was interesting to notice, were seldom given to the hatred and malice of those who stayed at home. Yet the war was a fact, and because the decision of it would depend on might, the men of the North would be most unwise to call the victory they fought for "right." "We are to triumph," Seymour warned his hearers, "only by virtue of superior numbers, of greater resources, and a juster cause." The arrangement of his words is significant.

Slavery, he insisted, was not the cause of the Civil War, for slavery had always existed in the land; it was present when the Union was formed, and the people had prospered before it became a matter of dispute. Causes and subjects of contention were frequently distinct: the main cause of the war was the agitation and arguments over slavery. At this point Seymour made a statement which was often to be used against him thereafter, for he hit the nail on the head, and nicely: "If it is true that slavery must be abolished to save this Union *then the people of the South should be allowed to withdraw themselves from that government* which cannot give them the protection guaranteed by its terms." [18] At the base of the national misfortune, he believed, lay indolence and neglect of politics. It was coming to be thought respectable to take no interest in public affairs. The ignorance of the South as to the North was no more "dense and disreputable" than the ignorance of the North as to the South. To grant immediate freedom to four million uneducated Africans would disorganize, even if it did not destroy, the southern states.

Yet hatred of the South, he observed, was becoming a para-

18. See the Cooper Institute speech of Daniel S. Dickinson, October 9, 1862, in Dickinson, *Dickinson*, II, 197.

mount issue in the North — as witness the curious coöperation of men of opposite opinions in choosing the state ticket which had been put up at Syracuse. Never had politics made stranger bed-fellows; the men who were now working together for the conquest of the South recalled the " 'happy family' of the travelling menageries," where "animals of the most opposite character" were "penned together in one cage . . . birds, beasts, and reptiles living in apparent harmony." When he closed the central argument of his address at Utica in 1861, Seymour predicted the future better than he knew — the future which he must have hoped would never arrive.

> I shall not attempt to foreshadow the consequences of this war. I do not claim a spirit of prophecy. We have had too much of the irreverence that treats the finger of God like the fingers upon the guide-posts, and makes it point to the paths which men wish to have pursued. But I believe that we are either to be restored to our former position, with the Constitution unweakened, and the powers of the States unimpaired, and the fireside rights of our citizens duly protected, or that our whole system of government is to fail. If this contest is to end in a revolution; if a more arbitrary government is to grow out of its ruins, I do not believe that even then the wishes of ultra and violent men will be gratified. Let them remember the teachings of history. Despotic governments do not love the agitators that call them into existence. When Cromwell drove out from Parliament the latter-day saints and higher-law men of his day, and "bade them cease their vain babblings"; and when Napoleon scattered at the point of the bayonet the Council of Five Hundred, and crushed revolution beneath his iron heel, they taught a lesson which should be heeded this day by men who are animated by a vindictive piety or a malignant philanthropy.[19]

The shrewd warning of these prophetic words availed nothing in the North in the autumn of 1861. The Civil War was still something of a glorious adventure; blood and taxes had not yet made it monotonous and discouraging. The Democrats were overwhelmed at the state election, saving out of the wreck only the two canal commissioners on which the high moral purpose of the coalitionists could not unite. Seymour's speech at Utica, however, laid the foundation for an honest, if ineffectual, constitutional opposition in New York. Old Governor Throop, who

19. Seymour, *Public Record*, 40–41.

had succeeded to the office Van Buren had resigned in 1829 to become secretary of state and was subsequently elected in his own right, considered that speech "profound, patriotic, fearless, statesmanlike, and eminently Democratic":

It has been to me the most satisfactory document, which the times have brought forth, and highly as I have always thought of your talents, this document raises you still higher in my estimation, and places you in the front rank of eminent Statesmen. You cannot fail to do me the justice to believe that I can have no sordid views in thus addressing you — My only desire is to do something, if I can, to strengthen your resolution to serve your Country in the present deplorable condition of its affairs. Men of shallow minds, who constitute a great majority of the masses, and of whom are many brilliant minds, have formed that public opinion which has brought us into these difficulties, and holds us there still — and there is no hope of change until the condition of the country is far worse — But a time will come when even they will feel and see and become alarmed, and then men of sense will be allowed to act, and will be called upon to bring affairs into order. I heartily concur in your views that those, even of highest position, should be called to account and brought to punishment, who in the pride of place and power have spurned all the guarantees of the Constitution, and oppressed private citizens. History affords no evidence of a greater abuse of despotic power.[20]

Throop was only one man and an old one at that but he was typical of the conservative Democrats who had governed New York for years. Although resentment against the management at Washington was gaining headway, the war was still a holiday; but if things were not to go well, men like Throop would cast the deciding votes at the next election. By December, 1861, there seems to have been anxiety lest Lincoln should fall into the clutches of the radicals among his supporters, and the Democrats of New York went so far as to plan a descent on Washington to back up the President in case he should have the courage to clean out his Cabinet. Seymour was kept informed of these plans.

Perhaps I should advise you that Mr. Richmond was here yesterday on business; and that he thinks it important that you and others should go to Washington *some time* early in the Session. . . .

20. New York Historical Society: Seymour Papers: Copy of a letter of Enos T. Throop to Horatio Seymour, November 23, 1861.

Now that there is likely to be a split in the Administration, I think it vastly important that you and Mr. Richmond should be where your influence would be felt by the President — as it would certainly stiffen him up in opposition to the radicals. I wish you would appeal to Mr. Cassidy to go on at [the] same time.[21]

About the middle of December the flurry of fear over the possibility of war with Great Britain led Seymour to offer his services to Governor Morgan. The state was stripped of troops, and popular imagination had conjured up a plot for an invasion from Canada. The moment Lincoln quite properly overrode the excitable Seward and backed down on the outrageous seizure of Mason and Slidell from the *Trent*, the North awoke from its nightmare, but Seymour's letter is interesting evidence of his readiness to lend a hand to Lincoln at a time when the Civil War seemed about to be lost for ever through the folly of the very men who hoped to save the Union.

In view of the threatening aspect of Foreign affairs it is important to have an efficient organisation of the Militia of this State. A war with Great Britain would expose our Northern Borders to assault and would also endanger our great Commercial interests upon the Lakes. . . .

I therefore tender you my services in aid of any plan which you may deem advisable to adopt to meet the threatened dangers and I will accept any position in the Militia however subordinate in which I can strengthen the authority of our State or National Government.[22]

Governor Morgan sent Seymour his thanks indirectly on Christmas Eve; the Confederate envoys to France and England were released, and the reckless act of an officious subordinate was forgotten as quickly as possible — most quickly and completely, perhaps, by Lincoln himself. Less than two years later, however, Seymour had the painful opportunity of comparing the President's frank conduct in the affair of the *Trent* with his oblique if playful dodge in releasing Clement Vallandigham. It was one thing for a nuisance like Captain Wilkes to kidnap two

21. New York Historical Society: Seymour Papers: Letter of Isaac Butts to Horatio Seymour, December 5, 1861.

22. New York Historical Society: Seymour Papers: Letter of Horatio Seymour to E. D. Morgan, December 17, 1861.

rebels from a British vessel on the high seas; it was quite another, apparently, for the marplot of Fredericksburg to drag a "Copperhead" out of his home in Ohio.[23]

The Democrats were determined to be on their guard. Before long it became apparent that the government at Washington was not at all to their liking. Lincoln was losing the moderate vote. In March, 1862, Seymour received a long, confidential letter from William Kelly, who had been the "Soft" candidate for governor in 1860. Kelly was a respectable and prosperous farmer of Rhinebeck, in Dutchess County. He was eager to associate himself with Dean Richmond and Horatio Seymour, "*the foremost Democrats* in our State," in a visit to Washington to prevent the removal of McClellan, for, if McClellan were to give place to a "radical," the demagogues who were determined to crush slavery, whatever the consequences, would add command of the army to their control of the Cabinet. Once this were to happen, it would be quite impossible "to win back to their allegiance the great mass of Southern men, such as have remained quiet during the war, or have reluctantly taken up arms against the Union." Kelly had only recently got private word from Washington and thither he repaired to save the day.[24]

Partly as a consequence, perhaps, of Kelly's visit Seymour was invited about this time to give a public lecture in the Smithsonian Institution at Washington, "at such time as shall suit your convenience." The formal invitation which was sent to him bears the signatures of twenty representatives in the Con-

23. As to the origin of the term "Copperhead" readers should consult the *American Historical Review*, XXXII, 4 (July, 1927), 799–800. James Ford Rhodes could not trace the word further back than the issue of the Cincinnati *Commercial* for October 1, 1862 (*History*, IV, 224, note). Albert Matthews went back as far as an issue of the Chicago *Tribune* for September 24, 1862, which described the term as current in Indiana: *Publications*, Colonial Society of Massachusetts, XX (1917), 207. Paul S. Smith quotes the Cincinnati *Gazette* for July 30, 1862: "The Copperhead Bright Convention meets in Indianapolis today." The word caught hold and circulated widely throughout the Middle West and then the whole North.

24. New York Historical Society: Seymour Papers: Letter of William Kelly to Horatio Seymour, March 8, 1862.

gress, and among the names are those of George H. Pendleton, Erastus Corning, and Clement L. Vallandigham.[25] Just about this time Seymour visited Washington and "went to the camp of our soldiers" apparently to see McClellan.[26] Lincoln got wind of the meeting and spoke of it with suspicion a year or more later. Then, in the summer of 1862, Governor Morgan put Seymour in charge of the work of recruiting in Oneida County. Even business visits to the West were now impossible, and by June, 1862, John F. Seymour, or "Little Pomp," had taken the place of his brother as president of the Fox and Wisconsin Improvement Company.[27]

As the time for the autumn elections came round, Governor Morgan let it be understood that he was not available for a third term. The Democrats decided to put up the strongest candidate they could lay hold of, for Horace Greeley's nagging of the President and the bloody defeats in the field were weakening the prestige of the administration and making the war unpopular. If the conservatives could carry the state of New York, so it was argued in 1862, they could bring pressure to bear on Lincoln and smoke the radicals out of the Cabinet and Washington. The New York *Herald* urged the Democrats to nominate General Dix, and the Republicans (by way of inaugurating their policy of always trying to choose the candidate for their opponents whenever their own cause is quite hopeless) echoed Bennett's endorsement of the commander of Fortress Monroe. Dean Richmond, however, felt confident that he could carry his state without acting on the advice of his foes, and

25. New York Historical Society: Seymour Papers: Letter of April 1, 1862.

26. Seymour, *Public Record*, 47.

27. New York Historical Society: Seymour Papers: "John F. Seymour, Esq., of Utica, New York," was issued a pass to go in and out of Wisconsin "without detention," by William Johnson, mayor of Appleton, on August 15, 1862. For one of Seymour's recruiting speeches in Utica, see Seymour, *Public Record*, 43–45. Seymour urged a suppression of the rebellion before foreign nations should have the chance to intervene: "Ours is a border State, and we must not lose sight of our liability to invasion in case of foreign intervention, which may be expected if the rebellion is not speedily brought to its death-bed." These words are substantially verified by the report in the Utica *Morning Herald* of July 15, 1862.

Greeley was to justify that confidence. Seymour urged Richmond to put up Sanford E. Church, but the state chairman had other plans. On September 9, 1862, there assembled at Troy what was called a Constitutional Union convention. Richmond commissioned James Brooks of New York City to round up the "Silver Gray" Whigs — the old Fillmore men — and Seymour himself was duly nominated on an informal ballot.[28] The next day a Democratic convention assembled at Albany and ratified the action of the Troy convention by a unanimous vote. Richmond had so managed affairs as to give the Democrats the appearance and advantage of rising above partisanship to accept a nomination made by old Whigs. Seymour himself was present as a delegate at Albany, earnestly supporting the naming of Church, but Richmond insisted on his own choice as the strongest of all possible candidates. Although some historians have refused to pin the label of "War Democrat" on any but men who became Republicans in fact, the good generalship in the choosing of Seymour in 1862 can not be successfully denied.[29]

For many years the conventional character of Seymour among his enemies was that of an ambitious and plausible intriguer, constantly in search of office. Radical Republicans like Horace Greeley, for instance, were angry at his nomination in 1862 and infuriated by his election. If they did not cry fraud, they pretended to think that the greatest state of the nation had deserted the North and the Union. Few men, however, who said these things or thought them could really have believed them. In the first place, Seymour himself was too shrewd to suppose that two years as governor of New York in the midst of the Civil War would be a bed of roses for a Democrat. His sensational victory, moreover, pushed him into the

28. Brummer, *History*, 212–213. The vote stood: Horatio Seymour, 32; John A. Dix, 20; Millard Fillmore, 6; scattering, 3.

29. Brummer, *History*, 217–218. Even Gerrit Smith, abolitionist, described Seymour as "a gentleman of commanding talents, high culture . . . of bland and winning manners, admired social and domestic life": New York *Tribune*, January 23, 1863.

position of the leader of the opposition to the forces that were swiftly and surely getting control of both the Congress and the Cabinet. Alexander has described Seymour's state of mind during the summer and autumn of 1862 with skill and vision:

> Seymour sincerely preferred another. Early in August he travelled from Utica to Buffalo to resist the friendship and the arguments of Dean Richmond. It cannot be said that he had outlived ambition. He possessed wealth, he was advancing in his political career, and he aspired to higher honours, but he did not desire to become governor again, even though the party indicated a willingness to follow his leadership and give him free rein to inaugurate such a policy as his wisdom and conservatism might dictate. He clearly recognized the difficulties in the way. . . . These reasons were carefully presented to Richmond. Moreover, Seymour was conscious of inherent defects of temperament. He did not belong to the class of politicians, described by Victor Hugo, who mistake a weather-cock for a flag. He was a gentleman of culture, of public experience, and of moral purpose, representing the best quality of his party; but possessed of a sensitive and eager temper, he was too often influenced by the men immediately about him, and too often inclined to have about him men whose influence did not strengthen his own better judgment.
>
> Richmond knew of this weakness and regretted it, but the man of iron, grasping the political situation with the shrewdness of a phenomenally successful business man, wanted a candidate who could win.[30]

Americans are familiar with the statesman who is publicly unwilling and privately eager to receive a nomination and an office. A certain course of conduct is so commonly expected of a candidate in the United States that it has become almost conventional. There is no evidence, however, that Seymour said one thing and thought another in 1862 or 1868. Writing to his sister and her husband, the Ledyard Lincklaens of Cazenovia, he set down his judgment of the situation and his own relation to it.

> I feared my Cazenovia friends when they heard of my nomination would think me a hopeless vagrant. I did what I could to avoid it but I was forced on. I do not pretend to be indifferent to the feeling shown by the Convention. It certainly surprised and excited me. In many respects it is very injurious to me to be nominated, but now that I am in the field, I want a sharp bitter fight. I do not care about my election. That is not probable. But I want the opponents of the bad men who have brought our country into its deplorable condition to be so much aroused as to make them-

30. Alexander, *History*, III, 38–39.

DEAN RICHMOND

JAMES S. WADSWORTH

selves felt and respected. If this is done we shall have a strong, compact party that can defy violence and can keep fanatics in check. We live in a fighting world and in times like these they are most safe who take strong grounds and call around them strong friends. I enjoy abuse at this time, for I mean to indulge in it. Remember me to all in Cazenovia.[31]

To this letter Seymour's wife added a postscript in her own hand, one sentence of which reads as follows: "I believe there is but little chance of his election; so I give myself no uneasiness about it." If this sentiment was characteristic of Mrs. Seymour, it may be that his wife's lack of enthusiasm for the political activity of her husband partly explains his repeatedly expressed reluctance to run for office. Just a month later, however, Seymour's letter to his brother-in-law shows that having got into the fight, he was eager to win it:

I regretted my nomination but I shall spare neither my time nor my health in my efforts to carry the State. If we save New York we save the Union. This I know. I am hopeful. Our meetings are immense and the feeling deep and strong. . . . I have made appointments to speak in different parts of the State. Between speaking and writing I am hard at work but my health holds out well.[32]

In his belief that the voters "wanted to read," Seymour arranged for the circulation of documents published by the Democrats by means of hiring men to carry them from house to house throughout the state. In 1862 he even became a prophet in his own country or — what is more difficult still — in his own family. Two of his sisters, Mrs. Miller, of Utica and Mrs. Shonnard, of Yonkers, had gone over to the Republicans with their husbands — just as men join the churches of their wives. In 1862, however, Mrs. Shonnard began to weaken and was suspected of urging her husband to go to the extreme of voting for a Democrat.

The Democratic platform as prepared by Dean Richmond at Albany on September 10 contained a definite bid for the support of conservative opinion by declaring against all proposals

31. New York Historical Society: Seymour Papers: Horatio Seymour to Helen Seymour Lincklaen, September 18, 1862.

32. New York Historical Society: Seymour Papers: Horatio Seymour to Ledyard Lincklaen, October 18, 1862.

for the emancipation of slaves and urging the government "to use all legitimate means to suppress rebellion, restore the Union as it was, and maintain the Constitution as it is."[33] "The Union as it was, and the Constitution as it is" became the campaign slogan of the jubilant Democrats. They had chosen their man and had published their platform in advance of their opponents, and it looked as if the tide of public opinion were turning in their favor. The Republican nomination for governor was to cap the climax. Having failed to foist Dix on the Democrats, the optimistic friends of the general now urged him on the Unionists. Secretary Seward and Thurlow Weed both supported this plan, but Horace Greeley, working with the decisive aid of Governor Morgan, negotiated the nomination of General James S. Wadsworth, a former disciple of Silas Wright, who now sat at the active hand of Secretary Stanton.[34] Lincoln's preliminary Emancipation Proclamation, which was made public on September 23, helped Greeley to his victory in the Republican convention on September 25, and the receptive Dix went down and out on the first ballot. Yet if hope for emancipation nominated Wadsworth, fear of it probably defeated him, as well.

The campaign which followed was full of sound and fury. Once Richmond had dictated his act of sacrifice, Seymour threw himself into the fight for office with unusual vigor. He stumped the state from one end to the other — not a common practice in those days — declaring that the Union must be restored and the Constitution respected. The Republicans were anything now but "the happy family" of snakes and rabbits lying side by side. A conspicuous quarrel between Bennett of the *Herald* and Greeley of the *Tribune* added to the interest of the campaign. If Bennett ever denied that he was a bit of a blackguard, his denial must have been lost or forgotten. Greeley, however, was always eager to have it supposed that he was "high-minded." Blown about by every gust of opinion, victim of

33. Johnson and Smith, *History*, II, 462. According to these authors A. B. Laning prepared this platform.

34. For a good life of the Republican candidate, see Henry G. Pearson, *James S. Wadsworth of Geneseo* (New York, 1913).

any pseudo-scientific humbug, gentle in appearance, he was habitually violent toward every one who differed with him, a nuisance and a nag to his allies, and something of a common scold. In 1860 he had helped to defeat Seward at Chicago, and in 1861 Weed took his revenge by beating him for the senatorship. In 1862 Greeley got the upper hand again and nominated Wadsworth; if he could elect him, he would have his deputy as governor in Albany, at last. He laid the failure of his fine plan to a general conspiracy. He publicly accused Weed of treachery, for one thing. The mutual spite which these two political editors spilled into their respective journals made fun for less pretentious men for years.[35]

Seymour's speech to the convention at Albany accepting the nomination the day it was made was the first big gun of the campaign in New York State.[36] Referring to his visit to Washington in the spring of 1862, he declared that every one who visited the capital "could see and feel we were upon the verge of disaster." Only in the camp of the soldiers could he find "devotion to our Constitution, and love" of the "flag." This was no time, in his opinion, to let government continue unchecked by intelligent and active opposition. "Let the two great parties be honest and honorable enough to meet in fair and open discussion with well-defined principles and politics. Then each will serve our country as well out of power as in power. The vigilance kept alive by party contest guards against corruption or oppression." The Democrats, he promised, had no desire to embarrass President Lincoln; they protested, in fact, against insubordinate and disrespectful abuse of him. After eighteen

35. Thurlow Weed was long suspected of the treachery he denied by letter to the New York *Tribune* of November 4, 1862. Henry B. Stanton, in *Random Recollections*, 216, declares that Seward was "dead against" Wadsworth "all through the campaign." W. C. Bryant wrote Lincoln what is "generally agreed to be the major cause of this great reversal": Bryant thought Seymour's election would be a public calamity but might happen if the army were kept idle: Godwin, *Bryant*, II, 176. The Chicago *Times* of May 19, 1864, thought too many loyal voters were in the armies, an explanation which Brummer, *History*, 251–254, seems to support. Out of thirty-one congressional districts in New York State, the Democrats carried seventeen: Alexander, *History*, III, 52.

36. Seymour, *Public Record*, 45–58.

months of war, it was obvious that the Republicans could not save the country, for they were plagued by men who believed that the Civil War was "irrepressible" — and to believe that was to acknowledge that "our fathers formed a government which could not stand."

We charge that this rebellion is most wicked because it is against the best government that ever existed. It is the excellence of our Government that makes resistance a crime. Rebellion is not necessarily wrong. It may be an act of the highest virtue — it may be one of the deepest depravity. The rebellion of our fathers is our proudest boast — the rebellion of our brothers is the humiliation of our nation — is our national disgrace. To resist a bad government is patriotism — to resist a good one is the greatest guilt. The first is patriotism, the last is treason.[37]

According to Seymour the hopeless difficulty of the administration was the mutual hatred among the various kinds of men who professed to support the President. He declared that Lincoln's "hands would be strengthened by a democratic victory," for if the radicals were to force him forward into the rash policy foreshadowed by his preliminary Emancipation Proclamation, they would invite the intervention of Europe. The weight of taxation and debt, moreover, served to remind Americans that the war could not end too soon. It was not the Democrats who made Lincoln's obedience the condition of their support of him; quite the contrary — it was the radical Republicans:

We ask the public to mark our policy and our position. Opposed to the election of Mr. Lincoln, we have loyally sustained him. Differing from the Administration as to the course and the conduct of the war, we have cheerfully responded to every demand made upon us. To-day we are putting forth our utmost efforts to re-enforce our armies in the field. Without conditions or threats we are exerting our energies to strengthen the hands of Government, and to replace it in the commanding position it held in the eyes of the world before recent disasters.[38]

General Wadsworth remained conspicuously absent at the front all during the campaign of 1862; so Seymour exchanged the compliments of debate chiefly with old "Hards" like Dickinson

37. Seymour, *Public Record*, 52.
38. Seymour, *Public Record*, 58.

and Tremaine, not Barnburners like Dix. The Democratic candidate was effectively adroit in pointing out how absurd it was for him to be called a traitor by the very men who had not only voted for Breckinridge in 1860 but sat on the platform of Tweddle Hall during the first days of secession.[39] He reminded the public that many of the most furious foes of secession had broken up abolition meetings in the days before the Civil War, and had even heckled one in a church in Utica against his own protest. He did not deny to a man who had once been a proslavery Democrat the right to change his mind, but he felt that honest "penitence should make men modest, not abusive." The radicals had much to answer for, also: it was their meddling and intrigue which had demanded the removal of McClellan and brought on a series of disastrous defeats.

Though the President might defy the Supreme Court for the time being, Seymour pointed out, his suspension of habeas corpus and the threatened policy of emancipation would both have to stand the test of constitutionality at last. Neither the rights nor the property of loyal men North or South could be destroyed legally by a mere proclamation. The first thought for the moment, however, must be given to the war, for rebellion faced both Republicans and Democrats alike.

> We must accept facts as they stand. Overlooking all the past, we find the armed strength of the Government and of the rebellion engaged in deadly conflict. The sword is now the arbiter. Not only are the ranks of the armies arrayed in the defence of our flag filled by our friends and relatives, but we know that upon the results of battles hang the destinies of our country. Its greatness, its prosperity, its glory, are poised upon the turn of the conflict.[40]

A victory for the Democrats in New York, he believed, would bring the government at Washington to its senses by reminding men that the Civil War was being waged to crush a revolution — not to change the social system of the states which insisted on trying to secede.

39. Seymour, *Public Record*, 58–74: Speech at the Cooper Institute, New York, October 13, 1862.

40. Seymour, *Public Record*, 73.

We have all felt that we were entering upon a gloomy, uncertain future. A popular expression in favor of the objects avowed in the President's Inaugural Address, and solemnly pledged in the Congressional resolutions of 1861, would at once put us upon that ground which would stop Congressional controversies, would restore the energy of the Union men of the South, would strengthen the nation's credit by making a definite issue upon which we can succeed, instead of those whose success would disorganize one-half of our land, even if success could be attained by the means thus proposed.[41]

It was the speech at the Academy of Music in Brooklyn, on October 22, which gained for Seymour the subsequent blessing and good will of Thurlow Weed. The peroration of that speech was prepared in substance by none other than Samuel Jones Tilden. Thus when he spoke at Brooklyn, Seymour expressed the sentiments of a lifelong Whig, a famous Van Buren Barnburner Democrat, and presumably himself.[42] Shortly after Seymour's election, Weed wrote to him as follows:

If I go away without seeing you, let me entreat you to use the power and position the people have confided to you in such a way as will promote the interests of our whole country, and make your name illustrious and your memory blessed. Your Brooklyn speech contains all that is needful. Only stand by it, and our government can be preserved.[43]

At Brooklyn Seymour tried to chasten his hearers by reminding them that if northerners and southerners had taken the trouble to know each other well, the Civil War could never have occurred. Now, of course, it was too late to lament; yet if the rebellion were to end at once and slavery itself be forgotten, the North would have lost the war as certainly as if the armies of the enemy had captured Washington, for the government was rotten with corruption. Two great objects were equally important: to restore the Union, and to restore it as it was — not as it might be. The business of tinkering with the Constitution was easy to begin and hard to put a stop to. If the country were to allow Horace Greeley to tack all his pet theories on to the common instrument of government, other people, also, might rise up and ask to take their turn at making changes.

41. Seymour, *Public Record*, 74. 42. Seymour, *Public Record*, 75–84.
43. *Memoirs of Thurlow Weed*, T. W. Barnes, Editor, (Boston, 1884), 427: Letter from Thurlow Weed to Horatio Seymour, November 10, 1862.

Seymour realized that there was great force in the argument of his opponents that a political reaction in the North was liable to misinterpretation in the South. Would Davis and his generals read a hope for independence in a victory of the Democrats? Tilden, it will be remembered, had warned the whole country during the campaign of 1860 that the election of Lincoln without the support of one state in the South would be a national calamity, and for that reason he had urged his preference for Douglas on his fellow citizens. Tilden was a Free Soil Democrat, a devoted follower of Van Buren, and an active agent in the feud of 1848 which took the presidency from Cass of Michigan and gave it to General Taylor of Louisiana. It was to Tilden, therefore, that Seymour turned for the words with which to close his speech at Brooklyn — words that were spoken and printed as a direct message to the South. Tilden felt that the Democrats of New York had not made their purpose plain there: the war must go on until the eleven states which had tried to go out of the Union were ready to acknowledge that they could not. He put his message in writing and left it with Seymour on the morning of October 22. A comparison of what Tilden wrote with what Seymour spoke shows that the candidate for governor improved the language and omitted the definite pledge to restore home rule to the South.

> I wish that my voice could be heard throughout every Southern State. I would say, mistake not the conservative triumphs of the North. Listen not to the teachings of those who say we are not true to the Union, true to the Constitution. You know that we are those who battled for the Constitution, including your rights, when they were assailed and denounced. You know that at a time when you were safe within its folds you deserted your country's flag, and you deserted us, too, who had been true to the principles of your Constitution. Read those triumphs aright, and they will tell you they bring into power men who love the Constitution as a tradition; men who inherited it from their fathers.[44]

These words left no excuse to southerners for misunderstanding the intentions of the man who would soon be governor of New York. Both Davis and the Republicans were deaf to them.

44. Seymour, *Public Record*, 84; Tilden, *Letters and Literary Memorials*, I, 166–167.

Critics of Seymour's second term conveniently forget the scene and circumstances of it. The fierce battles of the summer and autumn of 1862 had been bloody and indecisive. Although Antietam was by no means a victory for Lee, the result held out little hope for an easy conquest of the South. General Wadsworth's record as a radical abolitionist counted heavily against him with the very body of independent voters who would decide the election. He had been constantly in trouble because of his failure to return fugitive slaves after he became governor of the District of Columbia early in 1862. When the district court sustained the property rights of the owners, Wadsworth flouted the decision publicly.[45] Anxiety in the North as to the possible intervention of Great Britain became active: Gladstone delivered his speech at Newcastle on October 7, 1862, and followed it up with his famous letter of November to Cyrus W. Field. If we are to believe the son of that Charles Francis Adams who represented the United States in England, this fear "contributed to conservative reaction through the North."[46]

Lincoln's policy, moreover, seemed puzzling and perverse to many of his supporters. In September, 1862, he had sent up the trial balloon of emancipation and had suspended habeas corpus. Although his administration suffered heavy defeats throughout all the loyal states in November, he affirmed emancipation on January 1, 1863, the very day Seymour was inaugurated as governor of New York, and signed the Habeas Corpus and Conscription acts which were rushed through a dying Congress in the last days of its session. Seymour had declared for a reaffirmation of the language of the President's first inaugural address and he refused to believe that the struggle to restore the Union could not be continued successfully without a proclamation of abolition. If emancipation was designed to weaken the southern will to victory, the success of the policy was not apparent. If it was paid as the price the abolitionists demanded

45. *Proceedings*, Massachusetts Historical Society, XLIV, 666.

46. See 2 *Proceedings*, Massachusetts Historical Society, XX, 470. Gladstone's letter to Field was published in *Harper's Monthly Magazine*, XCII (May, 1896), 847–848.

for continuing the war for the Union, it was used to purchase the support of men who were no longer loyal at heart. Were radicals who insisted on immediate abolition any less dangerous to Union than Copperheads who demanded immediate compromise? It is significant that a scholar like Rhodes was unable to discover any sound reason for the fear and abuse of Horatio Seymour in 1862.[47]

Seymour's election was by no means overwhelming; he polled 306,649 to Wadsworth's 295,897.[48] The Democrats did not control the legislature, and for the first time in a contest for the governorship Seymour failed to carry Utica and his home county of Oneida. Lack of support by a majority of his neighbors must have been discouraging, but there was consolation in the fact that his friend Francis Kernan replaced his brother-in-law, the magnificent Roscoe Conkling, in the House of Representatives. This husband of his little sister had always opposed him even ostentatiously and was to continue to do so. Good friends of Conkling thought him vain and arrogant, and some of his allies found him impossible. He supplied the House of Seymour with all those masculine virtues which the whimsical Horatio was supposed to lack.

Millard Fillmore's declaration in favor of Seymour may have had a little to do with the result.[49] Having analyzed the elections of 1862 with care, however, Rhodes came to the conclusion that disappointment with the course of the war was the chief cause of the political reaction of that autumn.[50] The strenuous Stanton, writing on November 11, 1862, blamed the retention of General McClellan.[51] Dickinson, though he hinted his suspicion of Seward and Weed, was so shocked and humiliated by what he called perfidy to the Union ticket that he found himself in the unique, if only temporary, position of being

47. Rhodes, *History*, IV, 168.
48. Werner, *Civil List*, 167.
49. Albany *Atlas and Argus*, October 27, 1862.
50. Benton, *Voting in the Field*, 19–26. Benton examined the ebb and flow of Republican and Democratic votes during the four years (1860–1863) in New York and six other big states. The total vote varied greatly, the even years always bringing out the largest numbers.
51. Frank A. Flower, *Edwin McMasters Stanton* (Akron, Ohio, 1905), 194.

unable to say anything.[52] Rutherford Birchard Hayes, in writing to his uncle, on the other hand, took Seymour's election with composure and ventured the prediction that once in power the Democrats would have to support the war.[53]

The pamphlet, *Executive Power*, in which Benjamin R. Curtis severely criticized Lincoln's proceedings of September 22 and 24, circulated widely in the North and doubtless had effect with some few thousands of intelligent and independent voters. Only a slight knowledge of politics, however, makes questionable the conclusion that Seymour won in 1862 because he was the better man with the better cause. It was Lee who did most to elect Seymour in 1862; Seward and Stanton between them could not send northerners to prison quite so rapidly as the generals of Lincoln were putting them in their graves. A few more speeches from Gladstone, however, might very well have reversed the result by means of inflaming resentment in the North.[54] Two letters from the victor afford an interesting contrast of a man's sense of fact and his fancy. On November 10, Seymour wrote to one of his sisters:

> I wish my troubles ended with the election. The result is very gratifying but I dread going to Albany again. I was about getting myself into comfortable home habits.[55]

Two days later, however, he treated himself to a vision of the imaginary benefits which might follow from what had happened.

> I hope the results of the late elections in the Northern States will do much towards the restoration of our Union — We now shew loyal men at [the] South that they will be safe within the limits of the Confederacy.[56]

Not long after, his cousin, Thomas H. Seymour, former governor of Connecticut, wrote to congratulate him on his triumph.

52. Dickinson, *Dickinson*, II, 599.

53. See letters of November 12, 1862, and January 12, 1863, in Hayes, *Diary and Letters*, II, 364–388. Referring to Seymour's first annual message, Hayes wrote: "I am perfectly willing to trust him."

54. Rhodes, *History*, IV, 339–343.

55. New York Historical Society: Seymour Papers: Horatio Seymour to Helen Seymour Lincklaen, November 10, 1862.

56. New York State Library: Manuscript Section: Horatio Seymour to Thomas A. Goodman, November 12, 1862.

In view of the resentment which Seymour aroused with his vigorous criticism of certain New Englanders and Puritans, it is interesting to find that his Yankee relative was in cordial agreement with him on that subject.

You are right, Governor, about the *Puritans*; I have seen enough of them. The *isms* all come from that stock. From that stock also comes [*sic*] hatred and strife. I don't know how bad they are your way, but here the puritan declaimers are about as near total depravity as you can well imagine. They stop at nothing, however bad, which can be used to serve their purposes. I did say to Mr. Miller that I believed the original Seymours were Catholics. My Grandfather, Thomas Seymour, had some story of this, and we have an old picture in the family, which was sent to him from England, in which I believe a Seymour family are represented attending mass. I will look it up and tell you more about it.[57]

Perhaps it is to the credit of New England that some of the harshest criticism of its people often comes from its own dissenting sons.

Immediately before he was inaugurated for the second time, Seymour made a gesture of coöperation in the direction of Washington: he tendered to Major Sprague, of the United States Army, the position of adjutant-general of the state. In writing Sprague to ask him to assume the duties of this office, he expressed his wish to have on his staff some one who would act in harmony with the federal government, some man whose practical acquaintance with military affairs would enable New York to maintain her proud preëminence in the work of preserving both the Union and the Constitution. Henry J. Raymond, the editor of the New York *Times*, who had declared during the campaign that a vote for Seymour was a vote for treason, climbed down as gracefully as he could when he printed this letter, acknowledging that it indicated "anything but the purpose of obstructing the war which has been attributed to Governor Seymour by some of his political friends as well as by many of his opponents." [58]

Any quick end to the Civil War, however, implied a nego-

57. New York Historical Society: Seymour Papers: Thomas H. Seymour to Horatio Seymour, November 26, 1862.

58. New York *Times*, December 24, 1862.

tiated peace. Seymour's victory in 1862, like Wilson's reëlection in 1916, was fatally in danger of misinterpretation — the South was set on independence, and Germany decided that the United States would never go to war. If the South was not winning, it was far from conquered, and the leaders of the seceded states lacked the wit to make the best use of the good fight they had put up while there was still time to do so. If we recall the arguments Seymour had used during the campaign, it is obvious that he was lost if the South should fail to offer peace to the North on the basis of reunion within the fateful three months of October, November, and December — that is, before the Emancipation Proclamation should be declared in full effect in all the states still in rebellion.

The stubbornness of the South robbed men like Seymour of their power to bring the Civil War to as good an end as was humanly possible in 1862. The day he took office for the second time it was already too late, for with emancipation the hope and the alternative of a negotiated peace was gone for ever. Lincoln's threat had failed; now he was irrevocably committed to abolition and conquest. Because Dean Richmond wished to pick a winner in 1862, and Jefferson Davis was determined to be a second George Washington, Horatio Seymour was to pass the next two years of his life in fierce argument and ceaseless anxiety, the hard-working object of unjust suspicion and long-lived slander.

XIII

"FORCE, DISSOLUTION, OR COMPROMISE"

1863–1864

SEYMOUR took his spectacular victory with decorum. Those who heard and read his speech at Utica on November 6 knew that he realized the darkness of the days which lay before him and the heavy responsibility which he would have to shoulder during the next two years.[1] His task was the same as that of Lincoln — he must take care lest he perish between the two extremes of opinion. He would live and work at the centre of a triangle of hostile abolitionists, secessionists, and Copperheads. His was the double burden of any war governor; he must manage his own state, as well as coöperate with the federal administration at a time of emergency and strain. Nor were his supporters in control of the legislature, for the assembly was evenly divided, each party having elected exactly sixty-four members. Many of the state officials, moreover — several of them elected in the off-year of 1861 — were openly unfriendly to him: Dickinson, for instance, was attorney-general. Those who were bitterly disappointed at the defeat of General Wadsworth insisted on supposing that he was determined to effect the independence of the South. Such men did not need evidence or reason in order to arrive at their accusation; rancor and a desire for revenge fed their argument. Yet Seymour's problem was insoluble, for after the Emancipation Proclamation all hope of restoring the Union by compromise rather than conquest was past. Shortly after Gettysburg President Lincoln declared that only three choices lay before the people of the North — "force, dissolution, or compromise" — that is, they must overcome the South, acknowledge its independence, or

1. Seymour, *Public Record*, 85–87: November 6, 1862.

find a middle way to peace and union.[2] What kind of compromise, he asked, would keep the Confederate soldiers out of Pennsylvania? By the summer of 1863, however, no middle course remained. Seymour had favored that way from the first; now he was the leader of an opposition which could not function.

Immediately after election-day he set to work to shape his policy. Through S. L. M. Barlow he got into communication with General McClellan, who was then staying at Trenton, New Jersey.[3] At Barlow's home in New York City he conferred with the deposed commander of the Army of the Potomac, whose unknown words were hardly likely to improve the new governor's opinion of Abraham Lincoln. It is interesting, in this connection, to observe that Seymour did not favor the nomination of a general by the Democrats in 1864, urging the choice of a civilian on the national convention over which he presided at Chicago. He seems never quite to have trusted the military mind: Jefferson was more to his liking than Jackson.

A far more important influence was brought to bear by John Dean Caton, late chief-justice of Illinois, a follower and great friend of Douglas. Caton had been born and reared in New York and had spent part of his youth at Utica. He enjoyed a considerable reputation in his day and real prestige throughout his own state. About the middle of December, 1862, Seymour had a long talk with him, chiefly on the subject of popular feeling in the Middle West. Caton assured Seymour that the people of his own part of the country would never consent to southern independence, reminding him that they held the balance of power in the United States. Seymour asked him to put his opinions in writing, and the letter Caton sent the governor-elect was subsequently published with his permission. This letter appeared in all the papers of the day, and if Jefferson Davis ever saw it, he would have done well to read, mark, and inwardly digest its contents, for if Caton judged correctly, the

2. Lincoln, *Complete Works*, II, 396–399.

3. New York Historical Society: Seymour Papers: Letter of Samuel L. M. Barlow to Horatio Seymour, December 2, 1862.

HORATIO SEYMOUR'S HOME IN ALBANY
1863–1864

hope for a Confederate States of America was doomed.[4] Dissolution of the Union, then, was out of the question. It is important to remember that when he began his second term as governor, Seymour accepted Judge Caton's opinion as the authentic voice of the North West.

Caton's letter shows that the meeting of the two men in December had been the occasion for a conference and not a lecture. These men began and ended by agreeing with each other. Seymour was unquestionably correct, he wrote, in assuming that the northwestern states would never consent to a division of the Union. The interests of the people of Illinois and their neighbors, he observed, were agricultural, and their very existence depended on the free navigation of the Mississippi River. Indeed, the financial stringency in that part of the country was chiefly due to the loss of southern markets, and, even if radical abolitionists might prefer division of the Union to the restoration of it as it had been, the states of the North West could not consent. The North, then, must prosecute the war "earnestly and to the last — not to crush and conquer the South but to crush and conquer the rebellion." This distinction without a difference may remind some readers of President Wilson's adroit separation of the German government from its people in 1918.

True policy, according to Caton, would wield the sword with one hand and offer peace with the other.[5] Many loyal supporters of the Union, he believed, had voted the Democratic ticket in the autumn of 1862 because they feared that the administration no longer represented their views — that abolition and conquest were crowding compromise out of the councils at Washington. If President Lincoln could be brought under moderate influence, the South might offer the new Congress a proposal to return to the Union — as soon as it saw that rebellion would receive no aid from northerners like Caton and Seymour.

4. Caton, *Miscellanies*, 17–31.

5. Professor Channing liked to say of the Civil War that the North fought the South with its left hand and built up the West with its right.

The President, he thought, was opposed at heart to the violent doctrines of many of his supporters and the warnings of his own proclamations. He had resisted the radicals until the gathering of governors at Altoona had forced his hand.

Those citizens who had lost faith in the integrity of Lincoln should remember, thought Caton, the enormous pressure to which he had been subjected. If the elections of 1862 showed a reaction of feeling toward the government, the Democrats ought to seize their chance to rescue the President from the wild men who held him captive. It was suspicion of the motives of these very men — an alarmed belief as to their power and prestige in the North — which had provoked the South to secession in the first place. To continue them in positions of importance and trust would destroy the Union by making its restoration for ever impossible. The proper and immediate object of moderates in the North should be to restore President Lincoln to complete control of his own administration — to give him the power to discard the advice of those men who would not support him except at the price of his endorsement of their own pet policies.

Caton's letter was widely circulated as a political tract, Thurlow Weed, in particular, lending all his influence to its distribution. As the doctrine of a Douglas War Democrat its importance for an understanding of Seymour's policy during the next two years can not be exaggerated. A feeling of general alarm throughout the North was no fiction of discontented partisans, for as late as February, 1863, no less a person than Weed himself feared that abolitionists and fanatics between them might yet lead the North to lose the Civil War.[6] Lincoln relied on the binding strength of the Mississippi River, the only power in the world greater than the London *Times*: what we now call the Middle West would never tolerate a separate South.[7]

When Seymour took office for the second time, he placed

6. New York *Commercial Advertiser:* Letter of Thurlow Weed, February 16, 1863.

7. Russell, *My Diary North and South*, I, 56–57.

significant emphasis on the fact that he was taking two oaths on one and the same day: the first, to support the Constitution of the United States; and the second, to maintain the constitution of New York. To a "strict-construction" Democrat, this double aspect of the office was important. Throughout the first two years of the Civil War the central government had been careful to defer to the states in the matter of raising troops, and soldiers were supplied to the Union by the several members of it, acting as such. Defeat in the field, however, and the apparently startling success of conscription in the South were to cause this cautious policy to be laid aside. If Democrats found the dual nature of the government important, certain Republican officials found it convenient. As regards the assigning and filling of quotas for the northern armies, it is interesting to notice that the so-called Copperhead Seymour squabbled over soldiers with Stanton rather less than governors like Andrew, of Massachusetts, and Curtin, of Pennsylvania — both Republicans. Joel Parker became governor of New Jersey on the same wave of conservative reaction which put Seymour in office, and not even Stanton found him an object of suspicion. Though Seymour was sincere in his lifelong distrust of the allocation of power to what he called a "central," as distinguished from a federal government, he never squarely faced the fact that, no matter how magnificent the Constitution might be, it could not remain for ever a theological mystery — if two men ride one horse together, somebody sits behind.

Seymour's first annual message was watched for far and wide. Men praised it or denounced it according to their preconceived notions of the author. We now know something of how this once famous document was prepared. On Wednesday, the last day of 1862, the governor-elect spent nearly two hours at the home of his intimate friend, John V. L. Pruyn, one of the most distinguished lawyers in the state. The two men talked through the evening, and the next morning Pruyn attended service at St. Peter's and then walked over to the old capitol to witness the second inauguration of the man he loved and admired. "The day was bright and beautiful," Pruyn recorded in his diary, "but there was no spirit in the celebration as if the condition of the country had weighed on the minds of all." A "great crowd" awaited the new governor in the assembly chamber; "he was warmly received and made a good speech." [8] What Seymour is reported to have said on that gloomy but momentous occasion is interesting as a forecast of his conduct for the next two years.

Fellow-citizens: In your presence I have solemnly sworn to support the Constitution of the United States with all its grants, restrictions and guarantees, and I shall support it. I have also sworn to support another Constitution — the Constitution of the State of New York — with all its powers and rights. I shall uphold it. I have sworn faithfully to perform the duties of the office of the Governor of this State, and with your aid they shall be faithfully performed. These constitutions and laws are meant for the guidance of official conduct and for your protection and welfare. The first law I find recorded for my observation is that which declares it shall be the duty of the Governor to *maintain* and *defend* the *sovereignty* and *jurisdiction* of this State — and the most marked injunction of the Constitution to the Executive that he shall take care that the laws are faithfully executed.

These Constitutions *do not conflict;* the line of separation between the responsibilities and obligations which each imposes is well defined. They do not embarrass us in the performance of our duties as citizens and officials.

I shall not, on this occasion, dwell upon the condition of our country. The power and the position of our own State had been happily alluded to by my predecessor. My views upon this subject will be laid before you in a few days in my Message to the Legislature.

This occasion, fellow-citizens, when official power is so courteously transferred from the hands of one political organization to those of another holding opposite sentiments upon public affairs, is not only a striking exemplification of the spirit of our institutions, but highly honorable to the minority party. Had our misguided fellow-citizens of the South acted as the minority of the citizens of our own State (a minority but little inferior in numbers to the majority) are now acting in this surrender of power the nation would not now be involved in Civil War.

While fully aware that I shall have but little control of public affairs in the position to which I have been called and can not do much to shape events, I yet venture to trust that before the end of my term of service, the country will again be great, glorious and united as it once was; and in conclusion, I now offer to Almighty God my fervent prayer that the clouds which overhang us may be scattered, and that the close of my official term

8. Journal of John V. L. Pruyn, December 31, 1862, and January 1, 1863.

may find our people united in peace and fraternal affection, and the Union restored to what it was while we listened to the advice of our fathers.

Fellow-citizens, I thank you for this kind reception — I thank those who differ with me politically, for their presence here and participation in this scene — for it affords emphatic testimony to the constitutional obligations yet felt by the people of this great State.[9]

After several hours of shaking hands, the new governor walked home with Mr. Pruyn and stayed for dinner. For several weeks the two men had been talking over the President's proclamation suspending habeas corpus and imposing martial law, and Pruyn's opinions had a most important influence on Seymour's policies. The strain of the war and the exceptionally angry feelings which attended the election of 1862 had produced a dangerous state of mind in New York.[10] On January 3, for instance, the New York *Herald* was so sanguine as to predict that Seymour's coming into office would "be likely to inaugurate a new era, in which the outraged Constitution will be vindicated, and that sacred instrument elevated to its proper position, where the founders of the government placed it, high above all executive or legislative authority, whether in peace or in war." New York would now be rescued from "a system of despotism meaner and viler than ever prevailed in Naples or Austria." Only the day before, Thurlow Weed's Albany *Evening Journal* had observed of Seymour's going into office that, although "nearly one half the electors of the State voted against him,

9. New York *Freeman's Journal and Catholic Register*, January 10, 1863. The Chicago *Times* carried an amusing account of the inauguration, which "grand event" transferred the "Empire State of the Union" from the hands of a representative of sectional hypocrites into the "safe keeping of a gentleman, a statesman, and a scholar, whose pure patriotism has never been questioned by the honest masses of his countrymen." The *Times* reporter got a seat in the assembly chamber only with difficulty; at eleven, the salutes began, one gun for each state of the Union; at half-past eleven, "the two distinguished gentlemen" (Morgan and Seymour) took a "conspicuous position under the dingy canopy, which shades and almost hides a full-length portrait of Washington." Seymour was sworn in by Horatio Ballard, secretary of state, and, "holding his right hand toward heaven," bowed down low in response to the requirements of the oath. The crowd seems to have been far from complimentary to the out-going governor: Chicago *Times*, January 3, 1863.

10. New York Historical Society: Seymour Papers: Letter of John V. L. Pruyn to Horatio Seymour, December 20, 1862.

every one of them" wished him well "in his avowed purpose to stand by the State and Nation in the pending conflict." [11] Complaints and outcries against violation of the Constitution have confronted every active President in every period of national emergency. Jefferson and Jackson, Lincoln and both the Roosevelts — all have had the same experience. Yet sovereignty in the United States rests with the power to amend that Constitution: the people can do as they please — if they persist.

Seymour was surrounded by men who felt sure that they knew how to do the right thing the right way. Rebellion was wrong, but the northern radicals were wrong, also, in the measures they were using against it. Lincoln, however, faced the practical problem of restoring the authority of the Union in eleven states, though it must be acknowledged that some of the methods of his men were crude. Repetition of legend by his blind admirers can not obscure the fact that no people can deprive another people of liberty without losing its own. Despotism in the North was the inevitable result first of the desire and then the determination to conquer the South. Seymour sensed the dilemma and hoped for compromise.

Such were the feelings of the gentlemen who met for an important conference at Pruyn's home in Albany.

January 3rd. Several gentlemen met at my house this evening at the request of Governor Seymour to discuss with him informally the points to be presented in his message to be sent to the Legislature on its opening next week. The Governor did not read the draft of the message but stated its substance especially on the material points of such absorbing interest now — the war — rather the rebellion — and the state of the country. In view of the present condition of things this message will probably be the most important document which ever emanated from a state government; if of the right tone, it will draw the country to its positions and conclusions and may do much to bring about some close of the present dreadful struggle. It was considered that the Emancipation Proclamation of President Lincoln just out ought to be noticed and its unconstitutionality pointed out and the opinion of all present seemed to be in favor of taking bold and strong ground, rather more so than that laid down by the Governor, as being de-

11. New York *Herald*, January 3, 1863; Albany *Evening Journal*, January 2, 1863.

manded by the present condition of affairs and expected by the people. The other persons present were Mr. Sherman, who is with me; Judge Parker; Mr. Stryker of Rome; Mr. Tucker of New York, late Secretary of State; Dean Richmond; Peter Cagger; Mr. Greene of Syracuse; August Belmont; E. B. Hart of New York; Walter S. Church; Mr. S. J. Tilden of New York, and Mr. Cassidy of the Atlas and Argus, being fourteen in all.

I urged the Governor to say that New York would give everything and do everything necessary to carry on the war on constitutional grounds but that she had neither men nor money with which to wage war to subvert the constitution.[12]

It is noticeable that Seymour did not read the draft of the message he proposed to send to the legislature but "stated its substance," and that friends like Dean Richmond, August Belmont, and Samuel J. Tilden urged on him the necessity of "taking bold and strong ground, rather more so than" the new governor seemed likely to do.

On Wednesday, January 7, Seymour sent into the legislature the first annual message of his second term.[13] More than two-thirds of this message were devoted to national affairs — to a discussion of the causes of the Civil War and to the use of federal powers by the Lincoln government. The spread of martial law and arbitrary arrest were pointed out as sources of the greatest uneasiness and anxiety in the North. According to the governor the elections of the autumn of 1862 not only were evidence of this state of mind but showed plainly that the central and the western states held the balance of power between the radicals of both New England and the South. If the Union were ever to be restored "as it was," sectional interest must be disregarded or denied a voice in the federal government. The mass of the voters would support neither secession nor abolition. Yet the naked fact of war could not reasonably be avoided:

12. Journal of John V. L. Pruyn, January 3, 1863.

13. For the full text of this message, see Lincoln, *Messages*, v, 445–484. Of the forty pages covered in this message, thirteen were devoted to business of the state, and twenty-seven to national affairs. The substance of the message is to be found in Seymour, *Public Record*, 88–105. Gerrit Smith's reply — a sincere abolitionist protest which called the Crittenden Compromise "satanic" — was printed in pamphlet form. This remarkable document bears the date of January 12, 1863, and was written from Peterboro.

We must accept the condition of affairs as they stand. At this moment the fortunes of our country are influenced by the results of battles. Our armies in the field must be supported; all constitutional demands of our General Government must be promptly responded to.

But war alone will not save the Union. The rule of action which is used to put down an ordinary insurrection is not applicable to a wide-spread armed resistance of great communities. It is weakness and folly to shut our eyes to this truth.

Under no circumstances can the division of the Union be conceded. We will put forth every exertion of power; we will use every policy of conciliation; we will hold out every inducement to the people of the South, to return to their allegiance, consistent with honor; we will guarantee them every right, every consideration demanded by the Constitution, and by that fraternal regard which must prevail in a common country; but we can never voluntarily consent to the breaking up of the Union of these States, or the destruction of the Constitution.[14]

Comment and criticism in the press were widespread and various. The New York *Times* of January 8 found Seymour's essay "remarkably innocent and commonplace," but the very next issue contained a long editorial attack on the suavity of treason and secession, which wound up with the compliment, "So Satan tempted Eve." Bryant, in the *Evening Post* of January 7, objected to having the business of the state crowded into one-quarter of the governor's message, but added: "What Governor Seymour says of arbitrary arrests and martial law has a great deal of truth in it and will commend itself to the approval of a majority of all parties." Yet Maryland, Missouri, and Kentucky, Bryant pointed out, had been saved for the Union "by the use of these very arbitrary powers which are now complained of." In other words, Bryant acknowledged that fourteen, and not eleven, states had wished to secede in the winter of 1860–1861. One must, however, fight fire with fire — rebellion with conquest. A restoration of the Union on the old basis, the learned editor concluded, was no longer possible. Several days later Bryant decided that Seymour would have made an "admirable metaphysician, if he had been born in that line of life, as Samuel Weller says." He took exception to Seymour's

14. Seymour, *Public Record*, 105.

declaration that slavery was not the cause but the occasion of the war.

Ten days later, while still unwilling to condone "illegal arrests," the author of "Thanatopsis" published a long article under the challenging caption of "The Perversions and Errors of Governor Seymour's Message."

> The message of Governor Seymour deserves the consideration which it receives, not because of its originality or profundity, but because of the importance which attaches to it as a political manifesto from a partisan Governor of the great State of New York, bent upon opposing the Administration of the general government in this time of rebellion and war. . . .
>
> Governor Seymour is a politician; not an inexperienced politician, with his position yet to select, his lessons yet to learn — but a trained politician, too far advanced to willingly change his theories or practices. He has "learned the ropes" of the system as it is, or, rather, as it was while he was undergoing his political education. Had the Charleston Convention compromised its difficulties, no man in the land was so likely to be its nominee for President as Horatio Seymour of New York. . . .
>
> He is doubtless perfectly sincere in desiring the Union to be preserved, especially if he can share largely in the honor of preserving it. Besides, its preservation is essential to his political purposes. Another thing, also, is essential to them — very essential — and that is *slavery*.[15]

Horace Greeley paid his compliments to the governor on January 8 and 9. His language was characteristic of a man whose very friends lamented his pride of opinion. According to the *Tribune* the message was filled with "dexterous dishonesty," "impudent though adroit sophistry," and altogether was a document concocted by "the demagogue whom cowardice, drunkenness, and masked disloyalty, have, in the absence of One Hundred Thousand of her noblest sons in the defense of their country, foisted into the Governorship of our State." Greeley took great care and much space in order that he should not be misunderstood: "We have regretted and censured some of the arrests made on the orders of the Secretaries of State and War — or rather, the failure to follow these arrests by indictment and trial." Even if it were not right, however, that men who might be innocent should languish in prison, the most important

15. New York *Evening Post*, January 12 and 22, 1863.

fact was that on the subjects of slavery and rebellion Governor Seymour wrote "for the meridian of Japan." The President had been more than patient with both: for eighteen months he had followed the "border-state policy" of not striking at slavery, and now he had proclaimed emancipation after a fair warning of three months. It was high time for this act of righteousness and war. In reference to the vexing charge that Abraham Lincoln was, after all, only a minority President, Greeley proclaimed his belief that the division of the Democratic vote in the national election of 1860 was the result of a definite conspiracy to find an excuse for secession. If he really believed what he tried to make other people believe, then his state of mind shows how little real understanding he had of the great problems of his time.

The comment of the *Herald* was favorable.[16] The *Atlas and Argus* of Albany reprinted the choice bits of praise which the message evoked through the North.[17] On January 22, the New York *Journal of Commerce* printed extracts on the subject of military arrest from the messages of the governors of Kentucky, Delaware, New Jersey, and Illinois. The consensus was that armies must be subject to civil authority, and that the American people were becoming anxious for their liberties. The legislature of Indiana thanked Governor Seymour for his message by means of a joint resolution passed by a vote of fifty-three to thirty-five.[18]

16. New York *Herald*, January 9, 1863.

17. Albany *Atlas and Argus*, January 20, 1863. These quotations are taken from editorials as far west as Milwaukee and from the Boston *Post*, the Pittsfield *Sun*, the Hartford (Connecticut) *Daily Times*, and the Trenton (New Jersey) *American*.

18. Resolved, By the House (the Senate concurring) that the thanks of the General Assembly of the State of Indiana are due, and are hereby tendered to the Honorable Horatio Seymour, Governor of New York for the able and patriotic defense of the Constitution, the laws and liberties of the American citizen, contained in his late message to the Legislature of that State, and *particularly* for his just and high appreciation of the interests, position, and patriotism of the great Northwest. And that we assure him that the conservative people of our own beloved State are looking with deep solicitude and confidence to his executive action, believing that they will find in it a firm and determined resistance to the encroachments of a despotic Administration upon the liberties of the American people, as well as a bold defense of the independent sover-

Professional historians have examined Seymour's message from various angles. Brummer concludes that the only influence which this "most conspicuous Democratic leader in the North" could exert on the government at Washington was the "indirect one of hostile criticism." In the face of war he was powerless to defend the full rights of the state of New York, although men like Fernando Wood and James Brooks counted on him to "call out, if necessary, the whole militia of our State as a *posse* to enforce the writ of *habeas corpus*." Wood used the words, "federal usurpation."[19] Brummer allows that "the conclusion of the message was more reassuring to those who believed in supporting the National authorities" than some of Seymour's words might have indicated. The hostile critics of the governor dwelt on two significant paragraphs:

> I shall not inquire what rights States in rebellion have forfeited, but I deny that this rebellion can suspend a single right of the citizens of loyal States. I denounce the doctrine that civil war in the South takes away from the loyal North the benefits of one principle of civil liberty. . . .
>
> "Martial law" defines itself to be a law where war is. It limits its own jurisdiction by its very term. But this new and strange doctrine holds that the loyal North lost their constitutional rights when the South rebelled, and all are now governed by a military dictation. Loyalty is thus less secure than rebellion, for it stands without means to resist outrages or to resent tyranny.[20]

The seasoned judgment of two able historians, Rhodes and Schouler, on the content of the message and the character and policy of the man who signed his name to it is of the greatest significance.[21] Pointing to Seymour as the natural leader of the eastern Democrats just as Vallandigham was for those in the West, Rhodes thought that the course of action which the new governor laid out was "in the main the right one for the opposi-

---

eignty of the several states of the Union; and that such action will receive the warm sympathies and hearty coöperation of all the conservative citizens of this State.

Resolved, That the Speaker of the House be directed to forward copies of these concurrent resolutions to his Excellency, Governor Seymour, and to the Legislature of that State: Albany *Atlas and Argus*, January 29, 1863.

19. Brummer, *History*, 255–258 and 261.
20. Lincoln, *Messages*, v, 466 and 469.
21. Rhodes, *History*, IV, 225–228; Schouler, *History*, VI, 417.

tion." Although the South had no thought of compromise in January, 1863, and Lincoln had been brought to "his decree against slavery by the logic of events," and the message was "exasperating to the Republicans," Rhodes could find "little in it that ought to receive condemnation at the judgment bar of history."

To Schouler, again, Seymour was not only "a man of integrity, and loyal, doubtless, to the Union," but committed by the support of those who were displeased "with the radical tendency of things at Washington" to a policy "obstructive" to the wishes of Lincoln. Earnest opposition to conscription led Seymour to make "accusations . . . unworthy of the grave occasion." Andrew Dickson White, the first president of Cornell, sat in the upper house of the legislature of 1863 as the senator from Syracuse. To White, his friend, the governor was "a patriotic man, after his fashion," whose hatred of the Lincoln administration was "evidently deep," a man, moreover, who did not believe that the war for the Union "could be brought to a successful termination." Governor and senator remained good friends, for White could never persuade himself to attack Seymour's "character or his motives."[22] Discussion of the message occupied the time of both the senate and the assembly for many days; "night after night" they sat in committee of the whole.[23]

Horace White believed that the victory of the Democrats in New York in 1862 led Secretary Stanton to fall "into a panic."[24] However this may be, the heavy defeats of the administration did not lead to any noticeable swing of policy toward the conservative side. President Lincoln read this message of 1863 and if he disapproved of its contents, then the private and confidential letter which he directed to the new governor on March 23 of the same year must have been disingenuous. How could he ask or even hope for the sincere co-

22. A. D. White, *The Autobiography of Andrew Dickson White* (New York, 1907), I, 105–106.

23. Brummer, *History*, 274–275.

24. Horace White, *The Life of Lyman Trumbull* (Boston and New York, 1913), 197.

operation of a man who was a traitor at heart? If the policies advocated by the governor in his message of January were impossible, then the substance of the President's letter of March was nonsense, or worse.

You and I are substantially strangers, and I write this chiefly that we may become better acquainted. I, for the time being, am at the head of a nation which is in great peril; and you are at the head of the greatest State of that nation. As to maintaining the nation's life and integrity, I assume and believe there cannot be a difference of purpose between you and me. If we should differ as to the means it is important that such difference should be as small as possible; that it should not be enhanced by unjust suspicions on one side or the other. In the performance of my duty the co-operation of your State, as that of others, is needed, — in fact, is indispensable. This alone is a sufficient reason why I should wish to be at a good understanding with you. Please write me at least as long a letter as this, of course saying in it just what you think fit.[25]

Thurlow Weed used to tell "in his later years" how President Lincoln once commissioned him to act as a messenger between himself and Seymour on a very important matter. Lincoln, according to Weed, gave him authority to say that if the governor would back the administration heart and soul for the suppression of the rebellion, the President would support him for the Union nomination as his successor in 1864.[26] Weed remembered the offer as having been made during a conversation which took place in the White House one evening in December, 1862. When he returned to Albany, he approached Seymour on the subject, but the governor preferred to administer his office "as an irreconcilable and conscientious partisan."[27] Nicolay and Hay suggest that Weed probably exaggerated the implication of Lincoln's words — "as is customary with elderly men." Yet Weed was making use of this story as early as 1864, and in one form or another it has persisted to this day.[28]

25. Nicolay and Hay, *Lincoln,* VII, 10–11. It was to Lincoln's credit that he refused to believe the absurd stories of Greeley and his like that Seymour had deliberately stripped New York City of troops in July, 1863, in order that the draft rioters might cut loose without interference. *Ibid.*, VII, 26.

26. Weed, *Memoirs,* II, 428.

27. Nicolay and Hay, *Lincoln,* VII, 12–13.

28. C. E. Macartney, *Lincoln and His Cabinet* (New York, 1931), 53; New York *Standard and Statesman,* April 12, 1864. The editor of the *Standard and*

Whoever was the author of Seymour's obituary in the Utica *Morning Herald* (1886) stated that Secretary Stanton himself favored the succession of Seymour to the presidency on a Union nomination in 1864, that is, at the outset — that Stanton had told him as much with "his own lips." However that may be, there is good reason to believe that the government at Washington was ready and willing to make advances in the direction of Albany. Merely because these negotiations came to nothing Seymour has been accused of coldness and even disrespect in regard to the President. The correspondence about policy which passed between the men has become confused with the story about the offer of political support. Writing in 1895, the governor's nephew, Horatio Seymour, Jr., thought that his uncle sent his answer to Lincoln's letter of March 23 privately by means of his own father, John F. Seymour, "who visited the President on purpose to convey his reply." He did not know "of any letter which passed between [his] uncle, Horatio Seymour, and President Lincoln relating to his acceptance of the nomination for the Presidency." [29]

In regard to his correspondence with Lincoln early in 1863, it is only fair to remember that Seymour was trained in the politics of the Albany Regency — Van Buren and Marcy (like

Statesman sneered at Weed for spreading a story calculated to give Lincoln indirect warning to "bow down again and worship" the Albany editor, or see Weed put Seymour in the White House — just as he had sent him to Albany. The story appeared in the Albany *Evening Journal*, over the initials "T. W."

Soon after the election of 1862, Mr. Lincoln remarked to me that, as the Governor of the Empire State, and the Representative Man of the Democratic Party, Governor Seymour had the power to render great public service, and that if he exerted that power against the Rebellion and for his Country, he would be our next President. I think Mr. Lincoln authorized me to say so, for him, to Governor Seymour. At any rate, I did repeat the conversation to him: New York State Library: Seymour Papers.

The *Atlas and Argus* commented on April 16, 1864: "Who would accept the succession to President Lincoln, except as his enemy, and as the antagonist of all his wicked, dishonest, destructive measures?"

29. New York Historical Society: Seymour Papers: Horatio Seymour, Jr., to Rufus R. Wilson, August 25, 1895. For the story that Lincoln sent Seymour his promise to support him in 1864 in writing, see the Saratoga *Eagle*, February 27, 1886.

William McKinley) preferred to talk rather than write. Letters could be lost or stolen, but conversations were "off the record" and susceptible of more than one interpretation. The new governor, as has already been noticed, chose for his adjutant-general Major John T. Sprague of the United States Army, who was then stationed at Albany as mustering and disbursing officer. Sprague was picked, it will be remembered, because of his "supposed familiarity with conditions in New York State," and with the hope of keeping "Stanton and Lincoln fully informed of what was going on."[30] He was expected to form the connecting link between Albany and Washington, and on one occasion, at least, we know that he was delegated to carry a verbal message directly from Seymour to Lincoln. This was during July, 1863, when the governor commanded him to ask Stanton and Lincoln to postpone the draft. Sprague called first on Provost-Marshal-General Fry, who, somewhat arrogantly, so it may seem to laymen, forbade him to appeal to the secretary of war or the President. Sprague, being only a major, did not dare to disobey a general. When he returned to Albany and confessed to Seymour why he had not delivered his message, the governor "simply waved him out of the office, accompanied by a look which expressed volumes."[31] Thereafter he addressed all communications pertaining to the adjutant-general's office to Colonel Charles Evans. Sprague's ridiculous regard for military rank was the cause of the first of the only two times that Horatio Seymour showed a loss of temper in public; the second resulted from the Democratic nomination of Horace Greeley in 1872.

For personal matters and important business the governor's younger brother acted as the liaison officer with Washington. According to the manuscript biography of Horatio Seymour prepared by his nephew, President Lincoln had definite and ample assurance of the opinions, the policies, and, above all, the

30. New York Historical Society: Seymour Papers: William Kidd to Mrs. Helen Lincklaen Fairchild, February 3, 1912.

31. New York Historical Society: Seymour Papers: William Kidd to Henry S. Miller, January 3, 1893.

sincerity of the new governor of New York as early as January 9, 1863. Writing from Washington on that date, John F. Seymour sent his older brother a full account of his recent visit to the White House. "General Hallock [*sic*]" took "Little Pomp" up to the library, where Lincoln was engaged in conversation with Senator Lyman Trumbull of Illinois. As soon as the senator had taken his leave and the general had left them alone, the two men talked over the political and military situation, referring to a former interview, of which no record remains. The President declared that he had the same stake in the life of the country as the governor — that, if the Union were broken up, there would be no "next President" of the United States. Although most of the officers of his army were Democrats, when the army failed, every one, Lincoln observed, was ready to complain. The record of his next remark corroborates the language of the letter, quoted above, which the President made public shortly after Gettysburg. He believed, he told Mr. Seymour, that there were but three courses possible in the circumstances: the first, to fight until the leaders of the rebellion were overthrown; the second, to give up the contest altogether and permit a division of the Union; and the third, to negotiate for compromise. This third course was impossible so long as Jefferson Davis was in power.

Continuing his report to the governor, John F. Seymour wrote:

> To this I replied . . . that you had no aspirations for the Presidency; that when you were here with me several years ago you said you did not envy the occupant of the White House; that there was too much trouble and responsibility, and no peace there; that you, and those who believed with you, were determined to sustain and maintain this Government and keep the country unbroken, and considered the ballot box the only remedy for evils; that you contended for respect for those in authority, and that while holding him responsible, you would sustain him against any unconstitutional attempts against his administration from any quarter; that these were the doctrines of your message. He said he would read it. I also said that although you did not indulge in loud denunciation of the rebellion as that was not your manner, yet it was a very great grief to you; that you were especially vexed at some of the Republican party who claimed to have a patent right for all the patriotism. That our all was at stake, and if you

and the Democratic party differed with him respecting military arrests, it was with the same view, and that was the benefit of the country.[32]

In the light of our knowledge of the private and personal means of communication between the governor and the President, much of the criticism of Seymour's delay in acknowledging Lincoln's letter of March 23 and of the tone of that acknowledgment is idle.[33] The content of the letter he sent to Washington is concise, and the import of the words he used in that letter is clear. He has been accused of failing to send a second letter as he promised, but an examination of the text of what he wrote shows that he stated merely that he would "give" the President his opinions and purposes with regard to the condition of "our unhappy country." There is no reason to suppose that he did not keep that promise by word of mouth. Worship of Abraham Lincoln has damaged the reputations of all those who dared to differ with him. Now, at last, time is taking its revenge, and what threatens to be a strong reaction toward the other extreme of opinion has begun to tell against Lincoln himself. Those who find Seymour's reply cold and lacking in confidence should remember that the President persisted in three policies which Seymour — and not he alone by any means — thought unconstitutional and arbitrary, as well as dangerous to the restoration of the Union.

In spite of what his critics chose to call the warnings of the elections of 1862, Lincoln had issued the Emancipation Proclamation and thereafter proceeded to sign the Habeas Corpus Act and the bill which was to put conscription into effect. The draft, we know, was none too nice in plan and operation, but to Seymour it seemed "iniquitous." As a candidate for governor he had publicly denounced wholesale arrest and imprisonment

32. Wall, *Seymour*, 30–31. In March, 1886, John F. Seymour called on President Cleveland in company with his niece, Helen Lincklaen Fairchild, wife of the man who was soon to become secretary of the treasury in succession to Daniel Manning. Mrs. Fairchild remembered her uncle remarking that his last preceding visit had been in 1863, when he carried Mr. Lincoln "assurance of all support from the State of New York," and from its governor.

33. Brummer, *History*, 256–257; Alexander, *History*, III, 63–67; Rhodes, *History*, IV, 331–332.

without trial and declared that emancipation would prolong the war. The tidal wave of Democratic victories during the autumn of 1862, of which his own election was the most sensational, was certainly no unlikely reason for his firm belief that a majority of the northerners thought Lincoln was ill-advised in his methods. Seymour was conscious, moreover, of the tug-of-war for control at Washington, and it was hardly probable that he would be willing to commit himself to the unqualified support of a man who might yet go over to the radicals — as, in fact, he did. Seymour believed that emancipation, conscription, and the suspension of habeas corpus were completely unsound policies; therefore to expect him to identify himself with the sponsors of these measures was absurd.

It was a time of wild thoughts, and Seymour, like Lincoln, was the victim of inconsiderate criticism and irresponsible advice. As is always the case in years of emergency the extremes of opinion attracted attention. If Garrison would have sacrificed the Union for abolition, if Vallandigham would have sacrificed it for peace, it is still doubtful whether any dangerously large number of northerners would have followed either man in 1863. Seymour, it has been pointed out, had attracted conservative support in 1862, especially among the "Cotton" Whigs like Millard Fillmore. Before he had been in office two months he received a significant letter from a man whose fame as a lawyer far exceeded his own. George Ticknor Curtis was a brother of Benjamin R. Curtis and took for his first wife the daughter of Joseph Story. He had followed Webster in the old days, had argued the case of Dred Scott before the Supreme Court, and had published a constitutional history of the United States. Curtis came out against the policies of Lincoln in an oration delivered in Boston on the Fourth of July in 1862, shortly before the time he gave up his residence in Watertown, Massachusetts, and moved to New York.

To judge by the letter he wrote Seymour, Curtis had persuaded himself that it was the duty of the governors of the northern states to issue proclamations which would limit the ill effects of President Lincoln's violations of the Constitution. He put the word "private" at the top of his letter, and when Seymour filed it with his papers, he endorsed it with the one significant word "political."

I am inclined to believe that the Bill pending in Congress, *called* a bill for the discharge of State prisoners, contains provisions grossly violating the Constitution, and undertaking to legalise the same kind of action which has hitherto been pursued without legislation. Probably this and other measures of this Congress will admit of an analysis so clear and sharp, in respect to infractions of the Constitution, as to make those infractions palpable to the apprehension of the people; and as they will touch the rights of both States and citizens, and will require some attention from the State Executives, I beg leave with the utmost respect and deference to suggest an Executive Proclamation defining the duties of the State officers in reference to these measures.

This suggestion — I hope you will excuse the request — is made in the hope that you will not allow it to go beyond your own mind. If I can be of any service to you in arriving at a correct appreciation of these measures, I beg you to command me at all times.

P.S.

I do not include the Banking Law, which is in direct conflict with the law of the State, and will therefore be capable of being reached by judicial proceedure [*sic*].

G. T. C.[34]

If former Whigs were ready to urge the governor to defy the President, men who called themselves followers of Jefferson and Jackson found his speeches and his message most devious and dangerous. An interesting specimen of the hostile criticism to which Seymour was subjected by these "War Democrats" is a pamphlet of five letters written during April, 1863, by an anonymous resident of Rural Vale, New York, who called himself "Junius."[35] For "Junius," whoever he was, the Civil War was the result of a carefully planned conspiracy, and James Buchanan, still living at "Wheatland," was, by the way, an "imbecile old dotard." Pointing out to Seymour that his elec-

34. George T. Curtis to Horatio Seymour, February 24, 1863. Letter in possession of the author.

35. A copy of this pamphlet, *Letters to his Excellency Horatio Seymour, Governor of the State of New York, by Junius*, is in the Boston Public Library. It was printed at the office of the *Commercial Times*, Oswego, New York.

tion as governor had been owing to a combination of liquor-dealers, northern traitors, and the off-scourings of the slums of New York City (which he politely called a "Sodom") taken in conjunction with the absence of the soldiers from the state, "Junius" urged the governor to give up his "negrophobia" and thus avoid the fate of Benedict Arnold and Aaron Burr.

To Seymour's protests against what "Junius" called the declaration of freedom, that is emancipation, and his insistence on "the Constitution as it is, and the Union as it was," the author concluded that no one asked for a change in the Constitution, but that to demand the Union as it was — with slavery — would be to ask the doctor to cure his patient without cutting out the cancer. Because he would not sacrifice slavery for the sake of the Union, Seymour (according to "Junius") was engaged in the dangerous diplomacy of trying to array the central and the western states against New England. Shrewd northern Democrats had seen in secession not only rebellion but freedom from the shackles which the power of slavery had fastened on their party. If the Union survived in spite of Seymour, treason would cling to his name "like the poison tunic of Nessus to Hercules."

Something of this strenuous spirit which can pass judgment on all differences among men as simply as it distinguishes between black and white survives in a more respectable form in a book by William Babcock Weeden.[36] Starting with the thesis that "The State is over all and in all,"[37] and writing as a vigorous admirer of Theodore Roosevelt,[38] Weeden professed to examine the management of the governments of Massachusetts, New York, Pennsylvania, and Indiana during the course of the

36. William B. Weeden (1834–1912), a graduate of Brown University, became a woollen manufacturer and an author. In 1875 he published *The Morality of Prohibitory Liquor Laws*, but he is best known for his *The Economic and Social History of New England, 1620–1789*, which appeared in 1890. Although he joined the Union army as a volunteer captain in the artillery in 1861, the gloomy outlook for the northern cause did not prevent him from resigning his commission to enter business in August, 1862. It is only fair to add that the book under discussion, *War Government, Federal and State . . . 1861–1865*, came out in 1906 — five years before the first edition of the *Diary of Gideon Welles*.

37. Weeden, *War Government*, xxiv.

38. Weeden, *War Government*, 269–270.

Civil War. He was chiefly concerned with the character and conduct of six men: John Albion Andrew, Edwin D. Morgan, Andrew G. Curtin, Oliver P. Morton, Horatio Seymour, and Abraham Lincoln. It need hardly be added that Seymour ranked a very poor sixth in his esteem, although the complaints and insubordinations of the governors of Massachusetts and Pennsylvania were embarrassing to Weeden's blind faith in the supremacy of the Union. The author of *War Government* was an ideologist who trusted the voice of the people only when it spoke his own desire. For justification of Governor Morton's having ruled Indiana in defiance of its legislature Weeden turned, for example, to what he called the "wholesome tyranny" of "the early Greek kingdoms."[39] The direct draft of 1863 was significant to him chiefly as an act of national consciousness.

Unable, according to his own confession, to "rise to the heights of [the] sedate charitableness" of James Ford Rhodes, Weeden, as late as 1906, arrived at the astonishing conclusion that there "was no essential difference between the position advocated by Horatio Seymour in 1863 and that of Robert E. Lee when he resigned his commission in the army of the Union."[40] Yet Edwin D. Morgan, a Republican, had called Seymour to his aid in the business of recruiting in 1862; both Stanton and Lincoln thanked him for his speedy and generous help at Gettysburg in 1863; and Grover Cleveland considered himself his disciple as late as 1884. Admiration of Lincoln and detestation of the Copperheads impaired Weeden's judgment in regard to all that lay between his love and hate. His scorn for the "Constitutional Democrats" was extreme, something like Dante's contempt for the trimmers who had no fixed place even in Hell. Horatio Seymour, however, was the serpent in the garden, for, try as he would, Weeden could not avoid the evidence in favor of his charm and his distinction. There was, he concluded, "no more incomprehensible personality in our history"; "he was not a vulgar partisan," yet only a "half-developed statesman," who "dropped back into a very musty and

39. Weeden, *War Government*, 260–261.
40. Weeden, *War Government*, xiv.

stale state sovereignty." Still, Greeley, according to Weeden, was "a greater fool than Seymour," for the editor created his paradise out of his immediate surroundings; whereas the governor dreamed his way to delusion.

Weeden's portrait of Seymour and his verdict on his character and conduct are striking examples of writing history from hindsight. Working over the result of his researches in the archives at Boston and Albany and Harrisburg, the author of *War Government* seemed unable to imagine the doubts, the dissensions, the honest differences of opinion, and the immense practical difficulties which bedevilled the men who lived through the crowded days of the Civil War. He was generous enough to admire and praise the genius and the courage of the generals who did their best to destroy the Union, but the "amiable Copperhead" was beyond his comprehension. He was probably one of those safe citizens who are so happy as to be able to conclude that the Civil War was, on the whole, "a good thing for the country"—it made the United States "a nation." He took his last leave of the dauntless governor as follows:

> Horatio Seymour, though extraordinary and not easily comprehended, was not an anomalous character. . . . He has been charged with "inordinate ambition" by some who ought to have known him well; but there was never a greater error in analyzing character. While he possessed some of the better traits of an ambitious demagogue, he was too much refined, in heredity and essence, to sink to the level of a vulgar populace. And something more kept him from the great ambition which controls heroes, for he had not the fibre of the forcible men of history. . . . Seymour was not a mere factious agitator . . . his intellect was duly perceptive. There was some reason for his discordant acts as governor from day to day. The cause was not in his own creative reason, but in the errant, disturbing forces of a powerful social faction, which sent his wits wool-gathering, instead of into the calm, considered action of a statesman. . . . He was moved by sentiment, when he ought to have been anchored by solid thought.[41]

To Weeden, Seymour was a case of "morbid conscience" coupled with "talent," a man "most dangerous in the crises of great affairs." That he and "Robert C. Winthrop should have been muddled . . . by events [was] a curiosity of history."

41. Weeden, *War Government*, 303–305 and 257.

Seymour heard and read harsher words in his own time, but he most of all, perhaps, would have enjoyed this hostile glance into the depth and gloom of his character. He was always a hard-working office-holder and during his second term he had to divide his industrious attention between the business of the war for the Union and the government of New York. The assembly was tied and tumultuous. A majority of twelve in the state senate which held over from the election of 1861 gave the Republicans the power to choose a successor to Senator Preston King on joint ballot, but the houses could not meet together until both were organized. Not until January 26, after the assembly had been in session nineteen days, was Callicott, a Brooklyn Democrat, made speaker on the ninety-third ballot. Then, for the first time, the governor's message was officially received. As part of the trade which put Callicott in the chair of the assembly, the Republicans sent Edwin D. Morgan to the Senate of the United States.[42]

In spite of the common belief that Seymour was defeated for governor in 1864 because of what was supposed to be his attitude toward Lincoln and the Civil War, it is probable that his failure to secure a third term was owing chiefly, if not wholly, to his having alienated powerful support within his party by certain acts connected with state policy. In the autumn of 1862 the Democrats of New York City were united for the moment because their defeat in the mayoralty election of 1861 had robbed them of patronage, the perennial reason for their quarrels. As often as they held office they fell into feuds over the spoils. In 1862, however, the two great factions in the city composed their differences and put up a fusion ticket, backed by Nelson J. Waterbury of Tammany, and Fernando Wood of

42. Morgan had made money as a grocer in Hartford, Connecticut, and then moved to New York City, where he became a millionaire merchant. He served as governor of New York from 1859 to 1863. Horace Greeley bitterly opposed his election as senator, but Thurlow Weed succeeded with his scheme and, having humiliated the editor of the *Tribune* for the third time, he withdrew from the control of the Albany *Evening Journal*. He had settled the score at last for Greeley's part in the defeat of Seward at Chicago in 1860. See Alexander, *History*, III, 53–57.

Mozart Hall. As a consequence of this truce Wood went to Washington as a representative in the Congress, and Seymour carried the city for governor by 31,309.[43]

His first official act was to set about removing the police commissioners of New York City — Thomas C. Acton and three others. On January 1, 1863, he summoned the commissioners to Albany to answer the accusation of having permitted the police to make arbitrary arrests of citizens and of allowing the prisons to be used for the illegal incarceration of persons against whom no charges had been preferred. During the election Superintendent Kennedy had issued an order threatening the arrest of any aliens who tried to vote after having claimed exemption from being called on to fill up the quota of soldiers assigned to the state by the federal government. The order was Kennedy's way of publishing the accusation that the Democratic machine of the city voted persons who were not citizens. The Democrats denied this, and declared that the Republican organization at Albany was using its control of the police commission to carry the state for General Wadsworth. Kennedy, so it was said, was merely trying to intimidate voters who could give no good reason for not having joined the army.

To many New Yorkers Seymour's action in calling the commissioners to Albany was simply carrying into effect the Democratic victory at the polls in November: it was high time for the Republicans to be taught a lesson. To other citizens, it was an act of revenge and political place-making pure and simple. The commissioners refused to go into Albany County for trial, declaring that any charges must be sent to the district attorney of New York County, whose duty it was to examine witnesses in the court of common pleas and certify to the governor the evidence taken. Seymour's lifelong defense of the doctrine that communities should govern themselves whenever possible came home to roost at last. It is pleasant to remember that he had the good grace to yield.[44]

43. Myers, *Tammany Hall*, 202–205.
44. Brummer, *History*, 261–263; New York *Times*, January 3, 1863.

The commissioners did not go to Albany, but the dispute between them and the governor was a complicated one and had grave consequences. The real difference went back to 1857, at which time the legislature had taken the control of the board of commissioners out of the hands of the head of the city and placed it with the state government at Albany. This act, of course, was directly contrary to Seymour's notions of what was fitting and proper, but the Republicans were determined to have the whip-hand of a community which was nearly always Democratic. The election of George Opdyke as mayor in 1861, however, had placed a member of their party in the city hall itself. The commissioners had been riding high and seemed pleased to act without the sympathy and coöperation of the politicians of the city. The moment a Democratic governor tried to call the commissioners to account the Republican members of the legislature rushed to their assistance. As a consequence of his failure to remove the commissioners, Seymour had a hostile board on his hands during the days of the draft riots, and Mr. Hawley, the chief clerk of the commission, acted as the channel of communication between the governor and the men he had tried to remove.[45] James Buchanan, who watched Seymour during his second term with attention and nearly always with sympathy, regretted that the governor had been obliged to "back out" in regard to his proposed removal of the board.[46]

In 1864, a compromise was negotiated at Albany with a view to setting up bi-partisan control of the commissioners of police. The Democrats at once began to quarrel among themselves as to who should have the two places assigned to their party. Tammany insisted on Elijah F. Purdy and Samuel Jones, but Seymour was determined that Bosworth and McMurray, the men he had previously tried to appoint to the commission, should go on the board. A bill went through the legislature designating Bosworth, McMurray, Acton, and Bergen as the four members of the new commission — the last two men being those

45. Headley, *Riots of New York*, 226–227.
46. Buchanan, *Works*, XI, 327–328.

whom the governor had tried to remove in 1863. Seymour signed this measure, and his enemy, Acton, remained president of the board. Acton continued Kennedy in the office of superintendent. The newspapers of New York indulged in an editorial rough-and-tumble over the question for the better part of two years, and Bennett's *Herald* finally came to the conclusion that the governor had "no back-bone whatever." Seymour's course disgusted Tammany.[47]

The Wigwam had still another reason for resentment. In the spring of 1863 Peter B. Sweeny, a friend and associate of William Marcy Tweed, went up to Albany to lobby in the legislature for the Broadway Railroad bill. The object of this bill was the granting of the traction rights on Broadway, in New York City, for ten years. Writing to Seymour on January 4, 1863, Tweed told him that Sweeny would call at his office "to explain the views" of the general committee of which Tweed was chairman. Dating his letter from Tammany Hall, Tweed concluded significantly: "We ask from you a fair consideration *of and on* all matters pertaining to the City as our organizations must be duly recognized to preserve our strength."[48] The traction bill came along soon after Sweeny's visit. On hearing what was proposed, a group of merchant-princes of New York offered to accept the projected franchise under conditions more favorable to the public. These volunteers were ready to restrict the company they planned to form to a passenger fare of three cents — or to pay the city or the state two hundred thousand dollars annually in lieu of all license fees if they were authorized to charge a fare of five cents in accordance with

47. Brummer, *History*, 368–370. On December 31, 1863, Seymour had notified Acton and Bergen that he would remove them on the charges of the district attorney. On January 2, 1864, the commissioners replied that the governor had no authority to remove them without an investigation of the charges as presented. Seymour appointed three new commissioners, but the old ones refused to give way. The effect of the legislative act a few weeks later was to leave four men in office — the first two of Seymour's three going on the board. For a description of the new police bill, see the New York *Times*, January 9, 1864.

48. New York Historical Society: Seymour Papers: William M. Tweed to Horatio Seymour, January 4, 1863.

the terms of the bill which had been reported out by the legislative committee on railroads. The merchants were ready to insert a clause providing for recapture by the city.

The scramble for favors was complicated by a quarrel among capitalists. On April 21, 1863, Commodore Vanderbilt persuaded the common council of the city to grant him the right to extend the Harlem Railroad, which he controlled, from Fourth Avenue down Manhattan Island to the Battery by a traction line on Broadway. His angry rivals at Tammany Hall determined to get a franchise from the superior power of the state, according to which they could lay their own tracks on Broadway or compel Vanderbilt to buy them out. Dean Richmond and Peter Cagger, two of the most powerful men in the councils of the Democratic party of the state, had long been bitter rivals of Vanderbilt in the business of handling the freight which went up and down the Hudson Valley. Naturally enough, Richmond and Cagger were pleased to make trouble for Vanderbilt by helping Sweeny to push his franchise through the legislature.

Thus Governor Seymour was confronted with another difficult and delicate problem. Richmond was state chairman of his party, and Vanderbilt was the rival of his friends. The city had granted one franchise, and the state had granted another. Whatever principle was involved in the dispute rested on the old question of the right of a community to home rule. The governor called Samuel J. Tilden to Albany and, having talked the matter over with him, vetoed the Broadway Railroad bill on the basis of the expert advice of the latter. According to Tilden:

> As early as 1863 some of them [the Tweed Ring] became deeply embittered because, being summoned by Governor Seymour to a consultation about the Broadway Railroad Bill, I advised him to veto it.[49]

Seymour based his veto, after "a full and patient hearing," on a respect for the power of local government: the city itself should grant its traction franchises, and not the legislature. Although it was argued that the council's grant to Vanderbilt

49. Tilden, *Public Writings*, I, 563.

had been improperly negotiated, nevertheless for him to sign the bill before him was to suppose that a second wrong could right the first.[50] The squabble gave him great anxiety, and his conduct required character and courage. John Pruyn found him exhausted with the fatigue of the fight:

> Returned from New York in the early train. On coming up to my house about three o'clock found Governor Seymour in the library. He had come here to get out of the crowd and excitement at his office. I found that he had just vetoed the Broadway Railroad bill, which has been the subject of so much anxiety and feeling.
>
> A cheerful fire and a cup of tea helped to recruit him. He dined with me and remained till [late] in the evening.[51]

Still another veto was called for by the governor's respect for the constitution of his state. The result of the election of 1862, as well as the example of other states, had determined the Republicans to give votes to the soldiers absent in service against the South. They felt that they could have elected Wadsworth if the men in the army could have taken part in the poll. By 1863 it was calculated that almost two hundred thousand citizens (or nearly one-third of the total number of electors) were out of the state — or not present in their precincts. On January 6, 1863, a bill to permit absent voting was introduced into the legislature. On April 8 a resolution to amend the constitution of 1846 so that soldiers might vote was also brought in, and on April 13 Governor Seymour sent in a special message recommending that this method be followed as more proper. The next day a bill for a constitutional amendment was submitted to the senate, but in the meantime the first bill, giving the vote to soldiers by mere legislative action, was making its way through the two houses. This bill passed on April 22–23, 1863, and Seymour promptly vetoed it as unconstitutional. By putting the act ahead of the amendment, Republican political strategy loaded Seymour with the blame for having denied a vote to the soldiers of New York. This charge damaged the

50. Lincoln, *Messages*, v, 517–520.

51. Journal of John V. L. Pruyn, May 7, 1863.

Democrats at the next election for the assembly in the autumn of 1863.[52]

The subsequent history of the granting of the franchise to soldiers is worthy of note. The constitutional amendment on which Seymour had insisted first and last was ratified at a special election on March 8, 1864. Then a new bill was brought into the legislature, permitting the soldiers to receive and mark their ballots in camp and mail them to the districts where they lived. Proxies were to cast them on election day. The Australian ballot, it will be remembered, was still a reform of the future; therefore it was provided that the tickets for the rival candidates should be distributed throughout the armies by special agents, to be designated by each party. Governor Seymour signed this bill on April 21, 1864, and the New York soldiers voted in the state and national elections in that year. It remains to be seen what use was made of this measure.

As if disputes within the state were not sufficiently vexatious for the leader of the Democratic opposition, a sudden political explosion in Ohio drove Seymour into public criticism of Lincoln. Early in the spring of 1863 Clement Laird Vallandigham, whose term in the House of Representatives had expired on March 3, visited Albany for a conference with the governor and the leaders of his party.[53] The objects of this conference were two: the first purpose was to discuss conscription and the suspension of habeas corpus, both of which measures Vallandigham had vigorously opposed during the last days of the expiring Congress. The second object was to unite the Democrats of the nation on a reasoned policy of opposition to what they called the radical government of Lincoln. The eastern Democrats,

52. Lincoln, *Constitutional History*, II, 235–240; and Benton, *Voting in the Field*, 132–170. Seymour's veto ran directly counter to the opinion of his inveterate enemy, Daniel S. Dickinson, who declared the bill was constitutional — his advice having been asked by resolution of the senate. Dickinson served as attorney-general of New York in 1862 and 1863. The veto, which was sustained in the assembly but not in the senate, was based upon the constitutional objection to proxy voting. In order to embarrass Seymour, no bill for actual voting in the field was brought in at the time.

53. Brummer, *History*, 303.

who preached respect for the Constitution, were lining up behind the leadership of Seymour; while those in the West talked peace and were reviled as Copperheads. Vallandigham was their most spectacular spokesman. After spending several days in Albany the dramatic gentleman from Dayton set out for his home country in Ohio.

Very soon thereafter two distinctly positive characters came into sensational collision on the soil of that state. Vallandigham was a remarkable man in more than one way, and the memory of his person and his power of speech was a long time dying in the land where he lived and moved and had his being. Son of a Presbyterian clergyman and part-time school-teacher, brought up as an apostle of the gospel of temperance (which meant total abstinence), Vallandigham had fought his own way up the ladder in both politics and law. The youth was father to the man: at one time he threatened to kill himself rather than swallow the glass of liquor which certain of his less abstemious friends tried to force down his throat. He quarrelled with the president of the college where he studied over the matter of a recitation on the subject of constitutional law and stubbornly declined to apply for his diploma. He was a fierce and even fanatical opponent of the use of force — so much so, that when the fever of the Maine laws for compulsory prohibition swept through the country in the fifties, he refused to support the cause of "temperance" any longer. If present-day knowledge of Clement Laird Vallandigham had been at the disposal of the public, President Lincoln might well have hesitated before allowing his government to become embroiled with a man so brave, so honest, and so determined as he.[54]

Vallandigham went back to Ohio by way of an excursion into Connecticut, arriving at Dayton on March 13. He was a private citizen for the moment, although he was probably planning the candidacy for governor which he undertook in the autumn. At Cincinnati General Ambrose E. Burnside of Rhode

54. James L. Vallandigham, *A Life of C. L. Vallandigham* (Baltimore, 1872).

CLEMENT L. VALLANDIGHAM

FRANCIS KERNAN

Island sat enthroned as commander of the Department of the Ohio. His dreadful failure at Fredericksburg had caused his removal to a good, safe distance from the field, where he could rule civilians instead of fighting soldiers. The sense that he was in disgrace made Burnside authoritative, touchy, and ferocious. With the suspension of habeas corpus this discredited general began to govern the citizens of Ohio, Kentucky, Indiana, and Illinois by means of general orders which he contrived at his headquarters with the same stubborn indiscretion he had shown at Fredericksburg. Order Number Nine, for instance, forbade all criticism of the civil or military policy of the administration; Order Fifteen prohibited the people from keeping or bearing arms; Order Thirty-Eight proclaimed the new crime of *implied* treason. The thunderbolts of this dusty Jupiter made the air of the North West electric. Vallandigham was just the sort of man who was destined to defy him.

On March 21 at Hamilton and on April 30 at Columbus the former representative made speeches which repeated the criticism he had hurled at the government of Lincoln from the floor of the House. He was fond of telling the public that if it was treason to discourage enlistments, then the generals of Lincoln were the most conspicuous of all traitors. Having read the speeches at Hamilton and Columbus, Burnside put several of his officers into plain clothes with orders to attend a meeting at Mount Vernon, where Vallandigham was scheduled to speak on the first of May. The spies were present according to command and took "fragmentary notes" of what was said and returned to headquarters. On the basis of this evidence Vallandigham was dragged from his home in Dayton at half-past two in the morning of May 5 by Captain Hutton, a member of Burnside's staff.[55] This spectacular arrest, accompanied as it was by words and gestures of defiance from the victim and the

55. For Vallandigham's speech, see Vallandigham, *Vallandigham*, 248–253. A detailed account of the arrest and trial of Vallandigham and the letters to and from Lincoln, with editorial comment, will be found in S. D. Carpenter, *Logic of History. Five Hundred Political Texts* (Madison, Wisconsin, 1864), 190–222.

blowing of bugles by Hutton's military escort, was carried out in comic-opera style, but raised an uproar through the North.[56] The act was worse than a crime; it was a blunder, and Secretary Welles confided to his diary the grave embarrassment and the concern which it caused the Cabinet.[57] Yet the President himself, according to his attorney-general, became noticeably ill-tempered at the suing out of writs of habeas corpus for the release of men his generals had arrested.[58]

The sequence of the case is well known: Vallandigham refused to plead before the court-martial, and Humphrey H. Leavitt, the United States district judge, denied his attorneys a writ of habeas corpus. Appeal was carried to the Supreme Court, but the justices decided that they could not function in cases of military law or commission. Thus this coördinate branch of the federal government, which is sometimes supposed to be the guardian of the ark of our independence in fair weather and foul, abdicated its great office during the Civil War. A little more than two years, however, after it discreetly refused to order that Vallandigham be set free, the Supreme Court practically reversed itself on the subject in the Milligan Case, the final decision of which declared that the Congress had no power to authorize military commissions, and that martial law could be proclaimed only in cases of actual invasion or disorder which closed the courts and deposed civil administration.[59] Burnside and the lawyers left Lincoln holding a bomb, and before it should explode in his hands, the President sent his

56. For the great meeting of protest in Union Square, New York City, see the New York *Herald*, May 19, 1863.

57. Welles, *Diary*, I, 306; *Official Records of the Rebellion*, Second Series, V, 717. For Rhodes on the subject of arbitrary arrest, see *History*, III, 442–443. A year later, when the unhappy Burnside launched another drive for the conquest of the South by the arbitrary suppression of the Chicago *Times*, in accordance with General Order 84, Secretary Stanton was forced to check the general's ardor by directing him to revoke the order and to take care to make no more military arrests or seizures of newspapers without previous consultation with the President. See Randall, *Constitutional Problems*, 493–496.

58. Bates, *Diary*, 306.

59. Randall, *Constitutional Problems*, 176–179 and 179–183; Warren, *Supreme Court in United States History*, III, 146–149; see, also, Rhodes, *History*, IV, 247–253.

unwelcome political prisoner through the lines and into the South. The act was artful — but evasion, pure and simple; a Seymour would have returned Vallandigham to the home from which he had been kidnaped.

On May 14 the governor of New York first gave public expression to his vigorous and pointed disapproval of the outrage.

I do not hesitate to denounce the whole transaction as cowardly, brutal, and infamous. Unless the case shall assume some new aspect, I shall take an early public occasion to express my views upon the subject.[60]

On Saturday, May 16, a mass meeting to protest against the rash folly of Burnside was held in the capitol at Albany. Seymour was unable to be present but he sent the chairman of the meeting a letter which was printed and circulated and read all through the North.

I cannot attend the meeting at the capitol this evening, but I wish to state my opinion in regard to the arrest of Mr. Vallandigham. It is an act which has brought dishonor upon our country. It is full of danger to our persons and our homes. It bears upon its front a conscious violation of law and justice.

Acting upon the evidence of detailed informers, shrinking from the light of day, in the darkness of night, armed men violated the home of an American citizen, and furtively bore him away to military trial, conducted without those safeguards known in the proceedings of our judicial tribunals. The transaction involved a series of offenses against our most sacred rights.

It interfered with the freedom of speech; it violated our rights to be secure in our homes against unreasonable searches and seizures; it pronounced sentence without trial, save one which was a mockery, which insulted as well as wronged. The perpetrators now seek to impose punishment, not for an offense against law, but for the disregard of an invalid order put forth in the utter disregard of the principles of civil liberty.

If this proceeding is approved by the government, and sanctioned by the people, it is not merely a step toward revolution, it is revolution; it will not only lead to military despotism, it establishes military despotism. In this aspect it must be accepted, or in this aspect rejected. If it is upheld, our liberties are overthrown; the safety of our persons, security of our property, will hereafter depend upon the arbitrary will of such military rulers as may be placed over us; while our Constitutional guarantees will be broken down.

Even now, the governors and courts of some of the great Western States

60. New York State Library: Seymour Papers: Horatio Seymour to George H. Pendleton, May 14, 1863.

have sunk into insignificance before the despotic powers claimed and exercised by military men who have been sent into their borders. It is a fearful thing to increase the danger which now overhangs us, by treating the law, the judiciary, and the State authorities with contempt.

The people of this country now wait with the deepest anxiety the decisions of the administration upon these acts. Having given it a generous support in the conduct of the war, we pause to see what kind of government it is for which we are asked to pour out our blood and our treasures.

The action of the administration will determine in the minds of more than one half of the people of the loyal States, whether the war is waged to put down rebellion at the South or destroy free institutions at the North. We look for its decision with most solemn solicitude.[61]

In this matter of Vallandigham Seymour's consistency was sounder than Lincoln's logic.[62] He continued to call attention to the violent wrong which had been done and even went so far as to hope that Vallandigham would be elected governor of Ohio in the campaign of the autumn of 1863, at which time he was defeated by more than 100,000 votes by Brough, another Democrat, whom the Unionists drafted to run against him.[63] Lincoln's central charge against Vallandigham was baseless, nor was that charge ever brought against him. The President "saw Burnside through" at no little cost to his own reputation in the long run.[64] He had quite properly given up Mason and Slidell in 1861; to have sent Vallandigham back home in 1863 would have added to his honor. Seymour's letter to the meeting at Albany became the text of Lincoln's constitutional opponents in the North. The Democratic state committee declared a "lack of confidence in the Administration's ability to bring about a peace beneficial to the whole Union," and endorsed the governor's denunciation of the kidnaping of Vallandigham. On June 3 a mass-meeting or state convention for "peace and

61. New York *Herald*, May 19, 1863. The conservative character of the men who presided and spoke at this protest meeting in Albany is clearly shown in Brummer. A gathering at Buffalo endorsed Seymour's letter and adopted the resolutions approved at Albany. The Union Square meeting, however, was radical and stormy: Brummer, *History*, 311–315.

62. Charnwood, *Lincoln*, 383–384.

63. New York State Library: Seymour Papers: Horatio Seymour to J. F. McKinney, September 14, 1863.

64. Vallandigham, *Vallandigham*, 312–313.

reunion" crowded the Cooper Institute and jammed the surrounding streets for blocks. The New York *Herald* estimated that thirty thousand people were in the neighborhood. The roar of cheers at the governor's arrival, the shouts for McClellan and Vallandigham, showed how far apart Lincoln and Seymour had drifted during five months.[65]

For two years, and in the very midst of civil war, Governor Seymour tried to maintain the integrity of the Constitution according to his honest understanding of it. This effort brought him into collision with the hasty and arrogant men in the service of Abraham Lincoln. The points of policy in dispute, moreover, were emancipation, conscription, and arbitrary arrest. There is no good reason for believing that either leader was not sincere. Lincoln's position was precarious to the extreme: his motley supporters were by no means united. Thurlow Weed, for instance, thought Horace Greeley was a public nuisance and a danger to the cause of union. All the Blairs despised Charles Sumner. Members of the Cabinet quarrelled and conspired one against the other. Lincoln had to work as well as he could with them all. More than one of his acts is open to serious question. Only the distance of time and his tragic death have lent enchantment to the view.

Yet Seymour led men who lacked a sense of reality. He protested that a constitution was not "a fair-weather thing"—that it was precisely in times of stress and violence that men needed most the common protection of their solemn agreements as to government. The "father of liberty," he declared, was not peace but war. To him, the sight of a Supreme Court which could not, or would not, function was disgraceful. The governor was never so careful or so anxious a lawyer as when he criticized the more surprising deeds of Lincoln. Centuries of experience, he should have remembered, had taught the Romans that in the midst of arms the laws are silent. If Lincoln had kept a strict eye on the Constitution, the North could not have conquered the South.

65. Brummer, *History*, 316–317.

Seymour chose his words far better than he knew — "fair-weather thing" is an apt description of the Constitution, as every national emergency has proved; each storm has twisted it into some new shape. People like to believe that the Supreme Court can protect Americans (even against themselves), but this notion is a snare and a delusion. As the government of the United States exists, only the Congress is supreme during any period of two years. Two-thirds of its members can oust a President and pack the highest court of the land. A mere majority, moreover, could add to the number of the justices — if the President should give his assent.

There is, in fact, a less sensational way by which the Congress can assert its actual supremacy whenever it may please. The late James M. Beck coveted the distinction of being called "the defender of the Constitution," which stood in dire need, so it seemed to him, of all the eloquence and wisdom that could be enlisted in its behalf. Yet in what was to be the last speech of his life he sounded this warning to the lawyers of Boston:

> Remember that the vulnerable point in the heel of our Achilles is that section of the judiciary article of the Constitution which in vague but sweeping language confers upon Congress the power to determine what exceptions there shall be to the appellate jurisdiction of the Supreme Court, and what regulations shall guide them in their procedure.[66]

Some Americans vaguely remember that long ago a President was impeached; they conveniently forget that only one heroic Republican, Ross of Kansas, stood between Andrew Johnson and the complete success of his persecutors. In 1868 the Congress showed its teeth; some day it may bite. They who trust that public opinion will always block a packing of the highest

66. The *Bar Bulletin* (May, 1936): James M. Beck, "The Supreme Court — Today and Tomorrow?" Boston, March 26, 1936. Even in a time of "profound peace and prosperity" the Constitution has been flouted. In 1921, and repeatedly for ten years thereafter, the Congress brazenly declined to reapportion representatives among the states according to the first purpose of the federal census. Thus the electoral vote in the presidential campaigns of 1924 and 1928 was distributed unconstitutionally, for it was based on the population of the states according to the census of 1910, not that of 1920. Had either of these two contests been very close, there might have been trouble — if an under-represented state like California, for instance, had happened to find itself on the losing side.

court fail to recall that the Congress once reversed this very process by abolishing a justiceship in order that Andrew Johnson should not have the filling of it. No decision of the Supreme Court, furthermore, has ever defeated the will of a determined majority of Americans; unpopular verdicts have been negatived by amendments.

Constitutions come and go — more rapidly than ever, nowadays — for whether they know it or not people incline towards Jefferson's opinion that "the world belongs to the living and not to the dead." Too much respect for the past, too great concern for the future, is bound to provoke ridicule among healthy people. If Seymour were alive to-day, he would hesitate, perhaps, to stake his reputation and career on the security of any written compact of government. Life taught him the bitter lesson he had not learned from history: that war — civil war and revolution soonest of all — drives even good men to extremes, leaving those who plead for reason to perish in the cross-fire from passionate partisans of contending wrongs.

XIV

"MY FRIENDS"

1863

AT no time after the foolhardy firing on the *Star of the West* and Fort Sumter did Horatio Seymour support the southern hope for independence. By its fearful choice of secession the South cut loose from the friends of the whole nation in the North; by an ill-considered act of war it gave its enemies the chance to work their will. Lincoln and Seymour were not headed in opposite directions; the difficulty was that the governor of the greatest state in the Union could not accept or endorse all the measures which the radical Republicans pushed through the Congress and extorted from the President. The common goal of the two men was the defeat of the rebellion. Although Seymour had doubted the effectiveness of coercion, after Sumter and Bull Run he saw that conquest was the alternative to compromise. A war for independence, however, can not be compromised. If Seymour ever feared for the Union, Caton confirmed his own opinion that the Middle West would never allow the mouth of the Mississippi River to pass into the hands of an independent power. Dickinson and Greeley persisted in calling Seymour a Copperhead, for it was easier to lump critics and traitors together than to try to do the right thing the right way. It is highly unlikely that either the orator or the editor looked for any evidence on which to convict Seymour of treason.

After eighteen months of war President Lincoln decided that the support of northern radicals was essential to the success of his determination to restore the Union. These radicals demanded their price — something which the much-criticized conservatives of the North never did. By September, 1862, the President shifted sharply from the position he had taken in his first inaugural — the restoration of the Union as it was — and issued his provisional Emancipation Proclamation. Six weeks later, however, his party met spectacular reverses all over the loyal states. Able jurists like Benjamin R. Curtis, for instance, questioned the validity of that proclamation publicly in a pamphlet, *Executive Power*, which was enormously popular throughout the North. There was much force in the argument that for Lincoln to threaten to free the slaves would stiffen and not weaken the resistance of the South. The shift in position would seem to verify the long-lived suspicions of die-hard secessionists of the years 1850–1860.

Yet the great question in regard to the policy which Seymour and his conservative friends urged on the government remains unanswered — would the South ever have returned to the Union voluntarily? The cost of conquest in blood and treasure was ghastly to both victor and vanquished, and the reunited nation was never again to be quite the country of the days before the Civil War. Jefferson Davis played at being a George Washington to the bitter end of his lost cause. He was still dreaming and demanding independence on the eve of the fall of Richmond. The one chance for a negotiated peace was that short period which elapsed between the elections of 1862 and the final Emancipation Proclamation of January, 1863. It was Davis and his generals who let that opportunity go by.

Lee probably elected Seymour governor of New York in 1862, although the unlucky nomination of Wadsworth by the Republicans was, it will be remembered, an important contributing cause to the result. Thus the man who put him in the office put him out, as well, for the invasion of Pennsylvania led directly to the indiscreet speed of the draft of 1863 and the riots of July. At the time of Gettysburg Seymour already had his hands full, for of all the war governors, his position was the most delicate and difficult. By the end of September, 1863, he had been able to get back to Utica only once in eight months because of the "engrossing" duties which held him at Albany.[1]

1. New York State Library: Seymour Papers: Letter from Horatio Seymour to J. F. McKinney, September 14, 1863: Clipping from an unidentified newspaper.

He was working desperately to fill up the quota of New York and was working with exceptional success. One of the unfortunate squabbles which hampered his complete coöperation in military matters is typical, if trifling.

The Union League Club of New York City was founded in 1863. That same year it asked Seymour for permission to recruit a negro regiment in New York, but the governor refused the authority on the ground that he had no power to grant the request. The club promptly appealed directly to Secretary Stanton, who was glad to give the members what they asked for. The regiment was raised, and eighteen thousand dollars were collected for its expenses. In due course the negro soldiers were paraded on Broadway and marched off to the front in January, 1864. Edward Channing called attention to the painful practice of rounding up black men as a means of filling quotas after the signing of the Enrollment Act on March 3, 1863. There is no reason to suppose that the ladies who presented the colors to that regiment and the gentlemen who paid its bills did not know that every negro in it counted to the credit of the quota of the state at Washington and diminished the drain on white men by just so much.[2]

The campaign of Gettysburg forced the governor of New York into the most exciting circumstances of his whole life — a time of crisis and ill will. As late as June 26, when Seymour was sending thousands of soldiers into Pennsylvania, Colonel John Dash Van Buren, who served on his staff, was carrying messages to Lincoln for him urging the President "to pay no attention to newspaper statements as to the Governor's unfriendliness."[3] Secretary Stanton had first called for help with

2. Benson J. Lossing, *The Empire State* (Hartford, Connecticut, 1888), 535. For Seymour's failure to become a member of the Union League Club, see Alexander, *History*, III, 61.

3. *Century Magazine* (February, 1907), 501: Colonel Silas W. Burt, "Lincoln on His Own Story-Telling." Colonel Burt's description of the visit of Van Buren is interesting from more than one point of view. Mrs. C. S. Fairchild, niece of Governor Seymour, resented Burt's invention of a wholly "mythical cousin" who drank too much whiskey: New York Historical Society: Seymour Papers: Colonel Van Buren, a member of the assembly from Orange County, had been appointed

a telegram dated June 15, and on the same day Seymour wired him twice and immediately began to rush troops to the aid of General Meade.[4] Governor Curtin of Pennsylvania joined in what became a clamor for help. There can be no question that Seymour did his best, and did well, all during the terrible two weeks and more when Lee had got behind Washington and seemed to be heading for Philadelphia. Four persons intimately concerned with the campaign which ended at Gettysburg have left direct and indisputable evidence of his invaluable services to the cause of the Union — Lincoln, Stanton, Charles Anderson Dana, who was then assistant secretary of war, and Governor Curtin. The press echoed Lincoln and Stanton in praise of the governor of New York. If the *National Intelligencer* is to be believed, John Albion Andrew did not do nearly so well in 1862 as Seymour in 1863.[5] As late as 1868 Curtin rebuked Stanton and his fellows for calling Seymour's loyalty to the North into question. According to Curtin, the Democrats held the "trump card" in that matter.[6]

George Opdyke, the Republican mayor of New York, protested when he learned that all the troops had been ordered to leave the city for the front, but Major-General Sandford declared that the governor must be obeyed.[7] Seymour planned to replace the soldiers who had left with militia from the interior of the state, but General Wool requested him to countermand his order to this effect.[8] This very important alteration of plans seems to have been called for by the refusal of regular army

paymaster-general by Seymour, on May 26, 1863. This same Van Buren acted as go-between for Seymour and Chief-Justice Chase in 1868.

4. For this Gettysburg correspondence, see Seymour, *Public Record*, 111–117.

5. *National Intelligencer*, July 16, 1864. This item refers to Andrew's response to Stanton's request for aid in 1862 when "Stonewall" Jackson was invading the valley of the Shenandoah.

6. *National Intelligencer*, August 22, 1868. The letters of Stanton for the President and himself are in Seymour, *Public Record*, 113, 116, and 117; Dana's evidence will be found in the New York *Sun* of February 14, 1886. For messages not in the *Public Record*, see *Official Records of the Rebellion*, Series One, XXVII, parts 2 and 3, serial numbers 44 and 45.

7. Opdyke, *Official Documents*, 264.

8. Lincoln, *Messages*, V, 549.

officers to station militia in the federal forts of the harbor. Between sixteen and twenty thousand troops left New York State during June and July of 1863.[9] There was a general agreement as to the fact of Seymour's prompt coöperation.[10] Later on, it was convenient, for one reason or another, for certain people to forget this fact.

The Civil War was decided at Gettysburg, and Seymour not only played an important part in the victory but acted a minor rôle in the famous aftermath of the battle. When the national cemetery was dedicated in November, 1863, he represented New York at the exercises. A correspondent of the Philadelphia *Press*, who watched the governors of the loyal states walking to and fro and talking together in the railroad station at York on their way to the ceremonies, thought Seymour, "with his quick eyes, gentlemanly bearing, and bland and polished manners," divided with Governor Curtin the honor of being the handsomest man in the group. It was noticed, also, that when the governor of New York greeted John Brough, of Ohio, he asked after Vallandigham with "dry pleasantry" and received the laconic reply that Ambrose Burnside's prisoner of state was then "in Canada."

Everybody remembers the circumstances — how Edward Everett of Harvard, who was expected to be the grand orator of the occasion, filled an hour with noble sentiments and glittering phrases, and how Lincoln followed him and made the day immortal in five minutes. Seymour spoke, too, but his short address to the soldiers of his state was nothing but a side-show to the main tent. He did not try hard like Everett or triumph like Lincoln; but his few words were also plain and to the point.

Sergeant, I place these colors in your hand in the firm confidence that they will be borne through every field of triumph, of trial, and of danger, in a way that will do honor to yourselves; to the great State which you represent, and the still greater country to which you belong. May God bless you

9. The Seneca *Observer*, November 2, 1864; Brummer, *History*, 320.

10. Alexander, *History*, III, 66; Brummer, *History*, 320; Rhodes, *History*, IV, 273–276: "No response was so prompt, no action so effective, as that of Horatio Seymour of New York."

as you serve your country in the distant fields of danger. We find in those glorious fields you left behind you, many who are not indifferent to this conflict — who are not indifferent to the welfare of the whole Union. I do not doubt, therefore, that when you shall return from your dangerous fields of duty, you will bring back this standard to place among the archives of our State with honorable mention of the services her sons have performed. I do not doubt that, though it may perhaps be returned torn and stained, yet it will be still more glorious, and with glorious recollections clustering around it.[11]

The day after Gettysburg, Governor Seymour went to the Academy of Music in Brooklyn to speak at a celebration of the Fourth of July. As regards the time of its delivery this speech was probably the most unfortunate of his whole career.[12] If it be true that the repulse of Lee at Gettysburg had so filled "Copperheads with dismay" that Seymour was "compelled to omit from his speech . . . a fierce attack upon the war management of the Government and its generals and an eulogy of McClellan,"[13] the orator of the day might have been wiser if he had edited his speech even more thoroughly than he did. He opened by referring to the "broken promises" of victory — this the day after Lee had been checked in his invasion of Pennsylvania, and Vicksburg had opened its gates to General Grant. If the satisfaction of saving Philadelphia seemed only negative at the time when the decisive battle of the Civil War had been fought on northern soil, the opening of the Mississippi River was a major triumph for the North. The tide had turned, but Seymour was not quick to see the shift of it. He missed his chance to get his share of credit for helping to drive Lee out of Pennsylvania.

Fellow-Citizens: — When I accepted the invitation to speak, with others at this meeting, we were promised the downfall of Vicksburg, the opening of the Mississippi, the probable capture of the confederate capital, and the exhaustion of the rebellion. By common consent all parties had fixed upon this day when the results of the campaign should be known, to mark out

11. Seymour, *Public Record*, 370.

12. Seymour, *Public Record*, 118–124. See the New York *Tribune*, July 6, 1863, for a part of this speech.

13. *Official Records of the Rebellion*, Series One, XXVII, part 3, serial number 45, 552–553.

that line of policy which they felt that our country should pursue. But in the moment of expected victory there came the midnight cry for help from Pennsylvania, to save its despoiled fields from the invading foe, and, almost within sight of this great commercial metropolis, the ships of your merchants were burned to the water's edge.[14]

Because the draft riots broke out nine days later certain suspicious people tried to lay part of the blame for them on the governor's speech in Brooklyn. An examination of the text of Seymour's address will show that there is no ground for any such charge.[15] Stripped of incidental criticism the governor's words were mainly a repetition of opinions which he had expressed publicly in both 1861 and 1862. Thomas H. Seymour, who had been governor of Connecticut, and Senator George H. Pendleton of Ohio spoke from the same platform. The comment of the New York *Herald* was caustic, but thereby hangs a tale. Bennett had a grievance against the governor of New York and he made the most of his chance to jeer at the goings-on in Brooklyn.

On the Fourth of July Governor Seymour of this State, ex-Governor Seymour, of Connecticut, and the Honorable Mr. Pendleton, of Ohio, delivered speeches at the Academy of Music before a new democratic club, composed of politicians as small and unappreciative as the speakers themselves. We took the trouble to publish these addresses in yesterday's *Herald*, and are almost sorry that we wasted so much valuable space upon such trashy productions. In the midst of the greatest crisis the world ever saw — with the news of the greatest victory of the war just electrifying the country — these political trimmers spent the precious hours of our national anniversary in talking about the arrest of Vallandigham and the suppression of a few tuppenny papers, and the awful despotism which these actions of the administration had imposed upon the country. . . . The more these small fry politicians chatter, the firmer becomes our conviction that if a couple of hundred niggerhead and copperhead organs had been suppressed, and about 5000 niggerhead and copperhead leaders thrown into a common prison, long ago, the country would have been in a far better position to-day and in the future.

The two Seymours and Mr. Pendleton, or Peddlington, did well to select the Academy of Music for their exhibition. Mozart Hall has sunk com-

14. Seymour, *Public Record*, 118.

15. July 4, 1863, fell on Saturday. Seymour spoke at the Society of Tammany at half-past one; about half-past two he addressed the "large assemblage," "nearly one half of them ladies," in Brooklyn.

pletely out of sight, and Tammany Hall, covered with ivy and redolent of Jacksonian memories, was celebrating the glorious victory won by the brave Army of the Potomac over Jeff. Davis' best generals and best soldiers. It is most curious and remarkable that the Academy of Music orators had nothing to say about this victory.[16]

Now it is obvious that the *Herald* either had undergone a complete change of heart since it had chuckled over the defeat of Wadsworth in November, 1862, or that some unhappy incident had intervened between election day and the Fourth of July. James Gordon Bennett was a very practical man and whenever he failed to get what he wanted, he got nasty. In July, 1863, he had his own good reason for roasting Seymour, for the governor had refused to put their joint friend on the board of commissioners of the metropolitan police. The editor had asked for the appointment directly, and immediately after Seymour's inauguration. He had pressed for favorable and speedy action.[17] Thus, by the middle of the summer of 1863, both the *Tribune* and the *Herald* were sniping at Seymour.

The Fourth of July speech at the Brooklyn Academy of Music is an unexceptionable plea for the long-sighted wisdom which respects civil rights of citizens in time of war. Defeat of the rebellion demanded a united North, and hunting Copperheads, or so it seemed to the speakers in Brooklyn, was hardly an effective method of arriving at the goal. The administration, thought Seymour, should take care to set a good example, for the "bloody," "treasonable," and "revolutionary" doctrine of "public necessity" could be used "by a mob as well as by a government." Against the excuse that national emergency knew no law Seymour brought his favorite counsel of perfection: "Liberty," he declared, "was born in war; it does not die in war." It took the experience of four bitter years to teach him

16. New York *Herald*, July 7, 1863.

17. "Your note a few days ago was received and is satisfactory. The bearer of this letter is Judge Russell, an old friend of mine and of yours. . . . In the proposed removal of the Police Commissioners, I would be much gratified if you could give him one of the vacant seats. . . . *If possible I hope you will consider of this speedily.*" New York Historical Society: Seymour Papers: James G. Bennett to Horatio Seymour, January 2, 1863.

that if war begets liberty, peace gives it birth. The best section of the Brooklyn speech is made up of those words with which the governor prophesied the dreary and disgraceful years of reconstruction.

No victory can restore greatness, and glory, and power to a people who are unworthy of liberty. No peace will bring back prosperity to a land which cannot understand the great principles upon which governments should be protected and the great objects for which governments are instituted.[18]

The hostile criticism called forth by the Brooklyn speech was little or nothing compared with what was to come after. Within two weeks Seymour was to face the charge which would dog his footsteps as long as he lived. The Civil War seems far off now to men and women who live in a world which took its present shape in the summer of 1914; yet people who would hesitate to try to name the Democrat who ran for President in 1868 are likely to remember that once upon a time a governor of New York called a gang of the rioters his "friends." The fact remains, however, that the man who polled a handsome popular vote against General Grant in 1868 and was not improbably the choice of the white men of the country, never even so much as saw one of those rioters. The uprising against the draft was magnified until it became a political myth, a convenient source of abuse during the presidential campaign of 1868. Even Edward Channing did not get the story quite straight sixty years later — though the "several persons" he reports as having been killed is far nearer the probable total of about eighteen than the fat round figure of one thousand, which became fastened in the records of the time.[19]

Seymour spent the week-end before "the great draft riots" with relatives of his wife, a Mr. and Mrs. James Neilson, who lived in northern New Jersey. He had come down from Albany to inspect the defenses of New York City and after making a tour of the forts in and about the harbor, he left for the country

18. Seymour, *Public Record*, 118–124. In the report of Seymour's speech in the New York *Herald* of July 6, 1863, the word "protected," as given above, reads "predicated."

19. Channing, *United States*, VI, 424.

on the evening of Friday, July 10. The machinery for the first federal draft had been put in order: the enrollment had been made in the spring; the quotas had been assigned to congressional districts, and everything was ready for the drawing of names in "the lottery of life." Then Lee invaded Pennsylvania, and every available soldier was rushed off to Meade's army. Having given up every soldier he could find, Seymour urged the government at Washington to postpone the drawing of names until fresh troops should arrive in the city and complaints against the quotas assigned to certain districts could be heard and adjusted. A more unfavorable moment for the publication of the names of conscripts could hardly have been found, but the federal officials had made their plans, and the decisions of the military were not to be changed.

The gross exaggeration of the New York riots of July was not wholly intentional or malicious. There were unquestionably people who hoped that putting the worst face possible on the affair would give President Lincoln an excuse for proclaiming martial law in the city, and these people made the most of the disturbance. Even friends of Governor Seymour, however, have gone out of their way to praise his cool head and courage in the very midst of what are said to have been terrifying scenes of slaughter. The *Herald* had no love for either Lincoln or Seymour by this time; therefore its comments may be taken as those of a neutral observer of the scene. According to Bennett "a single regiment of militia" could have quelled the whole disturbance on the morning of Monday, July 14, but the call for men to go to Gettysburg is sufficient explanation for the fact that the "single regiment" was not there.

> Now that the smoke and the dust and the noise and confusion of the late riots in this city have cleared away, we may without much difficulty get at their true character, their causes and the elements involved in them. We are all satisfied that while under the general panic which they created throughout Manhattan Island they were greatly magnified — that, in brief, what was supposed to be a prodigious mountain has dwindled down to a contemptible molehill.[20]

20. New York *Herald*, July 24, 1863.

Horace Greeley, for instance, played up the riots for all they were worth in the pages of the *Tribune*. He became so excited on the subject that his journalistic rivals, who were never tired of poking fun at the peculiarities of his person, began to spread the story that the great editor had fled from the city during what his paper called the "bloody week." Bennett made so much sport of him on this score that he goaded Greeley into publishing a detailed account of his goings and comings during the three days of July 13 to 15. Although the soul of the *Tribune* lived well uptown, the long and short of the story amounts to this: on Wednesday, July 15, Greeley, according to his own statement, was compelled to hire a carriage in which to drive to and from his office because there were no street-cars running on that day.[21] The headquarters of the *Tribune* were directly across the street to the east of the city hall from the front steps of which Seymour is believed to have faced a howling and murderous mob. The editor acknowledged that he had armed the staff of his newspaper — he always thought of himself as a shining mark — but declared that right through "bloody week" he took his luncheon daily at the restaurant where he always ate at noon. By way of rebutting Bennett's vexing charge that he had scampered out of the city he solemnly accused the *Herald* of complicity in this quietly planned "rebellion" behind the lines.[22]

Idleness, too much liquor over the week-end, a spirit of mischief, the simian desire to destroy, a bitter feeling against negro labor on the docks, and last but not least, the stubbornly stupid choice of Saturday as the day on which the drawing of the names should begin in New York City — these were the

21. New York *Tribune*, July 16, 1863.

22. New York *Tribune*, August 21, 1863. The arrangement of the news in the *Tribune* during the "bloody week" is interesting. On the morning of Tuesday, July 14, the *Tribune* devoted the whole of the first page to the riots. In the issue of Wednesday morning, July 15, a complete story of the fall of Vicksburg took up five of the six columns on the first page. On the right was a single column with the caption, "The Riot Continued." Vicksburg had surrendered on July 4, 1863; therefore this account of the capitulation was not the "news" but the "story."

circumstances which combined to provoke the lawlessness which Horace Greeley thought was a deep plot to strike the armies of the Union from the rear. Crowds of tipsy citizens paraded with banners bearing the legend, "No draft," built barricades of wagons, held up the horse-cars, cut down telegraph poles, and went through the second-best store of Brooks Brothers like a swarm of locusts. A good-for-nothing Virginian named Andrews — the cheap kind of leader who always comes to the front when rowdies fight with the police — gave the necessary "copper" color to the whole proceeding. That a major was killed and a colored orphan asylum was burned is quite true, but the *Journal of Commerce* called the attention of its readers to the fact that the crowds at every point in the city during the trouble contained thousands of mere "spectators." [23] Within a week of the act for which Seymour has been abused for half a century the New York *Atlas* had printed a statement of the fact that when the governor stood on the steps of the city hall at noon on Tuesday, July 14, he spoke to "the populace in the park, — not to the riotous mob." [24] Yet because the truth has never overtaken the lie the legend lives on like that of the witches who were "burned" at Salem.

To persist in the plan to draw the names of the drafted men on Saturday with full realization that those names would be published in the papers on Sunday — and this in a city stripped of troops for Gettysburg — such want of tact, such lack of a knowledge of human nature, was hardly to be expected, even of soldiers. Yet General Fry could see nothing wrong with what he had done even after he had thought the matter over for twenty years.[25] The draft was a new departure and full of dynamite. More than one of Fry's enrolling officers was shot dead from ambush in Indiana. The astonishing fact is that the law of 1863 did not arouse more resentment than there is any record of. After Lincoln signed the bill much of his time was

23. New York *Journal of Commerce*, July 20, 1863.
24. New York *Atlas*, July 18, 1863.
25. Fry, *New York and Conscription*, 28–31.

devoted to correcting or alleviating the pedantic enforcement of this law by Secretary Stanton and Provost-Marshal-General Fry.

Although federal conscription was a leap in the dark, the Enrollment bill was hustled through an expiring Congress in less than one month. On February 9, 1863, Henry Wilson, of Massachusetts, chairman of the military committee of the Senate, brought in his draft of S. 511 after a preliminary squabble in the Congress over the national use of the militia. On Saturday, February 14, Senator Wilson moved that his bill be taken up on Monday, February 16, when it passed the Senate, matters having been managed in such a way that there was no definite vote on the principle of the measure. It was sent over to the House of Representatives on February 17 and passed on the twenty-fifth by a vote of 115 to 49. It is not true that the "lame ducks" decided the result, for if all the defeated members who were leaving on March 3, 1863, had refrained from voting, the law would have passed both houses just the same.[26] On February 28 the Senate concurred in amendments made by the House, and the enactment was engrossed and signed by the Vice-President and the Speaker on the second of March. President Lincoln approved it on March 3, 1863.

Although the votes of "lame ducks," or members defeated for reëlection, did not decide the result in the House of Representatives, an examination of the division on this important bill is interesting. On February 25, 1863, the House consisted of 181 members.[27] Of these, 105 were going out of office on March 3, 1863 — 59 because they had been beaten in November, 1862, and 46 because they had not offered themselves as candidates. Of the 59 "lame ducks," 43 voted for the bill, and 10

26. For details of the vote in both Senate and House, see the author's manuscript biography of Horatio Seymour in the Harvard College Library, III, 1078–1083: Appendix II, "Congressional Vote on the Enrollment Act, 1863." The complete text of the act is in the *Congressional Globe . . . Third Session of the Thirty-Seventh Congress*, Part II, Appendix (Washington, 1863), 209–211. For the decisive vote in the House, see the *Congressional Globe*, Part II, 1293.

27. *Biographical Directory of the American Congress, 1774–1927* (Washington, 1928), 266–273.

voted against it. Of the 46 who were not candidates in 1862, 35 voted for the bill, and 6 voted against it. Thus, of the 115 representatives who voted for conscription, almost at the end of the Thirty-Seventh Congress, not less than 78 knew that they were no longer responsible to their constituents after March 3, 1863. Only 37 of the men who made up the majority for the bill were in the position of having to "face the music" in November, 1864.

The Senate (48 members) was overwhelmingly Republican, and the changes impending as a result of the elections of 1862 were negligible. As noted above, moreover, parliamentary procedure was used to prevent a clear expression of opinion. The closest vote there occurred on the proposal to amend the bill so as not to exempt governors, judges, and justices of the peace from the operation of the act. This amendment was lost by a vote of 19 to 17. Senator Bayard's motion for the indefinite postponement of consideration of the Enrollment bill as amended by the House was voted down by 35 to 11.

"An Act for Enrolling and Calling out the National Forces, and for other Purposes" ordered the listing of all male citizens of military age; the drawing of sufficient names from these lists to fill up quotas already assigned in such congressional districts as had failed to fill these quotas; and provided for the federal arrest of deserters. This law was a change of policy in so far as it substituted direct action by the national government for the various independent systems of the several states. James Barnet Fry, of Illinois, was chosen to manage both the enrollment and drafting of citizens and given the title of provost-marshal-general of the United States. One of Fry's deputies — an assistant provost-marshal-general — was stationed in the capital of every state. New York was made an exception, three assistants being assigned to that state, one at Albany, one at New York City, and a third at Elmira.[28] For every congressional district there

28. In the northern division (Albany), Major Frederick Townsend, 18th United States Infantry, a resident of Albany; in the southern division (New York City), Colonel Robert Nugent, 69th New York Volunteers, an Irishman, a Democrat, and a resident of the city; in the western division (Elmira), Major A. S. Diven, 107th New York Volunteers, Republican member of the Congress (1861–1863),

was appointed a provost-marshal together with a commissioner and a surgeon, and this board of three men selected the enrolling officers for the district. In describing how the provost-marshals were chosen for the congressional districts of New York, General Fry protested against the charge that politics had had any influence with him. Any one who has a casual acquaintance with the history of New York will find his protest surprising after examining the list of sponsors for the men he named to office. New York, it will be remembered, had gone Democratic in November, 1862; yet the names General Fry offers as evidence of his complete disregard for politics are nearly all those of prominent, active, and partisan Republicans.[29]

New York and the Conscription of 1863, the book which General Fry published the year before Seymour died, is a small, apparently impartial volume, which careful students will not take long in discovering must be used with caution. The author begins his work with an expression of regret at New York's choice of Seymour as governor in 1862 and closes with a chuckle at his defeat for reëlection in 1864. Fry had good reason not to love the governor or his family. As late as 1867 Seymour had referred to him in public as "the weak head of the Enrolling Bureau."[30] A year before, moreover, Senator Roscoe Conkling made Fry the object of a famous attack on the floor of the House, in replying to which a certain James G. Blaine so far forgot himself as to be sorry for what he had said — eighteen years afterward. Conkling opposed Fry's promotion in 1866, calling him a worthless public servant, and denouncing him with all his fascinating power of speech. As soon as Fry had left the army and turned author he set about trying to mend the reputation which Seymour and his decisive brother-in-law had damaged. His book is the dry disquisition of a man accustomed to obey and command — not to reason and persuade.

but recommended by Seward as a friend of Seymour. Townsend had been adjutant-general to Governor John A. King, and later served as presidential elector for Garfield in 1880: Fry, *New York and Conscription*, 14–15.

29. Fry, *New York and Conscription*, 13–15.

30. Seymour, *Public Record*, 300.

It was the success of the South with conscription that decided the North to make this new departure into federal control of the drafting of soldiers. Compulsory service, it was believed, had built up the armies with which Lee wrought havoc during 1862. Directly or indirectly, the system brought three hundred thousand men into the southern ranks. If it won battles, it did not win hearts; yet only North Carolina fought the law through its own courts.[31] There is something amusing and puzzling about the difficulties which both the Union and the Confederacy experienced in trying to persuade or force Americans to go on fighting one another during the four years which decided the fate of secession. The South had not provided for a Supreme Court, and the Enrollment Act of 1863 never came before Chief-Justice Taney and his associates. The constitutionality of forced military service was not passed on by the highest court of the United States until 1918, when the legality of the Selective Service Act of 1917 was unanimously affirmed. In reporting the decision it is interesting to notice that Chief-Justice White, a Democrat, leaned heavily on the Fourteenth Amendment, which, he declared, had made citizenship of the United States "paramount and dominant" instead of subordinate and derivative. [32] The Fourteenth Amendment, it will be remembered, was added to the Constitution after the Civil War.

Governor Seymour was a vigorous opponent of federal conscription, first and last.[33] To begin with, he thought the law was unnecessary — which it would have been if all the states had done as well at finding soldiers as New York. In the second place, he thought the act evasive and dishonest — as indeed it was. Once it was a law, however, he publicly declared that it would never work and ought to be tested in the courts.[34] This opinion carried him beyond the position of many people who approved his course of conduct as a whole. Buchanan, for instance, though he believed that the Enrollment Act was "un-

31. For a thorough study of conscription in the Confederacy, see Albert B. Moore, *Conscription and Conflict in the Confederacy* (New York, 1924).

32. Randall, *Constitutional Problems*, 268–274.

33. Seymour, *Public Record*, 164.

34. Seymour, *Public Record*, 366.

wise and unjust in many of its provisions," thought Seymour was wrong in saying that the law was not constitutional.[35] Early in the spring and summer of 1863 the governor conferred with Major Diven, who was the assistant provost-marshal-general at Elmira.[36] The men exchanged several letters on the subject of the draft and on May 22 had a long and confidential interview at Albany, in the course of which the governor asked the major to assure President Lincoln that there could be no question of his support in putting down the rebellion, but that he was "extremely tenacious in relation to the question of arbitrary arrests" and doubted the constitutionality of the Enrollment Act. On August 6, Major Diven informed Seymour that he had gone to Washington as he had promised him and was ordered to report that the executive officers of the government of the United States "will do nothing to assume that these laws are invalid, particularly as in this case they entertained no doubts as to the constitutionality of the law providing for the draft." Major Diven urged Governor Seymour to promote an application for a writ of habeas corpus directly to one of the justices of the Supreme Court.

Seymour was not alone in what sounds like a strange opinion in view of the plain words of the Constitution. The supreme court of Pennsylvania declared the Enrollment Act unconstitutional by a vote of three to two but reversed its decision by the same vote in 1864 after an election. The United States circuit courts in Pennsylvania and Illinois, on the other hand, upheld the law in two important decisions.[37] Horace Greeley added to the confusion by vigorously protesting against conscription in a letter to Secretary Stanton dated June 12, 1863.[38] Just one week later Seymour wrote Lincoln that he had enlisted the services of Tilden, who was going on to Washington for the purpose of stating his "views and wishes" with regard to the affairs of

35. Buchanan, *Works*, XI, 341–342.
36. Fry, *New York and Conscription*, 73–76.
37. Nicolay and Hay, *Lincoln*, VII, 13, note.
38. Randall, *Constitutional Problems*, 268.

New York.[39] Although a great many people agreed with Governor Seymour that a direct federal draft was beyond the powers of the Constitution, it is difficult to see why they should have done so. The biographers of Lincoln published an argument which the President drew up as an appeal to the northern Democrats, but never printed. This paper is really the rough draft of a letter to Seymour. Lincoln pointed out that the system of volunteering seemed to have run its course and that the power "to raise and support armies" was granted to the Congress by the Constitution. Therefore he believed the Enrollment Act was both expedient and legal.

The central argument for him was necessity; the draft, he declared, was substantially fair and honestly administered, and the commutation of three hundred dollars would keep down the cost to men who wished to purchase substitutes. Two sentences of Lincoln's statement of the case for the new law would have distressed the opponents of slavery and amused its supporters. "The principle of the draft, which simply is involuntary or enforced service," he wrote, "is not new. It has been practised in all ages of the world."[40] Both governor and President were equally illogical: the real difference of opinion was a disagreement as to the necessity for federal control of dragging men into the army.

Seymour continued to insist that whether constitutional or not the Enrollment Act was neither necessary nor wise. When the bill was before the House of Representatives, Congressman Steele of New York spoke against it and defended the governor of his state from the attacks of Thaddeus Stevens, who had angrily called him a traitor. Steele pointed out that Seymour had recommended to a legislature in which the Republicans had half the members of the assembly and controlled the senate measures which would have got ten men for every one which Senator Wilson's bill would bring into the armies of the Union.[41]

39. Fry, *New York and Conscription*, 33–34.
40. Nicolay and Hay, *Lincoln*, VII, 49–57.
41. *Congressional Globe*, 37 Congress, Third Session, 1263–1264.

The most conscientious student of the draft during the Civil War was forced to conclude that Henry Wilson of Massachusetts was "never a real friend of conscription." His official statement that the prime object of the measure was to produce soldiers is belied, according to Shannon, by all his conduct in connection with the act and its enforcement. In the eyes of the author of *The Organization and Administration of the Union Army*, the measure was passed by the Congress not to get men, but to give the federal government a whip which it could use on the states. Shannon's hard words must have brought a smile to the lips of the shade of Horatio Seymour. The law he fought bitterly "was not a conscription bill in any sense; it was merely a piece of class legislation designed, even in the last resort, merely to stimulate mercenary enlistments and to match the rich man's dollars with the poor man's life."[42]

Professor Shannon made a patient study of the final reports of the bureau of the provost-marshal-general.[43] The net result of the federal draft, so far as he could discover, was startling.

> For all practical purposes, it may be said that the two years of almost constant drafting and preparation for draft produced 170,000 men, of whom nearly 120,000 were substitutes.[44]

Of all the men whose names were drawn for service, then, only about fifty thousand actually went into the army. Drafted men paid the United States an aggregate of $10,500,000 for the purchase of substitutes.[45] Of the enrolling officers, moreover, thirty-eight were killed; sixty were wounded; and twelve were injured in property, according to General Fry's final report to

42. Shannon, *Union Army*, I, 308. See Shannon's description of the law, I, 305; men liable to draft were divided into two classes. The first consisted of all men, married or single, between twenty and thirty-five, and all unmarried men from thirty-five to forty-five. The second class included only the married men from thirty-five to forty-five. This second class was not to be called out until the first was exhausted.

43. *Official Records of the Rebellion*, Series Three, V, serial number 126, 803–842.

44. Shannon, *Union Army*, II, 137.

45. New York *Times*, July 22, 1917.

the government.[46] The real force of the Enrollment Act appears in the by-product of the more than one million men who volunteered for service in the army and navy of the North. Commutation had to be abolished within eighteen months, for the war department found that it was getting money but not men.

Senator Wilson was shrewd enough to realize that the shifty system which he made a law would frighten men into voluntary service. The lessons the government learned about raising armies during the last years of the Civil War were incorporated in a final report on the draft which was filed away in Washington. Long afterward this report was pulled out of a pigeon-hole and applied to the drawing and enforcement of the Selective Service Act of 1917—a lame endeavor to disguise conscription with a new name. President Wilson had to learn by trial and error what Senator Wilson knew by instinct: no amount of expert advice could make forced military service popular among Americans. To draft citizens for the ranks of an expeditionary army was a surprising new departure, to say the least—if not, in fact, the straw which broke the camel's back of the President's power with the people.

As late as December 23, 1864, almost two months after he knew he would soon have no more responsible interest in conscription, Governor Seymour drew up a circular in regard to the enrollment, which was sent out from the executive office in Albany.[47] The object of this circular was to call attention to a comparison between the quotas assigned by counties in New York and New England according to the call for five hundred thousand men which Lincoln made on July 18, 1864. Every one of the thirty-one congressional districts was listed except the eight in and around the cities of New York and Brooklyn. The state had been directed to supply 39,318 men, and the governor who was going out of office showed the citizens of New York that the average excess required of their state, district

46. *Official Records of the Rebellion*, Series Three, v, serial number 126, 599–932.

47. Seymour, *Public Record*, 265–266.

by district, over those of New England was 507 men. The bounty had risen to seven hundred dollars for each purchased volunteer — commutation at three hundred dollars a head having been abolished on July 4, 1864. On the basis of the government's own figures, then, Seymour showed that New York had been asked for an excess of almost ten thousand men in thirty-one congressional districts, the bounties of whom would have added up to $6,750,000. Dwelling on the injustice of federal conscription, he concluded, "the excess of the quota of these districts of this State over those of New England is not due to any difference in the character of population, but mainly to the activity of town officials in the latter States, in cutting down the enrolments to the number of persons liable to do duty." Quotas for the draft, it will be remembered, were assigned on the basis of the enrollment of men liable, and not on population.

Many of those who voted against Seymour in 1864 probably thought that wrangling about the raising of soldiers would cease with the inauguration of his successor, Reuben E. Fenton, but such was not the case. On December 1, 1864, after having sent over 156,000 soldiers and sailors into the army and navy during the year, the state over which a so-called "Copperhead" governor had presided since January 1, 1863, had an excess on credits with the federal government of 5,301 men, according to the report of the Republican who followed him in office.[48] On December 19, 1864, Lincoln called for 300,000 troops, and about January 7, 1865, it was learned that the quota of New York would be 46,861. As soon as he had looked over the list of the men required of the thirty-one congressional districts Fenton found the assignments so unequal that he sent two of his aides to Washington to protest. One of these, Colonel George W. Palmer, left with Fry a careful explanation of the governor's plan for the complicated business of crediting one and three-year enlistments properly to the several districts.[49]

General Fry's answer was a bombshell. On January 20 he

48. Lincoln, *Messages*, v, 607–608.
49. Lincoln, *Messages*, v, 626–628.

telegraphed that revised quotas would be sent forward in a day or two, but that the quota of New York would be increased by the revision from 46,000 to over 60,000.[50] Fenton took the first train to Washington in order to argue or wheedle a reduction out of Fry or Stanton. Not only was he unable to understand the war department's use of figures, but the "large increase" of the quotas in New York City seemed to him "extraordinary."[51] When Fry sent on the corrected lists for the congressional districts on January 24, it was found that the six districts in New York and Brooklyn were called on for three and often four times as many men as the outlying districts.[52] In talking with Fenton, General Fry laid the confusing inequalities and revisions to the carelessness of mustering officers and ignorance of the law on the part of the local officials.

On January 26 the legislature took a hand when a delegation of angry senators and assemblymen waited on Governor Fenton, who had returned to Albany three days before. This delegation set out for Washington on January 27. On January 30 the assembly "respectfully requested" the governor to communicate to the house all information as to the unexplained increase of the quota of New York from 46,000 to 62,000 men.[53] The governor submitted all the correspondence and figures in a special message. That same day he asked the federal authorities to postpone the draft until these figures could be checked and corrected or popular feeling reconciled to them.[54] Finally, on February 2, President Lincoln reduced the quota of the state by one-quarter "subject to further examination and action," but Lee had surrendered before another call for soldiers was thought necessary.[55] Thus opposition to the draft, in New York at least, was, it will be seen, persistent, non-partisan, and probably in a large measure justified. Horatio Seymour's protests

50. Lincoln, *Messages*, v, 628.
51. Lincoln, *Messages*, v, 630.
52. Lincoln, *Messages*, v, 621–622.
53. Lincoln, *Messages*, v, 624 and 632.
54. Lincoln, *Messages*, v, 633.
55. Lincoln, *Messages*, v, 634.

do not suffer by comparison with those of Reuben E. Fenton; on the contrary, they gain character and strength.

People who like to believe that Horatio Seymour's opposition to the draft was partisan and opportunistic ought to read a speech he made at Seneca Falls, New York, on November 1, 1865. Almost one year after he had retired from office and a full six months after Appomattox he denounced the draft as a notion "repugnant to the genius of our institutions." In spite of all the powers of a despotism, the federal machinery for conscription had "produced no men." Senator Wilson would probably have acknowledged privately that it was never supposed to — such was the conclusion of Professor Shannon. By the time the government was willing to have recourse to the proper officials, that is the county supervisors, declared Seymour, the soldiers whom the draft brought into the army cost more money than they would have cost without it. Forgetting or ignoring the enormous indirect force of the Enrollment Act of 1863, Seymour continued to believe long after the surrender of the South that "the draft failed because it was contrary to the theory of our government."

As in the South, then, forced military service was the subject of wrangling and ill will. People duped or defied the enrolling officers and even killed three or four dozen of them. The fever of fight had died out on both sides, and the vague feeling that this draft meant one thing for the rich man and another for the poor was, so Professor Shannon found, substantially correct. That this resentment came to a head with the drawing of names in New York on July 11, 1863, was largely accidental. The city was inadequately garrisoned, but General Wool had refused reinforcements. What troops were on the scene could not be used promptly, moreover, for Colonel Harvey Brown, of the Fifth United States Artillery, who commanded the soldiers in the forts of the harbor, and was a brigadier-general by brevet, refused to obey General Wool's command to come to the aid of Major-General Sandford of the National Guard until the question of rank should be decided in his favor.

It was Tuesday before the intervention of Governor Seymour persuaded him to bring his men to police headquarters. Thus, while the disorderly elements of the city were drifting about New York breaking windows, fighting the police, and setting fire to houses, one general protested another's claim to superior rank until a mild-mannered man of peace hit on the *modus operandi* of keeping the two commanders apart.

There were six congressional districts in New York City: the fourth, fifth, sixth, seventh, eighth, and ninth. Charles E. Jenkins was provost-marshal of the last, and it was at his headquarters at the corner of Third Avenue and 46th Street — at that time a region of vacant lots and shanties — that the drawing of names began on the morning of Saturday, July 11, 1863. After a Sunday at home looking over the lists of the names of those who had been drafted, a crowd of residents in the district held a secret meeting of protest. On Monday, July 13, just as the work of the morning was getting under way, a group of laborers began to stone the headquarters of Jenkins, which were ultimately broken into and set on fire. A whole block of suburban buildings was burned to the ground. The neighborhood was very much uptown in 1863, not by any means respectable, and more than three miles as the crow flies from the city hall, then situated at the centre of New York.[56]

Mayor Opdyke got word of the trouble at about a quarter to ten in the morning and telegraphed to Governor Seymour three times in the one day, trying to reach him by way of Albany. Seymour, it will be remembered, was staying at the home of James Neilson, who lived at "Woodlawn" in New Brunswick, New Jersey. About noon on Monday, while the governor was driving over to Long Branch, he got out of his carriage at the station at Old Bridge on the South River and was surprised to be handed a telegram addressed to himself by Inspector-General Miller of the National Guard and Brigadier-General Wool, commander of the Department of the East. This message informed him that New York City was in a state of riot and ad-

56. For Rhodes's account, see *History*, IV, 321–322.

vised his immediate return. Refusing to allow his nephew, young Neilson, to go with him, Seymour caught the first train he could find.[57] According to his own account he did not reach New York until the morning of Tuesday, July 14; thus he must have spent the night of Monday on the way.[58] Mayor Opdyke saw him at noon on Tuesday,[59] when he found him at the St. Nicholas Hotel, where the governor always put up when he came down to the city.[60]

Seymour has been criticized for having been absent from New York over the very week-end when the federal draft was first to be put in operation. When he stated some time later that he had not been officially informed of the day on which the drawing of names was to begin, General Fry declared that due notice had been sent to him in ample time and wrote a book to prove his case. As is not unusual in such disputes the governor and the general were talking about different things. Official notice of the government's intention to set the draft in motion was undoubtedly sent to Seymour, and the receipt of this notice he did not deny. Discretion as to the drawing of names, however, was left to the boards of the several districts, and the governor insisted that he had never been specifically informed that such a drawing would be held in the ninth congressional district on the morning of Saturday, July 11. General Fry had ordered his provost-marshals to start drawing names whenever the enrollments in their districts were completed. Thus Seymour could never have learned the precise day chosen for the ninth district from any one but Charles E. Jenkins. Fry acknowledged that Seymour had not been given this information but blamed the governor for not having asked Provost-Marshal Jenkins for it!

57. New York Historical Society: Seymour Papers: Letter of James Neilson to Mrs. C. S. Fairchild, July 26, 1920.

58. Lincoln, *Messages*, v, 545–546.

59. Opdyke, *Official Documents*, 273–274.

60. Commenting on Seymour's movements, General Fry (*New York and Conscription*, 28) shows the spirit which informs his book: "The *New York Times* says [1879] that when Governor Seymour heard at Long Branch of the disturbances in New York City, 'he hurried to the metropolis without having tasted food.' Why the Governor fasted at Long Branch is a mystery."

The governor was a meticulously truthful man. Any one who read the New York newspapers had no good reason for not knowing that the head of the state was stopping at the St. Nicholas Hotel and would sleep there on the night of Thursday, July 9. He had come down from Albany on official business and had made a tour of inspection of the defenses of the harbor. If Seymour had been told that the first drawing of names would take place at Third Avenue and 46th Street on Saturday morning, July 11, he would hardly have left the city on the evening of Friday, July 10, for a quiet week-end in the country. Even Mayor Opdyke, a Republican, stated that he advised the authorities "to postpone the draft a few days" until troops would be returning to the city from Gettysburg. But his suggestion "was deemed unadvisable." [61]

After a conference with Mayor Opdyke and General Wool, who also made his headquarters at the St. Nicholas Hotel, Governor Seymour issued the first of his two proclamations, which stated in substance that "riotous proceedings must and shall be put down." In the afternoon he gave out a second, which declared "the city and county of New York to be in a state of insurrection." [62] Then he set out for the city hall, something less than a mile away. He covered the distance on foot, walking with two companions. His friends have called this act courageous, but in view of the fact that all the disturbances in the streets were uptown more than a mile north of the St. Nicholas, the compliment is quite superfluous.[63] These three gentlemen seemed to have found no reason for not being in the streets of New York at noon on Tuesday. The last disturbance in City Hall Park had occurred about two o'clock that morning, when Captain Greer and the police of the third precinct drove a noisy gang of rowdies away from the buildings of the *Times* and the *Tribune*, in Park Row. The store of Brooks Brothers, situated at the northwest corner of Catharine and Cherry

61. Opdyke, *Official Documents*, 265.
62. Seymour, *Public Record*, 126–127.
63. See an account of this incident by Miss Blandina Dudley Miller, Seymour's niece: New York Historical Society: Seymour Papers.

streets, on the East Side, was not pillaged until that evening. This store was half a mile in a straight line from the steps of the city hall, and actually, of course, much farther away.[64]

On reaching the city hall Seymour went directly to the governor's room. As the people poured out of their offices at lunch hour the news spread that the governor was at hand, and shouts and cheers went up and calls for a speech. The mayor and the other officials who were with him begged him to show himself and say something to the crowd which was collecting in the park. There was no disorder or sign of disorder, it must be remembered, within a radius of a mile from the steps on which the governor appeared.

In reading what Seymour is supposed to have said during the next few minutes which his political enemies never allowed him to forget, it is necessary to notice that only one version of this impromptu address, Greeley's, begins with what was thought to be the notorious formal salutation of "My Friends." It is well to remember, also, that blood-thirsty rioters, roaming through a city on a second day of evil deeds, are hardly likely to stop and listen to a speech. The partisan side of what is said to have happened is best represented by a broadside in the Library of Congress which shows a large-eyed, dapper Seymour facing a gang of ruffians with a negro swinging from a branch of a tree in the background. The racial animus of such disorder as actually occurred came out in the chasing and beating of negroes and the burning of the colored orphan asylum on Fifth Avenue, far uptown. Seymour never denied that he had introduced himself to his audience with the words, "My Friends," for he never pretended to remember what he had said. Later in the day he drove down and spoke in Wall Street, and then went uptown, where he made a third short speech, presumably repeating each time the substance of what he said at the city hall at noon. No complete report of any one of the

64. Barnes, *Draft Riots*, 32. Barnes's account is nothing if not dramatic. On Monday night a "terrific thunder-storm" broke over the city, deluging the streets with water and scattering the crowds: Headley, *Riots of New York*, 183.

Library of Congress

"MY FRIENDS"

three speeches is in existence.[65] A notice in the New York *Times*, however, is interesting:

During the afternoon the Governor addressed a large concourse of people in Wall-street. His speech was the same in substance as that delivered from the City Hall steps. He said he had sent to Washington to ask that the draft in this State might be suspended until the Courts could decide upon its legality. To the decision, when it came, all owed obedience. If they decided it to be legal, he would use every exertion to make it as equal as possible upon all citizens. The Governor's remarks were well received. . . . Subsequently the Governor addressed the people in the upper part of the City — the tenor of his remarks being substantially the same.[66]

Of the six reports of the speech Seymour made from the steps of the city hall only one was printed in a paper definitely friendly to the governor — the New York *World*; three appeared in papers openly hostile to him — Bryant's *Evening Post*, Bennett's *Herald*, and Greeley's *Tribune*. The earliest accounts came out in the *Express* and *Evening Post*, on the afternoon of the speech.[67] Of the six newspapers concerned, only the *Express* and the *Times* may fairly be called neutral in regard to Seymour, for, although Henry J. Raymond of the latter paper had no great love for the governor, he hated Horace Greeley both politically and personally. The account in the *Express*, it will be noticed, is innocuous but did not profess to be complete. The reporter for Bryant's *Evening Post* managed to get nearer to the speaker, it would seem, for his story was livelier than that of the *Express:* "Shortly afterward, a crowd having concentrated near the City Hall, Governor Seymour, who was in the building, appeared on the steps and briefly addressed the

65. Readers of Nicolay and Hay, *Lincoln*, will find (VII, 22–23) an oddly incorrect account of Seymour's actions on July 14, 1863. We are told that Seymour returned from Long Branch (a point he did not reach) "a prey to the most terrible agitation"; whereupon "he was hurried by his friends to the City Hall, where a great crowd soon gathered." His speech was a "venial fault, pardonable in view of his extreme agitation." "The serious matter was his intimation that the draft justified the riot, and that if the rioters would cease from their violence the draft should be stopped." Just where the future secretary of state and his editorial assistant found this statement does not appear, for it does not occur in any of the reports.

66. New York *Times*, July 15, 1863.

67. See Appendix.

mob." It will be observed that the "crowd" of the first part of this sentence becomes a "mob" in the second part. The spirit of the third paragraph and the last sentence of the report in the *Evening Post* is obvious.

It was William Cullen Bryant, then, who, on the evening of Tuesday, July 14, gave the cue to Horace Greeley for the legend which the latter started in the *Tribune* on the morning of July 15. Greeley wished to believe that the disorders in New York were part of a Copperhead conspiracy in which Seymour himself was involved.[68] Lee was to invade the North, and when New York was stripped of troops, a rebellion would break out behind the Union lines. It is charitable to suppose that Greeley was the victim of his own imagination, but he played up the disloyalty of Seymour in cold blood as late as 1868. In the meantime Bennett of the *Herald*, nursing his political grudge against the governor, looked on with a malicious grin.

Only five of the six reports pretended to be complete. The common denominator of these five is not large. The speaker began by remarking that he had come in from the country on hearing of trouble in the city; that he had sent his adjutant-general to Washington to find out if the draft might be postponed; that both persons and property must be protected; and that if the conscription law were declared constitutional, the people could rely on him to see that it should bear equally upon the rich and the poor. Variations in, and additions to, these statements are

68. On July 15, the *Tribune* published an editorial with the heading "A General Wanted." In this editorial, Greeley used his accusation that Seymour had "called these savage rioters his 'friends'—as indeed they are—" as a reason for the government's declaring the city "in a state of revolution." New York City needed a general with unlimited authority. On Thursday, July 16, Mayor Opdyke issued a proclamation to the effect that "the insurrection was practically ended": Headley, *Riots of New York*, 245. Just after daylight, according to Headley, the Seventh Regiment (New York) came in across New Jersey, marched along Canal Street and drew up in front of the St. Nicholas Hotel. Rhodes (*History*, IV, 328) says the riot ended in a fight near Gramercy Park on the evening of Thursday, July 16. For a speech to the "rioters" made on Friday, July 17, by Archbishop John Hughes, as a result of a letter Governor Seymour wrote him on July 14, see Hassard, *Hughes*, 499–500.

personal and partisan. Even Greeley's paper printed the following words on the morning of July 15:

I wish you to take good care of all property as good citizens, and see that every person is safe. The safe-keeping of property and persons rests with you, and I charge you to disturb neither. It is your duty to maintain the good order of the city, and I know you will do it. I wish you now to separate as good citizens, and you can assemble again whenever you wish to do so.[69]

One has only to read the *Tribune* report carefully to realize how the editor had to embroider his story for use in the campaign five years later.

Seymour was an experienced public speaker and ought to have been able to tell a mob from a crowd by 1863. The man who issued the two proclamations one of which he had already signed was hardly likely to plead with rioters — or even suppose he was addressing them when he was not. The phrase, "My Friends," has been foolishly haggled over. If Seymour used it (and it is by no means certain that he did), it meant no more than the "Ladies and Gentlemen" used extravagantly in our own day. President Lincoln was bitterly complained of as long as he was alive; yet no one has seen fit to object to the fact that he closed his first inaugural with these words: "We are not enemies, but friends. We must not be enemies." Now the "dissatisfied fellow-countrymen" to whom Lincoln directed those two sentences were the people of the South, and seven of the southern states had already seceded from the Union. Should Lincoln be charged with condoning secession because he addressed the southerners as "friends" as late as March 4, 1861?[70]

Seymour always laughingly denied that he had called "rioters" his "friends," because he could not remember that he had ever seen one. The good evidence of two eye-witnesses seems

69. See Appendix.

70. Lincoln, *Complete Works*, II, 1–7. The reference is to the last two paragraphs of the first inaugural. Seven states had already seceded from the Union: South Carolina, December 20, 1860; Mississippi, January 9, 1861; Florida, January 10; Alabama, January 11; Georgia, January 19; Louisiana, January 24; and Texas, February 1, an action which was ratified by the people on February 23.

to bear him out in this matter. Thirty years after the event William Kidd, who served as Seymour's military secretary during his second term and stood beside him on the steps of the city hall at noon of July 14, wrote as follows:

The wilful misrepresentation of the Governor's speech to the crowd in front of the City Hall by the republican journals was cruel and unjust, as he never addressed the crowd as "my friends," but when he came forward to order them to disband and obey the laws, some in the crowd called out "Governor, we are your friends." He then said, "If you are my friends, you will go to your homes like peaceable citizens," and then continued his speech.[71]

In 1896 a second eye-witness, after he had read a speech made at Saratoga by the man who was soon to become Governor Black, offered his testimony as to what actually had happened.

This eye-witness, S. W. Benedict, happened to be walking up Broadway at noon on July 14. He had reached a point just opposite the city hall when he saw a crowd dispersing and asked a man what was going on — this, be it remembered, at the very centre of a city supposedly in the throes of a riot. Benedict received for reply: "Governor Seymour has just made a speech counselling law and order" — or "some words to that effect." "This," wrote Mr. Benedict to the governor's niece, "was the remarkable speech of which you wish an explanation!" It is pertinent to add his comment: "There was no riot or semblance of one at that time and place; the rioters were miles away uptown."[72] The people who were leaving the park at the moment Mr. Benedict happened along looked to him like clerks and artisans; he had gone out to get his luncheon, and so, he gathered, had they. Such was the "blood-thirsty mob" which Seymour faced from the steps of the city hall — orderly men, whom he may have been so wicked as to call his friends. It is easy to understand why Horace Greeley did not "scamper" out of the city but went to and from his office without interruption

71. New York Historical Society: Seymour Papers: Kidd wrote down his report in 1893; this report was certified to on February 3, 1912, in Washington, D. C.

72. New York Historical Society: Seymour Papers: S. W. Benedict to Mrs. C. S. Fairchild, October 30, 1896.

during the whole week, ate his dinner at his regular restaurant, and without having to protect his well-known figure with a "disguise."

Some time before the drawing of the names was to begin in New York, Governor Seymour sent Adjutant-General Sprague to Washington to ask Lincoln and Stanton to postpone the draft. Sprague failed to carry out his commission because he dared not disobey his superior, Provost-Marshal-General Fry, who arrogantly forbade him to speak to the President or the secretary of war.[73] It was more than a week before the governor learned that his message had never been delivered. Not long after, Greeley charged Seymour with having sent Tilden to the capital for the express purpose of getting the draft suspended because he was afraid that the Irish servant girls would burn down the houses of their masters and mistresses if the law which took their men away from them were put into effect.[74]

The actual postponement of the draft gave rise to contradiction and ill will. Mr. Wall states that Stanton ordered a temporary suspension on Wednesday, July 15.[75] Rhodes told a somewhat different story. According to him, Assistant Provost-Marshal-General Robert Nugent acknowledged to Governor Seymour and Mayor Opdyke at the St. Nicholas Hotel on Wednesday, July 15, that General Fry had telegraphed him to suspend the draft. Colonel Nugent declared that he had no authority to make this order public, but Seymour and Opdyke finally persuaded him to write a notice over his own name: "The draft has been suspended in New York City and Brooklyn." Rhodes states that this notice was printed in nearly all the newspapers and undoubtedly was the cause of the rioters retiring to their homes and employments.[76]

Then the city took a hand. Within a few days both boards of the council unanimously passed an ordinance which granted

73. New York Historical Society: Seymour Papers: Letter of William Kidd to Henry S. Miller, January 3, 1893.

74. New York *Tribune*, July 24, 1863.

75. Wall, *Seymour*, 45.

76. Rhodes, *History*, IV, 327.

three hundred dollars to any drafted person "who shall be found to be unable to pay the said sum." A further provision of the same ordinance gave three hundred dollars to any drafted person who would volunteer for three years or the duration of the war. This measure would have relieved New York City of conscription at an estimated cost of about $2,500,000. When Mayor Opdyke vetoed the bill, he called attention to the "fact" that a "great proportion" of the rioters were "persons under twenty years of age." [77] If the mayor is to be believed, then, many of the "rioters" were boys.

Disorder occurred in certain parts of Manhattan Island during only three days at most, Monday to Wednesday, July 13 to 15, and not four, as is often stated. The crowd which wrecked and burned the provost-marshal's office at 46th Street and Third Avenue on the morning of Monday at a point more than three miles northeast of the city hall moved down Third Avenue, stalling the horse-cars on its way. Collisions with the police occurred along the line of march, and it was this mob that attacked and murdered Major O'Brien. In the afternoon of Monday an army of policemen attacked and broke up a parade which had come down Broadway just north of police headquarters, which were situated in Mulberry Street exactly a mile from the city hall. On the night of Monday a violent summer thunder-storm broke over New York, and the downpour of rain drenched and scattered the crowds. Thus nature did quite as much, if not more, than the forces of law and order in restoring the city to temporary quiet.

For the description of the kind of people who burned the colored orphan asylum between 43rd and 44th Streets just west of Fifth Avenue on that day one should turn to Edward P. Mitchell's *Memoirs of an Editor*. Mitchell as a boy stood at a window of his father's house on Monday night and watched a procession of shouting, drunken men and women carrying torches and banners go by — bent on mischief but headed nowhere in particular. Respectable people took care to stay in-

77. Opdyke, *Official Documents*, 284–294.

doors that night.[78] There was sporadic disorder in outlying parts of the city during Tuesday. On the evening of that day Brooks Brothers' store at Catharine and Cherry streets was broken into and sacked, and more than three miles away to the north and west police and soldiers stormed the barricades which had been thrown across Eighth Avenue at West 38th Street. General Sandford's post of command was just a little to the southeast in the armory at the corner of Seventh Avenue and 35th Street. By nightfall the "great draft riots" were at an end.

The moment he arrived in the city on July 14, Governor Seymour authorized the arming first of the police and then of citizens who were called to their assistance.[79] Superintendent Kennedy had three generals to help him: Wool, of the Department of the East; Sandford, of the National Guard; and Brown, of the regular army, commanding in all about twelve hundred soldiers.[80] Wool stayed at the St. Nicholas Hotel with Seymour; Sandford was stationed at the arsenal, uptown; and Brown, whose headquarters were at Fort Hamilton in the harbor, joined Kennedy at police headquarters in Mulberry Street — but not until Tuesday, July 14 — bringing with him three companies of regulars.[81]

It is often stated that sending troops back to New York to suppress the draft riots impaired Meade's pursuit of Lee after Gettysburg. Reference to Mr. Freeman's great biography of the southern commander will cast more than a shadow of doubt on this belief. General Lee crossed the Potomac, heading north into Maryland, on June 25; the Battle of Gettysburg was fought on July 1, 2, and 3. Lee left the field on the fourth, in the midst of a torrential rain, which lasted until July 6. At five o'clock on the afternoon of that day Longstreet and he rode into Hagerstown. From July 7 to July 12 Lee rested on the defen-

78. Edward P. Mitchell, *Memoirs of an Editor* (New York, 1924), 58–63.

79. Opdyke, *Official Documents*, 272–273, and 276; see, also, Rhodes, *History*, IV, 326–327.

80. Lincoln, *Messages*, V, 548; Seymour, *Public Record*, 125–139.

81. Headley, *Riots of New York*, 176–178, is not quite accurate on this point.

sive at Williamsport, on the north side of the Potomac, sending his wounded and his prisoners across the river, and waiting for it to subside to a fordable depth. A crazy bridge was thrown across the stream. On July 13 the flood dropped, and by the evening of that day the Confederates were back in Virginia. The first rioting in New York City occurred on that very morning. Whether the northern criticism of Meade was just or not is beside the point; the fact is that fully nine days elapsed between the end of Gettysburg and the beginning of the riots. Therefore any pursuit of Lee which could have been impaired by the trouble in New York would have been polite, not to say considerate.

In view of what actually happened on July 13 and 14, 1863, the magnifying of the reports may be thought mysterious. More than one person, however, had good reasons for exaggerating the extent and damage of these riots. The people for whom Horace Greeley was spokesman hoped that if Lincoln were only sufficiently alarmed, he would proclaim martial law, and then the city could be governed with ease. Troops were sent into New York to insure safety at the resumption of the draft in August. Governor Seymour and his friends, on the other hand, had no desire to minimize popular discontent with the quotas assigned to the six congressional districts of New York and Brooklyn. Lincoln, it was believed, might be persuaded to revise the demands — as, indeed, he did when confronted with the figures which Seymour submitted to him. The governor made another point, moreover: all the violence and disorder of the week had been put down by the metropolitan police with very little aid from the military.[82] New York, it was implied, both city and state, was quite able to manage its own affairs. A third group of persons, if not most numerous, was most important in swelling the total of the casualties and damages. A very large group of citizens were not long in awaking to the fact that they could make money by making the most of the riots.

The small number of people who lost their lives in the riots

82. Lincoln, *Messages*, v, 584.

can not be determined exactly. On July 20, the New York *Tribune* published a "list of persons killed in the late riots, for whose burials certificates have been obtained." Seventy-four names were printed, nine of these of children between two and sixteen years of age. Many bodies, it was stated, were still concealed in boxes in the cellars uptown "awaiting removal." Four days later the *Tribune* estimated the total number of killed at from three to five hundred. The metropolitan police reported that one thousand persons had perished, and Seymour carelessly let this round figure go into his second annual message to the legislature.[83] By 1891 Theodore Roosevelt had swelled the total to twelve hundred.[84] A careful examination of the death records of the city from 1853 to 1867 shows that if anything like a thousand people died in New York during the week of July 13 to 20, 1863, their corpses must have disappeared in some miraculous manner. The summer increase in mortality was regular for 1863, and whenever causes are given in the record, it is found that the increase was owing to the death of children.[85] There is no evidence that any more than seventy-four possible victims of the violence of three days died anywhere but in the columns of partisan newspapers.

Claims for damage to property became a scandal the moment it was discovered that the county would have to pay for the losses. On July 18 the *Tribune* estimated the total damage at $400,000, and by July 27 twenty-six claims had been filed with the comptroller, whose duty it was to present these claims to the board of supervisors of the county of New York at the expiration of sixty days. The claims ranged from one of eighteen dollars to another of more than $25,000, and the grand total amounted to $92,001.24. On August 4 the *Times* declared that payments for damages would cost $1,100,000. Obviously

83. Lincoln, *Messages*, v, 548.

84. Theodore Roosevelt, *New York* (London and New York, 1891), 203–205.

85. Valentine, *Manual of New York*, 200: Valentine gives the percentage of deaths in New York City as follows: 1860, 2.79; 1861, 2.553; 1862, 2.304; 1863, 2.592; 1864, 2.367. In 1863, 25,196 people died in New York; in 1864, the deaths totalled 25,645; in 1866, 26,815. In July, 1863, 2,682 people died; in July, 1864, 2,552; in July, 1865, 2,624; in July, 1866, 3,903.

word had got round that the riots would pay dividends to all those who knew how to get them. As claims poured in they were referred to a special committee of the county supervisors. This committee advertized its meetings in the newspapers and sat for the first time on September 7 at the city hall. Claimants were supposed to prove ownership of property, the fact of destruction, and the value involved. The chairman of this special committee was Elijah F. Purdy, a colleague of Peter B. Sweeny and William Marcy Tweed.

Up to December 31, 1863, the county had paid out $713,-589.33 because of the riots of July. According to the itemized account only $421,447.22 had been spent for damages; the county had paid $261,757.50 for "state militia on duty"; $13,-729.00 for the salaries of clerks and examiners; $10,006.18 for meals and supplies, and, among other things, $86.73 for the purchase of furniture for the "riot committee."[86] Claims continued to be filed and met during 1864, in which year warrants were drawn for $643,560.80, of which $550,176.74 was for damages. Over forty-five thousand dollars was paid out for rations for the militia and the police, and more than twenty-eight thousand dollars went for the services of clerks. The only credit entry in the whole story was for $457.52, received from the sale of "property taken from rioters." By the last day of December, 1864, the riots had cost New York County $1,356,669.61.[87] The comptroller paid the warrants out of a fund which resulted from the sale of "Riot Damages Indemnity Bonds of the County of New York." During 1865 warrants were drawn for $159,-731.38, of which payment on claims accounted for $151,-181.53. Thus the riots had cost the county a grand total of $1,516,423.99.[88]

On August 4, 1863, the grand jury of the county of New

86. *Fifth Annual Report of the Comptroller . . . of the County Government . . . 1863*, 130.
87. *Sixth Annual Report of the Comptroller . . . of the County Government . . . 1864*, 50 and 164.
88. *Seventh Annual Report of the Comptroller . . . of the County Government . . . 1865*, 31.

York brought in twenty indictments, most of them for crimes connected with the riot. The trials of those indicted were held in the court of general sessions, August 5 to 11. One man was sentenced to imprisonment for ten years; two others were found guilty of robbery and each was condemned to be locked up for fifteen years. The records of the courts of oyer and terminer and general sessions in the county show no increase of trials, acquittals, or convictions for the year 1863.[89]

The net result of the "great draft riots" was three days' disorder, possibly seventy-four deaths at most, and probably eighteen, the burning of a colored orphan asylum, an orgy of journalism, and a scramble for fictitious damages. To believe with the excited Greeley that hundreds of bodies were buried in back-yards or "smuggled across the ferries" to be laid away "secretly" out of the city would be absurd. Friends of Governor Seymour wrote in such a way as to magnify his cool good nature, his sleepless industry, and his power of quick decision, when it was still a matter of doubt as to how far the disturbances of Monday and Tuesday would spread and how serious they would become. His enemies made political capital of his casual speech to curious citizens from the steps of the city hall. The only significant part of that speech, and the only possible source of misunderstanding, must have been a repetition of the proclamation he had issued that very morning. The legend did good service in 1868, and the persistent libel of his cowardly and "disloyal" language followed him to the grave.

Some time before the presidential election of that year the whole question of the riots was debated fiercely in the constitutional convention of which former Mayor Opdyke was a member. All those who would like to believe the "old, stale, stereotyped slander" that Horatio Seymour ever called rioters against the draft his "friends" would do well to consult the proceedings of this convention for January 29, 1868. There they will find the explicit evidence of yet another eye-witness who stood by the governor's side at noon of Tuesday, July 14, 1863.

89. Valentine, *Manual of New York*, 131.

Edward Channing was always cautioning his students against the unreliability of the "rickety memories of old men." Opdyke, however, was not an old man at the time he spoke; the incident to which he referred was less than five years off, and he did not belong to the political party of the governor whose conduct he was honorable enough to defend. According to him there was not the slightest sign of disorder in the neighborhood when Seymour spoke at the city hall — not a rioter in sight, or any reason to suppose there was.[90]

Thus the recorded testimony of those who were present reduces the story of Horatio Seymour's ever having pleaded with a mob to a simple case of what reputable journalists call "editing the news." Bryant's *Evening Post* planted the seed of it, and Greeley's *Tribune* peddled the poisonous fruit. Historians have been led astray merely because the governor was too busy at the time, too much the thoroughbred, thereafter, to dignify the slander with denial.

90. *Proceedings and Debates of the Constitutional Convention of New York*, IV, 3106–3108.

XV

THE DEVIL AND THE DEEP SEA

1864

SEYMOUR saw the approach of the presidential election of 1864 with almost as much anxiety as did Lincoln. It looked for a time as if there would be a change at Washington, and the governor of New York was wise enough to know that a successor to Lincoln might be far less satisfactory than the President. Suppose the radicals were to put a creature of their own in his place? The schemes of these Republicans to replace Lincoln at the head of affairs were as unwelcome to the governor as to the President himself. Nevertheless, when Seymour urged his party to put up a civilian, and a conservative civilian, his enemies accused him of talking for himself. The two men he mentioned most frequently were Justice Samuel Nelson, a New Yorker, and a member of the Supreme Court, and James Guthrie, of Kentucky, who had served Pierce as secretary of the treasury. Defiant as he was in regard to the arrest of Vallandigham, Seymour made reunion the indispensable basis for peace; there could be no negotiation without it. He stood up valiantly for the rights of the man who had been kidnaped from his house but he never subscribed to his plan for an unconditional cessation of war. The first business at Chicago would be to prevent the party's being put in the position of seeming to endorse such a scheme.

It was, however, as the leader of the opposition to certain of the acts of Lincoln, Seward, and Stanton that Seymour provoked most of the unreasoning resentment which has been handed down to our own day. Cato may have loved the lost cause, but historians do not; failure would have made Washington a traitor and Lincoln a tyrant. The death of the latter relieved him of the grave responsibility for the choice of means he made in 1862 — that autumn when he decided that the Union could not be saved without the ungrudging support of those very radicals who were the last to wish to see it restored. A negotiated peace would have ruined the plans of these vindictive men, for if Davis had accepted Lincoln's terms at any time after the elections of 1862, the Democrats would have recovered complete control of the Congress. The reëlection of Lincoln, his untimely death, and the honest ineptitude of Andrew Johnson gave these radicals all they had dreamed of and had hardly dared to hope for. As a result the South did not regain home rule until 1877.

The bullet which took Lincoln's life left a legend in his place — a myth of perfect greatness which has distorted history and given rise to such reactions as the bitter biography by Masters. Even the dead are likely to suffer just as soon as all men speak well of them. Lord Charnwood, for instance, produced what promises to be the most popular biography of Booth's illustrious victim, and because he was beyond the battle of petty American politics, Charnwood's comments on the character and conduct of Seymour are far more important than partisan complaint and mere repetition. The governor of New York, he acknowledged, was a loyal supporter of the Union, a bitter critic of corruption in the management of the war, and, if a relentless foe of abolition, "a more presentable antagonist than Vallandigham." Many of Seymour's speeches seemed "fair enough" to this British biographer and much of his conduct "patriotic enough"; he was, moreover, a "gentleman." Yet the chief opponent of Lincoln, according to Charnwood, harangued a "defiled mob" in gentle terms and "persecuted" the President with protests against conscription.[1]

Because the book appeared in the midst of the World War it was not until 1921 that a friend of the memory of Seymour challenged the biographer's charges and recommended that he look into the works of James Ford Rhodes in order to shape for

1. Charnwood, *Lincoln*, 384–387.

himself a more nearly accurate idea of the man who had the ungrateful task of differing with Lincoln. Charnwood read Rhodes and graciously acknowledged his error, adding that he had begun his biography before 1914 and had finished it in 1916 as "a sort of tract for the times for English people." "It looks," he continued, "as if I had done him [Seymour] grave injustice for which I should be very sorry, and when the time comes that I can systematically revise my book, I must look into the matter carefully." [2] As late as 1917, then, it was the fate of Horatio Seymour to be criticized for conduct which resembled most uncomfortably that of men like Morley, MacDonald, and Lansdowne, all of whom made the conquest of Germany rather more unreasonable than it might otherwise have seemed.

Even if Seymour's hope for a negotiated peace was baseless, the talking-point of his criticism of the government of Lincoln was strong: rebellion in the South was no excuse for any one's ruling with a high hand in the North. The very acts he complained of, however, pleased those radicals who had voted for Lincoln in 1860, much as they desired to get rid of him by 1864. Seymour's words of warning and reconciliation enraged these men, for they hated Lincoln only less than they hated him. The more considerate the critic the more inconvenient he made himself. Gerrit Smith, for instance, could not find it in his heart to "murmur at the providence" which had brought Seymour into "high political power" in 1863; he was prepared to take him as "part of the penalty of the American people for their oppressions of the poor" — in so many words, a punishment. A good many persons would have agreed with this rich abolitionist that the sooner the country got rid of this governor the better.[3] Their refusal to believe that he was ready and even eager to leave office is hardly to be wondered at. It is not easy to think that a man whom you hate is willing to step out of your way. To explain Seymour's desire to go back to private

2. New York Historical Society: Seymour Papers: Copy of a letter to Admiral Stockton, May 1, 1921.

3. Letter of Gerrit Smith to Horatio Seymour, January 12, 1863: Pamphlet in possession of the author.

life in 1864 it is necessary to turn to the state of affairs in New York.

Immediately after the riots of July a cloud somewhat bigger than a man's hand appeared on the horizon in the person of John Adams Dix, for on Friday, July 18, 1863, Secretary Stanton relieved General Wool of the command of the Department of the East and put Dix in his place. Troops were sent into the city in preparation for the levy planned for August. The choice of this new commander was unfortunate, for Seymour and he had never been good friends. The governor saw in the general an adroit politician who had so managed his conscience that he could bolt with Van Buren in 1848 and vote for Breckinridge in 1860. Dix, it will be recollected, had been pushed hard for the nomination which Seymour received in 1862. Gideon Welles found the mercenary staff of the commander of Fortress Monroe a source of annoyance and vexation. Dix was supposed to be very popular in his state but although he ran for governor three times, his one election to that office coincided with the defeat of Greeley in 1872, when his Democratic opponent was Kernan, a Catholic. As soon as he was stationed in a well-garrisoned city Dix felt himself firmly seated in the saddle. A clash with the governor was likely, if not certain.

On July 30 Dix wrote Seymour that the draft would be "resumed" in New York "at an early day," and went on to say that if the governor would promise him troops enough to make the city safe, he would not have to call on Washington for aid.[4] Seymour wrote at once to General Fry asking for definite information as to the date of the draft, which, he had been promised, "would not be made in New York and Brooklyn without some notice being given to me." He added that he was preparing a letter to Lincoln on the subject, which letter ought to reach the President "next week."[5] On August 3 he put it in

4. Seymour, *Public Record*, 140.

5. New York State Library: Seymour Papers: Horatio Seymour Letter-Book, 1863–1864.

the mail and thus opened a complicated controversy.[6] On the same day he wrote General Dix that he believed Lincoln's answer would "relieve you and me from the painful questions growing out of an armed enforcement of the conscription law in this patriotic State, which has contributed so largely and freely to the support of the National cause during the existing war." [7] He promised Dix that he would write him again as soon as he heard from Washington. Within one month, however, the general was lecturing the governor on the wickedness of using the word "conscription" when everybody knew that the Congress had passed what was properly called "An Act for Enrolling and Calling Out the National Forces." [8]

Seymour saw no reason for a draft in New York, for according to his figures the state had a surplus of men to her credit. If the war department is to be believed, there was, in fact, a shortage. The scrambling for and the squabbling over man-power among the several states only added to Lincoln's burden during the next eighteen months. The fact that Connecticut, for instance, hired recruits in New York City did not simplify the figures which the rival and reluctant governors juggled before the eyes of the administration. The office of provost-marshal-general was the kind of unpopular post that some one always has to fill, but the odd aspect in the case of Fry is that he seems actually to have liked his work. Just as often as two greedy states tried to claim credit for one and the same man, this desk general would come to judgment like a Daniel. The incidental fact that his decision usually succeeded in exasperating both governors at once annoyed him not at all. Against Seymour he nursed a grudge for twenty years, and yet the record shows that Seymour's Republican successor was no less of a "nuisance" than he. It would be difficult to clear Fry of partisan feeling in this one relationship.

6. Seymour, *Public Record*, 148–155.

7. Seymour, *Public Record*, 140–141.

8. Seymour, *Public Record*, 141–143: Letter of John A. Dix to Horatio Seymour, August 8, 1863.

Fry probably secretly resented Governor Seymour's having written directly to President Lincoln instead of sending his letter through what the army likes to call "channels." His arrogant refusal to permit the timid Major Sprague to speak with Stanton and Lincoln on behalf of Seymour's proposal in July is ground for suspecting that he was annoyed at the governor's direct intervention. Like many soldiers he had scant regard for politicians and even less tact in concealing his opinion. Men who make it their business to obey in the hope of being able to command one day, rarely, if ever, learn how to persuade. Professor Shannon discovered a strange want of candor in Fry's official report on the subject of popular opposition to the enrollment and the draft of 1863. "Both in the matter of extent and of the amount of personal violence," he writes, "this statement by Fry is far short of the truth."[9] This "want of candor" should be kept in mind by readers of the apology which Fry published in 1885. The spirit of the book is none too sweet, and the conscious effort to seem impersonal provokes suspicion.

Seymour had opposed the draft in principle; now his letter to Lincoln questioned the accuracy of the enrollment. Although the governor was careful to write that he did not suspect the motives of the men who prepared the figures, Fry took pride in the efficiency of his staff so long as he faced a Democratic governor. When Fenton confronted him with puzzling comparisons in 1865, he humbly sought refuge in the ignorance and carelessness of enrolling officers, and confusion as to the proper application of the law. The tables of figures which Seymour sent to Lincoln require artful explanation even at this day. The fourth congressional district, for example, had a population of 131,854 and cast a vote of 12,363 in 1862. This district was asked for 5,881 men in the first draft; whereas an upstate district like the fifteenth, with a population of 132,232 and a vote of 23,165, was called on for only 2,260.[10] The contrast between the figures for five of the congressional districts in New

9. Shannon, *Union Army*, II, 204.
10. Seymour, *Public Record*, 155.

York and Brooklyn and seven of those elsewhere is subject, however, to two possible qualifications.

The first of these is the fact that great cities like New York and Brooklyn contained large numbers of males who were not yet qualified to vote but who were liable to enrollment by virtue of having taken out their first papers. Their intention of becoming citizens subjected them to the risk or opportunity of never living long enough to do so. In the country areas, on the other hand, most of the men liable to enrollment were voters. The second qualification is an assertion based on a measure of probability. Critics of Seymour's figures declared that enlistments had reduced the number of males available for military service far more upstate than in New York and Brooklyn. There were, however, two sides to this second explanation; for the rural areas, and even neighboring states like Connecticut and New Jersey, had perfected a free-and-easy way of buying recruits in the slums of these cities and thus filling up their quotas by means of taxes and not levies of men.

Years after the protest to Lincoln, General Fry wrote that Governor Seymour's real object in sending his letter to the President was not to correct the enrollment or equalize the execution of the draft, but to obstruct and postpone any federal demand for troops in New York.[11] According to Fry it was only because Lincoln was conscious of the governor's real motive that he made an arbitrary reduction of the quotas in certain districts in New York — a curious defense of his act, indeed. The President's reply was plain: "I cannot consent to suspend the draft in New York, as you request, because among other reasons time is too important." In view of the fact that as late as February 2, 1865, Lincoln cut down the quota of New York by one-quarter for Governor Fenton, whose loyalty to the administration was never in doubt, Fry's explanation of the reduction of August, 1863, hardly seems adequate.

Lincoln acknowledged that the "disparity of the quotas for the draft" as submitted to him was "certainly very striking,"

11. Fry, *New York and Conscription*, 35–36.

but added that recent immigration since the time of the census of 1860 might possibly account for much of the apparent unfairness of the figures. Because the armies were desperately in need of men, the President went on, the draft must continue in all the congressional districts of the state, but only 2,200 men would be drawn from the second, fourth, sixth, and eighth districts — the average of the other districts in New York. These four districts, together with the seventeenth and twenty-ninth, would be enrolled a second time by presidential order. This concession was gall and wormwood to General Fry. Lincoln closed his letter with a promise that he was ready and willing to forward any action to get an opinion on the constitutionality of the Enrollment Act from the Supreme Court.[12] The opinion was never obtained, but it is difficult to see how Buchanan and Lincoln could have been found in error on that question.

On August 6, 1863, Seymour wrote Tilden a letter which shows his deep distrust of the administration and, in particular, the motives of Seward and Stanton. "I am satisfied," he stated, that the federal government "means to go on in a spirit of hostility to this State; that it is governed by a spirit of malice in all things small and great. . . . This conscription will make the administration odious and contemptible. It will fail as a measure to raise men." According to Professor Shannon, Seymour was right in his prediction; it is doubtful, however, if the unpopular measure was ever designed to "raise men." In referring to the letter he had sent to Lincoln, Seymour told Tilden that he had questioned the fairness of the enrollment and the policy on conscription "in calm and respectful terms" and had asked for a test of its constitutionality. The governor's last paragraph was prophetic: "It will do no good, except making up a record. I look for nothing but hostility, but I shall do my duty, and demand my rights, and let consequences take care of themselves. I feel no uneasiness."[13] No governor of any loyal state did more, or less. It can not be denied that the draft was hated in both North and South.

12. Seymour, *Public Record*, 155–156.
13. Tilden, *Letters and Literary Memorials*, I, 183–184.

The very next day Seymour sent off a vigorous letter to General Dix in which he stated that he thought he had "discovered the process by which the frauds have been perpetrated." [14] The word "conscription," as we have seen, was too much for the general, who replied with an essay to point out that the term should be confined to Europe, where it properly belonged. Calling attention to the fact that the South was drafting rebels into its ranks far more strenuously than the North was calling loyal men to the colors, Dix closed his letter with a useless lecture on the crime of secession and repeated his request for assistance in view of the approaching draft.[15] A further exchange of letters between the two men led Dix to ask the war department for ten thousand troops. Stanton sent the soldiers back from Maryland, and the drawing of names took place quietly in August.

A last letter from Seymour put on record the haphazard fashion in which he was given notice of the two drafts of July and August, 1863.[16] John Adams Dix could not confine himself to the business of his command, for on September 9, 1863, he prepared a long defense of the constitutionality of the Enrollment Act for a gathering of War Democrats in Wisconsin. In spite of the style and redundancy of this message the argument is sound.[17] Seymour, like many Americans before and since, rationalized his dislike of a law into a conviction that it was contrary to the Constitution. He believed the draft was inexpedient and he persuaded himself that it was illegal. When he wrote Lincoln on August 8, he expressed his regret at the President's refusal to suspend the draft. New York, he pointed out, had never been delinquent in supplying soldiers for the armies of the Union; the state could and would fill up its regiments more easily without federal interference. He enclosed a full report on the enrollment which Judge-Advocate Nelson J. Waterbury had prepared for him. In calling attention to the

14. New York State Library: Seymour Papers: Horatio Seymour Letter-Book, 1863–1864.

15. Seymour, *Public Record*, 141–143.

16. Seymour, *Public Record*, 145.

17. Dix, *Memoirs*, II, 343–352.

figures he submitted, Seymour concluded, "You cannot and will not fail to right these gross wrongs." [18]

Waterbury's report on the enrollment, together with another call for soldiers in the autumn of 1863, prompted a comparison of the quota of New York with those of other states. When a committee of distinguished citizens appealed to him on the subject, Secretary Stanton realized that public opinion was turning against him so strongly that something would have to be done. With the approval of the President a commission of three was appointed to pass on the facts and figures in regard to New York. William F. Allen, the chairman of this commission, was a resident of New York City, a Democrat, and a friend of Governor Seymour. Serving with him were two men who were probably expected to arrive at a decision rather different from the official report of the commission — John Love, a War Democrat from Indiana, and Chauncey Smith, a Massachusetts lawyer. General Fry referred to Smith as "probably" a man of no party, which was Fry's way of describing a New England Republican who, it developed, would disagree with him.

The unanimous decision of this commission was a feather in the cap of Governor Seymour. After acquitting the enrolling officers of intentional unfairness, the report condemned the system by which these officers had worked. The enrollment, the commissioners found, was clearly inaccurate and imperfect, and the figures for the cities of New York and Brooklyn were "excessive." [19] The official biographers of Lincoln stated that "Judge Allen clearly dominated the commission." [20] Lincoln believed that the commission was so busy trying to find loopholes in the law that it had no time to "find men" but he accepted the report as final. Seymour had the satisfaction of receiving a unanimous vote of thanks from a Republican legislature for his "prompt and efficient efforts in procuring a cor-

18. Seymour, *Public Record*, 157–158.
19. Fry, *New York and Conscription*, 48–51.
20. Nicolay and Hay, *Lincoln*, VII, 41.

rection" of the "errors in the apportionment of the quota" of New York.[21] The net result was an adjustment of inequalities among the districts and a saving of almost 25,000 men to New York. The governor's victory came too late, however, to save him from the reverses of the state election in November, 1863.[22]

Seymour's correspondence with Lincoln and Dix found its way into the newspapers and caused widespread editorial comment. Members of the assembly and a secretary of state were to be elected in the "off year," and the Republicans hoped that they could repair the political damage of 1862. Because Seymour had vetoed the bill giving the votes to soldiers absent in the field he entered the campaign under a cloud. The constitutional amendment on which he insisted did not authorize absentee voting until the election of 1864. As November approached, the Republicans besieged Stanton for furloughs which would permit soldiers to return to the state in order to cast their ballots there. "The number of those who left Washington for middle and central New York was estimated at from sixteen thousand to eighteen thousand. The Democrats denounced this." [23] Secretary Seward stooped low enough to justify this dangerous weakening of the armies on the basis of the fact that

21. Seymour, *Public Record*, 158–159. This special commission was created by order of the war department on December 5, 1863. Its task was to correct enrollments in New York State. Lincoln objected that the commission did not go out to "find men," but devoted itself to examining the principles of the draft. The President directed Stanton to accept the commission's table of figures for New York State in this way: where the table called for increases, the quota was to stand; where the table called for decreases, the quota was to be reduced accordingly: Fry, *New York and Conscription*, 55–57.

22. The decision of Stanton's special commission included two recommendations which aroused a disagreement over method. It was proposed to adjust quotas "upon the basis and in proportion to the entire population." A call for soldiers was a direct tax. In the second place, it was suggested that any state or district furnishing its full, just share, and proportion of men required under any call or order for a draft in proportion to population should be relieved of the draft. But General Fry stood out for quotas based not on population but enrollment, and insisted that the figures of 1863 were more satisfactory than the census of 1860. The "amended act" (approved on February 24, 1864) made the basis of the district quotas the number of men of military age therein resident: Fry, *New York and Conscription*, 54–55.

23. Brummer, *History*, 351–352.

Seymour had vetoed a bill which he also was well-informed enough to know was not constitutional.[24]

In June, 1863, before the draft riots of July, Seymour still hoped that the radicals of the North would lose out at the elections in the autumn and thus put the control of the loyal states safely in the hands of the conservatives. His letter to a correspondent in Chicago shows how important he felt these elections would be.

> I hope the results of the elections in the great central states will save our country. If the conservative men in the central parts of the Union will act in concert, they can control the policy of the government. We can never live under a Gulf State or a New England system of laws. The great populous and powerful central states, which are free from sectional passions and prejudices must give the tone of popular sentiment. . . . I am very much obliged to you for your kind expression with regard to myself. I shall try to meet the expectations of my friends in dealing with the great questions of the day, but I fear they are of a magnitude beyond the grasp of any living man. Our friends in Chicago bore themselves nobly during the trials and excitements growing out of General Burnside's insane conduct. They won a victory for themselves and the country. I believe the aroused spirit of the American people, in behalf of their "home rights" will yet save us from despotism.[25]

It began to look as if the issues were indeed beyond "the grasp of any living man." When the Republicans held their "union" convention at Utica on September 2, leaders took care to avoid the split between radicals and conservatives which had wrecked the candidacy of General Wadsworth in 1862. Seymour's strictly correct conduct in regard to the bill giving votes to absent soldiers was branded as unpatriotic, invidious, and unjust.[26]

The Democratic state convention met at Albany on September 9. Governor Seymour addressed the evening session in what has been called "a dreary speech."[27] The Albany *Evening*

24. New York *Herald*, November 6, 1863.

25. Schenectady, New York, *Democrat and Reflector*, July 9, 1863, quoting the Chicago *Times*.

26. Brummer, *History*, 280–283 and 337–339. Some Unionists voted against the concurrent resolutions to amend the constitution for soldiers' votes because they insisted that the bill Seymour vetoed was constitutional.

27. Alexander, *History*, III, 79–80; see, also, Seymour, *Public Record*, 365–369.

Journal thought the governor ought to be indicted under the law forbidding "indecent exhibitions."[28] Beginning by expressing the hope that his "friends" were not confined to the tumultuous people of New York City, Seymour defended his correspondence with Dix and Lincoln on the subject of the draft and declared that the great victories at Vicksburg and Gettysburg made opportune an offer of peace to the South. He would never willingly embarrass the administration; he would never consent to a dissolution of the Union; and he had never doubted that it would be restored. Both emancipation and conscription, he believed, had been unwise, and against the immediate injustices of the draft he would not cease to protest so long as he was governor of the state. His words in regard to the proclamation of Lincoln which Chief-Justice Taney did not live long enough to declare unconstitutional were conciliatory; for after all, that question would not press for an answer until the war was over.

> I am willing to leave the emancipation proclamation just where he has left it, to stand valid if the courts pronounce it valid, and to fall if invalid; and it must fall because it is invalid. I agree with him when he proposes to leave it where he knows it must die, without regret.[29]

The convention adjourned with cheers for McClellan and Seymour, after having adopted resolutions which endorsed the conduct of the governor and "the vigour which he displayed in putting down a lawless and reckless mob."

The governor was under still another handicap, for he had been forced to take the unpopular side of the question of how the debt of the state should be redeemed. It was the old bitter dispute over paper and gold, the controversy which invariably comes to the surface in times of emergency. In the spring of 1863 the legislature had to determine whether the interest on the bonds of the state should be paid in specie or in greenbacks. The Republicans, who controlled the senate and made just one-half of the assembly, favored the use of greenbacks because,

28. Albany *Evening Journal*, September 10, 1863.
29. Seymour, *Public Record*, 369.

so they said, payment in specie would look like a slur on the financial policy of Secretary Chase. Most of the Democrats stood out for payment in coin, and the bankers of New York City declared that the use of greenbacks would amount to repudiation. Seymour incorporated their views in a message to both houses.[30] A small number of the Republicans joined with the Democrats and saved the day for what was thought to be the honor of the state, by voting that persons residing out of the United States should be paid in gold or its equivalent. Seymour, however, had to bear the burden of allowing greenbacks to be paid to the American people and gold to the bankers of foreign creditors.

On April 22, 1864, the governor had to face the question again at a time when he was thought to be a "repudiated" executive. The assembly was now heavily Republican, and a concurrent resolution had passed both houses of the legislature according to which the debt of New York, both principal and interest, was to be paid in "currency"—no distinction being made betwen foreign and domestic holders of the bonds of the state. A special message had no effect on the legislature, and the governor was forced to send out his famous circular letter to the merchants and bankers of New York under the date of April 23, 1864. This letter asked them to collect sufficient money to pay the foreign creditors in gold. The last paragraph is significant: "I have faith that whatever money may be so contributed will be only lent. Better counsels will prevail among our legislators, and the State will repay what is now advanced."[31] Thus, when a Republican legislature went back

30. Brummer, *History*, 276–277.

31. Greenbacks were the second most important issue of the national election of 1868. The Democratic platform was not sound on this financial heresy. Horatio Seymour not only talked gold, but paid it in the crisis of 1864. In view of his conduct, the accusations Dix brought in his letter from France in September, 1868, are a damaging reflection on the general's character. For Governor Seymour's two special messages on the payment of interest on the state debt, see Lincoln, *Messages*, v, 490–493 and 578–581; and Seymour, *Public Record*, 215–218. For one of Seymour's letters of thanks addressed to Howland and Aspinwall, New York City, on May 11, 1864, see the Seymour Papers in the New York Historical Society: "There is little doubt now, I think, that my re-

on its promise to pay debts with honest dollars the governor who was called a Copperhead had to go out and borrow gold from the pockets of the prosperous citizens of the state. On September 22, 1863, it is interesting to notice in this connection, Peter Cooper, emancipationist — and Greenback candidate for President in 1876 — threw the great influence of his good name against Governor Seymour with a long open letter on the evils of slavery.[32]

By the autumn of 1863 Seymour had been governor for less than a year but he had raised up enemies on every side. His pressure for recruiting disappointed the comparatively small Copperhead element in the state; his opposition to the draft and its enforcement led many men to class him with the lukewarm friends of the Union. He had blocked, with his veto, the bill giving votes to soldiers, insisting that the constitution of the state must be amended for that express purpose. He had forced the legislature to pay foreign creditors of New York in gold, and easy-money men denounced him as a tool of the bankers. Bennett, of the powerful *Herald*, had failed to place a friend on the metropolitan board of police; Greeley, of the *Tribune*, accused him of conspiracy in the riots of July. Tammany had lost a valuable traction franchise by his veto — a grant by means of which Tweed and his associates hoped to hold up Vanderbilt and make him pay their price. The drafts of August and October proved that the governor's opposition to the hated policy of conscription was ineffective, and Stanton's special commission would not vindicate Seymour's claim for a correction of the figures until long after election day. The adroitness of dishonesty was not his to use in his own defense, and the wily Chauncey Mitchell Depew, who had let his party

liance on the New York merchants to secure payment of the State's interest (so much, at least, as is due to foreigners), in coin was just and well founded." For Greeley's characteristically specious argument against Seymour's stand for paying state banks gold on the New York debt, see the *Tribune* of May 3, 1864. This threatened repudiation by New York State was noticed in the London *Daily News*. The New York *Times* and the *Evening Post* applauded the governor's policy. From the approved point of view of the present day Seymour was wrong.

32. New York *Evening Post*, September 26, 1863.

trade him out of the speakership of the evenly divided assembly in order that Governor Morgan might go to the Senate of the United States in 1863, was beginning his long and prosperous political career — as Republican candidate for secretary of state.

Surrounded by grudges and suspicions, as in 1854, Seymour took the stump and made four speeches which were, as he acknowledged long afterward, "sharp and defiant."[33] Shortly before the first of these he sent a letter to the Democrats of Milwaukee, who had invited him to address them on October 25, as if to counteract the effect of the learned disquisition which General Dix had sent into the state. This letter describes Seymour's position in national politics in the autumn of 1863 concisely.

In the gloomy night which overshadows the nation, there is no hope but in the restoration to power of the democratic conservative party. The fanatical leaders who precipitated this bloody conflict by underrating the South, its resources and military ability, who scoffed at the Crittenden compromise and all other efforts to avert civil war — who rejected the measures of the Peace Convention, and who, after war was forced upon us, have persistently created obstacles to its vigorous and successful prosecution, by perverting it from its original purpose, the restoration of the Union, as solemnly avowed in our National Congress, into a hopeless Emancipation crusade, and by driving from the army through abolition intrigues, General McClellan and other officers of military capacity, to make place for political adventurers — have, by their entire policy exhibited alike their incapacity to carry on war or inaugurate peace.

Failing to crush the southern rebellion, their entire energies seem now directed to the destruction of popular rights and personal freedom throughout the North. Safeguards of Liberty wrested from despotism after a struggle of centuries, are by them ignored or swept away. The substitution of an irresponsible military tyranny in place of law, the suppression of free speech — the muzzling of the press, the mid-night seizure, mock trial and illegal banishment of a distinguished citizen of Ohio, and that too in a loyal district, where the civil law is in unobstructed operation, — are among the

33. Alexander, *History*, III, 81, praises the oratorical ability which Seymour showed on this tour, although he finds himself in disagreement with the governor's point of view. See Seymour, *Public Record*, 160–197. The finest of these speeches — the address at Cooper Institute, October 31, 1863 — was so good as to be particularly annoying. In Seymour's alternative to the offer of an immediate negotiated peace with the South can be read an accurate prophecy of the scandals of reconstruction.

mad acts, by which all constitutional government and every principle dear to freedom, are sought to be crushed and destroyed.

While we will freely expend blood and treasure to overcome southern traitors, we must with equal spirit and similar sacrifices resist such treasonable usurpation at the North. The latter formidable and dangerous, because secret and insidious in its advance, must be expelled at all hazards.[34]

Friendly newspapers were few and far between. The Albany *Atlas and Argus* did its best to defend the governor from the charge of having betrayed the peace party which elected him by becoming an "indispensable ally of Lincoln."[35] Bryant, of the *Evening Post*, described the Democratic state convention as the ghost of "Twaddle" Hall.[36] The well dressed gentleman from Utica was solemnly likened in both character and career to Robespierre.[37] Greeley bobbed up with the declaration that Seymour was a nepotist — his brother Jonathan drew two hundred dollars a month from the treasury as state agent; a nephew was paid one hundred and fifty dollars a month as an officer; and a cousin and two other nephews each received one thousand dollars annually as clerks in the executive department.[38] The governor was described as a man whom rebels delighted to honor — who had called rioters, with torch and bludgeon in hand, his "friends."[39] The October elections went against the Democrats all over the North; Lincoln was drawing dividends from the triumphs at Vicksburg and Gettysburg. On the night before election Seward spoke at Auburn, according to his custom, urging the people to make his chief the President of all the United States — *de facto* as well as *de jure*. Was it to be supposed, he asked his neighbors, that if Lincoln were not returned in 1864 the "majority" who elected him in 1860 would "acquiesce, without rioting and without bloodshed, to the elec-

34. New York State Library: Seymour Papers: Letter of October 20, 1863.

35. Albany *Atlas and Argus*, September 19, 1863.

36. New York *Evening Post*, September 12, 1863.

37. Rochester *Union*, October 3, 1863. See page 554.

38. New York *Tribune*, October 9; and Alexander, *History*, III, 80. John F. Seymour served as state agent for the relief of New York soldiers during his elder brother's second term.

39. New York *Tribune*, October 1, 1863. The New York *Herald* (September 26, 1863) accused Seymour of hobnobbing with Copperheads in Connecticut, endorsing Vallandigham in Ohio, and doing nothing but talk in the riots.

tion of Jefferson Davis, or John C. Breckinridge, or Horatio Seymour?"[40] What the Republicans called the "Union Ticket" triumphed in New York by majorities of thirty thousand. As compared with the returns of 1862 the Democratic totals showed a loss of over twenty-one thousand votes; the majority by which Seymour had been elected governor was wiped out in New York City alone. The Republicans gained eighteen thousand votes. "The result was regarded as a rebuke to Governor Seymour."[41]

Seymour took his great disappointment calmly. So far as he could know he had made his last campaign. During the second year of his second term he faced a definitely hostile legislature. The annual message he sent to it on January 5, 1864, shows a change in emphasis. The business of the state, including his report on the riots of July, 1863, occupied thirty pages of print; while a discussion of federal affairs filled only eleven.[42] Into that space, however, the determined governor crowded a vigorous and detailed criticism of the policies of the government at Washington. Overlooking the fact that conscription was being used as a club to force recruiting, he complained that the Enrollment Act brought in "money and not men." He put his objection to it into one paragraph: "It not only fails to fill our armies, but it produces discontent in the service; it is opposed to the genius of our political system; it alienates our people from the Government; it is injurious to the industrial pursuits of the country."[43]

Pointing out that the federal government had asked for nearly "two millions of men" by January, 1864, Seymour insisted that its effort "to make itself independent of popular and local influences" had not only "impaired its power to get recruits" but had raised a hostile feeling against "coercion."

40. New York State Library: Seymour Papers: Scrap-Books, VI, 173. This shameful speech can not be found in *Works of William Henry Seward*, George E. Baker, Editor, (New York, 1883–1884).

41. Rhodes, *History*, IV, 416.

42. Lincoln, *Messages*, V, 520–561.

43. Lincoln, *Messages*, V, 538.

If it were asked why a draft should not succeed in the North as well as in the South, the answer was that the soldiers of the Union "would cheerfully undergo the hardships not only of a coerced but of an unpaid service, if the condition of the country demanded these sacrifices." Upon the same principle, however, they had a right to share in the prosperity of a country where the men who stayed at home were making money or getting "unusual wages." So long as the people were financially prosperous, the governor declared, the armies of the Union ought to be filled by bounties and not by compulsion. Soldiers should receive the same pay as labor earned at home. Yet the depreciation of the currency robbed them of one-third of the value of what they were paid.

If the Enrollment Act had been designed to keep up the number of men in the field with the least possible public expense, the workings of the law had been just the reverse. It had proved a levy on property rather than a draft on persons. Sudden and irregular calls for soldiers embarrassed the business of the country, and the indiscriminate drawing of men from any community disrupted industry. The cure for these evils was "a permanent plan for recruiting" and "reasonable bounties" which would encourage volunteering. The militia of the several states should be armed and equipped in the manner set forth by the Constitution. The negligence and false economy which led the governments of the states and the nation to allow the militia to decay had been "fearfully punished" in 1861. An army of conscripts, on the other hand, would become estranged from the people and a peril to the republic. The "unanimous political action" of such an army could make a President. Of all the dangers which threatened to separate soldiers from citizens the draft was the greatest.[44]

Seymour brought his second annual message to a close with a cogent criticism of the ill-advised policies which were not to be liquidated for twelve years. As late as January, 1864, the governor of the greatest state of the Union found that he could

44. Lincoln, *Messages*, v, 539–543.

not in his heart "agree with those upon the one hand who insist upon an unconditional peace, or with those, upon the other extreme, who would use only unqualified force in putting down this rebellion." He demanded "a fair, dispassionate and respectful hearing" for the middle course he begged his fellow citizens to follow while there was time. There were two antagonistic theories before the American people for bringing an end to the "destructive contest." The first was the resolution which "consecrated the energies of war and the policy of government to the restoration of the Union, the support of our Constitution." Faith in that resolution had supplied men and money "without distinction of party."

The opposite theory would prevent the immediate return of the revolted states upon the condition of laying down their arms. Not only was it absurd to insist that states which could not secede were not in the Union the moment they were ready to acknowledge the fact; it was dangerous to the point of inviting disaster. To maintain that the eleven states of the Confederacy must be "reëstablished" was to turn rebellion into revolution. According to this plan the whole population of a third of the Union would be stripped of all political rights until they were purged by presidential clemency. Yet the "disorganization and destruction of the South" would demand a standing army and a continued drain upon the persons and property of the American people. It was, continued Seymour, "a fact full of significance that every measure to convert the war against armed rebellion into one against private property and personal rights at the South" had been "accompanied by claims to exercise military power in the loyal states of the North." Seymour knew that no man can rob another man of liberty without losing his own.

What especially alarmed him was the fact that new and extreme claims to arbitrary power should be advanced at the very time it was declared the strength of the rebellion was broken. Once the vice of victory got into the veins of loyal men, it would poison peace and restoration. The armies and navies of the

North had won "signal victories"; they had done their part with "courage, skill, and success." Now was the time, according to the "usage of the civilized world," when "statesmanship must . . . exert its influence." The great object of battles was to place the North in a position from which an invitation to the rebellious states to acknowledge the Union could be offered with "dignity and magnanimity." Belligerent rights had been conceded to the South from the beginning, and the "mutual respect" which the fearful struggle had taught the contestants forbade the thought of denying the South self-government at the end. Over thirteen years later President Hayes was forced to realize that the radical experiment of reconstruction was the total failure Seymour predicted it would be.[45]

In its dual aspect as a criticism of the acts of the administration and a warning against the plans of the radical Republicans Seymour's second annual message attracted national attention. The editors of New York City divided along the usual line: Bryant, Greeley, and Raymond attacked it as an expression of sympathy with the South and a pat on the back for Jefferson Davis. Although Seymour's words were not to have effect, for men absorbed in a given task are always scornful or resentful toward advice, the message caused much favorable comment through the country.[46] Yet arguments rarely end fights, no

45. Lincoln, *Messages*, v, 552–561.

46. For a surprisingly long list of complimentary editorial paragraphs, see the Seymour Scrap-Books, VIII, 6–12: New York State Library. The tenor of the message was approved, among many others, by the Providence *Daily Post*, the Chicago *Times*, the Milwaukee *News*, the Harrisburg, Pennsylvania, *Patriot and Union*, the Pittsfield *Sun*, the Brooklyn *Daily Eagle*, the Boston *Post*, the Hartford *Times*, the Newark, New Jersey, *Journal*, and, of course, the New York *World*. For the opinion of a famous observer, supposedly neutral, see the London *Times* of January 22, 1864: "If anything will rouse them from it, it will be the employment of the army as a machinery for the election of Presidents. This danger Mr. Seymour thinks is by no means remote. Supposing any of the federal states are conquered or occupied, the army by which they are held must be still maintained. Then, under the condition of Mr. Lincoln's last proclamation, one-tenth of the population in any such state may by taking the vote of allegiance bring it into the Union again, or fix new boundaries, and come in as a new state carved out of the old one. As such, it will have two votes in the federal senate, and political influence equal to the State of New York itself."

matter how often they begin them. To the mind of Brummer,

> Governor Seymour was a conscientious man, and he doubtless intended that his message should be a solemn warning to those in power. Instead, it served as a text for many partisan speeches in the Legislature, and whatever influence the document had in moulding public opinion among the mass of Democrats was not in the direction of holding them firm in the support of the war.[47]

In the spring of 1864 Governor Seymour became embroiled in another dispute with General Dix. This time the question at issue was the freedom of the press. On May 18 the New York *World* published a bogus proclamation according to which President Lincoln was supposed to have called for a day of fasting and prayer and, what was more important still, four hundred thousand men. The *Journal of Commerce* copied the false news. The furious Stanton secured an executive order by virtue of which the commander of the Department of the East was given authority to suppress both papers. The editors, proprietors, and publishers were to be arrested and imprisoned; the establishments were to be occupied "by military force" and held "until further orders"; publication was to be stopped. After both Lincoln and Seward had signed this extraordinary document General Dix "reluctantly executed" the order. Soldiers descended on the offices of the newspapers and, seizing the men they found, held them under military guard for three days.[48] Four days after the outrage Governor Seymour instructed A. Oakey Hall, the district attorney of the county of New York, to bring the raid to the attention of the grand jury. The jury not only refused to find an indictment but passed a formal resolution that it was "inexpedient" to examine into the matter. Then the governor directed Hall to appeal to "some proper magistrate," promising him assistance "in the prosecu-

47. Brummer, *History*, 358–359.

48. A concise and careful account of this disgraceful incident will be found in Randall, *Constitutional Problems*, 496–499. Lincoln assumed full responsibility for the suspension (Welles, *Diary*, II, 67), but Randall justly concludes: "The order was a hasty one, based upon mere suspicion of wrongful intent, and the Administration itself felt that the action was ill-advised."

tion of these investigations."[49] A judge named Russell issued a warrant at the request of Hall, and both General Dix and his second in command were arrested and then released on their own recognizance.

The case of the "People versus John A. Dix and Others" was tried before Judge Russell on August 7, 1864, the commander of the Department of the East standing accused of kidnaping and inciting to riot. The sensational case "was elaborately argued by distinguished counsel and it involved legal principles of great importance." The prosecution maintained that the Indemnity Act of March 3, 1863, was unconstitutional. The defense argued that the law was fully vindicated because the grand jury had failed to indict Dix or his subordinates. Judge Russell rendered what has been called a "harmless decision," affirming the unconstitutionality of the Indemnity Act and decreeing that Dix and the others who had executed Lincoln's order should be held "subject to the action of the grand jury of the city and county." No action was ever taken. Dix, however, became the implacable enemy of Seymour. He would wait four years and more for his revenge. Thus, as in the case of the arrest of Vallandigham in 1863, the governor of New York publicly defied what he believed to be an act of tyranny. To ardent advocates of the radical doctrines which postponed the liquidation of the Civil War, Horatio Seymour had become a public nuisance.

With the summer of 1864 came the time for the national conventions. Lincoln was by no means certain of renomination. Accident and intention had established a tradition in favor of a single term. Since the days of Andrew Jackson no President had served eight years. Between 1836 and 1860 six men had been elected to the office, two of whom died in the White House, neither of the successors securing an election in his own right. Van Buren had been renominated and defeated; Polk, Pierce,

49. Seymour, *Public Record*, 218–221: Letters of Horatio Seymour to A. Oakey Hall, May 23 and June 26, 1864.

and Buchanan had not been named a second time — Polk because he would not be. There was more than tradition at stake, however. The growing legend of Lincoln's perfection has consigned much contemporary opinion of him to convenient oblivion. For contemptuous and poisonous words in regard to his character and conduct one need not turn to Confederates or Copperheads; the radical Republicans were full of scorn and hatred of him. For these men Chase was the heir-apparent in 1864. No one has questioned the ability or loyalty of Murat Halstead, proprietor and editor of the Cincinnati *Daily Commercial*. This man had a thorough knowledge of American politics as early as 1860; his mind was nimble; his pen was skillful, and his principles were prominent. Yet in 1863 Halstead was writing to John Sherman: "If Lincoln was not a damned fool, we could get along yet. He is an awful, woeful ass." "Can't you take him by the throat," Halstead begged Secretary Chase, "and knock his head against a wall until he is brought to his senses on the war business? I do not speak wantonly when I say there are persons who feel that it was [*sic*] doing God's service to kill him, if it were not feared that Hamlin is a bigger fool than he is."[50] Such opinions were not rare, by any means; to the self-righteousness of the radicals Abraham Lincoln was, at best, a trifler. One searches the speeches and letters of Seymour for such words as these in vain.

It was a tipsy actor who pushed Lincoln from the path of the northerners who shared the sentiments of men like Halstead. Immediately after the President's proclamation of amnesty on December 8, 1863, the movement to replace him with his secretary of the treasury became menacing. Senator Samuel C. Pomeroy, of Kansas, and John Sherman aided and abetted the ambition of Chase until such time as the action of the legisla-

50. *Mississippi Valley Historical Review*, XXIII (June, 1936): Charles R. Wilson, "The Original Chase Organization Meeting and *The Next Presidential Election*," 62.

ture of Ohio made it obvious that the secretary could not swing even his own state against Lincoln. The drive for a change of leaders in 1864 had the secret support of three-quarters of the Republicans in the Senate of the United States at one time, but bitterness and double-dealing proved a boomerang. The conspirators outdid themselves, and public opinion began to take notice. The plot blew up, and the intended beneficiary of it bowed himself out of the Cabinet. Before long it was plain that the President would be named for reëlection.

Seymour was between the devil and the deep sea. On the one hand stood the radical Republicans, who seemed to gain influence and power day by day. Time after time Lincoln was forced to give way to them in order to insure his nomination and election. The President was not all right, but the most potent of his supporters were certainly all wrong. On the other hand stood those impractical Democrats who followed Vallandigham and his program of "immediate peace." Although this dramatic son of Ohio had been beaten for governor in the autumn of 1863, two circumstances had qualified the chilling effect of that defeat. When General John H. Morgan led his raid into Ohio in July, the indiscriminate destruction of the property of both loyal and disaffected people had reacted against the interest of the Copperheads. In selecting a candidate to oppose him, moreover, the Republicans had found it prudent to name a War Democrat, John Brough. One Democrat routed another. When Vallandigham returned to the United States from Canada in June, 1864, he found his prestige practically unharmed in his own part of the country.

He was allowed to move about the North very much as he pleased, although a year of exile in Canada had not cooled his ardor or curbed his tongue. It has been unusually difficult for students of the period to pass sane judgment on this remarkable man. One author who asserts that Vallandigham skated on "the thin ice of near-treason," whatever that may mean, acknowledges on the same page that "it is certain" that "he had no real sympathy with the rebellion." This writer's summing up of the character of Vallandigham is more nearly neutral than most:

> He was of Huguenot and Scotch descent; the scion of families early transplanted to Virginia, and thence to Ohio; Presbyterian and Democrat by forces as immutable in such minds as any laws of nature. He inherited a fixed philosophy of life. His was one of those minds that instinctively fear innovation, whose eyes were on the past, whose faith clung to established institutions and time worn customs. The dogmatic assurance and inflexible purpose of his kind were entrenched in a cold and selfish personality. . . . And yet somehow he possessed a grace of bearing and powers of address which captivated those who came within his sphere. College education, legal studies and practice in the courts, and editorial experience on the Dayton Empire failed to liberalize his ways of thinking, but from their training he developed a power of expression, the eloquence of the political platform, in which few of his generation surpassed him.[51]

His forced tour of the South, his conferences with Confederates in Canada, and the fiasco of Greeley's visit to Niagara Falls in July, 1864, did not shake Vallandigham's conviction that immediate peace was not only possible but probable. His dramatic appearance before the district convention of Democrats at Hamilton, Ohio, led to his election as a delegate to the national convention of the party at Chicago.

Among critics of Lincoln's military management the name of McClellan became increasingly important. Seymour faced a dilemma. His interest in blocking the policy of one man and heading off the nomination of the other drew attention to the difficult position of his party in 1864. It put up a man who complained that he had not been allowed to conduct the war properly on the platform of another man who believed that the war should end at once. McClellan, in the eyes of Seymour, had been guilty of arbitrary acts in Maryland in 1861; Vallandigham was a visionary. Both Guthrie and Nelson, moreover, conservative Democrats of unblemished reputation, were

51. See *Collections*, Western Reserve Historical Society, XCIX (December, 1918), for an interesting paper: Elbert J. Benton, "The Movement for Peace Without a Victory During the Civil War." The words cited will be found on pages 38 and 12–14.

seventy-one years of age in 1864. By 1880 Seymour had come to believe that a man of seventy was too old for public life.

Guthrie and Nelson are now forgotten, but neither was a nonentity in his day. Although the first was an irascible son of Kentucky who made himself rich, he had reformed the treasury during his tenure of office (1853–1857), weeding out waste and fraud with a reckless hand. He it was who changed the basis of pay for the collector of the port at New York from commissions to salary, thus mortally offending Greene C. Bronson, who got his revenge by splitting the assembly ticket in 1853 and running as the "Hard" candidate for governor in 1854. At the outbreak of the Civil War, Guthrie was president of the Louisville and Nashville Railroad, and his loyalty to the Union not only helped to keep Kentucky "neutral" but furthered the winning of the great campaigns in the West. The railroad was as important a factor in the outcome as the Mississippi River. Guthrie took himself out of the field in 1864, however, by standing for election as a delegate to the national convention of the Democrats at Chicago.

Samuel Nelson had already had a distinguished career on the bench of New York when President Tyler appointed him to the Supreme Court during the last days of his administration. Nelson made a name for himself at the time of the fierce dissension over the Dred Scott Decision. The first intention of the majority of the court had been to dismiss the case for lack of jurisdiction, but rumors of the plans of the dissenting justices, Curtis and McLean, led to an unfortunate change of front. Taney took command and prepared one set of questionable *obiter dicta* to match another. Nelson read his own opinion, which seems, after eighty years, the most reasonable and judicious of the three. That his mental vigor was unimpaired as late as 1871 is shown by his service in the business of the *Alabama* claims. The next year he resigned from the Supreme Court and died in 1873 at the age of eighty-one. Men much less able than Samuel Nelson have reached the head of affairs in the United States.

The Democratic state convention assembled at Tweddle Hall, in Albany, on February 23, 1864. It named no issues and mentioned no candidate. Seymour, Richmond, Belmont, and Isaac Butts, of Rochester, were made delegates-at-large, with instructions for the unit rule. The first plan of the Democrats had been to hold their national convention on July 4, but the plots and counter-plots in the ranks of the Republicans had tempted their opponents to postpone the choice of their nominee until they should know whether or not Lincoln was to be the candidate. Oddly enough, Seymour himself was drawn into contact with a scheme for providing a better nominee than the President, and that through no less a person than Governor John Albion Andrew.[52]

Republican opponents of Lincoln resented what they called the "snap nomination" at Baltimore, and, in looking around for a more popular or pliable person, Governor Andrew asked Seymour for his aid and counsel. He proposed that the chief executives of the two states should meet quietly in New York City for an informal and confidential talk on the best and quickest means to "conquer a peace." Andrew had been conferring with Colonel Jaquess, who had returned only recently from Richmond. He offered to meet Seymour "at such house" in New York as he might suggest. The regency training of the pupil of Marcy was too ingrained for the New Yorker to commit his opinions to paper: on August 16 he scribbled a note of three lines to the governor of Massachusetts and turned up in his office in Boston on the nineteenth.[53] What these two men said to each other is known only at second hand and that by recollection, for their conference was strictly private. After two hours of conversation they separated, each man impressed by the other but neither persuaded. According to Colonel Henry Lee, Andrew remarked to him at the time: "I hardly know what to make of Governor Seymour; he seemed very sincere.

52. Pearson, *John A. Andrew*, II, 157–158. Andrew's letter to Seymour is dated August 11, 1864.

53. Massachusetts Historical Society: Andrew Papers.

I think he is carried away by his own subtlety, perhaps."[54] Shortly after returning to Albany, Seymour set out for Chicago.

To block the program of Vallandigham, on the one hand, and the nomination of McClellan, on the other, he had nothing more than his own prestige and the name of Samuel Nelson. As the obvious leader of the constitutional opposition to the policies of the radical Republicans Seymour was a person of importance and promise. He might easily have managed his own nomination; that he was unwilling to do so is proved first, by his going to the convention as a delegate, and second, by his acceptance of the permanent chairmanship. His journey into the West was marked with a series of ovations at every stop, and "especially at Detroit, crowds, cheers, speeches, and salvos of firearms greeted him."[55]

> There was also much in Seymour himself as well as in his words to attract the attention of the convention. Added years gave him a more stately, almost a picturesque bearing, while a strikingly intelligent face changed its expression with the ease and swiftness of an actor's.[56]

When he went up to take his place as presiding officer of the convention, a storm of cheers followed him from the floor. Not only could he have headed the ticket if he had been willing,

54. Readers of Pearson, *John A. Andrew*, II, 158, footnote, and John T. Morse, Jr., *Memoir of Colonel Henry Lee*, 237, will observe that the two stories of the meeting of the governors do not agree in all details. Professor Pearson drew on Lee's story as it appeared in "Random Recollections" in the Newton *Circuit* for June 19, 1896. When Mr. Morse published his memoir in 1905, he quoted Colonel Lee directly. According to this account, Seymour arrived at Governor Andrew's office unannounced and told him, among other things: "I have read everything you have said or written; I don't agree with you about anything, but I like you because you have convictions. I can't get along with Seward because he has no convictions."

55. Alexander, *History*, III, 107.

56. Alexander, *History*, III, 111–112. Depew's opinion of Seymour, as given by Alexander, is interesting: "Governor Seymour was an elegant and an accomplished gentleman with a high-bred manner which never unbent, and he was always faultlessly dressed. He looked the ideal of an aristocrat, and yet he was and continued to be until his death the idol of the Democracy." The Detroit *Free Press* of September 1, 1864, described Seymour as "middle-aged," with "a frank and open countenance," "stately in form," and "straight as an arrow," always affable except when "the passions" darted "rapid flashes from his piercing eyes" — a man whose brain was "evidently wearing out the body."

but, what is more important still, he might have written the platform. Defeat in the assembly elections of 1863 and the stubborn accusation that he was working all the while for himself in 1864 seem to have made him the victim of his own indecision.[57]

August Belmont called the convention to order at noon on Monday, August 29, in the Amphitheatre at Chicago. Former Governor Bigler of Pennsylvania was chosen temporary chairman, and the committee on permanent organization chose the governor of New York as president. In taking the chair on Tuesday, Seymour expressed the hope that the Democrats would act in such a way as to cause the Republican party to "die here where it was born." The one way, however, was to follow the middle course between the men who talked with Vallandigham and those who sulked with McClellan. That middle course Seymour himself made impossible. He saw no man before him who did not "love the Union"; he saw no man who did not "desire peace" — no man who was "not resolved to uphold the great principles of constitutional freedom." The administration could not "now save this Union, if it would": its proclamations, its vindictive legislation, its "displays of hate and passion" had "hampered" its "freedom of action." The soldiers were not to be blamed for the "ruin" of the country; it was those who stayed at home who cried havoc and demanded "that no mercy . . . be shown." If the administration could not save the Union, the Democrats must do so. "Mr. Lincoln values many things above the Union; we put it first of all. He thinks a proclamation worth more than peace; we think the blood of our people more precious than the edicts of the President." [58]

It is often said that the Chicago platform was Vallandigham's, and that the second paragraph sealed the doom of the Democrats in 1864. This is not strictly true. Twenty-three states

57. See, for instance, a dispatch dated August 28, 1864, in the New York *Evening Post* of September 1, 1864.

58. *Official Proceedings, Democratic National Convention*, 22–24; and Seymour, *Public Record*, 230–233.

had sent delegates to the convention; among them was Tilden, one of two men who represented the ninth congressional district of New York. Tilden went on the committee of resolutions, opposed Vallandigham as chairman, and managed the election of Guthrie by the close vote of 13 to 11. Guthrie made John B. Weller, of California, chairman of the sub-committee which was to draw up the platform. This sub-committee met after dinner on Monday, August 29, sat until one o'clock in the morning of Tuesday, and was not ready to report until four that afternoon.[59] Then it brought in a platform of six paragraphs, the second of which Vallandigham had written and forced through the committee of resolutions by a narrow vote. It received the wildest welcome, and when the uproar had subsided, all six paragraphs were adopted by a voice vote of the convention.[60]

In 1880, former Senator James R. Doolittle, of Wisconsin, a War Democrat, drew up an explanation of the defeats of his party in the four presidential elections from 1864 to 1876. Doolittle stumped the country for Seymour in 1868, but twelve years later he declared that the Democratic candidate was doomed from the very first, "though a majority of the people did not want General Grant for president." According to Doolittle, Seymour was defeated in 1868 not because of the much-exaggerated speech to the so-called "rioters" but rather because he "presided at that convention in 1864, which passed that suicidal platform of surrender to the Rebellion."[61] The head and front of offense, if we are to believe Senator Doolittle, was the following paragraph, second of the six:

Resolved, That this convention does explicitly declare, as the sense of the American people, that after four years of failure to restore the Union by the experiment of war, during which, under the pretence of a military necessity, or war power higher than the Constitution, the Constitution itself has been disregarded in every part, and public liberty and private right alike

59. *Official Proceedings, Democratic National Convention*, 25.
60. *Official Proceedings, Democratic National Convention*, 27–29.
61. *Wisconsin Magazine of History*, VI, 1 (September, 1922), 96–97: Letter of James Rood Doolittle to C. A. Dana, April 16, 1880.

trodden down, and the material prosperity of the country essentially impaired, — justice, humanity, liberty, and the public welfare demand that immediate efforts be made for a cessation of hostilities, with a view to an ultimate convention of the States, or other peaceable means, to the end that, at the earliest practicable moment, peace may be restored on the basis of the federal Union of the States.[62]

In view of the fact that Tilden, with the aid of August Belmont, the national chairman, and William Cassidy of the *Atlas and Argus*, had defeated Vallandigham for chairmanship of the committee on resolutions, it is natural to wonder why he did not fight the famous second paragraph on the floor of the convention. What was thought to be the fatal section had passed the committee by only a "slight majority." Alexander has called attention to the fact that John Bigelow saw fit to omit all mention of Tilden's presence at Chicago in 1864.[63] He suggests that Tilden feared a fight — a split such as had wrecked the national convention at Charleston in 1860. He had defeated the person but not his idea. The future would show that if one word can ever describe a man, "circuitous" would be the term for Tilden. His devious conduct in 1877, for instance, was the despair of his supporters. Lacking the power of personal appeal, he was probably afraid to face the magnetic Vallandigham before that wild crowd at Chicago.

Historians have thought that it was absurd for this convention to declare the war a failure and then nominate a general for President. It was Vallandigham himself, it is not always remembered, who moved that the choice be made unanimous. The selection of McClellan can be taken to imply, however, that if he had been continued in command of the Army of the Potomac, the war might not have been a "failure" by 1864. The first mention of his name raised a row. After New Jersey had offered him as her candidate, Delaware nominated Senator Powell, of Kentucky, who promptly withdrew. Then Michael Stuart, of Ohio, put up Governor T. H. Seymour, of Connecticut. In rising to second this nomination, Benjamin G. Harris, of

62. Stanwood, *History of the Presidency*, 304.
63. Alexander, *History*, III, 113–114.

Maryland, took the opportunity to launch a violent attack on McClellan for having arrested the legislature of that state in September, 1861. Amid noisy protests from the galleries and the floor (Seymour all the while insisting that Harris should have a hearing) the angry delegate from Maryland aired his opinion of McClellan. He asked the convention if they thought Antietam was a "victory" and concluded by declaring, "Why, as a military man, he has been defeated everywhere." When Alexander Long, of Ohio, pleaded with the delegates not to name McClellan, his plaintive words "I beg of you to give us another candidate" were greeted with cries of "Seymour of New York!"[64]

As the roll was called for the first ballot five votes from Iowa, four and one-half from Missouri, two from Ohio, and one-half from Massachusetts were recorded in favor of the presiding officer.[65] If Seymour had the itch for office from which he is supposed to have suffered all his life, now or never was the chance to scratch it. If the leading candidate had been the man of his choice, it would have been easy for him to make the self-denial which he did. Such was not the case, however.

> . . . deep in his heart Seymour did not fancy McClellan. His public life had been brief, and his accomplishment little either as a soldier or civilian. Besides, his arrest of the Maryland Legislature, and his indifference to the sacredness of the writ of *habeas corpus*, classing him among those whom the Governor had bitterly denounced, tended to destroy the latter's strongest argument against the Lincoln administration.
>
> Dean Richmond, now a vigorous supporter of McClellan, could not be confused as to the General's strength or the Governor's weakness, and he attempted at an early hour to silence the appeal for Seymour by solidifying the New York delegation for McClellan; but in these efforts he found it difficult to subdue the personal independence and outspoken ways of the Governor, whose opposition to McClellan was more than a passing cloud-shadow.[66]

Twice the convention trampled on the better judgment of its presiding officer; at Albany in September he would sacrifice his convictions to the needs of his party for the third time.

64. *Official Proceedings, Democratic National Convention*, 39.
65. *Official Proceedings, Democratic National Convention*, 43.
66. Alexander, *History*, III, 107–108.

When Amasa J. Parker rose to report for New York, he announced that his state, "regretfully passing by her favorite son, who disclaims the candidacy," gave all its thirty-three votes to McClellan. Without these the general could not have been chosen on the first ballot.[67] Under the unit rule a majority of one, that is seventeen delegates, would have been sufficient to swing all thirty-three to the governor. For this he would have to give nothing but his nod of assent. The name of Samuel Nelson, however, was not strong enough to sway the delegates to Seymour's will. Ohio having retired to revise its vote, the presiding officer took advantage of the interval of waiting. The final decision still hung in the balance. His last renunciation of the nomination was coupled with the best apology possible for the act of McClellan in Maryland in 1861.

The PRESIDENT: Some gentlemen have done me the honor to present my name in connection with the office of President of these United States. It would be affectation on my part to say that these evidences of regard did not give me great pleasure; but many months since I announced to my friends in the State of New York that I could not, for reasons of both public and private character, be a candidate for that high office. Having thus advised life-long friends of my purposes, those to whom I have been under so many great and enduring obligations, it would not be honorable on my part to allow my name to be brought forward under circumstances of apparent antagonism to them, when their views and commitments led them in another direction. [Cheers.] As a member of the New York delegation, I thought it would be advisable to place in nomination for the Presidency, an eminent jurist of that State. [Cheers.] I was led to that conclusion, not by any doubt of the ability and patriotism of General McClellan, or from any want of regard for his person or character, for I cherish a warm attachment for both. I know that General McClellan never sought the nomination now conferred upon him. [Cheers.] I know from his declaration to myself and others that it would be more agreeable to him to resume his connection with the army of his country, than to occupy the Presidential chair; but the wishes of the people have decided that it should be otherwise. [Applause.]

I wish to say a few words with regard to the objections which have been urged against his nomination, and which have caused some excitement in this convention. I speak more particularly of the objections urged by the delegation from Maryland. I did to one of its members an act of injustice

67. *Official Proceedings, Democratic National Convention*, 43. McClellan received 174 on the first, unrevised ballot, with 151 necessary to nominate.

by a decision, because I did not understand the purport of his remarks. It is due to him, that I should say, that I am confident that he never meant to take part in the proceedings of this body, without submitting in an honorable manner to its decisions. [Cheers.] With respect to the orders issued by General McClellan affecting the citizens of that State, I must say that I do not approve of them; but they must not be viewed in the light which events have since thrown upon the policy of the administration. At that time the wisest and best men of our country had confidence in its purposes. Then, the President denounced measures which he has since adopted; then the friends of the Union in the border States were listened to by him, with every appearance of respect and deference. The mask had not been thrown off, and obedience to his orders did not imply hostility to the rights of States. We must bear in mind how at that moment the public was convulsed by a condition of affairs without precedent, and by questions which were suddenly forced upon the public attention, and with regard to which, public men were compelled to act without time for reflection. What man can say after looking back over his own action during the past three years, that he had not fallen into many and grave errors with respect to his duty? God knows, I cannot, after reviewing my own official conduct, which was ever governed with an earnest and prayerful desire to do what was right. [Cheers.] I cannot say that all my official action has been such, as at this time to commend itself even to my own approval.

This is no time to ask, who have been right in the past; but who are right now, and who will act in the future with a single purpose to save our Union, our Constitution and our liberty. [Cheers.] We are now appealing to all classes of citizens to unite with us in this great object. It would be unjust to a multitude of men who voted to put Abraham Lincoln into the presidential chair and who mean by their votes to put him out of it, to look backward, and to canvass past differences of opinions. [Loud cheering.] Would that we were able to draw a veil over the last three years' history of this country! Let us forget the past, and devote ourselves in the future to the salvation of our country. [Cheers.]

It is but just to say, of the distinguished general, whom we have in effect already placed in nomination, that there is no man living, who feels more keenly than he does, the wrongs which have been heaped on the State of Maryland, a State whose history is honorable, and which has ever been identified with all that is glorious, in the history of our Union, in the better days of the Republic. [Cheers.] While I did not, in the delegation of which I am a member, vote for placing him in nomination, I cannot refrain from saying in behalf of General McClellan what in my heart I feel to be true, that when he is elected to the Presidential office, he will reflect with fidelity, boldness and zeal, the sentiments of patriotism and love of liberty and law, which animate the hearts of those who are here now assembled. [Long and continued cheering.] [68]

68. *Official Proceedings*, *Democratic National Convention*, 44–45.

Then the convention nominated McClellan on the first ballot.

The nominee's repudiation of the peace plank has been cited as proof of the inconsistency between the words and the acts of the convention, but it is well known now that General McClellan wavered for at least a week, undecided as to what he ought to do. Seymour had been made chairman of the committee of notification, and he it was who wrote the letter which was drawn up at the St. Nicholas Hotel in New York City and dispatched at one o'clock in the afternoon of Thursday, September 8. McClellan's acceptance was written as if it came from Orange, New Jersey, and bore the same date. Both letters were talked over on the spot by the committee and the candidate before they were given to the press. Vallandigham had put peace before reunion; McClellan reversed the order: "The reëstablishment of the Union in all its integrity is, and must continue to be, the indispensable condition in any settlement. . . . The Union is the one condition of peace — we ask no more." [69]

A week before, Seymour had endorsed the action of the convention in a speech at Milwaukee on September 1, when he declared that the nation could not do worse than elect Lincoln for a second time, for to return him to office offered no hope for the future. Unequal representation in the Senate, he reminded his hearers, made every new addition to the power of the central government more dangerous than the last. Before long, a minority might impose its will on the majority. To check this dangerous drift in national affairs he begged the North, while there was yet time, to negotiate a peace with the South before taxation and tyranny should ruin them both.[70] Then he went East to work over the letter which would notify McClellan of his nomination.

As soon as he returned to New York, Seymour found that his unwillingness to accept another, that is a fifth, nomination for governor was laid to his disappointment at having failed to win

69. *Official Proceedings, Democratic National Convention*, 59–61.

70. Seymour, *Public Record*, 234–241.

the first place at Chicago. He might very well have allowed his political enemies to accuse him of sulking in his tent, for he felt that he had worked to very little purpose for two years and he was eager to retire from office. A quarrel within the party was to checkmate him. Dean Richmond, who had forced his nomination on him in 1862, would have been glad to let him go, for the state chairman had backed McClellan and wished to choose a candidate who would fit in with the general. He had his eye on William F. Allen, who had served as chairman of Stanton's committee to correct the figures for the enrollment in New York. Those friends of the governor who resented Richmond's failure to force him to accept the nomination at Chicago now took pleasure in crossing their leader from Buffalo. The state chairman had given them McClellan; they would give him Seymour.

The Democratic convention met at Albany on September 14, and it was soon plain that a majority of the delegates wished the governor to run again. Although a member withdrew his name from consideration, he was nominated by acclamation from the floor in spite of the fact that one hour before he had positively refused to be a candidate. To the committee which came to his office to notify him of his fifth nomination he pleaded his poor health and the demands of his private business and requested that some one else be named. He did not say he would not run.[71] The story goes that Seymour was persuaded to allow a "complimentary vote" to be introduced into the convention, and that this vote was so worded by its sponsors as to spell his nomination.[72] It is interesting to notice that when the Republicans gathered at Syracuse on September 7 to nominate Reuben E. Fenton for governor, they did not see fit to attack the record of Seymour's second term.[73]

He faced a dreary prospect in the autumn of 1864. In the first place, as the tide of Union victory rose, all talk of a ne-

71. Brummer, *History*, 417–418.
72. Alexander, *History*, III, 117–120.
73. Brummer, *History*, 397.

gotiated peace became increasingly unpopular in the North. The return to an age of reason was further off than even Seymour realized. Neither the platform nor the candidate of the Democratic convention at Chicago was to his taste. Nor was it only in the North that he found himself abused. If Seymour is supposed to have courted the good opinion of the South before and after 1861, he must have been discouraged to read such paragraphs as the following from the Savannah *Republican* for 1864:

> If there are two men in all Lincoln's dominions who deserve universal contempt, they are the Governors of New York and Kentucky. Seymour went into office with many furious threats of what he intended to do in case Lincoln should attempt to carry out his tyrannical and unconstitutional policy within the limits of New York, but no sooner was he seated in the gubernatorial chair than he showed the white feather, and instead of resisting Lincoln, went to work to help him! Bramlette wrote Lincoln a blood and thunder letter, declaring that slaves should not be enlisted in Kentucky without the consent of their owners, but Lincoln went on with the business, and the wretched apology for a Governor now cools down and issues a proclamation, in which he talks about taking the enrolling officers before a court martial, where he knows Lincoln will get just any decision he wants! [74]

Copperhead in the eyes of the extreme men of the North, coward and trimmer to the die-hards of the South, sick at heart, and ill, Seymour went down to Philadelphia early in October to make his one long speech in what he felt would be his last campaign.[75] It was no time, he declared, to ask "what brought the war about"; the pressing question was how the country could "preserve its existence and perpetuate its liberties." The armies of the North had done their work; now "rebellious discontent" was travelling northward as the soldiers "fought their way south." He was willing to assume that "in the next thirty days the army of Lee" would be "destroyed" and "that of Hood annihilated." Then, and only then, would the deluded people of the North "see, for the first time, the full measure of the im-

74. New York State Library: Manuscript Room: Seymour Scrap-Books, VIII, 107.

75. Seymour, *Public Record*, 248–261.

policy of the acts of the Administration." The price of conquest would be a government by bayonets.

> These victories will only establish military governments at the South, to be upheld at the expense of northern lives and treasure. They will bring no real peace if they only introduce a system of wild theories, which will waste as war wastes; theories which will bring us to bankruptcy and ruin. The Administration cannot give us union or peace after victories.[76]

His prediction came true, even though the Lincoln he could not agree with would give way to Andrew Johnson. Calling attention to the fact that Senator Sumner would "reduce the southern states to the condition of colonies" — whereas the President planned to receive them back into the Union whenever one-tenth of the population should declare itself loyal — Seymour foresaw the stubborn conflict which followed the murder of one President and provoked the brazen plan to remove another. Pointing to the words and acts of members of the Congress like Thaddeus Stevens, he declared that "neither Mr. Lincoln nor his cabinet" now had "control over National affairs." They were powerless to induce the Congress to undo all it had done; the President's hands were now "manacled."

If the voters returned the Republicans to power, they would learn two bitter lessons: first, that it "is dangerous for a government to have more power than it can exercise wisely and well," and second, that they could not "trample upon the rights of the people of another State without trampling on [their] own as well." He himself sought no office; least of all did he desire the short satisfaction of a "political triumph":

> What is a political triumph? I stand before you to-night a candidate in my own State for an honorable office. What matters it if politics alone were to be considered, whether I am elected or beaten? A few brief years, and I shall pass away and slumber in the grave; in a little time we, with all our passions, our hopes, and our fears, shall be no more. In the issues of this contest are the destiny of our country, the liberty of our land, the preservation of the Constitution, the union of the States.[77]

76. Seymour, *Public Record*, 253.
77. Seymour, *Public Record*, 258.

When men of the North accused him and his friends of sympathizing with the South, what they really said was this: "You can make peace with the South better than we."

Tammany had endorsed the choice of McClellan before his nomination at Chicago, and when it was found that Fenton had polled over eight thousand votes more than Seymour, the New York *World* and half a dozen other Democratic papers cried "treachery": the organization, it was whispered — and then shouted — had traded votes in the hope of electing a Democratic President as a reward for letting in a Republican governor. In New York City alone twenty thousand Democratic voters, it was said, were unable to get ballots, "notwithstanding all the exertions in their power." [78] So much for political gossip. The most likely reason for Seymour's failure to return to Albany for a third term lies farther afield. Fenton, a former Democrat who had opposed the Kansas–Nebraska bill of 1854, had become a Republican in 1856. For some years he had been sent to the House of Representatives for the congressional district which included his own county of Chautauqua. He had constantly courted the favor of Horace Greeley and, once he had been elected chief executive, proceeded to build up one of the smoothest political machines the state of New York has seen. He made a respectable governor and an acceptable senator, but he never enjoyed a personal or political popularity comparable to that of Horatio Seymour. The election of 1864 was probably determined not by the casting of votes but by the counting of them.

In 1863, it will be remembered, the constitution of the state had been amended so as to allow soldiers to vote without returning home. The Australian ballot, of course, was still a thing of the future; each party printed its own ticket, and every voter had to ask for the one he desired. According to the law the

78. New York *World*, November 15, 1864. This charge of treachery is not well founded. Tammany was not enthusiastic for Seymour at any time; McClellan was the first winner the Wigwam had picked since 1840: Myers, *Tammany Hall*, 205–206. The vote in New York County, in 1864, stood: McClellan, 73,716; Seymour, 73,537; Lincoln, 36,687; Fenton, 36,310: Valentine, *Manual of New York*.

ballots were to be carried into the camps, given to the soldiers who should ask for them, and, when marked, sworn to, and sealed, were to be mailed back to the precinct in which the soldier lived, there to be cast by the neighbor he should choose. The process by which a soldier could vote from camp was so elaborate [79] that John Cochrane, attorney-general of the state, warned the election officials that if any one of nineteen steps should be omitted the vote would have to be rejected.[80] It was up to each party to put the ballots in the hands of the soldiers. Seymour probably expected trouble, for on October 4 he asked Secretary Stanton to grant as many furloughs as he could in order that the soldiers might "repair to their respective homes to cast their votes personally at the coming election." To this request Stanton immediately replied that granting the maximum number of furloughs to voters had been the policy of the department in 1863 and would be the policy in 1864, as well.[81]

Chauncey M. Depew had been elected secretary of state for New York in November, 1863, however, and Depew was not in the hands of Seymour's friends. In regard to the problem of sending ballots to the soldiers who could not get furloughs Seymour wrote the secretary twice but failed to receive an acknowledgment of either letter. Late in September he informed him:

> I shall send a set of ballots to every regiment from New York. I will send them for both political parties, if you or any other person, will furnish me those for the candidates of the Republican party — or if you prefer to send them, I will give you any facility in my power.[82]

In a second letter, dated October 1, the governor again called the management of the matter of the soldier vote to the attention of Depew, to whom the legislature had delegated the task of distributing Republican ballots:

> Some days since I spoke with you, concerning the appointment by you and myself of joint Commissioners to proceed to the several United States Hospitals, and to visit the armies in the field, for the purpose of distributing

79. Benton, *Voting in the Field*, 144–145.
80. New York *Tribune*, November 1, 1864.
81. Seymour, *Public Record*, 247.
82. New York State Library: Manuscript Room: Seymour Scrap-Books, VII.

ballots to our New York soldiers, now in the United States service, and to carry out the purposes of the law for soldiers voting.

As the day for the election approaches, every delay becomes injurious to our soldiers — and as I have heard nothing from you, with reference to a co-operation in making such appointments, I have selected several Commissioners to proceed to Washington and the Army of the Potomac to this end.

I shall be happy to add others if you will name them.

I have directed them to carry ballots for any parties that may see fit to put them into their hands.[83]

Thus the secretary knew the plans of the governor, whom he left in the dark as to his own. Depew's schemes threatened to go to smash against the stubbornness of Stanton, who stoutly refused to give him information as to the situation of regiments from New York for fear the newspapers would get hold of the facts and print them for the Confederates to read. Depew was in despair and appealed to Elihu Washburne, who had as much influence on Lincoln as any man alive. Washburne is said to have persuaded the President that Stanton's refusal would cost the Republicans the electoral vote of New York. However that may be, Lincoln spoke to his secretary of war, who gave Depew the information he desired, but only after an executive order directed him to do so. The American Express Company carried the Republican ballots to the camps.[84]

Having failed to secure non-partisan coöperation from his secretary of state, Seymour sent the Democratic ballots to the camps by means of fifty or sixty agents, each of whom was armed with a commission signed by himself. Peter Cagger, of Albany, has been blamed for the choice of certain of the men whom Seymour selected. Cagger, however, though a politician, seems to have been a reputable lawyer; nothing to the contrary, at least, has ever got into print.[85] The fate, if not the character, of some of these agents was unfortunate. Mr. Mott, for instance, died suddenly one night at the Avenue House, a

83. New York State Library: Seymour Papers: Letter of Horatio Seymour to Chauncey M. Depew, October 1, 1864.

84. Benton, *Voting in the Field*, 154–156.

85. Benton, *Voting in the Field*, 159–161; and Amasa J. Parker, 2nd, *Landmarks of Albany County* (Syracuse, 1897), 155. "Hill, Cagger and Porter" became one of the great law firms in New York State.

hotel in Washington, soon after having been seen "out and well at eight o'clock." [86]

Worse, still, was to come, however: on October 26 a Democratic state agent, together with three of his inspectors, was arrested at Baltimore, and the office of the state agency in that city was closed. The next day Colonel Samuel North, the New York State agent in Washington, was seized and locked up with two of his deputies. Secretary Stanton ordered these arrests at the urgent request of Judge-Advocate Holt, to whom compaints had been made by Major-General Wallace, one day to be the author of *Ben Hur*, and a Colonel Seward, special judge-advocate. In view of the fact that the governor's brother had charge of all the work of the New York State agency, Seymour himself must have had reasonably definite knowledge of the character and conduct of the men who had been seized. Yet the charge on which they were arrested was that of having concocted "a carefully matured plan for defrauding the soldiers of the State of New York, now in the field, of their votes at the approaching Presidential election." Ferry, one of the arrested agents, pleaded guilty of forgery; Edward Donohue, Jr., another, was tried on October 28. Both men were sentenced to imprisonment for life, and these harsh sentences were confirmed by Abraham Lincoln.[87] Nelson J. Waterbury, judge-advocate-general of New York, publicly denounced Ferry as "a sanctimonious villain" and called two men by the names of Wood and Newcomb, both of whom had turned "state's evidence," a pair of "abolition stool-pigeons." [88]

86. New York *Tribune*, October 13, 1864.

87. Benton, *Voting in the Field*, 161–165; and New York *World*, November 2, 1864. More than three years afterward Seymour showed his faith in Donohue by writing to the attorney of the New York Central Railroad in an effort to get him a job. His language is interesting: "I mean Edward Donohue, Jr., who was imprisoned at Baltimore at the election of 1864. I feel bound to stand by men who were then wronged and to make their cause my own": New York Historical Society: Seymour Papers: Horatio Seymour to Sidney T. Fairchild, December 20, 1867.

In spite of his sentence to "imprisonment for life" Donohue was at liberty a little more than three years later.

88. New York *World*, November 1, 1864.

On October 30 Seymour appointed a commission of three prominent Democrats, Amasa J. Parker, William F. Allen, and William Kelly to go to Washington and enquire as to the facts and circumstances of the arrest of the agents of New York.[89] These commissioners saw Secretary Stanton and visited Colonel North, who was under lock and key together with an assistant named Cohn, in the Old Capitol Prison, which then stood on the site of the new Supreme Court Building. After talking with North the commissioners demanded the release of the two prisoners, but Judge Holt countered with a flat refusal. Then they appealed to Lincoln, who was cordial but would give them no satisfaction: the arrested agents must await their trial. Parker and his associates returned to Albany. Long after the election — on January 6, 1865 — North, Cohn, and a third agent, by the name of Jones, were brought up for trial before a military commission. All three prisoners were acquitted and turned loose. An apologist for this proceeding acknowledges that the state law was both "complicated and foolish" and "full of opportunities for mistake and fraud." The same author asserts that Colonel North was a man of high character and may fairly be believed to have been innocent of any wrong-doing whatever. He had merely spent a little more than two months in one of Stanton's jails.[90]

On November 18, 1864, Amasa J. Parker wrote of the treatment of the agents who had tried to carry Democratic ballots to the Union soldiers:

> In answer to your letter of yesterday, I would state that I have no doubt in the least, thousands of honest soldiers' votes were lost by the course pursued at Washington in arresting our agents without cause. The proceedings had the effect to intimidate our agents elsewhere, and nearly suspended all operations in taking Democratic votes. Added to that, the delay to forward our votes by mail until after election was such as to make a difference of thousands more. On a fair vote, I have no doubt we had at least 20,000 Democratic majority in this State.[91]

89. Seymour, *Public Record*, 262.

90. Benton, *Voting in the Field*, 167–168.

91. Albany *Evening Journal*, December 14, 1864; see, also, New York Historical Society: Seymour Papers: A private letter from Judge Parker to Governor Seymour, Albany, November 7, 1864.

From this distance it looks as if Stanton, or some one who could excite his suspicions, had decided that no soldier should receive a Democratic ballot if he could help it. Such conduct, we know, would not have been out of character, for the man who sat in the Cabinet of President Johnson for three years was to prove himself sadly wanting in both honesty and self-respect. While it will not do to say that a fair count of the soldier vote would have reëlected Seymour in 1864, it is nevertheless certain that the count was not complete or fair.

Once the official returns were in, Governor Seymour showed himself to be more serene than his supporters. He was genuinely happy not to have to go on for another two years, for he had worked hard and to very little purpose. Two letters he wrote on November 24 are characteristic of his public and private feelings in regard to the triumph of the Republicans. The first was to a political correspondent. Expressing himself as "entirely satisfied with the result of the election," Seymour declared that "a majority of the people" were with his party when they acted "freely." Yet, "the change in the public mind should be overwhelming" before the Democrats could hope to "control affairs with success." "The financial and political fallacies of the administration" would, he believed, "die out on their hands." Political change would have to "begin at the bottom, not at the top." He was "confident" that the Democrats would carry the state election in the autumn of 1865, which they did, and capture a majority of the House of Representatives in 1866, which they did not, and "gain full power in 1868." "Mr. Lincoln . . . only reflected popular vices, errors, and delusions."

I have no fear about the end. We must suffer much within four years but we must be patient, forbearing, and hopeful. I am encouraged by the stout-hearted way the Democrats meet the results. More than ever they are sure they are right. In this state they would go into an election tomorrow and win a victory in the face of the success of Mr. Lincoln; on the other hand the Republicans are thoughtful and doubtful. The change begun in the public mind will not stop short of a political revolution.[92]

92. November 24, 1864: A. L. S. in possession of the author.

The second letter was a private one, addressed to his sister, Mrs. Ledyard Lincklaen.

> I am very much gratified with your kind letter and your invitation to visit Cazenovia — I shall do so in the course of the Winter or Spring — I cannot leave here until after the 1 of January — Mary and myself will then go to New Jersey for a while. I mean to get rest during the months of Winter — My health is excellent. Your rose bush makes true auguries. My enjoyment in the prospect of relief from the hard duties of this office is perfect. I am satisfied with the result of the election. We had a large majority of the real voters of the State but it is better to give the Republicans the whole responsibility — I am very glad I was a candidate, that I went into the canvass and that I have been deprived of the office.
>
> I enclose for Helen a paper which has on it the autographs of four Generals.[93]

A week or so before his death, long after the time when he could feel anger or ambition, Seymour wrote thus of the problems and perplexities of his troublesome second term as governor of New York: "The greatest question which grew up during the late war was the power claimed by Mr. Lincoln's administration that a state of war gave to it the right under any circumstances to set aside the laws and the Constitution." [94] A statement of his brother confirms this impersonal point of view. Twenty-three years after he had called on President Lincoln at the request of the governor, John F. Seymour entered the White House for a second time in order to present his niece to Grover Cleveland. As they crossed the threshold, her uncle reminded her of the occasion of his former visit and then remarked that the only reproachful words he had ever heard his dead brother speak of the President with whom he had felt it was his duty to differ were these: "Mr. Lincoln was not fair to me." [95] The simple statement rings true, even in its lack of resentment — perhaps, after all, Mr. Lincoln was not quite fair.

93. New York Historical Society: Seymour Papers: Horatio Seymour to Mrs. Ledyard Lincklaen, November 24, 1864.

94. New York State Library: Seymour Papers: Quoted in a letter of L. B. Proctor to Horatio Seymour, January 17, 1886.

95. New York Historical Society: Seymour Papers: Memorandum of Mrs. Helen Lincklaen Fairchild, wife of Charles S. Fairchild, secretary of the treasury, 1887–1889.

XVI

CHASE OR HENDRICKS

1865–1868

IN 1864 Seymour predicted that the men who had made war could not make peace, and the twelve years between Appomattox and the inauguration of President Hayes were to vindicate him as a prophet. Lincoln, although the gunfire of hard fact forced the granting of belligerent rights to the South, never allowed himself to speak as if the Confederate states were not part of the Union: more than once he had to rebuke those of his generals who were indiscreet enough to boast of having driven the "rebels" back to their "own territory" — the United States, he would remind them, still extended to the Gulf of Mexico and the Rio Grande. Once Lee had surrendered and Abraham Lincoln was dead, however, the southern states discovered that they could "come back" into the Union — which they were supposed never to have left — only on conditions. The Congress which made those conditions had been elected by the northern states and was firmly in the clutches of the radical Republicans. The animus of this change of policy was obvious: to restore the southern states to the representation they enjoyed in 1860 would deprive those radicals of their power to govern the Union.

Professor Randall has described the cruel absurdity of the situation aptly:

> The period was prolific in ironic inconsistencies: the inconsistency of using the word "reconstruction" for a period in which restoration was deliberately prevented; the inconsistency of counting southern states in the ratification of the thirteenth amendment, yet holding these states out of the Union; the inconsistency of passing the Civil Rights Act and subsequently launching a constitutional amendment to give the federal government the power which by the Civil Rights Act had already been exercised;

the inconsistency of saying that the fourteenth amendment was submitted to the southern states, when in reality the matter was submitted to fabricated carpetbag governments, after native white governments in ten seceded states had rejected it, and the action of these fabricated governments was not to be recognized unless they voted yes. The ratification of the fourteenth amendment, when stated in its simplest form, sounds like an Irish bull or a huge joke: the southern states could not qualify as members of the Union until after they had performed a function which only members of the Union can perform. Nor even then could they qualify unless enough states affirmatively acted to put the amendment into force. There was the further inconsistency of denying representation to the South because of the withholding of negro suffrage while extending no such penalty to those northern states in which a similar discrimination existed, also the inconsistency of seeming to imply that negro suffrage might be denied, yet linking the fourteenth amendment with a compulsory imposition of negro suffrage by requiring that only negro-suffrage governments could be recognized in the ratification. The people of the southern states were inconsistently required to pay federal taxes and were for certain purposes treated as within the United States, while at the same time they were for other purposes held to be outside the Union and subject to a form of military rule which the Milligan decision declared to be illegal within the limits of the United States even in war time. In one sense they were deemed to be within the country, in another sense enemies.[1]

It would be unfair to call this change of front a breach of faith, for only men who inspire faith can be said to break it.

That this usurpation should have lasted twelve years might seem strange if one did not take into account the bias and the bitterness of many of the "best minds" among the victors. The North had conquered the South against the better judgment of its cooler minds, and that conquest brought with it a responsibility which was borne without great honor. The sudden removal of Lincoln from the scene is now generally regarded as having been a misfortune in a much more significant sense than was realized at the time. Then opinion was by no means unanimous.

It would be wise for Americans to admire Lincoln for what he was, and not make him a national myth. George Washington seems likely to last long enough, even without the school-book

1. *Mississippi Valley Historical Review*, XIX, 3 (December, 1932): J. G. Randall, "John Sherman and Reconstruction," 383–384.

story of the cherry tree. When Lincoln was first inaugurated, he could feel his country breaking up under his feet. Like Pitt the Younger, this uncertain son of the Middle West was made for peace, and met war. Had he been less patient with the vanity of soldiers and more scrupulous as to the rights of civilians, the South would probably have won a fatal freedom from a divided North. He perished on the eve of what would have been his greatest service to the Union. To write of him as if he were without faults, to consider every critic a crank or a Copperhead is to push the whole period out of focus. Like every statesman who aspires to real success, Lincoln had to serve the time. It would seem that he knew himself far better than many of his friends and biographers knew him.

Speaking noble praise of Lincoln at the funeral services held in his honor at Concord, Massachusetts, on April 19, 1865, Ralph Waldo Emerson, as serene a spirit as the North could boast of, uttered words which might well have alarmed the hearts of lesser men:

> And what if it should turn out, in the unfolding of the web, that he [Lincoln] had reached the term; that this heroic deliverer could no longer serve us; that the rebellion had touched its natural conclusion, and what remained to be done required new and uncommitted hands, — a new spirit born out of the ashes of the war; and that Heaven, wishing to show the world a completed benefactor, shall make him serve his country even more by his death than by his life? Nations, like kings, are not good by facility and complaisance. "The kindness of kings consists in justice and strength." Easy good nature has been the dangerous foible of the Republic, and it was necessary that its enemies should outrage it, and drive us to unwonted firmness, to secure the salvation of this country in the next ages.[2]

There is something fascinating about the intellectual lapses of wise men. In just what way the "unwonted firmness" of the "new spirit born out of the ashes of the war" secured from "uncommitted hands" "the salvation of this country in the next ages" would require a greater philosopher than Emerson to explain. One thing, however, the dark words he spoke at Concord do explain — the savage spirit which made recon-

2. Emerson, *Complete Works*, I, 329–338: "Abraham Lincoln," 336–337.

struction respectable. Lincoln was indeed lucky in the moment of his taking-off, for the men who had got the upper hand in the North by 1865 would have broken his heart. Death was better — even at the hands of Booth. So far as is known Seymour said nothing at the time of the murder of Lincoln, but he could not have missed the dreadful implication of the loss more blindly than did Emerson.

Lincoln and Emerson saw each other just once, Charles Sumner being the means of their meeting. That these three northerners should shake hands in one room augured ill for the conquered South. The notions of the unhappy senator and his confederates in the Congress poisoned the domestic and foreign policy of the Union until President Grant found Sumner insufferable, and Hayes firmly put the Senate back in its place. By that time, however, the mischief had been done, and the eleven secession states were definitely committed to the unfortunate device of the single-party system which they still maintain. Northern vindictiveness defeated itself in the long run: until 1861 only three-fifths of the southern negroes were counted for representation; now all of them are. Thus the South gained strength in the Congress and the electoral college. As the policy of reconstruction took shape, once again the conservatives were caught between the two extremes; but this time it was the conservatives of the Republican party. That the triumphant outcome of the Civil War justified his worst suspicions could have been only cold comfort to so kind a man as Seymour, and he said little for a time. Then, in the autumn of 1865 he made two speeches, one at Buffalo in October and the second on November 1 at Seneca Falls.[3] His theme was the dangerous centralization of the government of the Union — the transformation of a "confederacy" into a "consolidated

3. The place Seymour chose for the second speech is significant. In every one of his six campaigns (1850–1868) Seneca County remained faithful to him with a single exception: Ullman, the American candidate, carried it in 1854. In 1864, Seneca was the only county to support him in the west centre of the state. In 1868, Seymour was to carry no county north of Albany or west of Sullivan, but Seneca.

government." The best cure for the confusion of the times, he declared, was to take away the temptation of arbitrary power by the quickest possible return of home rule to one third of the Union.

Although General McClellan was titular leader of the Democratic party, Seymour took the lead against the radicals in New York State. The situation was confused, for the murder which put a Union Democrat in the White House threatened to make reconstruction a partisan issue. When all else failed, Sumner and Stevens could rail at Johnson as a man disloyal to the coalition which had put him in second place on the ticket. The new President believed that the sole object of the war had been to restore the Union, and as often as he said so and acted as if he meant it, Seymour and his friends found him on their side. Both North and South had already suffered enough, and the wisest course was restoration. The former governor charted his course for twelve years in his speech at Seneca Falls in the autumn of 1865.

> In 1864 I ventured a prediction, in speeches that were published at the time, that when victory should crown our arms it would be seen that the policy of those who assumed power in the Administration was such that they could not bring back the Union. The Union is not truly restored until every State is governed by its own population, controlled by its own laws, and until its people, returning to their own proper pursuits, are toiling with us to lift the burden of debt which now oppresses us, and to advance the prosperity of the common country.[4]

In passing on to the discussion of the financial policy of the government, the delusive prosperity of inflation, and the curse of quick riches, Seymour called in as witness to his warnings the Republican secretary of the treasury, Hugh McCulloch. The debt amounted to three thousand millions of dollars, and either expansion or contraction of the currency was certain to cause further hardship. It was doubtful if there was enough left of the national credit, thought Seymour, to hold the southern states as conquered provinces, quite apart from the ethics or danger of the policy. People who held the bonds of the United States

4. Seymour, *Public Record*, 276.

had a right to require that its government should be economical, for cutting down expenses was the best safeguard against repudiation. To keep faith to the last dollar would cost enough in taxes; now it was proposed to hold a standing army in the South. This was a new kind of Union, indeed. In the days before the war and debt, Seymour reminded his hearers, a man could support himself with six hours of daily toil; in 1865, he had to add two hours a day to provide for his share of the cost of what had happened in five years.[5]

Seymour was never more persuasive than when he was explaining the relation of public government to private life. If people complained of the high cost of living in 1865, the answer, he pointed out, was open to their eyes. Five months had passed since May 26, when the last of the southern armies had surrendered, and yet in New York State alone there were still five major-generals on the federal pay roll whose annual salaries added up to one hundred thousand dollars. They were all superfluous, for most of the half-million private soldiers from the state had been mustered out of the service. This, he reminded his fellow citizens, was only one specimen of the management which was still costing millions of money that no one had to spare. The one escape from a government caught in the coils of its own policy was to clean house.

Turning to the question of negro suffrage, Seymour argued that to try to settle the matter by national action was against the very genius of the Union. If the Constitution were to stipulate who might vote in southern states, the same was true of northern states. What seemed interesting to him was the fact that the very class of men who now demanded that the federal government should establish "universal suffrage" in the South was the same that insisted, as late as 1856, that no "foreigner" ought to vote in the North. No part of the Union could lay hands on the rights of any other part without imperilling its own rights at the same time. The American experiment which the Old World had scouted in 1788 had been

5. Seymour, *Public Record*, 274–288.

successful over a huge expanse of territory chiefly because the "minute details of local affairs" had not been left to one central government. The venture would have been unworkable otherwise, and the only hope for continued success was to respect the spirit of it. Power must be spread thin. The quickest way to recover from the Civil War would be to liquidate elaborate government. New Yorkers could make their state election a referendum on the issue of continued war or peace.

> We go into this contest for home rights. The mistake of our Republican friend is that he begins wrong. He looks upon government as something splendid, remote, and grand, holding in its grasp the destinies of the people; while the truth is that the only strength of government is in the people, and that National honor and National dignity spring from the fireside happiness of the citizens.

Apart from national issues, the only real excitement of the state campaign of 1865 was the reappearance on the public scene of John Van Buren, the "itinerant orator" whose career of travelling on the great name of his father and trading on his own tongue would come to an end the very next year. This mercurial man was the Democratic candidate for attorney-general and flung himself into the campaign with his customary fury. In 1862, he had backed Seymour against Wadsworth, but by 1863 he affected to have been betrayed by the governor's "passion for peace" and deserted him. By 1864 trouble-makers were telling people that Prince John thought Seymour was "a damned fool . . . who had spoiled everything at Chicago . . . and [had] been the cause of most of the disasters of the Democratic party." If he and Vallandigham, so these gossips heard, had been "kicked out of the national convention it would have been a good thing for the party." [6] Many of the disasters of the Democratic party in New York State, it might have been objected, had followed repeated refusals to nominate John Van Buren for one office or another. In the year 1865 one of his rare candidacies on the Democratic ticket resulted in his being badly beaten. During the campaign he indignantly denied the

6. Alexander, *History*, III, 134–135.

words which had been put into his mouth by Depew, who repeated them years later to Alexander. The obvious way to beat Van Buren in 1865 was to sow trouble between him and Seymour. Prince John saw the point: "No person understands better than Governor Seymour the differences between him and myself," he wrote from Buffalo when Republican papers began to print the gossip, "but whatever they may have been, they have never led me, in public or private, to deny his great intelligence and his singular personal and official purity." [7]

In 1865, according to Alexander, "Seymour's prophetic gift was in eclipse. Nothing had happened which he predicted—everything had transpired which he opposed." [8] This is to take the short view of the Civil War: if the South was conquered, the Union had yet to be restored. Just as soon as the component parts of the Republican majority began to fall asunder the government at Washington was "a house divided against itself." Like the Whigs in 1841 the Republicans of 1865 discovered that nominating a dissident Democrat for second place was a dangerous experiment. Coalitions have been talked of since that day but never once have they been tried by a major party for a third time. At the congressional elections of 1866 the split between the President and the Congress was wide and notorious. While Johnson did the best that could be expected of him to carry on the policies of Lincoln, and Seward stood at his right hand, Stanton from within the Cabinet, Sumner in the Senate, and Stevens in the House, worked their will in spite of him.

If Seymour had been vindictive, he would have laughed to see his country stewing in its own juice. Although he stayed away from the state convention at Albany in September, 1865, he spoke in the campaign and made no comment on what must have seemed to him the disappointing result. The death of Dean Richmond and John Van Buren the next year, however, changed the face of things in New York. Richmond was succeeded as state chairman by Tilden, a tireless worker behind

7. New York State Library: Seymour Papers: Albany *Evening Journal*: Letter of October 28, 1865.

8. Alexander, *History*, III, 127.

scenes. His great reputation as a lawyer, his wealth, the high respect in which he was held by numbers of men whose loyalty to the Union had never been questioned, added strength to the Democratic opposition in New York. In just ten years he was to become a safe presidential alternative to a comfortable majority of the American people. Thousands of the men who preferred him to Hayes had probably voted for Lincoln in 1860 and 1864. Lucius Robinson was only one of many who went back to the Democrats after the Civil War; before long he became governor of New York. The party of Jefferson and Jackson was gaining recruits once more. The days of its long decline were past.

The excitement of the congressional elections of 1866 drew Seymour out of his retirement. On October 30 he spoke at the Cooper Institute in New York City.[9] Europe supplied him with a timely object-lesson for his fellow citizens. Prussia had defeated Austria during the summer, and the contrast between Bismarck's work of reconciliation among Germans and the treatment of the conquered South was too startling to be overlooked. His dwelling on it could hardly have made comfortable reading for thoughtful Americans. Seymour called himself a conservative, and conservative he was on the subjects of abolition and paper money, but he put a fundamentally liberal doctrine into words at the Cooper Institute in October. "We have more to fear from the South if it accepts the doctrine of subjugation than we ever had to fear from its armed rebellion; we cannot enslave them without enslaving ourselves." [10] "To-day," he went on, "the power of Great Britain is paralyzed by its harsh, unjust, and contemptuous treatment of Ireland." He urged Americans to look first at Germany and then at England and learn that as often as people are treated as enemies and outlaws they will bide their time and wait their chance to act the part assigned to them.

Seymour opposed the Fourteenth Amendment for what appeared to him the sound reason that the make-up of the Senate

9. Seymour, *Public Record*, 280–298.
10. Seymour, *Public Record*, 290.

— the gross inequalities of representation among the several states — spelled the negation of the notion that questions of citizenship and suffrage were properly matters of national concern. Referendums in great Republican states of the North had denied negroes suffrage within the year; to force this "reform" on the South was the very insanity of power. Little did he guess the relative strength which that policy would give, one day, to the party he served and loved. The amendment was pushed through in spite of his warning and almost since the day of its adoption has been so used as to protect the rights of property, not human beings. Hard times, he warned his audience, were ahead of them all: taxation meant toil, and the burden of the great national debt was neglected only because the full pressure of it was "cushioned" with an inflated currency. His closing words contained a warning to the reckless leadership at Washington:

> A party which is unchecked in its power loses control of its own action. . . . The theory of our Government is, that parties will be so balanced that neither [Republicans or Democrats] can go beyond safe limits. Those who framed our Constitution contemplated minorities as essential to the public good, and tried to secure for them a share in Government.[11]

The elections went against the conservatives; the Democrats were defeated in New York, and Andrew Johnson saw the radical Republicans win a two-thirds majority in the House of Representatives. As soon as the new Congress assembled the veto would no longer protect the President or the people. The vengeful spirit of Sumner and Stevens had triumphed. Matters went from bad to worse in Washington, and before long the country began to grow weary of the spectacle of strife and hatred. The President was deprived of that executive power to remove officials which all his predecessors had exercised. Stanton persuaded himself that he was properly responsible to the Congress. The arrogance of the radicals grew by what it fed on: once they had robbed the President of his authority

11. Seymour, *Public Record*, 297–298.

to remove men from office, they went on to take away his right to appoint to office. When an associate justice of the Supreme Court died, the Congress abolished the post in order that Andrew Johnson should not have the filling of the vacancy. The leaders of the South had tried rebellion; now the leaders of the North were lighting the fires of revolution. Sane men had to sit back for the time being, and wait.

By the autumn of 1867 Tilden's ability as an organizer began to show results. When the Democrats gathered at Albany on October 3, Seymour was on hand to give them their cue. Yet all was not peace and plenty in the party. Tammany came into the convention hostile to the former governor, who, so it was said, had managed matters long enough. The delegates from upstate, however, lined up behind him, and though Mayor John T. Hoffman was made temporary chairman, the former governor was chosen as permanent president. His welcome from the floor was "spontaneous and effusive": "If it was noisy, it was also hearty. It had the ring of real joy, mingled with an admiration that is bestowed only upon a leader who captivates the imagination by recalling glorious victory and exciting high hopes of future success." [12]

The issue was not place but principle, and Seymour met it gladly. "We have put down rebellion," he told the delegates, "we are now struggling with revolution. The first was sectional; the last is universal. The first sought to divide our country; the last threatens to destroy it." After describing legal tender as an invisible tax and dwelling on the fact of federal extravagance, Seymour closed his speech to the convention with a call to arms:

> As the shadow of coming defeat falls upon the Republicans, they even promise to become honest; and in their zeal they have pitched overboard all of their officials who have not robbed the treasury. We will end the good work they began, by throwing the rogues after them. Let us lift up the Democratic standard, and lift it high. Let us fight for fireside rights, for

12. Alexander, *History*, III, 178–179.

freedom of opinion, for an honest management of public affairs. Above all, let us battle for the restoration of the Union, and may God defend the right.[13]

"Perhaps no American," remarks Alexander of this speech, "ever possessed a more irritating way of presenting the frailties of an opposite party." It was Democratic policy to let dog eat dog at Washington; Andrew Johnson had made his bed and he must lie in it alone — so long as he kept Seward in his service. Seymour is supposed to have persuaded the convention to keep hands off; however that may be, no endorsement of the President went into the records at Albany. Alexander observes of the proceedings that they contained no evidence that Andrew Johnson existed; the silence was "remorseless." "Divested of respect, stripped of support, and plucked of offices," the chief executive, if we are to believe Alexander, had been "coolly dropped" by the Democrats of New York.[14] Even if it be argued that support might have given him courage, it could hardly have helped him out of his predicament. Samson was in the hands of the Philistines. Silence in 1867 surely was no greater crime than voting to impeach the chief executive in the vain effort to remove him the following spring — an effort in which both senators from the Empire State participated.

Seymour's hopes were helped in 1867 by what he would have called "a spasm of virtue." All during the Civil War the Republicans had done their best to make the system of canals profitable to their party. Contracts and jobs were handed round among friends for five years. Just when public opinion was becoming restless on the subject, the politicians who showed deep concern for the happiness of mankind in the South made the foolish mistake of refusing renominations to those state senators of their own party who had been most active in exposing corruption in the maintenance and control of the canals. The New York *World* played up the exposures in its best style, and one petty thief after another was put in the pillory of the press. Seymour made fun of the victims in his speech of October 3

13. Seymour, *Public Record*, 298 and 309.
14. Alexander, *History*, III, 181–182.

and got keen satisfaction from helping to put to rout a whole crew of Republicans whom even Horace Greeley had gulped down and then endorsed.[15] The cry of graft was one millstone, and the proposal to give the vote to negroes was another; the Democrats swept the state by a majority of fifty thousand. Now that the Civil War was over, New York was growing tired of statesmen who scolded and squabbled and politicians who did nothing but scramble for office and steal. This off-year election forecast the Democratic victory of 1868. And once again Horatio Seymour was at the centre of the stage.

Another development of this campaign was important: George Hunt Pendleton and Seymour got in touch with each other again. Pendleton hoped to head the ticket in 1868, and the feeling that he was the coming man in the party was widespread in the West. There were doubts about Pendleton among conservative Democrats, however, for he had come out in support of what was called the "Ohio Idea," the proposal to pay off at least the first federal bonds which would soon fall due by printing greenbacks — that is, borrowing money without interest. Ohio voted in October, and as soon as he had read the election returns Seymour wrote the senator a letter of congratulation. Pendleton's reply shows that he was already scanning the East for new friends.

> I am rejoiced to hear your confirmation of all the reports we get from New York. I hear also good news from Wisconsin and Minnesota. If our hopes shall be realized — our labor will just have begun, for then comes the question of administering the power which will be confided to our hands. As you say, this is indeed a grave responsibility and will require all the wisdom and firmness and virtues which our party can command.
>
> We must deserve the public confidence in order to possess it. I shall be glad to confer with you on this subject when the smoke of the battles of next month shall pass away, and if I am in New York I will let you know, that we may meet. I cannot refrain from expressing my admiration of your very splendid speech before the Convention. It was the most comprehensive and able opening of an offensive canvass which I have read.[16]

15. See the New York *World* of October 16 and 22, 1867, and the New York *Tribune* for September 26, 1867.

16. New York Historical Society: Seymour Papers: Letter of George H. Pendleton to Horatio Seymour, October 21, 1867.

After the autumn of 1867 it soon became obvious that if Pendleton and repudiation were ever to be headed off, the Democrats must give up their hope of winning or find some one to put in his way. The party was not of one mind by any means on the question of money: men like Belmont and Tilden found themselves opposed by Cyrus McCormick, for instance, who believed that inflation would cost the country less than continued control by the radicals. As between the two evils of paper money and reconstruction this successful man of business urged his party to choose the former. Nor were Republicans united on the issue.

As Pendleton gathered strength in the West the East began to cast about for a candidate of its own to pit against him. There were English, of Connecticut, and Parker, of New Jersey, both small states. A southerner was out of the question; Hancock of Pennsylvania might do; perhaps the wisest course of all would be to pick a "sound money" man from Pendleton's own part of the country. Of the three men who directed the Democratic party in New York, Belmont had been born abroad, Tilden had never held office, and Seymour was thought to be unwilling to do so again. Perhaps he could be smoked out of retirement.

Late in November, 1867, the editor of the *Democratic Union* of Oneida County placed the name of the former governor at the head of the editorial column of his paper as that of the proper candidate of his party for President in 1868. Seymour was always an industrious reader of newspapers and as soon as he saw that the suggestion was taking hold, he wrote directly to the author of it.

> These marks of good-will and confidence give me great pleasure, but I am compelled to say that I am not and cannot be a candidate for the Presidency. As my reasons for saying this are personal, it is not necessary to state them. They in no degree grow out of a waning interest in the great and serious questions which divide parties in this country. . . . In trying in the future, as I have in the past, to uphold principles which I deem to be right, I can do battle with more vigor when I am not a candidate for official position.[17]

17. Seymour, *Public Record*, 339. For Seymour's private explanation of his move, see his letter to Tilden, November 29, 1867, in Tilden, *Letters and Literary Memorials*, I, 211–212.

In a letter he wrote to Tilden a few days later Seymour touched on the "personal" reasons to which he had referred — he hoped to "save what little property" he had. He expected "now to be let alone." If he thought he had taken himself out of the field, he was doomed to disappointment. His refusal only attracted attention and protests. In January, 1868, he sent a second letter to a friend, who got his permission to print it in the Syracuse *Courier and Union*. By this time Seymour was embarrassed and a little angry: Republicans doubted his honesty, and Democrats questioned his judgment.

> I assure you I am not a candidate for the office of President. In my letter, I said what I meant; and I am annoyed to find it is looked upon by some as a strategic movement. I have had a large number of letters from leading men in the North-West. I have written to them that my name would never go before the National Convention. I am very much gratified that my friends are willing to support me for the office of President — as much pleased as if I wished the office. I do not know when I can go to Albany, but have told all my friends there my purposes, whenever I could do so without exposing myself to the imputation of declining what might be beyond my reach.[18]

No word of proof that Seymour was not sincere has ever been produced. To confuse his earnest interest in politics with a lust for office simply will not do. When Alexander wrote that "Seymour was never without ambition, for he loved politics and public affairs, and the Presidency captivated him,"[19] he must have been drawing on the purely private opinion of Chauncey Depew. For those critics who have objected that Alexander leaned too much on the senator's memory in preparing his political history of New York this very statement is a case in point. To believe it one must suppose that Seymour played the hypocrite for more than twenty years. Among his friends John Pruyn, for one, knew better as early as December, 1859, when Seymour told him that he would not be President if he could.[20]

His two letters refusing to allow his name to come before the next national convention were reprinted and read outside his

18. Seymour, *Public Record*, 339.
19. Alexander, *History*, III, 100.
20. Journal of John V. L. Pruyn, December 6, 1859. See page 188.

own state. The opinion one man expressed of his decision is of considerable importance. Late in 1867 Seymour's friend, Hiram Ketchum, went down to Washington to talk with President Johnson. He carried with him a letter of introduction from the former governor. Ketchum read that letter to Johnson, who seemed to be astonished at two sentences in it: "I do not know if my letter will help or hurt you. He [Johnson] has never done anything I asked him to do." According to Ketchum, the President spoke of Seymour "in the kindest and most flattering terms," and then went on to voice the regret he felt when he read the news of his refusal to be considered as a candidate in 1868. It seemed to Johnson, so he told Ketchum, that any citizen "should be willing to serve the country in any position where he would be useful." The close of Ketchum's letter shows that Seymour had set a difficult task for himself:

> I have read your very manly and patriotic letter to the Editor of the Democratic Union of the 25 ult. I have only to say that I have not heard any other name so often spoken of as the Candidate to be supported by the Anti-radicals as yours, and to add with perfect candor that there could no nomination be made which I should take greater pleasure in supporting. I consider nothing settled on this point; you have done nothing to impair your popularity, or to diminish the desire of your friends to make you the next president.[21]

Even the people who believed that Seymour meant what he said were apt at inventing unworthy motives for his decision. In March, 1868, the *Ohio State Journal* began to circulate a story that the former governor of New York did not dare to run for President in that year because the state department had in its possession evidence that he had carried on a confidential correspondence with the Confederate commissioners who went to Canada in 1864 — the men who vainly offered money to Vallandigham.[22] When the Utica *Daily Observer* was so naïve as to wonder why he took no notice of this story, Seymour wrote

21. New York Historical Society: Seymour Papers: Letter of Hiram Ketchum to Horatio Seymour, December 12, 1867.

22. For the story of the offer of this money, see Benton, "The Movement for Peace Without a Victory During the Civil War," 65–66.

the editor a letter in which he stated that the charge was "absurd on its face." Though Seward's hostility to him, he continued, was "well known," and the department of state had not since 1860 troubled itself about suborning perjury just as long as an accusation was barely plausible, experience had taught him that "putting down one slander" always gave "rise to another." The whole business, he concluded, was typical of the activity of the national government "during the past seven years." Any persons who may have given such evidence were the same kind as those who had testified against Colonel North and the state agents of New York in the matter of collecting the votes of the soldiers in 1864.[23] When Seymour was nominated against his wish and expectation, Seward, it is interesting to notice, did not produce the treasonable evidence the *Ohio State Journal* said he possessed.

Seymour waited a month after the Democratic landslide in the elections during the autumn of 1867 and then sat down one "bitter cold morning" and wrote a long letter to Tilden, manager of their party in New York. His purpose was to chart a course to follow in New York and the nation. The Democrats had won control of the legislature, but there was rough water ahead in Washington, for the Congress was beginning that session during which the radicals were to impeach the President. Writing before "the bright wood fire" which was "blazing on the hearth-stone" of his "farm-house," Seymour reviewed "seven years of war or of discord, of corruption, of hate, of taxation and tyranny" since their party had gone "out of power." The cordial tone of the letter is interesting in view of the gossip, then and since, that these two men were never so friendly as they might have been. Although John Bigelow saw fit to embalm this chatter in the biography of the man he made his one and only hero, there is no good reason for believing it. Tilden was a cold man who wasted as little time as possible on the simpler human emotions; he lacked Seymour's gracious ways. His brain was a tool and a very fine tool; he handled men like

23. Utica *Daily Observer*, March 28, 1868.

machines. He never took the trouble to learn how to get under their skins. That two such dissimilar men as Seymour and Tilden should have worked together in confidence and loyalty for more than fourteen years is evidence enough to silence idle suspicions.

Looking forward from that winter day to a time when "right and truth" should "conquer," Seymour stressed the dangers which lay between themselves and victory. Little did he think that they must wait for success no less than eighteen years.

> But all conditions have their dangers. The time-servers and spoil-hunters are seeking to come back to our party, not as penitents, but as leaders. They may in time forgive us for not joining in their treachery, but it will always be counted against us that we did not go out with them to gather spoils. There is danger that these men may divide those who stood together in the years of trial and of trouble. They hatch schemes to draw off some who have strength, and thus break up the band that held together in the dark days.[24]

Men like Dix and his fellows were now eager to worm their way back into the Democratic party, "generals without troops," hoping to return like conquering heroes bringing not strength but discord. "We do not want more leaders," warned Seymour; "we have the public with us." Those "men of nerve and of truth" who had stood "the tests of the last seven years" ought to get together and plan to "train up as many new men" as they could find and "fit them for places of honor and trust" — not suffer those who came in sunshine and left in storms to walk back into Democratic councils and scheme for their own gain. The rival candidates for President, he cautioned the state chairman, would try to enlist supporters wherever they could be found. "Let us keep our power," he concluded, "by holding ourselves free."

Within less than three months, however, he was looking around for a likely candidate; Pendleton was picking up delegates in the West, and the surest way to prove the sincerity of his own unwillingness to run was to find a suitable man who could and would run. On March 4, 1868, scribbling a short note

24. Tilden, *Letters and Literary Memorials*, I, 214–215.

to Tilden in regard to an engagement to meet him in Albany, Seymour expressed the opinion that Hendricks would be "as good a candidate for the Presidency" as the Democrats could get. He had "thought the thing over and looked through the country" and did not see how the party could "do better."[25] This was in March, but before long a dramatic turn in events would put the senator from Indiana in second place, so far as Seymour was concerned. Oddly enough, just a week before the date of this message to Tilden, John Bigelow told Gideon Welles, at the time of the meeting of the Democratic national committee in Washington, that the plan was to nominate Seymour — that the state chairman thought he would "run stronger than any man in New York," and did not "look beyond it."[26] Welles had watched the radical Republicans at close range for years and had learned to hate them at first hand; he was eager to see the Democrats win in 1868. The name of Seymour left him cold, however, for he believed that any one of three men would run better than the former governor — Hendricks, Hancock, or Charles Francis Adams. In his first choice, then, he agreed with Seymour, whom he grudgingly supported, in the long run, against Grant.

Senator Hendricks would have made a strong candidate; he was able and affable, and there would have been no trouble in persuading the southern delegates to support him in the convention — as would have been the case with a man like Adams. He was popular and had fought arbitrary government without ever having had his loyalty called into question. He was, moreover, what is called "sound" on the financial issues of the day. A conservative candidate from the Middle West looked like the best man to block Pendleton and his greenback theories. Vallandigham had thrown his support to "Gentleman George," and at one time it seemed certain that he would win. Eastern Democrats like Tilden and August Belmont were determined that he should not. The plan to put up Hendricks was wrecked

25. Tilden, *Letters and Literary Memorials*, I, 221.
26. Welles, *Diary*, III, 295.

by the political rivalry of the candidates from Indiana and Ohio. A feud grew out of the skirmishing for delegates when friends of Hendricks accused the Pendleton men of sharp practice. Before long, supporters of each of these two men were determined that the other should not be the candidate at New York. The quarrel got into the newspapers and spread far and wide. Seymour got wind of it and began to look elsewhere for a leader. The business of the Democrats was to elect a successor to Andrew Johnson — not to defeat Pendleton or Hendricks.

The sensational impeachment of the President provided him with his man. This extraordinary proceeding monopolized the political interest of the United States during the spring and led some Democrats to believe that the best thing they could do would be to put Johnson at the head of their ticket. It is well known that he would not have refused the nomination, for even after his acquittal he was eager for what he hoped would be a "vindication." In New York, however, his close association with Seward made him wholly unacceptable to Democrats of real influence like Belmont, Seymour, and Tilden. He had a negative effect on the campaign, for the desperate effort to remove him from office alarmed men of moderate opinions and made more friends for him than he had ever been able to acquire for himself. It was plain, at last, that he was the victim of persecution. Respectable citizens knew that articles of impeachment which Benjamin F. Butler, of Massachusetts, had a hand in preparing could have little or no principle connected with them.

That this outrageous plan should have come within an ace of success lights up the whole landscape of the period of the Civil War. The sight of Secretary Stanton clinging to his office — of Benjamin Wade, of Ohio, voting to remove the man whom he would have succeeded — was shocking enough to disgust even more people than it did. Eight men emerged from that sad spectacle with credit. Thirty-five of the Republican senators venomously voted to convict the President, and all twelve

Democrats had decided to acquit him. Seven Republican senators, and seven only, followed the dictates of conscience and courage, and their names make up the roll of honor in the dramatic poll which was taken at noon on May 16 — Fessenden, of Maine; Fowler, of Tennessee; Grimes, of Iowa; Henderson, of Missouri; Ross, of Kansas; Trumbull, of Illinois; and Van Winkle, of West Virginia. The fate of Ross is one of the minor tragedies of American history.[27]

Thus, the most discreditable chapter in the constitutional history of the United States was written by the "best minds" of the Republican party — many of them men of education, ability, and good birth. It would be difficult to prove that any one of them did not know better. According to gossip, three votes in Johnson's favor were held in reserve — Morgan, of New York; Sprague, of Rhode Island; and Willey, of West Virginia. The story is no credit to the three; it subtracts, rather, from what respect one can muster up for the sincere, if unbalanced, enemies of Johnson. For these three men to vote one way while they thought another was a wanton violation of their oath of office.

Never has the Senate of the United States sunk so low as during the spring when it sat as a jury at the trial of Andrew Johnson. Senator George F. Edmunds, of Vermont, for instance, was commonly supposed to be a man of character. He was still being talked of as a presidential possibility as late as 1884. In 1877 his party put him on the electoral commission which seated Hayes. Edmunds voted to find Johnson guilty although at the time the Tenure of Office Act was being debated in the Senate he had argued that members of the Cabinet should be excluded from its terms because it would not be proper for the Congress to put a President at the mercy of an

27. Edmund Gibson Ross was born in Ashland, Ohio, in 1826, and died in Albuquerque, New Mexico, in 1907. He was apprenticed to a printer, worked in Milwaukee, and settled in Kansas in 1856, where he became editor of the *Tribune*. He entered the Union army as a private and became a major. From 1866 to 1871 he sat as a senator from Kansas. Defeated as a Democratic candidate for governor in 1880, he removed to New Mexico, of which he was appointed territorial governor by Grover Cleveland in 1885.

"irremovable" head of any department of the government. One of the articles of impeachment, however, dealt with the "violation" of this very act. Perhaps Charles Francis Adams, 2nd, was not wholly wrong when, after years of personal experience, he formed the opinion that the senator from Vermont was a corrupt hypocrite.[28] The long, closely-reasoned opinion with which Edmunds justified his vote to remove Johnson is a striking specimen of what a man can do with words.[29] Much has been made of the wickedness of William Marcy Tweed, and few there are who would dispute the statement that he was a vulgar, arrogant thief. Yet the distinction between a man like Tweed and a man like Edmunds is real and important: the first was frank even in wrong-doing; the second was not. One man stole from the public; the other man lied to himself.

Apart from the seven Republicans who voted to acquit the President, an eighth man emerged from the impeachment trial with distinction—Chief-Justice Chase, who sat as the presiding officer. Chase is something of a puzzle to students of character; great things were hoped of him, and hoped for too often in vain; Lincoln believed that he was insane on the subject of the presidency; less generous persons have called him a sneak. Shelley's lines on Byron are not inappropriate for this New Englander who went out to the Middle West and spent much of his adult life endeavoring to live up to the dreams of an adoring daughter:

> The sense that he was greater than his kind
> Had struck, methinks, his eagle spirit blind
> By gazing on its own exceeding light.

Chase was the sort of man whom great office edifies; had he ever reached the goal of his desire, his name would be remembered among the first Americans. As he sat in the Senate chamber during that spring of 1868 with the eyes of the whole nation

28. *Charles Francis Adams: an Autobiography* (Boston, 1916), 192.

29. *Congressional Globe*, 40 Congress, Second Session, *Supplement*: "The Trial of Andrew Johnson," 424–428: "The Opinion of the Honorable George F. Edmunds."

on him, his dignity, his force of character, and his even-handed justice pushed him to the front of praise and gratitude. Before long Seymour had made up his mind as to the best course for the Democrats to follow in 1868: Chase was the man to heal the wounds of war.

With this in mind he established contact with Colonel John Dash Van Buren, a joint friend, who was in and out of Washington all during the spring of 1868.[30] Van Buren kept Seymour in touch with the political gossip of the capital. In April, so he wrote, there was "strong talk" for General Hancock, and everybody was eager to know what Seymour thought of him. The colonel assured enquirers that the former governor was "for serving the country and for any Democrat who could be surest to win." By the first of May the movement for Hancock was "loud and noisy," and even President Johnson was said to be in favor of him. Hendricks, "the brightest, clearest mind" in Washington, so Van Buren thought, preferred to go back to the Senate. He told Seymour that he had talked with Chase, who believed that negro suffrage was "beyond reversal," but that universal amnesty would "put the native whites in the lead" at the South.[31] The last two sentences of the letter of May 1 are significant: "Your declination is regarded in Washington as sincere. As you said to me some time ago, the next Presidency, if to be got by us, must be got by diplomacy — do you see any opening?"[32]

30. For the letters of John Dash Van Buren to Horatio Seymour, see the Seymour Papers in the New York Historical Society.

31. According to the Fourteenth Amendment, which was passed by the Congress on June 16, 1866, and proclaimed as ratified on July 28, 1868, any state which denied the right to vote to adult male citizens "except for participation in rebellion, or other crime" was to have its representation in the Congress reduced in proportion. The Fifteenth Amendment, which passed the Congress on February 27, 1869, and was proclaimed as ratified on March 30, 1870, forbade any state to deny or abridge the right of citizens of the United States to vote "on account of race, color, or previous condition of servitude." Until 1870, then, adult male negroes could be denied the right to vote by any state which was willing to undergo the penalty provided by the Fourteenth Amendment.

32. New York Historical Society: Seymour Papers: John D. Van Buren to Horatio Seymour, May 1, 1868.

Writing from New York on May 20, Van Buren reported that he had seen the chief backers of George H. Pendleton — Washington McLean, publisher of the Cincinnati *Enquirer*, and Vallandigham. McLean had gone to Deerfield to talk with the former governor and told Van Buren that he was pleased with the interview and still believed that Pendleton could be nominated. When Van Buren took a "*general* look," he wrote Seymour, he was inclined to agree with him that the Democrats could "carry any one," but as soon as he began to count by states, he thought "otherwise." "Wall Street" believed that Grant would not accept the Republican nomination, and as the fear of Grant declined the stock of Hancock went down accordingly. Van Buren's postscript is important: "If the game was regarded as a safe one, you would be nominated in spite of yourself." In a second letter which he wrote the same day and marked "private" Van Buren suggested Chase at the head of a new party on the basis of "*Universal suffrage of whites and blacks in voting for new constitutions in the South* and refusing admission [to seceded states] till the vote is thus taken and for *universal amnesty*." Such, apparently, was the platform on which Chase might be expected to be willing to stand for the presidency.

By June 19, however, Colonel Van Buren was writing Seymour that he did not "know what to make of the Chase matter." His ignorance seems to have been due to the fact that the Chief-Justice was ready to take either nomination in 1868. The Van Buren–Seymour correspondence shows that at least two of his supporters for the Democratic nomination were obviously in earnest. For them the goal of the game was immediate reunion and lasting peace. The former Free Soil Democrat whom they hoped to honor at New York had drifted away from his Republican affiliations during the three years and more that he had served as Chief-Justice. He had helped to checkmate the radicals and save the day for Johnson and justice by the narrowest of margins. Would the party take him back now after twelve years and put its standard in his hands? All the southern states, however, were sending delegates to the national convention in New York, and it was more than doubtful if these delegates could ever be persuaded to vote for the nomination of Chase. Perhaps Van Buren led Seymour to underestimate the difficulty which they faced.

It seems pretty clear we shall have no difficulty in carrying our troops over to him — the rank and file are over-anxious to run that way, so much so that they will suffer a disappointment. The officers, as you see by the *World*, kick. I have seen a Washington private letter saying that Wade Hampton and other prominent Southern men favor Mr. Chase. I should not wonder; for he would be able to take Southern men into full council at once.[33]

Postponing, for the moment, the question of Seymour's honesty in regard to his support of Chase in 1868, it is important to discover just how earnest the Chief-Justice was in dallying with the Democrats that year. The sum and substance of the letters published by the first of his biographers is this: Chase would not have refused the Democratic nomination if it had been offered to him on a platform of universal amnesty and universal suffrage.[34] The last paragraph of a letter of May 30 to August Belmont shows that Chase was not unwilling to be drafted on his own terms:

I have now answered your letter as I think I ought to answer it. I beg you to believe me — for I say it in all sincerity — that I do not desire the office of President nor a nomination for it. Nor do I know that, with my views and convictions, I am a suitable candidate for any party. Of that my countrymen must judge. If they think fit to require such services as I can render, they are, without doubt, entitled to them. If they have no requisition to make upon me, I shall be entirely content.[35]

He refused, however, to encourage his friends who took an interest in the outcome. Early in June, William Cullen Bryant thought the tide in New York was running so strongly in favor of Chase that it seemed to him impossible for the convention

33. New York Historical Society: Seymour Papers: John D. Van Buren to Horatio Seymour, June 19, 1868.

34. J. W. Schuckers, *The Life and Public Services of Salmon Portland Chase* (New York, 1874), 574–590.

35. Schuckers, *Chase*, 586.

to avoid nominating him for the presidency. In a letter of June 19 the Chief-Justice threw cold water on the hopes of the editor, who had to acknowledge that he had "surveyed the ground from a higher point of view and with a more comprehensive vision." [36]

As late as the day the Democratic platform was adopted, Chase was in communication with delegates to the convention. When J. P. Tucker sent him a portion of the financial plank, he wired, on July 7, that he would have to see all the resolutions.[37] The next day he wrote Colonel Van Buren that he had seen only a telegraphic abstract of the platform, which was "in the main, very good." He took it for granted that the general government contemplated no action to overthrow governments in any states from which senators and representatives had been admitted to seats in the Congress, but he did not wish to be understood "as expressing any opinion on questions of constitutional law which might come before the courts." He would be gratified if the convention chose any one of "the distinguished names before it" rather than his own.[38] Thus, up to the last moment, Chase did not refuse to accept the Democratic nomination in 1868. Nor could Seymour's efforts in his behalf have been a source of embarrassment to him, if we are to believe Henry B. Stanton, who said that he had "seen some of the private correspondence that passed between the ex-governor and the chief-justice at this period, wherein the latter warmly thanked the former for the efforts he had made to give him the nomination." [39]

Because Seymour failed to do what he hoped to do, his enemies, and in particular certain friends of Chase, made themselves believe that his support of the Chief-Justice had not been sincere. He was accused of the tactics which William Jennings Bryan made notorious at a later day — of urging the name of some impossible person for the very nomination he himself

36. *Annual Report of the American Historical Association, 1902*, II, 519–520.
37. R. B. Warden, *An Account of the Private Life and Public Services of Salmon Portland Chase* (Cincinnati, 1874), 706.
38. Warden, *Chase*, 707.
39. Stanton, *Random Recollections*, 239.

hoped to get. Three bits of evidence make this cynical explanation of what happened at New York in 1868 extremely improbable. Over five years after the convention Seymour wrote a long letter in response to the request of one of the early biographers of Chase. The delegation of which he had been a member had decided to support Sanford E. Church if a New Yorker were to be chosen — or Senator Hendricks if the choice were to go elsewhere. Behind questions of political preference there arose "grave doubts," according to Seymour, "if any one could be elected by the unaided strength" of the Democratic party.

Even were a Democrat to go into office as such, he would find himself in a position worse than that of Johnson, "who had struggled with ability and vigor, but vainly, to uphold the executive rights and powers." The welfare of the whole country required that the radicals should be checked, and the best way to promote that policy, he had argued, was to sink party differences in a national nomination. The first need in 1868, so Seymour wrote in 1873, was to restore constitutional government — discussions about tariffs or state rights or finances could be postponed for the time being. The name of Chase occurred inevitably in this connection to men who were primarily concerned for government by law as against government by force. His conduct of the impeachment trial, his "marked ability, and stainless private character, made him prominent as a fit standard-bearer in the contest betwen civil rights and the military power."

The nomination of Chase was discussed in private, but so far as Seymour knew in 1873, no delegate to the convention had ever communicated with the Chief-Justice on the subject. It was he, himself, who "first suggested the propriety of his nomination if . . . expedient."

As the difficulty in the way of agreeing upon a Democratic candidate became apparent, the name of Mr. Chase was looked upon with more favor. The delegation from New York decided upon presenting it to the convention unless it could secure the nomination of Mr. Hendricks. There would have been a strong opposition to Mr. Chase at the outset, but I think in the end he would have been nominated. But time was needed to bring this about, and the delegates were impatient to return to their homes. Many of them could not afford the expense of a long stay in the city of New York, and none of them had made arrangements for a protracted session. Impatience to close the work of the convention had much to do with its final unconsidered action.

"I believe," concluded Seymour, "that if Mr. Chase had been made President in 1868, the difficulties and dangers which now perplex our country would have been at this time satisfactorily adjusted." He believed, too, that Chase could have beaten Grant.[40]

In 1876 he was still of this opinion. "I think with you," he wrote that year, "that our friends made a mistake in not nominating Judge Chase in 1868." There remains a third bit of evidence. Thirty years after the convention Abram S. Hewitt described how he had dined with Tilden, John Kelly, and Governor Seymour at the Manhattan Club in New York City on the evening of July 8, the day before the latter was chosen suddenly to head the ticket. According to Hewitt "There was a unanimous agreement that Chief-Justice Chase was to receive the nomination the next day," but the convention was "carried off its feet," and the presiding officer was drafted "in spite of all his efforts to prevent this action."[41] If the sentiments of the diners are significant for Seymour's reputation for sincerity, the date of the dinner, it will be seen later on, is just as important for the good character of Tilden.

There is every reason for believing that Chase was willing and Seymour was sincere up to the last moment before the stampede which wrecked a plausible plan. Seymour never found or acknowledged any reason for concealing what he had hoped to do. Hendricks remained his second choice, and Hendricks stood at the top of the ballot when the delegates broke and turned in tumult toward himself. That neither his first choice nor his second was made the nominee at New York is best explained by the fact that each man was cordially hated by the powerful delegation from Ohio.

40. Schuckers, *Chase*, 570–573: Horatio Seymour to J. W. Schuckers, September 12, 1873.

41. Nevins, *Hewitt*, 265–266, quoting a letter from Abram Hewitt to George L. Miller dated December 8, 1898.

SALMON P. CHASE

THOMAS A. HENDRICKS

XVII

CANDIDATE BY COMPULSION

1868

IT was at noon on Saturday, the Fourth of July, 1868, that August Belmont, chairman of the national committee, called the Democratic convention to order in the auditorium of what was thought to be a "magnificent temple" — the brand-new headquarters which Tammany Hall had built for itself on the north side of East Fourteenth Street. The conscious effort to assemble on the birthday of the nation brought the delegates into New York City fully two days earlier than was necessary, for the convention did not get down to real business until Monday, July 6. In his speech of welcome Belmont "pointed with pride" to the sweeping victory which the party had won in New York State at the autumn elections of 1867; dwelt briefly on the unrest and resentments of reconstruction; and called attention to the fact that the Republican party had made the dangerous choice of a general in selecting its nominee for President.[1] The remarks on Grant were odd coming from the national chairman of the party, for Hancock became one of the strongest candidates in the balloting which followed, a great number of Democrats, many of them southerners, believing that they could not do better than match one northern general with another.

Then Henry L. Palmer, of Wisconsin, took his place as temporary chairman and congratulated the members on the fact that every one of the thirty-seven states of the Union was

1. *Official Proceedings . . . National Democratic Convention*, 3–5. The names of the delegates and detailed votes by ballots, together with a picture of the seating of the delegates, can be found most conveniently in Shannon, *Manual of the Corporation of the City of New York, 1868*, 781–803. A good account of the convention can be found in Stebbins, *Political History of New York State, 1865–1869*, 325–350.

fully represented on the floor. Immediately thereafter it was pointedly decided not to adopt the rules of the "present" House of Representatives, after which Francis Kernan moved that the rules of 1864 should serve. The three important committees on credentials, organization, and resolutions having been appointed, the convention adjourned until Monday morning. Of the thirty-seven members of the last committee only three are remembered to-day: James A. Bayard sat for Delaware; Henry Cruse Murphy for New York; and Wade Hampton for South Carolina. Although Vallandigham was very much in evidence as a vehement supporter of Pendleton, Ohio's place on the committee was filled by William J. Gilmore.

The convention met for the second time at half-past ten on Monday, when the business-like Tilden proposed that the reading of the journal be dispensed with. Then Hiester Clymer, of Pennsylvania, offered the name of Horatio Seymour for permanent chairman, and Murphy got permission for the committee on resolutions to sit during sessions of the convention. The presiding officer was greeted with the "wildest enthusiasm" as he took the chair to thank his fellow delegates for their "kind partiality." [2] Reminding them that they should not seek "a mere party triumph," he begged them to act in such a way as to liberate the business and labor of the land from the shackles of "bad laws" and "crushing taxation." The great task was to save those sections of their common country which were suffering "from the unhappy events of the last eight years."

In spite of the fact that he believed that the delegates would do well to avoid "harsh invective against men" they would be forced to meet the assertions in the resolutions adopted by the late Republican convention. There was no man in the hall, he thought, who had it in his heart to excite so much of angry feeling against that party as would be stirred up in the minds of all who read its declarations "in the light of recent events" and the condition of the country. Burdened taxpayers were

2. *Official Proceedings . . . National Democratic Convention*, 24–27; and Seymour, *Public Record*, 335–338.

asked to congratulate themselves on the success of that policy of reconstruction which had saddled the cost of a "military despotism" on them. All forms of repudiation were denounced as national crimes by the very party which had made paper money legal tender. Creditors who had been forced to accept a currency often worth no more than forty cents on the dollar in repayment for sterling coin would hardly take these pious promises at their face value. The men who called for a reduction of the public debt had already wasted half a billion dollars trying to govern one-third of the Union without its consent. After seven years of Republican policies the once excellent credit of the United States was "tainted in the markets of the world."

According to Seymour the "crowning indictment against the follies and crimes of those in power" was the resolution which endorsed the principles of the Declaration of Independence as "the true foundation of democratic government." The fact was that within ten states of the Union any American citizen who dared to quote that declaration in his own defense "would be tried and punished by a military tribunal." If a citizen of the state where the ashes of Washington lay buried were to remind his rulers that "the military should ever be subordinate to the civil authority," he could be "dragged to prison" even from the grave of the man who wrote the declaration. Surely this was no time for Democrats to "suffer any prejudices growing out of past differences of opinion" to hinder them from acting together to rescue their country from the danger of being turned over to the untried hands of "a military chieftain." Evidently it was the hope of New York to make an issue of General Grant. They were met, he continued, in the very city where, amid "glad processions of men" and "manifestations of great joy," the federal government had begun to function:

> I thank God that the strife of arms has ceased, and that once more in the great conventions of our party we can call through the whole roll of states, and find men to answer to each. Time and events in the great cycles have brought us to this spot to renew and reinvigorate that constitutional government which nearly eighty years ago was inaugurated in this city. It was

> here that George Washington, the first President, swore to "preserve, protect and defend" the Constitution of these United States. And here this day we as solemnly pledge ourselves to uphold the rights and liberties of the American people. Then, as now, a great war which had desolated our land had ceased. Then, as now, there was in every patriotic breast a longing for the blessings of good government, for the protection of laws, and for sentiments of fraternal regard and affection among the inhabitants of all the States of this Union.

It was in the spirit of George Washington, then, that the delegates should reinaugurate their government and "start it once again on its course to greatness and prosperity."

At the conclusion of his speech Seymour was handed two petitions, which were read to the convention by a secretary. The first was presented by Erastus Brooks, a delegate from New York, and came from representatives of the National Labor Union. If its language sounded radical to men of that day, it probably pleased the supporters of Pendleton. Pointing out that legislation and monopoly tended to "purloin" the "earnings of industry," the signers went on to declare that the producing classes were of first importance; while "distributors, financiers, and statesmen" were of "secondary consequence." Although the national honor required the paying of public debt "in good faith," every obligation of the United States "not specifically contracted to be paid in gold" ought in fairness to be met with "lawful currency." Government bonds, it was urged, should be redeemed with "legal tender notes" or exchanged, at the option of the owners, for other bonds bearing interest at three per cent.

The notes of the national banks in circulation should be replaced by legal-tender treasury certificates. Taxes must be made equal and collected "on every species of property, according to its real value." No more of the public domain should be granted to any corporation "under any pretext whatever," and lands not yet disposed of ought to be withdrawn from sale and "granted to actual settlers." The representatives of the union tendered their thanks to the Congress and to those state legislatures which had passed the Eight-Hour Law. They declared that the low wages, the long hours, and the damaging service of "working girls and women" were a "standing reproach to civilization" and urged these new competitors to learn trades, engage in business, join labor unions, or use "any other honorable means" to obtain fair treatment from their employers. Calling attention to the mass meetings held in Chicago during August, 1867, to ratify the principles of the National Labor Union, the signers of this petition warned the industrial classes to exact pledges of support from every candidate for public office.[3]

The second petition came from the Woman's Suffrage Association of America. It had been signed by a central committee of four women in New York City on July 4, 1868. It asked for the privilege of appearance before the convention, reminding the members that although women had both "property and education" and that taxation without representation was tyranny, the one qualification for suffrage which they lacked was that of sex, which was "insurmountable." The statement of this fact roused laughter on the floor and in the galleries. Although women had borne their fair share of the burdens of the war, the party in power had not only failed to heed "the innumerable petitions" of the association, but after having voted to give the suffrage to two million black men was now entertaining the proposal to insert the word "male" in the federal Constitution where it had never been and thus leave fifteen million white women "dethroned."

A "minority party," the petitioners pleaded, not quite tactfully, perhaps, was in a position to "consider principles," and inasmuch as the Democrats had "perpetuated" their power early in the nineteenth century by extending the franchise by repealing property qualifications, they should go with the "tide of progress" which was "setting" in all countries and assure their dominance for "decades to come," by endorsing suffrage for women. The Civil War had been a struggle between capital and labor, the same struggle which had "convulsed the race through the ages," but labor had still to be protected from

3. *Official Proceedings . . . National Democratic Convention*, 27–28.

"bondholders and monopolists." The petition concluded with an appeal to the delegates to vote for "universal suffrage" and "universal amnesty."[4]

According to the record "applause greeted various portions of the document," and when the laughter died down, Seymour remarked, "I may mention that this document is signed by Susan B. Anthony." Although he called attention only to one name, the first and second signers were Elizabeth Cady Stanton and Mrs. Horace Greeley, and the fourth, Abby Hopper Gibbons. It is interesting to notice that the petition of the National Labor Union went to the committee on resolutions; while that submitted by the ladies was referred to the committee on credentials.

In the afternoon of July 6 a committee from the convention of "Conservative Soldiers and Sailors," then in session in New York City, was welcomed to the floor and its formal address read to the delegates by a clerk. Twenty signatures were attached to this document, which declared against suffrage for "ignorant negroes," calling attention, at the same time, to the recent adverse votes of several great northern states on the question. Endeavors to influence senators to find President Johnson guilty were denounced, and the policy which denied aid and government positions to veterans was contrasted with their loyal service and sacrifices during the war. In making Grant independent of Johnson, the radical Republicans, according to these soldiers and sailors, had put the life of the republic in jeopardy. Among the twenty signers of this address were General H. W. Slocum, John A. McClernand, Thomas Kirby Smith, and Thomas Ewing, Jr., the last of whom was called on for a speech in which he praised the rapid reunion of the North and South as evidenced in the friendly relations in a gathering of two thousand men who had served on opposite sides in the Civil War. Then the convention adjourned for the day, after a long parliamentary wrangle over the very important question as to whether or not candidates should be put in nomination before the platform had been drawn up, read, and adopted.

4. *Official Proceedings . . . National Democratic Convention*, 29–30.

On the morning of Tuesday, July 7, Thomas L. Price, of Missouri, called the convention to order as president *pro tempore*, for although Seymour was present on the platform, it was stated that he was "slightly indisposed." Mr. Wright, of Delaware, began the day by reading, between punctuations of applause, five paragraphs of resolutions which had been sent to him by Alexander Hamilton Stephens, of Georgia. According to the late vice-president of the Confederacy the only Union which could last must rest on the Constitution, and the Constitution expressly provided for the "political integrity" of the states. Inasmuch as the "venerable teachings" of Jefferson, Madison, and Jackson were against the abolitionists, and in view of the fact that the Democratic party had supported the federal government during "the late unhappy conflict of arms" for the precise purpose of maintaining the Union and not to subjugate the states, the right to grant suffrage should continue to remain where it properly belonged.

The obvious aim of these resolutions offered in behalf of Stephens was to head off the Fourteenth Amendment, which was proclaimed as ratified just three weeks later, as well as to forestall the Fifteenth Amendment, which was started on its strange career early in 1869. After the message had been referred to the committee on resolutions, Bigler, of California, asked for a reading of those adopted at the Democratic convention of his state, when it was found that the patriotic duty and deliberate purpose of the party was "never to submit to be governed by the negro nor by those claiming to be elected by negro suffrage." The California Democrats declared, moreover, that the Eight-Hour Law was "a Democratic measure." [5]

The list of delegates, as certified by the committee on credentials, contains no more than a dozen interesting names. New York was strongest in brains and influence, as well as in numbers: August Belmont was a delegate-at-large, and Henry Cruse Murphy, a scholar and a statesman, was chairman of the key committee on resolutions. The permanent president was

5. *Official Proceedings . . . National Democratic Convention*, 57. John Bigler (1805–1871) was governor of California from 1852 to 1856; William Bigler

a New Yorker, and Samuel J. Tilden, Augustus Schell, William Cassidy, and Francis Kernan sat as party representatives from various districts. Three men were present whose reputations were not improved by time — Peter B. Sweeny, A. Oakey Hall, and William Marcy Tweed. From Indiana came Daniel W. Voorhees, "the tall sycamore of the Wabash"; Benjamin F. Buckner and John G. Carlisle sat for Kentucky; Maryland had elected Montgomery Blair, and Missouri, James O. Broadhead. Among the men from North Carolina was Zebulon B. Vance, and Vallandigham helped represent Ohio together with General George W. McCook, of the well-known family of "The Fighting McCooks." Former Governor Bigler sat for Pennsylvania; and South Carolina, characteristically enough, had sent two complete sets of delegates, the first chosen in April and the second in June. Apart from General Wade Hampton of that state, the names of the southern delegates are those of men unknown to-day.

Amid calls for order in the hall and quiet in the noisy galleries, Murphy took the floor about noon on July 7 to read the platform to the delegates. Differences of opinion, he declared, had been resolved in the committee, the members of which had given their "unanimous approval" to the resolutions he submitted — eight paragraphs in all headed by a preamble, which acknowledged that the two questions of negro slavery and the right of a state to secede were settled for all time. The first resolution called for the immediate restoration of all thirty-seven states to the Union and the government itself to the American people. The second recommended amnesty for all offenses and regulation of the elective franchise by the several states.

The third and fourth resolutions were the most important in the light of future events, for they demanded that the national debt be redeemed in "lawful money of the United States" where there was no express statement to the contrary and called for

(1814–1880) was governor of Pennsylvania from 1852 to 1855 and senator from 1856 to 1861. Both Biglers sat in the Democratic national convention of 1868.

equal taxation on all property, including government bonds and other securities. The next plank proposed one and the same currency for both government and people, laborer and office-holder, pensioner and soldier, producer and bond-holder. The sixth resolution urged economy in the national administration, a reduction of the army and navy, and abolition of the Freedmen's Bureau and "all political instrumentalities designed to secure negro supremacy." The system of internal revenue must be simplified, and the enactments for enrolling state militia in national forces during a time of peace must be repealed. The committee went on to declare for a tariff for revenue on foreign imports "such as will afford incidental protection to domestic manufactures."[6]

In calling for a complete reform of the administration, the makers of the platform urged the voters to bring an end to the "usurpations of Congress and the despotism of the sword," and announced themselves as favoring equal rights and protection for both naturalized and native-born citizens. The bulk of this eighth resolution consists of an arraignment of the policies and performances of the radical Republicans, not the least of which was subjecting the "learned Chief Justice" to the "most atrocious calumnies" for having refused to do less than his duty as presiding officer at the trial of President Johnson. Declaring that suffrage was a state question and that attempts by the Congress to control it were a "flagrant usurpation of power," the resolutions proceeded to promise to carry out all pledges to soldiers and sailors. Public lands should be given to the people, and proceeds from the sale of lands, and not the lands themselves, should be applied to public improvements. Andrew Johnson, it was declared, was "entitled to the gratitude of the whole American people." The last plank called on every patriot, "including the conservative element," to come to the support of the Constitution and help "restore the Union."[7]

After a great demonstration during which the delegates rose

6. *Official Proceedings . . . National Democratic Convention*, 59.
7. *Official Proceedings . . . National Democratic Convention*, 58–60.

and adopted the platform "without a dissenting voice," Seymour resumed the chair. There were three important matters to be cleared up before the making of nominations. The first had to do with the famous two-thirds rule. In order to avoid any misunderstanding the president stated that he desired every delegate to know the proper use of that rule. The convention of 1868 had adopted the rules of that of 1864, and the Chicago convention had voted to follow those of 1860. Because he had not been present at Charleston or Baltimore Seymour stated that he had gone through the proceedings of the two conventions carefully and asked the clerk to read the decisions of the chair at that time. It was clear, he proceeded to explain, that the two-thirds rule required that the nominee of the convention should receive the votes of two-thirds of all members — not merely two-thirds of those voting.

At this point Richardson, of Illinois, rose to protest that the proper interpretation of the two-thirds rule called only for two-thirds of the votes cast and urged the delegates to recommend a repeal of the mischievous measure to the convention of 1872. Kernan, of New York, opposed this motion and was backed by Clymer, of Pennsylvania, chairman of the committee on organization. When Richardson withdrew his motion, Seymour ruled that the convention would act according to the decisions of the chair at Charleston and Baltimore. When the secretary read the two decisions of 1860, and the president had stated the electoral vote as 317, it was formally announced that 211½ votes would be necessary for the nomination of the candidate. Owing to the two sets of delegates from South Carolina the convention was slightly more than twice as large as the electoral college, but the states were counted on the ballots in proportion to their relative strength there.

After another plea for quiet in the galleries, during which he reminded the audience that the noise they made was an act of inhospitality to the Democratic party, Seymour ruled that "this Convention has a right, at any time, to bring forward any new candidate it may see fit."[8] In providing that candidacies should not be closed after the states had made their nominations, the president was looking forward to the use of the name of Chief-Justice Chase when the proper time should come. In fact, the first move in favor of the Chief-Justice had already been made a day or two before at the moment when A. Oakey Hall, from the eighth congressional district in New York City, had introduced a resolution which thanked Chase for his "ability, impartiality, and fidelity" in presiding at the court of impeachment. Hall's resolution was received with cheers and referred to the committee.[9] Oddly enough, however, Seymour himself became the victim of the rule by means of which he hoped to see Chase chosen to lead the party.

A third question came up for discussion when Thurman, of Ohio, called attention to the resolution unanimously passed the day before, according to which any candidate was supposed to be pledged to support the nominee of the convention. Seymour pointed out a distinction: the vote of July 6 committed all the delegates to the support of the man whom two-thirds should choose, "but," continued the president, "how far candidates themselves may be regarded as pledged I do not know." His statement that there ought to be no doubt but that any one who allowed his name to be used would support the nominee of the convention was greeted with cheers. Laughter met Tilden's proposal that exceptions ought, in honor, to be mentioned.

Of the thirty-seven states represented, New York with 33 votes, Pennsylvania with 26, Ohio with 21, and Illinois with 16 were the four important centres of power. Senator Pendleton entered the convention with the enthusiastic support of the third and fourth states; while New York and Pennsylvania hid their influence during the early ballots by supporting favorite, if somewhat obscure, sons. There were more than two of such, however: Senator Doolittle, of Wisconsin, held the eight votes

8. *Official Proceedings . . . National Democratic Convention*, 65.
9. *Official Proceedings . . . National Democratic Convention*, 41.

of his state together with the four of Rhode Island through many ballots; New Jersey cast her seven for Joel Parker; and Connecticut supported its governor, James E. English, a rich manufacturer of New Haven. Each delegation, it was decided, should have five minutes in which to present a candidate. After Connecticut had named her favorite son, Maine offered the name of Hancock, "a general obedient to civil authority." Because the delegation did not act under the unit rule the minority spoke and voted for Pendleton, expressing the hope that the convention would select a man who would lift the burden of debt and taxation from the shoulders of the people. Then New Jersey nominated Parker, a governor who had helped sustain the Union without permitting federal encroachment.

After Tilden had announced that Sanford E. Church was the unanimous choice of New York, General McCook put up Pendleton for Ohio, and when Oregon was called, the chairman declared that his state had no candidate but intended to vote for the senator from Ohio. Pennsylvania was the next to be heard from. Judge George W. Woodward gave a speech so long-winded as to provoke shouts and interruptions before he could wind up with his eulogy of Asa Packer, whom he was pleased to describe as a large taxpayer, a builder of railroads, a business man, an Episcopalian, and a lifelong Democrat. Then Tennessee brought in the name of Andrew Johnson amid enthusiastic cheering, and when Wisconsin had declared for James R. Doolittle, the minority shouting for Pendleton in the meantime, the roll of nominations was complete — eight men, in all. Just before the balloting began, Seymour ruled that according to the previous vote of the convention delegates from territories could not take part; whereupon a Mr. Cavanaugh, of Montana, begged the convention not to act "like the Radical Congress." [10]

The name of Seymour, it will be noticed, did not go before the convention. The presiding officer had taken care that it should not. When the delegates from New York assembled for

10. *Official Proceedings . . . National Democratic Convention*, 74.

a caucus on Thursday, July 2, Mr. Hardenburgh, of Ulster County, moved that they should offer their former governor as their candidate and frankly invite the other states to cast their votes for him. Seymour, of course, was present, and promptly protested, stating that he could no longer remain silent now that his name had been "used by two of his friends." He was not a candidate for the office of President, "a place far above his merits and beyond his aspirations." To allow his name to be offered by a delegation of which he was a part, he added, "did not seem to him to be right." He begged his friends to have regard for his "private honor" even if they could not respect his "former inclination." [11] Thus he made his third explicit refusal to allow his name to be voted on at New York.

The first ballot was taken just before noon on Tuesday, July 7, and most of the delegates probably hoped to set out for home that evening. Pendleton led off with 105, most of them from the Middle West. The second man was Johnson with 65, the bulk of his votes coming from the southern states. Church was third, with 34, the delegation of New York and one other vote, and Hancock was fourth with 33½ — fourteen of these from the solid delegations of Louisiana and Mississippi. The fifth man was Packer, with the 26 votes of Pennsylvania. Aside from English, who had 16 votes, and Doolittle and Parker with 13 each, Reverdy Johnson of Maryland got 8½, Hendricks of Indiana 2½, and Francis P. Blair, Jr., of Missouri, one-half.

On the second ballot, which followed immediately, Pendleton lost one vote; Johnson lost thirteen; and Hancock picked up seven. The third ballot was taken after a recess and showed 119½ for Pendleton, 45½ for Hancock, and 34½ for Johnson. Although the thirteen votes of Indiana were instructed and still cast for Pendleton, Senator Hendricks received 9½ votes on this ballot. By the fourth ballot, Church, of New York, had taken third place from the President. During the calling of this roll the chairman of the delegation from North Carolina suddenly and without comment cast all the nine votes of that

11. Seymour, *Public Record*, 339–340.

state for Horatio Seymour. The record has it that this act was followed by "loud and enthusiastic cheering, participated in by the galleries." When Tilden warned the presiding officer that he would move to clear the galleries if the audience would not keep quiet, Richardson of Illinois put in, "I move to clear them now." A delegate from Michigan persuaded Richardson to withdraw his motion, after which Seymour came forward and asked the convention to permit him to "make a single remark."

Very much to my surprise my name has been mentioned. I must not be nominated by this Convention, as I could not accept the nomination if tendered, which I do not expect. My own inclinations prompted me to decline at the outset; my honor compels me to do so now. I am grateful for any expression of kindness. It must be distinctly understood, it is impossible, consistently with my position, to allow my name to be mentioned in this Convention against my protest. The clerk will proceed with the call.[12]

Immediately after the fourth ballot a motion to adjourn was made and lost, and the convention proceeded with its business. Pendleton continued to climb slowly, Hancock following at a distance; while Hendricks worked up gradually into third place. The strength of Johnson melted away until his name disappeared for the first time on the fourteenth ballot. In the meantime the great states of New York and Pennsylvania still held off, steadily casting their solid votes of 33 and 26 for Church and Packer. After the sixth ballot the convention voted down the proposal to take a recess until six o'clock by 218 to 99, and then, by exactly the same vote, decided to adjourn until ten o'clock in the morning of Wednesday, July 8.

The fourth day brought a surprise, when Indiana broke her instructions for Pendleton and put Hendricks in nomination, Fitch announcing that the majority would cast their votes for him without claiming any authority to coerce the others. The minority felt that it could not leave Pendleton in view of the action of the state committee at Indianapolis on January 5, 1868; so the vote of the state stood divided on the seventh ballot — Hendricks 9½, Pendleton 3½. The change had been discussed

12. *Official Proceedings . . . National Democratic Convention*, 83–84; and Seymour, *Public Record*, 340.

in conferences overnight and was long and bitterly resented by other supporters of the senator from Ohio, who was still far ahead, with 137½. On the next, and eighth ballot, Pendleton reached his peak, 156½, at the very time when New York changed from Church to Hendricks. The fight between the East and West was out in the open at last: the conservatives would beat the senator from Ohio with the senator from Indiana. From this point on the supporters of Pendleton resolved that whoever might get the nomination, it should not be Hendricks.

The high total of Pendleton was assembled from twenty-six states. No less than 49½ of his votes came from the eleven states of the Confederacy: the delegations of five, Alabama, Georgia, Louisiana, Mississippi, and South Carolina, were solid for him. While Pendleton was slowly sliding back from his high of 156½, Hendricks took second place from Hancock and held it for eight ballots. On the fifteenth, Pennsylvania finally came out from under cover and dropped Packer to throw her twenty-six votes to Hancock, who not only forged ahead of Hendricks on the sixteenth, but Pendleton, as well. On this ballot the vote stood: Hancock, 113½; Pendleton, 107½; Hendricks, 70½; Doolittle, 12; Parker, 7; and Johnson, 5½. One delegate from California and another from Indiana, each with half a vote, were not recorded.

Just why Hancock had to wait twelve years for the presidential nomination of the Democratic party is something of a mystery. The southern states were not unwilling to support him; he had won the powerful backing of Pennsylvania; and he had not incurred the hatred of the men who had hoped to put Pendleton over. His war record was distinguished, and his conduct in regard to President Johnson and reconstruction had been correct and honorable. Robert J. Walker, of Mississippi, who had sat in the Senate and served Polk as secretary of the treasury, in writing Tilden from Washington in 1868, named Hancock as the strongest possible candidate of their party. Walker gave six reasons for his opinion: Hancock could carry

Pennsylvania; the Democrats must match Grant with a general; the South admired him as a gallant Unionist; he had always been loyal to the party; he would make a good President; and as commander-in-chief of the army he would be able to manage General Grant.[13] He was, to be sure, only forty-four, but the sole interest against him was the desire of the Democrats to make a political issue of the fact that the Republicans had nominated "a military chieftain." Seymour worked for his election in 1880 and was much disappointed by his defeat; a little more than a year after the New York convention he stated that he would have been glad to see him named.

Hancock picked up twenty-four votes on the seventeenth ballot, and continued at the head of the list through the twenty-first ballot, Hendricks creeping up on him slowly and surely. On this seventeenth ballot, moreover, the name of Chase appeared for the first time, when the Chief-Justice received one-half a vote from California. Tilden's motion to adjourn was then lost by 174½ to 142½. The chairman of the New York delegation probably hoped for an opportunity to talk over the respective chances of the two men that state was willing to see nominated — Hendricks openly and Chase in secret. On the seventeenth ballot the strength of Pendleton in Illinois began to crumble; Richardson, the chairman, allowing the sixteen votes to break for the first time as follows: Pendleton, 8½; Hendricks, 7; and Johnson, ½. When the chairman, in accordance with the vote of the majority, cast all sixteen votes for Hendricks in the course of the eighteenth ballot, his action produced a protest from one of his associates, by the name of Malony. The cause of the trouble was the famous unit rule. The delegates from Illinois had been instructed for Pendleton, and Malony now asked that the rule be discarded by the convention. Seymour declared that such a change required a day's notice; that every delegation was its own master; and that according to the decision of 1860 the vote of every state was to be announced by its chairman.

13. Tilden, *Letters and Literary Memorials*, I, 233–236: R. J. Walker to Samuel J. Tilden, May 30, 1868.

When Mr. Malony continued to demand that his vote be recorded for Pendleton, Bayard, of Delaware, put in his oar with the observation that the unit rule made a farce of a deliberative body; whereupon Seymour had the clerk read to the convention the decision of the chair in 1860. Then Clymer, of Pennsylvania, joined the argument by announcing that the convention at Charleston had voted: "That in any state which has not provided or directed by its state convention how its vote shall be given, the Convention will recognize the right of each delegate to cast his individual vote." [14] When Seymour had the clerk read the vote cited by Clymer, the restless and noisy delegates voted to adjourn.

The two-thirds rule under which Democratic national conventions made nominations for more than a century was, it is often forgotten, a very necessary protection against the use of the unit rule by the states. A moment's thought will show that under the operation of this unit rule an actual minority of any convention might cast what would only appear to be a majority vote. The fact that all states did not see fit to enjoin the unit rule on their delegations added a further complication. In 1860, for instance, as President Buchanan pointed out, the lesser number of the delegates voted down the greater number on the question of the platform. The two rules should, in justice, stand or fall together. In 1936, however, the Democratic national convention abolished the two-thirds rule without any reference to the unit rule, although it softened the decision to take a "veto power" from the South by recommending to the convention of 1940 the weighting of representation according to the size of the Democratic vote in the several states. If the size of that vote be gauged by national elections rather than primaries, however, the single-party South will stand to lose even more, for the fact that in nine states of the Union the choice of officials is made within one party robs election-day of the interest it holds for the voters in close, or two-party states.

On the morning of July 9, the fifth day of the convention,

14. *Official Proceedings . . . National Democratic Convention*, 139.

Thomas L. Price, of Missouri, was in the chair, Seymour being busy in the caucus of New York. When Mr. Broadhead of that state had put Francis P. Blair, Jr., in nomination, California followed with the name of Stephen J. Field, an associate-justice of the Supreme Court. Then Vallandigham got the floor to withdraw the name of Pendleton. His action could not have been much of a surprise. On the last ballot of the day before, the eighteenth, the candidate from Ohio had shown a net loss of exactly one hundred votes from his highest total — 156½, on the eighth. He had entered the convention with the largest block of delegates but the field had been against him, and it was evident by Wednesday evening that his chance to be the nominee in 1868 was gone. When Vallandigham had read a letter which Pendleton had written Washington McLean, of the Cincinnati *Enquirer*, just a week before, the convention proceeded to the nineteenth ballot.[15] The twenty-one votes of Ohio, it is interesting to notice, were cast for Asa Packer, whom Pennsylvania had dropped for Hancock long before. The disappointed supporters of Pendleton in his own state refused to give their votes to the general at the very moment when their action might have brought him the nomination. On this nineteenth ballot, Richardson cast the sixteen votes of Illinois for Hendricks, once again over the loud protests of delegate Malony.

On the twentieth and twenty-first ballots Ohio divided her vote, giving eleven to Hancock and ten to English. The twenty-first ballot was the beginning of the end, for Hancock's vote fell off by seven, his first loss since he had taken the lead on the sixteenth. He and Hendricks were neck and neck now — 135½ for the general and 132 for the senator. New York had come into the convention on the morning of July 9 with the plan of springing the name of Chase if and when the vote of Hendricks began to decline. This was the limit of the discretion which the persuasive Seymour had obtained for the chairman of the delegation by a small majority. If Tilden had interpreted his power

15. *Official Proceedings . . . National Democratic Convention*, 143.

freely, Chase probably could have been chosen. Hendricks continued to gather strength, however, going from 107½ on the nineteenth ballot to 132 on the twenty-first, when the Chief-Justice got four votes from Massachusetts. This was the moment for the astute but timid Tilden to act: when New York was called on the twenty-second ballot, he should have thrown its thirty-three votes to Chase, acting on the knowledge he must have had that the embittered supporters of Pendleton, seeing Hancock could not win, would never let the prize go to Hendricks. Tilden was too slow, however, and Ohio got in ahead of him at the decisive moment.

As the twenty-second ballot was in process of being taken, it became obvious that Hendricks would easily win first place. He had rolled up 145½ to 103½ for Hancock when young General McCook, of Ohio, threw twenty-one votes to Horatio Seymour, and one delegate from Tennessee followed suit. In announcing the sensational shift of Ohio, McCook declared that he acted "at the unanimous request and demand of the delegation . . . and with the consent and approval of every public man in the state, including . . . Pendleton." Amid rousing cheers and applause he placed the president in nomination "against his inclination, but no longer against his honor." He asked the convention to vote "for a man whom the Presidency has sought, but who has not sought the Presidency" — the one man who could drive the "Vandals" from power at Washington. He closed his remarks amid "tremendous excitement, and nine cheers" for Seymour.[16] Seymour, who had taken the chair again some time during the morning, walked to the front of the stage, and, as soon as he could make himself heard above the uproar, protested for the fifth and last time against the use of his name by his party.

> The motion just made by the gentleman from Ohio excites in my mind the most mingled emotions. (Applause.) I have no terms in which to express my gratitude (Cheers) for the magnanimity of his State, and for the generosity of this Convention. (Cheers.) I have no terms in which to

16. *Official Proceedings . . . National Democratic Convention*, 152–153.

tell of my regret that my name has been brought before this Convention. God knows that my life and all that I value most in life I would give for the good of my country, which I believe to be identified with that of the Democratic party. (Applause, and cries of "Take the nomination then.") I do not stand here as a man proud of his opinions, or obstinate in his purposes; but upon a question of duty and of honor I must stand upon my own convictions against the world. (Applause, and a voice, "God bless you, Horatio Seymour.") Gentlemen, when I said here at an early day, that honor forbade my accepting a nomination by this Convention, I *meant* it. When, in the course of my intercourse with those of my own delegation and my friends, I said to them that I could not be a candidate, I *meant* it. And now permit me here to say that I know, after all that has taken place, I could not receive the nomination without placing, not only myself, but the great Democratic party, in a false position. But, gentlemen of the Convention, more than that, we have had to-day an exhibition, from the distinguished citizen of Ohio, that has touched my heart, as it has touched yours. (Cheers.) I thank God and I congratulate this country, that there is in the great State of Ohio, whose magnificent position gives it so great a control over the action of our country, a young man, rising fast into fame, whose future is all glorious, who has told the world that he could tread beneath his feet every other consideration than that of duty; and when he expressed to his delegation, and expressed in more direct terms, that he was willing that I should be nominated, who had stood in such a position of marked opposition to his own nomination, I should feel a dishonored man if I could not tread, in the far distance, and in a feeble way, the same honorable pathway which he has marked out. (Great applause.) Gentlemen, I thank you, and may God bless you for your kindness to me, but your candidate I cannot be. (Three cheers for Horatio Seymour.) [17]

Having surrendered the chair to Price, of Missouri, in order to confer with the delegation of his own state, Seymour left the platform of the hall. As he did so Vallandigham got the floor to declare that Ohio could not and would not accept the declination. "The safety of the people," he shouted, "is the supreme law, and the safety of the American Republic demands the nomination of Horatio Seymour, of New York." Cheers interrupted him as he called on the other states to make unanimous the nomination which Ohio had proposed. At this point Francis Kernan, of Utica, rose to seal the fate of the unhappy president of the convention. Declaring that New York "had neither lot

17. *Official Proceedings . . . National Democratic Convention,* 153; and Seymour, *Public Record,* 340–341.

nor part in the motion," Kernan pointed out that two or three days of balloting had proved that none of the candidates before the convention could obtain the votes of two-thirds of the delegates. The honor of Seymour was "entirely safe" in the eyes of his friend and fellow townsman:

> No one can doubt that he has steadily and in good faith declined; but, now that his honor is safe, his duty to his country, his duty to his fellow-citizens, to all that shall come after us, requires that he shall let the judgment of the delegates of this Convention prevail if they should select him as the standard-bearer most certain, in their opinion, to win a triumph for the country next November.[18]

When Kernan sat down, the states began to revise their votes, one after another, New York holding off to the last. Then Tilden took the floor to ask if there were any delegation which had not yet voted, explaining that motives of delicacy made it impossible for his state to act until every one of the other thirty-six had done so. Although he could not have believed "last evening" that what he had just now seen would take place the following day, the choice of the convention was the very best it could have made. He had thought over the question during several months and had discovered that the only obstacle to naming Seymour was his refusal to allow it. The demand of Ohio was compelling at the moment it was made; the choice of Seymour would resolve all differences of opinion and bring peace and victory to the party.[19] Seymour having been unanimously nominated, the convention voted at twenty minutes past two to take an hour's recess. When the unwilling candidate was pushed out of the hall, he supposed that he would have a chance to decline for a sixth time, but General Blair was unanimously nominated for Vice-President on the first ballot of the afternoon, after which the convention broke up, and the delegates went home.

There is a striking parallel between the Democratic conventions of 1864 and 1868. Seymour was president of both; in

18. *Official Proceedings . . . National Democratic Convention*, 154–155.
19. *Official Proceedings . . . National Democratic Convention*, 158.

neither case was the candidate the man of his own choice; in each case the plank of the platform which had to be repudiated was prepared in Ohio; and lastly, Vallandigham was the chief agent in the outcome. Senator Hendricks was going ahead rapidly when Ohio moved, and, except for the unfortunate feud over delegates, Hendricks would have made an acceptable candidate. The Pendleton managers had adroitly secured the thirteen votes of Indiana for their man, although Hendricks was really the first choice of the state, and Chase the second.[20] According to the New York *Sun*, Vallandigham and his associates discovered evidence, at the crucial moment, of a trade for mutual support between Indiana and Pennsylvania in favor of a Hendricks–Hancock ticket.[21] The immediate result of this discovery was the stampede to Seymour. There was another reason for the sudden act of McCook and Vallandigham: Ohio did not fancy Chase. He had been governor and then deserted the party in the dark days before the Civil War. The plan of New York had probably been whispered about; Vallandigham would kill two birds with one stone.

No other American has ever received the nomination of a major party against his will. Within a period of eight months Seymour had declined no less than five times to allow his name to be used: twice by letters published in the papers; once by personal protest in the caucus of the New York delegation on July 2; and twice from the stage of the convention — when North Carolina announced nine votes for him on July 7, and just before he surrendered the chair early in the afternoon of July 9. His fate was strange indeed for a son of his state. The long list of notable New Yorkers who have lost the presidency begins with Aaron Burr and ends with Alfred Smith. Time and again, moreover, major parties have passed New York by in choosing their leaders, feuds within the state usually accounting for their going elsewhere. If we remember how many of its citizens have fallen short of nomination or election, it is odd that

20. Warden, *Chase*, 708–709.
21. New York *Sun*, July 11, 1868.

New York should have been the home of the one and only American who has ever been compelled to run for President in spite of himself.

In view of the fact that this was not the first time that Seymour had refused to let his name be used for a nomination which he later accepted, the question of his sincerity deserves careful consideration. Most of the stories that Seymour connived at his own nomination are partisan tittle-tattle based on nothing more than journalistic guess-work. The situation was singular, and some people wished to make it mysterious. A seasoned politician like Blaine, it is interesting to notice, thought that Seymour neither sought nor expected the outcome; in his opinion the platform was prepared expressly for Pendleton, whose managers refused to see him defeated by the hated Hendricks.[22]

George L. Miller, of Omaha, a friend and frequent correspondent of Horatio Seymour, stopped off at Utica on his way to the national convention. He went out to Deerfield and had a long talk with Seymour late in June. Miller was instructed for Pendleton, whom Seymour acknowledged that he liked personally, but whose greenback doctrines he opposed with what seemed to Miller decisive logic and convincing reason. The New Yorker thought that his delegation would go for Hendricks, and added, "I shall certainly favor that choice."[23] Miller slept at Deerfield, and the two men took a parlor car to Albany the next day. There the upstate delegates foregathered to go down to the city together. Thus Seymour named Hendricks as his first choice in a letter he wrote Tilden in March, and late in June was still agreeable to his nomination, although after the impeachment trial, he believed that for the Democrats to nominate Chase would split the Republican party and win the election.

22. See Blaine's clear and plausible account of the convention in *Twenty Years of Congress*, II, 391–403. A good report of the proceedings is to be found in Smith, *A Political History of Slavery*, II, 351–361.

23. New York Historical Society: Seymour Papers: A memorandum of G. L. Miller.

If there were any real basis for the gossip that Seymour was secretly not unwilling to accept the nomination, D. S. Alexander, a gentleman learned in the lore of New York politics if any one ever was, would have stumbled, sooner or later, on some evidence for the suspicion. Alexander's testimony, however, is all the other way:

To an intimate friend he spoke of family griefs, domestic troubles, impaired health, and the impossibility of an election. Besides, if chosen, he said, he would be as powerless as Johnson, a situation that "would put him in his grave in less than a year." In the whole convention there was not a man who could truthfully say that the Governor, by look, or gesture, or inflection of voice, had encouraged the hope of a change of mind. Within forty-eight hours every Democrat of influence had sounded him and gone away sorrowful. Now, when order was restored, he declined again. His expressions of gratitude seemed only to make the declaration stronger.[24]

This historian blamed Tilden. The charge is interesting, for Seymour himself thought Tilden had got him into a scrape—probably because he believed that the chairman of the delegation had not seized the psychological moment for springing the name of Chase on the convention. The accusation that he had plotted the nomination of Seymour drew a letter of express denial from Tilden.

I had no agency in getting Governor Seymour into his present scrape, though I should have been glad of his nomination if his consent could have been freely given. I yielded to his wishes out of tender regard for him, and I feel now that I am the last man who can with delicacy bring a pressure to bear upon him; but my judgment is, that acceptance under present circumstances would not compromise his repute for sincerity or be really misunderstood by the people; that the case is not analogous to the former instances which have made criticism possible; that the true nature of the sacrifice would be appreciated, while on the other hand the opposite course would be more likely to incite animadversion; that, on the whole, acceptance is the best thing.[25]

According to Alexander, Tilden was a liar, for he desired Seymour above any other man. Although it was doubtful if any one could defeat General Grant, the former governor of New

24. Alexander, *History*, III, 200.

25. Bigelow, *Tilden*, I, 211–212: Letter of S. J. Tilden to Francis Kernan [July —, 1868].

New York Historical Society

HORATIO SEYMOUR

1868

York was sound on the financial question and would probably carry the state. On the evening of Wednesday, July 8, according to this story, Tilden entertained Ohio's most influential delegates at Delmonico's, and there completed the plan which was carried out with success on Thursday. With five men, Allen G. Thurman, George E. Pugh, Washington McLean, General G. W. McCook, and George W. Morgan, so it is said, Tilden concocted a scheme by which the Ohio delegation would retire for consultation and then return to force Seymour's name on the convention. According to Abram S. Hewitt, however, Tilden dined that very night with Seymour, John Kelly, and himself at the Manhattan Club, in order to perfect the strategy for the nomination of Chase.[26] It is hardly likely that Tilden ate two dinners with two quite different groups of men and made two opposing plots on the one night of Wednesday, July 8, 1868. Although Alexander does not divulge the source of this story, it was probably told him by Chauncey Depew. Against one man's tale of what he heard we must set Hewitt's written record of the dinner he himself attended.

Two keepers of diaries, only one of which has been published, were not quite certain that Seymour meant what he said. One of them, indeed, was sure that he did not. In making an entry dated Tuesday, July 7, Gideon Welles wrote in regard to the proceedings of the convention in New York:

> The vote of New York was given for Sanford E. Church. This, I told those present [at the President's], was a blind and meant Seymour, that the New-Yorkers intended Seymour should be the candidate, and Seymour also intended it, provided he became satisfied he would secure the nomination; but, unless certain, he would persist in declining.[27]

The fact that this suspicion, for which no shred of evidence can be found, stands in that record raises the question of how far diaries and journals can be relied on in the writing of history and biography. Welles, it is now well known from a study of his manuscript, tampered with his text from time to time. Some

26. Nevins, *Hewitt*, 265–266.
27. Welles, *Diary*, III, 396.

portions were worked over at a later date. Is it just possible that the busy secretary failed to post his diary until after the compulsory nomination of Seymour was an accomplished fact? Did he, by any chance, writing on the ninth of July, or even later, persuade himself that he had foreseen what happened?

The same doubt, without casting any aspersion on the honesty of the author, will occur to some who might otherwise be puzzled by an entry in the diary of a loyal friend of Seymour who was close at hand — John V. L. Pruyn. After talking with the former governor in New York City on July 2, the very day he refused to let the New York delegation use his name in the convention, Pruyn, either then or possibly later, wrote as follows:

> I saw Governor Seymour and had a frank and direct conversation with him about the Presidency. He is not a candidate and will not consent to be. *As to this he is positive.* Should the Convention finally offer him the nomination, that will put the matter on another ground. It is fair to infer that in such an event he would accept.[28]

Is it likely that Pruyn carried his journal with him when he went down to New York from Albany in July, 1868? Did he post it the night of the day he talked with Seymour or did he write from memory later — perhaps after he returned home? Was he tempted — reading partisan criticism of Seymour and the accusation that his nomination was a plot — to try to excuse his conduct in a way that was not the wisest? If Pruyn interpreted any part of that talk in such fashion as to explain Seymour's acceptance of the accomplished fact, then he innocently cast doubt on the sincerity of his friend. The New York *Sun* had questioned this sincerity openly under date of June 30. It was just that article, perhaps, which prompted the conversation to which Pruyn referred. The evidence of both these witnesses — one at a distance, the other close at hand — is open to grave doubt. Welles wrote in the rôle of a prophet, Pruyn as the apologist.

It has been said again that Seymour was the secret prefer-

28. Journal of John V. L. Pruyn, Albany, New York, July 2, 1868.

ence of Tammany Hall — probably because the national convention was held in the new home of the organization. Having let the South and the West dictate the platform, the New York politicians, if we are to believe this story, packed the galleries of the hall and shouted till they got the man they desired. "There was a general suspicion," writes Myers, "that the organization, hopeless of the election of the Democratic President, had forced Seymour's nomination for the purpose of trading votes for its State and local ticket."[29] The shrewd James Schouler fell in with this notion: Seymour was put forward in 1868 "not to defeat Grant, but to help the Democrats to carry New York State."[30] The theory is plausible, especially in view of the fact that the Democrats elected Hoffman governor — and that Hoffman ran ahead of Seymour.

Nelson J. Waterbury, however, was in a position to know rather well just what was being said and thought in Democratic headquarters on East Fourteenth Street. Exactly a week after the nomination Waterbury wrote Seymour from Albany that the talk in New York City left him with the impression that Tammany Hall was none too pleased with the outcome, "but they will have to shout with the loudest and can do nothing against the current." According to Waterbury, the fact that sentiment for Chase had been strong in Wall Street led to rumors that there would be plenty of money to spend if the Chief-Justice were nominated — that the hope of getting this money had been very tempting, and the loss of it was deeply lamented.[31] At no time in his life, it must be remembered, was Seymour the servant, or even the ally, of Tammany Hall; more than once he openly defied its rulers, and though he laughed at the righteous indignation of the men whose laziness made William Marcy Tweed the power he became, he joined with Tilden to drive him from power.

It was the mature judgment of Rhodes, one of the best

29. Myers, *Tammany Hall*, 216–218.
30. Schouler, *History*, VII, 125–126.
31. New York State Library: Seymour Papers: Nelson J. Waterbury to Horatio Seymour, July 16, 1868.

historians of the period, that in making the nomination it did, the convention avoided two pitfalls: Pendleton would have meant repudiation, and for Chase to have accepted a nomination would have stained his honor and the reputation of the office he held. "Chase or Seymour was the only solution. . . . In Seymour ability, breeding, character were each conspicuous: all knew him for an honour to his party and to his country." [32] If the latter part of this generous statement be true, many orators and voters spoke and acted oddly in 1868. Although even the writer who reported the convention for the *Nation* acknowledged that no man could have stood up against the demonstration which forced the hand of Seymour in spite of his better judgment,[33] the ferocity with which his character and conduct were assailed during the presidential campaign has never been exceeded. Although he made a surprising showing at the polls, millions of Americans were of the set opinion that Horatio Seymour was an "honor" to neither his party nor his country.

Not one of the avowed candidates for the Democratic nomination failed to support Seymour in the campaign. The attitude of Chase is particularly interesting, for he did not seek the first place of either party openly. For many years, however, the Chief-Justice was bitterly abused because it was believed that he was willing to "soil his ermine" in 1868 by going back into politics. After 1916 the force of this criticism lost favor: Hughes made a hot potato of it. One can only imagine the dilemma of James Ford Rhodes in the latter year: could he vote for a former associate-justice or must he stay at home?

According to a nephew of Seymour, Henry S. Miller, of Utica:

Governor Chase always thought that Mr. Seymour cheated him in securing the nomination to the Presidency in 1868. His principal foundation for this belief was the fact that just as soon as the nominations were made, a banner was in readiness with Seymour's portrait painted upon it. The fact is that the transparency was made with a vacant place for the portrait of

32. Rhodes, *History*, VI, 278–279.
33. New York *Nation*, VII, 160 (July 23, 1868), 64.

any one who should happen to be nominated. This information I received from Martin T. McMahon.[34]

Although Chase long lived in the belief that he was headed for the White House, the words quoted above do not fairly represent his state of mind during the summer and autumn of 1868. It is true that his disappointed and indiscreet friends went about the country accusing the Democratic candidate of treachery to their hero. On August 23, Colonel Van Buren wrote Seymour that a letter of support from the Chief-Justice would be most valuable and important and that he gathered that Chase desired to express a preference for him "by his vote." [35] In the Middle West, however, certain men who had hoped to see Chase chosen complained of what seemed to them the manipulation of the delegates at New York. As the campaign wore on Seymour was driven to protest to Van Buren against the "indecent attacks" of those who spoke as the "active supporters" of the Chief-Justice.[36] He felt he had a right to rely on the loyalty of the colonel, whom he had made paymaster-general of the state of New York when he became governor for the second time. He reminded Van Buren that he had thought "it would be well to nominate [Chase] for the presidency," and had persuaded the delegation of his own state to support his opinion with their votes whenever it became obvious that Hendricks could not win.

When Van Buren received this letter, he wrote to Chase, telling him that the Democratic candidate for President was pained and hurt by the accusation that he had outwitted his supporters in July. The Chief-Justice promptly rebuked his friends for what seemed to him their unfortunate, if not "regrettable" statements, writing at least one of them that he did not believe that Seymour had sought the nomination for him-

34. New York Historical Society: Seymour Papers.

35. New York Historical Society: Seymour Papers: John D. Van Buren to Horatio Seymour, August 23, 1868.

36. New York Historical Society: Seymour Papers: Horatio Seymour to John D. Van Buren, September 8, 1868.

self and that any declarations to the contrary would vex and embarrass joint friends of them both.[37] In the course of this triangular correspondence, Colonel Van Buren reminded Seymour of a very important fact: "You have a letter from Chase to me, which I gave you in convention — you put it in your breast pocket and did not return it — take care of it — *it recommends you to take the nomination* — look it up, for it may be of use." [38]

Two days later Chase assured the colonel that he had called off his embarrassingly loyal supporters by reminding them that "justice to Governor Seymour is duty from us." [39] He begged Van Buren to believe that he took pleasure on all occasions in expressing his opinion that the Democratic candidate for President was "an accomplished statesman, an upright citizen, and in all his private relations irreproachable." He added that it was his private opinion that Seymour's acceptance of the nomination was "to be regretted," but "not to be censured." Although he preferred him to General Grant, the Chief-Justice believed that his own "convictions" restrained him from taking any part in the campaign. The failure of the convention to endorse negro suffrage was the loop-hole by which he preserved his judicial dignity as between the two candidates for the presidency. On election-day, according to Dr. Coleman, he failed to vote for either one because he "swallowed hook, line and sinker the Republican ranting about Blair." [40]

"The victim of his own popularity, power, and strength," Seymour, wrote his friend George L. Miller, in 1893, was drafted by the convention of 1868 in two minutes as he "fled

37. Schuckers, *Chase*, 592–593: S. P. Chase to Colonel William Brown, September 29, 1868.

38. New York Historical Society: Seymour Papers: John D. Van Buren to Horatio Seymour, September 22, 1868.

39. On August 23, 1868, Chase wrote privately to Whitelaw Reid: "I do not want to be understood as having any sentiment but respect and general concurrence of sentiment for Mr. Seymour. Without a platform, and free from the influences of violent and rash men, I [*sic*] believe the national administration will be safe in his hands. I have known him, more through mutual friends than personally, for a good while, and have always had very kindly feelings toward him. When we differed most, I have never heard of an unkind or an ungracious expression from him": Smith, *Political History of Slavery*, II, 362–363.

40. Coleman, *Election of 1868*, 102–104 and 371–372.

from the platform in dismay." Miller followed him into an anteroom of the hall as quickly as he could force his way through the crowd, only to find that the president of the convention had left the building. He had, in fact, sought refuge in the home of Colonel Van Buren on Ninth Street, where Miller found him "perfectly cool, still hoping that some other solution of the problem could be made, but it was a foregone conclusion that he must be the leader of the party." [41]

A little more than a year later, in the course of an interview with a reporter from the New York *Sun*, Seymour went over the story of his plans and his emotions at noon on July 9, 1868. He denied that he had intended to bring forward Mr. Chase's name himself, adding that when the convention came "to a sort of deadlock," he supported the claims of the Chief-Justice in a caucus of the New York delegation. After "an animated discussion, it was decided by a small majority" that New York should vote for Chase as soon as "Mr. Hendricks began to drop off." When the sudden shift toward himself occurred, Seymour, according to his own account, "became so bewildered and embarrassed" that he left the hall. He expected that the convention would take a recess (as, indeed, it did) before proceeding with the nomination of a candidate for Vice-President, when it was his intention to "refuse the nomination." He had had no correspondence whatever with Chase, whom he supported because he "deemed him the best and strongest candidate we could select."

> It is true that Mr. Chase did not suit our principles in some respects, but in the main he was found acceptable. I would have cheerfully acquiesced in the selection of Hendricks, Hancock, or even Pendleton. With the latter I differed on the financial question; otherwise I was in accord with him. . . . I can say one thing with candor and sincerity. I did not seek that nomination, nor did I desire it. I was forced, compelled by the very peculiar circumstances in which I was placed to accept it.[42]

This unique victim of his own political popularity regretted his good nature to the last of his days. "The failure to insist on my declination of the nomination then," he said long after-

41. New York Historical Society: Seymour Papers.
42. New York *Sun*, October 5, 1869.

ward, "was the mistake of my life." [43] In 1876 he was given the opportunity to show that he always had meant what he said. Once again the circumstances were sensational and even embarrassing. The Democratic state convention sitting at Saratoga nominated him for governor a sixth time over his express refusal to be considered as a candidate or be made the nominee. He was in a tight place, for Governor Tilden had been put up for President, and if he would not run, Tammany, so he was told, could force the choice of its own man. Thus he faced the risk of being accused of hurting Tilden's chances in the election and at the same time handing his party over to the control of the New York City machine.

While the decision was thought to be trembling in the balance a reporter from Utica dashed out to the farmhouse at Deerfield in the middle of the night. Seymour, quite unaware of what had happened, was in bed and sound asleep, but when he was awakened, he got up and received his unwelcome guest courteously. A moment later a telegram arrived confirming the news of his nomination. As he wrote a receipt for the message he bade the bearer wait and then asked the reporter if the convention had adjourned. On being told — inaccurately, as it so happened — that it would meet at ten o'clock that very morning, he sat down by the light of a candle and sent off his final refusal by telegraph. Some people were tempted to suspect that Horatio Seymour did not mean what he said. Time and again he had refused nominations and then accepted them. Good luck had given him a last chance; he would not let it slip for all the world. In 1868 he had tried to be firm, but he was tired and slow. "But this will rub that out, will it not?" he asked his midnight visitor as the latter took his leave; and the reporter was ready to acknowledge that he thought it would.[44]

43. Utica *Herald*, February 13, 1886.

44. Utica *Herald*, August 31, 1876.

XVIII

"DISGUISED AS A GENTLEMAN"

1868

PEOPLE look back at the result of the national election of 1868 as if the outcome had been a foregone conclusion from the very first. The vigor with which that campaign was conducted, however, implies that such was not the case. To be sure, the excitement and strain of four years of civil war, the murder of one President, and the impeachment and threatened removal of another seem to have tired out the attention of the public so that the very important contest which put Grant in the White House came as an anti-climax to eight years of upheaval and hatred. Not many Americans could even recall to-day the name of the Democratic candidate for President in 1868; yet the nomination of the party did not go begging that year. Any one of five eminent men would have been happy to have it. When a shrewd politician like Blaine, moreover, had looked at the returns of the election, he was uncomfortably astonished at the narrow margin between the parties. He was at a loss to explain the size of the Democratic vote. Although a glance at the electoral count seems to verify the popular notion that Grant's victory was overwhelming, a study of the figures will show that this notion is not accurate. The electoral college has never been a reliable index to the respective strength of winners and losers; rather has it served to conceal the proportion of nays to yeas in the choice of a President.

Not long ago Charles H. Coleman confirmed the fact that the Republicans were anxious in 1868, at least as late as the October elections.[1] Naturally enough, their leaders pretended to be confident of victory, but even the New York *Nation* called attention to the figures which Horace Greeley had published in the

1. Coleman, *Election of 1868*, 308–309.

Tribune, according to which a change of 36,000 in the popular vote in 1864, properly distributed of course, would have made McClellan President.[2] Such calculations are the playthings of politicians, for according to defeated candidates votes are never "properly distributed." Many people felt that the radicals had overreached themselves in their endeavor to remove Andrew Johnson; seven Republican senators had broken with the party on that issue. In fact, the failure of impeachment had made the persecutors of the President feel the shift of the sands of public opinion under their feet. They had made use of every advantage, both fair and unfair, on which they could lay their hands; politics allied itself with piety, and yet all failed. Nothing in American history so nearly approaches the gloomy, apprehensive spirit of Tacitus as the pages in which Gideon Welles reported the gossip and rumors which filled Washington during the month of April 18 to May 18, 1868.[3] Once their victim had slipped from their grasp the radicals forgot Andrew Johnson and set about the business of preventing their expulsion from power.

The Republican nomination was dictated by the need of hiding a coalition of hatreds behind the glamour of what was still a great name. So far as he had been anything before the Civil War, the inarticulate Grant was a Democrat — he had voted for Buchanan in 1856 and he had tried to vote for Douglas in 1860.[4] On the commission of Johnson he had travelled through the South during the disputes over reconstruction and had made a magnanimous report which seemed to justify the presidential policy of wishing to forgive and forget.[5] He had supported Johnson until the bitter quarrel over Stanton's tenure of office had tempted him to tie himself up with the men who were planning the President's impeachment and removal.[6] Gideon Welles, who began by being ready to trust Grant, even against

2. New York *Nation*, VII, 159 (July 16, 1868), 41.
3. Welles, *Diary*, III, 334–370.
4. Rhodes, *History*, VI, 188.
5. Commager, *Documents*, 10–11.
6. McCulloch, *Men and Measures*, 403.

his own better judgment, set down a most unpleasant picture of the general's verbosity, arrogance, and duplicity while he was sitting in the Cabinet of the tactless but honest and able successor to Abraham Lincoln.[7] Still, as late as the spring of 1868 certain Democrats of New York hoped to capture Grant as the candidate of their own party and carry the country with him — as they had won with Andrew Jackson forty years before.[8]

As soon as the open quarrel between the general and the President made Grant an impossible selection for the convention which was to assemble at New York, the Republicans were shrewd enough to take advantage of their opportunity: the doubters swallowed the hero like a dose of medicine — much to the disgust of Chief-Justice Chase, who was Horace Greeley's choice to head the ticket. The convention which nominated him contained delegates from every state but Texas, and Grant's father was seated on the rostrum. The Republicans were lucky: they shelved the greenback issue and four words of their nominee, "Let us have peace," became their slogan.

Some of the admirers of Grant have been so hard put to it to explain his character that they have sought refuge in the theory of a dual personality. If good luck saved his skin at Shiloh, if he escaped the misfortune of ever having to face Stonewall Jackson on the field of battle, he showed himself to advantage at least twice in his life — he was a gracious victor at Appomattox and determined beyond admiration on the deathbed where he spent his last days. As head of the nation, however, Grant was a striking example of Dean Inge's paradox that nothing fails like success. Keeping Washington and Jackson in mind, apparently, he seems to have looked on the presidency as nothing more than a fitting reward for his great service to the Union. The most charitable explanation of his eight years in office is the lame apology that it never occurred to him to regard either of his elections as a challenge to his character and courage. He was content to rest on his laurels, and the leaves of

7. Welles, *Diary*, III, 169, 176–181, 182–183, 187, 196–197, 259–261, 267, 273–274, and 363–364.

8. Coleman, *Election of 1868*, 84–88.

those laurels soon withered in the stale air of party politics and high finance.

From this distance the wiser preference between Grant and Seymour is hardly difficult to arrive at. To complain of the unhappy outcome in 1868 is to forget that the hatreds of the Civil War died hard. To multitudes of respectable people the Democratic candidate was a discredited traitor or, at best, a temporizing trouble-maker. For those who gulped at the thought of Grant, Seymour was out of the question. Not even the conquest of the South or the abolition of slavery could restore the rule of reason in the North. Take Whittier, for example. Writing to the *Nation* to deny the rumor that he was planning to compose a battle-hymn for the campaign, the poet dwelt on the importance of securing a Republican victory at the "coming election" with these words: "Nothing short of the harp of Orpheus which 'drew iron tears down Pluto's cheek,' could exorcise or charm to sleep the evil spirits of Democracy." [9] Thus the gentle-hearted Quaker who had libelled Daniel Webster's love of the Union with "Ichabod" eighteen years before passed over a man of peace and charity to help make a good general into a bad President.

The Republicans had two strong arguments in 1868. In the first place, whatever happened to the House of Representatives the Senate was certain to remain firmly in their control for two, and probably four, years. The election of a Democratic President, therefore, would merely continue the deadlock which had followed the death of Lincoln. This deadlock seemed desirable to the Democratic candidate. In the second place, if the North believed in reconstruction, as the elections of 1866 had seemed to indicate, then the policies of that system ought surely to remain in the hands of its friends. The editors of even the more respectable Republican newspapers and periodicals played up reports of race riots and "massacres" throughout the South. The *Nation*, for instance, referred to "partisan murder-

9. New York *Nation*, VII, 169 (September 24, 1868), 248: Letter dated Amesbury, September 11, 1868.

ing," and printed lurid reports of the bloody goings-on in Arkansas.[10] The election of a Democratic President, these gentlemen warned the public, would mean the reopening of the Civil War. Seymour was not the man to be feared — that success would "put him in his grave" was the one prediction on which his opponents and he were in agreement — the real danger to the peace of the land was General Blair.

Although collisions between whites and blacks were not uncommon during reconstruction, Dr. Coleman came to the conclusion that the stories of violence through the South were grossly and malignantly exaggerated.[11] According to Rhodes, the disorder was "sporadic and not universal," and, considering the effect of four years of war and the sudden new status of the former slaves, was hardly a matter for surprise.[12] Anthony Trollope visited the United States, travelling through the South during the suffocating heat of the summer of 1868 in the capacity of a correspondent of a London paper. His letter dwelling on the unhappy aspects of reconstruction appeared in the *Pall Mall Gazette* for July 11, 1868.[13] During August and September of 1868, moreover, General Howard, head of the Freedmen's Bureau, toured every southern state except Arkansas and Florida, addressing, in all, twenty public meetings. In New Orleans, for instance, he witnessed the presentation of a flag by one Seymour club made up of white men to another composed of negroes. As late as September 29 Howard brought back no alarming stories of riot and uproar from the South.[14] Any intimidation of blacks by whites could not have been very effective, for General Grant received the electoral votes of six of the former Confederate States.

Nevertheless the Republicans dwelt on the dangerous proclivities of the Democratic nominee for Vice-President. Francis

10. New York *Nation*, VII, 174 (October 29, 1868), 341; and 175 (November 5, 1868), 361. See, also, the editorial in the *Nation* for October 22, 1868.
11. Coleman, *Election of 1868*, 320–326.
12. Rhodes, *History*, VI, 307–308.
13. *Daily National Intelligencer*, July 25, 1868.
14. Washington *Daily Chronicle*, October 1, 1868.

Preston Blair, commonly called Frank, was a son of the able political editor on whom Andrew Jackson liked to rely and the brother of Montgomery, who sat in Lincoln's Cabinet until the radical Republicans forced the President to put him out. The military member of this trio had struck out boldly to keep Missouri in the Union during the winter of 1860–1861 and had served with success and some distinction in the Civil War. He was forthright in action — so much so that his proclamation freeing slaves in conquered territory embarrassed Lincoln's careful policy of courting the loyalty of the border states. Gossips said that Blair drank to excess, but the only real objection to him as a politician was his explosive taste for speaking plainly. Not long before the Democratic convention assembled in New York, Blair wrote what became a notorious letter to one of the delegates, Colonel James O. Broadhead, of Missouri. Hoping to draw the line of battle for 1868, and perhaps to head the ticket himself, the general stated that the "real and only issue in this contest was the overthrow of reconstruction, as the radical Republicans had forced it in the South." The President inaugurated in 1869 should, he continued, declare these methods unconstitutional and trample "into dust the usurpations of Congress." [15] The letter was a fire-brand, so Republicans insisted; if Blair were ever President, the whole country would soon be in flames.

The Democratic candidate for second place was not lacking in good references. In 1863 Lincoln referred to him as "still young" but possessed of "abundant talent." [16] Tilden thought him "a gallant young man . . . of very popular manners" who would have to encounter the "antagonism created by other members of his family — not by himself." [17] In view of the issue which the Republicans were sharp enough to make of the Broadhead Letter, Blair's campaign speeches in 1868 seem

15. New York *World*, July 3, 1868.

16. Lincoln, *Complete Works*, II, 433–434: Abraham Lincoln to Montgomery Blair, November 2, 1863.

17. New York Historical Society: Seymour Papers: S. J. Tilden to Horatio Seymour, May 11, 1868.

FRANCIS P. BLAIR, JR.

harmless and even inoffensive.[18] He travelled widely and talked freely. At Omaha, for instance, he declared that the Democrats stood for "free government and constitutional government in this country," as against "a minority in both sections composed of the white race." The nation would never submit, he hoped, to the subjection of the South; there would be no peace until the government of the defeated states had been given back to their white inhabitants.[19] Republican orators and editors harped on the probability that Blair would replace the delicate Seymour in the White House before long if the Democrats should happen to win.

The reception of Seymour's nomination by the South must have been a source of wonder to those northerners who had sincerely believed that the former governor of New York had been a Copperhead. General Rosecrans spent the summer of 1868 at White Sulphur Springs, in West Virginia, where he was in communication with a number of former generals and statesmen of the Confederacy. It was his impression that these southerners were honest in accepting their defeat in 1865.[20] The election of Grant would mean universal suffrage, but the victory of Seymour, they argued, would put an end to reconstruction. The removal of one evil would lessen the effect of the other. General Wade Hampton felt called upon to deny that he had "dictated" that plank of the Democratic platform which denounced reconstruction as "unconstitutional, revolutionary and void," declaring that it had been introduced and backed by a New Englander.[21] Hampton campaigned for Seymour openly, and Robert J. Walker, of Mississippi, Polk's secretary of the treasury, came out in support of the candidate.[22] Most of the men who were or had been leaders of the South, however, kept out of the election of 1868 — any genuine enthusiasm which the

18. *National Intelligencer*, July 14, 1868.

19. *Daily National Intelligencer*, July 24, 1868.

20. New York *Express*, September 5, 1868.

21. *National Intelligencer*, October 27, 1868: Letter of Wade Hampton to G. L. Park, October 17, 1868.

22. See the *Mississippi Valley Historical Review*, XIX, 362–381: H. D. Jordan, "A Politician of Expansion: Robert J. Walker."

New Yorker's name raised in the eleven conquered states can not now be traced. Southerners in 1868, like Governor David B. Hill, of New York, after the first nomination of Bryan, were "Democrats still, but very still." Whatever support he did receive there, however, probably hurt Seymour in the North:

> Robert Toombs, Benjamin H. Hill, General Forrest, "Pirate" Semmes, Howell Cobb, Wade Hampton, Zebulon Vance, and many others, some of them delegates to the New York convention, all known as leaders in the war on the Southern side, were speaking for Seymour. Nothing that they said was allowed to escape the readers of Republican newspapers.[23]

The Republicans had two advantages more in 1868. In the first place, they were free of certain cranks and chronic trouble-makers in their own ranks. William Lloyd Garrison, for instance, refused to sign up and work for General Grant.[24] Thaddeus Stevens, who had angrily declared that he would "vote for Frank Blair, even if a worse man than Seymour headed the ticket" rather than support the "swindle" of paying government bonds in gold, conveniently died in Washington at midnight on August 11.[25] The bitter man whose iron-works had been burned when Lee invaded Pennsylvania in 1863 was gone sooner than might have been hoped, and with his spirit went the evil genius of the radical Republicans. On the other hand, more than the usual number of persons eminent for respectability and success declared for the Republicans. Henry Ward Beecher plumped the weight of the most famous American political parson onto their side of the scale, certain that Grant's civil administration would be "as remarkable as his military career." Though his power to look into the future was hardly such as to win him reputation as a prophet, Beecher believed it fitting that all the men who had stood up for the Union should flock to the standard of the conqueror of Lee. When the reverend gentleman went on to state that "a chance to vote for such a man as Grant" was an "honor" that could not "happen twice in a man's lifetime," he must indeed have

23. Oberholtzer, *New York Since the Civil War*, II, 188.
24. Garrison, *Garrison*, IV, Part II, 259.
25. J. A. Woodburn, *Thaddeus Stevens* (Indianapolis, 1913), 570–571.

puzzled the ambitious if unhappy warrior he was trying to praise. Grant did his best to make that "honor" happen more than twice. This clergyman's opinion of the Democratic candidate was quite definite, as all his opinions were likely to be: Seymour was a man "who, through all the years from 1860 to 1868, studied how to help Southern treason without incurring the risks and pains of overt and courageous treasonable acts." [26]

For Seward, who had stood up wisely at the side of Andrew Johnson and worked well enough in times of storm and stress, the election of Grant seemed "the most practicable and easy solution of the national embarrassments." [27] This influential pronouncement was awaited with wide interest and was given out at Auburn on the last day of October, almost on the eve of the election. The surest guide to Seward's character and policy, however, is the one word "easy." As governor of New York his reputation for seizing opportunity was notorious. Once Lincoln was dead, Welles found him shifty and unreliable. The way he chose was always the shortest and the smoothest. Schurz and Stanton were in another class: they worked up their hatred for Seymour into something like a love for Grant. The predicament of Schurz must have been particularly trying for a man of irreproachable principles, for by 1872 his hero had become his villain. In 1868, however, the Democratic candidate seemed to Schurz nothing more than respectable, pleasant, and plausible — a man whose "sickly shrinking from great responsibilities" and "lack of true manhood" he saw fit to deride. "I believe he has not moral force enough to distinguish truth from falsehood," Schurz told his audiences — the sly New Yorker was always seeking refuge by the surf at Newport or in the perfume of the pine trees of Wisconsin.[28]

Stanton was still smarting from the overthrow of May; he pitched into the campaign in order to repair his reputation. When Seymour denounced his management of the armies as both arrogant and extravagant, the blood rushed to his head

26. *Daily National Intelligencer*, September 5, 1868: Letter of August 13, 1868.
27. *National Intelligencer*, November 3, 1868.
28. Schurz, *Speeches, Correspondence and Political Papers*, I, 462–463.

—as it would do once too often in December, 1869. The Democratic candidate, he scolded, had been "travelling" on his "pass" for years—"the only certificate of character he ever had." He found himself forced to take the stump in order to explain that embarrassing telegram of cordial thanks for military aid which Lincoln had directed him to send to the governor of New York just before Gettysburg. When Stanton protested against thanking a Copperhead governor to the exclusion of the loyal "war governors," the President (if we are to believe his secretary of war) had replied: "They do not need it, and Seymour does." [29]

Even Senator Roscoe Conkling hurried East from Colorado to join in the campaign against his own brother-in-law, using all his arts and energy to carry Oneida County against its more distinguished son.[30] It was Seymour's triumph in 1862 that had given Conkling's seat in the House to Francis Kernan. Never was the senator more vain and vindictive, however firmly and frequently he felt forced to deny the taint of insanity in his wife's blood.[31] Elsewhere things were not so simple: Governor Curtin, of Pennsylvania, remembering how desperately he had begged for the soldiers Seymour sent into his state before Gettysburg, advised his fellow Republicans to "give up" attacking the "loyalty" of the Democratic candidate for President.[32]

Of all the Republican editors in 1868, only Greeley, of the *Tribune*, and Godkin, of the *Nation*, seem to have tried to outdo each other. The famous weekly never circulated widely at any time, for Godkin was sniffed at as an imported Anglo-Irishman. Greeley's influence, however, was immense, and only his lifelong lack of good judgment can save him from the suspicion of malice in 1868. Immediately after Seymour's nomination he confined his objections to the Democratic candidate to a denunciation of two of his well-known speeches—the plea he

29. Flower, *Stanton*, 396–398. But see Seymour, *Public Record*, 117, for Stanton's cordial letter to Seymour dated June 27, 1863.

30. Alexander, *History*, III, 212.

31. Coleman, *Election of 1868*, 258.

32. *National Intelligencer*, August 22, 1868. See page 301.

made at Tweddle Hall in 1861 and the unlucky address on the Fourth of July in 1863. He derided the opponent of Grant for having doubted if secession could be met by force — a curious charge, in view of his own suggestion that the wayward sisters be allowed to depart in peace.[33] Greeley went from strength to strength. The seed of the story that the governor had called draft rioters his "friends" had been sown by Bryant five years before; now it was to sprout and flourish and bear fruit.[34] The legend had been fashioned into what is called fact, and fastened on American history. Dr. Coleman has told how quickly and frankly the Democratic candidate met the charge in an interview in the *Sun*, yet always without making it plain that no rioters were present when he spoke.[35] Cartoons were spread about the country picturing Grant demanding "unconditional surrender" at Vicksburg as compared with Seymour pleading for peace with ruffians and rowdies.[36] "Scratch a Democrat and you'll find a rebel under his skin," was the war-cry of the *Tribune*.[37] Seymour always took Greeley's passionate abuse with unexcelled composure. When his friend, G. L. Miller, asked him what he thought of the *Tribune's* wild attack on the speech he made at the Cooper Institute on June 25, 1868, the object of the editor's fury glanced at him as they strode up Broadway together and remarked with a smile, "Mr. Greeley is mad." [38] Four years later Seymour voted for this same man for President and even spoke in his favor.

Seymour, or some one of his household, clipped and saved all

33. See the New York *Tribune* for July 20, 21, and 25, 1868.
34. See, for instance, the Hartford *Post*, October 8, 1868.
35. Coleman, *Election of 1868*, 255. At least three able scholars of the present time have been led astray by what would seem to have been exaggerated accounts of the draft riots of July, 1863. Dr. Coleman refers to Seymour's attempt "to placate the mob"; while both Randall and Shannon have printed excessive totals for casualties. See J. G. Randall, *The Civil War and Reconstruction* (Boston, 1937), 414, note, quoting Shannon, *Union Army*, II, 213. Edward Channing's "several" is nearer the truth.
36. Alexander, *History*, III, 210.
37. New York *Tribune*, August 4, 1868.
38. New York Historical Society: Seymour Papers: Memorandum of G. L. Miller, written down in 1893.

the printed comment on himself in 1868 which he could find — good, bad, and indifferent. The collection assembled seems to show that the press of the United States was overwhelmingly against him in 1868. Oddly enough, one of the pleasantest extracts — a despatch to the New York *Sun*, dated Utica, July 20 — was overlooked. According to the writer "this very anxious aspirant for presidential honors" was engaged in making hay with his laborers, quite unlike the "country gentleman of leisure" he was commonly believed to be. When his professional visitor remarked on the "enthusiasm with which his nomination had been received," the suave gentleman from Deerfield wondered how people could get excited about any thing in the heat of a hot summer, and went on to suggest that it would be wiser to postpone politics until cooler weather. Heat, he warned his hearer, was responsible for his own "unfortunate predicament." "Had I been as cool as I am now, I should have declined." After some general conversation which drew forth no promise of so much as a post-office from a possible President, the reporter took his leave.

Two other close views of this amiable candidate are distinguished for both skill and venom. As samples of political journalism of half a century ago, George Alfred Townsend's letter to the New York *Evening Post* and a communication to the Chicago *Tribune* signed "Gath" — "Horatio Seymour at Home: His Origin, Family, Character, and History" are noteworthy.[39] The opinions about Seymour which the reporter for the *Post* got in Utica were "unfavorable ones." He was praised for "his manners and his connections," was "well to do, childless, scheming, not studious, in bad health . . . intensely selfish, very stealthy, earnest of power, reckless of fame." He was

> . . . a slender, bronchial looking man, with a small chest, a bald head, low round the neck with some ruffles of grey hair, and of a bloodless complexion. His mouth is large, and his nose is straight and knobby at the nostril. He has a good, clear, vigilant eye and a spherical forehead; the expression below

39. Hartford *Post*, quoting the New York *Evening Post*, July 21, 1868, and the Chicago *Tribune*, July 20, 1868.

the eyes is indecision and self-introspection. In his dress he is particular, and in his address saying very little more than Grant and meaning a good deal less.

This "clammy dictator of the wills and ballots of the Democratic party" had no joy of "love, children, society, woman"; his nature was "too feeble to make him eminent even in insincerity"; other men made "enemies by their earnestness, but Mr. Seymour only waits." He led "a dull life" at Deerfield, where he was "so fortunate in his selection of farmers that he has the repute of possessing some of the finest fields in the Mohawk valley." This "timid lawyer who gave up the profession because he had neither nimble nor profound qualities to give him a biding place among his competitors" quit the bar "from sheer want of pluck and conscious ineptitude." Even his "desire to grow rich" had failed him, for he "stands to-day with, perhaps, $200,000, when his ambition did not stop short of many millions." He was, nevertheless, "a close-fisted man," able to be stingy, but "too weak to be enterprising."

James Buchanan had died at "Wheatland" on June 1, 1868. Some able journalist who looked in on his funeral decided to be struck with the resemblance between the dead man who had been President and the living Democratic candidate for that office. Utica and Lancaster were towns of about the same size; both men gave up the practice of law and settled in suburbs; Seymour's home was almost as much a bachelor's as Buchanan's; he was, indeed, "almost as much of a corpse" as the former occupant of the White House. "The old man in his coffin — large, distinguished, composed — was, though a failure," a man who died still in possession of his self-respect.

Seymour is a little creation. His face is an outlined wriggle. Its expression is a dodge. He looks like a boned man, after the method of the boned turkey. In physical as in moral dignity he is not up to the level of recent Democratic Presidents. Frank Pierce was hearty, downright, constant. Tyler was at least obstinate. Polk was sturdy and sincere. Van Buren was a man of wide accomplishments and with the courage to face his party and break it in half. Horatio Seymour . . . is . . . a slender little man with a smooth tongue, feeble health, and a constant fear of aberration, whose art it is to wheedle the vain, promise the ambitious, and charm the religious. His three great monuments have been the veto of the prohibitory law, the New York riots, and the conquest of the Democratic convention.[40]

Godkin, of the *Nation*, was honorable enough to acknowledge that Seymour had magnetism, dignity, and great skill at appealing to the public.[41] It remained for an editor no less respectable, the author of "Thanatopsis," to introduce the subject of insanity into the campaign. William Cullen Bryant presided at the New York *Evening Post*, and before long that paper was calling for legislation to cover the case of a President who might go mad. The fire was not long in spreading: soon and late the mental stability of the whole Seymour family was dragged into doubt and discussion. There could be no question that Henry Seymour had committed suicide, and that his wife had survived her faculties by five or six years. A partisan press used half the truth and laid his act to a threatened exposure of his "malpractices" as canal commissioner. The story grew in the telling. Seymour's mother had died "violently insane"; a brother had blown out his brains; and he himself was said to realize that he would end his days in a mad-house. He was reduced to avoiding all "excitement and severe labor." So far as can be discovered Seymour never publicly referred to any of these exaggerations and falsehoods.

Chase, as we have seen, so managed his conscience as to wriggle out from under the responsibility of supporting the choice of either of the conventions from which he was ready and willing to accept a nomination; he did not vote in 1868. The conduct of the leaders of the Democratic party in regard to Seymour does not bear out the baseless charge that he had tricked them all to get what he had secretly desired from the very first. General McClellan, titular leader of the party during four years, sent a letter of endorsement to a New York mass meeting on October third.[42] The Ohio men were loyal:

40. Hartford *Post*, August 1, 1868, quoting the Troy *Times*.
41. New York *Nation*, VII, 169 (September 24, 1868).
42. *National Intelligencer*, October 8, 1868.

Pendleton spoke in support of the ticket at Grafton, West Virginia, as early as July 16.[43] The substance of his remarks was an attack on the financial management of the United States, a plea for amnesty for the South, and praise of both Seymour and Blair. Two weeks after the election, Pendleton sent Seymour a cordial letter in reply to one written him on November 20. In this letter, the senator deprecated the "after-election grumblings" and "fault findings" and "threats" which were dividing the defeated Democrats. He put himself at Seymour's service, and, asking him to visit him in Cincinnati, expressed the hope of getting from him his opinion of the proper guidance of the party for the future.[44] A friend of Seymour wrote him from Columbus, Ohio, in August that though he detected "a trifle of disappointment here at Mr. Pendleton's defeat," observation led him to believe that it was "*less* with him than with many of his admirers."[45] Judge Thurman, speaking at Columbus on his return from New York, regretted that "Ohio's great son did not receive the nomination," but denied that the choice of Seymour was a "New York trick," declaring that the head of the ticket was "a high-minded, honorable man"— "one of the greatest and purest of the public men of our times."[46]

The endorsement of a third man from Ohio may have hurt Seymour rather than helped him. Speaking at Dayton, on July 28, Vallandigham declared:

For President we have nominated Horatio Seymour, an eloquent orator, an able and experienced statesman, an accomplished gentleman, sober and righteous in the enlarged, catholic sense of the term; a man of the strictest pecuniary integrity; the candidate of no "ring" or faction, and one who will neither himself steal, nor permit theft in others. . . . Nominated, to my personal knowledge, against his will, and without a pledge or promise to any one upon any subject, he is under no obligation of any sort other than that

43. New York *Tribune*, July 18, 1868.

44. New York Historical Society: Seymour Papers: G. H. Pendleton to Horatio Seymour, November 25, 1868.

45. New York State Library: Manuscript Section: N. E. Paine to Horatio Seymour, August 16, 1868.

46. *Daily National Intelligencer*, July 16, 1868.

which binds the patriot and gentleman. And if he be "insane," as little creatures with false, malicious tongues insinuate, I would that the same method were in the madness of all other public men.[47]

Winfield Scott Hancock had been the second, if not the first favorite son of Pennsylvania at New York, and partisan gossips insisted that he was sulking in his tent. No sooner had the general got wind of the rumor than he wrote from Newport on July 17, "Those who suppose that I do not acquiesce in the work of the National Democratic Convention, or that I do not sincerely desire the election of its nominees, know very little of my character."[48] Tilden's participation in the campaign took the form of raising funds and drawing up cold-blooded indictments of the extravagance of the seven years during which the Republicans had controlled the administration. Seymour was in correspondence with the state chairman throughout the whole campaign. In ability to organize, in detailed analysis of error, Tilden was surpassed by no politician of his day; three years later he and Seymour made a team that was the despair and the undoing of William Marcy Tweed. It would have taken more than management and money to beat Grant in 1868, and Tilden was not the man to set a river on fire. At the state convention in September he was so encouraging as to declare that if the Democracy did their duty, as he knew they would, the party would elect Seymour and Blair.[49] Earlier in the summer, he sent a long letter to the grand ratification meeting which was held at Washington on July 18. Senator Doolittle was the orator of the occasion, and there were telegrams from Pendleton, English, and Parker. According to Tilden the "political contest" of 1868 was "the most important ever waged upon this continent." It presented two great issues — justice to the people and economy in government.[50]

Senator Hendricks, it will be remembered, was Seymour's

47. *National Intelligencer*, August 4, 1868.

48. New York State Library: Seymour Papers.

49. *National Intelligencer*, September 5, 1868.

50. Bigelow, *Tilden*, I, 215–217; and *Daily National Intelligencer*, July 20, 1868.

second choice for the Democratic nomination in case the name of Chase should fail to win the support for which he hoped. Fear of Hendricks had forced the embittered friends of Pendleton to the recourse of drafting Seymour. That neither candidate was nominated at New York does not seem to have reconciled the mutually hostile friends of each. The smoke of battle still hung low over the Middle West. During the summer the New York *Sun* published an anonymous article on the convention, which was commonly attributed to a Dr. Pierce, who was a brother-in-law of Hendricks. Both Indiana and Ohio were October states in 1868, together with Pennsylvania and Iowa, only the last of which the Democrats openly conceded to Grant. It was important, therefore, for the Republicans to stir up all the mischief they could, for the vote in these states had all the fly-blown reputation for prophecy which now attaches to the silly September election in Maine. Apparently a member of the Hendricks family thought that there had been double dealing at New York and that Seymour's friendship for Hendricks was false. On September 5, therefore, the senator from Indiana wrote to Seymour directly and frankly:

> My attention has been called to an anonymous article in the New York Sun, upon the New York convention, which has been attributed to Dr. Pierce. I have not seen Dr. P. since I heard of the article, and do not know anything about it from him. Of course I need not disclaim all sympathy with any doubt or suspicion of the utmost candor of conduct on your part at the convention. I believed every word you said in your letter to me written soon after your nomination, and I think Dr. Pierce is now entirely satisfied. My own desire for your election amounts to a profound anxiety, for I feel that the highest interests of the country are involved in it.
>
> I have now been in the northern part of our state for several days. The changes in our favor are not so numerous as in southern Indiana, yet they are found in every county — with none against us — and I am encouraged.[51]

It would not be enough, however, to hold the northern Democrats in line. Seymour's only hope was to recover the voters his party had lost in 1860 and 1864. The most important defection from the Republican ranks was that of Senator John

51. T. A. Hendricks to Horatio Seymour, September 5, 1868: A. L. S. in possession of the author.

R. Doolittle, of Wisconsin, who had been a militant supporter of the Union. Reconstruction had made Doolittle a Democrat again, and he did his best to carry Wisconsin for the national ticket. In a letter he sent the senator early in August, Seymour showed how much he relied for success on the conversion of men like Doolittle. The tone of the letter leads a reader to suspect that the enthusiasm of those who surrounded him had persuaded Seymour to hope that he might win in 1868. All his plans, he declared, had been "thrown into confusion" by his nomination, and he had put off his letter of acceptance to the last moment, with the "vague idea that in some way the political programme might be changed." But the uprising in the state of New York had been amazing. Democratic meetings were "spontaneous, unanimous and enthusiastic." "I find I must go into the work," wrote Seymour, and expressed the hope that Doolittle would approve the sentiments of his letter of acceptance. The reaction was now so "deep and strong" that the Democrats must "teach moderation." He would leave "affairs at Washington" to the "sole management" of the senator, who alone, he knew, had "stopped the formation of a third party." Having been "jerked" into the nomination, he was completely free, as the senator knew, of "a single promise to redeem" and could "shape the canvass as shall be deemed best." President Johnson was surrounded by men "very hostile" to himself and had been misled as to Seymour's "views and feelings." Early in August, therefore, Seymour did not wish to believe that his defeat was a foregone conclusion. The task of gaining the support of the Johnson men he left to Senator Doolittle.[52]

This letter to Doolittle offers an odd contrast to another which Seymour had already written ten days earlier to a personal friend in New Haven — C. M. Ingersoll. Complaining that his friends had plunged him into "a sea of trouble," Seymour expressed doubts as to the result of the campaign. He had been forced into the fight, however, and would do the best he could. This indiscreet letter to Ingersoll was published "with

52. *Magazine of History*, XVII, 1 (July, 1913), 57–58.

much gusto" in the New York *Tribune* and copied by the New York *Herald*. It seems to have been stolen from Ingersoll's private papers, but Horace Greeley gleefully refused to tell how he came by it and declined to restore it to its rightful owner.[53]

Immediately after his nomination, Seymour had implied, in a short speech at Tammany Hall on July 10, that the platform was acceptable to him, and that though he had hoped to "take an active part . . . in the great struggle going on for the restoration of good government, of peace and prosperity to our country," his nomination now "excluded" him from doing so. The harmony and the forbearance of the delegates were "the sure tokens of a coming victory."[54] In 1868, it may be remembered, popular opinion was not yet quite accustomed to a candidate's stumping the country for his own election as President. Nominees were supposed to accept votes but not seek them. Politics were still polite. Seymour's last-minute departure from what he himself considered good taste provoked unfavorable comment among conservative Democrats even in the South.

October 22, 1868: Mr. Seymour, so says the telegram of this morning [the author is writing in Paris] has started on a political tour — that is in vulgar terms, commenced stumping the country. This I have always looked upon with contempt, let the candidate be who he may. He is deserving of defeat. In the year 1860 the system of electioneering was resorted to by all parties, Breckinridge possibly less than any of the others — still he made some speeches in his own state. Douglas stumped and Lincoln stumped and Bell stumped and Everett stumped — they all resorted to this singularly disgusting and immoralizing mode of currying success . . . every dirty wretch is at full liberty to pull, haul, and traduce the man who thus makes a spectacle of himself. . . . The stumping of Mr. Seymour will benefit him nothing — he is a condemned man and Grant will be the next president.[55]

Seymour dated his letter of acceptance August fourth.[56] He apologized for his delay in sending a formal acknowledgement of his nomination with the statement that he had waited

53. Coleman, *Election of 1868*, 261.

54. Seymour, *Public Record*, 341–342.

55. Manuscript diary of Daniel Henry Holmes (1816–1898), of New Orleans, now in the possession of his daughter, Mrs. Georgine Holmes Thomas, of New York City.

56. Seymour, *Public Record*, 342–347.

to see "what light the action of Congress would throw upon the interests of the country." His private explanation to Senator Doolittle was, it will be noticed, quite different. The "violence of congressional action" was to be deplored, for it would continue the "discord in our country." The "minds of business men" were "perplexed by uncertainties," and the hours of labor were "lengthened by the costs of living made by the direct and indirect exactions of Government." It was only carpet-bag senators and representatives who demanded protection from the people they professed to represent. Home rule should be restored to the South, where "the chiefs of the late rebellion" had "submitted to the results of the war." Good government required opposition, but it had been the misfortune of the Republican party that "events of the past few years" had given it the chance to "shackle the Executive, to trammel the judiciary, and to carry out the views of the most unwise and violent of its members." Republicans, as well as Democrats, were "interested in putting some check upon this violence." To elect a Democratic President and a majority of Democratic members of the House of Representatives was the surest way to supply such a check. Republicans would still control the Senate, and the federal government would thus be safe from both extremes of opinion. The office of President was not inviting to an honest man, for he must undergo not only "the falsehoods and abuse of the bad," but "suffer from the censure of the good who are misled by prejudices and misrepresentations." Closing with a reference to the spontaneous enthusiasm he encountered everywhere, Seymour declared that he could not "doubt we shall gain a political triumph which will restore our Union."

It was the third and fourth planks — proposals to redeem the debt in "lawful money" and tax federal bonds — which made the most trouble for Seymour among conservative Democrats. Eventually he practically discarded them. His attitude was consistent with his record during his second term as governor, when he protested against the proposal to pay the bonds of New York in "coin." Foreign investors, he insisted, must be paid in gold, but there was no just basis for any distinction between them and the domestic holders of the bonds of the state.[57] In 1868 the Democratic candidate was accused of coming out for gold merely because he himself held bonds of the United States. The moment it was denied that he held any he was denounced for lack of patriotism in not having bought them.[58]

Belmont and Tilden, between them, managed the finances of the Democratic campaign in 1868. Augustus Schell, a prominent citizen of New York City, was made chairman of the national executive committee. On August 15, eight men agreed among themselves to give ten thousand dollars each for the just and lawful expenses of Seymour and Blair, any unexpended surplus to be refunded.[59] H. T. Helmbold, a patent-medicine advertizer of New York, contributed $40,000, much to the scorn of the Republicans, and published a notice to the effect that he was willing to bet a million dollars on the election of the Democratic candidate. William Corcoran, of Washington, was also a generous contributor. Both parties levied on wages and salaries received from the government.[60] Belmont arranged for the preparation of what was practically a complete record of Seymour's public career from the speech at Springfield for Buchanan, in 1856, to a letter written as late as July 21, 1868, in which Seymour's secretary rashly denied that the nominee had ever owned a bond of the United States. This *Public Record*, as it was called, was compiled and edited in the office of the New York *Sun*, where it was published by I. W. England. It contained a good index and was obviously designed for the use of speakers and editors. The latter were charged one hundred dollars a copy. Seymour himself paid eighty dollars for ten copies.

It is interesting to notice that this record contained no refer-

57. Seymour, *Public Record*, 215–218.

58. Seymour, *Public Record*, 347.

59. Tilden, *Letters and Literary Memorials*, I, 245. These eight contributors were: August Belmont, Thomas C. Durant, George I. Magee, C. H. McCormick, Charles O'Conor, Augustus Schell, Richard Schell, and Samuel J. Tilden.

60. Coleman, *Election of 1868*, 299–300.

ence to the famous struggle over prohibition in the spring of 1854. The cause was dead, or sleeping, rather, for the national need for what Carrie Nation liked to call "infernal revenue" from taxes on alcoholic beverages took the subject out of politics for the time being. As the war debt began to diminish, prohibition came to the fore. Two campaign biographies put in their appearance — the first was prepared by David Croly, of the New York *World*, and the second came from the hand of Edward Winslow Martin, a native of Richmond, Virginia, who lived in Brooklyn after 1865 and chose to write under the name of "James D. McCabe, Jr." Both these books put into circulation what is probably the very poorest of the many pictures of Horatio Seymour — a grim Horace Greeley without glasses.

These two books came out late in August, by which time the campaign was getting under way. Although Seymour received the usual landslide of letters from people asking for loans which they promised to pay back twice over out of their winnings at betting on him, and was urged to stir up the feelings of the Jews against Grant, he seems to have rested inactive at Utica.[61] On September 10 he delivered a characteristic address at the agricultural fair at Saratoga, making no mention of politics and appropriately confining himself to the problems of farmers and discussing the true pleasures and rewards of life. He was still an old-fashioned candidate.[62] Visitors crowded in on him with their familiar flattery, their false confidence, and their schemes for gaining office if he should win. John Dash Van Buren, who had gone to and fro between Chase and Seymour during the spring and early summer of 1868, wrote that he hoped the candidate was "serene" and confident, for his supporters were not. The reports from the South were better than those from the North, but Van Buren himself was ill and unable to take part in the campaign. Mr. Chase was still in the woods of New Brunswick. One sentence from Van Buren spoke volumes: "I have a letter from Belmont — he is discouraged." This was at

61. New York Historical Society: Seymour Papers: Hiram Ketchum to Horatio Seymour, July 24, 1868.

62. New York *World*, September 11, 1868.

the end of September. The heat of the summer of 1868 had been intense all over the country. The Congress had not left Washington until the last of July, when the whole nation had "rejoiced" at its adjournment.

The day after Colonel Van Buren wrote Seymour, a remarkable letter from France appeared in the American newspapers. John Adams Dix was just past seventy; he had sat for four years as a Barnburner Democratic senator from New York during the days of the masterful Polk. For years thereafter he hankered to get back into federal office, but in vain. He understood that Pierce had promised to make him minister to France, but another went to Paris in his place. He dabbled in business and spent part of his ample leisure at sketching and painting. Then on the eve of the Civil War Buchanan called him to take the post of secretary of the treasury in his collapsing Cabinet. There Dix spent a few hectic months. When the Civil War broke out he became one of the many political generals whose services to the Union threatened to make a fact of southern independence. In 1866 Johnson and Seward sent him to Paris, where he served as American minister for three years. The circumstance that he was the representative of the head of the government does not seem to have had much weight with Dix. Charles Francis Adams, for instance, returning from England the same year, quite correctly declined to take any part in the campaign, although his eldest and his favorite son was the Democratic nominee for governor of Massachusetts — and he himself would ultimately vote for Grant.[63]

Remembering his fierce difference of opinion with Governor Seymour during the latter's second term, Dix struck from Paris with the speed and poison of a snake. He had "reluctantly" suppressed the *Journal of Commerce* and the *World* five years before; whereupon Seymour had promptly had him placed under arrest, and the editors of these opposition papers were quickly released. The letter Dix wrote on September 4, 1868, was addressed to a friend in New York City, and "not intended

63. Coleman, *Election of 1868*, 253 and 289.

for publication." No sooner had it reached America, however, than it appeared at full length in the papers. Although the minister professed to regret that his "distance from home" had not saved him from taking part in the campaign, he found himself unwilling to swallow the "imputation" that he was "heart and hand with Mr. Seymour." He had been acquainted with the Democratic candidate for President for more than a quarter of a century, and knew that this "amiable gentleman" of "respectable talents" had not "a single qualification" for the great office to which he aspired. He was "deficient" in "firmness of purpose." Twice as governor, according to Dix, he had failed to hold the Democratic party together. He had stated his belief that the national debt should be paid in specie and had promptly accepted a nomination on a platform which favored payment in paper. General Dix declared that he would be "greatly surprised" if the American people were to prefer as their President the man who was speaking without "love of country," at the Academy of Music in Brooklyn on July 4, 1863, at the very moment when General Grant was accepting the surrender of Vicksburg, and General Lee was fleeing from his defeat at Gettysburg.[64]

The Democratic newspapers criticized an American minister's meddling in politics, contrasted his partisan attitude with the caution of Adams, and laid his letter to a personal hatred of Seymour and the desire to hold on to his seventeen-thousand-dollar salary when Grant should become President.[65] If staying in Paris was his desire, Dix was doomed to disappointment. President Grant did not see fit to continue him in that office from which President Johnson should have removed him at once. Yet the malice of the minister to France struck Seymour in his heel. The inopportune speech on the Fourth of July coincided with the great victories of Gettysburg and Vicksburg. When the governor protested that "the bloody and treasonable and revolutionary doctrine of public necessity" could be "pro-

64. New York *Herald*, September 23, 1868.
65. *National Intelligencer*, September 26, 1868.

claimed by a mob as well as by a government," ten days later the draft rioters in New York could be said to have taken him at his own word. In view of the advantage open at this point, it is not surprising that the Republicans made the most of Seymour's unlucky language on that day.[66]

During September, 1868, Seymour wrote three interesting letters to Tilden. He was at the head of the party in New York, and on Belmont and him, next to the candidate himself, rested the responsibility for the direction of the campaign. By September 26, Seymour thought that a "fresh presentation" of purposes in a way that would "arrest public attention" was necessary.[67] He had been talking over the matter with Cyrus H. McCormick, in whose judgment he had "great confidence." Every candidate for the presidency, he thought, must make up a "privy council" — a number of men upon whom he could lean, statesmen who would help him "shape out before election a line of policy" which would "carry the country through its difficulties," in the event of the success of the Democrats. He was eager to talk with Tilden, for he felt he was in danger of being "isolated" too long, and promised to write him soon about "taking the field" himself. He had been advised to do so the very day he wrote.[68]

Tilden replied on September 30, and Seymour acknowledged the letter at once, urging him to persuade Generals McClellan, Hancock, and Slocum to go down to Philadelphia and speak at the meeting which the Democrats were planning for the following week. A great audience would surely greet them, for the soldiers throughout the country were waiting to see what the "popular generals" would do. The party could make its "best show in that way"; it had "neglected the soldiers too much." Seymour's anxiety as to the outcome in Pennsylvania and the importance he attached to it are proved by the letter he wrote the very next day. He told Tilden that he himself had written

66. See Oberholtzer, *New York Since the Civil War*, II, 180–181.

67. Tilden, *Letters and Literary Memorials*, 247.

68. New York Historical Society: Seymour Papers: Thomas C. Fields to Horatio Seymour, September 26, 1868.

McClellan asking him to go into that state (although he "felt a delicacy in doing so"), for McClellan had "more power in Pennsylvania than any living man," so Seymour thought, judging from his own experience in the campaign of 1864. The general's visit would offset the effect of the soldiers' convention which had been got up by the Republicans, for with "many thousands of them McClellan's words [would be] words of command." Men from the army would hardly be inclined to vote for Grant — "he slaughtered them too ruthlessly." [69]

After the October elections, when all four states of Pennsylvania, Ohio, Indiana, and Iowa went Republican, the New York *World* came out with its sensational demand for a change in the ticket. According to Dr. Coleman, who has studied the history of this surprising proposal, new candidates had been talked of before the defeats in October, and, after those elections, the suggestion was revived by friends of Chief-Justice Chase, on the one hand, and President Johnson, on the other. The position of the latter was made all the more difficult because of his close association with conservative Republicans like Seward. Not until Johnson sent his telegram to Seymour at the beginning of the latter's speaking tour did the President seem quite to have given up hope of having himself made the opponent of Grant. Both Belmont, as head of the national committee, and Tilden, as New York state chairman, threw all their private and public influence against this eleventh-hour demand for a change.[70] Seymour, according to Manton Marble, was thought a Copperhead, and the danger of Blair was the threat of revolution; the two candidates should at once retire and allow the national committee of the party to replace them with more popular men.

Professor Hutchinson's biography of Cyrus Hall McCormick has lately added some intimate details to the story of this negotiation. McCormick was a loyal and a liberal Democrat, and a

69. See the letters of October 1 and 2, 1868, in Tilden, *Letters and Literary Memorials*, I, 247–249.

70. Coleman, *Election of 1868*, 348–359.

very good friend of Seymour. He failed to be elected as a delegate from Illinois to the Democratic national convention of 1868, but he attended the convention and did his best to influence its action. According to McCormick, the great issue in 1868 was radical Republican misrule of the Senate. Although he was a "gold" Democrat, McCormick thought it was sheer folly for his party to quarrel over the question of the currency and thus lose their chance to win the votes of the conservative Republicans. He was ready to support the taxing of federal bonds and the "issuance of several millions more of greenbacks," in order to present a solid front against the radicals. He favored a compromise policy on "greenbacks," and tried to persuade the southern delegates to support the nomination of Chase. He lamented the selection of his friend, Seymour, and was alarmed by the latter's repudiation of the "easy" money plank in his letter of acceptance. On September 15, Seymour wrote McCormick, "this election is in the hands of the business men. It will go as their judgment shall dictate." Disappointed as he was, McCormick served on the finance committee with Belmont and contributed twelve thousand dollars to the cost of the campaign.

On October 15, McCormick, without Tilden's approval, wrote Seymour to ask him if he would retire from the head of the ticket if Chase could be persuaded to accept the designation of the national committee. The results in the four October states had made the rout of the Democrats inevitable. Seymour answered his letter five days later, telling McCormick that he did not wish to seem to shrink from defeat, that he must be governed in his action by the national committee and that he, for one, did not believe that Chase would take the nomination. Tilden, we know, and Belmont, it is to be suspected, did not endorse the desire or the scheme for a change in the ticket. All things considered, it would have been well to keep the plan for a shift of front secret, but it got into the papers.[71]

The New York *World* came out for the change on the very

71. Hutchinson, *McCormick*, II, 311–314.

day McCormick wrote to Seymour. On the sixteenth, Senator Eaton, of Connecticut, wrote a "confidential" letter to Seymour, in which he declared that such a shift would be political suicide, that November might yet save New York, New Jersey, Connecticut, and the South, and that when Chase "was approached yesterday" for the use of his name, he had "scouted the idea of any such change," "like a man of sense."[72] General Blair wrote his father from Washington, leaving it to him and Tilden to decide whether the scheme was necessary. The elder Blair wrote Tilden asking him to let him know by wire if he ought to come up to New York. According to the old adviser of Andrew Jackson, it was only intrigue which was making difficulties for the Democrats. If the ticket were to be altered, why not McClellan and Pendleton, or Hancock and Hendricks, for the "copulation of Seward and Chase" would bring not only defeat, but eternal disgrace on the Democracy.[73] Old age had not impaired the judgment of Jackson's editor — Hancock and Hendricks, for instance, would have made the very best ticket the Democrats could have offered the country in 1868. The choice had been made, and by October it was too late to think of change. Seymour himself told Colonel Van Buren that now he felt it was his duty to stick and not try "to shift his misfortunes" onto the shoulders of some one else.[74]

After the middle of October General Blair went to the rear, and Seymour was prevailed upon to tour the North in search of votes. Apparently he had the tacit approval of Tilden, who had already delivered at Chatham, in Columbia County, New York, late in September, an elaborate and reasoned arraignment of the Republican management of the finances of the government. This prosperous railroad lawyer presented his cogent case much

72. New York Historical Society: Seymour Papers: William Wallace Eaton to Horatio Seymour, October 16, 1868.

73. Tilden, *Letters and Literary Memorials*, I, 198–199: F. P. Blair to S. J. Tilden, October 19, 1868. The letter is misdated "1865" in this volume.

74. Historical Society of Pennsylvania: Chase Papers: John D. Van Buren to S. P. Chase, October 24, 1868.

in the bloodless manner of Edmund Burke. In closing "Taxation in the United States," he declared:

I have confidence that if you elect Governor Seymour and give him adequate support, he will to a large extent redress the evils under which you suffer; and I am free to say that if I did not believe he would exert every power and every faculty of intellect and of body to accomplish these results, I would take no interest in his election. I believe he will have at his service the best minds that the country affords, and best opportunities. I believe that his election is the best chance and the best hope for American constitutional government on this continent.[75]

Already before the October elections, Tilden had written a long letter on "the waste of war," which the New York *World* printed five days later.[76] By October 14, however, it seemed plain that the Republicans would carry the country. One desperate effort yet remained, and Seymour was "goaded into activity." He was already at Buffalo on his way to the field of battle when he received from President Johnson a telegram which urged him to appeal to the country with an "inspired tongue" against "the despotic power now ready to enter the very gates of the citadel of liberty."[77] From Buffalo Seymour went on to Cleveland and thence to Chicago, where he spoke on October 24. Then he appeared at Detroit and came back to the East by way of Indianapolis, Columbus, Pittsburgh, and

75. Tilden, *Public Writings*, I, 422–452.

76. Tilden, *Public Writings*, I, 453–466: Samuel J. Tilden to the editor of the New York *World*, October 12, 1868.

77. This message from President Johnson deserves to be given in full:

I see it announced in the papers of this morning that you will enter the Presidential canvass in person. I trust this may be so, as the present position of public affairs justifies and demands it. It is hoped and believed by your friends that all the enemies of constitutional government, whether secret or avowed, will not be spared; and that their arbitrary and unjust usurpations, together with their wasteful, profligate and corrupt uses of the people's treasure will be signally exposed and rebuked. The mass of the people should be aroused and warned against the encroachments of the despotic power now ready to enter the very gates of the citadel of liberty. I trust you may speak with an inspired tongue, and that your voice may penetrate every just and patriotic heart throughout the land. Let the living principles of a violated Constitution be proclaimed and restored, that peace, prosperity and fraternal feeling may return to a divided and oppressed nation.

New York State Library: Seymour Papers: Andrew Johnson to Horatio Seymour, October 22, 1868.

Philadelphia, speaking at all these cities and at many places on the road. At the end of his energetic swing around the circle, he was much too tired to accept invitations to stump in New Jersey and New York, and returned to Utica through Wilkes-Barre. During much of the trip he suffered from speaker's sore throat. Alexander describes him as preaching the "gospel of peace" in the vain attempt to talk down the great prestige of Grant.[78] His strongest argument was the obvious wisdom of heading off complete control of the federal government by the radical Republicans. The quickest way to peace, he argued, was to forestall revenge.

The speeches of this tour are very much alike in form and substance. The radio had not yet put politicians on their mettle. One speech would still do for a campaign. At Chicago, however, the candidate had got into his stride and was not yet worn out with travelling and talking. He began at the suppression of the "rebellion" and examined the policy of reconstruction, provoking laughter by remarking that Mr. Colfax, the Republican candidate for Vice-President, had retreated from the discussion of current questions to the Kansas troubles of 1855 and the Dred Scott Decision of 1857. Restoration of the South, Seymour insisted, must employ the negro profitably and thus improve his condition in life. It would also give the South the power to contribute its fair share to paying off the huge cost of the Civil War.

At Chicago, Seymour felt safe in emphasizing what he called the unequal distribution of the currency.[79] It is interesting to

78. Alexander, *History*, III, 211. For a complete list of the speeches of this tour in October, 1868, see Wall, *Seymour*, 100–101.

79. Seymour's speeches on the currency reflect the discontent of certain financial policies of the government after the Civil War. On January 30, 1864, $449,-338,902 of greenbacks were outstanding — $450,000,000 having been authorized by the Congress in 1862 and 1863. An act of April 12, 1866, provided for the retirement of United States notes at the rate of $10,000,000 a month for the ensuing six months, and thereafter at $4,000,000 a month. About $40,000,000 of notes were retired, but widespread complaint led to the suspension of the act on February 4, 1868. As greenbacks were issued, prices rose rapidly, but after April 12, 1866, they declined faster than they had advanced. The acute discontent caused by deflation is reflected in Seymour's campaign of 1868: New York *Times*, June 17, 1935.

notice that he seems to have discovered the difference between the important power of coining money and the equally great power of controlling credit. Most of the quarrels over finance arise from a failure to see this significant distinction. It was the national banking act, he declared, which had concentrated money at the East to the detriment of the agricultural states of the West. The privilege of putting out bank bills "became a valuable monopoly under this law," and the South and the West, where banks were few and far between, had to borrow money at high interest. "More than fifty-seven millions of this currency was given to the state of Massachusetts and less than ten millions to the state of Illinois, yet you have twice the population of Massachusetts."

The banking system, however, was not the only burden on the West: the cost of transportation deprived the farmers of a reasonable profit on what they raised. Heavy taxes for the huge federal debt should persuade a genuinely patriotic administration to reduce the cost of government as quickly and surely as possible. American national credit in 1868 was "lower than that of the Turk." Merely to contract the volume of currency would crush every debtor and business man in the country. It was impossible to make a bond which did not bear interest worth more than a bond which secured it — and paid more than ten per cent. The way to lift American currency to its normal value was to raise the bonds of the United States to par in the markets of the world. In other words, without openly saying so, Seymour declared for redemption in gold and thus adroitly repudiated the Pendleton plank of the platform on which he was supposed to stand. In view of his record in the matter of the bonds of his own state in 1864, the Democratic candidate in 1868 was thoroughly consistent in supporting what the whole-hearted Thaddeus Stevens had been pleased to call a "swindle." [80]

Seymour's disdain for violent language in the face of almost certain defeat redounds to his credit. It would have been easy for him to yield to the temptation to collect all the elements of discontent in the country and enlist them in his own sup-

80. Albany *Argus*, October 27, 1868.

port. On the contrary, he kept his eye on the one good object in view — the vain hope of checking the policy of the radical Republicans. James Ford Rhodes describes the speeches of this middle-western tour as "excellent and moderate."[81] Nine years later, President Hayes quietly acknowledged that reconstruction had been a failure by taking the federal troops out of the secession states. The South had traded a President for home rule in 1877, and slowly but surely negro suffrage sank down out of sight.

If the defeat of the Democrats was not so overwhelming as thought, it was decisive. Grant polled 3,012,833 votes against 2,703,249 for Seymour. Of the eleven Confederate States the Democrat received the electoral votes of only Louisiana and Georgia, and the return from the latter state was contested when the official figures were presented to the Congress. Although Seymour would not have had a majority of the college even with the support of these eleven states, three of them — Virginia, Mississippi, and Texas — were not allowed to take any part in the election, and the remaining six were "carried" for General Grant. The very narrow margin by which Seymour lost several of the northern states and the use of the new negro vote provoked the suspicion — or the guess — that a majority of the white men of the nation probably preferred him to Grant.

That Grant should lose New York to Seymour by a majority of ten thousand was a source of shame and anger to Republicans. Although Conkling swung their home county of Oneida into line against his brother-in-law, the Democratic candidate carried fourteen counties out of sixty and lost eleven others by less than five hundred votes apiece. Chemung, for instance, went for Grant by one vote.[82] It is commonly said that Tammany, which was running Mayor John T. Hoffman for governor, cared nothing for the presidential ticket, and was intent only on securing the state.[83] Seymour's majority of an even 10,000 was supposed to have been adjusted to suit bets on the election, but

81. Rhodes, *History*, VI, 306–307.
82. *Evening Journal Almanac* (Albany, 1869), 52. See map.
83. Alexander, *History*, III, 206.

Hoffman beat Griswold for governor by 27,946.[84] It is generally assumed that the election was decided in the cities of New York and Brooklyn, but a glance at the map will show that Seymour carried a solid block of four counties stretching from Albany southwest to the border of Pennsylvania, to which Schoharie was attached on the west and Columbia County on the east. Beyond these two groups of counties — seven of them in the lower valley of the Hudson and around New York Harbor and six of them forming the group mentioned above, Seymour carried but one other, Seneca, halfway out toward the western end of the state. Even if his victory in the cities of New York and Brooklyn be laid to organized corruption, there is still to be explained his strength in counties like Westchester, Putnam, Columbia, and Ulster. In 1868, it must be remembered, the organization called Tammany was confined, even as it is to-day, to the island of Manhattan, and the rival machines of the other boroughs of the city as it now exists had little or none of the smooth power they have come to possess. Tammany itself, moreover, was frequently torn by rivalry and faction. Tweed was already at work, but the first election of Hoffman was only the beginning of his three fattest years of success.

Seymour's victory in New York was made the subject of a federal investigation. On November 4, Horace Greeley spoke at the Union League Club, which promptly petitioned the Congress to look into the vote of the state. This petition was presented to the House of Representatives by Mr. Lawrence, of Ohio, on December 14, and accepted by a vote of 134 to 35 — 52 abstaining. Thereupon Speaker Colfax, the Republican candidate for Vice-President, appointed a committee of seven: five Republicans and two Democrats — Kerr, of Indiana, and Ross, of Illinois. Lawrence was made chairman of the committee, which met first in Washington on December 18, and moved up to New York the next day. It reported to the House of Representatives on Febuary 23, 1869. As printed, this report fills nine hundred pages.[85] A minority report denounced the findings

84. Alexander, *History*, III, 214–215; Werner, *Civil List*, 167.
85. *House of Representatives, Reports of Committees, 1868–1869:* Number 31.

as "stale slanders," but neither of the two representatives who signed it had any direct interest in the affairs of the state.

A study of the printed record prompts the suspicion that the work of the committee and the report of the majority can hardly be said to have been wholly free from partisan bias. The charge of fraud was not new. There was a tradition that the pivotal vote of New York in 1844 had been gained by corruption. Neither Whigs nor Republicans could lose the state without a protest. In 1884, for instance, Conkling got the votes which gave Cleveland the election, but Tammany got the blame. Many years afterward Theodore Roosevelt wrote of Seymour's victory:

> The majorities by which the city was carried for the Democratic presidential candidate . . . represented the worst electoral frauds which the country ever witnessed, — far surpassing even those by which Polk had been elected over Clay.[86]

If we look back for a moment we shall find a parallel not quite so plain as Roosevelt wished to believe. Silas Wright, it will be remembered, was running for governor in 1844; like Seymour, he came from upstate and was put on the ticket for the express purpose of making use of his great power to draw votes. Like Seymour, too, he was personally above suspicion, and, like John T. Hoffman in 1868, he ran ahead of the presidential candidate. Nor did the Whig machine lack oil and eager hands. "Charges of wholesale frauds were made by both parties," according to McCormac, "but it may be doubted," he concludes, "that such frauds materially affected the election results."[87]

John I. Davenport served as clerk of the congressional committee appointed by Colfax. Subsequently he became chief supervisor of elections for the southern district of the state. In 1894, he published *The Election Frauds of New York City and Their Prevention*, dedicating his book to the Union League Club, the Republican Party, and, with some lack of humor, to President Grant. Davenport's volume purports to be a history of the frauds practised from 1837 to 1870, though more than

86. Roosevelt, *New York*, 207.
87. McCormac, *Polk*, 281.

one third of the book is devoted to the election of 1868. Partly, perhaps, because the Democrats carried Philadelphia also in October of that year, the author begins his discussion with a description of the means by which vagrant voters were imported into Pennsylvania from New York. There was more than one good reason for this digression — not only had Philadelphia gone against Grant, but the figures assembled by the congressional committee and used by its clerk years afterward proved far too much.

If Tammany padded the lists of voters to the extent alleged, then the actual vote received by Seymour and Hoffman must have been almost wholly fraudulent or thousands of persons who were carefully prepared for the purpose did not go to the polls on the day appointed. A third explanation is possible: perhaps more than one of the thousands of new citizens voted for Grant and Griswold — if only by mistake. Though the Republicans had their own very active state and city machines in New York in 1868, Davenport could hardly have been expected to suppose that they gleaned any gain in fields of corruption. Seymour's strength in the city makes it extremely unlikely that the whole, or even the larger part, of the 108,316 votes which he received there in November, 1868, was fraudulent. Hoffman, who was mayor and candidate for governor at one and the same time, outran Seymour in the city by over four thousand votes, but he did so in the state as well, carrying fifteen counties in all. Even in Oneida he polled nineteen votes more than Seymour; his surplus over Griswold, it has been seen, was almost 28,000.[88]

The total vote of New York City in the presidential election of 1868 is not so remarkable as it may seem at first sight.[89] It is true that the Democrats added approximately fifty per cent. to

88. Werner, *Civil List*, 167; *Evening Journal Almanac*, 52.

89. Davenport, *Election Frauds*, tables 3 and 5:

	Total Vote	Democratic Vote
1860	96,023	62,611
1864	110,433	73,709
1868	156,288	108,316
1872	132,481	77,814
1876	171,689	112,621
1880	205,381	123,015

their vote of 1864; while the Republicans made a gain of only thirty per cent. In 1864, however, thousands of voters were absent in the army, and the arrangements for collecting votes in the camps were far from satisfactory. The method was cumbersome, and the manner was suspicious. There are good reasons for believing that Seymour was counted out that year by manipulation of the soldier vote. When Seymour ran for governor in 1862, moreover, he received 54,312 votes in the city, slightly more than half the total he rolled up there in 1868. Grant's vote in the city in 1868, however, more than doubled that received by General Wadsworth, whom Seymour defeated in 1862. Practically the same percentages hold for Brooklyn.[90]

The falling-off of the Democratic vote in 1872 is partly to be accounted for by the strange nomination of Greeley, who did only a little better than McClellan had done eight years before. In 1880, when the Democrats put up Hancock and lost the state to Garfield, the figures show that they polled almost eleven thousand votes more than when they carried it for Tilden in 1876. To assert that all the profits of corruption in 1868 were Democratic is to assume a huge falling-off in the "respectable" support for Seymour. This explanation would be hard to prove — in view of the great vote he got throughout the country. He carried Kentucky, for instance, by over 76,000, and the only majority which excelled his in that state was the margin of 77,000 which Massachusetts gave Grant. If he won Oregon by only 164 votes out of a total poll of 22,000, he lost California by only 514 votes out of an aggregate of more than 108,000.[91]

Davenport's endeavor to estimate the percentage of votes cast in New York City in relation to the number of actual voters led him to the interesting conclusion that the total vote of the city in 1868 was 108 per cent. of the persons who could possibly have been entitled to suffrage.[92] On this basis he calculated a total fraudulent poll, in 1868, of 27,554, which would have left

90. See map.
91. Coleman, *Election of 1868*, 384.
92. Davenport, *Election Frauds*, 220–222.

Governor Hoffman the slender plurality of 392, and have given the state to Grant by 17,000. But the violent disputes over the honesty and the adequacy of the federal census of 1860 and 1870 and the state census of 1865 and 1875 leave Davenport's estimates open to question. The state census of New York, it will be remembered, lists citizens separately from aliens as a means of apportioning the assembly. When the Democrats complained of the federal census of 1870, they declared that the Republicans used one set of figures as the basis for representation in the Congress, and quite another set of figures when they were assigning quotas for the drafts of 1863 and 1864. However that may be, statements as to the percentage of votes actually cast as compared with potential voters do not prove which party was the more successful at fraud. Chiefly as a result of the enquiry, the legislature passed a reform bill in May, 1869, which Governor Hoffman refused to sign. In 1870, according to Davenport, a state law was passed by means of a bargain between Tweed and the Republican senators: he backed the bill they desired, and they, in turn, voted for the infamous "Tweed charter" for the city of New York.[93]

The most important ground for the charge of fraud in the election of 1868 was the wholesale naturalization of aliens. There is no doubt that this work went on helter-skelter for many months, chiefly in three courts. The sudden rise in the rate at which foreigners were made citizens that year was not only suspicious but spectacular. Two judges were chiefly active, and both had unsavory reputations — John H. McCunn, justice of the superior court of New York City, 1863–1872, who died in office, and George G. Barnard, justice of the supreme court, first district, who was elected in 1860 and removed twelve years later.[94] Laughable stories are told of how the eager aliens were herded through their courts in droves; new citizens were sworn in very much as Spanish priests once christened Mohammedans — in crowds. Eye-witnesses declared that applicants took the

93. Davenport, *Election Frauds*, 243–268.
94. Werner, *Civil List*, 345 and 354.

oath on any old volumes that happened to be lying about the court-rooms. According to Davenport, of 33,318 naturalizations in these courts, over 30,000 were pushed through in the one month of October.[95]

It is only fair to remember, however, that there were two good reasons for a rise in naturalization. In the first place, so long as the Civil War lasted, it was obviously to the advantage of aliens not to become citizens, for, by remaining foreigners, they could evade military service. That people fresh from Ireland and Germany should have shown no great desire to fight in a war about which they could have known little or nothing is hardly a matter for surprise. Many native Americans shared their reluctance. Up to the time of the Enrollment Act of March, 1863, the state was using every effort to fill up the quotas assigned to it, and thereafter national conscription made American citizenship a liability in the eyes of able-bodied men who were not already in the army. In the second place, 1868 was the first presidential election after the end of the war.

As far as the actual tabulating of the vote is concerned, the story goes that Tweed asked for telegraphic information as to the results upstate so that he might adjust the count in the city accordingly. In order to keep the Republicans off the wires, Tweed sent all kinds of trivial messages during the evening and was ready, so it was alleged, to telegraph the whole Bible, if necessary.[96] Davenport was wanting in either intelligence or

95. Davenport, *Election Frauds*, 139–140. Davenport's figures show the following record of naturalization in the city of New York:

1850–1859	60,000
1860–1867	70,604
1868	65,000 (October, 57,217)

For an interesting partisan popular digest of the frauds of 1868, see Post, *The Wig and the Jimmy*. The author prepared his pamphlet, which sold for twenty-five cents, because the voluminous report of the congressional committee had been issued in an edition of only two thousand copies and was not, therefore, available to the public.

96. *Documents of the Board of Aldermen*, Part II, Number 8, 226. Myers, in *Tammany Hall*, writes that in 1877, when Tweed was under examination and had no reason for lying, he stated, "that he *thought* the Inspectors of Elections 'lumped' the votes and declared them without counting, in order to overcome the result in the rest of the State and give the electoral vote to Seymour."

honesty, however, and seems not to have realized that he made his case too good to be true. Immediately after his election as governor, Mayor Hoffman resigned, and a special election followed on the first Tuesday in December, 1868, when A. Oakey Hall defeated Frederick A. Conkling by a vote of 75,109 to 20,835.[97] The office in question was of first importance to Tammany, which might have been expected to do its very best to make sure of holding on to it. If the Democrats added 65,000 voters to the lists in 1868, Hall's vote ought to have been much larger than it was, even in a special election. Although neither Tweed nor his puppet, Hall, was ever a credit to New York, it is not quite safe to fasten on these men as early as 1868 the evil reputations they did not attain until three years later. The skill and arrogance of Tweed grew by what they fed on. A falling-off of almost forty thousand Democratic votes between November and December in 1868 was not surprising, for millions of Americans who come out to vote in presidential elections can not be prevailed upon to take the trouble to go to the polls at any other time.

In 1870, at the time of the first appearance of the figures of the federal census for that year, Seymour himself returned to the charge that fraud had given him the electoral vote of New York in 1868. In a speech at Rome on October 18, in the course of which he went so far as to refer to Greeley's *Tribune* as a "leprous journal," the titular leader of the Democratic party presented a careful comparison of mutually contradictory estimates of people and voters in New York City.[98] Going back to his quarrel with the administration in 1864 over the accuracy of the enrollment in certain congressional districts, Seymour showed that, according to the Republicans, New York City was "very populous for the purpose of fighting, but very thinly settled for the purpose of voting." If citizens of the state wished to judge of the principles of the party which was trying to "recon-

97. Myers, *Tammany Hall*, 218–219.

98. Speech at Rome, October 18, 1870, in the Utica *Observer* for October 20, 1870.

struct" the South, a reasonable basis for a sound decision was the conduct of that party in New York, for if Republicans were dishonest and unjust in the North, it was not unfair to suppose that they were very much the same in the South. Thus, questions growing out of the census returns for the cities of New York and Brooklyn were "of more than mere local importance." The federal census of 1870 showed that the population of New York City was just under one million, but the largest vote ever given in that city — 1868 — was less than 156,000. The population of Oneida County, however, was about 109,000, and its vote was about 24,000. The total vote of the whole state added up to more than 850,000. If, then, the figures for the city showed fraud, there was "fraud all over our land." Those who brought charges of corruption by giving detailed descriptions of just how cheating was used at elections, knew far "too much for the good of their reputations."

Complaints against the census returns for 1870 were widespread, and there were "proofs that the work has been badly done." Census-takers were paid the same sum that was given in 1860 for each person enumerated, with the consequence that they listed persons easy to get at and left those whose entry on the rolls would cost more than the reward. Thus they had not only "strong political reasons" for doing their work carelessly, but a "moneyed interest" as well. In forcing down the figures for the city in 1870, however, the Republicans were convicting themselves of fraud in 1864. In the sixth congressional district of New York, for instance, the vote, according to partisan papers, was "unduly large in comparison with census returns." In 1870, this district was said to contain only 118,000 people, a falling-off of more than 16,000 in ten years. This district was overwhelmingly Democratic. In 1864, there were charged against it more than 30,000 men as liable to military duty, when, in the county of Oneida, with approximately the same population, only 9,190 were enrolled. An enrollment of 30,000, however, postulated a population of about 300,000. As a result of the governor's protests, the enrollment of the sixth district was reduced to about 20,000 — which still implied a population of about 200,000. Now which set of federal figures was honest — the enrollment of 1863 or the census of 1870? In 1868, Seymour reminded his audience, the vote in the sixth district of the state was "no greater in proportion to the population than that of the county of Oneida."

A study of the statistics would show that the enrollments of 1863 and 1864 invariably approximated one half of the voters. The figure for New York City fell short "only six of 128,000." In 1864, then, there should have been 256,000 voters within the city limits — such "was the showing of the Republican authorities . . . who protested [the enrollment] had been fairly and carefully made." If so, how could a vote of 156,000 in 1868 be called excessive? Even if New York had added nothing to its population in six years, the official statements of the Republicans in 1864 and 1870 "overthrew and destroyed" each other.

> All agree that New York has increased since 1864. How does it happen, then, that at that time it was so crowded with voters who were liable to military duty, while now there are so few who have a right to the elective franchise?

The best way to learn the temper of men who asked the voters to make them their representatives in the councils of the state or nation was to watch their conduct at home. In reading Davenport's statement that 108 per cent. of those entitled to vote in 1868 went to the polls, it is well to keep in mind a reasonable doubt as to the accuracy of the enrollment for conscription in 1863, as well as the census of 1870. Both sets of figures could not possibly have been true, and it is not unlikely that neither accorded with the facts. If the city vote was unduly large in 1868, then the Republican districts of the state, on the basis of their own returns, were "steeped in fraud to their very eyelids." Seymour was never unwilling to return to this subject as long as he lived.

Writing in 1886, Blaine thought that the slender popular majority for Grant in 1868 was "a very startling fact." A solid South, he feared, would doom the Republicans to perpetual defeat, but he did not go on to observe that it was precisely negro suffrage which would make the South solid. "Considering the time of the election," continued Blaine, "considering the record and the achievements of the rival candidates, the Presidential election of 1868 must be regarded as the most remarkable and the most unaccountable in our political annals." [99] It was Senator Doolittle's considered opinion, on the other hand, that "a majority of the people did not want General Grant for president." It was the "suicidal platform" of the Chicago convention of 1864, he thought, which made Seymour, who had presided there, a man marked out for suspicion.[100]

Hancock and Hendricks, perhaps, would have made a better showing for the Democrats in 1868, but even if they had carried all four of the October states, the Congress "would have acted to prevent the possibility of any Southern States supporting the Democratic ticket." [101] The only way the Democrats could have elected a President in 1868 would have been to carry every close state in the North and hold both Georgia and Louisiana as well. The vote of Georgia, it will be recalled, was contested at the electoral count, and it most certainly would have been disallowed if it had been decisive. The party which claimed the credit for having saved the Union was bound, bent, and determined to continue to rule it, even after ignoring the one honest way to its desire — the building up of white support in the South. Twelve years of reconstruction were to close this way, apparently for ever, and fasten on eleven, or nine, states the tedious tyranny of a single-party system tempered by faction and murder. A solid South provoked a solid North, and this geographical division of parties confused the world-old issue as between conservatives and liberals. To-day the conservative party finds in its ranks radicals who call themselves Republicans, and the liberal party has to suffer Democrats who are

99. Blaine, *Twenty Years of Congress*, II, 408.

100. *Wisconsin Magazine of History*, VI, 1 (September, 1922), 95–99: James Rood Doolittle to C. A. Dana, April 16, 1880.

101. Coleman, *Election of 1868*, 378.

Republicans in everything but name. The real battle-ground of opinion in the nation is limited to the states which lie between these unchangeable extremes — the so-called "doubtful" states.

In the one respect that no man but Horatio Seymour has ever received the national nomination of a major party against his will, the campaign of 1868 is unique in the history of the United States. To believe that he secretly desired this nomination, to think that it was worthless and went to him by default, will not do, for such were not the circumstances. The etiquette of American politics keeps presidential aspirants away from national conventions of their party. Seymour not only allowed himself to be made a delegate-at-large but accepted the post of permanent presiding officer. When he silenced the proposal in the state caucus of July 2 that New York support him as its favorite son, he pointed out that it would be improper for a member of the convention to permit his name to go before it. His very presence at New York, he fondly believed, removed him from consideration as the candidate. It was the rivalry of East and West, of conservatives and radicals, that made him the victim of his own merits.

Although any one of five men — Johnson, Chase, Pendleton, Hendricks, and Hancock — would have been glad to accept what Seymour did his best to refuse, it is safe to say that no nominee of the Democrats could have been elected President of the United States in 1868. The Republicans were resolved to retain control of the country they said they had saved, and the lesson they learned from the figures of 1868 was the fact that they would have to look about them to win in 1872 and 1876. They did. The choice of Greeley relieved them of worry as to how they would get a second term for Grant, but the great panic of 1873 and the rising tide of Tilden three years later proved that they had been wise to take warning.

It is doubtful, however, if any other candidate could have run a better race than Seymour — Chase, perhaps, and probably Hancock. Not even his enemies suggested that he would have failed so dismally in the great office as did General Grant. As to those of his opponents who were frank enough to acknowledge that no genuine objection could be brought against his character or his ability, the worst that they could say of Seymour in 1868 was this — that he was "a Democrat disguised as a gentleman."[102]

102. Philadelphia *Press*, September 17, 1868.

XIX

"THREE TROUBLESOME OLD FOOLS"

1869–1875

IN 1868 Seymour accepted his first and his last national nomination, if the empty honor of having his name put up for senator by the Democrats in 1861 be taken for the legislative formality which it was. The Democratic victory in the state the year he ran for President left Tweed the apparent master of the situation. Governor John T. Hoffman was preëminently his man, and by 1869 the party controlled both houses of the legislature and had elected the state officials for the third consecutive time. Seymour, as nominal leader of the national party, and Tilden, as chairman of the state organization, were, for the moment, little more than figureheads.[1] Ultimately, however, it was the prestige and power of these men, together with the invaluable aid of Nast and Kernan, which worked the final ruin of the crudest, if not the worst, of the leaders of Tammany Hall.

In the autumn of 1869 a polite reporter from the New York *Sun* dropped in on Seymour at Deerfield. He found him standing erect near the centre of his living-room, dressed in "a suit of deep black" and "holding a small ornamental china cup" which the reporter took care to make clear contained nothing more harmful than coffee. About a dozen persons were scattered around the room, most of them visitors, and the ex-governor was in good form. The conversation turned from the nomination of the year before to prospects for the future. When asked if he believed that Chief-Justice Chase would ever sleep easily outside the White House, Seymour laughed and answered: "Well, if Mr. Chase runs for president just once, and gets defeated, his ambition will be satisfied, I can assure you." As for himself, he was cured of the taste for public life which he had

1. Alexander, *History*, III, 228.

once enjoyed; he was converted to the love of the country, and his farm of five hundred acres kept him busy. As soon as he could arrange all his affairs, he planned to spend "some time abroad." Just why the Seymours never went to Europe is something of a mystery. It may have been the Macedonian cry of Tilden which put off the trip until it was too late.[2]

Seymour's correspondence during two quiet years shows that he had by no means lost interest in public affairs, although he knew that he was through for ever with the holding of public office. The letters he sent at this period to his old friend, George L. Miller, of Omaha, whose loyalty was always on the look-out for chances for Seymour's advancement, are full of references to the political anxieties of the time. Thanking Miller for a saddle of antelope, Seymour observed that his knowledge that he had "disinterested friends" was his "one great advantage over General Grant." Apparently he was quick to sense the fault of character which was to cost the President much, if not all, of the good name with which he entered the White House. Eight years in office were not to add anything to the general's reputation, however deeply they entrenched in Washington the party which made a national hero a partisan, too. Seymour's suspicion is all the more significant in view of the fact that the best of his friends among Republicans, Hamilton Fish, was Grant's secretary of state.

It amused Seymour in 1869 to read speeches of Senator Morton and others, in which opponents of his during the past year made use of "the figures and almost the facts which they denounced so savagely when we pressed them upon public attention in 1868."[3] The majority in the House and Senate were by no means united, and hardly had Grant been inaugurated before the difficult question of currency began to split the government in the Congress. Discussing the dilemma of the Republicans, Seymour expressed the opinion that if the Democrats

2. New York *Sun*, October 5, 1869.

3. New York Historical Society: Seymour Papers: Horatio Seymour to G. L. Miller, February 3, 1870.

had held in 1868 to the position which they took in New York in 1867, they would have "swept the country." In adopting a platform which threatened the standard of values of a great business community, the supporters of Pendleton, thought Seymour, had alarmed all creditors, both public and private. The greenback craze was "like Satan's flight into Chaos." Seymour's opinion seems odd when it is remembered that he carried the "hard money" states like New York, New Jersey, and Maryland, and lost Ohio, where Pendleton was especially powerful.[4] It recalls the stubborn belief of Van Buren, expert politician though he was, that not the panic of 1837 but the campaign tactics of the Whigs defeated him for reëlection in 1840.

Now, at last, the Republicans were compelled to meet the problem which the Democrats had for a time "saved them from confronting." They it was who must change the standard of value as set by the emergency of the Civil War, whenever they dared to resume specie payments. What they had done so far had already filled New York with "bankrupt merchants," for goods had shrunk in value; while their debts stood unchanged. Seymour believed the Republicans would have to "back down," for the West was beginning to get excited over what the Democrats had warned the people of a year before. Debtors or creditors had to suffer, and great numbers would be ruined either way, for the nation could not "stand still." Seymour's conclusion is characteristic:

> No one can see how the thing will end. We must wait and watch. In the meantime I hope our friends at the West will not make issues without consulting us at the East. We who have with infinite labor held New York against the fiercest attacks ought not to be assailed without a hearing.[5]

By the summer of 1870 Seymour had to return to the defense of the canals. The question was the proposed reduction of tolls, and a convention was called at Rochester for July. Naturally, the interests of the New York Central and the Erie rail-

4. See Rhodes's observations on the apparent contradiction in the election results of the campaign of 1868.

5. New York Historical Society: Seymour Papers: Horatio Seymour to G. L. Miller, December 20, 1869.

roads would oppose any measure which would take freight from their lines. By an act of April 25, the legislature had submitted to the people the proposal to fund the canal debt of the state. The measure was lost at a referendum, just as the new constitution of 1867 had been turned down by the electors the year before.[6] Largely owing to the influence of Seymour, the reduction of tolls was put through the legislature; no act in many years, he thought, would do so much good not only to his own state but to the whole West. New York could take pride in building up the trade of the country by "a bold and wise act," which enabled the farmers to get their grain to the seaboard. The state might lose a million dollars of tolls in 1870, but the people would gain many times that sum in other ways. Low tolls on the canals would make low charges on the railroads — the state did well to show as much "pluck and vigor in cutting down charges" as the railroads did when they waged war upon one another. Henceforth, the canals of the state would be used in the interests of labor and commerce — and not merely as a means of squeezing taxes out of traffic.[7] Seymour was shrewd enough to see that once the Erie Canal had paid back the cost of its construction and improvement, it should be looked on as a free waterway, like the Hudson River. Twelve years later, by an amendment to the constitution, all tolls were abolished.[8]

Hoffman was renominated at the Democratic state convention at Rochester, in September, 1870. This convention was controlled by Tweed, and as Tilden called it to order in the capacity of state chairman, he quite appropriately had his pocket picked. Meanwhile, the Republicans were torn asunder by the rivalry of two former governors, Morgan and Fenton. Fenton, who had succeeded Morgan in the Senate in 1869, at the end of two terms at Albany, was one of the ablest political organizers the state had ever seen. As Fenton gained control of the party in New York, President Grant grew weary of his perpetual de-

6. Werner, *Civil List*, 133.

7. New York State Library: Seymour Papers: Horatio Seymour to A. E. Culver, June 16, 1870.

8. Werner, *Civil List*, 225.

mands for offices, and began to turn to his colleague, Conkling, who had entered the Senate in 1867. Conkling was both politically helpful and personally amusing, and the means by which he took the leadership from Fenton were dramatic, oratorical, and sarcastic. Before long, Seymour saw his magnificently masculine brother-in-law acting as deputy for the President in the state — arrogantly, but always with an eye to becoming Grant's successor.

So long as the Republicans exercised their greatest skill in plotting against one another, the Democrats continued to win the elections. So it turned out in 1870. Speaking as a guest of honor at the final rally of the campaign in Tammany Hall, Seymour devoted his address to the new legislation on canals. Tweed's ways, he was not long in discovering, were not his, and when the time for getting rid of him arrived, he joined with Tilden to clean the party without allowing the Republicans to reap the benefits of the reform. To oust Tweed and beat their opponents at the same time required supremely skillful generalship. Seymour and Tilden worked together at this delicate task for three years. Whenever a party long in control is put out of office, the political profits of the change generally accrue to traditional opponents not one bit better than the discredited victims of public virtue. In fighting Tweed, therefore, Seymour kept in the minds of his companions the fact that very little would be gained by allowing the spoilsmen of Conkling and Fenton to ride into power on the bad name of Tammany.

In the autumn of 1870, however, Tweed was still in his glory: the entertainment at the final rally was lavish, and the Wigwam was filled with jubilation. The guests were treated to speeches by Governor Hoffman, Tweed, and Jim Fisk, the shady partner of Jay Gould.[9] Seymour was in strange company, indeed, but there was a deep gulf fixed between the men of the days before and after the Civil War. For a quarter of a century the political spirit of the American people wavered. Emergency contracts for the army and the navy and the quick acquisition of wealth

9. Myers, *Tammany Hall*, 229–230.

aroused the greed and the envy of little men and big ones. In the strange circle of President Grant, scholars and gentlemen rubbed shoulders and elbows with rogues and thieves. There was nothing like it again in the United States until the government which followed a futile foreign war and the fall of Woodrow Wilson. The defeat of Blaine in 1884 put an end to an interval.

It was the hot autumn of Sedan and the stormy sunset of the Second Empire. That very month Louis Napoleon was to come to the end of his great adventure. Tweed could well have learned a lesson from over-weening confidence, if he had ever given himself the trouble to look beyond the horizons of New York. By taking thought he might have spared himself the inconvenience of a sudden trip to Spain. Reaction was already under way in the devoted city he plundered. In 1870 disaffected Democrats had joined forces with the independents and the Republicans to unite on a candidate for mayor in opposition to A. Oakey Hall. Ledwith, their nominee, polled only 46,392 votes against the 71,037 received by the office-boy of Tweed, but an analysis of the result showed a significant shift in sentiment. Governor Hoffman's vote in the city exceeded the total for Hall by 15,631, and the Republican candidate for mayor ran nearly 12,000 votes ahead of the party's nominee for governor.[10] When the Tweed "Secret Accounts" were published at the end of July, 1871, it was obvious that either Tweed or Tilden would have to go.

The story of the state chairman's war on the boss of New York is the most courageous chapter of a singular career. Tilden laid his plans upstate, first meeting Francis Kernan, fellow townsman and friend of Seymour, at Albany, on the fourth of August. Ten days later, the two men went to Utica, where they held consultations with Seymour, who expressed his full sympathy with what was about to be done.[11] His memory ran back far into the history of New York politics, as is shown by the

10. Myers, *Tammany Hall*, 230.
11. Tilden, *Public Writings*, I, 588.

letter he wrote Tilden before they talked together. There was no better time, he thought, for "Republican surgeons" to hack and cut away at corruption, for when the public mind was once turned to the question of frauds, there would be "a call for the books at Washington as well as in the city of New York."

> I think a spasm of virtue will run through the body politic. Business is dull. The farmers are getting poor, with no look ahead of better times. Immigration, railroads, and machinery are crowding the markets with provisions and breadstuffs. Taxes are now felt as they have not been since 1860. The corruption in our party is local. In the Republican party it is pervading. We can lose nothing by stirring up questions of frauds.[12]

The first assault on Tweed was planned for the state convention in the autumn of 1871. Tilden sent out letters to thousands of Democrats, declaring that "wherever the gangrene of corruption had reached the Democratic party we must take a knife and cut it out by the roots." By September 22, one of his letters appeared in the New York *Tribune*. The state convention was to meet at Rochester on October 4, and, working in conjunction with the reformers led by Tilden, Seymour went on from Utica to act as its presiding officer. The opponents of Tweed claimed a majority, but once the boss arrived from the city, the upstate delegates began to weaken. Tweed did not have to enter the convention hall. Although Tilden would not compromise, Alexander declares that his opening speech dealt with the frauds in New York City, with all the "delicacy of a surgeon examining an abscess."[13] Supremely confident of its power, Tammany waived its right to participate in the proceedings and completely out-generalled the reformers by this tactful semblance of self-sacrifice. Thereupon the convention determined to treat fraud as "a local matter" and thus keep it out of the state campaign.

When he came into the hall, Horatio Seymour was hailed, "amid tumultuous cheers," as the "future president in 1872." Looking around him, he saw Francis Kernan seated beyond the

12. Tilden, *Letters and Literary Memorials*, I, 274.
13. Alexander, *History*, III, 266 and 269.

rail, and immediately moved his admission to the floor of the convention, as a Democrat "whose very presence was a sufficient credential to his title to a seat." Kernan, it was well known, was the joint friend of Seymour and Tilden, and Tammany hated him.[14] Immediately a delegate from Kings County offered the name of another to block him — a man who was not only regularly elected, but "the friend of that great Democrat, John T. Hoffman." Mention of the governor's name produced the roar of cheers it was supposed to, and the national leader of the Democrats, standing before the convention of his party in his own state, saw another man preferred before his friend.

> Seymour had lived long in years, in fame, and in the esteem of his party. He could hardly have had any personal enemies. He possessed no capricious dislikes, and his kindly heart, in spite of a stateliness of bearing, won all the people who came near him. To be thus opposed and bantered in a Democratic assembly was a deep humiliation, and after expressing the hope that the Tammany man would fight for the Democratic party as gallantly in future as he had fought against it in the past, the illustrious statesman withdrew his motion.[15]

There was more than rhetoric in Seymour's attitude. Tweed had control of the convention, but the man who was expected to serve as its presiding officer had brought with him from Utica a prepared speech in which he denounced the corruption in the government of New York City. Although the reformers had failed to hold their ranks together, and those who would not compromise had been refused seats in the hall, Seymour was determined to say what he had intended. He would be presiding officer only on his own terms. Once he was given to understand that he could not be president of the convention unless he would forego his "philippic against the Tammany thieves,"

14. People acquainted with the long and honorable careers of Francis Kernan, of Utica, and Henry Cruse Murphy, of Brooklyn, may be surprised to find the former called the "henchman" of Horatio Seymour in the *Dictionary of American Biography*. Murphy was not only eminently successful in business, but he was a scholar and a gentleman, and so, in fact, was Kernan. It was unreasonable to blame Kernan for the political misfortunes of Murphy: *Dictionary of American Biography*, XIII (1934), 351.

15. Alexander, *History*, III, 271.

he declined the doubtful honor which was offered him and went home abruptly.[16] He laid his leaving to illness. His sudden disappearance caused dismay, for Tweed's men were insolent enough to suppose that they could bully Seymour and trade on his name at the same time. In the exultation and anger with which he rode to his fall, however, the boss of New York could not conceal his contempt. Seymour, Tilden, and Kernan were "three troublesome old fools."[17] And yet their day was not over, by any means: four years later Tilden was to go to Albany as governor and Kernan to Washington as senator. A year thereafter Seymour himself was nominated to succeed Tilden.

Four days after he got home, Seymour wrote Tilden a long and remarkable letter which tells much to students of the time. When he set out to preside over the convention, he believed that the Democrats were determined to clean house, but the moment he arrived in Rochester he saw that "the switch had been changed" — and knew that a party had been made up to which Tilden, Kernan, and he were not to be invited. "Of that," he writes, "I am proud." Even Cassidy, of the *Argus*, had turned against him, for the simple reason that Tweed was the first man in the party to pay him fairly for his long and faithful service. The editor of the *Argus* had swung the upstate men into line for Tweed, but Seymour's judgment was philosophical.

> It is not in my heart to say an unkind word of Cassidy. In many ways he has had a hard time. His fine mind has been used by others while he was left poor. It was the strange policy of the Central Railroad men to give wealth to Weed and others, who fought them if they did not, while Cassidy was helped to live by loans and in other ways which kept him poor. When Tweed went to Albany he turned a stream of patronage into the *Argus* office which made it strong and rich. I think Cassidy means, in the main, to stand up for the right, but it is hard for him to strike men who have lifted him into wealth and when all about him shrink back.

This letter contains one of the rare bits of evidence as to the skill with which men of the regency had learned to estimate and manage others. The pupils of Van Buren, once having

16. New York *Times*, October 9, 1871.
17. New York *Tribune*, October 6, 1871.

learned to watch men and divine their motives, never lost that valuable art. "We may forgive others," writes Seymour of the split in the convention at Rochester, "but the men who have left us will not forgive us."

They have yielded to temptation, and now they are like church members who have fallen from grace; they not only hate to meet their minister, but they learn to hate him. . . . They were glad to hit us, and the young men would have done more if the wiser ones had not held them back. . . . I made up my mind to go home. I told Mr. Warren I would not act as president of the convention.

Referring to his sensational departure, Seymour shows that he realized he had made a mistake in seeming to have played sick. Not for the first, but for the last time in his life he had done the right thing in the wrong way. What his enemies called weakness of character was a psychological, perhaps an hereditary, defect. In a tense moment he faltered, subject to the state of mind, perhaps, which killed his father during the exciting summer of 1837. His own words are the best commentary on the manner of his leaving Rochester.

In the evening I was very ill, and when the committee called upon me I said I was not well enough to go into convention. This was true, but I am sorry I put that reason out. I was in so much pain that I had not my wits about me. I should have said to them, as I did to Warren, simply that I would not preside.[18]

Seymour saw the party which he preferred to trust enter the state campaign under the handicap of the evil reputation of Tweed. His position was made all the more difficult because he had the good sense to realize that when Republicans and Democrats rail at each other for corruption they are merely playing at pot and kettle. "By what right," Seymour asked, did "the plunderers of the nation denounce the robbers of a city?" These thrusts and parries were well enough in the game of professional politicians, for they brought to light the misdeeds of public men on both sides and served to check abuses in the interest of the people. Political fencing, however, even if skillful, could not

18. Tilden, *Letters and Literary Memorials*, I, 283–285.

quiet honest men in either party. What the public demanded, according to Seymour, was positive, not comparative, honesty in its leaders. A reputable party must punish the wrong-doers in its own ranks. The question for the voters to answer in 1871 was this: which of the two great parties arraigned its own corruption the more plainly? In pointing out this contrast, and in drawing attention to the unsavory reputation of the government of Grant, Seymour laid his finger on the essential hypocrisy of what was to become a whole generation of journalistic complaint against the crimes of Tammany Hall.[19]

In protesting against the Republican desire to dwell on the issues of the Civil War, Seymour recalls Samuel Johnson's definition of patriotism as "the last refuge of a scoundrel." In spite of his suspicion of the purity of the motives of his traditional opponents, he joined with Kernan to help Tilden in the hard work to be done. Once the New York *Times* had published its exposures of the impudent and greedy crowd which governed New York City, Tilden grimly set about the destruction of Tweed. He organized reform and he raised the money for the expense of it. Tweed, like any scandalous political boss in any part of the country, was a party man only in name: the words "Democrat" and "Republican" have never been anything more than conveniences of locality to the various gangs which have plundered the cities of the United States. Tweed, for instance, could always count in a crisis on a definite number of Republican votes in the state senate. In 1870 eight Republican senators helped him to block the measures of Tilden, and these senators Tweed did his best to reëlect. He even went so far, in 1871, as to offer to let Tilden name the delegates to the state convention and all the candidates on the ticket, if his nominations for the legislature were not interfered with.[20]

The scandal of Tweed's reign led to one of the most interesting, and not the last, effort to reform Tammany Hall from the inside. The first battle, however, had to be fought at Albany.

19. Utica *Observer*, October 31, 1871.
20. Alexander, *History*, III, 267.

Seymour had warned Tilden of the difficult work ahead. In the autumn of 1871 Tammany still had the advantage of the reformers. There was more uproar than resolution. Seymour urged caution on the eager and sanguine Tilden. "You know," he reminded him, "that I hold that all that a man does about politics after he is sixty years old is only meddling with other people's business."

But duty may force us to act, and then how do we stand? The Democratic leaders and organization are dead against us. The members of the convention went home pleased with the diplomacy of their leaders, but with lower tone of morality than they had when they left home. The young men we look to with hope in the future are debauched. They were willing to have Tammany coaxed out of the convention and then to slam the door in the face of the honest men who had unearthed crime in New York. When the leaders had done their work on Thursday noon the Tammany men stood in the light of having acted in a high-toned, generous way. The convention was grateful to them for allowing it to say stealing was wrong in a way that should hurt no one's feelings. . . . The majority of the convention wanted to leave matters in that shape, and they were angry when you and Kernan and West and others forced them to do a few decent acts. I think you saved the ticket by this. I know you saved your honor. . . . You are in the way. . . . I have stated all the odds against you, but you can whip the party back to right grounds if you wish to do so. It is on the defensive now.[21]

Tilden, however, had not "saved the ticket": in 1871 the Democrats went down to defeat under the burden of Tweed. Shortly after the election Seymour sent a private and characteristic letter to a friend in Bangor, Maine, having delayed writing until he should see the returns. The Democrats, in his opinion, deserved defeat, and could now "shake off bad men and put an end to many schemes all of which would have done harm." When Republicans talked of fraud, they encouraged the people to look at their own side of the house.

Our rogues are now all dead; theirs are all alive. No more can be said against us, but they cannot shut the gate that is now open and through which we can go to the field of debate we have long sought to enter. . . . I am sure this is a ground upon which all at the North and South can unite and stand and which I have not yet seen laid out. . . . I do not think we

21. Tilden, *Letters and Literary Memorials*, I, 284–285.

were wrong in the past, I do not mean to give an inch of ground in my faith nor to give up any of my works.[22]

Having forwarded to this correspondent the speech he had made at Utica on the last day of October, Seymour turned again to Tilden. The letter he wrote him on the day after Christmas presented a realistic, if gloomy, view of the situation at Albany. More than one-half of the members of the legislature would have good reason to hate Tilden, for they had got their nominations with a view to making money, and the nagging reformer had put them in the minority. Everywhere throughout the state, Seymour warned him, the active men of both parties had been given an interest, in one form or another, in the plunder of the Tweed Ring. These people were skillful in tactics and in making up combinations against those who threatened the profits they took out of politics. They would pretend to praise the exposure of grafters who were already known as such, but they would do their best to prevent any further revelations. "You can scarcely put your finger upon a clean spot in Albany."

Seymour had come to the conclusion that Tilden would do well to "take no more part in the business of legislation" than his duty demanded. He advised him not to make himself responsible for the new city charter, but to lift himself "above the squabbles and intrigues of the Legislature" by serving the public in the one way available to him. He must reform the judiciary of New York — at that work he could outwit his opponents, for they knew little and cared less about such matters. No one, in fact, would dare to oppose him, for all the business interests of the country were deeply concerned in this "grand question" which Tilden would do well to make his specialty. If he could lay his finger on the guilt of judges, he should "bring in articles of impeachment." The spectacular part of the destruction of Tweed was past.

The Ring is now dead. Its friends are squirming yet, but they are mortally hurt. They can be left to die in due time. You have in New York worse

22. Massachusetts Historical Society: Autograph Collection of the late Grenville Howland Norcross, of Boston: Horatio Seymour to Marcellus Emery, November 14, 1871.

men than Tweed. Men like Tweed, Fisk, and others, who have brought disgrace upon our country, could have done nothing without the help of the courts. To clean out the foul judiciary of your city is the only great work you can do this winter, and this you can do in a great way. It will excite the interest and attention not only of this State and nation, but of Europe as well. You will have the whole legal profession to uphold you in this work.[23]

If the Democrats were to make an issue of the evil reputation of the Grant administration at the national election in 1872, it was obvious that they would have to reform themselves not only at Albany but in New York. The best men in the party struck directly at Tammany Hall with the proud determination to try to make it law-abiding. When Tweed resigned as grand sachem, the respectable Augustus Schell was chosen as his successor. Schell and John Kelly were eager to draw in the support of all the prominent Democrats. At the annual meeting of the society in April, 1872, Tilden and Seymour, together with Charles O'Conor, Sanford E. Church, and August Belmont, were elected sachems — all of them because they were conspicuous members of the reform movement among the Democrats. An historian of Tammany Hall attributes the coöperation of these able and honest men to mixed motives — they would not only help to reform Tammany, but they would advance their own political fortunes. The suspicion of personal interest was obviously unjust in the case of Seymour, for two years later he declined to become a senator of the United States, and four years later he refused the certainty of succeeding Tilden as governor.[24]

What Seymour did in 1872 was to lend the influence of an honorable name to a sincere effort to capture and control the city organization of the Democratic party. It was the first of such efforts, and it was doomed to disappointment. Tammany's very reason for existence denied the possibility of permanent improvement in the character of the institution. The spoils of

23. New York State Library: Seymour Papers: Horatio Seymour to S. J. Tilden, December 26, 1871.

24. Myers, *Tammany Hall*, 252.

office were the profits which could be collected from all those people who were too busy at making money for themselves to give any time to, or take any trouble for, "public affairs." Seymour's final verdict on the disgraceful history of Tweed and his associates was shrewd and searching — corruption, he pointed out, flourished in every community where good men were too lazy or able men were too greedy to do their duty by the people. Tweed was not the creator of the system he had made infamous; quite the contrary: he himself was its creature.

> It is certain that in the worst days of [Tweed] Ring rule the Ring robbed the city, not by buying up the humble voters, but by getting the endorsement of rich men. The Ring purchased the state governments, not the voters that made them. Tweed was a man of little education, who worked himself up from an humble position, and who found that as he gained wealth he gained the respect of many rich men who denounced him when he was stealing in a small way, but were glad to be associated with him in railroad and other enterprises when he robbed on a large scale. He soon learned that the way to hold his power was not to deal with the humble voters, but to buy officials, gain the favor of heavy taxpayers and associate himself with those engaged in large enterprises. The men of wealth, not men of labor — public officers, not the mass of voters — made him what he was.[25]

The gallant effort against both Tammany and Grant was to come to nothing in 1872, chiefly because of the superb folly of the nomination of Horace Greeley. This strategy afforded what is perhaps the most absurd spectacle in the history of American politics. There is something dramatic in the futility with which the opportunity for change was thrown away. The bad judgment of the gentlemen who assembled at Cincinnati looks almost deliberate. The only excuse which historians have been able to discover was the frigid manner of Charles Francis Adams and Greeley's hope of amnesty for the South. On July 9 the Democratic convention at Baltimore ratified this unwise nomination. For the first time in many years, except for 1860, Seymour did not attend the national convention of his party. If we allow for the circumstances which made 1860 exceptional with him, his absence in 1872 was conspicuous and significant.

25. New York *Herald*, November 4, 1878.

Even a loyal leader like Senator Hendricks sent his regrets. Seymour had absented himself from the state convention at Rochester on May 15 which endorsed the Cincinnati platform.

Some years later an old and intimate friend of Seymour declared that the news of Greeley's nomination was the second and the last occasion on which he had ever seen Seymour lose his temper. It was in the library at Deerfield. George Miller had stopped off on his way back from Baltimore, where he had been sent from Omaha as a delegate instructed for Greeley. According to his story, his host got up from Daniel Webster's chair and "strode across the room with a sort of moderated rage," muttering "raw head and blood bones." [26] What was still worse, Seymour's dearest foe, General Dix, was put up for governor by the Republicans. They swept the state, Greeley falling 42,000 votes behind the total for Seymour in 1868.

Disgusted as he was with this whimsical new departure in politics, Seymour summoned all his powers of self-control in order not to seem to take revenge on Horace Greeley. For a generation the editor of the *Tribune* had reviled and ridiculed the Democrats. Only vanity could have persuaded him to accept what discretion, if not decency, should have compelled him to decline. He had "assailed Seymour with a violence that might well seem to have made any form of political reconciliation impossible. With equal skill he had aimed his epithets at every Democratic statesman and politician from Van Buren to Fernando Wood." [27] Association with him would have been intolerable, and support seemed like a mockery. Seymour was in a difficult position. In writing Tilden in order to return to him a loan of five thousand dollars, he confessed that he could not work up any enthusiasm over the campaign of 1872. He felt he was growing old very fast, and found it especially hard to go out to speak for Greeley, whose "abuse" had been "gross." If

26. New York Historical Society: Seymour Papers: Mr. Miller's account of this interview was set down in 1893.

27. Alexander, *History*, III, 287. In *The American Conflict*, I, 438, for instance, Horace Greeley makes the preposterous charge that Horatio Seymour urged New York to join the southern confederacy in 1861.

he could be employed in "driving negroes out of office," perhaps his nomination could be justified. He himself would vote for Greeley, but whatever he did he would do merely for the sake of Tilden and Kernan.[28]

Eventually Seymour spoke in support of Greeley, calling public attention to the fact that he was doing his best to put politics above personal resentment. At Clinton, in Oneida County, on November 2, he declared that the movement which began at Cincinnati and ended at Baltimore would be unworthy of support if it had been dictated by considerations of strategy alone. The great evil which confronted the public was the "social demoralization" which invariably resulted from war. It was high time that the young and active men should take control of both parties, for their faith and vigor were the one hope left to the old men. Referring to partisan discontent with the nomination, Seymour took occasion to heap coals of fire on the head of the famous editor. "No one has stronger reasons for personal dislike of Mr. Greeley than I have. But I must not let my personal feelings stand in the way of his being made a useful instrument in bringing about reforms." [29]

Seymour's public support of Greeley in 1872 raises the pertinent question as to whether the statesman did not give place to the politician. Andrew Dickson White, whose conscience was never too tender to remain Republican, believed that Seymour cherished an almost religious faith in the divine mission of his party. His liking for Democrats was inherited, perhaps congenital. To speak and vote for Greeley was, in one sense, a breach with the past. The Baltimore endorsement had caught his fingers between the bark and the tree. If he had bolted Greeley in 1872, it would have been only human of his critics to accuse him of personal spite — of having sacrified statesmanship to politics. On the other hand, it is hardly likely that so good a judge of men as Seymour could have honestly supposed

28. Tilden, *Letters and Literary Memorials*, I, 311: Letter of October 3, 1872.

29. New York State Library: Seymour Papers: Clinton, Oneida County, November 2, 1872.

that Horace Greeley would have made a better President than Grant. Whatever may be thought of the general's eight years in the White House, it is difficult to imagine the alternative. It was a heart-breaking decision, for the country had nothing to choose but one of two evils. Just as in the days of 1848, when Van Buren was flattered into costing Cass the presidency, Seymour saw once more the folly and futility of reform founded on hatred. A little less thought as to the disqualifications of Grant might have saved the liberal Republicans from their blunder. Seymour's course in 1872 does more credit to his heart than his head. It is good to remember that he could not vote for Grant, but it is painful to think of his having spoken in behalf of Greeley.

What Seymour did for Tilden, the state chairman, Democrats like Charles O'Conor flatly refused to do, even for the empty honor of being named for governor of New York.[30] The nomination went to Francis Kernan, and to Kernan Seymour gave the strength of his sincere support. Disgust with Greeley and a popular prejudice against Roman Catholics combined conveniently to elect John Adams Dix. The reformers had been too clever by half; their fine-spun schemes for defeating Grant came to nothing at last. The fly in the ointment was Greeley's lifelong aspiration. Tilden alone emerged triumphant among the Democrats, for in 1872 he won the friends who made him governor in 1874 and gave him his plurality at the national election of 1876. Dix, the devout Episcopalian, was a disappointment to his friends. His two years at Albany confirmed Seymour's harsh opinion of his character and his ability. According to the testy biographer of Tilden, Dix was one of those "passive instruments or victims of a class of parasitical politicians in whose eyes the chief, if not the only, use of a government was to enrich those who conducted it." General Dix, it will be remembered, had played no very creditable part in the campaign of 1868, launching a partisan attack on Seymour from Paris, while serving as minister to France by appointment

30. Bigelow, *Tilden*, I, 218–219.

of President Johnson, who was himself supporting Seymour. Gideon Welles formed a most unfavorable estimate of the general's service at Fortress Monroe during the Civil War. According to Welles, Dix "cuddled and favored intercourse with the Rebels, not, I think, for his own personal pecuniary benefit, but under the influence of Ludlow, his aide, and an unscrupulous intimate." Welles thought the general "avaricious," the sort of man who feared and conformed to "the opinions of men in power." [31]

The net result of the nomination of Greeley was a second term for Grant. In New York State the consequences were even more disheartening, for when Dix replaced Hoffman as governor, one gang of spoilsmen calling themselves Republicans succeeded to another gang who called themselves Democrats. There was no difference in principle between these opponents: their only arguments were offices. The Republicans promised little in the way of improvement and they performed less. At first sight, the defeat was most discouraging to the foes of Tweed. Democrats who had refused to work with him were left to the cold comfort of seeing the weight of his bad name drag the whole party down to defeat. The reformers, it is true, had captured Tammany Hall, but they were out of power at Albany. It was obvious that they must work hard to rebuild their party on the basis of their own reputations. Unwittingly, Dix was to contribute to their ultimate success. As governor he was no better, we have seen, than Seymour had supposed he would be. By the autumn of 1873 Seymour returned to the attack. He had been invited to attend a meeting of the new Tammany on the twenty-ninth of October, the annual rally in the campaign for elections to the assembly. In sending his regrets from Utica, on the twenty-seventh, he took advantage of the circumstances to denounce the administration at Washington. Hard times had caught the Republicans in power; for twelve years they had been in control of the government, and now a financial convulsion was following the civil convulsion of the war. Seymour

31. Welles, *Diary*, III, 442–443.

voiced what was already coming to be an old-fashioned alarm at the growth of the central government; it seemed to him as if the power of the states were doomed to disappear.

Reconstruction survived the Civil War twelve years; prosperity survived it eight. Reckoning could not be avoided. The boom of speculation was bound to break, for the country was full of soft money and wild adventure. Railroads were the pet bubbles of the hour, and profits from war-contracts with the government had put riches into the hands of men who could never have earned them honestly and were unable to manage them well. Crops failed in the valley of the Danube, and when Europe began suddenly to call home its investments, American credit caved in. Riches disappeared, and what was still worse, reputations followed after them. The immense ruin of 1873 left six years of gloom and suffering. Even the wolves died with the sheep. It would be sixty years before people lived through such bitter days again — when for a second time the false prosperity of war would work their misfortune. Four times in the history of American business public opinion has shifted suddenly from the extreme of confidence to the opposite extreme of cowardice. The cyclone of 1873 struck Grant at the very beginning of his second term.

The October elections of that year resulted in gains for the Democrats, and these gains Seymour chose to interpret as a warning to "those in power that they are going beyond the limits which will be tolerated by the American people." What those limits might be, he would have found increasingly difficult to determine had he lived much longer than he did. In spite of Seymour's optimistic understanding of the situation, the electorate of 1873 was not voting for state rights — it was voting against hard times. The usual reaction was setting in, and people were making local elections national referendums. In calling for a cutting down in the activity and expense of the federal government, he observed that, while there were "honest differences of opinion as to the constitutional powers of the General Government," that construction of the Constitution which reduced to a minimum the business managed from Washington was the safest. "The prayer to be delivered from temptation," he added, was "as wise in politics as in religion." In the fall of 1873, then, he urged the voters of his state to make their annual election a referendum on the declaration that the Republican party had "assured general stability and prosperity throughout the land" and furnished "a wise, economical and wholesome administration of public affairs both in the nation and in the state." In a trial of strength on that issue, he felt that the Democrats could go before the people of New York with confidence.[32]

By 1874 the panic was in full swing, and the Democrats stood to profit from its effects. Greeley was out of the way, and the disorganizing results of the Cincinnati nomination were being forgotten. A year or more of Governor Dix showed the voters of New York that a change of men had not meant a change of principles. There were rumors that the canal ring upstate had little to learn from the Tweed ring in the city. By pulling down Tweed, the Democrats had cleared the field for a decisive conflict in the state. The chastening effect of defeat and the long and honorable service of Tilden had made his nomination advisable, if not inevitable. In 1872 Dix had defeated Francis Kernan for governor by over 50,000 votes; two years later, the figures were to be almost exactly reversed against him. Just as soon as success hove in sight of the Democrats, his rivals tried to head off Tilden.

Seymour had more than one stake in this campaign, but first of all he felt that Dix should be retired from office. Late in August he was urging Tilden to try for the nomination for governor, even if it meant no more than a martyr's crown. He had a feeling that the Democrats were embarrassed with Tilden's passion for honesty, and would try to put up some one else in his place. The two men had been talking together in Utica in the familiar fashion of veterans of the days of the regency, and

32. New York State Library: Seymour Papers: Letter to the committee on invitations, Tammany Hall, October 27, 1873.

Seymour warned his friend that his views perhaps were "colored by the prejudices of an old man," and that his want of courage resulted less from the difficulties in the way than from the fact that he was "worn out and inefficient." He seems also to have grown cynical about the art of politics.

I feel it my duty to say what I think. The call for honest men is a new form of speech at this time. No *invasive* honesty will be upheld. Our people want men in office who will not steal, but who will not interfere with those who do.

Flattering himself that he enjoyed the ill will of the Tweed Ring almost as much as Tilden, Seymour promised to do his best in rounding up delegates to the state convention. Six sentences betray lost confidence and the vanished hope of youth:

Reformers are hated, and only bear sway when there is a tempest of popular rage against corruption. A new man will be brought out against you after a little time. I do not see any course for you but to go on and take a defeat. You have gained an honorable fame as one who has been sacrificed because you are honest, able, and fearless. The crown of martyrdom is a glorious one. Even those who hate you will be forced to praise you.[33]

Seymour lived up to his promise of doing his best for Tilden in a way that should not harm his friend. He attended the district convention in order to get it to send him as a delegate to the state convention. He had difficulty in identifying Tilden's enemies, but he felt that "every canal official" was "at work to keep" Tilden's "friends out of the convention." His opponents, he thought, were a great compliment to Tilden's character.[34] At Syracuse, on September 17, 1874, the desired nomination was put through on the first ballot, and reform became the issue of the state campaign. Three days later Seymour sent the candidate a letter of congratulation and advice, urging him to make no more speeches, for his only choice would be to talk about his services to the state or discuss national issues, which would alienate the votes of Republicans who might otherwise support him. The true policy was "to look after organizations."[35]

33. Bigelow, *Tilden*, I, 221–222.
34. Tilden, *Letters and Literary Memorials*, I, 335–336.
35. Tilden, *Letters and Literary Memorials*, I, 337–338.

The next day Seymour sent him another letter by means of Abram S. Hewitt. After warning Tilden of the strength of the granger movement in the state, he assured him that Francis Kernan was ready to ease the "soreness among the Irish" over his own defeat of two years before, by campaigning for the ticket at the first opportunity. Now that the nomination was safe in his hands, his first object should be the defeat of Dix. It is difficult not to believe that some personal feeling went into the glad assistance which Seymour offered at this task. In view of the overwhelming success of Tilden at the polls, it is only reasonable to suppose that Seymour might have spared himself the pains of the four letters he wrote during the autumn of 1874. Perhaps he could not deny himself the pleasure they gave him.

Dix, he believed, was a "mercenary man" who had "gained influence from political positions" and "rented it out to companies of doubtful characters for large pay." He had opposed the Civil War until Lincoln made him a general. If the facts of Dix's career could be given to Whitelaw Reid, the *Tribune* might be prevented from supporting him. Much as he valued "the quiet work of organization" within the party, Seymour urged the Democratic candidate to put "travelling merchants and tradesmen at work" in his behalf, for they went into every part of the state and learned what was going on. With this in mind, he sent to Tilden a man with influence among such itinerants to help him build up under his "own direct *private* control agencies" which would "cover the ground outside of the old political machinery." That Seymour was ever jealous of Tilden is very unlikely in view of his vigorous activity in this campaign and the offices he was yet to refuse for himself in 1875 and 1876. It is questionable, however, which motive was uppermost in his mind in 1874 — the wish to elect Tilden or the desire to defeat Dix.

Even though he had to go to Wisconsin on business, Seymour did not neglect the Republican governor. Writing from Appleton, in October, he urged Tilden to get "some of the bright writers of the *World*" to hold Dix up to good-natured "ridicule."

His sketch of the general's political career is a tribute to the power of memory, not charity.

Starting out with a view of being an Anti-Mason, he shifted to the Democratic party for the office of adjutant-general. He hesitated between Cass and Van Buren until he was nominated for governor by the Free-Soilers. He went back to the Democratic party for the New York Post Office under Pierce. He went over to Buchanan for a place in the Cabinet; and from his Free-Soil views he became so violent for the South that he would not vote for Douglas, but supported Breckinridge. After presiding at an anti-war meeting, he at once went over to Lincoln when he was made a major-general. To get a nomination for the French mission he took part with President Johnson. To get confirmed he left him for Grant. In 1868 he intrigued for a presidential nomination from the Democratic party, as in 1866 he had tried to be nominated by the same party for the office of governor. Not getting this nomination he held on to Grant, and in 1872 he got a nomination from the Republicans. I think this history shows that he valued his political principles at a high rate, and never sold them unless he got a round price and pay down.

Two days later Seymour sent Tilden a private letter to inform him as to just how Governor Dix had enlarged his staff and made his son his private secretary after boosting the salary of that office. The people thought the governor got $4,000 a year, but the Dix family managed to collect $17,500. "I do not object to liberal pay," concluded Seymour, "but it does not look well for a reformer to increase his own compensation under pretexts, and then try to get others to submit to retrenchment."[36]

Whatever one may think of these Parthian shafts which Seymour shot in secret from the ambush of his retirement, John Adams Dix was a likely target. The defeat of 1874 marked his exit from the stage of public life. He had served all men and parties with an impartial eye, for first and last he had served himself. Place and power had always meant much to him. Soft acquiescence had given him a nice eye for the art of getting on. When Dix welcomed his successor at the capitol in January, 1875, two disciples of Silas Wright faced each other for the last time. Between the death of the leader they loved,

36. For these four letters, see Bigelow, *Tilden*, I, 227–228 and 232–233; and Tilden, *Letters and Literary Memorials*, I, 341. For a more favorable picture of Dix, see Rhodes, *History*, III, 138–139.

and the day of their meeting again, lay the shadows of the Civil War. Both were dignified, even urbane. Tilden was sixty, and Dix, almost seventeen years his senior, greeted him with words in which the fretful Bigelow could find only "guarded commendation." Tilden, however, was equal to the occasion, though Seymour must have smiled at what was perhaps the unintentional sting of the new governor's statement that he had come to Albany to sustain the administration of their predecessor of thirty years before — the man they held in common admiration, Silas Wright. Again, almost forty years later, still another governor was to go up to Albany with that name on his lips — William Sulzer, the only chief executive of New York who has been impeached and removed.

Seymour had attended the state convention which had nominated Tilden, and his "conciliatory, tactful remarks" had probably prevented an open feud on the floor between the stalwarts and the reformers. He made his preference for Tilden plain, standing before the delegates as "a man loaded down with favors" from his party.[37] Seymour's position had been all the more difficult for the reason that the opponents of Tilden were working for the nomination of another of his friends, Judge Church. He drafted the platform, which, according to Alexander, a Republican, "abounded in short, clear, compact statements, without buncombe or the least equivocation. It demanded the payment of the public debt in coin, the resumption of specie payment, taxation for revenue only, local self-government, and state supervision of corporations. It also denounced sumptuary laws and the third term." [38] Rumors of the ambition of President Grant were already in the air, and six years later Senator Conkling was to fight hard to give him a third nomination, probably with the secret hope of landing a first for himself.

With Tilden as their leader the Democrats entered the campaign of 1874 with confidence. Seymour and Kernan spoke in Brooklyn and New York at the end of October. The former

37. Albany *Atlas and Argus*, September 18, 1874.
38. Alexander, *History*, III, 314.

governor reverted to 1868 and held up to ridicule the contrast between the Republican promises and performance in the matter of the currency. Dwelling on the consistency of Tilden's record as a gold Democrat, he observed that it had taken their opponents six years to grant the meaning of repudiation.[39] Seymour made his last speech of the campaign at Utica, on the Saturday before election-day. When the votes were counted, it was found that Tilden had swept the state and even carried the legislature. Fenton was doomed; for the first time in thirty years the Democrats would elect a senator from New York.

Seymour was at once urged to accept the nomination. His own brother-in-law, also a resident of Utica, would have been his colleague, but the doubtful propriety of taking two senators from one family and the same town seems to have had nothing to do with Seymour's quick and firm decision. Election-day fell on November 3, and before the week was out it was obvious that the Democrats were in complete control. The office was his, not for the asking, but merely the accepting. Not only did he resolve to decline it for himself; he determined to win it for Francis Kernan. On November 11, he wrote the editor of the *Freeman's Journal*, of Cooperstown, that the papers were accurate in declaring that he was not a candidate.

> I have made up my mind that if a man who has reached the age of sixty is not as influential out of office as he can be in official position, he has failed to make a good character and record. At and after that age he should hold an unselfish relation to affairs. I mean to take an interest in public affairs, and to serve my country to the extent of my abilities, but I shall do so in a private station. If my experience or counsels or exertions are of any value, they will be given to uphold those principles which I deem to be right.[40]

Three days later he wrote a second letter for the Utica *Observer* to publish on the fifteenth. Writing privately to a friend in the meantime, he asked his support for Kernan, and

39. New York State Library: Seymour Papers: Speeches of October 26 and 28, 1874.

40. New York State Library: Seymour Papers: Horatio Seymour to S. M. Shaw, November 11, 1874.

called his attention to the letter to be published the next day.[41] A fourth letter, to the Schenectady *Evening Star*, also advocating the choice of Francis Kernan, referred to his own infirm health.[42] According to Henry B. Stanton, one of the reasons for Seymour's resolute refusal was his gradual loss of hearing; he did not care to enter the Senate with "waning powers." [43] Once he had made it evident that he would not take the office, Seymour spent the early winter making sure of success for Kernan. As the time for the caucus approached, he was urged to go to Albany and exert his personal influence on the Democratic members of the legislature.[44]

Kernan, it will be remembered, was a Roman Catholic. In Seymour's eyes this fact added to his availability. Writing to R. A. Parmenter, a legislator who had publicly declared his intention of voting for Seymour, the "great decliner" argued the question carefully and at length. If Mr. Parmenter preferred to throw his vote away, he might do so, but it was high time for the Democrats to recognize the services of what some people still insisted on calling foreigners. The Republicans had appointed Catholics as collector and postmaster in New York City; while the Democrats were open to the suspicion of having no interest in anything but Catholic votes. Kernan had reluctantly accepted the nomination for governor in 1872 in order to counteract partisan appeals to religious feelings, and he had gone down to defeat under the burden of Greeley's candidacy.

In 1874, the Republicans had tried to make a sectarian issue of Kernan's sacrifice, but he had campaigned loyally through the state and without any expectation of reward in view of the fact that the formation of districts for the legislature made it almost impossible for the Democrats to gain control. Now that

41. Horatio Seymour to an unnamed correspondent, November 14, 1874: Letter in possession of the author.

42. New York Historical Society: Seymour Papers: Horatio Seymour to J. J. Marlett, November 16, 1874.

43. Stanton, *Random Recollections*, 239–240.

44. New York Historical Society: Seymour Papers: R. W. Sherman to Horatio Seymour, January 11, 1875.

the victory was greater than had been hoped for, it was high time to take the opportunity to reward and honor Francis Kernan.

> As a Protestant, I repel the idea that those of my faith are ready to persecute those who differ from us in religious opinions; as a Democrat, I protest against any action which shall tell the Israelite, the Unitarian, the Methodist, the Catholic, or men of any other creed, that they are to be proscribed for their religious belief. Even in England, where Church and State are united, Mr. Gladstone, who is waging war with the Catholics, declares that he does not wish to shut them out of the British Senate. The morals and the glory of a State are promoted when every man feels that all its honors are within his reach and that of his children, if they have a right to claim them by virtue of their abilities and good conduct. A religious test is treason to the spirit of our Government. . . . This question is forced upon us and we must meet it in a clear, sharp way. If we fail to do this, we shall be overthrown. Not one thing has been urged against Mr. Kernan but the fact that he has a religion. His morals, his ability and his patriotism are unassailable. Let us meet this question boldly. It can never come in a fairer shape. . . . I did not withdraw my name from the canvass for personal reasons alone, nor to advance the interests of Mr. Kernan. . . . I have no interests which can mislead me in this matter. An honorable office is a temptation to a different conclusion.[45]

Although his health was not good, Seymour went on to Albany in the depth of winter to see the fight through. He was faithful to his word and successful, but making a senator cost him a bad cold. Once Kernan was safely elected, Seymour went back to Deerfield happy at the thought that he would soon be "cut off from Utica by the floods in the Mohawk," hopeful of "a quiet time after the rows in Albany." [46] The canal policy of Governor Tilden was his only political anxiety. Writing him on the eve of his first annual message, Seymour urged the governor to postpone the question of canals to a special message, in order to avoid undue length in his first communication to the legisla-

45. See the two versions of this letter, dated January 8 and January 12, 1875, respectively, in the Seymour Scrap-Books, New York State Library, Albany. The short version of the letter, that of January 12, was published in the press. It contained no reference to religion, but merely restated Seymour's refusal to accept the senatorship and his belief that Kernan should be chosen.

46. New York Historical Society: Seymour Papers: Horatio Seymour to Helen Lincklaen, March 31, 1875.

ture. Having cleaned up New York City, for the time being, Tilden set out on the trail of the contractors who plundered the state by means of the canals. Seymour advised the governor to go slowly for fear of harming the whole system of canals with eagerness to punish those who were in control. He had his own "fixed and settled opinion about the canals," and, because this opinion was a matter of tradition and common knowledge, he did not care to be thought to differ with the governor.[47] The canal ring, it will be remembered, had tried hard to head Tilden off with Church in 1874.

Tilden, however, went ahead in his own way. His reforms led to much ugly gossip as to a coolness between Seymour and himself. Seymour's silence is fully explained by the frequent mention of illness in his correspondence. As a matter of fact, he had two ties of affection to hold his interest to state politics: his nephew, Horatio Seymour, Jr., and Charles Stebbins Fairchild, the husband of his favorite niece, Helen Lincklaen, were both planning careers for themselves at Albany. Fairchild, who was one day to succeed Daniel Manning as Cleveland's secretary of the treasury, was elected attorney-general of the state in November, 1875. Two years later, Seymour's nephew, Horatio Seymour, Jr., won the first of his two terms as state engineer. In the collapse of 1879, he was the only Democrat elected on the state ticket.

By the autumn of 1875, however, the ex-governor felt "too ill and too old to do much" toward campaigning for Tilden's canal reforms. Promising to help all he could, and wondering if his fears did not "spring from the distrust which old men have of the future," he warned Tilden not to be too confident.[48] The reform measures were put through, however, by 1876. The office of canal commissioner was abolished, and in 1878 the whole system of canals was turned over to a superintendent of public works. Through this centralization of authority it was

47. Tilden, *Letters and Literary Memorials*, I, 357.
48. Tilden, *Letters and Literary Memorials*, I, 387–388.

hoped to make grafting in contracts more difficult. Seymour's chief interest was not so much administration as abolition of tolls.

He supported Fairchild in his successful campaign for the office of attorney-general and spoke at Brooklyn in behalf of the state ticket and the policies of Tilden. Though the Democratic majority was cut down in 1875, Seymour believed that the outcome was "the greatest victory our party ever won."

> It leaves us in a perfect condition. The combinations against us were fearful. They are now scattered and crushed out. They cannot be renewed. After the Tweed exposures we were badly beaten. This time we were strong enough to beat our own wrong-doers and the Republican party besides. I do not know of any other instance where a party has been able to reform its ranks and punish the plunderers in the face of the enemy and yet win a victory.[49]

With Tilden at Albany and Kernan at Washington, and both with his blessing, Seymour may have smiled to think how "troublesome" an "old fool" he had been for Tweed since 1871. He had used all the power of his name in New York and brought all his skill to bear against the arrogant boss who had honored three independent and determined Democrats with his burly contempt. At times their good fight had seemed lost, for the enemies of honest government attacked not only in front; they fell on both flanks and the rear. The disciples of Marcy and Wright stood fast, and finally the day was theirs. They had showed Tweed and his kind that they had learned far better than he how to manage men. They had taken Tammany from his control and had driven him out in disgrace. Tilden and Kernan accepted the reward of office, but there remained for Seymour the pleasure of having proved to any one who cared to know that he could work to win without the spur of personal ambition.

49. New York Historical Society: Seymour Papers: Horatio Seymour to G. L. Miller, November 6, 1875.

XX

"ELDER STATESMAN"

1875–1880

TILDEN had retired Governor Dix to the private life which he was not to leave again except for the permanent repose of the churchyard of Trinity. As late as his seventy-ninth year, the inveterate vanity of Dix tempted him to take the Republican nomination for mayor of New York, but he was easily defeated by Smith Ely. It was 1876, the year that Tilden and Lucius Robinson swept the state. By that time General Grant was coming to the end of his eight years, and it began to look as if he were not unwilling to serve for twelve. The campaign of 1876 promised the first fair fight between the two great parties in twenty years. As it drew near, men began to leave their old allegiances. In the minds of hundreds of thousands of voters who had lived through the Civil War, the Republican party was no longer synonymous with the safety of the Union. Young men were impatient of the feuds of old men.

Republican government, moreover, was supposed to be good government; Republican finance was expected to promote prosperity and preserve it. For twelve years there had been no reasonable alternative to offer the voters: secession, the Civil War, the murder of Lincoln, the impeachment of Johnson, the nomination of Greeley — these mistakes had piled one impediment upon another. Since there was only one party "fit to govern," the real battles between honest men and rogues took place within its ranks. Grant forced men to consider the advisability of finding an effective check on that party's monopoly of power. The financial collapse of 1873 made a desire for change popular.

A year later Tilden's sensational defeat of Dix singled him out as the obvious man to change the scene at Washington. If Democrats could sweep before their own door at New York and Albany, it was time for them to go to work elsewhere. Two years as governor would test Tilden's character. The eyes of the hopeful people were fastened on the lean, husky-voiced, secretive, sickly millionaire bachelor of Greystone. Seldom has a national hero been less heroic in appearance and more cautious in conduct than Samuel Jones Tilden. His puzzling character raises a doubt as to whether he could have lived up to the hopes of the men who trusted and admired him. He was all brain and industry. His logic was inflexible and unassailable, but good presidents need more than reason for their great office. They must persuade men to do their will.

The off-year election of 1875 endorsed the canal reforms of Tilden and strengthened his hand in the government of the state. As a means of making improvement permanent, it was proposed to draw better men into the service of the state by raising the salaries of the legislators. Better pay, it was argued, would buy better men. Seymour's reaction to this suggestion was characteristic; his opposition to it was based on his love and respect for local government. Before long he got into print on the subject. His letter to the editor of the *Freeman's Journal* of Cooperstown declared that what was needed at Albany was not more pay but more men. If constituencies were small, he argued, good men would stand for election "at the request of their neighbors"; large districts compelled candidates to submit to the ordeal of an annual campaign among people they did not know.

The reasoning of Seymour makes interesting reading now that the drift is all in the other direction. To-day reformers urge the cutting down of city councils and state assemblies. Nebraska has turned to a unicameral legislature which is hardly more than a big committee. Large numbers of law-makers, thought Seymour, would be less liable to the influence of "the men who hang about the lobbies of the capitol and corrupt its legislation." Although he was commonly accused of an implacable hostility to New England, he thought New York would do well to take a lesson from the six states east of the Hudson. There the lower bodies of the legislatures were numerous, every member representing a relatively small number of citizens. People of consequence frequently took seats in these assemblies and not only lent dignity to their gatherings but attracted other men of ability.

Eventually New York decided to increase the salaries and not the numbers of her law-makers, and the apportionment of the senate and assembly seats has remained a scandal ever since. The state divides the dishonor of rotten boroughs with Rhode Island. Seymour argued that men of small means could go to Albany "without unreasonable sacrifices," if they knew that they would benefit from association with their betters; honest ambition would be encouraged, and the level of the candidates would be raised. He suspected that government could never compete with the rewards of private business, and sixty years have verified his judgment. Public service, he maintained, was a question of character and pride; the adequate reward of it was not money, but distinction.[1]

Every public appearance laid Seymour open to the charge of an itch for office. It was difficult for him to make men believe, especially as the year 1876 drew near, that his concern for politics was impersonal. There is something almost ridiculous in the repeated denials he was forced to put on record. When he refused to succeed Fenton in the Senate in 1875, he was accused of having his eye on the presidency. Even his friends were importunate: if Tilden were to go to the White House, Seymour could return to Albany. Just at this time an indiscreet outburst from Blaine tempted Seymour to contradict the gentleman from Maine publicly. It was a question of the campaign of eight years before. Blaine declared that the Democrats had favored inflation. To say that the national convention of that year had committed his party to inflation was false, wrote Seymour: "in truth, the record reads the other way." Blaine had attacked Pendleton as well as Seymour, and the latter wished to make

1. New York State Library: Seymour Papers: Letter to S. M. Shaw, December 7, 1875.

sure of the position of the senator from Ohio before he answered the orator from Maine.

Writing to his friend Miller, the editor of the Omaha *Daily Herald*, Seymour asked for definite information on the subject. In 1868 Miller had tried in vain to persuade Seymour to declare for the nomination of Pendleton, but Seymour refused to support a "soft money" man.[2]

> I do not know what Mr. Pendleton's position is. The fact that he thought a class of bonds were payable in "greenbacks" does not commit him for inflation nor does it make him an opponent of specie payment. You said in your conversation yesterday that you thought he was a hard money man in principle. Can you let me know if this is so? I hope it is, for I regard him as an important man in the political and public sense and I watch his course with interest. My political career is ended, but I am anxious for the future of the Democratic party and for the country. If Mr. Pendleton can keep out of the financial muddle, his future will be successful. I do not know what will be done at our national convention about finances, but I do know what will be the ultimate fate of all inflationists — all history teaches us that.[3]

During twelve years, his financial notions were consistent: at least he had convictions on the subject. In 1864 he had appealed to the bankers of New York over the head of the legislature in order to redeem the debt of the state in gold; in 1868 he had urged the bringing of the bonds of the United States back to par in the markets of the world; in 1876, he grimly faced the fact that the inflation of the Civil War would have to be paid for sooner or later out of the property and wages of the people. Resumption of specie payment would spell deflation.

At the time of the collapse of 1873 he wrote an interesting letter on the national outlook. He thought the "panic" had "come to stay a while," and stay it did, for six years. It was not really a "panic" at all; it was a fact. Americans had "made too many railroads, too much stock, too many bonds"; they were an "extravagant people"; yet the very policy of economy was go-

2. New York State Library: Seymour Papers: G. L. Miller to Horatio Seymour, May 17, 1868.

3. New York Historical Society: Seymour Papers: Horatio Seymour to G. L. Miller, February 28, 1876.

ing to make a good deal of trouble at the beginning. He was not sorry that the crash had come, for the longer these reckonings were put off the more mischief they worked. He was writing at the dreary dawn of the second of the four great financial misfortunes which have swept over the United States:

> I think we are to have a gradual settling down of prices and shrinking of fortunes. It may be that the government will step in and inflate the currency. In that case gold will go up, and we shall go out to sea again. The future is full of uncertainty. I look for troubled times. By and by it will clear up, and you and your contemporaries will gather in the fruits of the toils, the schemes and speculations, of this day. Increased population and production will in time float off the stranded ventures of the day. I may not live to see this, but you and others of your years will reap the benefit of this state of things.[4]

He drew a quiet satisfaction from the common-sense view of the situation, however clearly he realized that the Civil War had not come to an end at Appomattox. The North and South had done their best to ruin each other, and now the common country was meeting the cost of their unwisdom.

As the time for the national convention approached, the rise of Tilden's stock lifted two anxieties from Seymour's mind. In the face of the governor's availability he himself was relieved of the necessity of having to talk himself out of the picture. The sound-money record of Tilden left no doubt as to where the Democrats would stand at St. Louis. All was safe for the party, and even victory seemed certain. Immediately before the convention, Seymour declared that he would not accept another nomination for the governorship.[5] Once it was settled that Tilden would not be a candidate for a second term, pressure to push him into the place was resumed, for the Democrats knew that they would need the electoral votes of New York and felt that Tilden and Seymour would make an unbeatable combination. Seymour would kill off the candidates they wished to avoid. The state convention was not to meet until late in August,

4. New York State Library: Seymour Papers: Horatio Seymour to an unknown correspondent, September 27, 1873.

5. Horatio Seymour to James M. Thompson, June 5, 1876: Letter in possession of the author.

but as early as July the old governor did his best to prevent the fiasco which followed.

Complaints of illness run through his correspondence; it was the summer of the sun-stroke which took him out of the national campaign that autumn. Unable to write himself, on July 28 he dictated a letter to his old friend, Shaw, which that editor promptly published in his paper. In the four important paragraphs out of the five which comprise this letter, Seymour tried to make it plain that he would never accept a sixth nomination for governor. No more could he hold any office in the gift of Tilden, were the latter, as he hoped, elected President. He must remain in private life, and he only trusted that the state convention would meet in peace, for he did not see how the Democrats could "fail to carry the state." [6] He had declined to be considered a competitor of Tilden at St. Louis; he would not run for governor again; he could not serve in a Democratic Cabinet. Men who hated him said he was jealous; gentlemen who loved him hoped he would change his mind. From any other person three noes would have been enough.

When the Democrats chose their state delegation to the national convention at St. Louis, they assembled at Utica, where certain of the enemies of Tilden tried to use Seymour's name against his. There was gossip that the governor's canal policy had led to "strained relations" between the two men. Seymour countered by openly praising Tilden's canal message as "a great state paper," and came out for his nomination.[7] Tilden took him at his word and set about the hard work of nominating the lieutenant-governor, William Dorsheimer, of Buffalo, as his own successor at Albany. Tammany Hall and the canal ring, however, were determined to get the nomination for Clarkson N.

6. New York State Library: Seymour Papers: from the Cooperstown *Freeman's Journal:* Horatio Seymour to S. M. Shaw, July 28, 1876.

7. See Alexander, *History*, III, 341; and the written recollections deposited in the Seymour Papers, in the New York Historical Society, of George L. Miller, of the Omaha *Herald*; and Mrs. Walter J. Oakman, the daughter of Roscoe Conkling, at whose home in Utica Seymour stayed during the convention of April, 1876.

Portrait at "Marysland"

HORATIO SEYMOUR

Potter. When the state convention assembled at Saratoga on the morning of August 30, a hard fight was in prospect. The supporters of Potter were ready to shout down any suggestion from the Tildenites. Seymour's closest friend in the convention was Senator Francis Kernan, who must have known his mind. According to one story, Seymour telegraphed Kernan "that very afternoon," not to allow his name to be used.[8] The absurd result was a combination of bad management by Tilden's men and bad manners on the part of Potter's. One of the delegates from Utica was J. Thomas Spriggs, representative in the Congress and later the mayor. The Seymours were not quick to forgive his dubious activities on the last two days of August in 1876.

By the time the convention had assembled, it looked as if the only way for the reform element of the party to block the nomination of Potter was to force an acceptance from Seymour. Late in the afternoon he was chosen by acclamation. Then a committee of ten was appointed to negotiate for Seymour's assent. The act was impudent and hardly complimentary to his character. L. B. Faulkner, S. T. Fairchild, and J. Thomas Spriggs were made a visiting committee to call on the candidate at Deerfield. Fairchild was the father-in-law of Seymour's favorite niece. Faulkner, the chairman of the committee, stayed at Saratoga; while Fairchild and Spriggs set out on their diplomatic errand. They took a late train to Utica, arriving there at six o'clock on the morning of August 31. The victim, in the meantime, had got news of what had happened and telegraphed his flat refusal to the president of the convention at midnight on August 30. This telegram was published in the Utica *Herald* the next morning. Its language left no doubt as to Seymour's intentions, but Judge Gray, the man to whom it was directed, did not present it to the convention on the second day of the session.[9] He thought he had good reason for withholding it.

8. New York *Tribune*, September 2, 1876.

9. [Utica, August 30, 12 Midnight]: "To the President of the Democratic Convention: — I learn with surprise and regret that I have been nominated

Just what happened after Fairchild and Spriggs arrived at Utica on the morning of August 31, is not clear. In spite of the telegram which the *Herald* already had in type, Spriggs and the editor of the Utica *Observer* seem to have united in an effort to force Seymour's hand. Fairchild faded from the scene. Seymour's sixth nomination for governor was an accomplished fact. The *Observer* published an editorial which stated that, although the nominee "would prefer to retire to private life . . . he [had] never yet refused to respond to the call of duty" and would not decline the office.[10] Meanwhile, between sessions of the convention at Saratoga, Judge Gray had shown Seymour's telegram of refusal to Daniel Magone, Jr., chairman of the state committee, and Magone advised him to suppress it until word should come from Fairchild and Spriggs. Gray showed the message to the reading clerk, who concurred with the advice of the state chairman. For half an hour the president delayed calling the convention to order for the session of the second day. Then Colonel Faulkner, chairman of the visiting committee of three, received a despatch from Congressman Spriggs. "Go ahead and complete your ticket," read the message. The Democratic managers were delighted. Colonel Faulkner announced Seymour's acceptance from the platform of the convention; Dorsheimer was immediately renominated for lieutenant-governor, and the convention adjourned.[11]

Fairchild and Spriggs started back to Saratoga just before half-past eleven on the morning of August 31. They arrived there too late to prevent the result — whatever the message was which they intended to deliver to the committee and the convention. Seymour was left in a painful predicament: to accept would make him a laughing-stock, especially after 1868;

as a candidate for the office of Governor. While I am grateful for this mark of regard on the part of the Convention, I am compelled by obstacles which I cannot overcome to decline the proffered honor. I shall do all in my power to promote the success of the Democratic ticket at the election, but I cannot be a candidate for any office."

10. New York State Library: Seymour Papers: Utica *Observer*, August 31.
11. New York *Herald*, August 31, 1876.

to decline might be to hand over the governorship to the enemies of the reformers. He might not only make Potter governor; he ran the risk of costing Tilden the state. His best friends considered the "political trick" an "outrage" which would "recoil on its authors." There was much excitement over the situation.[12] Seymour kept his head and asserted himself. More than eight years before he had faced a similar dilemma. He had bitterly regretted his delay. Now, if ever, he had the chance to clear his record — no matter how ungracious his conduct might seem. Though Colonel Faulkner sent him assurance of the "good faith" of the convention, Seymour stood by his decision.[13]

The Democrats had scattered to their homes; he must act quickly if their campaign were not to become a farce. On September 4, he sent a long letter to the chairman of the state committee. Declaring that although he would "cheerfully sacrifice" himself in the circumstances, Seymour added that "a recent illness" had made him unable "to perform the duties devolving upon the Governor of New York." The reference was to his sun-stroke. The present inconvenience of his decision would prove an advantage in the end, he thought, to both his party and his state. There was no doubt about the result of the approaching election, and a change of management at Washington promised nothing but benefit to the United States. Republicanism would be the same under Hayes as under Grant, and the only way to reform public affairs at a time of "business distress and gloom" was to give the Democrats control of the presidency and the House of Representatives. Even though there was no hope of gaining the Senate, the "unchecked power" of one party would come to an end.[14] The letter was published on

12. Manuscript journal of J. V. L. Pruyn, August 31 to September 1, 1876.

13. New York *World*, September 2, 1876: Faulkner's message read as follows: "The state convention, including myself, acted towards you in the utmost good faith. The form of telegram received by me from Mr. Spriggs was agreed upon in the Committee of ten to signify, as its language indicates, your acceptance. I remained in Saratoga to more speedily convey your decision to the Convention."

14. New York State Library: Seymour Papers: Horatio Seymour to Daniel Magone, Jr., September 4, 1876.

September 5, and editorial comment in the press of the country was widespread and, on the whole, flattering. The Democrats were left in disappointment and distress. The Republicans believed that Seymour's refusal to run was a fatal blow to the hopes of their opponents. Even they could afford to be complimentary now to the man they had abused in 1868.[15]

Although the state committee had power to fill the vacancy left by Seymour, the confused situation gave the Tilden Democrats time to perfect their plans. It was decided to recall the delegates to Saratoga. On September 9, a reporter from the New York *Herald* found Seymour weak and ill. Declaring that he himself had never been what people called a "Seymour man," the old governor ventured the opinion that the American system of election "was a pitiful farce" if one man's unwillingness to run for an office were to expose his party to defeat. If the Democrats were prudent, they could even make capital of his refusal by taking note of the objections which had been brought against his name. They would do well to find a man quite unconnected with "the prejudices engendered by the war."[16] When the convention reassembled on September 13, Lucius Robinson was nominated over Potter on the first ballot, by one and a half votes more than were necessary to a choice.[17] As Wellington would have said: it was a "damned near thing." Seymour let his name go on the list of presidential electors. As chairman of the college he made a speech at Albany in December, of which more later.

Ill health prevented him from taking any active part in the campaign. From time to time he wrote to Tilden; reports of interviews with him appeared in the papers. Taxation was the burden of his criticism of the management of the government:

15. New York State Library: Seymour Papers: Scrap-Books, III, 28–32. The editorial comment of the Cincinnati *Enquirer* is characteristic: "When Mr. Seymour says, 'Your candidate I cannot be,' it doesn't seem to have any effect. His nomination, in spite of his declination, is evidence of the esteem in which he is held by the democracy of New York. No stronger nomination could have been made."

16. New York *Herald*, September 9, 1876.

17. Alexander, *History*, III, 346.

> If we can get a Democratic President and House of Representatives, with a Republican Senate, their controversies and efforts to show that each strives for economy will give us relief. Give each party a share of power and they will cut down the cost of government like a pair of shears. One party having all the power will never make reforms.[18]

He warned Tilden that his enemies counted on the large towns to defeat him. Although he was still "out of health" and wrote "with difficulty," he cautioned the candidate that "reform" was "not popular with working-men," for to them it meant "less money spent and less work." Most of these working-men were Catholics. Seymour would fight fire with fire:

> I think it important that some quiet, judicious person should visit the large towns and see the leading Irishmen and call their minds back to the hostility of Hayes and the Republicans to their nationality and religion. There is danger of a loss of vote among the class.[19]

On the eve of the election he put in an appearance at a rally in the Opera House at Utica. Speaking with difficulty, "at the sacrifice of [his] health and against the protests of [his] physicians," Seymour voiced his "intense anxiety" for the success of the Democratic party. Senator Kernan spoke from the same platform, and Charles Francis Adams sent a telegram of endorsement and support. Obviously the old Union party had begun to break up at last. Seymour had to sit until the uproar of his arrival had died down; his husky voice and his fatigue showed his fellow townsmen that his days of stump-speaking were almost over.

Lucius Robinson had worked faithfully with the Lincoln men throughout the Civil War; now he was the Democratic candidate for governor. In calling attention to this fact Seymour laid his finger on a shift in sentiment which was significant.[20] During the twenty years which were to follow until the first nomination of Bryan, the Republicans found that they had lost their "monopoly" of respectable opinion. This was disappointing and surprising. Yet the fact remains that in the five elec-

18. New York State Library: Seymour Papers: October 25, 1876.
19. Tilden, *Letters and Literary Memorials*, II, 470.
20. Utica *Observer*, September 30, 1876.

tions which followed (1876–1892) the Republican candidate for President collected the most votes in only one. In 1880 Garfield's total exceeded that for Hancock by about ten thousand.

Two governors were pitted against each other in the sensational campaign of 1876. As if to supply comic relief, Peter Cooper, the philanthropist, let himself be put up as the candidate of the Greenback party. Hayes, of Ohio, was a veteran of the Civil War; his unassailable record was distinct only for its lack of color. He had won the battle for hard money in his state and had made one of its many able governors.

Tilden, on the other hand, was almost as much of an object of argument as Blaine. The battle raged about his character and his career, and enemies even looked up the records of his private income. His shrewd opinion that it would be dangerous to elect Lincoln President in 1860 — his open support of Douglas at that time — were dragged out against him. During the Civil War he had gone about his own business; he had made money and had quietly reorganized the Democratic party throughout the state. In 1862, at the request of Seymour, he had written the peroration to the Brooklyn Academy of Music speech of October 22 — the speech which served notice on the South that the northern opponents of radicalism had no intention of accepting secession.[21] Working with both Seymour and Francis Kernan, Tilden had led the attack on Tweed. With Nast's aid he destroyed him. Going to Albany in 1875, he had carried reform into the government of the state, and very much to the annoyance of people who would have preferred that he confine his attention to the iniquities of Tammany. Tilden was able and ambitious and, like Hayes, he was honest. In the long run, however, it was just as well, perhaps, that he never became President of the United States.

Just one hundred years after independence there was danger

21. Tilden, *Letters and Literary Memorials*, I, 166–167. Seymour, as the better orator of the two, improved the language of Tilden's draft and significantly omitted pledges to restore home rule to the South.

that the American experiment would blow up. The outcome of the presidential contest of 1876 was a severe test for popular government. By 1870 all the secession states had been restored to their places in the electoral college, and the Republicans entered the campaign with very little private hope of carrying any one of them. They could win, they calculated, with the North and the West, just as they were able to do many times thereafter. As the returns came in, it looked as if a Democrat would go to the White House for the first time in twenty years, for Tilden had swept the doubtful states of the North. He had 184 electoral votes without question, and 185 was a majority of the whole number. Like Hughes in 1916, he went to bed on election night after the congratulations of those who were convinced that he would be the next President of the United States.

On the following day, however, it appeared that the returns from three states were disputed. The Republican managers claimed exactly 185 votes for Governor Hayes. It seemed unlikely that they could make good their claim, for they needed every electoral vote of all three states in question in order to arrive at their magical majority of one. Yet they had the upper hand, for only the House of Representatives was Democratic: Grant and the Senate, presumably, would work together. The longer the argument lasted the hotter it became. Supporters of both Hayes and Tilden consulted the Constitution for an accurate understanding of just how and by whom the electoral vote was to be counted. The Constitution, however, did not convince every one the same way, but it was not the first time or the last that it was found lacking in provision for an emergency. Never before had there been a disputed return from a state; never before had it been discovered that the Constitution contained no provision for such a dispute.

The electoral commission set up by the Congress was the only way out. Five senators, five representatives, and the five senior justices of the Supreme Court — eight Republicans and seven Democrats — examined the returns from four states and decided every case in favor of Hayes by a vote of eight to seven.

It is difficult not to believe that Florida had preferred Tilden. With tact as deplorable as that of Adams in 1825, Hayes offered the first place in his Cabinet to the chief of his lawyers, and with taste as poor as that of Clay, Evarts accepted the office.

Seymour's speech at the meeting of the electoral college at Albany in December, 1876, summed up his opinion of the exciting situation. Here, in the centennial year of the Declaration of Independence, the American people were confronted with the deliberate endeavor to defeat their will. They were "startled by the assertion that there had been discovered in remote Southern States, the exact number of electoral votes which would be given to and would elect the presidential candidate who was not the choice of the majority of the American people." Oddly enough, however, the Republicans had conducted their campaign on the assumption that the "solid South" would go for Tilden. Now they had in view an act of revolution. Their plots involved "anarchy, distress and dishonor." Their "first false steps forced a reluctant South into rebellion"; having almost destroyed the Union, they were now determined to control it by means of corruption. As he announced the vote of New York, Seymour professed to believe that the events of the day would be "recited through the centuries."

The proper way, in his opinion, to obtain the just decision in the great dispute before the nation, was to appeal respectfully to the "virtue and patriotism" of the "great Republican party." On that party rested the heavier responsibility for an honest outcome. He doubted if any honorable member of that party would be willing to snatch at a victory which would prove a curse. The Republicans were in control of the country, and the administration had used the government for partisan purposes at the late election. Nearly one hundred thousand official dependents had been forced to work in behalf of one part of the whole people. What was called politics in the North was denounced as "intimidation" in the South. The great danger was not so much what the Republicans wished to do in 1876, but what they would eventually have to do if any "trick or fraud" placed "the candidate of the minority" in the presidential chair against the wishes of the people. The great question was not which man was to be President but how long a majority could be kept out of power. In four years the Republican party had lost five hundred thousand votes in the North, and had failed to establish itself among the whites of the South. If the Democrats desired nothing more than partisan advantage, they would not regret any of the follies of reconstruction, for these were rapidly driving recruits into their own ranks.

Henry Watterson, of the Louisville *Courier-Journal*, printed threats of a march on Washington to seat Tilden by force. There were days when it seemed doubtful if all Tilden's supporters would accept the decisions which made his rival President. People who remember those wild words and tense days will not find Seymour's warning against violence untimely. The Democratic party was conscious of its strength and its position; it was too confident of the future — too strong, indeed — to use force. Fraud might cost Tilden the office to which he was entitled, but just punishment would surely follow, for the party which controlled the towns, the counties, and the states would ultimately control the country. The leading men of business, labor, and capital should warn the politicians not to go too far. Such men as these could, if they would, force a settlement in accordance with right. Even frenzied rulers would quail before public opinion — once it was aroused.

Seymour was scrupulously careful to speak respectfully of Hayes and Wheeler. He thought too highly of their characters to believe that they would wish to be put at the head of the United States "against the declared wishes of a majority of the American people." To take office from the hands of politicians of Louisiana would be to stand in a pillory, to advertize a fraud. If the Republicans decided their own case in their own favor against the majority of the American people on the certificate of Louisiana, the world at large would know well what to think of the decision. Mexican politics would mean Mexican finances and Mexican disorders. In yielding to the "majesty of the law," the Republicans would serve their own welfare, in the long run.

As he solemnly announced the electoral vote of the state of New York, Seymour performed what he believed would probably be the last official act of his life. Old age and infirmity had relieved him of suspicion, and though faith in the Democratic party may have clouded his judgment, withdrawal from the competition for public office made his love of country unselfish at the same time that it deepened his anxiety for its honor. The speech breathed no threatenings of fire and slaughter, nor did the speaker doom his country to perdition if the decision were to go against his opinion. Seymour still had confidence enough, after all the troubled times through which he had lived, to believe that Tilden would be seated. He overlooked or forgot one important fact. Hayes sincerely believed that an honest vote throughout the United States would have put him without question in the office he obtained.[22]

The merits of the electoral decision of 1877 will be argued to the end of time. Honest elections through the South, Hayes believed, would have given him a large number of its electoral votes. Rhodes thought that a full knowledge of the facts in Louisiana would have led Hayes to refuse the presidency; Schouler, an eye-witness of the electoral count at Washington and a careful student of both candidates and their methods, could not agree.[23] The disappointment of the Democrats was deep and bitter, and the curious conduct of their candidate

22. *Proceedings of the College of Presidential Electors of the State of New York*, 9–27. As Alexander J. Wall has pointed out in his *Sketch of the Life of Horatio Seymour*, 106, this address disproves the statements made by James G. Blaine in *Twenty Years of Congress*, II, 412. Blaine had taken Seymour to task, in the book published immediately after the latter's death, for never having repudiated the methods by which he received the vote of Louisiana in 1868. In 1876 Seymour referred to the politicians of that state as "men . . . of whom they [the Republicans] think as ill as we [the Democrats] do." The burden of Blaine's charge against Seymour seems to be this: that having been forced to swallow camels, he did not strain at gnats. Although it is difficult to determine which vote of Louisiana was more corrupt — the Democratic victory of 1868 or the Republican victory of 1876 — Seymour, at least, did not become President of the United States by virtue of such a vote.

23. Rhodes, *History*, VII, 236; Schouler, *History*, VII, 327, note.

during the exciting days of the canvass of the votes did nothing to lessen their sense of loss. It is doubtful if Tilden, in view of the lack of executive tact which he then displayed, would have made a better President than the deliberate Hayes. His course of conduct showed a rare combination of politics, pedantry, and indecision. The responsibility for the bad management of his case was his own. His faithful lieutenants were left in the dark. The final decision hung by a thread. Conkling, who would probably have voted at least once in such a way as to seat Tilden, was excluded from the commission; the ambitious David Davis dodged his duty by leaving the Supreme Court for the Senate; and Justice Bradley confirmed the sudden change of his opinion with prayer.[24]

It is refreshing to remember that only three senators of the United States share the distinction of having voted to remove one President and to seat another nine years later — Edmunds, of Vermont; Frelinghuysen, of New Jersey; and Morton, of Indiana. All three found Johnson guilty; all three sat on the electoral commission. Of these three Frelinghuysen, in 1877, was a "lame duck" who was to go out of office in March.[25] The gentlemen from Indiana and New Jersey were practical politicians who always went along with their party. Only Edmunds was put to the trouble of squaring his action with his famous reputation for having character and a conscience. The times called for an unimpassioned indictment of what was about to be done. Seymour's speech to the electoral college of New York supplied that indictment in advance of the decision.

By an amendment to the state constitution adopted on November 3, 1874, the term of office of the governor was fixed at

24. Nevins, *Hewitt*, 373.

25. New Jersey has sent four Frelinghuysens to the Senate of the United States: Frederick (1753–1804), who served from 1793 to 1796; Theodore (1787–1862), son of Frederick, who served from 1829 to 1835; Frederick Theodore (1817–1885), nephew and adopted son of Theodore, who served from 1866 to 1869 and from 1871 to 1877; and Joseph Sherman (1869–), nephew of Frederick Theodore, who served from 1917 to 1923: *Biographical Directory of the American Congress, 1774–1927*, 989.

three years.[26] In Lucius Robinson the Democrats elected an upright, if rather rigid, man who had worked with both parties. Robinson defeated former Governor Morgan by over 30,000 votes.[27] Stringent economy and a habit of doing the right thing the wrong way were to turn the tide against him. In the autumn of 1877, Fairchild, Seymour's nephew by marriage, came up for renomination as attorney-general, and was defeated. His ceaseless activity against the canal ring had aroused resentment. He had stood firm in refusing to release Tweed. Tammany and the canal ring united to take control of the state convention at Albany, in October. Although the very men who squeezed out Fairchild put up Horatio Seymour, Jr., for the office of state engineer, the Tildenites were routed. The autumn elections were encouraging, however, and in October even Ohio went Democratic. Republicans interpreted the results as a northern rebuke to Hayes for having withdrawn federal troops from the South. Their opponents chose to consider the vote as a referendum on the robbery of Tilden.

The canal commission had been abolished by amendment in 1876, and Governor Robinson was determined to reward the faithful Fairchild by appointing him to the new office of superintendent of public works. Seymour's letter of advice to Fairchild is characteristic of his caution. It was carefully marked "private." It shows how unwilling he was to have others face the wear and tear of the world from which he himself shrank. Referring to a newspaper notice of Fairchild's probable nomination for the new office, Seymour continued:

> You can best judge if it is best for you to take the place, and I do not wish to say anything on that point. But I hope you will not let anything be done if you do not feel sure that the Senate will confirm you. You have borne a great deal of abuse in the past, but time shows that you were right, and there is a change in the public mind. If you are named for this place, the flood-gates of abuse will open again. If you are confirmed, you can

26. In view of the recent decision to fix the term of office at four years, it is interesting to note that New York has changed its mind more than once on how long a governor should serve. From 1777 to 1822 the term was three years; from 1822 to 1876, two years; from 1876 to 1894, three years again. In 1894 the two-year term was restored; in 1937 it was made four years.

27. Werner, *Civil List*, 167.

shew that you are the man for the office, but if your name is thrown out, you will have no chance to shew that the charge made against you is false. You will rest under the odium excited by your enemies in the public mind. I do not know how the land lies nor what the chances are. You can learn about this. Do not be put up to be knocked down.[28]

Two weeks later Seymour went to Albany and spent three days on this business. He discovered that, owing to quarrels between the Democratic factions, Fairchild's confirmation depended on the Republicans. A second trip to Albany was unavailing, and the office went to another. The old governor had guessed right. A little more than seven years later President Cleveland made Fairchild his assistant secretary of the treasury.

Five years of high-mindedness at Albany — Robinson after Tilden — had worn down the patience of deserving Democrats. The renomination of Robinson split the party, and two tickets were put up in the autumn of 1879 with John Kelly at the head of the second. The result was not difficult to foresee: Alonzo B. Cornell went into the office on a minority vote.[29] Tammany had taken its revenge; the governorship had meant nothing to the Wigwam so long as Robinson was in Albany. According to Alexander, "every Democrat except the nephew of Horatio Seymour rested in the party morgue by the side of Lucius Robinson."[30] Of all the candidates on any one of the three state tickets, the largest vote was given to that nephew.

Seymour himself had been seriously suggested as a compromise candidate in 1879 by the men who knew that Tammany was determined to get rid of Robinson. In a private letter written in February, he had declared that he could not "be a candidate for any office nor . . . accept any nomination if made." Although he could not declare himself publicly for fear of exposing himself "to the charge of declining what would not be offered," he did his best to let it be known that he could not in "any circumstances take any official position."[31]

28. New York Historical Society: Seymour Papers: Horatio Seymour to Charles S. Fairchild, December 29, 1877.

29. Werner, *Civil List*, 167. The vote stood: Cornell, 418,567; Robinson, 375,790; Kelly, 77,566.

30. Alexander, *History*, III, 426.

31. Horatio Seymour to an unknown correspondent, February 24, 1879: Letter in possession of the author.

On April 7, a committee of six, headed by August Belmont, sent Seymour an official request that he allow his name to be offered to the state convention. The action of this committee was the result of "a meeting of Democrats from different parts of the State held in New York on the fifth."

> The reasons which lead your personal and political friends to ask you to reënter public life are obvious. While there are no differences among Democrats upon questions of principle, serious and distracting controversies of a personal character have arisen which threaten the organization of the party and imperil its success. These dangers will be avoided under your leadership. A very large majority of those present concurred in this view, without, however, intending any reflection upon the other gentlemen who have been mentioned in connection with the governorship.
>
> The undersigned believe that the general sentiment was well represented at the meeting referred to, and that the use of your name will prevent any controversy at the next convention, and put an end to all uncertainty as to the result of the election.[32]

Nothing more than a nod of approval from Seymour would have given him his seventh nomination, but he stood by Lucius Robinson.

Immediately after the defeat of 1879 there came a call for Seymour to act as receiver for the party. He alone could quiet quarrels and restore confidence. Seymour wrote to the New York *Herald* in the hope of denying the rumor that he was ready to act as arbiter.[33] Disclaiming any such "influence, wisdom, or impartiality" as was imputed to him, he recommended that factional troubles ought to be allowed to wait for the next state convention. The Republicans came to the aid of the Democrats. The folly of Arthur in trying to force Folger on the state brought the Democrats back with a bang in 1882.

It is difficult to believe, but Horatio Seymour was besieged with requests to become the Democratic candidate for President in 1880.[34] The shower of letters and petitions did not cease until

32. New York Historical Society: Seymour Papers: Among others, Augustus Schell and William Dorsheimer signed this letter, along with August Belmont.

33. New York State Library: Seymour Papers: Letter of November 18, 1879.

34. In the Seymour Papers in the New York State Library there is a large bundle of letters from correspondents all over the country, editors and local politicians among them, urging Seymour to allow delegates to be instructed for

June of that year. As late as June 14, the president of the Western Union Telegraph Company notified him that a special wire was to be placed at his disposal, "similar facilities" having been "tendered other prominent candidates." [35] According to Alexander, Seymour declared early in 1880 that if he had to choose between a funeral and a nomination, he would prefer the first.[36] His correspondence during the next six months supports this statement of his feelings. In December, 1879, John R. McLean, publisher of the powerful Cincinnati *Enquirer*, had approached Seymour on the subject of letting his name go before the public. The old governor thought over his long "private and confidential" answer carefully.[37] After stating that there were reasons why his nomination was "out of the question," Seymour continued:

> I do not like to expose myself to imputations of speaking as if there was danger that I should be forced to decline any honor of the kind. I am somewhat sensitive on that point. A few years back to allay some unreasonable suspicion I allowed myself to disclaim all desire for office, until the Republican papers said with some truth that I declined so much that it must be that I wanted something. I must say there was more declining on my part than was called for, and it has been a cause of some mortification to me.

Tilden refused to commit himself as to a second nomination, and it is not clear just how much of the sentiment for Seymour was stirred up in the hope of playing the old game of using one New Yorker to kill off another. Some of this sentiment, at least, was sincere. In December, 1879, Stilson Hutchins, editor of the Washington *Post*, began to push Seymour's name in that paper. On the third of January Seymour sent him a courteous explanation of his position. If Hutchins would do all he could to make

---

him at the next national convention. Nearly all these letters are endorsed as having been answered.

35. New York Historical Society: Seymour Papers: Letter of Norvin Green to Horatio Seymour, June 14, 1880.

36. Alexander, *History*, III, 451, citing a letter of Seymour to George L. Miller, New York *Tribune*, June 21, 1880.

37. New York State Library: Seymour Papers: Draft of a letter from Horatio Seymour to John R. McLean, December 17, 1879.

it plain that Seymour could not be a candidate and would not take the nomination, he would save him "from the embarrassment of saying anything publicly." Seymour gave his reason for wishing to avoid such action:

If I [make a statement], our opponents will charge that I am unwilling to go upon the Presidential ticket because I feel that the Democrats are to be defeated. This is not true, as I believe we can carry the next election if we are not unwise.[38]

Hutchins was a hard case. Writing him again on January 27 in reference to an article which appeared in the *Post* on the seventeenth, Seymour tried to convince him that the use of his name was inadvisable, quite apart from any personal considerations. He could not carry New York, and if Tilden were not nominated by the Democrats in 1880, then no New Yorker should be. To insist on Seymour's name would merely injure his friends in the party, for any suspicion that he was ready to run would impair what he hoped would be their disinterested influence in the convention.[39] At the suggestion of Seymour, Thomas Dunlap, a joint friend of himself and Tilden, called on the latter early in 1880. Dunlap's report of his visit makes amusing reading. According to the letter he sent Seymour, he found Tilden, who "enquired very particularly after your health and appearance," "quite reticent and full of secretiveness." Dunlap learned much which he was eager to tell but could not put on paper.[40]

As the time approached for the national convention to meet at Cincinnati on June 22, Seymour took the precaution of sending a letter to J. Thomas Spriggs, the delegate who was to repre-

38. New York Historical Society: Seymour Papers: Horatio Seymour to Stilson Hutchins, January 3, 1880.

39. Originals and drafts of the interesting letters and telegrams which passed between Stilson Hutchins and Horatio Seymour are to be found in the Seymour Papers in the New York State Library. Seymour's letter of January 3, 1880, was not only an unqualified refusal to allow the use of his name: he asked Hutchins to discourage in the Washington *Post* all talk of his acceptance. On January 15 he telegraphed Hutchins, who had declined to print his letter of the third.

40. New York State Library: Seymour Papers: Thomas Dunlap to Horatio Seymour, March 17, 1880.

sent the district in which he lived, lest any question should arise as to his "position or purposes." He did not seek the nomination and he would not accept it if made.[41] After the nomination of Garfield at Chicago, there was renewed talk among the Democrats that they should nominate a New Yorker. They needed New York in order to win but they did not all feel that they needed Tilden. Fernando Wood wrote to Seymour from the House of Representatives:

> The nomination at Chicago renders it more evident that the result of the presidential election is dependent upon the state of New York. Our own serious divisions in that state of course imperil success. There is but one way to unite us in New York and to save the party. And that is your nomination. It is the almost unanimous feeling in Congress that you cannot, in view of these facts, refuse to accept the nomination, which is now substantially settled. I do not ask for any reply.[42]

Seymour became less communicative as the day of the convention drew near. He felt that his sensational refusal in 1876 had taught Spriggs a lasting lesson; this time he could rely on him. Cincinnati would know that he meant what he said. The nomination of General Hancock pleased him, and his defeat at the election was a bitter disappointment — all the more so when he found that the difference in the popular vote was hardly more than ten thousand. His own state was to blame. In 1880, moreover, the electoral vote of New York was decisive, as it was to be twice again, in 1884 and 1888. Garfield, he thought,

41. The letter was published in the New York *Herald:*

> My name has been spoken of in connection with the nomination to be made at Cincinnati next week, and as you are the delegate from the district in which I live, I ask you in my behalf to state that I am not a candidate for any nomination to be made by that body, nor could I accept such nomination if the Convention should see fit to present my name to the public. I do not suppose that there is the least probability of such action or that my name will be presented. But I deem it proper to send you this letter to be used if any question should come up about my position or purposes.

Stanwood has condensed the story of this negotiation:

> A movement was begun in favor of Mr. Horatio Seymour, and it made not a little progress in a quiet way. Mr. Seymour was captured by an "interviewer" and expressed himself in such terms that it was believed that he really would not accept the nomination if it should be tendered; and although he received a few votes, there was no opportunity to test his actual strength in the convention: *History of the Presidency*, 412.

42. New York Historical Society: Seymour Papers: Fernando Wood to Horatio Seymour, June 10, 1880.

would have made a better senator than President. Although he felt very kindly toward him and wished him, somewhat later, a "prosperous administration," Seymour had the suspicion that Garfield hoped "to please others instead of making others please him." That, he thought, was certainly not "General Jackson's way." Moreover, the new President's "ideas of constitutional construction" were so "loose" that they invited "schemers." [43]

Seymour's satisfaction at the nomination of Hancock was not quite consistent with his opinions in the past. He had never favored military men for civil office. Washington was an exception, and Jackson had been blown into power by an explosion of popular will. At times, Seymour thought, he had acted dangerously like a dictator. The naming of Harrison and Taylor was unwise of the Whigs, and Scott was an obvious failure as a candidate. McClellan was not his first choice in 1864, and Grant had been an appalling disappointment. General Hancock, however, was also without experience in politics, and Seymour had to confine his praise of the nominee to his success as a soldier who had always been obedient to law.

In the campaign of 1880 the Democrats labored under a double disadvantage. In the first place, the return of prosperity made it difficult to deny the specious Republican claim to the credit for the recovery. Failures of the crops in Europe caused an unusual demand for the surplus products of the United States, and the increased purchasing power of the farmers which resulted restored confidence and cash to business. The panic of 1873 had worn itself out. In the second place, restoration of home rule to the South revived the sectional antagonisms of 1860. Republicans argued that the election of Hancock would put the South in the saddle again — as they insisted it had been before the Civil War.

Picking up the public utterances of Schurz and Sherman and Cameron, Seymour tried to show that the nationalism which Garfield openly acknowledged and desired was a snare and a delusion. The term "nation," he declared, had been selected

43. New York *Herald*, March 25, 1881.

because it was "a word of obscure and indefinite meaning" which would cover the intended change in the character of the Union and any partisan plan to retain control of it. If government were to gravitate to Washington, as Garfield hoped, then the Senate, which had been designed to protect the small states, would soon become a menace to the large ones. It was necessary only to compare their respective populations to discover that the loser in the long run would be the North, and not the South or West.[44]

If the South, moreover, were ever to combine with the new "rotten-borough" states of the West, the majority of this "nation" would find itself at the mercy of a minority. If, according to the congressional resolutions of 1876, "the Constitution was framed by the people acting in their primary and individual capacity through their representatives thereto duly constituted," then the people could change the Constitution in the way they made it — without regard to the states. Seymour scented danger. In 1880 he argued as if he believed that there were effective ways of protecting people from themselves. If such was his thought, time has shown that he was mistaken.

In comparing the attitudes of the two candidates Seymour imagined Garfield "communing with himself" and resorted to the dangerous expedient of putting words into his mouth, and printing the soliloquy between quotation marks. The context made the oratorical convention plain, and the words were not altogether unlikely for the expression of the sentiments of an ardent admirer of Hamilton. Garfield, however, indulged in some self-righteous indignation: Seymour had made him say what he had never said. It was outrageous to be accused of having stated, for instance, that "Hamilton was right when he said that Senators should hold [office] for life. I am glad that his opinions grow in favor. He did not like our Constitution, but said everything depended upon the way it was construed."

44. New York State Library: Seymour Papers: Speech delivered at the Utica Opera House, September 15, 1880: *The Purposes of the Republican Party Hurtful to the Rights and Interests of the People, and Most so to those of the North!*

Early in October Garfield wrote to a friend that Seymour's answer to his letter of acceptance was "a gross breach of honor" provoked by his praise of Hamilton and his affirmation of the nationality of the general government.[45] Seymour's intention was innocent, but his use of quotation marks was rash, if not dangerous.

Seymour's health never completely recovered from his exertions in the campaign of 1880. After his speech at Utica he attended a rally at the Academy of Music, on October 21, in Brooklyn; on the twenty-ninth he spoke at Little Falls. He spoke again at Watertown on Saturday, October 30, just before election-day, November 2.[46] The addresses at Brooklyn and Little Falls were devoted to the question of the tariff. State taxes, he pointed out, were levied on "property," but those for the support of the federal government fell, in fact, upon "persons," for the tariff was a tax upon what men used. As a rule, the largest families paid the most revenue. Both parties agreed that the federal government should raise the money necessary for its debts and current expenses from levies on imports, collections on which had amounted to about two billion dollars in fifteen years.

Beyond the need for revenue, however, the tariff should not go; deliberate protection would work harm to the whole country. Prosperity had returned to the United States largely as the result of the sale abroad of surplus crops, but the people of Europe would have to pay for the food they needed by means of the export of manufactures. If American industry were unwilling to allow these imports, if the Republicans were to carry what they called protection to the logical limit of exclusion, people who refused to buy in Europe would soon find they could not sell there. As the rates of the tariff were raised, moreover, the revenue would fall. Americans had seen Republican policy sweep their flag from "the oceans of the earth"; in twenty years

45. Smith, *Garfield*, II, 1028–1029: J. A. Garfield to J. C. Hamilton, October 5, 1880.

46. New York State Library: Seymour Papers.

the merchant marine had disappeared, and now it began to look as if the foreign markets would go, too.[47]

In the last of his four speeches Seymour returned to his attack on the Republican interpretation of the Constitution. Governments perished from two causes: violence from without and corruption from within. The theory and threat of secession had been argued and used almost from the foundation of the Union. Secession, however, had come to an end with the Civil War. The danger from corruption remained. If the federal government were to continue to usurp the functions of the states, that danger would increase. Every year of our history has made this argument sound more academic than the year before. Six weeks earlier, in answering Garfield, Seymour had dwelt on the ideal safety provided by a constitution of checks and balances. For him, the "President, the Congress, and the States" seemed designed to work together under the Olympian supervision of the judiciary. The Supreme Court was the last authority on "the supreme law of the land." Just where and how the Constitution gave that court the power to declare an act of the Congress unconstitutional, Seymour did not say. The only difficulty he acknowledged was one of spirit and not letter. Bad policy had made mischief since 1860:

> Until within the past twenty years, the Executive, the Legislative, and Judicial Departments, gave honest construction. . . . They did not seek to usurp power by strained definition. They sought to carry out its spirit.[48]

By implication, then, it was the Republicans who had perverted the federal government. The case was not quite so simple. There was more than one fly in the ointment of this theory, and Seymour could not or would not see it.

The Constitution was put together by men who had no mandate to make a new government, for they were delegated merely to revise the Articles of Confederation. Their new frame of government was accepted by the narrowest of margins. A workable union of the thirteen free states was the necessity which

47. See the Utica *Observer*, October 28, 1880.
48. New York State Library: Seymour Papers: September 15, 1880.

knew no law in 1788. Patrick Henry openly denounced the document of 1787 as a pig in a poke. Years later President Jefferson complained bitterly of the "twistifications" by which John Marshall adjusted the Constitution to his own ideal of government. Jackson simply defied the Supreme Court, and Taney's cold logic showed the alarming implications of a dubious assumption or extension of judicial power.

Americans who think of the Supreme Court as the last and safe protection of the Constitution are pleased to forget or wish to conceal two facts. Even if it be granted that the court was supposed to have the unwritten power to disallow laws of the national legislature,[49] there remain the two difficulties that the size of the court was not fixed, and the extent of its appellate jurisdiction is left to the Congress. President Grant has often been unjustly accused of having packed the court in order that it should reverse itself on the question of legal tender. Readers of Charles Warren will discover that this is not the whole story. The Senate itself did the packing by means of securing advance and secret information as to the opinions of the two men proposed for membership before it would agree to their appointments. The publication of Nevins's *Hamilton Fish* confirms this view of the facts.[50] The Supreme Court has always been used as a political tribunal.

Still again, in wrangling over the question of sovereignty as between the Union and the states, lawyers are likely to forget that only the people are sovereign, whether they act through the states or the nation. Washington had the good sense to foresee that the Constitution could be changed in whatever way the voters might desire. Ballots could abolish it. Sovereignty of states, moreover, was dealt its first blow when the citizens of thirteen acting together admitted (that is, made) the fourteenth. Vermont showed which way supremacy would shift. How could the creature be thought superior to the creator?

49. In this connection, see the *New Republic* (September 18, 1935), LXXXIV, Number 1085: Max Lerner, "John Marshall's Long Shadow," 148–152.

50. Allan Nevins, *Hamilton Fish* (New York, 1936), 305–307.

It was questionable, moreover, if the Union had authority to enlarge itself beyond the territory acknowledged as independent by Great Britain in 1783. New England was quick to see the import of Jefferson's purchase of Louisiana, and Yankees talked secession when the first state was set off in the great valley in April, 1812. In 1788 the population east of the Berkshires made up about one-third of that of the whole country; in 1930 it was less than one-twentieth. By 1880 twenty-five of the thirty-eight states had been established by federal act. Union was no longer a matter of law; it was a condition of mind. State rights became the refuge of lost causes.

On October 28 Seymour addressed an open letter on the tariff to William Dorsheimer, state chairman. It was his opinion that the commercial interests of the city, the state, and the whole country had never been in greater peril. During the past two years American exports had amounted to about $1,500,000,000 and the favorable balance of trade resulting had benefited every kind of industry. The only danger was that European countries might try to check American exports by heavy taxation. So far the desire for cheap food had prevented this policy, but the Republicans were making arguments for British landlords. "They contend that all countries should produce everything they need as far as possible within their own boundaries and should buy nothing of others if they can avoid it." The telegraph carried these words to Europe over night. If such doctrines were true in the United States, they were equally valid in Europe.

The chief income of the federal government was raised by taxes on imports. The object of a tariff for revenue was the maximum return. What was called a "protective" tariff would not protect until it became prohibitory. When owners of real estate and the stocks of railroads cheered Republican speeches in favor of protection, they gave their support to the very policy which would deprive the farmers first of their markets and then of their purchasing power.[51] Seymour's case against protection

51. New York State Library: Seymour Papers: Horatio Seymour to William Dorsheimer, October 28, 1880.

attracted favorable attention even after the defeat of General Hancock. Alexander Mitchell, for instance, president of the Chicago, Milwaukee and St. Paul Railroad, while laying the loss of the election to an "army of office-holders, the unprecedented use of money, and the prosperous times," praised Seymour's speech on the tariff and pointed out the political and popular confusion between free trade, which was impossible, and freer trade, without which the United States could not get along in the world.

Seymour's convictions on this subject were not trumped up for the campaign. In 1884 the Democrats of New York hoped to dodge protection as an inconvenient issue. Cleveland was to face it with misfortune four years later. Writing to the Honorable Fred A. Conkling, Seymour put his notion in a nutshell: "I do not see how we can hope to hold the position of declaring to the world that we expect to sell what we produce to all the world *free from duties*, while we intend to shut out from our country the products of other people."[52]

Although the popular vote of the nation was almost equally divided in 1880, the return of good times had saved the Republicans with the narrowest of margins. The part New York played in the result reflected very little credit on that state. Hancock himself believed that he had been "knifed" by "Honest" John Kelly. Late in November, in a letter acknowledging Cyrus Hall McCormick's protest that the Democrats had been cheated out of an election for a second time, he wrote: "There is no doubt we would have gotten through safely but for the peculiar results in the cities of New York and Brooklyn."[53] Garfield's nomination had soured the suspicious John Sherman; his election discouraged Horatio Seymour; his administration made a deadly enemy of Roscoe Conkling. On May 14, 1881, both the senators from New York State resigned as a protest against the President. The failure of the legislature to rebuke

52. New York Historical Society: Seymour Papers: Horatio Seymour to F. A. Conkling, April 3, 1884.

53. Hutchinson, *McCormick*, 356–357: W. S. Hancock to C. H. McCormick, November 28, 1880.

Garfield with their reëlection was a momentary triumph for the government at Washington. The secretary of state was Blaine, whose feud with Conkling was notorious. Days of anger were not over. Then Guiteau murdered Garfield, and Arthur made sport of the anxiety of his friends and the alarm of his enemies by making an excellent President. But he dabbled his way to a party defeat in New York and failed to get himself put up for election.

Then finally in 1884, it looked as if James Gillespie Blaine would come into what was thought to be his own at last. The end of his heart's desire was in sight: he was nominated for President of the United States. Once again it seemed likely that the election would turn on the result in New York. John Kelly of Tammany was predicting Cleveland's defeat. Conkling was in retirement. Ironically enough "the tattooed man" from Maine was just the kind of politician that the former Republican boss of New York could understand and might have admired — except for a little argument of eighteen years before.

It was April, 1866, and Blaine and Conkling were colleagues in the House of Representatives. James Barnet Fry had come up for promotion, and Conkling, who had quarrelled with the provost-marshal-general, rose to excoriate him in his special style. Blaine flew to his defence, accusing Conkling of having drawn two salaries from the federal treasury. The congressman from Maine had the last word, but he would live to regret it.

As to the gentleman's cruel sarcasm, I hope he will not be too severe. The contempt of that large-minded gentleman is so wilting; his haughty disdain, his grandiloquent swell, his majestic, supereminent, overpowering, turkey-gobbler strut has been so crushing to myself and all the members of this House that I know it was an act of the greatest temerity for me to venture upon a controversy with him. But, sir, I know who is responsible for all this. I know that within the last five weeks, as members of the House will recollect, an extra strut has characterized the gentleman's bearing. It is not his fault. It is the fault of another. That gifted and satirical writer, Theodore Tilton, of the New York Independent, spent some weeks recently in this city. His letters published in that paper embraced, with many serious statements, a little jocose satire, a part of which was the statement that the mantle of the late Winter Davis had fallen upon the member from New York. The gentleman took it seriously, and it has given his strut additional pomposity. The resemblance is great. It is striking. Hyperion to a satyr, Thersites to Hercules, mud to marble, dunghill to diamond, a singed cat to a Bengal tiger, a whining puppy to a roaring lion. Shade of the mighty Davis, forgive the almost profanation of that jocose satire! [54]

Conkling never forgot or forgave Blaine's sarcastic ridicule, and Blaine, again, was at Garfield's right hand in the battle over spoils in 1881. Asked if he would take the stump for the Republican candidate, Conkling replied: "No, thank you, I don't engage in criminal practice" — and might have added "any more." Two anonymous and savage attacks on Blaine's career appeared in the New York *World* for May 29 and August 12; Conkling was counsel for the *World*, and two years later the handwriting of one of the manuscripts was proved, so it was said, to be his.[55] He had beaten his brother-in-law Seymour in Oneida County time and again; surely he could beat Blaine. He had lost his seat in the Senate, but the man from Maine should lose even more. Oneida had gone for Garfield by 1946 votes in 1880; in 1884 Cleveland carried it by 33 votes.[56]

"That defection alone," writes Muzzey, "cost Blaine nearly double the number of votes necessary to affect Cleveland's plurality in the State." Whether or not Conkling's revenge was the decisive factor in the result, as Thomas Collier Platt and Charles Anderson Dana both believed, depends on one's definition of "decisive." If the election had not been close, the hate of Conkling would have been ineffective, to be sure, but consider-

54. *Congressional Globe*, April 30, 1866, 2299; and D. S. Muzzey, *James G. Blaine* (New York, 1935), 60–62; 307–308. According to Muzzey the quarrel had begun when Conkling, for mistakenly putting a couplet about Utica in Addison's *Cato*, had lost a bet of a case of champagne to Blaine; any dispute between these men over principles was said to be nothing more than a disguise for personal animosity.

55. Russell, *Blaine of Maine*, 403.

56. The record of Oneida County is interesting: 1880: Garfield, 14,546; Hancock, 12,600; 1882: Cleveland, 13,673; Folger, 8,741; 1884: Cleveland, 13,823; Blaine, 13,790; 1885: Hill (Democrat), 11,693; Davenport (Republican), 12,596; 1888: Harrison, 16,241; Cleveland, 14,276. Roscoe Conkling resigned his seat in the Senate on May 14, 1881; he died on April 18, 1888. The three presidential votes in Oneida County are significant: Garfield carried it by 1,946 and eight years later Harrison carried it by 1,965. The vote of 1884 was exceptional and decisive.

ing the circumstances, it is difficult not to think that except for this personal feud, Blaine, and not Cleveland, would have become President in 1885. The Mugwumps did the talking, but for once in his life Conkling and those independents he had always called "male milliners" had the same end in view — to impose the discipline of defeat on the "only party fit to govern."

Seymour's satisfaction at having a disciple in the White House must have been qualified by his knowledge of the motive of one man who helped to put him there. The Mugwumps took the credit for themselves; angry Republicans like George Frisbie Hoar blamed Burchard's indiscretion or John Kelly's frauds according as fancy directed. Democrats fondly believed that the election had turned on the public record of Grover Cleveland. The better man had won, and the better man ought to win sometimes. Now, for the first time in twenty-eight years, their candidate would become President. Yet the feather that shifted the scales in their favor had been plucked long before from the tail of a "turkey gobbler."

XXI

"OLD HUMBUG OF A FARMER"

1880–1886

TOWARD the end of the Civil War Seymour left the family home in Utica and moved two miles north into the country across the Mohawk. There a little west of the village of Deerfield he put up a plain wooden dwelling at the top of a low hill from which he could look southward over the rolling land of the valley. In 1864 the view was even more beautiful than now. This farm of five hundred acres was one part of his wife's share of the Bleecker quarter of Cosby's Manor. He named it "Marysland" and was proud of its soil and the simple comfort of the unpretentious house.[1] For almost a quarter of a century thereafter this place was to be his home. Whenever the deep snows of winter and floods of spring cut him off from Utica, Seymour and his wife had a chance to enjoy the rare pleasure of being alone. At the time he left town he turned over all the business of the family estate to his younger brother, who practised law and collected rents.

Horatio Seymour was only fifty-four, but reading, playing the farmer, and writing letters amply filled up the days when he was not called on to officiate at some local function. He was well known for miles about the country, and the whole community came to regard him as a convenience. He might just as well have been a clergyman. Young reporters in need of copy — even correspondents from the New York papers — seldom failed to stop off at Deerfield. Seymour could not only talk well; he was good at listening, and as he grew old his willingness to

1. In the autumn of 1871 he was so busy "rebuilding" this house that he had "no heart" for the work of writing an article on "House Adornment" for the New York *World*: Horatio Seymour to A. B. Crandell, October 10, 1871: Letter in the possession of the author.

HORATIO SEYMOUR'S HOME AT DEERFIELD

1864–1886

see people did not lessen. He was courteous and nearly always interesting or amusing. He would never play the social entertainer, however: "Unless the subject interested him, he would sit in dreamy silence, and was often a failure at dinner, where he could not 'talk to order.'"[2] Knowledge of books and men had taught him much, and his comments and not-too-frequent quotations show a wide acquaintance with American history and English literature. He knew the Bible well and shared with Charles II that amiable monarch's love of *Hudibras*.

As years passed he became a familiar figure all over central New York. He never had to stay at home, for he farmed his land by tenants, and his real delight in the country was his large garden, which he let run wild. He liked to go hunting in the Adirondacks in the autumn. Although he was fond of horses, he was a great walker by preference till he grew old, when he drove his own old-fashioned buggy. Every cause and every anniversary levied on his tongue and pocket-book.

Standing almost six feet, slender until the last years of his life, and noticeably erect, Seymour adorned scores of platforms, indoors and out, his voice clear and resonant, his hazel eyes lighting up and darkening as he spoke, his large, sensitive mouth always ready for a smile. Though he wrote out his speeches, he never read them, nor would he use notes. Multitudes of men admired the manner which some called charm and others guile.[3] Numbers of good citizens professed to see in Seymour the restless ambition of Satan; social climbers accused him of pride. Friendly descriptions of him dwell most often on his eyes and mouth, but perhaps the most striking feature of his appearance to the present generation was the fringe of beard which extended from one ear to the other beneath his chin in the fashion of

2. New York Historical Society: Seymour Papers. The words quoted are those of Miss Blandina Dudley Miller.

3. Chauncey Mitchell Depew was never at any time a friend of Seymour; he was, in fact, his political opponent at a very important moment (1864), but Depew's disciple, the historian Alexander, writes of Seymour's "handsome face," "luminous eyes," "fascinating manners," and "sound judgment": Alexander, *History*, II, 61.

Hamilton Fish and Horace Greeley. Except for the latter's spectacles there is a fleeting resemblance between Seymour and the implacable editor of the *Tribune*. In character these men were utterly dissimilar, for Greeley's ambition was the nightmare of his party, and his pride of opinion and verbal violence were the despair of those who had to disagree with him. To Hamilton Fish, on the other hand, the likeness both in manners and character was striking. Although these two men were always political opponents, they were always good friends. The enemies they had in common called them a couple of purse-proud aristocrats. Horatio Stevens White, the son of another lifelong Republican, Andrew Dickson White, was given his first name in honor of Seymour.

Except for business trips into the Middle West to look over his land in Illinois and Iowa and the development of his interest in the Fox and Wisconsin Canal, Seymour rarely left his native state by choice. Before the Civil War he and his wife would sometimes summer at Newport, where he made many good friends among southerners and gained a valuable understanding of their difficulties and their ideals. As a delegate to the national conventions of his party he visited various parts of the country, and his campaign tours of 1856, 1864, and 1868 took him all over the North at one time or another, from Massachusetts to Minnesota. Oddly enough, however, he had never been south of Washington before 1873, when he spent a part of the winter in Florida.

Although he was thinking of a trip abroad in 1869, the year after the fatigue and strain of the presidential campaign, he never carried out his plan. The chief reason was probably not lack of money, for while Seymour himself was not so rich as he was frequently supposed to be, his wife owned real estate and drew rent from Utica, Albany, and Troy. The governor could have had a foreign mission from Buchanan in 1857, but just at that time the Wisconsin venture was getting under way, and he preferred to stay at home. Occasional visits to New York City in the winter for tours of the shops and picture-galleries, with the St. Nicholas Hotel as headquarters, seem to have been the only desire which could draw man and wife from Deerfield. There were relatives to visit in northern New Jersey, and it was at their home that Seymour was staying for a week-end in 1863 when chance news of the riots made him hurry back alone at night to the city he had left three days before.

Seymour liked to take his ease with dignity. That he should be willing to sacrifice public fame for leisure was puzzling to his political opponents. The calm with which he met both good luck and bad, moreover, annoyed people with less experience and poise. Neither abuse nor defeat could ruffle his self-possession. Miss Murray could not forget how she had watched him at close range all through the strenuous days of the counting of the votes in 1854. The bitterness was unbelievable, and every new report seemed likely to change the result. Yet Seymour himself was the coolest and most unconcerned of all his household and supporters. If this was hypocrisy, it wore well, for ten years later, at the time when Reuben Fenton was declared governor in questionable circumstances, an intimate friend found the Democratic candidate "cheerful at the result — as a man from whose mind a load has been lifted." [4]

Seymour had the dangerous habit of making fun of himself — the kind of humor which goes with money and independence of mind. When Grant visited Utica for a reunion of the Army of the Cumberland in 1875, his former opponent was called on to perform the delicate task of introducing the President to the audience at the Opera House. After complimenting the distinguished guest on his military fame, Seymour went on to remark that although he himself had never sought success as a soldier, the fact was undeniable that on the one occasion when they two had met in conflict, the general had run much faster and much farther than he. Victors can afford to be generous; the conventions of politics require that they should be, but the poisonous campaigns of 1854, 1864, and 1868 put Seymour's strength of character to a genuine and a severe test.

Although the very best authority assures us that a soft answer

4. New York Historical Society: Seymour Papers: Sidney T. Fairchild to Mrs. Charles S. Fairchild. Copy from a blotter-book of 1864.

turns away wrath, Seymour was never successful at silencing all his critics. In 1864, for instance, when Cassidy, the editor of the *Atlas and Argus*, declared that Seymour was "as fascinating as a woman in the executive chamber," the angry editor of the rival *Knickerbocker* protested that, for all his winning ways, the governor of New York was "more dangerous than an angel who does improper things." [5] In October, 1863, the Rochester *Union* elaborately likened Seymour to Robespierre: both were "timid and nervous," "crafty," and "decorous," "as precise as a Puritan Minister"—neither was a "drunkard" or a "glutton," or "licentious"; each was a "busy man" of "spotless linen" and "dainty" abstractions. Readers were urged to look further into the striking similarity between their governor and the "smooth-spoken" Frenchman who had been his "lamented predecessor." [6] It may have amused the living part of this parallel to notice that it took nothing less than a civil war to clear him of the charge that love of drink had driven him to veto the Maine bill. The "tippler" of 1854 became the "traitor" of 1864.

Yet it was not alone the desire for leisure which drew Seymour away from his youthful interest in public life. The popular sentiments of the violent times through which he lived led him to distrust the immediate verdicts of voters. He came to believe that he would never live to see what he hoped for. He called the Lincoln draft a "lottery of life" and he learned to look on elections, also, as lotteries. Three of his nephews dabbled in state politics after his retirement, and he did his best to discourage them all. In 1881 he wrote a characteristic letter to the son of his older sister, Mrs. Rutger B. Miller:

> I do not like your idea of staying at Albany two years longer—I have been anxious to have you and Horatio come away. All the time you spend there is lost, and at the end of two years you will be worse off, for you will be older and less fitted for permanent pursuits. The older you grow the more difficult it will be to get any suitable occupation. A small compensation in private life is better than a larger one . . . which you hold at the good will of others and which you may lose at any moment. I urged Horatio

5. New York State Library: Seymour Papers: Scrap-Books, XI, 86.
6. Rochester *Union*, October 3, 1863. See page 353.

Seymour to give up his office if he could earn only five hundred dollars a year in some business. When you come to Utica, we will talk the matter over.[7]

Public service, he would have agreed, might be a duty, but too much of it for one man was a luxury. The strife was hard; the dust was thick, and the palm withered.

Apart from his low opinion of place-holding as a profession, Seymour cherished the ambition to succeed as a man of business. He bought heavily in land and held on. Most of the one or two hundred thousand dollars he was supposed to be worth at the time of his death was tied up in the West. He was never eminently successful as a money-maker, however, and according to his own report he suffered "severe" losses in Wisconsin — through no fault of his own. When his political enemies taunted him with being afraid to face the wear and tear of the world, they were talking of a man who honestly preferred his private business to the ornaments of office — especially after his one "respectable" term as governor. His father left politics to care for his fortune; why should he not do likewise? Although he had no children to inherit what he might leave, there were numbers of nieces and nephews in the offing, and Seymour himself is said to have been generous to a fault.

One story told of him is typical: in 1876 the Democrats of Oneida went in deep to carry the county for the party, working with the understanding that the cost of their campaign would be met by Tilden and his friends. Tons of documents arrived from New York, and the county committee's bill for postage alone amounted to more than four hundred dollars. At the end of the campaign the Democrats were still fifteen hundred dollars short. Bills had to be paid, but the cash from the state committee failed to arrive. As a last resort, the local leaders turned to

7. New York Historical Society: Seymour Papers: Horatio Seymour to Henry S. Miller, December 21, 1881. Horatio Seymour, Jr., served four years as state engineer, having been twice elected to that office, 1877 and 1879. The first time he received more votes than any other Democrat on the ticket; in 1879 he was the only nominee of his party to be elected. Many voters probably mistook the nephew for his uncle.

Seymour, asking him to use his influence with the party to get the promised money. When he heard their story, he drew his own check for the deficit and never mentioned the matter again.[8]

That Seymour's hobby was politics is not strictly true. Nor was farming his chief interest. According to the reminiscences of a neighbor, Seymour always called himself "an old humbug of a farmer" — he was, so this observer thought, "far more theoretical than practical." His real hobby was the Erie Canal.[9] Sooner or later he got back to "Clinton's ditch," the enterprise which had given his state its imperial place in the Union. "My interest," he told a reporter from the New York *Herald* in 1881, "has never flagged. . . . I may fairly say that the canals have kept me in their harness from my youth up."[10] The very next year Seymour was to prove his point with his vigorous support of the startling but shrewd proposal to abolish all tolls. For New York to continue to collect tolls on the Erie Canal would be as foolish, he declared, as for a city to levy a tax on those who used its streets. The canal had made New York the gate and the highway to the West, and for eight months of the year it would regulate the rates of railroads better than men could ever do. The whole state had profited from it ever since 1825. Within three years of his death he saw the Erie Canal a free waterway at last.

Amid all the alarm at the competition for the traffic in grain which passed through New York, Seymour, it is interesting to notice, had the foresight to predict that the real danger of rivalry would come, rather, from the direction of the St. Lawrence "after the enlargement of the Canadian canals." There were, he pointed out, only three great waterways from ice-free oceans into the heart of North America: the Mississippi, the St. Lawrence, and the Hudson.[11] The last two would one day compete for the freight to and from the Middle West. Only recently

8. Washington *Post*, April 27, 1880.

9. New York Historical Society: Seymour Papers: "Reminiscences" of David Gray, of Utica, 1886.

10. New York *Herald*, March 25, 1881.

11. New York *Herald*, March 26, 1881.

(1934) the Senate of the United States refused to ratify the St. Lawrence Treaty with Canada for this very reason, but then it was railroads and not canals that carried the day against an international plan for improving the northern route.

It was more than sixty years since his father, as superintendent of construction between Rome and Utica, had brought the first section of the "great canal" to completion. Fifty-seven years before, DeWitt Clinton had emptied a cask of Lake Erie water into New York Harbor. "Clinton's ditch" had been deepened and widened more than once; the locks had been lengthened; the branch canals, many of them wasteful, had been run out into almost every part of upper New York. Mules disappeared from the tow-paths, and by the seventies Seymour was offering a prize for the man who could produce a propellor which could be used on canals without stirring up the water to the damage of their banks. Forty years had passed since the young assemblyman from Utica had first crossed swords with Michael Hoffman at Albany; his canal report had made him speaker, and from the speakership he went to the office of governor. Eighty million dollars had gone into the trunk canal, and eighty million dollars had come out again. He was old, and the mantle of DeWitt Clinton which he had once worn proudly had indeed become a harness. Now he was ready to lay it aside.

Students of the present day are likely to test the souls of the generation of the Civil War by their views on slavery. Who was on the side of the angels, and who was against them? Seymour, when he was still a young man and serving as mayor of Utica, had used his office, it will be remembered, to defend the right of assembly and free speech for a convention of abolitionists in the city. He protested in person against the uproar raised by rowdies and bullies. He demanded the hospitality of his city for the rabid guests within its gates. The contempt he felt for the Garrisons and Birneys — shouting for abolition from the comparatively safe vantage of free soil — did not blind him to the importance of the issue of slavery and the danger it bore for the safety of the whole country. In 1845 he told Silas

Wright that he could not support any measure looking toward the extension of slavery into the territory which might be acquired from Mexico. At that moment he was speaker of the assembly and thus leader of the Democratic majority. He was talking to a Barnburner governor of the greatest state of the Union.

He believed, or wished to believe, that slavery would one day be abolished by the action of the southern states; he insisted, moreover, that it could never successfully compete with the spread of free labor through the North and West. Although the Kansas–Nebraska Act helped to defeat him in 1854, the delirious deed of John Brown convinced him that the people of the free states must walk warily. In 1860 he talked and worked and voted for Douglas — Douglas, who did not care whether slavery was "voted up or down." In 1862 and 1863 he declared that emancipation was unconstitutional, but so, indeed, did Chief-Justice Taney. From first to last on the subject of slavery Seymour was far too slow or too patient for the feelings of reformers and fanatics; never once did he defend the system and never once, on the other hand, did he urge its abolition otherwise than by the free choice of the southern people. The proper place to work for abolition, he maintained, was the South.

Yet Seymour was by no means a "let-well-enough-alone" man in his outlook on the world. During his first term as governor the pardoning power brought him into contact with the penal system of his state, and experience convinced him that this system was both ignorant and cruel. His granting of certain pardons and his refusal to give others angered both the friends and enemies of prison reform. Although, in one instance, he sent to the gallows a married man who had murdered his mistress (probably without intention and certainly without premeditation), he was accused of turning "hordes" of convicts loose on the community. Precisely the same charge was brought against him again during his second term.[12] For the remainder of his life

12. New York State Library: Seymour Papers: See the complaint of the Albany *Evening Journal* during the autumn of 1864.

he devoted much time and thought to the question of crime and punishment. His opinions on the subject sound reasonable enough for us to call them modern.

In 1854 he went down to New York City to make a speech at the opening of a new house of refuge on Randall's Island. Remarking on the fact that during the past two years as governor he had been "compelled to act upon more than two thousand applications for pardon," he observed that Milton, long before, had accurately described the problem which still vexed legislation: "Impunity and remissness are the bane of a commonwealth; but here the great art lies, to discern in what the law is to bid restraint and punishment, and on what things persuasion only is to work"—a task for Lord Acton and the "History of Liberty" he never wrote.

About four years later, Seymour sent a letter on the subject of the pardoning power to John A. King, who was just then beginning his one term as governor. King acknowledged the letter and asked Seymour's permission to publish it, together with his own reply, in the New York *Tribune*. He thought his predecessor had "placed the whole matter in a new and very strong light." [13] The occasion of the correspondence was the proposal to transfer the power to pardon from the governor to a commission. Seymour threw all the weight of his influence against the change. Writing in defense of his opinion that the criminal code should be softened, Seymour described his advanced position in two sentences:

> I am a strong believer in the influence of hope rather than that of fear. The longer I live and the more I see and learn of men, the more I am disposed to think well of their hearts and poorly of their heads.[14]

Complaint against Seymour's exercise of the pardoning power during his second term was largely political. These petty partisan squabbles were quite separate, however, from the great

13. New York State Library: Seymour Papers: John A. King to Horatio Seymour, January 29, 1859. Seymour's letter was dated January 7, 1859.

14. New York State Library: Seymour Papers: Horatio Seymour to M. H. Booce, April 4, 1859.

question which Seymour continued to study. In 1873 he went down to Baltimore as president of the Prison Congress and made a speech which was printed at Utica the same year.[15]

In 1878 Seymour's interest in the subject came up against the opposition to the use of convict labor. Hard times had caused a fall in the wages of free men, and there was widespread complaint against the states which made their convicts earn their keep with the production of goods. Seymour's tracts led one of his correspondents to ask for his advice as to legislative repeal in these states. Prisoners, thought the enquirer, should earn their maintenance by labor at public works; otherwise, the competition of convicts was as dangerous to free men as that of slaves had been.[16] In December, 1878, Seymour published "Crime and Tramps" in *Harper's New Monthly Magazine*. The prevalence of vagrancy had stirred up a fad of alarm after the crash of 1873, but Seymour urged a civilized approach to the trouble rather than the popular remedy of a resort to jails and fines. Alarmists, he observed, were calling for Delaware's whipping-post, but "the real evil" of a whipping-post, he pointed out, was "not the harm done to the criminal, but to the lookers-on."

The panic of 1873 did more than turn tramps out on the highways of the country; it made communists. Perhaps the desperate experience of Paris in 1871 helped to encourage demonstrations and to frighten those solid citizens who almost lost their wits with anxiety about them. The unemployed paraded with some show of strength, and there was talk of violence in the cities. A reporter from the New York *Herald* stopped off in Utica and found Seymour possessed of his habitual serenity. Did he not, then, fear trouble from "the communists or other socialistic parties" who sought "to divide property"? The old governor acknowledged that he did not: he thought they were "the most harmless of men" and would do "more good than

15. New York State Library: Seymour Papers: Speech of January 21, 1873. See, also, *Prison Reform Congress, Baltimore, 1873*.

16. New York Historical Society: Seymour Papers: Goldsmith B. West to Horatio Seymour, March 11, 1878. West was the editor of the *Western Shoe and Leather Review*, published in Chicago.

hurt." On the contrary, their very impotence showed the great strength of the American system of government. One had only to make a comparison. Look here upon this picture and on this:

> A madman may shoot a king and shake a state, but majorities cannot be assassinated. It is a blunder to interfere with their parades with arms in their hands. It would be a good thing if they were obliged to show themselves with all their weapons, and banners, and mottoes on frequent occasions. Not only are the majority of our people owners of property, but not one poor man out of a hundred in our country would give up his chance of gaining wealth for all that the communists could give him if they had full sway. Such parties are dangerous only in countries where society is so stratified that the laborer has no hope, no chance to lift himself above want, unless he can overturn the social and political condition under which he lives.[17]

Seymour could not break off without taking a parting shot at the politics of his more respectable opponents. The communists declared frankly that they would divide wealth, but did not the high-tariff men get riches by having taxes laid on others? Communist and capitalist agreed in their desires; their fierce disputes arose from nothing more than a difference of opinion as to who should have the wealth.

On July 4, 1879, Seymour accepted the difficult duty of presenting his theories of penal reform to men who had good reasons for knowing more about prisons than he. His short address to the convicts at Auburn, which he later referred to as "my talk with 'my friends' in prison walls," is a model of difficult good taste and tact. He aimed to hit the hearts of these unhappy men but he probably shot over their heads. It is doubtful if an experienced speaker ever faced a more exacting audience, for it must have tried his mettle to make sense without seeming to talk down to men who had failed in life.

In thinking over what he was going to say to them, he had tried to imagine himself possessed of the fabulous power of wiping out at least twenty errors in his past. So far as his own well-being was concerned he found to his surprise that he could spare the successes of his life much better than its failures.

17. New York *Herald*, August 10, 1878.

Character was tested not by the number of times a man fell but by the number of times he lifted himself up. For the truth of what he believed Seymour referred his audience to no less a person than Confucius. He spoke in the silver age of the seventies, when Tennyson had put the great words of St. Augustine into famous verse:

> I held it truth, with him who sings
> To one clear harp in divers tones,
> That men may rise on stepping-stones
> Of their dead selves to higher things.

Politics went off at a tangent from the real concern of the life of Horatio Seymour. He was past seventy-five when he died, but he had held elective office only eight years of his life — one as mayor of Utica, three as a member of the assembly, and four as governor. The library he collected was scattered after his death, but there was ample shelf-space for books in the cosy room at Deerfield, with its window from Faneuil Hall and the big desk-chair from the office of Daniel Webster. The variety of his interests amounted to a vice. Farming for him was chiefly supervising, but the continual calls on his time and his unfailing good nature must have taken him away from his books and his home more often than he should have liked.

Utica is situated nearly at the centre of New York and almost at the middle of the main highway through the state. The city was a favorite meeting-place for conventions, and no program was complete without words of welcome or advice from the old governor at Deerfield. The dairymen (of whom he counted himself one) must have been a nuisance. Until his health began to fail and he lost his hearing, he was infinitely obliging and always interesting. No subject touching on the history or commerce of the state left him cold, for his knowledge of its geography and its settlement and growth was more than merely respectable. He liked to dwell on the lasting contribution of Dutch law and manners and the influence of the Irish Catholics, who first came with the canal. In New York, he insisted, was to be found the significant and splendid scene of the meeting and mixing of three great peoples — the Dutch, the English, and the Irish. All three had shared in the building of the Empire State.[18]

The speeches of Webster, Burke, and Cicero are not the favorite study of school-boys, whatever teachers may choose to believe; yet Webster, we know, had an almost delirious effect on the men who happened to hear him. People who listened to the austere new style of Charles William Eliot or Woodrow Wilson still delight in reading over what those two men said largely because they will never forget the distinction and the power of their language. So is it, also, with sermons — witness Phillips Brooks. Seymour stands half way between the florid eloquence of a hundred years ago and the studied simplicity of the oratory of our own time. If he never drew tears, it was probably because he never tried to draw them. He appealed to heads, and heads he came at last to trust less than hearts. His model was Burke; yet he was more concise.

In his lecture, *The Use of Short Words*, Seymour expressed his theory that a man should speak and think at one and the same time. Short words, he insisted, were always best "for the teacher, the orator, and the poet." To see how well the preacher practised, one has only to turn to the text of Seymour's speech this very same year before the canal committee of the legislature of New York — April 9, 1878. On a much more famous occasion his failure was all the more conspicuous by contrast.[19]

Two essays contributed to the *North American Review*, "The Government of the United States" (1878) and "The Political Situation" (1883), sum up conveniently the political theories which Seymour defended during all his active life. The first article was prompted by a sweeping statement of Gladstone in a paper he called "Kin Across the Sea" and published in September, 1878: "The American Constitution is, so far as I can see,

18. Seymour's essay, "The Influence of New York on American Jurisprudence," is an interesting exposition of his ideas on the subject. He read this paper at Albany on February 12, 1879. It was published in the *Magazine of American History*, III, 4 (April, 1879), 217–230. It was circulated, also, in pamphlet form.

19. Seymour, *Public Record*, 370.

the most wonderful work ever struck off at a given time by the brain and purpose of man." The Constitution, Gladstone to the contrary, had never been "struck off at a given time": the fact was that it had grown up slowly in America from 1607 on, and the business of statesmen was to take good care that it should go on growing, and grow well. The compact of 1787 was the written record of political experience up to the time when it was made. It must serve the people or perish.

Neither of these essays by Seymour contains anything new, and each shows how consistently he held on to the gracious doctrine of what is now "old-fashioned liberalism." Protection of minorities and the primary importance of government by neighborhood were the simple principles which he warned his readers to keep in mind. At Springfield, twenty-two years before, he had quoted from the Bible to persuade his hearers that one man could judge better of his own affairs than "seven watchmen on a high tower." [20] Man had invariably lost self-government by a curious combination of lazy and magnificent notions. Remote control might seem far more majestic, but government at a distance meant lobbies and corruption: people like Tweed were the creatures and the servants of such systems. Washington had become "a city of parasites" — and this in his own lifetime. It seemed strange to him that Herbert Spencer should criticize the Constitution as the rigid work of theorists, for the Constitution was evolved under the stress of necessity by practical men who made their compromises out of circumstances.

Although the popular majority of American voters preferred the counsel of others, Seymour never howled calamity. As long as millions of people continued to tumble over one another getting out of the Old World and into the New, he had the good humor to believe that his country would survive its mistakes — even the misfortune of failing to follow his advice. He always viewed Europe in perspective: he was never one of those laughable Americans who are quite happy to be taken for Englishmen. When he was almost seventy, one of his nieces, who was

20. Seymour, *Public Record*, 5.

New York Historical Society

MRS. HORATIO SEYMOUR

living abroad, wrote him to ask for copies of his speeches for a foreign friend. When he sent them off to her, he urged her to come home to her own country:

I am glad to send you all the speeches you will take. It is hard in this country to get any one to read what you say as all are making speeches for themselves. Your friend is at liberty to translate all he sees fit. The more he uses of what I write the more I shall feel complimented. My excuse for saying so much is that I am getting too old to go away from home or to take an active part in affairs; so I take to giving advice, after the fashion of people who are of use in no other way. The most absurd thing I have agreed to do is to make an address to the young women who graduate in June from the college at Aurora. . . .

What is the use of your staying any longer in Europe? All the world is coming here. You will find three million more of American people than there were when you left. All the European statesmen are failures. Bismarck overtops the others, but his work will not stand. When a people want to run away from their homes, there is trouble brewing. We are getting along so well here that it is quite stupid. We have so little to quarrel about that we have to content ourselves with calling names and making faces. Both political parties are in confusion, and no one knows and but few care what will be the outcome.

Your Aunt Mary and myself are getting old and tired. We seldom leave home. Everything about us is old, shabby, and comfortable. I have made up my mind to stay by good wood fires in winter and to wander about the farm in summer.

He promised to "leave some space for . . . Aunt Mary," and Mrs. Seymour added a postscript of praise for the way in which her husband had "carried out his system of short words." There was nothing left for her to add.[21] "Bismarck overtops the others, but his work will not stand" — Seymour was never to know how well he had predicted the fate of the diplomacy of "blood and iron."

It was a peaceful picture Seymour drew of his days at "Marysland" as his life was coming to a close. He was spared all the practical anxieties of old age, but its physical infirmities brought with them caution and diffidence.

Mrs. Seymour and myself are lovers of country life. I have a great many theories on the subject which I have an old man's fondness for explaining

21. New York Historical Society: Seymour Papers: Horatio and Mary Seymour to Mrs. C. S. Fairchild, April 28, 1880.

to all who will listen to me. I wish we could have the pleasure of a visit from you at our farm house, for our building is nothing more than a plain wooden building. We think our views are very fine. I am sure you would sympathise with our ideas of rural beauty. We do nothing by force of men or money. I employ two artists who never fail to work out beautiful results. They are "*Nature* and *Neglect*." I am tired of artificial effects and I am trying to get back my farm of five hundred acres into the condition of a free growing park. I cherish all wild plants and animals. When my trees fall they are left to moulder into mosses and conservatories of native flowers. No fences can be seen from the front porch of my house. I am free from the tyranny of gardeners and the care of hothouse plants. I boast of my ferns and mosses and wild shrubs and climbing plants, but above all of a native forest which almost encircles the house. If you care to see an old couple who are living in an easy unpretending way, in the midst of scenes where there are no marks of toil but where nature does its own wayward work then you must make us a visit next summer.[22]

Some men have experienced more splendid evenings to life; very few have had one more serene. There was no need for work or worry, and there was time enough to grow wise.

Seymour's health had never been robust. As a boy of twenty he had a break-down, and late in the fall of 1830 his father sent him into the Adirondacks, where he spent three months with a guide, camping and hunting in the open wilderness, and "sleeping in the deep snows of the forest." According to the physician whom he habitually consulted during the last ten years of his life, Seymour was frequently ill but always "kept his engagements." It was difficult for him to be "prompt" and he "often seemed abstracted." "His occasional bilious or blue days were caused by a bad liver," but "severe depression," thought the doctor, would be a "misleading" description of his state of mind when he was not well.[23]

The real decline in Seymour's health, however, began in 1876. Deerfield had elected him path-master, "the only office," he was fond of saying, that "he ever asked for,"[24] and he went about

22. Letter from Horatio Seymour to Mrs. William Barnes, November 14, 1873, in possession of the author. Mrs. Barnes was the daughter of Thurlow Weed; she married William Barnes, a townsman of Horatio Seymour.

23. New York Historical Society: Seymour Papers: Memorandum of Dr. Willis E. Ford, and letter to Mrs. C. S. Fairchild, February 26, 1896.

24. Utica *Morning Herald*, February 13, 1886.

his work of supervising the repair of public roads "like any other farmer." On one of the hottest days of the summer he suffered sun-stroke and had to go to bed for several weeks. Walking was never easy for him afterward. In the early spring of 1880 a bad cold nearly carried him off, and he lay dangerously ill at the old house in Utica for more than a month. In May, 1883, he confessed to a friend: "My days of usefulness are all over and my years are behind me. I have entered upon the days when 'the Grasshopper is a burden.' I realize the force of the scriptural figure."[25] By mid-summer he apologized for the fact that his memory failed him "on many subjects and occasions."[26] Only the year before, however, a reporter from New York had found him just returning from a drive over his farm.

> He had been inspecting a meadow in the uplands, and what he had seen there evidently pleased him much. His eyes were bright, there was a little color in his cheeks, and he wore a silk traveling-cap even somewhat jauntily. He would not accept help to get out of the wagon, explaining that he felt so well this morning that a dozen years seem to have fallen from his shoulders. Nevertheless, age is telling upon the veteran statesman.[27]

His hard fight for Hancock had worn him out, and the decisive treachery of "Honest" John Kelly's Tammany had made all his good work go for nothing. He did not find it easy to be proud of New York in his old age, but he would live to be rewarded.

As late as March, 1884, still another interviewer found the governor in the old homestead in Utica seated before an open fire with his trim feet on a stool, characteristically studying a congressional speech on federal appropriations for rivers and harbors. His head was covered with a peaked cap of black silk — "a smoking cap if Mr. Seymour smoked" — which he did not. He wore eye-glasses, and a gold-headed cane stood by his chair. The most he could do by way of welcome was to bring his feet "spryly . . . to the floor" and offer the visitor a chair and his one good ear. The reporter got the impression that Seymour

25. New York Historical Society: Seymour Papers: Letter from Horatio Seymour to William L. Stone, May 15, 1883.

26. New York Historical Society: Seymour Papers: Letter of July 18, 1883.

27. New York *Herald* [June 30] 1882.

was conscious of his feebleness and made a point of underrating his strength for the pleasure of hearing himself politely contradicted.

Almost for the last time, now, the talk turned to politics. The disciple of Jefferson waved his weapon of logic, as of old. The "whole protective fabric" must "tumble" one day. Would Mr. Tilden be nominated again in 1884? He had heard that Tilden had lost his voice — well, that, it might be thought, was "a positive advantage" for any politician. The very best thing to do with a man who became President would be to "have his tongue cut off" the minute he entered the White House: "No man was ever yet hurt by what he didn't say." Francis E. Spinner, however, would have told him that there had been good reason to think otherwise during the fierce campaign of thirty years before. Then, at last, the tactful reporter drew the governor up to the real object of his errand. What did he think of young Mr. Roosevelt's "Czar Bill" for the reform of New York City? Was it a wise measure? Would it make a difference in favor of the cause of good government? His reply was printed at length in the New York *Mail and Express*:

> It makes no difference at all. The passage of such a bill signifies to the city of New York no more and no less purity than it had before. The situation resolves itself back to the virtue and intelligence of the people. The degree of virtue and intelligence in a constituency is marked by its choice of officers. As it now is the people of New York City may elect a good mayor or a bad one, and in the end the result will be the same. The constituencies that elected the Aldermen will elect the Mayor. It makes no difference at all.[28]

Nor did it, indeed.

Seymour had fired the sunset gun of his belief that no government could rise higher than the political morals of its several neighborhoods. It was idle to look to Albany, or even to Washington, for salvation — aldermen were more numerous and might seem less important than governors and presidents, but the choice of them was more significant to the welfare of the people. The alternative to democracy was authority imposed

28. New York *Mail and Express*, March 27, 1884.

from above. During the days when he was helping Tilden in his triumphant war on Tweed, Seymour described the infamous boss of New York City as the creature and the convenience of men who were too lazy, indifferent, or selfish to give any of their own time to the safe maintenance of the liberty they took for granted. They would leave government to men who made it a profitable profession and then cry out against corruption whenever things went too wrong or too recklessly. Democracy without the duty of direct responsibility, he said, would die. Seymour refused, however, to realize that in that very freedom which self-government gives to men lies the danger to it and, perhaps, its certain and tragic doom.

XXII

DEPARTURE IN PEACE

1886

THE nomination of Cleveland had stirred Seymour to a last pathetic effort. A son of New York and a Democrat had been named for President. That autumn he was visiting with relatives in Cazenovia. He was taking on weight and he was weak, but he toiled up a long flight of stairs to the rooms of the local Democratic club, and there he made what was to be his last political speech. Cleveland was the man of the hour — even in "self-seeking Oneida" wires were being pulled for him, for Conkling was at work under cover — perhaps the governor from Buffalo would get the better of Blaine, after all. Seymour's day was over, and he knew it. During the summer of 1885, however, a canal convention gathered at Utica; it was August, and Seymour paid for his kindliness at putting in an appearance by finding himself chosen chairman. He was quite deaf now, and it was only the courtesy of others which carried him through the few moments of formality. After warning his audience that the people would regret the folly of letting the railroads crowd the canals out of competition with themselves, he added:

> I love the State of New York and want to see its dignity preserved. . . . I am an old man; it concerns me no longer. My days have gone by, but I want to die with the conviction that the prosperity of the state will be sustained.[1]

Then he explained that he would have to leave the chair, for he could hear nothing that was being said. The mantle of DeWitt Clinton was no longer his. Never again did he appear officially in public.

During the spring and summer of 1885 his handwriting degenerated rapidly. The flowing script became crabbed and

1. New York *Sun*, February 14, 1886.

almost illegible, as in the letter of April 17, when he resigned from the board of trustees of Hamilton College, which had granted him the degree of doctor of laws in 1858. He had received a respectable share of the distinctions common to men of his kind: in 1877, through his old friend, Speaker Winthrop, he had been admitted to the carefully guarded ranks of the Massachusetts Historical Society as an honorary member — but Winthrop, too, had been called a Copperhead in 1862. At the request of the governor of New York, he served on a committee with Andrew Dickson White to look into the management and tuition at Cornell. A park was named for him as far west as Omaha, and in 1878 he had to write the aldermen of Albany to ask that historic Orange Street should not be changed to Seymour in his honor.[2] In 1873 he became the first chancellor of Union College. He was wise enough, however, in the ways of the world to realize that a man's distinctions lose their lustre as his friends and his enemies leave life.

Nearly all the men who had made history in his time had gone before him. At the beginning of the Civil War five former Presidents of the United States were still alive; twenty-four years later only two of all who had followed remained — Hayes and Arthur. Van Buren died at "Lindenwald" in the midst of the gloomy summer of 1862; Buchanan was buried at "Wheatland" just before the unlucky nomination of 1868. After that August the spirit of Thaddeus Stevens troubled the earth no more. Johnson had disappeared in 1875, and ten years later Grant was dictating the last lines of his autobiography from his death-bed. By 1870 Lee was already a memory, though Jefferson Davis would live with his despair till he was eighty-one. The lesser lights were going out, too, one by one.

It was all of twenty years since Daniel Stevens Dickinson had hurled Scripture at the heads of his enemies — the bobbed hair and the blazing eyes of the poet-senator were dust. McClellan, "Little Corporal" of the Potomac, had forgotten

2. New York State Library: Seymour Papers: Horatio Seymour to Alderman Cavanagh, February 22, 1878.

Napoleon to be governor of New Jersey and then died at fifty-eight — yet ten years older than was Douglas, whom men were a long time forgetting. Gettysburg and Bull Run echoed in the angry arguments of people who were growing old. Even the regency was nothing but a memory of great names — a Mr. Daniel Manning had succeeded William Cassidy in the office of that *Argus* where Edwin Croswell had worked at his spider-web for twenty years. Roscoe Conkling and Hamilton Fish remained, and Tilden, who warned Seymour that a call at "Greystone" would amount to nothing more than a meeting "between a dumb man and a deaf one." [3]

When Horatio Seymour was born, the magnificent Daniel D. Tompkins was governor of New York; when he died, the office was in the hands of David Bennett Hill, of Elmira. The sharp contrast between the manners and the methods of these two men measures the change which had come to American politics during a lifetime. From Hill to Governor Sulzer was not so far as from Tompkins to Hill. And much more than men had seemed to change in the course of seventy-five years. Seymour was fifteen when the great canal was opened for traffic; ten years later railroads had begun to creep over the maps of the eastern states. In 1844 the news of Polk's nomination was telegraphed from Baltimore to Washington; in 1859, the very year that drillers first struck oil in Pennsylvania, Queen Victoria had sent a cablegram to President Buchanan. Steamboats were still a novel sight on the Hudson when Seymour was a boy, but by 1885 they had seen their best days on both the Mississippi and the Ohio. Every new form of transportation and travel left new ways of speculation in its wake — turnpikes, canals, railroads, bank stocks, and real estate supplied constant sources of excitement, profit, and loss. In March, 1876, Alexander Graham Bell spoke the first audible sentence over his telephone; in a little more than a year people were talking to one another all the way from Boston to New York. Thomas Alva Edison patented his "speaking machine" in 1877; two years afterward

3. Bigelow, *Tilden,* II, 320–321.

he made his first incandescent bulb, after spending forty thousand dollars on experiments. Distance and darkness were no longer difficult and dangerous to human beings.

Yet all was not peace, progress, and plenty — even for Americans. Three social cyclones swept over the United States during Seymour's comfortable lifetime — the Civil War and the immense panics of 1837 and 1873. It was not so bad for wealth to vanish, for money is the ornament of men, but that reputation should perish and character should crumble under the strain of strife and misfortune — this was something to think about. Even more alarming than hard times and war was the disturbing instability of the people. Martin Van Buren was so blind as to lay his defeat in 1840 to the vulgar ballyhoo of the Whigs, but living longer would have taught him better. As late as 1904 Grover Cleveland was tempted to lament the fickleness of his fellow citizens in preferring Roosevelt to Parker.[4] Old age gave a touch of this same sour suspicion of men to Seymour, but he laughed it down as long as he lived. He died, however, in a very different world from that into which he was born. It is by no means certain that he saw the significance of the change. If he did, he was silent.

Almost to the last year of his life Seymour's shabby buggy was a familiar sight on the two or three miles of road between Deerfield and Utica. It was always moving slowly, for the horse was an old favorite, privileged to pick out his way and go as he pleased, and there were frequent stops for the exchange of greetings. If the old governor did not know every one in the neighborhood, every one knew him — the lively eyes and sensitive lips were the same, but those who begged a favor now often had to ask twice, for the obliging "governor" grew more hard of hearing year by year. On New Year's Day of 1886 his wife and he went to Utica to dine with Dr. Ford, who had married one of their nieces.

Then suddenly, not many days after their return to Deerfield, Mrs. Seymour fell ill, and the two old people were taken back

4. Nevins, *Correspondence of Grover Cleveland*, 590–591.

into town during the last week of January in the midst of a dense snow-storm and the fierce cold of mid-winter. They put up at the home of Mrs. Roscoe Conkling, thus finding their last refuge with that sister Julia whose marriage to a rising young criminal lawyer two years her junior Seymour had strenuously opposed long before. Whether or not she ever acknowledged that she had come to agree with the advice she had disregarded, to Julia Conkling her brother Horatio was always "the very best man in the world." They were housed happily together, the three of them, even though the more magnificent of the husbands was settled in New York City absorbed in his practice of law. January passed, and Mrs. Seymour was still unable to leave her bed.

The excitement of the removal from Deerfield and the strain of worry over his wife began to tell on Seymour. On Sunday, February 7, he suffered what was supposed to be a severe attack of indigestion followed by nausea. On Monday he seemed better again, and on Tuesday he was taken out for a drive — the day that Hancock, the hero of Gettysburg, died suddenly at Governors Island. It was too late now, however, for sunlight and fresh air to work their cure. Wednesday saw a return of his violent illness. On Friday, February 12, at three o'clock in the afternoon of the birthday of Abraham Lincoln, an "effusion of blood at the base of the brain" brought on a fainting spell. As soon as it was thought likely that he would not live, Mrs. Seymour was carried to his room from her own bed to bid him good-bye. There man and wife saw each other for the last time, really to separate for the first time in more than fifty years. At ten o'clock that night Horatio Seymour died.[5]

His body lay in state in the hall of the Conkling home on the morning of Tuesday, February 16, so that all those who loved him or merely wished to look at him might file by in the fashion of the day. Late that afternoon he was buried privately in Forest Hills Cemetery, after services at Trinity Church.[6] The

5. Albany *Express*, February 13, 1886.

6. At Pompey Hill, the Seymours had been Presbyterians, but Horatio was

SEYMOUR BUST AT UTICA

New York Historical Society

BUST OF SEYMOUR

big rough granite boulder which he himself found in the woods and had hauled to Utica for his tombstone was later cut down to a conventional oblong shape, on one side of which were carved his name and the places and full dates of his birth and his death, together with the fact that he had twice been elected governor of New York. Once again his desire for self-effacement was frustrated.[7] When his will was submitted for probate, it was found that he had left all his property to his brother and his sisters and their children.[8] In less than a month, his wife was buried beside him.

A flood of resolutions, obituaries, and speeches followed the news of his death. It was Dana, of all men, the cynical editor of the New York *Sun*, who tried to lay the ghost of Seymour's disloyalty to the Union — as former assistant to Stanton, he knew the facts at first hand.[9] The old governor was dead, and there was no longer any reason for printing lies about him. He had stood between the North and the South and he had perished without praise of either. But luckily for Seymour the world was a little larger than the United States. As far away as London, some friendly spirit sent this description of him to the *Times*:

> Horatio Seymour . . . was perhaps the best-loved man in America. In the race for power, in the field of achievement, he was easily outshone by others, but for the last ten years of his life, at least, it was true that the name of no other American could so surely touch the chord of popular feeling and enthusiasm, not only in his own section, but in the far West or the remote South as well. . . . With few exceptions he was the best of Amer-

---

confirmed at Trinity Church, Utica, September 4, 1831, and admitted to communion some time between October, 1838, and October, 1839. New York Historical Society: Seymour Papers: affidavit of the Reverend W. B. Maxim, May 26, 1892.

7. Seymour procured this boulder in 1879, in order to prevent his friends from setting up an expensive monument, which he thought would be a bad example. His hope was to find a good stone in his own county, but he stipulated that the contractor should "by no means go out of the state for it." When a suitable boulder was found in a swamp four miles north of Remsen, it took four yoke of oxen to drag the eight tons into Utica, and the transportation cost Seymour three hundred dollars. Utica *Morning Herald*, February 18, 1886.

8. Utica *Daily Press*, April 14, 1886. A list of the lands Seymour left and the approximate value of them will be found in the *American Rural Home*, of Rochester, New York, for October 2, 1886.

9. New York *Sun*, February 14, 1886.

ican orators, and was without any exception whatever the kindliest, most attractive, most valued of American publicists, alike in his utterances and his personality. His political career was full of self-abnegation. . . . His private life was so beneficent, so gracious in all its aspects, that the whole country came to know of it, and to take pride in it as exemplifying, at their very highest, the qualities of an American gentleman.[10]

Seymour liked to think of himself as a student of character — he drew strength from watching other men; the fact is, he was made for thought rather than action. Fallacy and fanaticism, brutality and hatred, all these broke against his steady power to think clearly. It was his bad luck to live through violent days when serenity seemed insincere to those who could not share it. His character, however, fits perfectly into his career. He doubted the value of much which happened in his time, and the penalty for doubt is to be called weak. Perhaps his great fault was his unwillingness to "live dangerously." His refusal to feel resentment was always philosophical; now and then it seemed feeble. Once when an angry sister asked him why he ignored the bitter abuse heaped on his head during the Civil War, he observed mildly, "Time will set all that right" — or "words to that effect." [11]

People who can even remember the Civil War are no longer many, and the ranks of those who took part in that disaster are thinning to the point of disappearance. To look back from the distance of seventy-five years is to see that neither North nor South was innocent of misconduct or guilt of the common misfortune. Rhodes and Channing did much to lead the way to an understanding of the accidents and ambitions which brought the two sections of the country into collision. Comparatively few men emerged from that war with undiminished credit. The rival forces were restless, militant, and malignant minorities, and thought of the wasted lands and ruined lives their frenzy left behind them helps one to appreciate the difficulty which Samuel Johnson faced as he tried to "settle the proportion of

10. London *Times*, February 16, 1886.

11. New York Historical Society: Seymour Papers: Memorandum in the handwriting of Seymour's niece, Helen Lincklaen Fairchild.

iniquity" between Rousseau and Voltaire. The barn had been burned down, but not all the rats were dead.

Rash men called Seymour a Copperhead because he hated the Civil War; yet if he was disloyal to the Union, the South seems never to have realized the fact. His well-reasoned protests against arbitrary government in the North roused little interest in the Confederacy, where he was known, if at all, as an ineffectual doctrinaire. In 1868 the secession states accepted his nomination for President without any enthusiasm. His failure to satisfy either North or South is most significant — now that the smoke of battle has blown away. Men of middle courses rarely incite a crisis, or survive it if they do.

Seymour's most serious misfortunes sprang from his grace, wisdom, and charm. Because he had none of the arrogance and bad manners which often go with a certain kind of ability and success, in spite of the fact that he never yielded to the temptation to persuade men by means of making the worse cause seem the better, shallow people underestimated the depth of his character. He had mastered with such skill the difficult art of managing men that they often overlooked his steadfast devotion to common sense, compromise, and peace. Much as he admired his own great state, often as he praised it wisely, he never thought of the Union other than in terms of the welfare of each and every part of it.

Whoever looks at the record will find it hard to doubt that Horatio Seymour loved his country quite as well as any of the brave men from either North or South who heard the guns of Gettysburg. It is not unlikely that he loved it even better.

APPENDIX

"MY FRIENDS"

THE SPEECH AT THE CITY HALL

July 14, 1863

NEW YORK *EXPRESS*

Tuesday Evening

[July 14]

About half past twelve o'clock, the crowd, numbering some ten or twelve thousand, called for the Governor and he appeared upon the steps, amid long and prolonged cheering.

The Governor said that he came here in haste, having heard of existing trouble. He regretted that this great city was so disturbed. (They've forced it upon us, Governor.) Let them go peacefully to their homes. (No. No. Yes.) He would be their leader. (Tremendous cheering, one stout fellow almost squeezing the Governor to death in his enthusiasm.) He would protect them in the exercise of their just rights at every hazard.

(Other things were said — but the Reporter could not get within fair hearing to make anything like a report.)

The Governor retired amid tremendous enthusiasm.[1]

NEW YORK *EVENING POST*

Tuesday Evening

[July 14]

About twelve o'clock this morning a large body of men assembled with violent demonstrations in front of the *Tribune* building, unmistakably indicating an assault, to which they were encouraged by a speaker who was haranguing them. Fortunately, however, a company of infantry at that moment appeared on the scene, and the rioters, alarmed, quickly dispersed, leaving the street almost deserted.

Shortly afterward, a crowd having concentrated near the City Hall, Governor Seymour, who was in the building, appeared on the steps and briefly addressed the mob. The gist of his address was that he had on Saturday last sent his adjutant-general to Washington with a request that the government would suspend the draft; that he desired to protect the people, and he implored the crowd, therefore, to respect the rights of person and of property, promising them that he would see that everything should be made satisfactory.

1. New York State Library: Seymour Scrap-Books, II, 167.

Governor Seymour did not command the mob to disperse; he merely "implored" them in dainty phrase to do him the kindness not to continue these violent proceedings, and at his side, while he was speaking, stood the man who had been encouraging the mob in an inflammatory address in front of the *Tribune* building.

The Governor's remarks seemed to give great satisfaction to the rioters.[2]

NEW YORK *WORLD*

WEDNESDAY MORNING

[July 15]

I left the country, on hearing of these disturbances in New York, for the purpose of sustaining the laws and upholding the authorities, and of inquiring personally into the difficulties. I come before you with confidence as my immediate constituents, and as one whose sentiments and principles have been tried and approved. (Cheers.) I call on the people to maintain law and order, to protect life, person, and property, for your salvation depends upon this. Anarchy will be ruin. On Saturday last I sent the Adjutant-General of the State to Washington for the purpose of requesting that the draft might be postponed, and I had every reason to believe that the request would be complied with. If the conscription law will not bear the test of the courts and the Constitution, it will not be enforced; but if upheld by the courts, then the State and City authorities will combine for the purpose of equalizing the tax and making it bear proportionately upon the rich and the poor. (Great cheering.)[3]

NEW YORK *TIMES*

WEDNESDAY MORNING

[July 15]

On taking the stand he was greeted with vehement and prolonged cheers. He said he had come from his quiet home to this scene of excitement, to do what he could to preserve the public peace.

A voice — "We want you to stay here."

I am going to stay here, my friends.

He implored the men whom he saw before him to refrain from all acts of violence, and from all destruction of property. They owed it to themselves and to the Government under which they lived, to assist with their strong arms in preserving peace and order. If they would only do this, and refrain from further riotous acts, he would see to it that all their rights were protected. (Cheers.) He was their friend and the friend of their families. He would say a word about the draft. And first he would state that on Saturday last he sent his Adjutant-General (Sprague) to Washington, to ask the Government to stop the draft in this city for the present. (Prolonged cheers.) There was no occasion for resistance, for the draft had not yet been enforced.

2. New York State Library: Seymour Scrap-Books, VI, 39.
3. Seymour, *Public Record*, 127–128.

If they would now quietly disperse to their homes and abstain from further acts of violence, he would promise them that no injustice should be done in the matter of the conscription, and that the rights of themselves and families should be fully protected. (Great applause, during which the Governor retired within the City Hall.)[4]

NEW YORK *HERALD*

WEDNESDAY MORNING

[July 15]

Fellow-Citizens: — Hearing that there was difficulty in the city, I came down here, leaving the quiet of the country, to do what I can to preserve the public peace. (A voice. — "We want you to stay here.") Governor Seymour continued: I come not only for the purpose of maintaining the laws, but also from a kind regard for the interest and the welfare of those who, under the influence of excitement and a feeling of supposed wrong, were in danger not only of inflicting serious blows to the good order of society, but to their own best interests. I beg you to listen to me as a friend, for I am your friend, and the friend of your families. I implore you to take care that no man's property or person is injured; for you owe it to yourselves and to the Government under which you live to assist with your strong arms in preserving peace and order. (Cheers.) I rely on you to defend the peace and good order of the city; and if you do this, and refrain from further riotous acts, I will see to it that all your rights shall be protected. (Renewed applause.) I will say a word about the draft: on Saturday last (before the outbreak occurred) I sent the Adjutant-General of the State to Washington, urging its postponement. The question of the legality of the conscription act will go to the courts, and the decision of those courts, whatever it may be, must be obeyed by rulers and people alike. If the conscription shall be declared to be legal, then I pledge myself to use every influence with the State and City authorities to see that there shall be no inequality between the rich and the poor. I pledge myself that money shall be raised for the purpose of relieving those who are unable to protect their own interests. There is no occasion for resisting the draft, for it has not yet been enforced. And now, in conclusion, I beg you to disperse; leave your interests in my hands, and I will take care that justice is done you, and that your families shall be fully protected.[5]

NEW YORK *TRIBUNE*

WEDNESDAY MORNING

[July 15]

My Friends: — I have come down from the quiet of the country to see what was the difficulty, to learn what all this trouble was concerning the draft. Let me assure you that I am your friend. (Uproarious cheering.)

4. Seymour, *Public Record*, 128–129.
5. Seymour, *Public Record*, 128.

You have been my friends. (Cries of "yes," "yes" — "that's so" — " we are, and will be again.") And now I assure you, my fellow-citizens, that I am here to show you a test of my friendship. (Cheers.) I wish to inform you that I have sent my Adjutant-General to Washington to confer with the authorities there, and to have this draft suspended and stopped. (Vociferous cheers.) I now ask you as good citizens to wait for his return, and I assure you that I will do all that I can to see that there is no inequality, and no wrong done any one. I wish you to take good care of all property as good citizens, and see that every person is safe. The safe-keeping of property and persons rests with you, and I charge you to disturb neither. It is your duty to maintain the good order of the city, and I know you will do it. I wish you now to separate as good citizens, and you can assemble again whenever you wish to do so. I ask you to leave all to me, now, and I will see to your rights. Wait until my Adjutant returns from Washington, and you shall be satisfied. Listen to me, and see that no harm is done to either persons or property, but retire peaceably. (Cheers.) Some of the crowd shouted: "Send away those bayonets," referring to a company of soldiers who were drawn up in front of the City Hall, but the Governor declined to interfere with the military, and bowing to the crowd, retired.[6]

6. Seymour, *Public Record*, 127.

BIBLIOGRAPHY

A SELECT BIBLIOGRAPHY

With several exceptions only little known or out-of-the-way books and other sources of reference are listed below. Readers who are interested will find a complete bibliography in the manuscript biography, Horatio Seymour, *in the Harvard College Library.*

MANUSCRIPTS

I. SEYMOUR PAPERS:

1. New York State Library, Albany, New York: A large collection, in thirty-one files, consisting of family records (genealogies and Bibles), business papers (account-books and receipts), letter-books, drafts of letters, and practically all the letters Horatio Seymour received and filed during a period of forty-five years (1841–1886).
2. New York Historical Society, New York City: Several hundred letters, most of them written by Horatio Seymour to political friends. This collection was assembled by Seymour's niece, Mrs. Helen Lincklaen Fairchild, widow of Charles Stebbins Fairchild. In this collection are to be found family pictures, photographs of dwellings, portraits, genealogies, drafts of speeches, and various memoranda.

II. MARCY PAPERS, Library of Congress, Washington, D. C., and New York State Library, Albany, New York: The papers dealing with William Learned Marcy's national service (Secretary of War, 1845–1849, and Secretary of State, 1853–1857) are in Washington. Much of the inside story of the disastrous split between the "Hards" and the "Softs" (1853–1854) which cost the Democrats the control of New York is to be found in the letters exchanged between Governor Seymour and Secretary of State Marcy (1853–1854).

III. JOURNAL OF JOHN VAN SCHAICK LANSING PRUYN (1811–1877), in the possession of his daughter, Mrs. William Gorham Rice, of Albany, New York. This journal covers the years from 1830 to 1877. Several paragraphs from this journal were published in the *Magazine of History* (New York, 1912–1913), XV, 77–79, 97–101; XVI, 24–28; XVII, 57–58. For a sketch of his life by John V. L. Pruyn, Jr., see the *New York Genealogical and Biographical Record*, XIV, 2 (April, 1883), 53–65.

BOOKS AND NEWSPAPERS

I. WORKS OF HORATIO SEYMOUR:

1. *Public Record of Horatio Seymour . . . 1856 to 1868.* Compiled and edited by Thomas M. Cook and Thomas W. Knox (New

York, 1868). This volume is most important for a study of Seymour's political career. It was promoted by the *Sun* of New York and the *Tribune* of Chicago, acting through their agent, Thomas M. Cook, at a cost of two thousand dollars. Cook collected the material and proposed to send it to Utica for correction by Mr. Noxon, Seymour's private secretary. The editors of the *Sun* and the *Tribune* objected because of the loss of time and their fear that Seymour would "doctor" the text. Cook, therefore, did his best to protect Seymour — as in the riot speeches — but planned a popular edition of the *Public Record*, the text of which should go to Seymour for revision. (See letters of Thomas M. Cook to Horatio Seymour, August 1, 1868: Seymour Papers, New York State Library, Albany.)

As stated in the "announcement" in the *Public Record*, every "speech, letter, proclamation, or order is printed in full," only messages to the legislature having been abridged. Persons of "opposite political sentiment" were employed in compiling the volume, and although Seymour "cheerfully furnished" such material as he had at hand, he deemed "many of his speeches incorrectly reported." The editors, however, let the speeches stand as they had appeared in the newspapers, and Seymour subsequently bought ten copies of the volume. Newspaper editors were taxed one hundred dollars a volume; Seymour paid eight dollars.

The three hundred and eighty-four pages and the index supply a reasonably accurate and thorough record of Seymour's public life from 1856 through the summer of 1868, with the single exception of the campaign of 1860.

2. Horatio Seymour, "Canal Report": *New York Assembly Documents*, 1844, VII, Number 177.
3. Speeches, Lectures, and Essays by Horatio Seymour: A complete file of all those ever published is to be found in the New York Historical Society. Using this file as a basis and the Seymour Scrap-Books at Albany, Alexander J. Wall published a complete list of these as an appendix to *A Sketch of the Life of Horatio Seymour, 1810–1886* (New York, 1929), 87–111. This list "comprises nearly two hundred items."
4. *A Lecture on the Topography and History of New York* (Utica, 1856). At the request of President White, of Cornell, this lecture was repeated, with some changes, at the Commencement on June 30, 1870 (Utica, 1870). This essay is the best statement of Seymour's favorite theory: the strategic importance of the Hudson and Mohawk rivers in the history of the United States.
5. "Address at Saratoga at the Celebration of the Centenary of the Surrender of Burgoyne, 1877": *Proceedings*, New York Historical Association, XII (1913), 206–225.

6. "Crime and Tramps": *Harper's New Monthly Magazine*, LVIII (December, 1878), 106–109.

7. "The Influence of New York on American Jurisprudence": *Magazine of American History*, III, 4 (April, 1879), 217–230.

8. "The Political Situation": *North American Review*, CXXXVI (February, 1883), 153–158.

II. SEYMOUR SCRAP-BOOKS, New York State Library, Albany, New York: Sixteen volumes of clippings from newspapers from all parts of the United States. Of these sixteen volumes, fifteen were the property of Horatio Seymour, "a close and constant reader of the public journals" (*Public Record of Horatio Seymour . . . 1856 to 1868*, 358), who collected the clippings himself. The sixteenth volume belonged to the governor's younger brother, Jonathan F. Seymour. The clippings in these sixteen volumes are both favorable and unfavorable. Mr. Willers, who was private secretary to the governor in 1864, described the collection as "the most complete for that period" and declared that Seymour "took considerable pride" in it. Seymour's nephew, Horatio Seymour, Jr., inherited this collection in 1886, using it as the basis for a biography of his uncle, which has never been published. The son of Horatio Seymour, Jr., sold the whole collection, and the New York State Library purchased it in Chicago.

III. AUTOBIOGRAPHIES, DIARIES, JOURNALS, LETTERS, AND SPEECHES:

1. *The Diary of Edward Bates, 1859–1866*, Howard K. Beale, Editor, (Washington, D. C., 1933).

2. John Dean Caton, *Miscellanies* (Boston, 1880).

3. Daniel S. Dickinson, *Speeches, Correspondence, etc., of the Late Daniel S. Dickinson of New York.* Edited, with a biography, by John R. Dickinson [his brother]: 2 volumes (New York, 1867).

4. Mrs. Basil Hall, *The Aristocratic Journey: Being the Outspoken Letters of Mrs. Basil Hall, written during a Fourteen Months' Sojourn in America, 1827–1828* (New York and London, 1931).

5. Murat Halstead, *Caucuses of 1860. A History of the National Political Conventions of the Current Presidential Campaign* (Columbus, 1860).

6. Honorable Amelia M. Murray, *Letters from the United States, Cuba and Canada* (New York, 1856).

7. George Opdyke, *Official Documents, Addresses, etc.* (New York, 1866).

8. Mrs. Anne Royall, *The Black Book: or a Continuation of Travels in the United States* (Washington, 1828).

9. William Howard Russell, *My Diary North and South* [1861] (Boston, 1863).

10. Henry B. Stanton, *Random Recollections* (New York, 1887). Henry B. Stanton was the husband of Elizabeth Cady, daughter of Daniel Cady.

11. "Van Buren-Bancroft Correspondence, 1830–1845": *Proceedings*, Massachusetts Historical Society, XLII.

12. Gideon Welles, *The Diary of Gideon Welles*: 3 volumes (Boston and New York, 1911). For a re-statement of the historical value of these volumes, readers are referred to the bibliographical note in James G. Randall, *Constitutional Problems Under Lincoln.* For an estimate of the character and work of Secretary Welles, see Schouler, *History of the United States, 1783–1877*, VII (1913), 1–2; 10–21.

IV. SEYMOUR AND HIS FAMILY:

1. Erastus Brooks, *Memorial Address on the Life, Character, and Services of Horatio Seymour* (New York, 1886).

2. Delano C. Calvin, *An Address in Memory of the Honorable Horatio Seymour, LL.D.*, (Geneva, New York, 1886).

3. Howard Carroll, *Twelve Americans: Their Lives and Times* (New York, 1883). The first of these essays is entitled, " 'The Farmer Statesman': Horatio Seymour," 1–47.

4. David G. Croly, *Seymour and Blair: Their Lives and Services* (New York, 1868).

5. Isaac S. Hartley, *Honorable Horatio Seymour, LL.D., Ex-Governor of the State of New York, . . .* (Utica, 1886). This appreciation was reprinted in the *Magazine of American History*, XV, 5 (May, 1886), 417–432.

6. Thomas P. Kettell, "Horatio Seymour of New York": *Democratic Review*, XXIX, 160 (October, 1851), 360–369.

7. James D. McCabe, Jr., [Edward Winslow Martin], *The Life and Public Services of Horatio Seymour, . . .* (New York, 1868).

8. William D. Murphy, *Biographical Sketches of the State Officers and Members of the Legislature, of the State of New York, in 1862 and 1863* (Albany, 1863): "Horatio Seymour, Governor," 5–15.

9. George Dudley Seymour, *The English Home and Ancestry of Richard Seamer or Semer of Hartford, Connecticut, Progenitor of the Seymours of Connecticut and New York* (Boston, 1917). Reprinted from the *New England Historical and Genealogical Register* for April, 1917.

10. Alexander J. Wall, *A Sketch of the Life of Horatio Seymour, 1810–1886, . . .* (New York, 1929).

V. Local Histories:

1. *History of Oneida County, New York, 1667–1878, with Illustrations and Biographical Sketches of Some of its Prominent Men and Pioneers*, Samuel W. Durant, Editor, (Philadelphia, 1878).
2. *Annals and Recollections of Oneida County*, Pomroy Jones (Rome, 1851).
3. *Our County and its People: A Descriptive Work on Oneida County, New York*, Daniel E. Wager, Editor, (Boston, 1896).
4. *Onondaga; or Reminiscences of Earlier and Later Times . . .*, Joshua V. H. Clark: 2 volumes (Syracuse, 1849).
5. *Re-Union of the Sons and Daughters of the Old Town of Pompey, held at Pompey Hill, June 29, 1871.* Published by William W. Van Brocklin, *et al.*, (Pompey, New York, 1875).
6. *The Pioneers of Utica*, Moses M. Bagg (Utica, New York, 1877).

VI. History of New York:

1. DeAlva Stanwood Alexander, *A Political History of the State of New York:* 3 volumes (New York, 1906). This admirable and popular history of New York is rich in pen portraits and character sketches. The narrative is always interesting. It must be remembered, however, that Alexander leaned on the memory of Chauncey M. Depew and served the principles of the Republican party in the Congress as a representative from New York for many years.
2. Sidney David Brummer, *Political History of New York State During the Period of the Civil War. Columbia University Studies in History, Economics and Public Law* (New York, 1911).
3. David H. Burr, *An Atlas of the State of New York, Containing a Map of the State and of the Several Counties* (New York, 1829) and (Ithaca, New York, 1839).
4. Edward P. Cheyney, "The Anti-Rent Agitation in the State of New York, 1839–1846": *Publications of the University of Pennsylvania. Political Economy and Public Law Series*, II (Philadelphia, 1887).
5. John I. Davenport, *The Election Frauds of New York City and Their Prevention* (New York, 1894).
6. J. H. French, *Gazetteer of the State of New York . . .* (Syracuse, 1859–1861).
7. James Barnet Fry, *New York and the Conscription of 1863* (New York, 1885).
8. Jabez D. Hammond, *The History of Political Parties in the State of New-York:* 2 volumes (Albany, 1842): Volume I, 1788–1820; Volume II, 1821–1840; *Political History of the State of New York* (Syracuse, 1852): Volume III, 1841–1847. The third

volume of Hammond consists of a biography of Silas Wright. Readers of Hammond's three very interesting volumes ought to inform themselves of his political prejudices and limitations. See the letter of Silas Wright to A. Hunt, September 20, 1844, in Ransom H. Gillet, *Silas Wright* (Albany, 1874), II, 1582–1586. Until 1826 Hammond was a devoted follower of DeWitt Clinton; in the thirties and forties Hammond favored the "Barnburner" section of the Democratic party. As late as 1844, it is interesting to note, an important Democratic leader like Silas Wright had never read the first two volumes of his own future biographer.

9. *Public Documents Relating to the New-York Canals . . . to Connect the Western and Northern Lakes with the Atlantic Ocean.* Introduction by Charles G. Haines (New York, 1821).
10. John S. Jenkins, *History of Political Parties in the State of New York* (Auburn, 1846). Second Edition, with Appendix, (Auburn, 1849).
    ——, *Lives of the Governors of the State of New York* (Syracuse, 1852). Jenkins must be used to supplement Hammond.
11. Peter Ploughshare [Samuel B. Beach], *Considerations Against Continuing the Great Canal* (Utica, 1819).
12. Eugene J. Post, *The Wig and the Jimmy: Or, A Leaf in the Political History of New York* (New York, 1869).
13. Louis Dow Scisco, *Political Nativism in New York State. Columbia University Studies in History, Economics and Public Law* (New York, 1901).
14. Homer Adolph Stebbins, *The Political History of the State of New York, 1865–1869. Columbia University Studies in History, Economics and Public Law* (New York, 1913).
15. William Trimble, "Diverging Tendencies in New York Democracy in the Period of the Locofocos": *American Historical Review,* XXIV, 3 (April, 1919), 396–421.
16. Edgar A. Werner, *Civil List and Constitutional History of the Colony and State of New York* (Albany, 1889).
17. Julius Winden, "The Influence of the Erie Canal upon the Population along its Course," a thesis submitted for the Degree of Bachelor of Philosophy in Pedagogy in the Philosophical Course, University of Wisconsin, 1900.

VII. Monographs and Separate Articles:

1. *The Barnburners,* Herbert D. A. Donovan (New York, 1925).
2. *The Democratic Machine, 1850–1854,* Roy Franklin Nichols. *Columbia University Studies in History, Economics and Public Law* (New York, 1923).

3. *The Election of 1868. The Democratic Effort to Regain Control*, Charles Hubert Coleman (New York, 1933).
4. "The Story of the Fox-Wisconsin Rivers Improvement," John Bell Sanborn: *Proceedings*, State Historical Society of Wisconsin (Madison, Wisconsin, 1900), 186–194.
5. *Constitutional Problems Under Lincoln*, James G. Randall (New York, 1926).
6. *The Organization and Administration of the Union Army, 1861–1865*, Fred Albert Shannon: 2 volumes (Cleveland, 1928).
7. "The Maine Law in New York Politics," John A. Krout: *New York History*, XVII, 3 (July, 1936).
8. "The Movement for Peace Without a Victory During the Civil War," Elbert J. Benton: *Collections*, Western Reserve Historical Society, XCIX (December, 1918).
9. *The Peaceable Americans of 1860–1861*, Mary Scrugham. *Columbia University Studies in History, Economics and Public Law* (New York, 1921).
10. *The Secession Movement, 1860–1861*, Dwight Lowell Dumond (New York, 1931).
11. "John Sherman and Reconstruction," James G. Randall: *Mississippi Valley Historical Review*, XIX, 3 (December, 1932).
12. *Voting in the Field*, Josiah Henry Benton (Boston, 1915).
13. "A Politician of Expansion: Robert J. Walker," H. D. Jordan: *Mississippi Valley Historical Review*, XIX, 3 (December, 1932).
14. *War Government Federal and State, in Massachusetts, New York, Pennsylvania and Indiana, 1861–1865*, William B. Weeden (Boston, 1906).
15. "The Motivation of the Wilmot Proviso," Richard R. Stenberg: *Mississippi Valley Historical Review*, XVIII, 4 (March, 1932).

VIII. BIOGRAPHIES:

1. *A Biographical Sketch of John Dean Caton, Ex-Chief Justice of Illinois*, Robert Fergus: *Fergus Historical Series*, Number 21 (Chicago, 1882).
2. *De Witt Clinton*, David Hosack (New York, 1829).
3. *The Life of John J. Crittenden, with Selections from his Correspondence and Speeches*, Mrs. Chapman Coleman, Editor, (Philadelphia, 1871).
4. *The Life of . . . John Hughes*, John R. G. Hassard (New York, 1866).
5. *Abraham Lincoln*, Lord Charnwood (London and New York, 1917). The great popularity of this book makes a word of caution necessary for some readers. It was well received even by

able critics (see the remarks of John T. Morse, Jr., *Proceedings*, Massachusetts Historical Society, LI, 90–105) but when friends of Seymour took exception to certain statements (see speech of Admiral Charles Stockton before the Loyal Legion, Washington, D. C., 1917), Lord Charnwood wrote a letter to his critics (Seymour Papers, New York Historical Society) in which he stated that he had brought his book to completion as a "tract for the times" to be read by the English people in 1916.

6. *Matthias and His Impostures*, William L. Stone (New York, 1835).
7. *Jemima Wilkinson*, David Hudson (Geneva, New York, 1821).
8. *The Life and Times of Silas Wright*, Ransom H. Gillet (Albany, 1874).

INDEX

INDEX

Abolitionism, xvii, 27, 146, 162, 178, 237, 239, 255, 261, 278, 557–558
Abolitionists, xviii, 44, 102–103, 155, 185, 206, 228, 254, 261–262; conventions of, at Utica, 67–70, 557
Acton, Thomas C., 284–286
Adams, Charles Francis (*d* 1886), 254, 401, 465; on Free Soil ticket, 109, 111; and Liberal Republican ticket, 501; endorses Tilden, 527
—— Charles Francis (*d* 1915), 404
—— John (*d* 1826), 58
—— John Quincy, 4, 26–27, 31, 33, 50*n*, 219, 530; his character, 32; describes travel by canal, 18–19; elected President, 47; receives students of Partridge's school, 31; his choice of Clay for secretary of state, 32, 47, 59
Alabama, secession of, 327*n*
Albany, N. Y., 13, 191; social life in, 35, 38; foreign population of, 64*n*; celebration of "wets" in, 157; Tweddle Hall convention in, 224–225; Hunker convention at (1848), 109; Democratic conventions at: (1862), 245, 249; (1863), 348; (1864), 364, 373; (1865), 390; (1867), 393; (1877), 534; Vallandigham protest meeting at, 293–294; Seymour's speech at (1876), 530–531
—— Eagle Tavern, 93
—— St. Peter's Cathedral, 158
Albany and Schenectady Railroad, 135
Albany *Argus*, 108*n*; merges with *Atlas*, 57, 66, 86, 149, 171; on canal commissioners, 12; on Seymour's candidacy (1850), 116–117; on election of 1852, 144
Albany *Atlas*, 108*n*; merges with *Argus*, 57, 66, 86, 149, 171; its analysis of Democratic defeat (1846), 105
Albany *Atlas and Argus*, defends Seymour (1863), 353; on Lincoln's offer to make Seymour his successor, 274*n*; on Seymour's winning ways, 554
Albany County, anti-rent disturbances in, 98
Albany *Evening Journal*, on Seymour's annual message (1854), 153*n*; on Seymour's inauguration (1863), 265; on Seymour's Utica speech (1863), 349
Albany *Knickerbocker*, on Seymour's trickery, 554
Albany Regency, 10, 12, 17, 26*n*, 33, 129, 142, 209, 237, 274, 572; heyday of, 48
Alexander the Great, conquests of, compared to settlement of New World, 183
Alexander, DeAlva S., 352*n*, 537; on Seymour's legislative skill and moral power, 74, 85; on Seymour's political ambitions, 397; on Seymour's personality and poise, 551*n*; on Seymour as Speaker of Assembly, 95; on Democratic truce (1848), 112, 115–116; on Myron Clark, 155; on Seymour's party leadership (1856), 174; on Seymour's moderate position (1861), 225–226; on Seymour's state of mind (1862), 246; on Chicago convention (1864), 365, 369; on Seymour's appearance (1864), 365*n*; on Seymour's position (1865), 390; on Seymour's position at state convention (1867), 393; on Johnson's position (1867), 394; on Seymour's refusal of nomination (1868), 434; on Tilden's part in Seymour's nomination (1868), 434–435; on Seymour's campaign (1868), 472; on Tilden's Rochester speech (1871), 493; on Seymour's humiliation at Rochester (1871), 494; on New York Democratic platform (1874), 511; on New York election (1879), 535
Aliens, influence of, on draft quotas of New York City, 343–344; naturalization of, 479
Allen, George W., maligns Seymour, 232
—— Rev. M., 68
—— William F., 373, 380; as commissioner to pass on New York quotas, 346
Altoona, Pa., meeting of governors at, 262
American Express Company, 378
American Literary Scientific and Military Academy, Middletown, Conn., life at, 29–30; students of, received by J. Q. Adams, 31–32
American party, 86, 93, 114–115, 161, 182, 187; national character of, 190. *See also* Know-Nothing party; Nativism
American Protestant Union, 159
American Revolution, 175

Amnesty, proclamation of, 360; Democratic platform on (1868), 418
Anderson, Maj. ——, 233
Andrew, Gov. John A., Mass., 159, 263, 281, 301; meeting of, with Seymour, 364–365
Andrews, ——, 309
Anthony, Susan B., petitions Democratic convention (1868), 416
"Anti-credit" men, 51
Antietam, Battle of, 254
Anti-renters, 65, 86, 93, 104–105, 132, 153*n*; grievances and riots of, 97–99; oppose Seymour's candidacy, 117, 119
Arbitrary arrest, 267–269, 277, 284, 295; complaints against, 270
Army, Union, bounties for enlistment in, 318, 330, 355; recruiting and enlisting of volunteers, 30, 160*n*, 232–234, 235*n*, 238, 263, 281, 300, 343, 355; Lincoln's call for men, 318; political generals in, 30, 236. *See also* Draft; Enrollment Act
Arnold, Benedict, 280
—— Matthew, 177; quoted, 168
Arthur, Chester A., 56, 177, 536, 547, 571
Austro-Prussian War, 391

Baird, Henry S., 233
Ballard, Horatio, 265*n*
Ballots, nature of, 134, 376
Baltimore, Md., Republican convention at (1864), 364; Democratic conventions at: (1844), 55, 77–83; (1848), 109; (1852), 124–129; (1860), 213–215, 420; (1872), 501; (1912), 81; meeting of prison congress at, 560
Bancroft, George, 79*n*, 88, 185*n*, 226
Bank of the United States (second), 27, 35, 48, 51
Banks, Gen. Nathaniel P., 30
Banks and banking, history of, in New York, 22, 35, 49, 73, 202, 228; "pet" banks, 46; in panic (1837), 22; national, 27, 35, 46, 48, 51–52, 473
Baptists, their attitude on slavery, 68
Barge Canal, N. Y., 13, 19. *See also* Erie Canal
Barker, James W., organizes Know-Nothings, 160–161
Barlow, Samuel L. M., 260
Barnard, George G., 479
"Barnburners," 34, 69, 71, 77, 82–83, 86, 89, 91–92, 94, 106–108, 117, 123, 125, 137, 143, 147–148, 150, 166, 251; definition of term, 35, 54*n*; policies of, 35, 52, 54–55, 66, 72; and Wilmot Proviso, 100, 109; choose independent ticket (1848), 109–111, 123
Barnes, Mrs. William, 566*n*
Barney, Hiram, 197
Bates, Edward, 208
—— Stephen, 8
Bayard, James A., 311; his part in Democratic convention (1868), 412, 427
Beardsley, Samuel, 33, 165
Beck, James M., on the Constitution, 296
Bedini, Monsignor, 158
Beecher, Henry Ward, 176; his stand on election of 1868, 450
Beekman, John P., 130
Bell, Alexander G., 572
—— John (*d* 1869), in election of 1860, 214, 217–218, 219*n*, 220, 221*n*, 461
Belmont, August, 209–210, 226, 267, 536; as delegate to Charleston convention, 211–212; as delegate to Chicago convention (1864), 364, 366, 368; activity of, in picking candidate (1868), 396, 401–402, 407, 417; his speech of welcome to convention (1868), 411; part of, in campaign (1868), 463–464, 467–469; elected Tammany sachem, 500
Benedict, S. W., testimony of, on Seymour's City Hall speech, 328
Bennett, James Gordon, 209–210, 248, 304, 326, 351; his estimate of Seymour, 207; supports Dix for nomination (1862), 244; quarrels with Seymour, 305. *See also* New York *Herald*
Benton, Elbert J., on Vallandigham, 362
—— Jessie. *See* Frémont
—— Thomas H., 27, 169
Bergen, James G., 285, 286*n*
Bigelow, John, 401; as biographer of Tilden, 205, 368, 399, 511
Bigler, Gov. John, Calif., 417
—— Gov. William, Pa., 222, 417*n*, 418
Birdsall, Samuel, 125
Birney, James, 557
Bismarck, Otto, Prince von, 391, 565
Black, Gov. Frank S., N. Y., 328
Black River Canal, 75, 90–91
Blaine, James G., 312, 433, 528; his attack on Conkling, 547–548; on election of 1868, 443, 483–484, 532*n*; in election of 1884, 492, 547–549, 570
Blair, Francis P., Jr. ("Frank"), 23, 236, 440, 450, 457–458, 463, 470; as a candidate for Democratic nomination (1868),

423, 428; nominated for vice-presidency, 431; as a campaign issue, 447–449, 468
Blair, Montgomery, 418, 448
Bleecker, John Rutger, 36
— Maria. *See* Miller, Mrs. Morris
— Mary. *See* Seymour
— Rutger, land holdings of, 36
Books, Charnwood's *Lincoln*, 338–339; Curtis's *Executive Power*, 256, 299; Davenport's *Election Frauds in New York City*, 476–477; Fry's *New York and the Conscription of 1863*, 312, 342; Hammond's *History*, 82; Lincoln's *Constitutional History*, 97; Nevins's *Hamilton Fish*, 544; Nicolay and Hay's *Lincoln*, 325*n*; Oliver's *Puritan Commonwealth*, 192; Post's *The Wig and the Jimmy*, 480*n*; Seymour's *Public Record*, 463–464; Shannon's *Organization and Administration of the Union Army*, 316; Stowe's *Uncle Tom's Cabin*, 103, 229; Weeden's *War Government*, 281–282
Booth, John Wilkes, 386
Born, Donald, ix
Boston *Post*, on Seymour's message (1864), 357*n*
Bosworth, Joseph S., 285
Bouck, Gov. William C., N. Y., 69–70, 72, 75, 83, 86–87, 92–93, 106, 130
Bradley, Joseph P., 533
Brady, James T., 215, 218, 238
Bramlette, Gov. Thomas E., Ky., 370
Breckinridge, John C., 34*n*, 110, 144, 340, 354, 510; as candidate for nomination at Charleston (1860), 208, 213; nominated (1860), 214; and election of 1860, 215, 217–218, 219*n*, 220, 221*n*, 461
Broadhead, James O., 448; his part in Democratic convention (1868), 418, 428
Bronson, Greene C., 33, 114, 123, 238, 363; and the collectorship of the port of New York, 149–152; candidacy of, for governor, 162, 164–165, 167
Brooklyn *Daily Eagle*, on Seymour's message (1864), 357*n*
Brooklyn, N. Y., Seymour's speeches at: (1862), 252–253; (1863), 303–306, 453, 466; (1874), 511–512; (1880), 542–543
Brooks, Erastus, 187*n*, 414
— James, 245, 271
— Phillips, 563
Broome County, N. Y., its vote in 1852, 134*n*
Brough, Gov. John, Ohio, 302; elected, 294, 361
Brown, Col. Harvey, conduct of, during draft riots, 320, 331
— Gen. Jacob, 7
— John (*d* 1859), the abolitionist, 188, 229, 558
— John W., 158
Browne, Charles F. *See* Ward, Artemus
Bruce, Marjorie M., ix
Brummer, Sidney D., on Seymour's annual messages: (1863), 271; (1864), 358
Bryan, William Jennings, 408, 450, 527
Bryant, William Cullen, 64, 176, 249*n*, 353, 357, 408, 453, 456; his reporting of draft riots, 326; and state printing, 66, 107; comments of, on Seymour's message (1863), 268–269. *See also* New York *Evening Post*
Bryce, James, Viscount Bryce, 227
Buchanan, James, 60, 70, 89*n*, 110, 114, 123, 171, 186, 189, 207, 210, 212, 214, 279, 285, 340, 360, 427, 444, 465, 510, 552, 571–572; an estimate of, 169–170; his party affiliations, 121; and Texas question, 80; seeks nomination (1852), 125, 127–128; his nomination (1856), 169, 172–173, 179, 186; his election, 182, 187; and federal patronage, 203–204; his record on slavery question, 221; his inaction (1860–1861), 221; on Enrollment Act, 313–314, 344; death of, 455
Buckner, Benjamin F., 418
Bucktail party, 8, 12, 51*n*
Buel, Jesse, 13, 108*n*
Buell, Deborah. *See* Marsh
Buffalo, N. Y., Free Soil convention at, 109; Vallandigham protest meeting at, 294*n*; Seymour's speech at (1865), 386–389
Burchard, Rev. S. D., 549
Burgoyne, Gen. John, 25, 175
Burke, Edmund, 180, 229, 563
Burnet, Gov. William (*d* 1729), N. Y., 14
Burnside, Gen. Ambrose E., 30, 302; his activities as commander of the Department of the Ohio, 290–294, 348
Burr, Aaron, 21–22, 38, 58–59, 219, 280, 432
Burt, Col. Silas W., 300*n*
Butler, Benjamin Franklin (*d* 1858),

N. Y., 20, 79*n*, 110, 197; declines Cabinet post, 88, 89*n*; manages Van Buren's campaign, 81–83
Butler, Gen. Benjamin Franklin (*d* 1893), Mass., 30, 210, 213; part of, in impeachment of Johnson, 402
—— Ebenezer, 5
—— Samuel (*d* 1680), 179
—— William A., 197, 200; on "crime" against Van Buren (1844), 79*n*
Butler's Hill, N. Y. *See* Pompey Hill, N. Y.
Butts, Isaac, as delegate to Chicago convention (1864), 364

Cady, Daniel, 74*n*
Caesar, Julius, conquests of, compared to settlement of New World, 183
Cagger, Peter, 209–210, 237, 267; railroad interests of, 287; and choice of agents to distribute ballots (1864), 378
Calhoun, John C., 27
California, in election of 1868, 478; under-representation of, 296*n*
Callicott, Theophilus C., 283
Calvin, Hon. Delano C., 28*n*
Cambreleng, Churchill C., advises Van Buren, 78–79
Cameron, James D., 540
Campbell, James, 145, 174
—— John A., 189*n*
Canada, 242; failure of United States to ratify treaty with, 201, 557
Canal Ring, xix, 508, 515, 522, 534
Canals, travel on, described, 18–19; promotion of, 49; New York investment in, 557; question of tolls on, 137, 489–490, 516, 556; in competition with railroads, 136, 194, 200, 490, 556, 570; lesser New York canals, 20, 52, 56, 75, 90; New York laws: (1819), 17; (1844), 72–75; (1850), 123; (1853), 146–148; (1875), 518; in Indiana, 196; Horatio Seymour's report on, 72–74; patronage and graft connected with, 11–12, 48, 55, 214, 237, 394; financing of, 15, 17, 53, 72–73, 75, 91, 135, 147–148, 557. *See also* Canal Ring; Erie Canal; Fox and Wisconsin Canal
Canaseraga Swamp, N.Y., 65
Carlisle, John G., 418
Carroll Hall ticket, 160
Cass, Lewis, 45, 71, 78, 112–113, 123–124, 152, 169, 216–217, 253, 504, 510; loses nomination (1844), 81–82; and Texas question, 80, 82; in election of 1848, 109–111; in Baltimore convention (1852), 125–128
Cassidy, William, 57, 66*n*, 86, 132, 149–150, 163, 207, 209–210, 242, 267, 368, 572; and state printing, 86, 107; at Democratic convention (1868), 418; supports Tweed, 495; on Seymour's winning ways, 554. *See also* Albany *Atlas*
Catholics. *See* Roman Catholics
Caton, John D., advice of, to Seymour, 260–262, 298
Catron, John, 189*n*
Cavanaugh, J. M., 422
Census, federal (1870), fairness of, 479, 482–483
—— New York, 479
Champlain Canal, 16, 52
Channing, Edward, xx, 261*n*, 306, 336, 576; on recruiting of negroes, 300
Charles II, King of England, 179, 551
Charleston, S. C., Democratic convention at, 207–213, 216, 420; Moultrie's defense of, 186*n*
Charlick, Oliver, 128
Charnwood, Godfrey Rathbone Benson, Baron, on Seymour, 338–339
Chase, Salmon P., 197, 301*n*, 350, 445, 459, 464, 487; as choice of radical Republicans (1864), 360–361; as a candidate for Democratic nomination (1868), xv, 404–410, 421, 426, 428–429, 432–435, 437–438, 441, 468–470, 485; his conduct during trial of Johnson, 404–405, 419; his feelings on Seymour's nomination (1868), 439–440, 456
Chemung County, N. Y., in election of 1868, 474
Chicago, Ill., canal convention at, 199; Republican conventions at: (1860), 208, 214; (1880), 539; Democratic convention at (1864), 260, 337, 366–371, 420; meetings in, to ratify principles of National Labor Union (1867), 415; Seymour's speech at (1868), 472–474
Chicago *Times*, on Seymour's inauguration (1863), 265*n*; suppressed, 292*n*; on Seymour's message (1864), 357*n*
Chicago *Tribune*, on Seymour (1868), 454
Choate, Rufus, 158
Church, Sanford E., 116–117, 130, 237, 245, 511, 515; as a candidate for Demo-

cratic nomination (1868), 422–425, 435; elected Tammany sachem, 500
Church, Walter S., 267
Cicero, 563
Cincinnati, Ohio, Democratic conventions at: (1856), 169, 172–173, 179, 186, 203, 211; (1880), 538–539; Liberal Republican convention at, 501
Cincinnati *Enquirer,* on Seymour's refusal to run for governor (1876), 526*n*
Citizenship, as a liability, 480. *See also* Aliens
Clancy, John M., 212
Clark, J. B. ("Champ"), 81
—— Gov. Myron Holley, N. Y., 114, 174; and temperance movement, 155–157, 161–162, 164–168
Clay, Henry, 26–27, 59, 65, 114, 121, 219, 476, 530; character of, 31–32; and Texas question, 78, 80; presidential candidacies of, 40, 47, 50*n*, 83–84
Cleveland, Grover, xviii–xix, 34, 56, 277*n*, 281, 382, 403, 515, 535, 546, 573; his election (1884), 476, 547–549, 570
Clinton, Gov. DeWitt, N. Y., 38, 49, 56, 58, 60–61, 76, 137, 153, 175, 192, 197, 201, 570; character of, 10; and Erie Canal, 12–20, 557; his feud with Van Buren, 8–13, 47; elected governor, 10, 47; political power of, 11; ousted as mayor of New York, 9; ousted from canal commission, 17*n*, 47; death of, 47
—— Gov. George, N. Y., 8, 58, 83*n*
Clinton, N. Y., Seymour's speech at (1872), 503
Clymer, Hiester, his part in Democratic convention (1868), 412, 420, 427
Cobb, Doris, ix
—— Howell, 227*n*, 450
Cochrane, John, 213, 377
Cohn, Maj. Levi, 380
Colden, Cadwallader, 14
Coleman, Charles H., on election of 1868, 440, 443, 453, 468; on violence in the South (1868), 447
Colfax, Schuyler, 472, 475–476
Columbia County, N. Y., anti-rent disturbances in, 98; in election of 1868, 475
Compromise of 1850, 79, 110, 114–115, 118, 120, 123, 127, 142; influence of, on Whig party, 114, 121, 161
Comstock, Calvert, Seymour's open letter to, 172–173
Congregationalists, 6
Conkling, Frederick A., 546; defeated for mayor of New York, 481
—— Julia Catherine (Seymour), 7, 24, 574
—— Roscoe, 7, 198, 522*n*, 533, 572; his estimate of Seymour, 130; letter to, from Seymour, 199; opposes Seymour, 255; his attack on Fry, 312; supports Grant, 452, 474, 511; finds favor with Grant, 491; his feud with Garfield, 546–548; his feud with Blaine, 312, 547–549; secretly supports Cleveland, 476, 548–549, 570
Connecticut, hiring of recruits by, 341
"Conscience" Whigs, 114, 161
Conscription. *See* Draft; Enrollment Act
Conservative Soldiers and Sailors, convention of, presents address to Democratic convention (1868), 416
Constitutional Union convention, 245
Conventions, party. *See under* names of parties
Cooper, Peter, on Seymour's gold policy, 351; as presidential candidate, 528
Copperheads, 282, 290, 305, 360–361; origin of term, 243*n*; policies of, 255, 290, 361; Seymour called one, xvi, 34*n*, 298, 351, 374, 449, 452, 468; in New York, 351; in Connecticut, 353*n*
Corcoran, William, 463
Cornell, Alonzo B., 535
Cornell University, Seymour's address before, 191–193; management committee of, 571
Corning, Erastus, 86, 130, 244; works for Marcy (1852), 126, 138–139; helps finance Democratic party, 209; his business ventures in Wisconsin, 194*n*, 197, 204–205
Cosby, Col. William, 36
Cosby's Manor, N. Y., 36, 550
"Cotton" Whigs, 114, 161, 278
Cowan, Richard D., ix
Crain, William C., 85, 93–94
Cram, Capt. Thomas J., 195
Cramer, John, 89*n*
Crawford, William H., 47, 50*n*, 58, 219
"Credit" men, 51
Crimean War, 170, 182
Crittenden, John J., 222, 225
Crittenden Compromise, 221, 224, 267*n*, 352; history of, 222–223
Crocker, Hugh, 104
Croly, David, his biography of Seymour, 464
Cromwell, Oliver, 240

Croswell, Edwin, 50, 51*n*, 54, 57, 82, 108, 113, 115, 130, 144, 149–150, 572; as Democratic boss, 48, 55, 71, 88; and state printing, 48, 66, 86, 107–108; supports Seymour, 85–86
Crowninshield, Benjamin W., 26
Currency, inflation of, 401, 488–489, 506; New York's attitude toward, 349–351; "Ohio Idea," 395; as campaign issue (1868), 350*n*, 396, 462–463, 469; stand of National Labor Union on, 414; Democratic platform (1868) on, 418–419, 519; Republican platform (1868) on, 445; New York Democratic platform (1874) on, 511; Seymour's attitude toward, 349–350, 355, 387–388, 391, 393, 413, 433, 462, 469, 472–473, 489, 511, 520–521
Curtin, Gov. Andrew G., Pa., 263, 281, 302; his call for troops, 301; defends Seymour (1868), 452
Curtis, Benjamin R., xvi, 190*n*, 278, 363; his *Executive Power*, 256, 299
—— George T., attacks policies of Lincoln, 278–279
Cushing, Caleb, 127–128, 146; on Pierce's handling of the patronage, 146*n*

Dallas, George M., 83, 171
Dana, Charles A., 301, 548; his eulogy of Seymour, vii, 575
Daniel, P. V., 189*n*
Davenport, Ira, 548*n*
—— John I., on election frauds in New York City, 476–480
Davis, David, 533
—— Jefferson, 211, 223, 253, 258, 260, 276, 299, 305, 354, 357, 571; rejects peace proposals, 338
—— Winter, 547–548
Dean, Gilbert, 126*n*
Delavan, E. C., 157, 204–205
Delaware County, N. Y., anti-rent disturbances in, 98–99
Democratic party, national, 50–51, 58–59, 65, 184, 289; dissension within, 110, 396; policy of, during Civil War, 217, 261, 268; influence of Kansas-Nebraska Act on, 121; platforms: (1864), 366–368, 372; (1868), 418–420; search of, for a candidate (1868), 395–402, 404–410; financing of campaign (1868), 463; movement in, to change ticket (1868), 468–470; contradictions in membership of, 484–485
—— Conventions, the two-thirds rule of, 81–82, 211–213, 420, 427; the use of the unit rule, 82, 128, 211–212, 216, 364, 370, 422, 426–428; (1844), 55, 77–83; (1848), 109; (1852), 124–129; (1856), 169, 172–173, 179, 186, 203, 211; (1860), 207–216, 420; (1864), 260, 337, 366–371, 420, 431; (1872), 501; (1876), 521–522; (1880), 538–539; (1912), 81; (1936), 427. *See also* Elections
—— Convention (1868), xv, 407–410, 445; Belmont's speech of welcome, 411; members of resolutions committee, 412; Seymour elected permanent chairman, 412; Seymour's speeches before, 412–413; receives petition from National Labor Union, 414–415; receives petition from Woman's Suffrage Association, 415–416; hears address from Conservative Soldiers and Sailors, 416; receives resolutions from Alexander Stephens, 417; platform adopted at, 418–420, 519; adoption of two-thirds rule by, 420; disputes over unit rule, 422, 426–428; leading candidates at, 421–422; balloting at, 423–426, 428–431; nomination of Seymour, 429–431; nomination of Blair, 431
Democratic party, New York, 53, 75, 144, 171, 179, 204, 389, 546; Albany manifesto of, 51*n*; committee of, 526; caucuses of, 66*n*, 85, 87; dissension within, 8–13, 34–35, 47, 50–52, 54–57, 60, 66, 69–72, 77, 85–86, 90, 105–106, 109, 113–114, 124–129, 140, 150, 162, 203, 207, 494–496, 535; re-establishment of harmony within: (1849), 106, 111–112, 123; (1850), 115; (1852), 132; (1856), 174; sends rival delegations to national conventions, 56, 106, 109, 173, 210–211; platforms of: (1862), 247–248; (1874), 511; and Free Soil issue, 144, 147; leaders of (1860), 209; supports fusion ticket (1860), 217–218; refuses to support a Union ticket (1861), 237; opposition of, to conduct of Civil War, 237, 240–241, 243, 247–248, 251, 253, 263, 266, 294–295; policy of, toward Johnson, 394; distribution of ballots by, to soldiers (1864), 378–380. *See also* Albany Regency; Barnburners; Hards; Hunkers; Softs
—— Conventions: (1846), 103–104; (1847), 109; (1849), 111; (1850), 116; (1851), 123; (1852), 125*n*, 130; (1853),

150; (1854), 163, 183; (1856), 174; (1857), 203; (1860), 212, 216; (1861), 236–237; (1862), 245, 249; (1863), 348; (1864), 364, 373; (1865), 390; (1867), 393; (1868), 458; (1870), 490; (1871), 493; (1872), 502; (1874), 508, 511; (1876), 521, 523–526; (1877), 534

Democratic party, New York City, dissension within, 118, 209–210; fusion ticket of (1862), 283–284. *See also* Tammany

Denio, Judge Hiram, 203

Denniston, Robert, 72–73

Depew, Chauncey M., 351; his estimate of Seymour, 365*n*; and the polling of soldier vote (1864), 377–378; as source of Alexander's information, 74, 390, 397, 435, 551*n*

De Peyster Case, 98*n*

Detroit *Free Press*, its description of Seymour (1864), 365*n*

DeWitt, Simeon, 14

Dickinson, Daniel S., 56, 63, 70, 95, 107, 115, 120, 131–132, 134, 144, 146, 152, 161–162, 165, 187, 204, 209, 211, 238, 255, 298, 571; and Erie Railroad, 122, 147; his political career, 122; his hatred of Seymour, 75, 118, 122, 130, 150, 200, 210, 231; elected to the Senate, 86–87; defeated for re-election to Senate, 34*n*, 118, 119*n*; and Wilmot Proviso, 100, 118; and Compromise of 1850, 34*n*, 118; opposes Marcy's presidential ambitions, 123–126, 128–129; as candidate for Cabinet post, 138–141; declines collectorship of port of New York, 149; as candidate for presidential nomination (1860), 207–208, 213; supports northern cause (1860), 228, 237; supports independent ticket (1860), 215–216; supports Union ticket (1862), 250; as attorney-general of New York, 259, 289*n*

Diven, Maj. A. S., 311*n*, 314

Dix, John A., 26*n*, 30, 34*n*, 51*n*, 56, 63, 71, 87, 100, 107, 114, 123–124, 149, 170, 210, 222, 251, 349, 350*n*, 352, 400; his political career, 465; Seymour's sketch of his career, 510; as a nepotist, 510; his program for New York Democrats, 52; on Free Soil ticket, 109–111; as candidate for Cabinet post, 138–141, 465; supports Breckinridge, 217, 238, 340; as secretary of treasury, 465; supports Lincoln in Civil War, 228; his war record, 30, 236, 505; as possible candidate for governor (1862), 244, 248; as commander of Department of the East, 236, 340–341, 345, 347, 465; and suppression of New York newspapers, 358–359; as minister to France, 465–466; his letter attacking Seymour (1868), 466; as governor, 502, 504–505, 507; defeated for re-election, 509–510; runs for mayor of New York, 517

Donohue, Edward, Jr., arrest of, 379

Donovan, Herbert C., on election of 1846, 105*n*

Doolittle, James R., 462; his explanation of Seymour's defeat (1868), 367, 484; as a candidate for Democratic nomination (1868), 421–423, 425; supports Seymour (1868), 458, 460

Dorsheimer, William, 536*n*, 545; as candidate for gubernatorial nomination (1876), 522, 524

Douglas, Stephen A., 81, 161, 170, 221, 223, 260, 444, 510, 528, 558, 572; his doctrine of popular sovereignty, 121–122, 146, 162, 182, 184, 190; his Freeport doctrine, 190; seeks presidential nomination: (1852), 125, 127–128; (1856), 173, 179; (1860), 208–209, 211, 213; in election of 1860, 214–218, 219*n*, 220, 253, 461

Dow, Neal, 133, 154

Downs, Solomon W., 125–126

Draft (conscription), 254, 277, 281; opposition to, 272, 278, 289, 295, 319, 338, 342, 344; resistance to, 309, 316, 320; in the South, 263, 313, 320, 344, 355. *See also* Army; Draft riots; Enrollment Act

Draft riots, New York City, 24, 202, 273*n*, 285, 299, 304; causes of, 308–309; drawing of names, 307–308, 321–322; events on Monday, 307, 309, 321, 330; events on Tuesday, 323–324, 331, 581; negroes attacked, 309, 324, 330, 335; Seymour's activities during, 321–329, 331, 335; activities of troops during, 320–321, 326*n*, 581, 584; suppression of, 326*n*, 329; damage done by rioters, 333–334; number killed during, 306, 332–333, 335; criminal indictments as result of, 335; myth of, 306, 309, 326, 332

Dred Scott Case, 189, 278, 363; significance of, 190

Dudley, Charles Edward, 34

Dumond, Dwight L., 227

Dunlap, Thomas, 538

Dutch, influence of, in New York, 70, 175, 191–193, 562

Dwight, Rev. Timothy (*d* 1817), 26

Eaton, William W., 470

Edgerton, Fay, 28

Edison, Thomas A., 572

Edmunds, George F., attitude of, toward Johnson's impeachment, 403–404; on Electoral Commission, 403, 533

Edward VI, King of England, 4

Elections, national: (1800), 58, 219; (1824), 47, 50*n*, 219; (1828), 50*n*; (1832), 50*n*; (1836), 50*n*; (1840), 40, 50*n*, 216, 489, 573; (1844), 84; (1846), 106; (1848), 109–111, 216; (1852), 131; (1856), 70, 182, 187, 189; (1860), 215, 218–220, 270; (1862), 310–311; (1864), 376, 444, 478; (1866), 390–392, 446; (1872), 478, 502; (1876), 478, 528–533; (1880), 478, 528, 539–540, 548; (1884), 528, 548; (1888), xix, 219, 528; (1892), 528; (1924), 296*n*; (1928), 296*n*. *See also* Conventions *under* names of several parties

—— (1868), 386*n*, 443; issues in, 350*n*, 446–449, 472–473; Seymour's speech accepting nomination, 461–462; movement to change Democratic ticket, 468–470; financing of Democratic campaign, 463; the line-up of prominent men in, 449–452, 456–460, 465; analysis of popular and electoral votes cast, 474–475, 478; fraud in, charged, 475–483

Elections, New York, polling of soldier vote (1864), 376–380; fraud in, charged, 475–477, 482; (1817), 10; (1828), 47; (1833), 35; (1836), 50; (1838), 46, 53; (1841), 53, 66; (1842), 69–70; (1844), 76, 84, 476; (1845), 35, 107; (1846), 97, 103–105, 107; (1849), 113; (1850), 65, 116–119; (1852), 131–134; (1853), 151; (1854), 114, 161–167, 386*n*; special (1854), 148; (1855), 173*n*, 187; (1856), 187; (1858), 204; (1860), 215–216, 218; (1861), 240, 259, 283; (1862), 245–257, 259, 284, 478; (1863), 353–354; (1864), 283, 373–376, 380–382, 386*n*, 482, 553; special (1864), 289; (1867), 395, 411; (1868), 475, 477; (1870), 491–492; (1872), 502; (1873), 507; (1874), 507–509, 512; (1875), 516, 518; (1876), 534; (1879), 535

Elections, New York City, fraud in, 475–483; (1850), 118; (1852), 134*n*; (1861), 283, 285; (1862), 283–284; (1868), 481; (1870), 492; (1876), 517

Eliot, Charles W., 563

Ellicott, Joseph, 12

Ely, Smith, elected mayor of New York, 517

Emancipation, xviii, 201, 248, 251, 254, 270, 278, 280; in conquered territories, 448

Emancipation Proclamation, 248, 250, 258–259, 277; question of constitutionality of, 266, 349, 558; effect of, on South, 299

Emerson, Ralph Waldo, 386; Concord speech of, at services in memory of Lincoln, 385

England, I. W., 463

English, Gov. James E., Conn., 458; as a candidate for Democratic nomination (1868), 396, 422–423, 428

Enrollment Act, 299–300, 480; analysis of congressional vote on, 310–311; provisions of, 311, 315, 316*n*, 347*n*; constitutionality of, 313–315, 344–345; administration of, 307, 309, 311, 318–319, 322, 340, 345–346; Lincoln and, 309–310, 314–315, 319, 329, 341–344; Seymour's opposition to, 307, 313–315, 318, 338, 340–344, 351, 354–355; true purpose of, 316–317, 320, 344; assignment of quotas under, 317–320, 341–346, 481–483; enforcement of, postponed, 307, 329; commutation of service under, 315–318; results of, 316, 320

Erie Canal, N. Y., xix, 52, 147, 193, 199, 572; early plans for, 13–15; construction of, 10–12, 16–17; opening of, 17–18, 20; opposition to, 8, 12, 15, 19–20; enlargement of, 75, 135*n*, 148; travel on, described, 18; traffic on and revenue from, 49, 73, 76*n*, 135–136; threatened by St. Lawrence route, 16, 201; decline of, 137. *See also* Canal Ring; Canals

Erie Railroad, 52, 147, 489; state support of, 49, 73, 122

Evans, Col. Charles, 275

Evarts, William M., 47, 530

Everett, Edward, 302; on Union ticket (1860), 214, 217, 461

Ewing, Thomas, Jr., 416

Fairchild, Charles S., xviii, 516; elected attorney-general, 515; defeated for reelection, 534; appointed superintendent

of public works, 534–535; appointed assistant secretary of treasury, 535
Fairchild, Mrs. Charles S. (Helen Lincklaen), ix, 7*n*, 277*n*, 300*n*, 382, 515
—— Sidney T., 199, 523–524
Farmer's Fire Insurance and Loan Co., 21*n*
Farmer's Loan and Trust Co., 21, 61
Farwell, Gov. Leonard J., Wisconsin, 195
Faulkner, L. B., 523–525
Federalism, 60
Fenton, Gov. Reuben E., New York, 491, 512, 519; objects to quotas under draft law, 318–320, 342–343; his nomination and election (1864), 373, 376, 553; his feud with Morgan, 490; his political career, 376
Ferry, Moses J., 379
Fessenden, William P., 403
Field, Cyrus W., 254
—— Stephen J., as a candidate for Democratic nomination (1868), 428
Fillmore, Millard, 56, 122–123, 126, 131, 170, 190, 214, 217–218, 278; and Fugitive Slave Law, 114; as presidential candidate (1856), 115, 161–162, 179, 182, 187
Fish, Hamilton (*d* 1893), 83*n*, 142, 488, 552, 572; his friendship for Seymour, 116; elected to Senate, 118, 119*n*
Fisk, James, 491, 500
Fitch, Graham N., 424
Fite, Prof. E. D., 212
Flagg, Azariah C., xix, 51*n*, 54, 66, 71–72, 88, 147–148
Florida, secession of, 327*n*; in election of 1876, 531
Folger, Charles J., 536, 548*n*
Foote, Henry S., 227*n*
Force, Peter, 31
Ford, Dr. W. E., 573
Forman, Col. Jonathan, 7
—— Mary Ledyard. *See* Seymour
Forrest, Gen. Nathan B., 450
Fort Orange. *See* Albany
Fort Schuyler, N.Y., 17*n*, 63
Fort Sumter, S. C., 30, 221, 226, 231
Foster, H. D., 227*n*
—— Henry A., 86
Fowler, Joseph S., 403
Fox and Wisconsin Canal, 153, 194–196; Seymour's connection with, 193, 197–200, 552
Fox River Improvement Company, 194*n*, 196, 244
France, danger of war with, 171
Franchise (suffrage), 284, 405*n*; demanded by women, 415–416; plank in Democratic platform on (1868), 419; extension of, in New York, 92, 97, 103, 288–289, 395; extension of, to negroes, 103, 388, 395, 415–416
Franco-Prussian War, 492
Free Soil movement, 99*n*, 100, 102–103, 144–145, 161–162, 178; splits New York Democrats, 71, 109–111, 113–114
Free Soil party, 115; convention of, 109; in elections: (1848), 109–111, 113; (1852), 131
Freedmen's Bureau, 419
Freeman, Douglas S., 331
Frelinghuysen, Frederick (*d* 1804), 533*n*
—— Frederick Theodore (*d* 1885), on Electoral Commission, 533
—— Joseph S., 533*n*
—— Theodore (*d* 1862), 533*n*
Frémont, Jessie (Benton), 169
—— John C., 115, 182, 186, 214; career of, 169; presidential candidacy of, 170, 179, 187
Fry, Gen. James B., 317, 340; his administration of the draft, 309–312, 318–319, 341–344, 346, 347*n*; his *New York and the Conscription of 1863*, 312, 342; on Seymour's activities concerning the draft, 322, 343; arrogance of, 275, 329, 342; defended by Blaine, 547
Fugitive Slave Law, 114, 120–121, 131
Fuller, J. C., 68
Gales, Joseph, 31
Gardiner, Addison, 104–105
Gardner, Gov. H. J., Mass., 161
Garfield, James, 312*n*, 543; his election (1880), 478, 528, 539–542, 546, 548; his interpretation of nationalism, 540–542; and the patronage, 546–548
Garrison, William Lloyd, 32, 68, 192, 229, 278, 557; attitude of, toward Grant (1868), 450
Gates, Gen. Horatio, 3, 25
Genesee Valley Canal, 75, 91
Geneva Academy (Hobart College), 28
Georgia, secession of, 327*n*; vote of, contested (1868), 484
Germans, in New York politics, 132, 217
Gettysburg, Battle of, xvi, 302–303; dedication of national cemetery at, 302–303
Gibbons, Abby Hopper, petitions Democratic convention (1868), 416

Gillet, Ransom H., on New York politics, 55; on the extension of slavery, 100; on Polk's relations with Wright, 89; on Polk's appointment of Marcy, 89*n*; on Wright's defeat (1846), 105*n*

Gilmore, William J., 412

Gladstone, William E., 254, 256, 514; on American Constitution, 563–564

Godkin, Edwin L., 456; opposes Seymour (1868), 452

Gould, Jay, 491

Granger, Francis, 119

Grant, Ulysses S., 24, 116, 303, 306, 367, 386, 401, 406, 410–411, 416, 426, 434, 437, 440, 476, 486, 491–492, 497, 500–501, 504, 506, 510, 525, 529, 540, 553, 571; his pre-presidential political record, 444–445; in elections: (1868), 443, 446–447, 450–451, 455, 458, 464–465, 468, 472, 474, 477–479, 484; (1872), 485, 505; as President, 445, 488, 490; ambitions of, for a third term, 511, 517; and packing of Supreme Court, 544

Gray, Judge Hiram, 523–524

Great Britain, in Crimean War, 170; strained relations with United States, 171, 242, 254; Irish policy of, 391

Greeley, Horace, 63, 118, 164, 185*n*, 214, 217, 225, 227, 248, 252, 332, 335, 376, 395, 464, 507, 552; an estimate of, 248–249; Weeden on, 282; his political ambitions, 167, 203, 231, 552; his stand on secession, 102; nags Lincoln, 244; his feud with Weed, 203, 238, 248–249, 283*n*, 295; his stand on prohibition, 133, 167; his estimate of Seymour, 120; as a critic of Seymour, 155, 202–203, 208, 217, 232, 298, 329, 351; opposes Seymour's candidacies: (1862), 245, 248; (1868), 452–453; his comments on Seymour's messages: (1854), 153*n*; (1863), 269–270; (1864), 357; accuses Seymour of nepotism (1863), 353; opposes conscription, 314; his actions during draft riots, 308, 328; his reporting of draft riots, 273*n*, 309, 324, 326; his analysis of popular vote (1864), 444; favors Chase (1868), 445; urges investigation of election (1868), 475; as presidential nominee, 275, 340, 478, 485, 501–502, 505, 513, 517. *See also* New York *Tribune*

—— Mrs. Horace, petitions Democratic convention (1868), 416

Green Bay and Mississippi Canal Company, 197, 200*n*, 202, 204, 232; partial liquidation of, 198

Greenback party, 528

Greenbacks. *See* Currency

Greene, ——, 267

Greer, Capt. James, N. Y. police (1863), 323

Grier, R. C., 190*n*

Grimes, James W., 403

Griswold, John A., 475, 477

Guiteau, C. J., 547

Guthrie, James, 208; his reforms of treasury department, 149, 151, 363; as candidate for Democratic nomination (1864), 337, 362–363; on resolutions committee at Chicago (1864), 367

Habeas corpus, writ of, 314; suspended, 251, 254, 265, 277–278, 289, 291, 369; denied, 292; enforcement of, 271, 292

Hale, John P., 131

Hall, A. Oakey, 358–359; his part in Democratic convention (1868), 418, 421; elected mayor of New York: (1868), 481; (1870), 492

—— Mrs. Basil, describes boarding-school, 29

Halleck, Gen. Henry W., 276

Halstead, Murat, 210; on Lincoln (1864), 360

Hamilton, Alexander, 21, 58, 98, 192; Garfield's admiration for, 541–542

Hamlin, Hannibal, 360

Hammet, William H., 80

Hammond, Jabez D., 12, 71, 105; his estimates of Henry Seymour, 10, 21; on Horatio Seymour as a lawyer, 33*n*; on Seymour's canal report, 75; on national Democratic convention (1844), 82; on Wright's canal bill veto, 91*n*; works for party truce (1848), 100, 111; his *History* criticized, 82

Hampton, Wade, 407; at Democratic convention (1868), 412, 418; campaigns for Seymour (1868), 449–450

Hancock, Gen. Winfield S., xix, 484, 567, 574; as candidate for Democratic nomination (1868), 396, 401, 405–406, 411, 422–426, 428–429, 441, 470, 485; endorses Seymour (1868), 458, 467; as presidential nominee (1880), 478, 528, 539–540, 546, 548*n*

Hardenbergh, Jacob, 423

Harding, Warren G., 140

"Hards," 34, 128, 132, 137, 143, 150–151,

161, 164, 166, 173, 203, 250; term explained, 113–114; choose independent ticket: (1853), 150, 152; (1854), 114, 162, 164; (1860), 215; support fusion ticket (1860), 218; support Union ticket (1862), 248
Harris, Benjamin G., attacks McClellan at Chicago (1864), 368–369
—— Ira, 231
Harrisburg *Patriot and Union*, on Seymour's message (1864), 357*n*
Harrison, Benjamin, 548*n*
—— William H., 46, 50*n*, 54, 65, 84, 540
Hart, E. B., 267
—— Ephraim, 12
Hartford, Conn., convention on New York lands at, 3
Hartford *Times*, on Seymour's message (1864), 357*n*
Hartley, Rev. Isaac S., on Seymour's distaste for the law, 33
Hawley, Jesse, on Clinton's part in planning Erie Canal, 14–15
—— Seth C., 285
Hayes, Rutherford B., 39, 256, 357, 383, 386, 391, 403, 474, 525, 534, 571; as presidential candidate, 528–529, 531–532; and Evarts, 47, 530
Head, Orson S., 196
Headley, Joel T., on draft riots, 326*n*
Helmbold, H. T., contributes to campaign fund of Democrats (1868), 463
Henderson, John Brooks, 403
Hendricks, Thomas A., 484, 502; his stand on inflation, 401; as a candidate for Democratic nomination (1868), xv, 401–402, 405, 409–410, 423–426, 428–429, 432–433, 439, 441, 470, 485; endorses Seymour (1868), 458–459
Henry, Patrick, 544
Herkimer, Gen. Nicholas, 192
Hewitt, Abram S., 231, 410, 435, 509
Hill, Benjamin H., 450
—— Gov. David B., New York, 450, 548*n*, 572
Hill, Cagger & Porter, firm of, 378*n*
"Hindoos," 160
Hitchcock, Mrs. Augusta B., ix
Hoar, George Frisbie, 549
Hobart College, 28
Hoffman, Gov. John T., 105, 393, 481, 494, 505; elected governor: (1868), 437, 474–477, 479, 487; (1870), 490–492; vetoes reform bill (1869), 479
—— Michael, xix, 66, 71–73, 93, 97, 557
Holland, as model for United States, 193
Holland Land Company, 12
"Holland Purchase," 3
Hollister, Frederick, 67
Holmes, Daniel H., his comment on Seymour's campaign (1868), 461
Holst, Hermann von, on New York election (1850), 118
Holt, Joseph, 379–380
Hood, Gen. Thomas, 374
Hooker, Rev. Thomas, 4
Hoover, Herbert C., 201
Hosack, Dr. David, 13–14
Howard, Gen. Oliver O., on conditions in the South (1868), 447
Howland & Aspinwall, 350*n*
Hudson, David, 41
Hudson River, 13, 190
Hudson River Railroad, 136
Hughes, Charles E., 115*n*, 529
—— Archbishop John, N. Y., 160; speech of, to "rioters," 326*n*
"Hunkers," 34, 69, 71, 77, 83, 86, 89, 97, 107, 113, 117, 122–123, 137, 143, 145, 147, 150, 166; term defined, 35, 54*n*; policies of, 35, 51*n*, 52, 54–55, 66, 72, 92, 95; desert Wright (1846), 106; and Wilmot Proviso, 109
Hunt, Gov. Washington, N. Y., 142, 217; elected governor (1850), 65, 116–117; his campaign for re-election, 131–134
Hunter, Robert M. T., 208, 213
Hutchins, Stilson, pushes Seymour for presidency (1880), 537–538
Hutchinson, Prof. William T., 468
Hutton, Capt. ——, Burnside's aide, 291–292

Indemnity Act (1863), constitutionality of, 359
Independent Treasury, 46, 51, 77, 104
Indiana, federal grants of land to, 196; resistance to draft in, 309; in election of 1868, 468
—— Legislature, its resolution of thanks to Seymour (1863), 270*n*–271*n*
Inge, William R., 445
Ingersoll, C. M., 460–461
Iowa, in election of 1868, 468
Ireland, criticism of British treatment of, 391
Irish, 175, 562; as canal diggers, 16, 63; importance of, in New York politics, 9, 64, 217, 509, 527; antagonism to, 159–160

Iroquois Indians, 190
Irving, Washington, 185*n*, 192

Jackson, Andrew, 34–35, 38, 46–50, 54, 58, 78, 87, 96, 114, 120, 122, 186, 189, 219, 260, 266, 279, 359, 391, 417, 445, 448, 470, 540, 544; an estimate of, 58–59; supports Polk, 80, 84
—— Gen. Thomas J. ("Stonewall"), 301*n*, 445
Jacobsen, Edna L., ix
Jameson, J. Franklin, ix, 84
Jaquess, Col. James F., 364
Jay, John (*d* 1829), 192
—— John (*d* 1894), 191
—— Peter Augustus, 20
Jefferson, Thomas, 5, 22, 38, 50, 58–59, 65, 96, 114, 119–121, 177, 186, 219, 260, 266, 279, 391, 417, 544–545, 568; Seymour's respect for, xvii
Jenkins, Charles E., and draft riots, 321–322
Jenne, Daniel C., 198
Jerome, Charles W., 7*n*
Jews, 464; jealousy of, 159
Johnson, ——, of the Albany *Argus*, 144*n*
—— Andrew, 122, 297, 338, 375, 381, 405–406, 409, 434, 451, 460, 465–466, 505, 510, 517, 571; his reconstruction policy, 387, 390; deprived of power by Congress, 392–393; his political isolation, 394; impeachment and trial of, 296, 399, 402–404, 419, 444, 533; on Seymour's unwillingness to be a candidate (1868), 398; as candidate for Democratic nomination (1868), 402, 422–426, 468, 485; his telegram to Seymour (1868), 471*n*
—— Cave, 82
—— Reverdy, as a candidate for Democratic nomination (1868), 423
—— Samuel, 576
—— William, 244
Jones, Morven M., 380
—— Samuel, 285
"Junius," attack of, on Seymour, 279–280

Kansas, Lecompton constitution, 221
Kansas-Nebraska Act, 145, 161–162, 558; influence of, on Whig party, 121; Seymour on, 145, 183–184
Kellogg, Spencer, 66
Kelly, John, 410, 435, 546; as a candidate for governor (1879), 535; his treachery (1880), 567; opposes Cleveland, 547, 549
—— William, 380; candidate for governor (1860), 216–218; alarmed by Lincoln's "radical" leanings, 243
Kennedy, John A., 284, 286, 331
Kentucky, in election of 1868, 478
Kernan, Francis, xviii, 64, 237, 255, 452, 503, 509, 511, 516, 528; his part in Democratic convention (1868), 412, 418, 420, 430–431; his opposition to Tammany, 487, 492, 497–498; excluded from floor of convention (1871), 493–494; defeated for governorship (1872), 340, 504, 507, 513; elected to Senate, 495, 512–514; works for Tilden (1876), 523, 527
Kerr, Michael C., 475
Ketchum, Hiram, 398
Kidd, William, testimony of, on Seymour's City Hall speech, 328
King, Gov. John A., N. Y., 57, 174, 187*n*, 202–203, 312*n*, 559
—— Preston, 283; and Wilmot Proviso, 100, 107
—— Rufus, 64
Kingsland, Ambrose C., 118
Know-Nothing party, 133, 160–162, 164–166, 179, 182, 192, 217, 228; in election of 1856, 187. *See also* American party; Nativism
Ku Klux Klan, 180

Land, Dutch leasehold system in New York, 97–99; federal grants of: to Indiana, 196; to Wisconsin, 194, 196; speculation in, 11, 22, 46, 49, 228; influence of Erie Canal on value of, 11, 50; price of, 195
Land reformers, in election of 1852, 131. *See also* Anti-renters
Lane, Joseph, 213; as candidate for vice-presidency (1860), 217
Laning, A. B., 248*n*
Lansdowne, 5th Marquess of, 339
Lawrence, William, 475
Leavitt, Judge Humphrey H., 292
Ledwith, Thomas A., 492
Lee, Ann, 39
—— Col. Henry, on Seymour-Andrew meeting (1864), 364, 365*n*
—— Robert E., xviii, 254, 256, 281, 299, 313, 319, 326, 374, 383, 450, 467, 571; his Gettysburg campaign, 301, 303, 307; his retreat after Gettysburg, 331–332

Leonard, Rev. Joshua, 7; as a schoolmaster, 27
Liberator, The, on Seymour's handling of convention disturbances (1842), 69
Lincklaen, Helen. *See* Fairchild, Mrs. Charles S.
—— Ledyard, 7; Seymour's letter to, 246–247
—— Mrs. Ledyard (Helen Clarissa Seymour), 7, 382; Seymour's letter to, 246–247
Lincoln, Abraham, xvi, 30, 50, 106, 119, 121, 160*n*, 169, 197, 208, 212, 222, 224, 226, 238–239, 241, 253, 259–260, 270, 281, 302, 307, 327, 332, 349, 371, 381, 390, 445–446, 451–452, 509–510, 517, 528, 554, 574; his nomination and election (1860), 214, 217–220, 225, 461; and Crittenden Compromise, 223; and patronage, 231; and Vallandigham, 242, 291–294; and *Trent* affair, 242; his "radical" policies, 241, 243, 249, 261–262, 272, 278, 289, 298; and emancipation, 248, 254, 277, 299; and habeas corpus, 251, 254, 265, 277, 292; and martial law, 265, 267; defies Supreme Court, 251; and conscription, 254, 277, 309–310, 314–315, 319, 329, 341–347; his call for troops (1864), 318; his extension of the executive power, 266–267, 277–279, 293–295, 337, 339; and suppression of newspapers, 358–359; and enlistment of slaves, 374; and polling of soldier vote (1864), 378–380; on status of rebellious states, 383; his reconstruction policy, 375; movement to replace (1864), 359–361; his relations with Seymour, 272–277, 300, 314, 341–343, 345, 347; criticism of, 256; on Frank Blair, 448; significance of his death, 338, 383–385
—— Charles Z., his *Constitutional History*, 97
Litchfield, Elisha, 71
Little Falls, N. Y., Seymour's speech at, 542–543
Livingston, Peter R., 10*n*
—— Robert B., 192
"Locofocos," 51*n*, 97*n*, 117, 228
London *Daily News*, 351*n*
London *Times*, on Seymour's message (1864), 357*n*; its eulogy of Seymour, 575–576
Long, Alexander, 369
Longstreet, Gen. James, 331
Louisiana, secession of, 327*n*; corruption in, 532*n*
Louisiana Purchase, importance of, 545
Love, John, as commissioner to pass on New York draft quotas, 346
Loy, J. F., 234*n*
Ludlow, W. H., 505
Lyon, ——, of the *Observer*, 144*n*

"McCabe, James D., Jr.," 464
McClellan, Gen. George B., 243–244, 255, 295, 303, 349, 352, 387, 470, 540, 571; removal of, from command, 251; confers with Seymour, 260; his nomination and candidacy, 362, 365–366, 368–371, 478; his actions in Maryland, 362, 369–371; repudiates party platform (1864), 372; endorses Seymour (1868), 456, 466–467
McClernand, John A., 416
McCook, Gen. George W., his part in Democratic convention (1868), 418, 422, 429, 432, 435
McCormac, Eugene I., 80, 476
McCormick, Cyrus H., 467, 546; on inflation, 396; his move to replace Seymour (1868), 468–470
McCulloch, Hugh, his estimate of Seymour, vii
McCunn, John H., 479
MacDonald, Ramsay, 339
McKinley, William, 275
McLean, John (*d* 1861), 26*n*, 190*n*, 363
—— John Roll, 537
—— Washington, 406, 428, 435, 537
McMahon, Martin T., 439
McMurray, ——, 285
Madison, James, 9, 153, 417
Magone, Daniel, Jr., 524
Maine, establishes prohibition, 133
Malony, R. S., fights unit rule at Democratic convention (1868), 426–428
Manning, Daniel, 277*n*, 515, 572
Marble, Manton, urges change in Democratic ticket (1868), 468
Marcy, William L. (*d* 1857), xviii, 20, 26, 56, 59, 61, 63, 71, 75, 111, 130, 132, 134, 161, 173, 195, 203, 274, 364, 516; association of, with Seymour, 33–34, 38, 45, 106, 143–146, 149, 152, 163–164, 170–171, 177; political ambitions of, 46, 90; as governor, 34–35, 48, 50–53; as secretary of war, 88–89, 95, 107; struggle of, for presidential nomination, 122–129; appointment of, to Pierce's Cabinet, 123,

129, 137–141; and patronage, 143–146, 149–150; his death, 187–188; Moore's estimate of, 188*n*
Marion, Gen. Francis, 186
Marsh, Clarissa (Seymour), 4
—— Deborah (Buell), 5*n*
—— Ebenezer, 5*n*
—— Mary. *See* Seymour
Marshall, John, 544
Martial law, imposed, 265, 267–268, 270–271; Supreme Court on, 292
Martin, Mrs. ——, 233
—— Edward W. ("James D. McCabe, Jr."), his biography of Seymour, 464
—— Morgan L., 195
Maryland, McClellan's actions in, 362, 369–371
"Marysland," Deerfield, N. Y., 550
Mason, James M., 242, 294
—— John Young (*d* 1859), 150*n*
Massachusetts, position of, at constitutional convention, 192; claims land in western New York, 3; protests against conditions in Kansas, 182; in election of 1868, 478
Masters, Edgar Lee, 338
Matthews, Albert, 243*n*
—— Robert, 42–43
Maxon, D. W., 234–235
Meade, Gen. George G., 301, 307; his pursuit of Lee, 331–332
Methodist church, split in, 103
Mexican War, 79, 99, 104
Mexico, abolition of slavery in, 100
Middletown, Conn., 29
Miller, ——, 170
—— Blandina D., 323*n*
—— George L., 434, 440–441, 453, 488, 502, 520
—— Henry S., on Seymour's nomination (1868), 438–439; Seymour's advice to, 554–555
—— Josiah T., 321
—— Morris S., 36, 178, 257
—— Mrs. Morris (Maria Bleecker), 27, 36
—— Rutger B., 90
—— Mrs. Rutger B., 247, 554
Milligan Case, 292, 384
Milton, John, quoted on crime and punishment, 559
Milwaukee *News*, on Seymour's message (1864), 357*n*
Mississippi, secession of, 327*n*; excluded from election (1868), 474
Missouri Compromise, 102, 114, 162, 225; repeal of, 121, 161, 183–184
Mitchell, Alexander, 546
—— Edward P., 330
Monroe, James, 11
Montgomery County, N. Y., Bleecker holdings in, 36
Moore, James B., his appraisal of Marcy, 188*n*
Morgan, Gov. Edwin D., N. Y., 30, 63, 97*n*, 214, 216, 235, 242, 244, 248, 265*n*, 281; elected governor: (1858), 204; (1860), 218; elected to Senate, 283, 352; position of, on impeachment of Johnson, 403; his rivalry with Fenton, 490; defeated for governorship (1876), 534
—— Gen. Daniel, 186
—— George W., 435
—— Gen. John H., 361
Morley, John, 339
Morris, Gouverneur, 14, 192
—— Robert H., mayor of N. Y., 160
Morse, Samuel F. B., 159
Morton, Gov. Oliver P., Indiana, 281, 488, 533
Mott, ——, 378
—— Lucretia, 68
Moultrie, Gen. William, 186*n*
Mozart Hall, 209–210, 217, 304
"Mugwumps," 549
Murphy, Henry Cruse, 494*n*; his part in Democratic convention (1868), 412, 417–418
Murray, Hon. Amelia, her acquaintance with the Seymours, 62, 101, 163, 165, 175–177, 553; review of her *Letters from the United States*, 101*n*
Muzzey, David S., on Blaine-Conkling feud, 548
Myers, Gustavus H., on Tammany's support of Seymour (1868), 437

Napoleon I, 43, 240
Napoleon III, 171, 492
Nast, Thomas, his fight against Tammany, 487, 528
Nation, Carrie A., 464
Nation. *See* New York *Nation*
National Intelligencer, *The*, on services of governors in supplying troops, 301
National Labor Union, presents petition to Democratic convention (1868), 414–416
Native American party. *See* American party

Nativism, 182; in New York, 155, 159–162, 192, 204; Seymour's hostility to, 154, 178; in Massachusetts, 161; in the nation, 162. *See also* American party; Know-Nothing party
Nebraska, 518
Negroes, 472; recruiting of, 300; orphanage of, burned, 309, 324, 330, 335; question of extending the suffrage to, 103, 388, 392, 395, 405*n*, 415–416, 440
Neilson, James, 306
Nelson, Samuel, in Dred Scott Case, 190*n*, 363; supported by Seymour for nomination (1864), 337, 362–363, 365, 370
Netherlands. *See* Holland
Newark *Journal*, on Seymour's message (1864), 357*n*
Newcomb, Edward, 379
Newell, George Washington, 134, 146
New Englanders, importance of, in New York, 44, 63, 70–71, 175; character of, 192, 257
New Jersey, boundary dispute, 20
Newspapers, suppression of, 292*n*, 304, 352, 358–359, 465
New York, position of, at constitutional convention (1787), 193; as a pivotal state in national elections, 5, 58, 70, 83, 96, 115, 140, 539; position and prominence of, 37–38, 43; industrial development in, 64; question of lands west of Seneca Lake, 3; New Jersey boundary of, 20; electoral college of, 47, 50*n*, 115*n*, 139, 530–531; electoral districts in, 8, 519; franchise in, 92, 97, 103, 284, 288–289; referendums in, 95, 97, 103, 148, 289, 490; "spoils system" and corruption in, 11–12, 48, 55, 59, 137–138, 143–146, 152, 162, 214, 237, 394, 507–508, 515, 522, 534; state printing of, 48, 53, 55, 66, 107–108, 187; foreign population in, 17, 44, 63–64, 70, 175, 191–192, 284; foreign language and parochial schools in, 159–160; anti-rent riots in, 98–99; political confusion in: (1854), 114, 166; (1860), 217–218; prohibition movement in, 132–134, 153*n*, 154–158; liquor laws of, 154–156; internal improvements, 10–20, 49, 52, 66, 72–74, 76, 90–91, 122, 147–148, 153, 228; religious fanatics in, 39–43; abolition of slavery by, xviii, 43; financial policies of, 17, 49, 51–53, 66, 72–75, 91–92, 147–148, 349–351, 490; borrowing power of, 97; debt of (1845), 53*n*; militia of, 235*n*; enrollment in, 345–347; number of troops supplied by, 318; furloughs granted voters of, 347, 377. *See also* Elections; Democratic party; Republican party; Whig party
— Assembly, committees of, 72
— Canal commissioners, 17*n*, 515, 534
— Comptroller, 54*n*
— Constitution of 1821, amended, 43, 93; question of revision of, 91–94
— Constitution of 1846, 97, 99, 135, 142; amended, 148, 289, 490, 533–534
— Constitutional convention (1846), 92–95
— Council of appointment, 9, 92
— Council of revision, 92
— Court of appeals, 97; decisions of, 98*n*, 158
— Court of first judicial district, decision of, 158
— Governor, 147; his power of appointment, 92, 97*n*; his veto power, 92; term of, 533–534; salary of, 43, 135, 510
— Legislature, reapportionment of seats in, 519
New York, N. Y., fire in (1835), 22; Democratic convention at (1868), xv, 407–431; patronage in, 150, 283; nativist riots in, 160; Pine Street meeting at, 222; Vallandigham protest meeting at, 294*n*; Conservative Soldiers and Sailors convention at (1868), 416; question of education of aliens in, 159–160; Seymour's quarrel with police commissioners of, 284–286; question of Broadway Railroad franchise, 286–288; Seymour's Cooper Institute speech, 391–392; the draft in, 340, 342–345, 351; votes bounties for drafted persons, 329–330; vital statistics of (1860–1866), 333*n*; "Tweed charter" for, 479. *See also* Draft riots; Elections; Tammany
New York *Atlas*, on Seymour's conduct during the draft riots, 309
— Battery, 42
— Brooks Brothers store, sacked by rioters, 309, 323, 331
— Bunker's Mansion House, 21
New York *Catholic Sentinel*, advice to Catholics (1855), 187*n*
New York Central Railroad, 49, 57, 137, 489; merger creating, 136
New York County, and claims for draft-riot damage, 333; criminal indictments in, because of draft riots, 335; prosecu-

tions in, arising from suppression of newspapers, 358–359; vote in (1864), 376*n*
New York *Evening Post*, on Seymour's annual message (1863), 268–269; on Seymour's City Hall speech, 325, 581–582; on Seymour's financial policy, 351*n*; on Democratic state convention (1853), 353; on insanity of the Seymours, 456
New York *Express*, 151; on Seymour's City Hall speech, 325, 581
New York *Herald*, on Seymour as possible candidate (1860), 207, 209–210, 213; on corruption in canal contracts, 214; urges nomination of Dix (1862), 244; on Seymour's inauguration, 265; on Seymour's Brooklyn speech (1863), 304; on draft riots, 307; on Seymour's City Hall speech, 325, 583; attack on Seymour (1863), 353*n*; opposes Seymour (1868), 461. *See also* Bennett, James Gordon
New York Historical and Geographical Society, Seymour's address before, 191–193
New York *Journal of Commerce*, on draft riots, 309; suppression of, 358–359, 465
New York Mills, N. Y., 64
New York *Nation*, on election of 1864, 443; on troubles in Arkansas (1868), 446; opposes Seymour (1868), 452, 456
New York *Standard and Statesman*, on Lincoln's offer to make Seymour his successor, 273*n*–274*n*
New York State Military Association, 235*n*
New York *Sun*, questions Seymour's sincerity in refusing nomination (1868), 436; on Seymour's attitude (1868), 454; attacks Seymour (1868), 459
New York Temperance Alliance, 133
New York *Times*, on Seymour's annual message (1863), 268; on Seymour's City Hall speech, 325, 582; on damage done in draft riots, 333; on Seymour's financial policy, 351*n*; opposes Seymour (1868), 461; exposes Tweed Ring, 497
New York *Tribune*, on Seymour's message (1854), 153*n*; accuses Seymour of duplicity (1857), 202–203; on Seymour as possible candidate (1860), 208; on Syracuse "juggle," 217–218; on Seymour's message (1863), 269–270; its treatment of draft-riot news, 308*n*; on Seymour's City Hall speech, 325, 326*n*, 327, 583–584; on number killed and damage done in draft riots, 333; on Seymour's financial policy, 351*n*; on election of 1864, 444; opposes Seymour (1868), 452–453. *See also* Greeley, Horace
New York *True Sun*, 86
New York *World*, on Seymour's City Hall speech, 325, 582; on Seymour's message (1864), 357*n*; suppression of, 358–359, 465; on election of 1864, 376; exposes corruption in management of canals (1867), 394; demands change in Democratic ticket (1868), 468–470; its attacks on Blaine (1884), 548
Nichols, R. F., on Marcy's presidential ambitions, 124, 138
Niskayuna, N. Y., 39
North, Col. Samuel, 379–380, 399
North Carolina, opposes southern conscription, 313
Northwestern Ship Canal convention, 199
Noyes, John Humphrey, 39
Nugent, Col. Robert, and the draft, 311*n*, 329

Oakman, Mrs. Walter J., 522*n*
O'Brien, Maj. Henry F., murdered by rioters, 330
O'Conor, Charles, 222; elected Tammany sachem, 500; bolts party (1872), 504
Oconto River Drivers (9th Wisconsin Battery), 233–234
Ohio, election in (1863), 294; in national election (1868), 468
"Ohio Idea," 395
Ohio State Journal, charges Seymour with treasonable conduct, 398
Oneida Community, N. Y., 39
Oneida County, N. Y., its record in elections, 91*n*, 119–120, 134, 255, 474, 477, 482, 548*n*; its quota under draft, 482; recruiting in, 30, 244
Oneida County *Democratic Union*, backs Seymour for nomination (1868), 396
Opdyke, Mayor George, New York City, 285; protests withdrawal of troops, 301, 323; activities of, during riots, 321–322, 329; proclaims riots ended, 326*n*; vetoes bounties for drafted persons, 330; on Seymour's City Hall speech, 335–336
Order of United Americans, 160

Oregon, in election of 1868, 478
Oregon Territory, 79; settlement concerning, 104
Oxford Academy, Utica, N. Y., 28

Packer, Asa, as a candidate for Democratic nomination (1868), 422–425, 428
Palmer, George W., 318
—— Henry L., 411
—— Waldo, ix
Panics, xix; (1837), 22, 46, 51, 53, 60, 229, 489, 573; (1857), 202; (1873), 485, 506–507, 517, 520–521, 540, 560, 573
Paris Commune (1871), 560
Parker, Alton B., 573
—— Amasa J., 174, 187*n*, 204, 267, 370; on treatment of New York election agents, 380
—— Gov. Joel, N. J., 263, 458; as a candidate for Democratic nomination (1868), 396, 422–423, 425
Parmenter, R. A., 513
Partridge, Capt. Alden, as school-master, 29–31
Patronage, in New York, 11–12, 48, 55, 59, 143, 305; in New York City, 150, 283; federal, 87–89, 107, 137–138, 144–146, 149–152, 162, 203–204, 231, 546–548
Peirce, J. L. O., ix
Pendleton, George H., 244, 459, 489; as speaker at Brooklyn (1863), 304; as candidate for Democratic nomination (1868), 395–396, 400–402, 406, 412, 414, 421–429, 432–433, 438, 441, 470, 485; supports Seymour (1868), 457–458; and the currency problem, 395, 438, 519–520
Pennsylvania, position of, at constitutional convention (1787), 193; in election of 1868, 468
—— Supreme court, decisions of, 314
People's convention, 237
People versus John A. Dix and Others, 359
Perry, Commodore Matthew C., 185*n*
Philadelphia, Pa., threatened by Lee, 301, 303; Seymour's speech at (1864), 374–375
Philadelphia *Press*, on Seymour at Gettysburg dedication, 302
Pierce, Dr. ——, 459
—— Franklin, 60, 70, 75, 110, 114, 120, 134, 143, 153, 163–164, 169–173, 179, 187, 189, 204, 337, 359, 445, 465, 510; an estimate of, 140; Seymour's opinion of, 164; nomination of, 129; selection of Cabinet by, 123, 129, 137–141; and the patronage, 144–146, 149–152, 162
Pierson, Elijah, 42–43
Pitt, William, (*d* 1806), 385
Pittsfield *Sun*, on Seymour's message (1864), 357*n*
Pius IX, 158
Platt, Thomas C., 548
Plumb, Rev. D., 69
Poland, rebellion in, 68
Politics, place of, in life, 40
Polk, James K., 34–35, 51, 54–55, 59–60, 64, 67, 70, 90, 95, 99, 104, 106–107, 110–112, 121–125, 146, 169, 186, 204, 221, 359–360, 425, 449, 455, 465, 476, 572; an estimate of, 80; nomination of, 79–83; career of, 84; selection of Cabinet by, 87–88, 89*n*; on New York Democratic politics, 89; his eulogy of Silas Wright, 108*n*
Pomeroy, Samuel C., 360
Pompey Academy, Pompey Hill, N. Y. 6, 27, 28*n*
Pompey Hill, N. Y., 5–6
Popular sovereignty, doctrine of, 121–122, 146, 162, 190; Seymour's attitude toward, 182, 184. *See also* Kansas-Nebraska Act
Portage Canal Company, 194
Portland, Maine, riots in, 154
Post, Eugene J., his *The Wig and the Jimmy*, 480*n*
Potter, Clarkson N., 523, 525–526
Poughkeepsie, N. Y., 191
Powell, Lazarus W., 368
Prentice, David H., 28
Price, Thomas L., his part in Democratic convention (1868), 417, 428, 430
Prohibition, xv, 114, 178, 181, 290, 464; established in Maine, 133, 154; as an issue in New York, xv–xvi, 132–134, 153*n*, 154–157, 161
Prohibition party, in New York, 166
Providence *Daily Post*, on Seymour's message (1864), 357*n*
Pruyn, John V. L., ix, 89*n*, 136, 190, 197, 206, 263, 265, 397; supports Marcy (1852), 125–126, 137–139; his diary quoted on Seymour's activities, 188, 264, 266–267, 288; reliability of his diary, 436

Public lands, Seymour's position on, 153–154; proposals of National Labor Union concerning, 414; plank in Democratic platform (1868) on, 419
Public School Society, 159
Pugh, George E., 435
Purdy, Elijah F., 285, 334
Puritans, Horatio Seymour's description of, 192; Thomas H. Seymour on, 257
Putnam County, N. Y., in election of 1868, 475

Quakers, their attitude toward slavery, 68

Railroads, 200–201, 572; consolidation of, 136; franchises for, 286–288; promotion of, 49; Seymour's criticism of, 199
Randall, J. G., 453*n*; on suppression of newspapers, 358*n*; on congressional reconstruction, 383–384
Raymond, Henry J., 167, 257, 325, 357. *See also* New York *Times*
Reconstruction, congressional, 484, 506; plan for, 383–384, 386; Grant's report on, 444; popular approval of, 446; Seymour's opposition to, 387–388, 391–392, 413, 462, 472; as campaign issue (1868), 446–449, 460, 472; failure of, 474
Reid, Whitelaw, 509
Religious fanatics, in New York, 39–43
Rensselaer County, N. Y., anti-rent disturbances in, 98
Republican party (first), 121
Republican party (second), 50, 57, 169, 178, 183, 187, 228; in election of 1856, 179; sectional character of, 57, 183, 186, 219–220; conventions of: (1856), 186; (1860), 208, 214; (1864), 364; and Crittenden Compromise, 223; dissension within, 390, 396; advantages of (1868), 446, 450; contradictions in membership of, 484–485. *See also* Elections
Republican party, New York, 216; conventions of: (1861), 237; (1862), 248; (1863), 348; (1864), 373; supports Union ticket (1861), 238; distribution of ballots to soldiers by, 378; dissension within (1870), 490–491. *See also* Elections
Republicans, radical, 242, 250–251, 298, 348, 361, 365, 401, 416, 419, 444, 448, 450, 469, 472, 474; policies of, 243, 255, 352; desire of, to replace Lincoln, 337, 339, 360; gain control of government, 338, 383, 392; quarrel of, with Johnson, 392–393
Rhode Island, 519; Dorr's Rebellion in, 94, 97*n*
Rhodes, James F., 84, 243*n*, 255, 281, 576; on Crittenden Compromise, 223; on Seymour's message (1863), 271–272; on the draft riots, 326*n*, 329; on Seymour's nomination (1868), 437–438; on violence in the South (1868), 447; on Seymour's campaign speeches, 474; on election of 1876, 532
Rice, Mrs. William G., ix, 188*n*, 397*n*, 525*n*
Richardson, W. A., his part in Democratic convention (1868), 420, 424, 426, 428
Richmond, Dean, 136, 147, 163, 236–237, 241–243, 246, 258, 267; at Charleston convention (1860), 207, 209–213, 216; at Albany convention (1862), 244–245, 247; at Chicago convention (1864), 364, 369, 373; his railroad interests, 287; his death, 390
Richmond, Va., fall of, 299
Rob Roy, canal boat, 18
Robespierre, Seymour likened to, 554
Robinson, Gov. Lucius, N. Y., 536; returns to Democratic party, 391, 527; his nomination and election, 517, 526, 534; defeated for reëlection, 535
Rochester, N. Y., Democratic state conventions at: (1851), 123; (1870), 490; (1871), 493; (1872), 502; canal convention at, 489–490
Rochester Bank, 61–62
Rockwell, William, 158
Roman Catholics, seek share in New York public-school fund, 159; hatred of, 102, 114, 160–161, 168, 178, 229, 504; their vote courted, 513, 527
Rome, N. Y., 63; Democratic state convention at, 111–113; Seymour's speeches at: (1862), 158; (1870), 481–483
Roosevelt, Franklin D., 56, 201, 266
—— Theodore, 56, 266, 280, 573; on number killed in the draft riots, 333; on fraud in election (1868), 476; his "Czar Bill," 568
Rosecrans, Gen. William S., on Seymour's candidacy (1868), 449
Ross, Edmund G., 296, 403
—— Lewis W., of Illinois, 475
Rousseau, Jean Jacques, 577

Royall, Mrs. Anne, describes life at boarding-school, 29–30
Ruscoe, Mercy. *See* Seamer
Russell, Judge A. D., 305*n*
—— William H., quoted, 226–227
Russia, in Crimean War, 170–171

Sabsworth. *See* Sawbridgeworth
St. Augustine and Tennyson, 562
St. Louis, Mo., Democratic convention at (1876), 521–522
St. Paul, Minn., Seymour's speech at, 205–206
Salina, N. Y., 6, 15. *See also* Syracuse
Sanders, ——, 150*n*
Sandford, Gen. Charles W., and the draft riots, 301, 320, 331
Saratoga, N. Y., Seymour's speech at (1868), 464; Democratic state convention at (1876), 523–526
Sault Sainte Marie Canal, 194*n*
Savage, John Y., 212
Savannah *Republican*, its attack on Seymour and Bramlette (1864), 374
Sawbridgeworth (Sabsworth), England, 4
Schell, Augustus, 418, 536*n*; part of, in campaign (1868), 463; elected grand sachem of Tammany, 500
Schlesinger, Arthur M., ix
Schoharie County, N. Y., in election of 1868, 475
Schouler, James, describes travel by canal, 18; on Seymour's message (1863), 271–272; his explanation of Seymour's nomination (1868), 437; on election of 1876, 532
Schurz, Carl, 540; opposes Seymour (1868), 451
Schuyler, Col. Peter, 17*n*
—— Gen. Philip, 14, 17*n*, 36, 192
Scisco, Louis D., on Nativism, 159, 161
Scott, Gen. Winfield, 88, 127, 185*n*, 540
Scrugham, Mary, 227; her study of election of 1860, 219–220
Seamer, Mercy (Ruscoe), wife of Richard, 4
—— Richard (*d* 1655), 4–5
Seaton, William W., 31
Secession, 251, 280, 327, 345, 453, 517, 528; of South, 170, 212, 220–222, 224; causes of southern secession, xvi, 239, 262, 270; Seymour's attitude toward, xviii, 34*n*, 206, 222–225, 239, 543; attitude of New York Democrats toward, 237; northern threats of, xvi, 206, 545
Selective Service Act (1917), 317; constitutionality of, 313
Semmes, Capt. Raphael, 450
Seneca County, N. Y., its record in elections, 386*n*, 475
Seneca Falls, N. Y., Seymour's speech at (1865), 320, 386–389
Seward, Col. Augustus H., 379
—— William H., 48, 66, 74, 77, 146, 167, 248, 255–256, 312*n*, 465, 470; Seymour's opinion of, 159, 365; defeated for governorship (1834), 50; elected governor: (1838), 46; (1840), 53; and foreign language schools, 159–160; and anti-rent disturbances, 98–99; and Compromise of 1850, 114, 118; his feud with Fillmore, 114, 126, 161; and Crittenden Compromise, 223; and Chicago convention (1860), 208, 214, 249, 283*n*; as secretary of state, 242, 337, 344, 347, 358, 399; his Auburn speech (1863), 353–354; his support of Johnson, 390, 394, 402, 451, 468; his stand on election of 1868, 451
Seymour, Clarissa. *See* Marsh
—— Epaphroditus, 4
—— Helen Clarissa. *See* Lincklaen, Mrs. Ledyard
—— Henry, 3, 25, 27, 61; at Pompey Hill, 5–6; his marriage, 7; his benefactions, 6; at Utica, 18–19; in War of 1812, 7–8; as a banker, 21, 61; his suicide, xix, 23, 456; Hammond's opinion of, 10, 21; as state senator, 8–9; his relations with Van Buren and the regency, 9–10, 17; on council of appointment, 9, 12; as Erie Canal commissioner, 12, 16–17, 20, 557; on boundary commission, 20; as mayor of Utica, 20
—— Horatio (*d* 1857), 145; character of, 26; career of, 3–4, 27
Seymour, Horatio (*d* 1886)
—— Family, 3–5, 7
—— Early life, baptism of, 7; education of, 27–29, 32–33; his practice of law, 33; death of his father, 23; his marriage, 36; his nickname, 25; his trip to Adirondacks, 566
—— Mayor (1842), 66, 557; and municipal finances, 67; protects abolitionists at Utica, 68–69, 557
—— Assemblyman (1842, 1844, 1845), 52, 76; elected, 66, 69–70, 84; as chairman of committee on canals, 72; his

report on canals, 72–75; supports canal law, 90–91; supports "stop and tax" law, 74–75; as speaker, 84–85, 90, 95; on committee on constitutional amendments, 93; his fight against a constitutional convention, 94–95

Seymour, period between assembly and governorship (1846–1853), at Syracuse convention (1846), 103–104; helps negotiate party truce (1849), 106, 111–112, 123; refuses to run for assembly (1849), 113; campaigns for governorship (1850), 65, 116–119; at Baltimore convention (1852), 124–129

—— Governor (1853–1855), campaign and election (1852), 105, 131–134; supports Marcy for Cabinet post, 138–140; his inaugural address, 146–147; his annual messages: (1853), 135; (1854), 153–154; his diligence, 135; signs act incorporating New York Central R.R., 136–137; and pardoning power, 135, 558–559; and patronage, 137–138, 143–146, 149; his fight for canal improvements, 146–148; vetoes prohibition bill, xvi, 155–157, 167, 172; and state election (1853), 150–152; entertains Mgr. Bedini, 158; as candidate for re-election, 33, 114, 161–167

—— Years between governorships (1855–1863), and a foreign mission, 70, 170–171; refuses membership on Kansas commission, 171–172, 189; his Tammany Hall speech (1855), 177–178; at Cincinnati convention (1856), 173; his Springfield speech (1856), 179–186; his address before New York Historical and Geographical Society (1856), 191–193; negotiates party truce (1856), 174; declines nomination for governor (1858), 188–189; his trips to Wisconsin, 37, 193, 200, 204–205, 231–233; his trip to Washington, 203–204; his St. Paul speech (1859), 205–206; as a possible choice of national convention (1860), 207–210, 212–215; supports Douglas, 215–216, 218, 558; at Syracuse convention (1860), 216–217; supports fusion ticket (1860), 216–218; supports Crittenden Compromise, 222–225; supports Union cause, 232–233, 238; recruiting activities of, 30, 234–235, 244; his Tweddle Hall speech (1861), 224–225, 453; his Utica speech (1861), 238–240; offers services to Gov. Morgan, 242; as senatorial candidate (1861), 231, 487; his speech at Rome (1862), 158

—— Governor (1863–1865), his nomination, campaign and election, 245–257; his acceptance speech, 249–252; his task, 259; and patronage, 305; his Brooklyn speeches: (1862), 252–253; (1863), 303–306, 453, 466; his conference with McClellan, 260; influenced by John D. Caton, 260–262, 298; his inaugural address, text, 264–265; his first annual message, 267–272, 349–350; his relations with Lincoln, 272–277, 300, 314, 340, 342–343, 345, 347; attacks on, by War Democrats, 279–282; tries to remove New York City police commissioners, 284–286; vetoes Broadway Railroad franchise bill, 205, 286–288; vetoes soldiers' franchise bill, 288, 347–348, 351; and Vallandigham, 293–294, 337–338, 359; supplies troops to Union army, 232, 263, 281, 300, 351; and Gettysburg call for troops, 300–302; his speech at dedication of Gettysburg cemetery, 302–303; his Utica speech (1863), 348–349; his letter to Milwaukee Democrats, 352–353; as a nepotist, 353; his second annual message (1864), 354–358; his letter to New York bankers, 350; and suppression of newspapers, 358–359; his position in national politics (1864), 361–363; at Chicago convention (1864), 260, 364–366, 368–369; his meeting with Gov. Andrew, 364–365; his Chicago convention speeches, 366, 370–371; supports McClellan's candidacy, 370–371; his defeat for re-election (1864), 283, 373–376, 380–382; his Philadelphia speech (1864), 374–375; and the polling of soldier vote (1864), 376–380; and the pardoning power, 560

—— Draft and draft riots, his opposition to draft, 272, 278, 289, 295, 313–315, 320, 338, 340–341, 354; his desire to postpone and test legality of draft, 275, 307, 313–314, 325–326, 329, 581–584; objects to New York quotas under draft, 307, 317–320, 342–347; his Seneca Falls speech (1865), 320; his movements during week-end before riots, 306, 321–322; reconciles generals in New York City, 321; proclaims state of insurrection in New York City, 323;

his City Hall speech, 324–328, 335–336, 581–584; authorizes arming of New York police, 331; on number killed in riots, 333; relations with Gen. Dix concerning draft, 340–341, 345, 347

Seymour, period between governorship and presidential candidacy (1865–1868), his Buffalo and Seneca Falls speeches (1865), 320, 386–389; his Cooper Institute speech (1866), 391–392; as chairman of state convention (1867), 393; his search for a candidate for 1868, 395–396, 400–402, 404–410; refuses to be candidate for nomination, 396–398, 423; outlines party program, 399–400; his speeches as permanent chairman of convention (1868), 412, 424, 429–430; his rulings as chairman of convention (1868), 420, 422; declines nomination, 423–424, 430; his sincerity in refusing nomination, 433–442; nomination of (1868), 396–398, 408–410, 429–431; ethics of his nomination, 485

—— Presidential candidate (1868), xv, 306; popular disapproval of, 446; southern support of, 449–450; newspaper attacks on, 452–456, 461; his Tammany Hall speech, 461; his acceptance speech, 461–462; his *Public Record*, 463–464; his Saratoga speech, 464; his campaign tactics, 467–468; movement to replace, as candidate, 468–470; his "swing around the circle," 461, 470–472; his Chicago speech, 472–474; analysis of the vote, 474–475, 478; on charges of fraud in election, 481–483

—— Later years (1868–1886), his explanation of Tweed's success, 501, 569; his influence on canal legislation, 489–490, 514–516; demand for, as convention speaker, 562; on management committee of Cornell University, 571; in fight against Tammany, xix, 487, 491, 498, 569; his Tammany Hall speech (1870), 491–493; his humiliation at and withdrawal from state convention (1871), 494–496; on convention and election (1871), 498–499; urges reform of judiciary (1871), 499–500; elected Tammany sachem (1872), 500; and Greeley's candidacy, 502–504; on panic of 1873, xix, 520–521; elected chancellor of Union College, 571; his trip South, 552; his speech at Prison Congress (1873), 560; his sketch of Dix's career, 510; supports Tilden's candidacy for governor, 507–512; at Syracuse convention (1874), 511; his Brooklyn speech (1874), 511–512; urges Kernan's election to Senate, 512–514; advises Tilden on canal policy, 514–516; refuses senatorship (1875), xviii, 500, 512, 519; his Utica speech, 553; as pathmaster of Deerfield, 119, 566–567; his quarrel with Blaine, 519; supports Tilden's candidacy for President, 522, 526; refuses nomination for governor (1876), 442, 495, 500, 521–526; on election of 1876, 530–531; his activities on behalf of C. S. Fairchild, 534–535; elected member of Massachusetts Historical Society, 571; publishes "Crime and Tramps," 560; publishes essays on government, 563–564; his speech before New York legislature (1878), 563; his speech at Auburn prison (1879), 561; refuses to be candidate for governorship (1879), 535–536; refuses to be candidate for presidency (1880), 536–539; supports Hancock (1880), 539–543; his speeches at Brooklyn and Little Falls (1880), 542–543; his speech at Watertown (1880), 543; on Roosevelt's "Czar Bill," 568; attends canal convention (1885), 570; resigns from board of trustees of Hamilton College, 571

—— Political life, general, his personality and oratorical skill, 57–58, 74, 143, 179, 352*n*, 456, 563; his renunciations of public life, 113, 172–173, 177, 188, 190, 215; called "Doughface" or "Copperhead," xvi, 34*n*, 298, 351, 374, 449, 452, 468; his interest in canals, xix, 19–20, 36–37, 56, 135–136, 146, 153, 193, 197–198, 489–491, 515–516, 556–557, 570; his association with Marcy, 33, 35, 38, 45, 56, 106, 123–130, 132, 134, 138–140, 142–146, 149, 152, 163–164, 170–171, 177; and federal patronage, 137–138, 144–145, 151–152, 163, 203–204; his relations with Tammany, xix, 177–178, 217, 285–288, 351, 376*n*, 437, 442, 461, 487, 491–493, 497–498, 500, 516, 569; his trips to Washington, 107, 125, 177, 203–204, 244; his relations with Tilden, 204–205, 252–253, 267, 287, 314, 344, 397, 399–401, 433–434, 437,

458, 467, 488, 491–492, 495, 497–499, 502–504, 507–512, 514–516, 522, 526–528, 538, 569, 572

Seymour, political ideas and philosophy, on slavery, xviii, 67, 100–101, 121, 184–185, 206, 226, 228–229, 239, 269–270, 280, 558; on abolition, xv, xvii, 44, 67, 101–102, 121–122, 146, 153, 178, 185, 391, 557–558; on Free Soil, 100, 144–145, 162, 178; on Kansas-Nebraska Act, 145, 162, 183–185; on popular sovereignty, 146, 182, 184; on Crittenden Compromise, 222–225; on secession, xviii, 34*n*, 206, 222–227, 239, 543; on emancipation, xviii, 102, 239, 252, 254, 278, 295, 349, 558; on conduct of Civil War and desirable terms of peace, 238–240, 244*n*, 250–251, 266, 268, 272, 298, 337, 339, 349, 352, 356–357, 366, 375, 387; on suspension of habeas corpus, 251, 278, 289, 293; on martial law, 267–268, 271, 293, 352; on arbitrary arrest, 267–268, 277, 284, 293, 295, 314; on conscription, 272, 278, 289, 295, 313–315, 320, 342, 345, 349; on suppression of newspapers, 352; on nature of federal constitution, 44, 153, 225, 227, 238, 295, 392, 543, 563–564; on local government, xvii, 180–181, 184, 205, 240, 263, 284, 389, 518–519, 564; on centralization of power in federal government, xvi–xvii, 181–182, 193, 204, 248, 252–253, 263–264, 270*n*, 271, 277–278, 293–296, 304–306, 315, 339, 352–354, 356, 359, 375, 382, 386, 506–507, 540–543; on congressional reconstruction, 386–389, 391–392, 413, 462, 472; on tariff question, xix, 153, 542, 545–546, 561, 564, 568; on management of public lands, 153–154; on sectionalism, 32, 57, 183, 186, 267, 473; on Nativism, xv, 154, 178, 180, 182, 192; on prohibition, xv, xviii, 132–134, 155–157, 178, 180–181; his faith in foreign population, 158, 182–183, 192; his dislike of party factions, 45, 57, 71; his hatred of hypocrisy, 185, 228–229; on currency problems, 349–350, 387–388, 391, 393, 413, 472–473, 489, 511, 519–521; on rewards of public service, 554; on penal reform, 558–561; on public speaking, xx, 563

—— Private life, his character and personality, 23–24, 44–45, 57–58, 143, 245*n*, 246, 551, 577; his education and culture, 365*n*, 551; his library, 562; his personal appearance, 28, 143, 365, 454–455, 551–552; his physical ailments, 119, 158, 205, 207, 235–236, 513, 522, 525, 562, 566–567, 570; his generosity, 555–556; his sense of humor, 553; his pride, 145; his failure to enlist, 30–31, 235–236; his wide range of interests, 28, 57, 62, 175, 190, 556, 562; his farming activities, 65, 455, 550, 562; his trips through the Adirondacks, 176–177, 566; his summers at Newport, 101, 145, 163, 213, 552; his proposed trip abroad, 163, 488, 552; his friendship for Hamilton Fish, 116; his acquaintance with Amelia Murray, 62, 101, 163, 165, 175–177, 553; his loan to Croswell, 85–86; his management of Seymour and Bleecker properties, 22, 24, 36, 61–62, 550; his business interests, 64; his investments in land, 36, 64–65, 198, 555; his speculations in Wisconsin, 190, 193, 197–200, 204, 509, 552, 555; his life at "Marysland," 550, 552–553, 565; his sectarian affiliations, 574*n*; his death, 574; his tombstone, 574–575; his will, 575; his estate, 137*n*, 555

—— Horatio, Jr., son of Jonathan F., 37, 232, 274, 554; elected state engineer, 515, 534–535, 555*n*

—— Horatio, son of Horatio (*d* 1857), 145

—— Horatio, grandson of Jonathan F., 232*n*

—— John (*d* 1713), 5

—— Jonathan F. ("John F."), 7, 25, 33, 37, 61, 64, 65*n*, 166, 194*n*, 197, 232*n*, 244; as messenger for Horatio Seymour, 274–277; as federal office-holder, 353; his connection with ballot distributors, 379; his visit to Cleveland, 382; as manager of family estates, 550

—— Julia Catherine. *See* Conkling

—— Mary (Bleecker), wife of Horatio (*d* 1886), 36, 142, 247, 565; her real estate holdings, 552; her illness and death, 573–575

—— Mary Forman, 7, 25, 27

—— Mary Ledyard (Forman), wife of Henry, 7, 34, 456

—— Mary (Marsh), wife of Moses (*d* 1827), 5–6

—— Mary (Watson), wife of John (*d* 1713), 5

Seymour, Maj. Moses (*d* 1827), 3, 5–6
—— Moses, son of Moses (*d* 1827), 4
—— Origen Storrs, Horatio's letter to, text, 61–62
—— Ozias, 4
—— Sophia Apollina, 7. *See also* Shonnard
—— Thomas, 4–5, 257
—— Gov. Thomas Hart, Conn., 29, 142, 256; on Puritans, 257; as speaker in Brooklyn (1863), 304; as a candidate at Chicago convention (1864), 368
Shakers, 39
Shannon, Fred A., 342, 453*n*; on the Enrollment Act, 316, 320, 344
Shaw, S. M., 522
Shelley, Percy B., quoted, 404
Sherman, Asa S., 267
—— John, 360, 540, 546
Shonnard, Sophia Apollina (Seymour), 247. *See also* Seymour.
"Silver-Grays," 161, 166, 245
Skinner, John B., supports Marcy (1852), 126
Slavery, as cause of Civil War, 103, 228, 239, 269; Seymour on, xviii, 67, 100–101, 121, 184–185, 206, 226, 228–229, 239, 269–270, 280, 558; opposition to, in New York, xviii, 43, 70, 229. *See also* Abolitionism; Compromise of 1850; Crittenden Compromise; Free soil movement; Kansas-Nebraska Act; Missouri Compromise
Slaves, stealing of, 67; trade in, 206; fugitive, 254; northern enlistment of, 374. *See also* Negroes
Slidell, John, 242, 294; withdraws name from Charleston convention, 213
Slocum, Gen. Henry W., 416, 467
Smith, Alfred E., 201, 432
—— Chauncey, as commissioner to pass on New York draft quotas, 346
—— Gerrit, 44, 67, 191, 229, 267*n*; his opinion of Seymour, 245*n*, 339
—— Jeffrey, 14
—— Paul S., 243*n*
—— Thomas Kirby, 416
Snyder, Jacob, 69
"Softs," 113–114, 122–123, 130, 132, 137, 140, 148, 150–151, 161, 166, 173–174, 177, 203, 211–212; and Kansas-Nebraska Act, 183–184; support fusion ticket (1860), 216–217
South Carolina, its ordinance of secession, 222, 327*n*
Speculation, 46, 49, 73, 152, 506. *See also* Land
Spencer, Judge Ambrose, 10*n*
—— Herbert, 564
Spinner, Francis E., 116, 568
Sprague, Maj. John T., 257; as Seymour's messenger, 275, 329, 342, 582
—— William, and impeachment of Johnson, 403
Spriggs, J. Thomas, 538–539; his part in nomination of Seymour (1876), 523–524, 525*n*
Stanton, Edward McM., 232, 248, 255–256, 263, 272, 274–275, 281, 314, 337, 342, 344, 373, 575; sanctions recruiting of negroes, 300; his Gettysburg call for troops, 300–301; and the draft, 310, 319, 329, 340, 345–346, 347*n*, 351; grants furloughs to voters, 347, 377; and suppression of newspapers, 292*n*, 358; and the polling of New York soldier vote (1864), 378–381; opposition of, to Johnson, 390, 392, 402, 444; his stand on election of 1868, 451–452; on Seymour's war record, 452
—— Elizabeth (Cady) 74*n*; petitions Democratic convention (1868), 416
—— Henry B., 128, 249*n*, 408, 513; his estimate of Seymour, 74
Stanwood, Edward 539
Star of the West, 298
Star Spangled Banner party. *See* American party; Know-Nothing party; Nativism
Steele, John B., 315
Stephens, Alexander H., 227*n*, 239; sends resolutions to Democratic convention (1868), 417
Steuben, Friedrich Wilhelm Baron von, 192
Stevens, Thaddeus, 375, 473, 571; attacks Seymour, 315; opposes Johnson, 387, 390, 392; opposes Grant (1868), 450
Story, Joseph, 278
Stowe, Harriet (Beecher), 103, 229
Strong, Selah B., 158
Stryker, John, 267
Stuart, Charles, 28
—— Michael, 368
Suffrage. *See* Franchise
Sullivan, Gen. James, 7
Sulzer, Gov. William, N. Y., 511, 572
Sumner, Charles, 32, 192, 295; his reconstruction policies, 375, 386; his opposition to Johnson, 387, 390, 392

Sumter, Thomas, 186
Supreme Court. *See under* United States
Sweeny, Peter B., 286, 334; at Democratic convention (1868), 418
Syracuse, N. Y., 6; Democratic conventions at: (1846), 103–104; (1847), 109; (1852), 130; (1853), 150; (1854), 163, 183; (1856), 174; (1857), 203; (1860), 216–217; (1861), 236–237; (1874), 508, 511; Whig convention at (1852), 131; Republican conventions at: (1861), 237; (1864), 373; People's convention at, 237
Syracuse "juggle," 217

Tallmadge, Nathaniel P., 77, 86–87; elected to Senate, 35; opposes independent treasury, 51
Tammany Society, xix, 118, 134*n*, 305, 393, 442, 476, 497, 522, 528; opposes Erie Canal, 8; Seymour's speeches before: (1855), 177–178; (1868), 461; (1870), 491–493; its quarrels with Gov. Seymour, 285–288, 351; its feud with Mozart Hall, 209–210, 217; endorses McClellan, 376; as host to convention (1868), 411; its attitude toward Seymour's candidacy (1868), 437; its fraud in election (1868), 474–477, 480–481; controls state, 487, 535; reform of, 492–493, 497–498, 500, 505, 569
Taney, Roger B., 189–190, 206, 313, 349, 363, 544, 558
Tariff, Seymour's views on, xix, 153, 542, 545–546, 561; Walker (1846), 99*n*, 104; Democratic platform on (1868), 419
Taylor, Jeremy, 95
—— Rev. John, 63*n*
—— John W., 26
—— Zachary, 78, 81, 84, 114–115, 123, 216, 253, 540
Temperance. *See* Prohibition
Temple, Gen. Robert E., 143
Tennyson, Alfred, Lord Tennyson, 562
Tenure of Office Act, 403
Texas, annexation question, 78, 80, 100, 107; secession of, 327*n*; excluded from election (1868), 474
Thomas, Mrs. Georgine (Holmes), 461*n*
Throop, Gov. Enos T., N. Y., 48, 119, 143; on Seymour's Utica speech (1861), 241
Thurman, Allen G., 421, 435; supports Seymour (1868), 457
Thwaites, Reuben G., 200
Tilden, Samuel J., xvi, xx, 140, 204–205, 209–210, 217, 226, 238, 267, 344, 397, 399–401, 410, 467, 488, 534–535, 555; his character, 391, 399–400, 518; his career, 528; explains Van Buren's stand on Texas question, 78–79; on election of 1846, 106, 109; opposes Lincoln's election (1860), 217, 220, 253, 528; contributes to Seymour's Brooklyn speech (1862), 252–253; advises Seymour on Broadway Railroad franchise, 287; as go-between for Seymour and Lincoln, 314, 329; on resolutions committee at Chicago (1864), 367–368; on question of inflation, 396; his preparation for and part in Democratic convention (1868), 390–391, 393, 399–402, 412, 418, 421–422, 424–426, 428–429, 431, 433–435; on Frank Blair, 448; his part in presidential campaign (1868), 458, 463, 467–471; at Rochester convention (1870), 490; his fight against Tammany, xix, 437, 487, 491–495, 497–498, 569; elected Tammany sachem, 500; elected governor, 495, 507–508, 511; his canal policy, 514–515, 522; his campaign for the presidency, 56, 115*n*, 442, 478, 485, 517, 521, 527–529, 531–532; his handling of electoral dispute (1876), 533; as possible presidential nominee (1880), 537–539, 568; his loss of voice, 568, 572
Tilton, Theodore, 547
Tompkins, Gov. Daniel D., N. Y., 8–9, 43, 56, 58, 131, 133, 572
—— Minthorne, 131, 133
Toombs, Robert, 223, 227*n*, 450
Townsend, Maj. Frederick, 311*n*
—— George Alfred, 454
Tremaine, Lyman, 251
Trent affair, 242
Trimble, William, 52
Trollope, Anthony, on reconstruction, 447
Troup, Col. Robert, 15
Troy, N. Y., Constitutional Union convention at, 245
Trumbull, Lyman, 276, 403
Tucker, Gideon J., 267
—— J. P., 408
Tweddle, John, 225
Tweddle Hall convention, 224–225
Tweed, William M., xix, 286, 334, 351, 437, 475, 491, 500, 505, 507, 516, 528, 534, 564; an appraisal of, 404; at Democratic convention (1868), 418; his

part in election (1868), 479–481; controls state, 487, 490–491, 494, 496; his "secret accounts," 492; his patronage of Cassidy, 495; works with Republicans, 497; his success explained, 501, 569; overthrow of, 458, 492–493, 500
Tweed Ring, 287, 499, 501, 507–508
Tyler, John, 54, 65, 77, 79, 100, 363, 455; on schism at Charleston (1860), 221*n*

Ullman, Daniel, his career, 160*n*; as Know-Nothing candidate, 114, 160–162, 164–165, 167–168, 386*n*
Ulster County, N. Y., in election of 1868, 475
Union League Club, New York, 475–476; recruiting activities of, 300
Union party, in election of 1860, 214, 217–218
United Society of Believers in Christ's Second Appearing. *See* Shakers
United States, 193; and St. Lawrence treaty, 201, 557; immigrants in, 182–183, 193; relations with England, 170–171, 242, 254; land grants of, 194, 196; relations with France, 171
—— Circuit court of Illinois, decision of, 314
—— Circuit court of Pennsylvania, decision of, 314
—— Congress, power of, 296–297
—— Constitution, great compromise in, 193; slavery compromise in, 102–103; Seymour's understanding of, 153, 225, 227, 238, 295, 392, 543, 564; J. M. Beck on, 296; Gladstone on, 563–564; inadequacy of, 529; proposed 13th amendment, 224; 14th amendment, 313, 391–392, 405*n*, 417; 15th amendment, 405*n*, 417
—— Electoral college, xix, 296*n*; an appraisal of, 219–220
—— Electoral Commission, 403, 529, 533
—— House of Representatives, election of President by, 219; investigates New York vote in election (1868), 475–476
—— Senate, committee of, on Crittenden Compromise, 223
—— Supreme Court, decisions of, 189–190, 224, 278, 292, 313, 363, 384; composition of (1857), 189*n*; size of, decreased, 393; packing of, 544; defied by Lincoln, 251; Seymour on, 543; true position of, 292, 295–297, 544
United States Bank. *See* Bank of the United States
United States Military Academy (West Point), 29
Utica, N. Y., 36; fire in, 22, 62; gas introduced, 64; industrial development of, 64; financial affairs of, 66–67; growth of, 62–63; foreign population of, 63–64; as a convention city, 63, 562; anti-slavery convention at, 67–69; Barnburner convention at, 109; Whig convention at, 116; Republican convention at, 348; Democratic convention at, 552; reunion of Army of the Cumberland at, 553; canal convention at, 570; Seymour's speech at (1861), 238–240; elections in: (1842), 66; (1843), 67; (1852), 134
Utica Anti-Slavery Society, convention of, 67–69
Utica *Observer*, warns against nomination of Wright (1846), 104*n*; attitude of, in election of 1852, 144; and charges of treason against Seymour, 398–399
Utica and Syracuse Railroad, 137*n*

Vallandigham, Clement L., 242, 244, 271, 278, 295, 304, 337–338, 353*n*, 359, 389, 398; his character, 362; his activities, 289–290; arrest and trial of, 291–294; exile of, 302, 361–362; defeat of, for governorship, 361; at national Democratic convention (1864), 362, 365–366, 412, 418, 428, 430, 432; his part in framing of platform (1864), 366–368, 372; backs Pendleton (1868), 401, 406, 412; endorses Seymour (1868), 457–458
Van Buren, "Prince" John (*d* 1866), son of Martin, 87, 103, 110, 130–132, 144–145, 150, 210; oratorical ability of, 74; his career, 103*n*; helps negotiate party truce (1849), 111–113; supports Lincoln in Civil War, 228, 389; his candidacy for attorney generalship, 389–390; death, 390
—— Col. John Dash, 104*n*, 441, 470; as go-between for Seymour and Lincoln, 300; as go-between for Seymour and Chase, 301*n*, 405–408, 439–440; and presidential campaign (1868), 464–465
—— Martin, 22, 27, 33, 34*n*, 38, 58–59, 61, 65, 71, 74, 84, 87–88, 104, 112–113, 123, 152, 185*n*, 197, 209, 211, 216–217, 241, 253, 274, 359, 455, 489, 495, 502, 504, 510, 571, 573; builds personal

party, 8–13; his alliance with Tammany, 8, 12; his feud with Clinton, 8–13, 47; as governor, 47; and political patronage, 11–13, 88; as President, 46–47, 50–54, 56; and Texas question, 78, 80–81; loses nomination (1844), 78–82; his relations with Polk, 79*n*, 88, 89*n*, 110; his feud with Cass, 45, 81–82, 125; on Free Soil ticket (1848), 78–82; his political "come-back," 55, 60, 69, 77–83
Vance, Zebulon B., 418, supports Seymour (1868), 450
Vanderbilt, Cornelius, 49; gains control of New York Central, 136; his Harlem Railroad franchise, 287, 351
Van Dyck, Henry H., 107
Van Rensselaer, Kiliaen, 98
—— Stephen, III, 98
—— Gen. Stephen, 47*n*
Van Winkle, Peter G., 403
Vermont, significance of its admission to the Union, 544
Vicksburg, capture of, 303
Victoria, Queen of England, 103, 171, 572
Virginia, position of, at constitutional convention (1787), 193; law of, concerning theft of slaves, 67; excluded from election (1868), 474
Virginia Dynasty, 8, 38, 58, 65, 183
Voltaire, Jean François Arouet de, 577
Voorhees, Daniel W., 418

Wabash and Erie Canal, 196
Wade, Benjamin, and impeachment of Johnson, 402
Wadsworth, James S., 109, 259, 284, 288, 299, 305, 348, 389; candidacy of, for governor, 248–250, 478; his handling of fugitive slaves, 254
Walker, Robert, 82; on Hancock's qualifications for presidency (1868), 425–426; supports Seymour (1868), 449
Wall, Alexander J., ix; on postponement of draft, 329
Wallace, Gen. Lewis, 379
Walworth, Reuben H., 110
War Democrats, 228, 245, 279
Ward, Artemus (Browne, Charles F.), 44, 101
Warren, Charles, 544
—— Joseph, 496
Washburne, Elihu, 378
Washington, George, 14, 186, 190, 219, 258, 299, 337, 385, 413–414, 445, 540, 544
Waterbury, Nelson J., 283; his report on enrollment, 345–346; denounces ballot distributors, 379; on Tammany's attitude toward Seymour's nomination (1868), 437
Watertown, N. Y., Seymour's speech at, 543
Watson, Mary. *See* Seymour
Watterson, Henry, 531
Wayne, James M., 189*n*
Webster, Daniel, 26, 110, 114, 121, 157, 180, 227*n*, 278, 446, 563
Weed, Thurlow, 53, 108, 119*n*, 129–130, 153*n*, 165*n*, 203, 218, 227, 231, 238, 248–249, 255, 262, 566*n*; as Whig boss, 48, 55, 167, 207; and state printing, 48, 53, 66, 107; encourages Seymour (1862), 252, 265; his feud with Greeley, 203, 249, 283*n*, 295; acts as go-between for Lincoln and Seymour, 273
Weeden, William B., his attack on Seymour, 280–282; his career, 280*n*
Weller, John B., on platform committee at Chicago (1864), 367
Welles, Gideon, 292, 340; the reliability of his diary questioned, 435–436; on Dix's war record, 236, 505; on possible Democratic candidate (1868), 401; on Grant, 444–445; on Seward, 451
Wesleyan University, Middletown, Conn., 29*n*
West, DeWitt C., 498
—— Goldsmith B., 560*n*
Westchester County, N. Y., in election of 1868, 475
Western Inland Lock and Navigation Company, 14
Western Union Telegraph Co., 537
Westervelt, Jacob A., 134
West Point. *See* United States Military Academy
Wheeler, W. A., 531
Whig party, national, 489; dissension within, 54, 65, 77, 114–115, 122, 126, 390; downfall of, 121. *See also* Elections
Whig party, New York, 48, 66, 123, 144, 476; conventions of: (1850), 116; (1852), 131; policies of, 50, 52; tactics of, 86, 90–93; dissension within, 114, 116–118, 161; adopts prohibition cause, 154–157; supports Nativism, 160. *See also* Elections

White, Andrew D., 191*n*, 272, 552, 571; on Seymour's party loyalty, 503
—— Chief-Justice Edward D., 313
—— Horace, 272
—— Horatio S., 552
—— Hugh, 63*n*
Whitesboro, N. Y., 63
Whittier, John Greenleaf, 108; supports Grant (1868), 446
Wilkes, Capt. Charles, 242
Wilkinson, Jemima, 40–42
Willey, Waitman T., and impeachment of Johnson, 403
Wilmot, David, 99, 230; his career, 99*n*
Wilmot Proviso, 79, 107, 114; disputes over, 99–100, 109
Wilson, Henry, and the Enrollment Act, 310, 315–317, 320
—— Woodrow, 258, 261, 317, 492, 563
Winthrop, Robert C., 282, 571
Wisconsin, financial policies of, 195–196; federal land grants to, 194, 196; and Fox and Wisconsin Canal, 194–200; volunteers from, 233–235
—— Constitution (1848), 195
Wise, Henry A., 127–128
Woman's Suffrage Association of America, petitions Democratic convention (1868), 415–416
Wood, ——, 379
—— Fernando, 118, 271, 502; his feud with Tammany, 209–211, 217, 283; his party at Delmonico's, 185*n*; elected to Congress, 284; supports northern cause, 236; urges Seymour to accept nomination (1880), 539
Woodward, Judge George W., 422
Wool, Gen. John E., 340; refuses to garrison New York City with militia, 301, 320; his activities during draft riots, 321, 323, 331
"Woolly-Heads," 161, 166
Wright, Curtis W., 417
—— Silas, 50, 54, 56, 63, 66, 71, 79*n*, 82, 85–86, 100, 109, 120, 125, 194, 248, 510–511, 516, 558; his character, 90; elected to Senate, 35; supports independent treasury, 51, 77; refuses vice-presidential nomination, 83; elected governor, 83–84, 476; refuses Cabinet post, 87; his relations with Polk, 87–89; Polk's eulogy of, 108*n*; and canal improvements, 90–91; and revision of New York constitution, 91, 93–95; and anti-renters, 98–99, 104; his defeat for re-election, 97, 103–105; death of, 108, 112

Yancey, William L., 221
Yates, Henry, Jr., 10*n*, 17
Young, John, 77, 97, 142; and anti-renters, 105, 108; elected governor, 104; reproaches Seymour, 94; his political tactics, 86, 91–95
—— Samuel, 17*n*

	DATE DUE		